POLITICS
IN THE
DEVELOPING
WORLD

Edited by
Peter Burnell | Vicky Randall | Lise Rakner

3rd Edition

OXFORD
UNIVERSITY PRESS

OXFORD

UNIVERSITY PRESS

Great Clarendon Street, Oxford OX2 6DP

Oxford University Press is a department of the University of Oxford.
It furthers the University's objective of excellence in research, scholarship,
and education by publishing worldwide in

Oxford New York

Auckland Cape Town Dar es Salaam Hong Kong Karachi
Kuala Lumpur Madrid Melbourne Mexico City Nairobi
New Delhi Shanghai Taipei Toronto

With offices in

Argentina Austria Brazil Chile Czech Republic France Greece
Guatemala Hungary Italy Japan Poland Portugal Singapore
South Korea Switzerland Thailand Turkey Ukraine Vietnam

Oxford is a registered trade mark of Oxford University Press
in the UK and in certain other countries

Published in the United States
by Oxford University Press Inc., New York

© Oxford University Press 2011

British Library Cataloguing in Publication Data
Data available

Library of Congress Cataloging in Publication Data
Data available

Typeset by Laserwords Private Limited, Chennai, India
Printed and bound by CPI Group (UK) Ltd, Croydon, CR0 4YY

ISBN 978–0–19–957083–6

10 9 8 7 6 5 4 3 2

Preface

This third edition of *Politics in the Developing World*, just like the previous editions, has benefitted substantially from feedback by referees and readers. The editors wish to thank all those who offered comments and also OUP for its decision to commission a third edition.

The most visible change is the addition of Professor Lise Rakner to the editorial team, a strategic decision aimed at broadening the international scope of the volume. In terms of content the third edition includes several newly commissioned chapters, including chapters on the contribution that institutionalist perspectives make to better understanding developing world politics, and on the dilemmas of states that are seeking to exit from violent internal conflict and build a more peaceful future. This last perspective is also illustrated by a new case study of Iraq. Other new additions include an account of contemporary China's growing significance for the developing world, and of India as another leading example of developing South–South relations. All the chapters retained from the second edition have been revised and updated. The edited chapters contain among other things fresh illustrative material and pedagogic content, which extends to new sample questions and guidance on further reading. Throughout, a conscious attempt has been made to emphasize gender issues more adequately, although doubtless there is scope to do even more. The overall composition of authors is both more international and closer to gender parity. Finally, the Online Resource Centre contains new extra material including case studies of politics in high-profile countries like Brazil and Iran. Readers of the book are urged to consult this invaluable resource.

New to this edition:

- two new chapters on 'Institutional approaches' and, 'From conflict to peace-building', and a remodelled chapter on governance, aid, and globalization;
- three new extended case studies are included in the text on India, Iraq, and China;
- all chapters have been updated to reflect the ongoing evolution of political regimes and development policies in the wake of recent events such as the global financial crisis;
- the Online Resource Centre has also been updated with new case studies, including Iran and Brazil.

Acknowledgements

The authors and publisher would like to thank UNCTAD for data presented in Tables 4.1, 4.2, and 4.3; and the World Bank for data presented in Tables 16.2, 22b.1, and 22b.2.

The data presented in Table 3.1 are taken from Helmke, Gretchen, and Steven Levitsky, eds, *Informal Institutions and Democracy: Lessons from Latin America*. p. 14, Fig. 1.1. © 2006 The Johns Hopkins University Press. Reprinted with permission of The Johns Hopkins University Press.

The publishers would be pleased to clear permission with any copyright holders that we have inadvertently failed, or been unable to contact.

Guided Tour of Textbook Features

This book is enriched with a number of learning tools to help you navigate the text and reinforce your knowledge of politics in the developing world. This guided tour shows you how to get the most out of your textbook package.

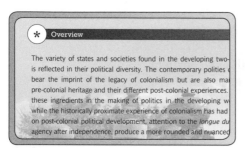

Overviews

Each chapter begins with an overview to set the scene for upcoming themes and issues to be discussed, and indicate the scope of coverage.

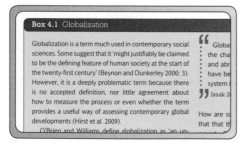

Boxes

Throughout the book, boxes provide you with extra information on particular topics to complement your understanding of the main chapter text.

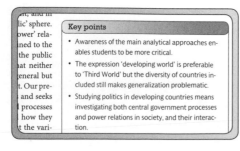

Key points

Each main chapter section ends with a set of key points that summarize the most important arguments developed.

Questions

A set of carefully devised questions have been provided to help you assess your understanding of core themes, and may also be used as the basis of seminar discussion or coursework.

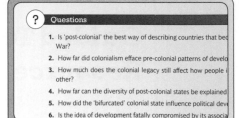

Further reading

Take your learning further by using the reading lists at the end of chapter to find the key literature in the field, or more detailed information on a specific topic.

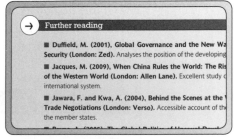

Web links

At the end of each chapter you will find an annotated summary of useful websites to help you with further research.

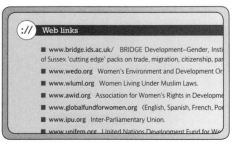

Glossary terms

Key terms appear in bold in the text and are defined in a glossary at the end of the book to aid you with exam revision.

Guided Tour of the Online Resource Centre

www.oxfordtextbooks.co.uk/orc/burnell3e/

The Online Resource Centre that accompanies this book provides students with ready-to-use teaching and learning materials. These resources are free of charge and designed to maximize the learning experience.

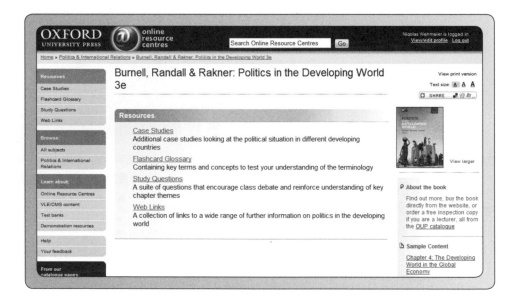

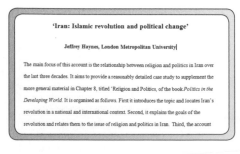

Case studies

Additional case studies have been included to invite you to compare and contrast the political situation in different developing countries, including Iran and Brazil.

Flashcard glossary

A series of interactive flashcards containing key terms allows you to test your knowledge of terminology.

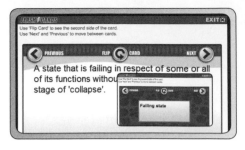

Study questions

A suite of study questions has been provided for revision purposes and to reinforce your understanding of the key themes.

1. How important are assumptions about the dominance of capitalism to the main approaches to theorising the politics of developing countries?

2. How if at all does dependency theory illuminate developing country politics in a globalizing world, and what are its main limitations?

3. Should there be a distinct developing world perspective on how to understand politics in the developing world? What is the most important contribution that scholars in the developing world could make to developing our analytical approaches now?

4. What important features of developing country politics does Marxism help us to understand better, that other theoretical insights either explain badly or alternatively ignore?

5. How do neo-patrimonialism and clientelism shape politics in developing countries and to what extent do they distinguish politics in the developing world from politics in the 'developed world'?

Web links

Click through to useful websites, selected by the book's authors, to find a wide range of further information on politics in the developing world.

www.freetrade.org
The site of the Center for Trade Policy Studies, Washington DC, whose 'mission' is to increase public understanding of the benefits of free trade and costs of protectionism.

www.twnside.org.sg/trade.htm
Third World Network page on trade issues, provides research critical of current global economic policies.

www.unctad.org
United Nations Conference on Trade and Development, containing voluminous data on trade and investment, and reports on the latest developments in the global economy.

www.oxfam.org
The site of the non-governmental organization Oxfam (UK), containing many of its reports on trade and protectionism.

Brief Contents

Detailed Contents

List of Maps

List of Boxes

List of Tables

Abbreviations

9/11	11 September 2001 terrorist attacks on the USA
ACP	Africa-Caribbean-Pacific states
AIDS	acquired immune deficiency syndrome
AKP	Justice and Development Party (Turkey)
ANC	African National Congress (South Africa)
AOSIS	Alliance of Small Island States
APRM	African Peer Review Mechanism
ARPCT	Alliance for the Restoration of Peace and Counter-Terrorism (Somalia)
ASEAN	Association of South-East Asian Nations
AU	African Union
AZAPO	Azanian People's Organization (South Africa)
BJP	Bharatiya Janata Party (India)
BRICs	rapidly developing emerging economies comprising Brazil, Russia, India, and China
BRICS	BRICs plus South Africa
BRICSAM	BRICs plus South Africa and Mexico
BSPP	Burma Socialist Programme Party
CACIF	Comité de Asociaciones Agrícolas, Comerciales, Industriales y Financieras (Guatemala)
CBO	community-based organization
CCP	Chinese Communist Party
CDB	China Development Bank
CEDAW	Convention on the Elimination of All Forms of Discrimination against Women
CFCs	chlorofluorocarbons
CIS	Commonwealth of Independent States
CNG	compressed natural gas
CODESA	Convention for a Democratic South Africa

COPE	Congress of the People (South Africa)
COSATU	Congress of Trade Unions (South Africa)
CPA	Coalition Provisional Authority (Iraq)
CPRC	Chronic Poverty Research Centre
CSGR	Centre for the Study of Globalisation and Regionalisation
CTAs	clandestine transnational activities
DAC	Development Assistance Committee (of the Organisation for Economic Co-operation and Development)
DLP	Democratic Liberal Party (South Korea)
DPKO	Department of Peacekeeping Operations (UN)
DPRK	Democratic People's Republic of Korea
DRC	Democratic Republic of the Congo (formerly Zaire)
DS	development studies (the discipline)
ECOSOC	Economic and Social Council (United Nations)
ECOWAS	Economic Community of West African States
ELN	National Liberation Army (Colombia)
EPB	Economic Planning Board (South Korea)
EU	European Union
EZLN	Zapatista Army of National Liberation (Mexico)
FARC	Revolutionary Armed Forces of Colombia
FDI	foreign direct investment
FH	Freedom House
FIS	Front Islamique du Salut
FOCAC	Forum on China Africa Cooperation
FOMWAN	Federation of Muslim Women's Associations in Nigeria
FRELIMO	Liberation Front of Mozambique
FRETILIN	Revolutionary Front for the Independence of East Timor
FRG	Frente Republicano Guatemalteco (Guatemala)
FSC	Forestry Stewardship Council
FTAA	Free Trade Area of the Americas

G8	Forum of of eight established industrial countries comprising Canada, France, Germany, Italy, Japan, Russia, UK, USA, plus European Union representation
G20	Forum of finance ministers and central bank governors of leading industrialized and developing economies
G77	Group of 77 least developed countries
GAM	Aceh Freedom Movement (Indonesia)
GATT	General Agreement on Tariffs and Trade
GDP	gross domestic product
GEF	Global Environment Facility
GM/GMOs	genetically modified organisms
GNI	gross national income
GNP	gross national product
GNU	Government of National Unity (South Africa)
H1N1	swine flu
H5N1	avian influenza virus
HCI	heavy and chemical industries
HDI	Human Development Index
HIPC	heavily indebted poor countries
HIP(I)C	Heavily Indebted Poor Countries (Initiative)
HIV	human immunodeficiency virus
IAU	Inter-Agency Information and Analysis Unit (on Iraq)
ICG	International Crisis Group
IDEA	International Institute for Democracy and Electoral Assistance
IFAI	Federal Institute for Access to Public Information (Mexico)
IFE	Federal Electoral Institute (Mexico)
IFP	Inkatha Freedom Party (South Africa)
IGC	Iraqi Governing Council
IMF	International Monetary Fund
IOC	international organized crime
IPU	Inter-Parliamentary Union
IR	international relations (the discipline)
ISI	import-substituting industrialization
ISO	International Organization for Standardization

IT	information technology
ITEC	Indian Technical and Economic Cooperation
KDP	Kurdish Democratic Party (Iraq)
LFO	Legal Framework Order (Pakistan)
LTTE	Liberation Tigers of Tamil Eelam (Sri Lanka)
MAD	mutually assured destruction
MAR	Minorities at Risk
MCA	Millennium Challenge Account (US government)
MDGs	Millennium Development Goals (of the United Nations)
MDP	Millennium Development Party (South Korea)
MEND	Movement for the Emancipation of the Delta (Nigeria)
MERCOSUR	Southern Common Market (Latin America)
MINUGUA	Misión de las Naciones Unidas en Guatemala
MKSS	Mazdoor Kisan Shakti Sangathan (India)
MNCs	multinational corporations
MST	Movimento dos Trabalhadores Rurais Sem Terra (Landless Rural Workers, Movement) (Brazil)
NAFTA	North American Free Trade Agreement
NAM	Non-Aligned Movement
NATO	North Atlantic Treaty Organization
NDA	National Democratic Alliance (India)
NDD	non-DAC donors
NEPAD	New Economic Partnership for Africa's Development
NGO	non-governmental organization
NIC	National Intelligence Council
NICs	newly industrialized countries (mainly East Asia)
NIE	new institutional economics
NLD	National League for Democracy (Myanmar)
NPT	non-proliferation treaty
NSSD	National Strategy for Sustainable Development

OAS	Organization of American States
OBCs	Other Backward Classes (India)
ODA	Official Development Assistance
OECD	Organisation for Economic Co-operation and Development
OPEC	Organization of the Petroleum Exporting Countries
ORHA	Office for Reconstruction and Humanitarian Assistance (in Iraq)
PAC	Pan Africanist Congress (South Africa)
PAN	National Action Party (Mexico)
PD	Democratic Party (Indonesia)
PDI-P	Indonesia Democratic Party–Struggle
PDP	People's Democratic Party (Nigeria)
PDPA	People's Democratic Party of Afghanistan
PFN	Pentecostal Fellowship of Nigeria
PKB	National Awakening Party (Indonesia)
PKI	Communist Party of Indonesia
PKS	Justice and Welfare Party
PML(Q)	Pakistan Muslim League (Quaid)
PNUD	Programa de las Naciones Unidas para el Desarollo
POPs	persistent organic compounds
PPC	People's Plan Campaign (India)
PPP	Pakistan People's Party
PPP	purchasing power parity
PRC	People's Republic of China
PRD	Party of the Democratic Revolution (Mexico)
PRI	Institutional Revolutionary Party (Mexico)
PRN	National Revolutionary Party (Mexico)
PRSP	Poverty Reduction Strategy Process
PUK	Patriotic Union of Kurdistan (Iraq)
RENAMO	Mozambican National Resistance
ROC	Republic of China
ROK	Republic of Korea (South Korea)
RSS	Rashtriya Swayamsevak Sangh (India)
RUF	Revolutionary United Front (Sierra Leone)

SA	South Africa
SACP	South African Communist Party
SALs	structural adjustment loans
SAPs	structural adjustment programmes
SARS	Severe Acute Respiratory Syndrome
SAVAK	Organization for Intelligence and National Security (Iran)
SCO	Shanghai Co-operation Organization
SLORC	State Law and Order Restoration Committee (Myanmar)
SME	small and medium-sized enterprises
TEAM-9	Techno-Economic Approach for Africa-India Movement
TEPJF	Electoral Tribunal of the Judicial Power of the Federation (Mexico)
TERI	The Energy and Resources Institute
TFG	Transitional Federal Government (Somalia)
TNA	Transitional National Assembly (Iraq)
TNCs	transnational corporations
TRC	Truth and Reconciliation Commission (South Africa)
UDF	United Democratic Front (South Africa)
UIC	Union of Islamic Courts (Somalia)
UK	United Kingdom
UN	United Nations
UNAIDS	Joint United Nations Programme on HIV/AIDS
UNAM	National Autonomous University (Mexico)
UNAMI	United Nations Assistance Mission for Iraq
UNCED	United Nations Conference on Environment and Development
UNCTAD	United Nations Conference on Trade and Development
UNDP	United Nations Development Programme
UNEP	United Nations Environment Programme
UNHCR	United Nations High Commissioner for Refugees
UNICEF	United Nations Children's Fund
UNIDO	United National Democratic Opposition (Philippines)

UNITA	National Union for Total Independence of Angola
UNMIT	United Nations Integrated Mission in Timor-Leste
UNMOGIP	United Nations Military Observer Group
UNOCHA	UN Office for the Coordination of Humanitarian Affairs
UNODC	United Nations Office on Drugs and Crime
UNRISD	United Nations Research Institute for Social Development
UNSC	United Nations Security Council
UNTAET	United Nations Transitional Authority in East Timor
UNU-WIDER	United Nations University's World Institute for Development Economics Research
UP	Uttar Pradesh (India)
URNG	Unidad Revolucionaria Nacional Guatemalteca (Guatemala)
US	United States
USA	United States of America
USAID	United States Agency for International Development
USSR	Union of Soviet Socialist Republics
WB	World Bank
WFP	World Food Programme
WGA	World Governance Assessment
WHO	World Health Organization
WMD	weapons of mass destruction
WSF	World Social Forum
WSSD	World Summit on Sustainable Development (2002)
WTO	World Trade Organization
WWF	World Wide Fund for Nature

About the Contributors

Tony Addison is the Chief Economist and Deputy Director of the United Nations University's World Institute for Development Economics Research (UNU-WIDER) in Helsinki, Finland.

Nadje Al-Ali is Professor of Gender Studies and Director of the Gender Studies Centre, School of Oriental and African Studies, University of London, UK.

Edward Aspinall is Senior Fellow and Head of the Department of Political and Social Change, School of International, Political, and Strategic Studies, Australian National University, Canberra, Australia.

Deborah Bräutigam is Professor, International Development Program, School of International Service, American University, Washington DC, USA.

Peter Burnell is a Professor in the Department of Politics and International Studies, University of Warwick, UK.

Torunn Wimpelmann Chaudhary is a researcher at the Chr. Michelsen Institute, Bergen, Norway.

James Chiriyankandath is a Senior Research Fellow with the Institute of Commonwealth Studies, School of Advanced Study, University of London, UK.

Peter Ferdinand is a Reader in the Department of Politics and International Studies, University of Warwick, UK.

Michael Freeman is a Research Professor in the Department of Government and was formerly Deputy Director of the Human Rights Centre, University of Essex, UK.

Jeff Haynes is a Professor in the Department of Law, Governance, and International Relations, London Metropolitan University, UK.

Stephen Hobden is a Senior Lecturer in International Politics in the School of Humanties and Social Sciences, University of East London, UK.

Nicole Jackson is Associate Professor in the School for International Studies, Simon Fraser University, Vancouver, Canada.

Adrian Leftwich is a Senior Lecturer in the Department of Politics, University of York, UK.

Emma Mawdsley is a Fellow of Newnham College and Senior Lecturer in the Department of Geography, University of Cambridge, UK.

Peter Newell is a Professor in the School of Development Studies, University of East Anglia, UK.

Marina Ottaway is Director of the Middle East Program, Senior Associate in the Democracy and Rule of Law Project, of the Carnegie Endowment for International Peace, Washington DC, USA.

Jenny Pearce is Professor of Latin American Politics in the Department of Peace Studies, University of Bradford, UK.

Nicola Pratt is Associate Professor, International Politics of the Middle East, in the Department of Politics and International Studies, University of Warwick, UK.

Lise Rakner is a Professor in the Department of Comparative Politics, University of Bergen and Senior Researcher at the Chr. Michelsen Institute, Bergen, Norway.

Vicky Randall is a Professor in the Department of Government, University of Essex, UK and Chair of the Political Studies Association, UK.

James R. Scarritt is Emeritus Professor in the Department of Political Science and formerly Faculty Research Associate in the Institute of Behavioral Science at the University of Colorado at Boulder, USA.

Andreas Schedler is Professor of Political Science at the Department of Political Studies, Centro de Investigación y Docencia Económicas (CIDE), Mexico City, Mexico.

Kurt Schock is Associate Professor of Sociology and Global Affairs in the Department of Sociology and Anthropology, Rutgers University, Newark, USA.

Robert A. Schrire is a Professor and Chair of the Political Studies Department, University of Cape Town, South Africa.

Rachel Sieder is Senior Researcher, CIESAS (Centro de Investigación y Educación Superior en Antropología School of Advanced Study), Mexico City, and Senior Lecturer in Latin American Politics, the Institute for the Study of the Americas, School of Advanced Study, University of London, UK.

Kathleen Staudt is Professor of Political Science, the University of Texas at El Paso, USA.

Astri Suhrke is Senior Researcher, Chr. Michelsen Institute, Bergen, Norway.

David Taylor is Senior Research Fellow at the Institute of Commonwealth Studies, University of London, UK.

Stephen Wright is Professor of Political Science, Northern Arizona University, Flagstaff, USA.

Introduction

Peter Burnell, Vicky Randall, and Lise Rakner

The aim of this book is to explore the changing nature of **politics** in the **developing world** in the twenty-first century. Both 'politics' and the 'developing world' are concepts that require further elaboration and which are discussed more fully below. By politics, we mean broadly activities associated with the process and institutions of government, or the state, but in the context of wider power relations and struggles. By the developing world, we are primarily referring to those regions that were formerly colonized by Western powers, have been late to industrialize, and sustain relatively high levels of poverty: Africa, Asia, the Middle East, and Latin America, including the Caribbean.

In our analysis of politics in the developing world, the complex and changing nexus between state and society has centre stage. This is because it is the reciprocal interaction of state and society and the influence that each one exerts on the other that most accounts for the distinctive character of developing countries' politics. Needless to say that influence varies in both degree and kind, over time, as between individual states and inside states. The book does not set out to present a case for saying the state is now marginal for the political analysis of developing countries. Nor does it argue that we must 'bring the state back in'. On the contrary, it recognizes that issues concerning the state have been, are, and will remain central to the political analysis, notwithstanding important developments—political, financial, economic, technological, and even social at the sub-state, regional, and especially global levels that are reshaping the nature, size, role, and performance of individual states.

A book about politics in the developing world is not the same thing as a book about development per se, or development studies. Indeed, the book does not have as its main objective to give emphasis to the politics *of* development where that means the elucidation of different development theories. There are other books that have been designed for this purpose. Certainly there has been a trend in the study of development to comprehend development in an increasingly holistic sense—one that emphasizes its multifaceted nature and the interconnectedness of the various parts, of which politics provides one very important element. And key relationships between politics and society and between politics and the economy are both explored in the chapters in the book, but without any mission to demonstrate that politics is in some sense the 'master science' that unlocks all other subjects. Instead the consequences that development can have for politics in the developing countries are as much a part of the analysis in this book as the implications that the politics have for development. So, although the book's primary focus is politics rather than development, we hope that its contents will still be of interest to anyone who is involved in development studies more generally.

A word is also needed explaining the geographical coverage of the book. As related below, the boundaries of the developing world are neither uncontentious nor unchanging. We have already suggested which regions have tended historically to be associated with it. However, this book's coverage, and more especially the case studies, does not include all the possible candidates, primarily for pragmatic reasons. Thus, Cuba, Vietnam, and some other countries that at one time claimed to be socialist, even Marxist–Leninist, are just as much part of the developing world as are the many countries that now defer to capitalism and adopt political pluralism. But notwithstanding the financial and economic traumas that hit the global system in 2008, such countries remain a small band. A few like Venezuela and Bolivia are currently pioneering redistributive social and economic policies but the forces of globalization in the post-Soviet, post-cold war world do seem to militate against a more widespread radical socialist transformation. Indeed, China, the credentials of which to be considered part of the developing world are open to debate, shows no intention of reverting to communism as an organizing principle for political economy even though it remains a one-party communist state. However, because contemporary China's relations with developing countries are increasingly significant and the distinctive combination of China's own politics with its rapid economic development appear to some to be a model for others to follow,

a chapter on China's relations with the developing world is included in this book.

There are other parts of the world, beyond the regions traditionally included, that might now be considered to fall into this developing world category. Although no express reference is made in the book to those elements of the post-communist world, a handful of the new European and Central Asian states that formerly belonged to the 'Second World' have certain characteristics long associated with the developing world. Some of them have come to acquire developing country status, in as much as the Organisation for Economic Co-operation and Development's (OECD) Development Assistance Committee (DAC) has made countries like Albania and Armenia eligible for official development assistance. By comparison, the post-communist world's more advanced members were styled 'countries in transition' and judged ineligible for such aid. Readers are free to apply the concepts and propositions in this book to an examination of all these other countries if they wish, just as area specialists seeking insights into those countries will find here material that resonates for their own subject. After all, the growing interdependence of states and rise of trans-territorial and supranational issues, such as those embraced by what might be called the new security agenda, certainly do not respect all the distinctions between categories of countries let alone national borders. The geopolitical unit of analysis that is most relevant to understanding the issues can easily straddle different states only some of which possess all main traits conventionally associated with developing countries. Similarly there are regions and localities inside the wealthiest countries ('the south in the north') that share certain 'southern' or 'Third World' characteristics, relative economic and social deprivation being one such characteristic, which the global economic recession in 2009 brought into sharper relief.

The developing world has been variously referred to as the Third World, the South, and the less developed countries, among other titles. Some of the members are rightly deemed 'emerging economies', and there is a distinctive group—the so-called BRICs (Brazil, Russia, India, China—occasionally supplemented by South Africa and Mexico to make up BRICSAM) that current debate singles out as rising powers, the harbingers of a new emerging multipolarity or more fragmented world. For example four of these countries—Brazil, South Africa, India, and China—played a key role alongside the US in negotiating the Copenhagen Accord of the United Nations Climate Change Conference (December 2009), and the same countries plus Argentina, Indonesia, Mexico, Saudi Arabia, South Korea, and Turkey also formally belong to the G20 group of the world's leading economies, taking part in, for example, the London Summit talks on tackling global economic crisis held in April 2009.

In fact the question of the meaningfulness of the Third World as an organizing concept has long been the subject of dispute, no less than the term's precise definition or true origins. Successive rationales for marking out a distinct Third World associated this world with a stance of non-alignment towards the capitalist and communist superpowers, with post-colonial status, with dependence on Western capitalism, and with poverty and economic 'backwardness'. All together this was a confusing melange of external as well as internal economic and political descriptors. Following the collapse of Soviet power, the disappearance of the 'Second World' served to hasten the decline of the 'Third World' as a category name. Here is not the place to revisit the history of the debates about a term that by and large have now been brought to a conclusion. An abundant literature exists (Wolf-Phillips 1979; Berger 1994; Randall 2004). In keeping with the general trend, then, we have preferred to use the term 'developing world'

for this book. In so doing we do not mean to imply that this term is entirely uncontroversial or unproblematic. Assuming a conventional understanding of 'development', there are many parts of the developing world where such a process is little in evidence and some where it might even seem to be in retreat. There are also those who question the validity of such conventional understandings of 'development', who indeed see development itself as an ideological construct subservient to the interests of Western donors, the international aid 'industry' and suchlike. We recognize the force of many of these arguments. At any rate, whatever term is favoured, there has also been a growing appreciation of the very considerable diversity to be found among and within those countries traditionally seen to come under its umbrella, and the widening of differences in their role and stance towards major issues in world politics.

Notwithstanding what in many instances has been a shared colonial past, some of the differences have always been there, like the enormous range in demographic and territorial size. Just at the lower end of the scale, the distinction between 'small' and 'micro' states that in total make up around 40 per cent of all developing countries and territories is a topic for debate. In contrast, in a regional context some of the larger developing countries now appear to be approaching almost superpower-like status, even while remaining vulnerable to major external shocks. Thus a country like India, a nuclear power with a population that exceeds 1 billion people, has very strong claims to be admitted to the permanent membership of the United Nations Security Council. Some people champion similar claims for Brazil and Nigeria, although the second is less stable politically and its fortunes continue to rest heavily on a very narrow base of energy exports.

Similarly the developing world has always been noted for considerable variety in terms of economic dynamism and technological progress, and recent decades have served only to make these contrasts more pronounced. Just as average incomes were in decline in many parts of Africa in the latter years of the twentieth century, so some of the so-called tiger economies in East Asia have become developed countries in all but name. South Korea, like Mexico, is a member of the OECD and South Korea now a member of the DAC. Their inclusion as case studies in this book illustrates how far and fast countries can develop, if political and other conditions are favourable. Yet in many parts of the developing world, including India as well as China, great inequalities persist alongside the growing prosperity of an emerging middle class and political elite.

Until the 1980s, despite the disparities in size and economic performance, it was possible to argue that most countries in the developing world had in common certain domestic political traits. These included a tendency towards authoritarian rule, whether based on the military, a single ruling party or personal dictatorship, or severe instability and internal conflict, and endemic corruption. But more recently political differences that were already there have become much more pronounced, nowhere more so than in the recognition that some states are failing or, even, are close to collapse. We are increasingly aware of the wide disparities in state strength and of the significance (not least

for development) of variations in the quality of governance. The role played by ethnic and religious identity in politics has also come more to the fore, with the misfortunes of Iraq since the fall of Saddam Hussein providing a vivid example. In contrast, in Latin America, ethnonationalism and religious conflict have been relatively minor themes, which is not to say they are absent: indigenous peoples have started to come out of the shadows. Examples of 'people power' and non-violent action by social movements are demanding increasing attention in this and some other parts of the developing world.

In sum, we are increasingly conscious of change, complexity, and diversity in the developing world and of significant disagreements that follow from differences such as those related to national power. Some common features among developing countries, such as the colonial experience, are now receding into history, which makes old manifestations of 'Third World solidarity' such as the Non-Aligned Movement harder to keep alive in their original form. This means the many differences within the developing world now appear in sharper relief even as new ways of constructing shared interests vis-à-vis the rich world and forging new South–South links among governments and non-governmental actors also proceed apace.

Politics as Independent or Dependent Variable?

Most people, still more so politics students, will have some idea of what is intended by the term 'politics'. Generally political scientists understand politics to refer to activities surrounding the process and institutions of government or the state and that is a focus we share in this book. However, there is another tradition, which some describe as 'sociological', that tends to identify politics with power relationships and structures, including but by no means confined to the state: they include, for instance, relationships

between socio-economic classes or other kinds of social group and between genders. When studying politics in the developing world, we believe it is particularly important to locate analysis of political processes in their narrower sense within the wider context of social relationships and conflicts. Here one of the themes and puzzles is the relationship between the more formal aspects of political processes and institutions that may have been to some degree imposed or modelled on Western prototypes, and their 'informal' aspects. The latter can be very resilient, and may even be regarded as more authentic. The informal hierarchies of power between patrons and clients are a specific example that applies especially although not exclusively to the developing world.

Despite our insistence on the need to understand politics in the wider power context, this does not rule out what is sometimes referred to as the **autonomy of the political**. That means the ability of politics to have independent and significant effects of its own. Thus any account of politics in the developing world that goes beyond the merely descriptive can have one or both of two objectives: to make sense of the politics; to disclose what else the politics itself helps us to understand better. Succinctly, politics can be treated as *explanandum* or *explanans*, and possibly as both.

For some decades there was a large movement in political science to view politics as the dependent variable. Analysts sought to advance our understanding of politics and gain some predictive potential in regard to future political developments by rooting it in some 'more fundamental' aspects of the human condition, sometimes called structural 'conditions'. This was nowhere more evident than in the tendency to argue that the kind of political regime — namely the relationship between rulers and ruled, usually depicted somewhere along the continuum from a highly authoritarian to a more liberal democratic polity — is a product largely of economic circumstance. The level of economic achievement, the nature and pace of economic change, and the social consequences were all considered highly important. It was not only Marxists who subscribed to broadly this kind of view. But there were also others who sought to explain politics, especially in some parts of the developing world, more as an outcome of certain cultural conditions. This invoked a matrix of social divisions much richer and potentially more confusing than a simple class-based analysis would allow. These and other inclinations that view politics as contingent are still very much in evidence in contemporary theorizing about politics in the developing world,

as several of the chapters in Parts 1 and 2 of the book will show.

However, over recent decades in political science, the larger study of comparative politics and area studies too have increased the weight given to the idea of politics as an independent variable, claiming in principle that politics matters: not only is it affected, but it too can have effects. Mair (1996) characterized this as a shift from an emphasis on asking what causes political systems to emerge, take shape, and possibly persist to questions about what outputs and outcomes result from the political processes and how well various political institutions perform. Making sense of the politics now goes beyond just explaining it. It extends also to an investigation of the impact of politics and its consequences. That includes the way in which contemporary politics is affected by the political history of a country, a proposition that is sometimes given the label of path dependence, which in its more narrow and most meaningful application suggests that institutional choices tend to become self-reinforcing (see Pierson 2000).

This move to view the more autonomous side of politics coincides with the rise of new institutionalism in political studies. New institutionalism has been described in a seminal article by March and Olsen (1984: 747) as neither a theory nor a coherent critique of one but instead 'simply an argument that the organisation of political life makes a difference'. The new institutionalism (explored more fully in Chapter 3) directs us to the study of political process and political design but not simply as outcomes or in terms of their contextual 'conditions'. This is not a completely new mood. As March and Olsen rightly say, historically, political science has emphasized the ways in which political behaviour is embedded in an institutional structure of norms, rules, expectations, and traditions that constrain the free play of individual will. The implications of this approach, and of tracing what political forms and political choices mean for a large set of issues of public concern, environmental issues for instance, are explored in Parts 3 and 4 of the book especially. In doing so, the chapters provide a bridge to studying the larger phenomenon of human development. Here we take our cue from the United Nations Development Programme, which said that its *Human Development Report 2002* is 'first and foremost about the idea that politics is as important to successful development as economics' (UNDP 2002: v). The UNDP's understanding is that human development, an idea that has grown in acceptance across a broad spectrum of development studies, aims to promote not simply higher material consumption but the freedom, well-being, and dignity of people everywhere. Development then has a political goal just as politics is integral to how we understand the meaning of development.

Global Trends

Notwithstanding the increasing differentiation within the developing world, it is a fact that over the last few decades there has also been a growing convergence. This is due to the presence of a number of major interconnected trends, political and economic, domestic and international. But these trends, far from reconfirming the more old-fashioned notions of the Third World, are instead ensuring that some of the most striking similarities emerging in the developing world today have a very different character from the Third World of old. This point is well worth illustrating before moving on.

One such trend, entrenched towards the end of the last century comprised pressures from within and without the societies to adopt the so-called Washington consensus of the Bretton Woods institutions—the International Monetary Fund and World Bank—on economic policy and national economic management. These developments have been held responsible in part for a near universal movement in the direction of neo-liberalism and marketization. There has been a shift from public ownership and the direct control of economic life by the state towards acceptance and encouragement of for-profit enterprise and growing opportunities for non-governmental development organizations. Although proceeding at a different pace in different places and experiencing widely varying degrees of success the implications of such changes for politics generally and the state specifically can be

quite profound. Ultimately the same might be true of the 'post-Washington consensus', which is now commonly said to have succeeded the earlier development, and which appears to give a bit more priority to tackling poverty as well as highlighting the developmental importance of attaining 'good governance'.

If *economic* liberalization has been one prong of a growing convergence among developing countries, then pressures towards *political* liberalization and democratization have been a second and, according to some accounts, symbiotically related development. The amount of substantive change that has actually taken place and its permanence are both open to discussion. Indeed, after a time in the early 1990s when the **third wave of democratization** seemed to have unstoppable momentum and some observers talked about the 'end of history', far more cautious claims are now much in evidence. By 2010 the reality has become more confused: authoritarian or semi-authoritarian persistence in some places sits alongside evidence of democratic reversal in yet others. While a number of the 'new democracies' are of questionable quality, the progress made by others has confounded the cynics. Yet irrespective of how truly liberal (in the political sense) or even democratic most developing countries really are and of how many possess market economies that are truly vibrant, recognition of the importance of governance in whatever way we define it (the definitions are many, some of them so vague or all-encompassing as to be almost useless) is ubiquitous. All these agendas have been driven strongly by developed world **institutions**, and notwithstanding the varied responses and reactions the developing world now looks a rather different place from the way in which the Third World was formerly understood.

Underpinning these and many other contemporary developments — such as the campaigns for gender equity, the salience of 'new security' issues, and international monitoring of human rights — there is the growing significance ascribed to **globalization**. Here globalization is understood at a minimum as 'the process of increasing interconnectedness between societies such that events in one part of the world more and more have effects on peoples and societies far away' (Baylis and Smith 2001: 7). The influence may be direct, and positive or negative, or both. It can also work indirectly. And of course, the developing countries are touched unevenly and in different ways — as is made clear in this book (and graphically illustrated by the data presented in Appendix 2). In purely economic terms, some are largely bystanders. They may share few of the claimed benefits even while incurring accidental and unintended costs. Their continuing vulnerability to fluctuations in the world market for their commodities is illustrative. Globalization theorists tell us the sites of power are becoming more dispersed, and some say power is leaking away from the state — more so in the case of many developing countries that are small or very poor or have weak governance structures than for big countries like the United States, Japan, Russia, China, or the other BRICs even. This unevenness is an unwritten assumption in much of the international political economy literature on globalization, which on its own admission biases attention towards the economically more developed parts of the world (see, for instance, Phillips 2005). It provides one more reason for arguing that treating the developing world as a distinct but not separate entity continues to make sense.

Thus while the old order summed up by First, Second, and Third Worlds has disappeared and the international system appears to be edging to a very uncertain future characterized by a greater dispersion of power compared to the cold war and its immediate aftermath, differences still exist between the developing world and its counterpart in the more affluent North. And if US foreign initiatives after 9/11, especially in the Middle East, caused widespread resentment in developing regions triggered by perceptions of a new imperialism reminiscent of older struggles for liberation from colonial rule, then claims to developing world solidarity might be credited with some purchase even now. A shared sensitivity to incursions or infringements of their sovereignty still supplies a common cause, one that China quite expressly promotes, although of course, unlike European Union member states, countries such as the US are hardly keen to surrender political autonomy either. Perhaps the dividing lines are nowhere more evident than in the North–South alignment over how to respond to global climate change. Most of the developed world sees a reduction in global greenhouse gas emissions as the priority, but many developing countries including India and China seem less convinced, and rather draw attention to the urgency of climate adaptation in developing countries and the rich world's obligation both to cut emissions and offer help. Interests and issues like these share with identities a responsibility for how the different worlds are constructed or construct themselves — sometimes expressly in opposition to one another.

Even so we should be continually challenging ourselves to distinguish between, on the one side what, how, and how far changes really are taking place in developing world politics, and on the other side the changes in our understanding that owe most to the lens through which we study the subject. Here history tells us that for the most part the lens tends to originate, or comes to be ground more finely outside and not inside the developing world. This is an important point: registering major developing world contributions to the way in which developing world politics is understood by observers in the developed world, while far from impossible, is crucial but not an easy or straightforward task.

PETER BURNELL, VICKY RANDALL AND LISE RAKNER

The book comprises five parts. Each part is introduced by its own brief survey of contents: short introductions can be read alongside this opening chapter. Part 1 on analytical approaches and the global context should be read first. The aim of this part is to provide an introduction to general theoretical approaches that offer different ways of making sense of the politics in the developing world. These simplifying devices enable us to bring some order to a great mass of facts. They are useful both for directing our inquiries and because they provide a lens or lenses through which to interpret the empirical information. They suggest explanations for what we find there. Ultimately, the point of theorizing is not simply to explain but to provide a gateway to prediction. And however tenuous are social science's claims to be able to predict with any confidence, the book aims both to assess the present of developing countries in the light of the past and to identify the major political uncertainties facing them in the foreseeable future.

So it is entirely appropriate that immediately following the analytical overview there is a chapter on colonialism and post-coloniality, themes that still resonate in so many different ways. Then special attention is given to institutional perspectives, followed by the changing international context. The glib conviction that now more than ever all of humanity resides in 'one world' betokens a very real fact of growing interconnectedness and interdependence, albeit highly asymmetric. There is increasing global economic integration at its core, but important political and other expressions of globalization, including new patterns in relationships among developing countries and China, should not be ignored either. The different analytical approaches these chapters offer should not be viewed as entirely mutually exclusive. Each can quite plausibly have something valuable to offer, even though the emphases may shift when applied to different country situations and historical epochs. Readers must

form their own judgements about which particular theoretical propositions offer most insight into specific issues and problems, or the more general condition of politics in developing countries. It is not the book's aim to be prescriptive in this regard, other than to restate that where possible notable perspectives from the developing world should be reflected.

Parts 2 and 3 set out to illuminate the changing nature, role, and situation of the state in relation to key social variables within developing countries. The two parts are a mirror image of one another. Together they explore both how the politics reflects or is affected by social context, and how states specifically have responded to the challenges posed by society, and the social effects. Particular attention is given to what this means in terms of the changing use and distribution of political power among state institutions and other actors. Thus Part 2 introduces the themes of inequality, ethnopolitics, and nationalism, religion, gender, civil society, and 'people power' movements, in that order. Part 3 proceeds to theorize the state, before going on to examine the distinctive features of states that are trying to escape violent conflict at home. This is followed by the condition of democratization, which after much impetus in the early 1990s now seems to be static or by some accounts is in decline, and by a discussion of governance, which is viewed against a background of globalization's impact and more especially the encouragement from international actors to undertake governance reforms in particular.

Part 4 identifies major policy issues that confront to greater or lesser degree all developing countries. In general terms, the issues are not peculiar to the developing world but they do have a special resonance and their own character there. And although the issues also belong to the larger discourse on development per se, Part 4 aims to uncover why and how they become expressly political. It compares different political responses and their consequences both for politics and development. The issues range from economic development and the environment to human rights and security. Some of these could just as well have been introduced in earlier chapters of the book. This is because the presentations in Part 4 do not concentrate purely on the *details* of policy, but rather out of necessity seek to locate the policies within the context of the policy *issues* as such. However, all these more policy-oriented chapters are grouped together because they are representative of major challenges for society and for government. Of course, where readers prefer to relate material from a chapter in Part 4 more closely to the material that comes earlier in the book, then there is no need to follow the chapters in strict numerical order.

Part 5 aims to illustrate in some depth, or by what is sometimes called 'thick description', principal themes raised in the earlier parts, so complementing the use there of examples drawn more widely from around the developing world. While space limitations mean that the case studies are not designed to cover all aspects of a country's politics, the cases have been selected both with an eye to their intrinsic interest and for the contrasts they provide in relation to one or more of the larger themes introduced earlier. Also, attention has been given not simply to illustrating developing country problems and weaknesses but also to highlighting cases that offer a more positive experience. A deliberate aim of the book is to show the developing world as a place of diversity, not primarily a region of despair. All the main geographical regions are represented in Part 5 together with the supplements offered by the book's Online Resource Centre. The particular selection of countries and the themes they illustrate is explained in more detail in the introduction to Part 5. Readers could usefully consult that introduction now. In total the country studies once again highlight the great range of experience in the developing world while at the same time drawing attention to new developments in South–South relations. They also demonstrate the benefit to be gained from a detailed historical knowledge of the

individual cases. But although the cases differ not least in respect of their relative success or failure regarding development in the widest sense and politics specifically, none of them offers a simple or straightforward picture. The case studies should be read in conjunction with the appropriate chapter or chapters from the earlier parts, and are not intended to be read in isolation.

The editors' view is that a final chapter headed 'Conclusions' is not needful. The chapters each contain their own summaries; such a large collected body of material is not easily reduced without making some arbitrary decisions; and, most importantly, readers should be encouraged to form their own conclusions. It is almost inevitable that readers will differ in terms of the themes, issues, and even the countries or regions about which they will most want to form conclusions. And it is in the nature of the subject that there is no single right set of answers that the editors can distil. On the contrary, studying politics in the developing world is so fascinating precisely because it is such a rich field of inquiry and constantly gives rise to new rounds of challenging questions.

So we finish here by posing some big overarching questions that you might want to keep in mind as you read the chapters. They can be used to help to structure the sort of general debate that often takes place towards the end of courses or study programmes that this book aims to serve. In principle, the subject of each and every one of the chapters and all the case studies merit further investigation as individual items. But for courses occupying a more limited number of weeks, one possibility is for lectures or presentations by tutors to concentrate on material drawn from Parts 1, 2, 3, and 4, and for the allotted student reading preparatory to each week to include relevant case study material as well.

- Is politics in the developing world so very different from elsewhere that understanding it requires a distinct theoretical framework?
- Is there a single theoretical framework adequate for the purpose of comprehending politics in all

countries of the developing world, or should we call on some combination of different frameworks?

- Are the main political trends experienced by the developing world in recent decades summed up best by increasing diversity or, alternatively, growing convergence, and are these trends likely to continue in the future?

- What are the advantages of applying a gendered framework of analysis to the study of politics in developing countries, and does one particular gendered framework offer equivalent insights in all countries?

- In what political respects is the developing world truly developing, and in what respects are significant parts of it not developing or, even, travelling in the opposite direction?

- What grounds are there for being optimistic, or alternatively pessimistic, about the ability of states to resolve conflict and manage change peacefully in the developing world?

- Are the role of the state and nature of the public policy process fundamentally changing in the developing world, and if so, in what respects?

- What principal forces, domestic or global, are creating incentives and pressures for fundamental political change and what forces are resisting or obstructing such change?

- How should developing countries' policies concerning the major public issues of our time differ from typical policies we see widely adopted in developed countries?

- What lessons most relevant to other societies can be learned by studying politics in the developing world, and to which countries or groups of countries are they most relevant?

- Drawing on what you understand about politics in the developing world, should China be included among the countries that are studied as part of the developing world?

 Web links

- http://blds.ids.ac.uk The British Library for Development Studies claims to be Europe's largest research collection on social and economic change in developing countries.

- www.eldis.org Thousands of online documents, organizations, and messages conveying information on development policy, practice, and research.

- www.gdnet.org The site of the Global Development Network, a worldwide network of research and policy institutes aiming to generate research at the local level in developing countries and to provide alternative perspectives to those originating in the more developed world.

PART 1

Approaches and Global Context

Politics in the developing world offers an enormously rich and fascinating canvas of material for investigation. If we are to make sense of what we find, we must approach the subject in a structured and orderly way, with a clear sense of purpose. That means having an adequate framework, or frameworks, of analysis comprising appropriate concepts lucidly defined together with a set of coherent organizing propositions. Propositions are advanced to explain the political phenomena in terms of their relationship with one another and their relations with other variables—both the influencing factors and the factors that are themselves influenced by, and demonstrate the importance of, politics. This part of the book introduces analytical approaches to the study of politics in the developing world. It sets out to situate that politics within both an historical and an international and increasingly globalizing environment, as befits the increase of interdependence ('one world') and supraterritoriality that appear so distinctive of modern times. It also reviews the contribution that can be made by a particular focus on institutions and the analytical purchase that adopting such a focus entails.

This part has two aims: *first* to identify whether the 'developing world' is a sufficiently distinct entity to warrant its own theory, as we seek to comprehend its politics in the light of both the past and the present. It compares the main broad-gauge theoretical frameworks that at different times have been offered for just this very purpose. Have the theoretical approaches that were pioneered in the early years of decolonization and post-colonial rule now been overtaken and made redundant by the other and more recent critical perspectives such as those offered by post-modern and post-structuralist thinking, Orientalism, and the like? Do some theories or perspectives work better for some cases than for others?

The *second* aim is to show why and in what ways it is becoming increasingly difficult to understand or even just describe politics within developing countries without employing at minimum an institutionalist perspective and taking account of factors in the contemporary international system, as well as the influence of any pre-colonial and colonial legacies. These are the inter-state and supra-state influences that originate in economic, financial, diplomatic, cultural, and other forums. Many of these influences can penetrate state borders without having either express consent or tacit approval from government. They collaborate and collide with a variety of intra- and non-state actors, reaching far down to the sub-state and sub-national levels. At the same time developing countries also participate in and seek to influence regional networks and wider international organization. The so-called BRICs is a good example: Even if the potential of this group of states to act as one in international affairs is not fully realized, recent changes on the international stage plus the emergence of China and India as new development donors suggest a paradigm shift in North–South as well as South–South relations. The nature of 'South–South' relations should be compared with 'North–South' relations before and since the end of the cold war. This part helps us to consider the developing world's place within the global system as a whole: such questions as how far are developing country politics conditioned by powerful constraints and pressures originating outside? Are those pressures and constraints and their impact in any sense comparable to 'neo-colonialism' or, indeed, the imperialism of old? Is power in the developing world now being ceded not so much to governments in the rich world as to a more diffuse and less controllable multilayered set of global commercial, financial, and economic forces and institutions? Or does their possession of valuable resources and growing presence enable at least some countries to be increasingly assertive in respect of their political autonomy and influencing world affairs? Readers are encouraged to read the introduction to Part 5 and to consult relevant case studies and in particular Chapter 23 on 'South–South Relations and the Changing Landscape of International Development Cooperation', alongside the chapters in Part 1.

Analytical Approaches to the Study of Politics in the Developing World

1

Vicky Randall

* Overview

Two contrasting broad approaches long dominated political analysis of developing countries. One was a politics of **modernization** that gave rise to **political development** theory, then to revised versions of that approach that stressed the continuing if changing role of tradition, and the need for strong government, respectively. Second was a Marxist-inspired approach that gave rise to **dependency theory** and subsequently to neo-Marxist analysis that focused on the relative autonomy of the state. By the 1980s both approaches were running out of steam but were partially subsumed in **globalization theory**, which emphasized the ongoing process, accelerated by developments in communications and the end of the cold war, of global economic integration and its cultural and political ramifications. Nowadays, the very concept of a developing world is increasingly hard to sustain and with it the possibility of identifying one distinct analytic approach as opposed to middle-range theories and a particular focus on the role of institutions more widely evident in contemporary political studies. In the absence of such an approach, certain key themes and agendas provide some degree of coherence. Similarly there is no distinctive set of methodological approaches but rather the application of approaches more generally available in the social sciences. Finally, whilst it is not possible to point to a systematic critique of prevailing or mainstream approaches, elements of a potential critique can be garnered from the literatures on orientalism and post-coloniality, and on post-development, and more generally from a post-structural perspective.

Introduction

This chapter provides an introduction to the main broad analytical approaches or frameworks of interpretation that have been employed in studying politics in the developing world. The 'developing world' is clearly a vast field, covering a great number of highly diverse political systems. To varying degrees those seeking to make sense of this field have felt a need for theories or frameworks of analysis to provide them with appropriate concepts or containers of information, and allow comparison and generalization across countries or regions. Some frameworks have been relatively modest or 'middle-range', but others have been much more ambitious in scope and claims. Moreover, despite aspirations to scientific objectivity and rigour, they have inevitably reflected the circumstances in which they were formulated—for instance political scientists' underlying values, domestic political pressures, and funding inducements, as well as perceived changes in the developing countries themselves. We all need to be aware of these approaches, and the surrounding debates, if we are to read the literature critically and form our own views.

We begin with what can be called the politics of modernization, emerging in the United States in the 1950s. This approach, including political development theory and its various 'revisions', operated from a mainstream, liberal, or, to its left critics, pro-capitalist perspective. The second and opposed approach, stemming from a critical, Marxist-inspired perspective, has taken the form first of dependency theory and then of a more state-focused Marxist approach. More recently the dominant, although by no means unchallenged, paradigm has been globalization theory, to some degree incorporating elements of both developmentalist and dependency perspectives. Globalization theory, however, has also served to problematize politics in the developing world as a coherent field, partly because it tends to undermine the premise of a distinct developing world. For this and other reasons, some have suggested that the field is currently in crisis. The last part of this chapter considers how far a distinctive and coherent approach to politics in the developing world is still discernible in the present day, and also asks whether such an approach would be desirable.

'Politics' and the 'Developing World'

Before considering the three main approaches themselves, we need briefly to revisit the notions of 'developing world' on the one hand and 'politics' on the other. This is because to understand and assess the approaches we need some idea of what it is that such analysis is supposed to make intelligible or explain. As noted in the introduction, the term 'developing world' has conventionally referred to the predominantly post-colonial regions of Africa, Asia, Latin America and the Caribbean, and the Middle East, perceived to be poorer, less economically advanced, and less 'modern' than the

developed world. 'Developing world' is preferred to 'Third World', because that latter term carries some particular historical connotations that make it especially problematic.

But even when we use the less problematic 'developing world', there have always been questions about what makes such a concept meaningful. What exactly are the defining features that these countries have in common and that distinguish them from the 'developed world', both generally and in terms of their politics? Are such common features more important than their differences? These questions, becoming more pressing as the differences have grown, have clear implications for both the need and the possibility for some kind of general approach to understanding and analysing them. More basically, some will want to question the assumptions underlying the notion of 'development'. From what to what are such countries supposed to be developing, and from whose perspective?

Similarly, 'politics' is a highly contested notion. Politics on one understanding is a kind of activity associated with the process of government, and in modern settings also linked with the 'public' sphere. On another understanding it is about 'power' relations and struggles, not necessarily confined to the process of government or restricted to the public domain. This volume takes the view that neither perspective on its own is sufficient, in general but particularly in a developing world context. Our preferred focus is on state–society relations and seeks to investigate both central governmental processes and power relations within society, and how they interact. One question to be asked about the various approaches to studying politics in developing countries, surveyed below, is how far they enable us to do this.

A further important question concerns the autonomy of politics: how far is politics as a level or sphere of social life determined by economic and/or social/cultural dimensions of society and how far does it independently impact on those dimensions? Is the autonomy of politics itself variable? The different approaches to be considered all address this question, more or less explicitly, but arrive at very different conclusions.

Key points

- Awareness of the main analytical approaches enables students to be more critical.

- The expression 'developing world' is preferable to 'Third World' but the diversity of countries included still makes generalization problematic.

- Studying politics in developing countries means investigating both central government processes and power relations in society, and their interaction.

- A further important question concerns the relative autonomy of politics.

Dominant Theoretical Approaches

It must be stressed that approaches to the study of politics in this vast swathe of the world's countries have in practice been extremely diverse. As discussed further below, most of the analytic and methodological toolkit of political science has been applied at one time or another. This includes statistical analysis, **rational choice theory**, and discourse theory. On the other hand, many country-based studies have not been explicitly theoretical at all. Nonetheless it is possible to argue that most studies of politics in developing countries have been informed to some degree by one or other of three main dominant approaches—modernization theory, Marxism-inspired theory, and globalization theory. These approaches or theoretical frameworks themselves have not necessarily been directly or centrally concerned with politics; however, both modernization theory and dependency theory have helped at least to generate more specifically political approaches.

The politics of modernization

The emergence of the 'politics of modernization' approach reflected both changing international political circumstances and developments within social science and specifically within political science.

Out of the Second World War a new world was born in which, first, two superpowers, the United States and the Soviet Union, confronted one another and, second, a process of decolonization was set in train leaving a succession of constitutionally independent states. Soon the two powers were vying for influence in these states. Within the United States, social scientists, and increasingly political scientists, were encouraged to study them.

For this, the field of comparative politics at that time was ill-equipped. It was: (i) highly parochial—focused on a narrow range of Western countries; (ii) typically concerned with the legal and historical development of governing institutions; and (iii) not systematically comparative at all. Responding to this new challenge, comparative politics drew on two developments in the social sciences. First, the 'behavioural revolution' encouraged a more 'scientific' approach that sought to build general social theories and test them empirically. Second, especially in sociology but also in economics, interest was growing in tracing and modelling processes of 'modernization'. Sociology has from its inception been concerned with the impact of industrialization on pre-industrial society, and modernization theory was able to draw on the insights of its founding fathers, such as Max Weber (1864–1920). Whilst modernization theory took different forms, its underlying assumption was that the process of modernization experienced in the West provided a valuable guide to what to expect in the developing world.

Political development theory

In this context interest grew in elaborating a specific concept and theory of political development. The Committee of Comparative Politics, set up in 1954 by the American Research Council and chaired by Gabriel Almond, and the funds at its disposal strongly influenced the emerging field of study. Whilst no one framework of analysis dominated, the one initially proposed and subsequently developed by Almond himself was both influential and highly representative.

Almond developed a structural-functional approach to compare politics in different countries and as a basis for his concept of political development. Drawing on Easton's (1965) systems theory and the 'structural-functionalism' of sociologist Talcott Parsons (1960), Almond's model distinguished a series of political functions and then examined their relationship with particular structures or institutions (see Box 1.1). There were four 'input' functions—political socialization (instilling attitudes towards the political system), political recruitment, and the 'articulation' and 'aggregation' of interests (demands). On the 'output' side three functions were identified—rule-making, rule implementation, and rule adjudication—and there was a more pervasive function of political communication.

Almond originally suggested that political development could be understood as the process through which these functions were increasingly associated with specialized structures—parties for interest aggregation, legislatures for rule-making, and so on—and with the emergence of modern styles of politics (achievement-based versus ascriptive and so forth). Later (1960) he identified five political system 'capabilities' (extractive, regulative, distributive, symbolic, and responsive), which were expected to grow as structures became more specialized and political styles more modern. These capabilities in turn would help the system to deal with four main problems (some writers later referred to these as 'crises')—of state-building (with the focus on state structures), nation-building (focusing on cultural integration), participation, and distribution.

Box 1.1 Almond's Framework for Comparative Analysis

Political system

INPUT FUNCTIONS	OUTPUT FUNCTIONS
and typical associated structures	*and typical associated structures*
Political socialization (family, schools, religious bodies, parties etc.)	*Rule-making* (legislatures)
Political recruitment (parties)	*Rule implementation* (bureaucracies)
Interest articulation (interest groups)	*Rule adjudication* (judicial system)
Interest aggregation (parties)	

Political communication

Political systems develop *five capabilities*:

- extractive (drawing material and human resources from environment);

- regulative (exercising control over individual and group behaviour);

- distributive (allocation of different kinds of 'good' to social groups);

- symbolic (flow of effective symbols, e.g. flags, statues, ceremony);

- responsive (responsiveness of inputs to outputs).

These help them to face *four kinds of problem*:

- state-building (need to build structures to penetrate society);

- nation-building (need to build culture of loyalty and commitment);

- participation (pressure from groups to participate in decision-making);

- distribution (pressure for redistribution or welfare).

(Almond and Powell 1966)

Almond's approach has been extensively and justly criticized, although it must be said that political scientists continue to use many of the concepts he developed, for instance state-building (see Chapter 12) and nation-building. It was argued that his political functions drew too heavily from American political experience, that his scheme was unilinear (assuming one general direction of change), teleological (holding out the goal of a modern, most of the time a liberal-democratic, polity), and ethnocentric. Similar criticisms were made of other attempts to conceptualize political development, with the added observation that they were excessively diverse, demonstrating a lack of consensus on what political development actually was (Pye 1966).

Political development theory, in this form, was in decline by the late 1960s, not least because supporting funding was drying up. But it has not entirely disappeared; indeed many of its characteristic themes resurfaced in the literature emerging from the 1980s concerning democratization and

governance. Before leaving political development theory, though, two further developments should be noted.

Modernization revisionism

One strand of criticism of political development theory—**modernization revisionism**—centred on its oversimplified notions of tradition, modernity, and their interrelationship. Taking up arguments voiced by social anthropologists against modernization theory, some political scientists questioned what they perceived as an assumption that political modernization would eliminate 'traditional' elements of politics such as **caste** and ethnicity (the topic of religion was largely ignored until the 1980s—see Chapter 8). Instead they suggested that aspects of political modernization could positively invigorate these traditional elements, albeit in a changed form, and also that these elements would invariably influence in some measure the form and pace of political change.

This perspective also drew attention to the ubiquity and role of **patron–client relationships**. In their 'traditional' form, local notables, typically landowners, acted as patrons to their dependent clients, typically peasants, in relationships that were personalized, clearly unequal, but framed in terms of reciprocity and affection. With greater 'modernization' and extension of state and market into the 'periphery', a modified kind of relationship emerged between peasant/clients and local 'brokers' who could mediate their dealings with the centre. But at the centre, emerging, seemingly modern political institutions—political parties and bureaucracies—also often operated on the basis of informal but powerful patron–client relationships, which moreover often linked into those at the periphery. This insight into the realities of **patronage** and **clientelism** was extremely valuable and has continuing relevance (see Box 1.2). Indeed, with the more recent emphasis on the role of political **institutions**, discussed further below and in Chapter 3, there has been renewed interest in these relationships, as part of the wider question of the relationship between formal and informal processes within institutions. Despite further criticisms that have been made of modernization revisionism in its turn, this perspective has greatly enhanced our understanding of political processes in the developing world.

Box 1.2 Patron–Client Relations (Two Illustrative Quotations)

An anthropological account of a traditional patron–client relationship between landlord and sharecropper:

A peasant might approach the landlord to ask a favour, perhaps a loan of money or help in some trouble with the law, or the landlord might offer his aid knowing of a problem. If the favour were granted or accepted, further favours were likely to be asked or offered at some later time. The peasant would reciprocate—at a time and in a context different from that of the acceptance of the favour in order to de-emphasize the material self-interest of the reciprocative action—by bringing the landlord especially choice offerings from the farm produce or by sending some members of the peasant family to perform services in the landlord's home, or refraining from cheating the landlord, or merely by speaking well of him in public and professing devotion to him.

(Silverman 1977: 296)

Patron–client relationships in Mexican party politics:

Given PRI monopolization of public office, for much of the post-revolutionary period the most important actors in the competition for elected and appointed positions have been political *camarillas* within the ruling elite. *Camarillas* are vertical groupings of patron–client relationships, linked at the top of the pyramid to the incumbent president. These networks are assembled by individual politicians and bureaucrats over a long period of time and reflect the alliance-building skill and family connections of the patron at the apex.

(Craig and Cornelius 1995: 259–60)

Politics of order

There is some disagreement as to how far the second development, referred to here as the **politics of order** thesis, was essentially part of the political development approach or represented a break with it. On the one hand, critics from the left have seen it as informed by the same underlying concern to promote capitalist interests (see Cammack, 1997) On the other, its leading exponent, Samuel Huntington, launched a scathing attack on political development theory (1971) for its unrealistic optimism, suggesting that rather than political development, it might be more relevant to talk about political decay.

Huntington criticized what he saw as a mistaken assumption in political development theory that in developing societies, economic growth would lead to social change (greater social pluralism, higher literacy rates, and so on) supportive of liberal democracy. Instead, rapid economic growth from low initial levels could be profoundly destabilizing, generating social dislocation and frustration that could convert into excessive pressures on fragile political institutions. In this context he maintained that what mattered was not what form of government existed (whether democratic or communist) but the degree of government. Huntington's search for the sources of strong government in developing societies even extended to the military, which he argued could provide stability and direction in countries at an early stage of development, although he saw strong ruling political parties, whether in one-party or multi-party systems, as the best means of providing legitimacy and coherence for government.

Critics accused this 'politics of order' perspective of inherent conservatism and authoritarianism. But it also injected a welcome dose of realism into the discussion; political development on Almond-type lines was just not happening. Second, it drew attention to the ability of political institutions not just to reflect economic and social development but themselves to make an active difference, that is, to the 'relative autonomy of the political'.

Marxist-inspired approaches

The second main category of approaches to be examined stems from a broadly Marxist perspective. As such, it has opposed the politics of modernization school, which it sees as driven by bourgeois or capitalist interests, and has stressed the determining role of processes of economic production and/or exchange and the social class relationships embedded in them. In fact, dependency theory, which emerged in the late 1960s, was primarily concerned to refute models of economic development and also modernization theory; its implications for politics, at least in the narrower governmental sense, were almost incidental, although it had considerable impact on the study of politics in the developing world.

One main reason was that it drew attention to a serious shortcoming of all forms of political development theory: their near-total neglect of the international context and implied assumption that politics in developing countries was shaped by purely domestic forces. Dependency theory originated in South America and reflected that continent's experience but was quickly applied to other parts of the developing world. It has taken numerous forms but will be briefly illustrated here through the arguments of a leading exponent, Gunder Frank (see also Chapters 2 and 5).

Frank (1969) maintained that the developing world had been increasingly incorporated into the capitalist world economy from the sixteenth century onwards. In fact, development of the developed world (known as the 'metropolis' or 'core') was premised upon 'underdevelopment' of the developing world (known as 'satellite economies' or the 'periphery'); development and underdevelopment were two sides of the same coin. Despite formal political independence, former colonies remained essentially dependent because the metropolis was able to extract most of their economic surplus through various forms of monopoly. Even when such economies appeared to be developing, this was only dependent and distorted development. Frank argued that the only way a satellite economy could end this dependence was to drastically reduce ties with the metropolis; later he recognized that even this was not really an option.

Whilst for a time dependency theory was extremely influential, it was also increasingly and justly criticized for the crude generalization and determinism of its economic analysis. Not all versions were quite as deterministic as Frank's. Wallerstein recognized a 'semi-periphery' of countries like the East Asian 'tigers' that over time had been able to improve their position within the overall 'world system', and by their example offered others on the periphery the hope of doing so too (Wallerstein 1979). Cardoso (1973) used the case of Brazil to argue that there could be meaningful 'associated dependent development'. By the 1980s, because of its weakness as economic theory but also because of the growing ascendancy of neo-liberal economic doctrine and developments in the world economy that appeared to contradict it, dependency theory was losing currency, although ironically the emerging 'debt crisis' of that same decade and imposition of structural adjustment requirements has seemed one of its best illustrations.

What did dependency theory have to say about politics in developing countries? Frank tended to minimize the independent effects of politics. He argued that both the state and the national political elite in such countries were identified with the 'comprador' economic class, which served as the local agent of metropolitan capital and consequently had a vested interest in the status quo. The only real possibility of change would be a revolution of those at the end of the chain of exploitation—the peasantry and urban poor—who had nothing to lose. Short of that, the different forms of politics, contests between political parties and so forth, had little significance. Again there were some variations in this position. Wallerstein had more to say about politics and a less reductionist view of the state but still ultimately saw strong states as a feature of the developed world and reinforcing capitalist interests. Even more exceptional were Cardoso and Faletto (1979), who used a comparison of Argentina and Brazil, two countries in which 'associated dependent development' had been possible, to develop a complex political analysis. This showed two things. First, politics was not simply about external processes of domination but also involved national processes of reconciling and incorporating newly mobilized social groups. Second, the actual content of domestic politics differed from one developing country to another, reflecting differing resource bases and levels of foreign intervention.

With the possible exception of Cardoso and Faletto, dependency theory shed little direct light on the political process as such within developing countries. Its real contributions were to insist on the intimate link between politics and economics, which had been largely neglected in the politics of modernization literature, and to demonstrate that the domestic politics of developing countries was incomprehensible without reference to their position within the world capitalist system.

Neo-Marxism rediscovers politics

Despite its Marxist associations, dependency theory had many neo-Marxist critics. In an argument paralleling modernization revisionists' criticism of modernization theory, they rejected its assumption that capitalism wiped out pre-capitalist forms. This view, they argued, was based on falsely equating capitalism with the market, rather than seeing it as a system of production. In fact capitalism as a dominant 'mode of production' could interact or 'articulate' with pre-capitalist modes. This further implied that different 'social formations' or countries on the periphery could have very different social systems (see Foster-Carter 1978).

At a more directly political level, neo-Marxist interest in developing societies was also stimulated by hopes that the socialist revolution that had failed to materialize in the West would begin there instead. Such hopes were raised by a 'third wave' of revolutionary developments (following a first wave centred on China, and a second wave from the late 1950s including Cuba and Algeria). The third wave from the late 1960s included communist victories in Vietnam, Cambodia, and Laos, revolution in Ethiopia, overthrow of Portuguese regimes in Africa, and revolution in Nicaragua (Cammack 1997). For these reasons neo-Marxists engaged in a much more detailed and rigorous analysis of social structure that was in some sense aimed at assessing the eligibility of different social categories—peasants, the lumpenproletariat (the urban poor who were not regular wage-earners), and so on—to inherit the role of revolutionary vanguard originally attributed to the industrial working class. As with 'modernization revisionism' this generated much valuable, careful research into what developing societies were actually like, although the appropriateness of the Marxist categories of social analysis imposed on them was often questionable.

As a corollary of this less determinist view of politics, there was a new interest in what Marxists typically referred to as the 'post-colonial state'. Marx himself generally depicted the state as a simple instrument of class domination—in the famous words of the *Communist Manifesto* (1872): 'The executive of the modern state is but a committee for managing the common affairs of the whole bourgeoisie.' But his writings sometimes alluded to a second possibility, as in France during the second empire under Louis Napoleon, when the weakness or divisions of the bourgeoisie allowed an authoritarian state to emerge that was 'relatively autonomous' from any particular social class. This notion was taken further by neo-Marxists such as Antonio Gramsci (1891–1937) and later Nicos Poulantzas (1936–79) analysing capitalist states in the West, but was also subsequently seized on to explore the relationship between the state and social classes in post-colonial societies. Hamza Alavi (1979), for instance, argued, with particular reference to Pakistan, that the post-colonial state enjoyed a high degree of autonomy. This was first because it had to mediate between no fewer than three ruling classes, but second because it had inherited a colonial state apparatus that was 'overdeveloped' in relation to society because its original role was holding down a subject people (others later questioned whether the post-colonial state in Africa could be described as overdeveloped, however). With reference to some African countries, there were also debates about whether the state itself could give rise to a new ruling class.

Globalization theory

By the early 1980s, and despite their diametrically opposed starting points, it is possible to argue that the lines of thought evolving out of early political development theory, on the one hand, and dependency theory, on the other, were converging around a reappreciation of the independent importance of 'the political' and an interest in strong government and/or the state. But both these lines of thought were also tending to run out of steam. Although strong government arguments gave the politics of modernization perspective a seeming new lease of life and, Higgott (1983) suggests, such

arguments persisted into the 1980s in the guise of a spate of public policy studies, this whole approach remained vulnerable to the charge of insufficient attention to the economic and international context. The Marxist-inspired approach never in any case enjoyed levels of research funding comparable with the more mainstream modernization approach; if dependency theory was increasingly challenged by the experience of oil-producing states in the Gulf, **newly industrializing countries** (NICs), and so forth, by the mid-1980s the neo-Marxist focus on socialist revolution in turn appeared increasingly anachronistic.

Reflecting these changes in the global environment, by the 1990s a new 'macro' approach was emerging, globalization theory, which tended both to absorb and displace the previous two (for a valuable overview, see McGrew 1992). Globalization theory (see Chapters 4 and 15) should more properly be referred to as globalization theories, since it takes many different forms. As with the previous two approaches, it can also often seem closer to an ideology or policy strategy than a theoretical framework. Globalization theory focuses on a process of accelerated communication and economic integration that transcends national boundaries and increasingly incorporates all parts of the world into a single social system. Although this process is often seen as originating in the distant past, there is general agreement that it accelerated in particular from the 1970s, spurred by developments in transport and communications and subsequently by the collapse of the Soviet bloc and end of the cold war.

Probably the most important dimension of this process is economic, with particular attention paid to developments in global trade, foreign direct investment, and finance (see Chapter 4). Associated with these economic trends, however, has been a significant cultural dimension of globalization that is increasing cultural awareness and interaction across national boundaries. Central to this process has been the remarkable development and expansion of information technology and the new electronic mass media, enormously extending the scope and immediacy of communication. The consequences of this process are undoubtedly complex and contentious. Despite the emergence of powerful media industries in a number of developing countries such as India, Brazil, and Mexico, it is questionable just how truly 'global', in the sense of multi-directional, cultural communications have yet become. For writers like Sklair (1991: 41) the predominance of US-based media conglomerates has meant the diffusion of images and lifestyles that promote the 'culture-ideology of consumerism'. By the same token, however, the perceived threat of cultural globalization has prompted complex counter-trends, including reassertion of local and national cultural identities (on religious identity, see Chapter 8).

Different forms of globalization theory emphasize different aspects—economic, cultural, and so on. They differ in what they understand to be the prime moving mechanism of the globalization process: some see it as driven by the underlying logic of unfolding capitalism; others as primarily a consequence of developments in communications; others as a combination of factors. Some accounts, echoing modernization theory, are essentially optimistic: they stress, for instance, the extent to which a globalizing economy, in which capital is increasingly mobile, hugely extends opportunities for investment and employment for those who are enterprising and adaptable. Others, echoing the mistrust and many of the arguments of dependency theory, are pessimistic; they depict an increasingly unfettered global capitalism, ruthlessly exploiting people and resources (such themes have of course been taken up by the so-called 'anti-globalization' movement).

Although the voluminous literature on globalization has relatively little directly to say about politics in the developing world, its implications are far-reaching. First, it suggests changes in the character of politics as a whole. While it would be premature to talk about a process of political globalization comparable with what is claimed in the economic and cultural spheres, one can point to a series of developments that incline that way, including the increasing perceived urgency of a number of issues—such as global warming, refugee flows, terrorism—the origins and solutions of which transcend national borders, the proliferation of international regulatory organizations, and non-governmental organizations, and the growth of transnational social movements.

At the same time, globalization theory emphasizes ways in which the nation-state is losing autonomy (see also Chapter 15). It is increasingly difficult for the individual state to control the flow of information across its borders or to protect its people from global security threats. Likewise, globalizing trends have greatly reduced its economic options, for instance, its ability to fend off the consequences of economic upheaval elsewhere, such as the 1997 East Asia financial crisis, or to successfully promote 'Keynesian' economic policies, to enhance welfare and protect employment, when these run counter to the logic of the global economy. With reduced autonomy comes reduction in the state's perceived competence and accordingly in its legitimacy. It comes under increasing pressure from within, as well as without, contributing to a process of 'hollowing out' the state.

Critics of the globalization thesis have long argued that this greatly overstates the threat posed to the nation-state, pointing out, for example, that many states, including the East Asian NICs, have actively promoted and benefited from the process of economic globalization, and suggesting that states may be able to invoke or harness nationalist reaction to globalizing pressures as an alternative source of legitimacy, as in India. More recently such debates have paid more systematic attention to the experience of developing countries. Mosley (2005) finds that in a number of the more developed countries in South America, and where there was the political will, the state has been better placed to resist these global pressures. Following the 1997 financial crisis and during the most recent global financial crisis (2008–09) it has been noted that a number of emerging economies, notably China and India but also others such as Malaysia and Indonesia, had retained sufficient protective regulation in place to withstand the worst economic consequences. However, these objections still seem less relevant for many of the poorer, smaller developing countries. Clapham (2002: 785) suggests that in such countries 'the logic of incorporation into the modern global system . . . has undermined the state's coercive capabilities, weakened its legitimacy and subverted its capacity to manage the inevitable engagement with the global economy'.

But globalization theory also creates difficulties for the notion of a distinct developing world. Even if we talk about a developing world rather than a Third World and are careful about which countries we include or exclude, this still implies a distinct geographic entity. However, globalization theorists like Berger argue that if we want to retain the idea of a third or developing world, this should be conceived of in sociological rather than geographic terms. The ongoing process of economic globalization means that economically based social classes are increasingly transnational or global in span. So, on this analysis, dominant classes in the developing world are more oriented, economically and culturally, to Western capitalist centres, where 'they have their bank accounts, maintain business links, own homes and send their children to school', than to their own countries (Berger 1994: 268). On the other hand, countries in the developed world, not least the United States, each have their own underclass (or 'Third' or developing world), even if there are few signs that such underclasses are coming together at a global level.

Overall, it is difficult to assess the globalization perspective as a framework for understanding politics in the developing world, because it takes such a variety of forms and reflects such a range of ideological positions, extending from a messianic optimism that echoes the crassest forms of modernization theory to doom-laden warnings that come close to the claustrophobic determinism of unmodified dependency theory. However, arguably even the left-wing version of globalization theory goes much further than dependency theory in recognizing the *inter*dependence of developed and developing economies. Globalization theory is much more open-ended than dependency theory; ultimately it envisages an integrated global economy but in the shorter term acknowledges developments are unpredictable and could include increasing differentiation between beneficiaries and losers. Perhaps the theory's most valuable contribution to understanding politics in the developing world is that, like dependency theory, it emphasizes the impact of global processes. But in other ways it poses problems for this field of study. First, it calls into question the concept of the 'developing world' as a geographically distinct entity. Second, whilst it does not discount the political level, it tends to depict economic and/or technological change as driving cultural and political change and thereby to downplay the importance of the independent effects or autonomy of the 'political' and certainly of the state.

Key points

- The politics of modernization approach emerged in the 1950s, initially taking the form of political development theory.
- Political development theory was criticized by 'revisionists' for simplifying and underestimating the role of tradition and by advocates of political order for excessive optimism.
- From the left, dependency theory criticized the modernization approach for ignoring former colonies' continuing economic and thus political dependence.

- Neo-Marxists criticized dependency theory's determinism and explored the relative autonomy of politics and the state.
- Globalization theory, drawing on both modernization and dependency theory, emphasizes increasing global economic integration.
- Globalization theory calls into question both the importance of the state (although revisionist arguments are emerging) and the existence of a distinct developing world.

It is more difficult to characterize the study of politics in the developing world today. The main emerging trends will become clearer in retrospect but some preliminary comments are in order.

A state of 'disarray'?

Both modernization-based approaches and Marxist-inspired approaches were found increasingly wanting by the 1980s. Although globalization theory incorporates significant elements of both, it too tends to undermine the rationale for studying politics in the developing world as a distinct field. Moreover, globalization theory reflects changes in the real world, including increasing differentiation amongst countries of the 'developing world', which pose further problems for meaningful generalization.

These developments within the field have coincided with a wider disillusionment with attempts at grand theory-building in the social sciences. (Globalization theory may well seem an obvious exception to this aversion, but it has been attacked precisely for its sweeping generalizations and also it nonetheless contrives to be extraordinarily open-ended and flexible.) One general school of thinking, originating in linguistics and philosophy, that has contributed to and helped to articulate such misgivings has been post-structuralism. The approach adopted by **post-structuralists**, discussed further below, questions the epistemological basis and claims of all the great theoretical approaches or 'meta-narratives' such as liberalism, Marxism, or indeed 'modernization'.

There has also been a steady growth of information about politics in different developing countries since the first attempts at generalization in the 1950s. Western governments, above all the US government, have funded research and teaching, some of it under the rubric of 'area studies'. Professional associations of area specialists, conferences,

and journals have proliferated. At the same time, political science expertise—concerning both the country in question and politics in developing countries more broadly—is expanding in a growing number of developing countries: not just in India where authors like Rajni Kothari have been challenging received thinking over many decades, but for instance in Mexico, Chile, Argentina, Brazil, Thailand, South Korea, Taiwan, and South Africa. Admittedly such indigenous authors often gravitate to the relative comfort and security of American universities; Africa for instance has its own 'academic diaspora'. The ranks of these indigenous authors are swelling all the time but include, for example, Guillermo O'Donnell, from Argentina, who devised the influential concept of 'delegative democracy' (see Chapter 14); Arturo Escobar from Colombia who is associated with the notion of 'post-development' (see below); Doh Chull Shin from South Korea who has written on democracy with special reference to that country's experience (see Chapter 22b) and Claude Ake, from Nigeria (who died in 1996).

Claude Ake is significant precisely for developing quite a powerful and influential argument against Western social science, and its approach to the developing world, including the theory of political development. He accused this approach of implicitly promoting capitalism and imperialist values (see Harris 2005). For instance in *Development and Democracy in Africa* (1996), Ake maintains that both national African political elites and Western agents have used the ideology of development to serve their own political ends and without heed to its relevance for Africa (see Box 1.3)—an argument that struck a responsive chord amongst African academics.

All of this has heightened awareness of the complexity and diversity of politics across this great tranche of the world's countries. Surveying all these developments, one might well conclude that politics in the developing world no longer even has pretensions to being a coherent field of study; rather, to quote Manor (1991: 1), it is 'in disarray'. Contributions to the debate that emphasise the distinctiveness of Asian values and the idea that Muslims have different political requirements compared to non-Muslims (both these contributions are discussed in Chapter 18) lend additional support to this finding.

> **Box 1.3** Claude Ake on the Ideology of Development
>
> . . .the paradigm was conveniently abstract. It paid little heed to historical specificity and treated the development process as something in no way connected to it cultural, institutional and political context . . . For the external patrons of the development paradigm, its abstract universalism allowed them to package their experience as universal and objectively necessary. For African leaders, it secured the liberty to use African culture selectively and opportunistically and to adopt whatever political institutions and practices suited their convenience. The problem was that the qualities that made the development paradigm so functional for those purposes also limited its usefulness as a tool of societal transformation and economic development.
>
> (Ake 1996: 17)

Themes and agendas

But a consideration of the general character of publication and research in the broad field of politics in the developing world over the last few years suggests that this is an exaggeration. Even though one of the logical implications of globalization theories may be to call the need for this distinct field into question, the frequent presence in such work of ideas about globalization does provide one significant element of theoretical common ground. Moreover, against this globalization background, three, partly overlapping, themes or research issues tend to predominate and shape lines of current comparative inquiry.

One is democratization (see Chapter 14). When the **third wave of democracy** broke in the mid-1970s, spreading through South America in the 1980s and much of tropical Africa in the 1990s, it served to confound the expectations of a generation of political scientists who had come to see political authoritarianism or decay as an intrinsic political feature of the developing world. Nonetheless, the global reach of democratization was extended not only as a consequence of pressures within developing countries, or of the collapse of the Soviet bloc and end of the cold war, but by more deliberate interventions of Western governments and intergovernmental organizations. As Chapter 14 describes, these included attaching political conditions to forms of economic assistance but also more direct international **democracy promotion** through financial and other forms of support to democracy projects. Linked to this drive, Western government and research foundation funding has helped to generate a huge literature apparently covering every aspect of democratic transition, including analysis of the effectiveness of international democracy assistance.

The second theme is the relationship between politics and economic development or growth. This overlaps with the theme of democratization since an influential strand of thinking now sees good governance and even democracy as a prerequisite of economic growth. As noted by Leftwich (1993), this represents an inversion of the early political development literature in which economic growth was generally assumed to be a condition of democracy. The concern with the politics of growth has also led to a reassessment of the importance of the state by bodies like the World Bank, which opened its 1997 report, *The State in a Changing World*, by declaring that the state is central to economic and social development, not so much as a direct provider of growth but rather as a partner, catalyst, and facilitator. The 2008–09 global financial crisis has reinforced this interest as observers debate which kinds of political arrangement have been associated with the most resilient economies. It has also led to an interest in the economic role played by civil society organizations and **social capital**. This theme, again, lacks a fully elaborated theoretical context but owes something to the strong government variant of the politics of modernization. But again, like the democratization theme, it is clearly partly driven by concerns of Western governments and intergovernmental organizations.

A third prominent theme concerns peace, stability, and security versus conflict and risk. Again this overlaps with the two previous themes: domestic conflict inhibits the emergence of political conditions conducive to economic growth, for instance, whilst many champions of democratization believe that democratic values and institutions provide the best guarantee both of domestic and of international security and order. The growing focus on causes and consequences of conflict and instability within developing countries is also, however, due to the perception that such conflict has been on the increase since the end of the cold war. An additional impetus has been the perceived need to combat international **terrorism**, heightened in the wake of September 11. In this context there has been particular interest, on the one hand, in the pathology of 'failing' and 'failed' or **collapsed states** and, on the other, in the 'politics of identity', especially ethnic and religious identity, in developing countries (see Chapters 7 and 8). Building on this theme, the most recent trend has been in analysis of the record and challenges of state-building in post-conflict societies (see Chapter 13).

These three themes do not amount to, or derive from, one coherent analytic framework, although they echo and incorporate elements of the earlier dominant paradigms as well as globalization ideas. But they do overlap in the sense that democratization, economic performance, and the presence or absence of internal conflict either do, or are seen to, significantly affect one another. These themes also clearly relate to observable trends in the developing world and resonate strongly with important constituencies there. At the same time, however, they reflect the concerns, interests, and research-funding priorities of international agencies, Western governments, and to a lesser extent **non-governmental organizations** (NGOs).

In pursuing these agendas of inquiry, then, political analysts have tended to eschew 'macro' political frameworks or narratives but, in keeping with trends in political science as a whole, have been more inclined to work with more modest 'middle-range' theories. These focus on particular issues or subsets of political structures or processes, for instance electoral systems, party systems, neo-patrimonial regimes, democratic **developmental states**, and corruption. And in many cases they involve applying or developing concepts and propositions that derive from reflection on experience in the developed world.

One further feature of much recent analysis of politics in developing countries, already alluded to in this volume's Introduction, is the importance attached to political institutions. This is again part of a broader trend in contemporary political science from the 1980s. The new institutionalism is only partly new of course, in that it is rearticulating what has been a longstanding concern in political science. But the new version has tended to adopt a very broad understanding of institutions as sets of rules that constrain individual behaviour, and there is an emphasis on informal as well as formal rules. Chapter 3 provides a greatly extended overview of this approach and the way it has been applied in analysing the politics of developing countries.

Strategies and Methods of Analysis

As noted earlier, the tendency when analysing the politics of developing countries has been to use the strategies and more specific methods of analysis that have been developed within 'mainstream' and Western political science. This was always to an extent the case but is even more noticeable now that the notion of a distinct 'developing world' is increasingly problematized. The politics of individual developing countries is studied in the context of area or regional studies (for instance centred on Latin America, the Caribbean, or South Asia), or as part of cross-national and regional thematic inquiries (for instance into executive–legislative relations or corruption). There has also latterly been some tendency to emphasize the international or global dimension of politics, for example the increasing salience of the religious dimension of politics (see Chapter 8), in individual developing countries, especially those in sub-Saharan Africa. The implicit argument is that, in such countries, external determinants are so powerful that apparently domestic political processes are best understood through the prism of international political economy and international relations approaches.

Most commonly, studies of developing country politics fall into the broad category of comparative politics. Accordingly we find a range of comparative 'strategies' deployed. First is the case study approach, in which the politics of a single country

is explored in some depth. In theory at least, such exploration should be informed by a research agenda reflecting a wider body of comparative research and should aim to test or generate propositions relating to that research. Case studies that simply celebrate the 'exceptionalism' of the country in question would not be considered proper social science, although of course even the idea of an 'exception' implies a broader pattern that is being deviated from. More middle-range comparative studies focus on particular questions. They may use a subset of cases (such as countries, local governments, parties) selected to illuminate the matter in question. In a methodological distinction going back to J. S. Mill (1888), cases in a 'most similar' design will be similar in a number of key respects whilst differing in regard to the variable being explored. In a 'most different' design they will differ in many key respects but not as regards that variable. In-depth qualitative analysis, often involving a historical perspective, will aim to identify particular factors associated with the variable under review. A good example of such an approach is Bratton and Van de Walle's study of *Democratic Experiments in Africa* (1997). Alternatively studies take a 'large N' of cases and use statistical methods to manipulate comparative data. The availability of such data is steadily growing. They include, for instance, election results and survey data collected through instruments like Latinobarometer and Afrobarometer, and the databases collected by Freedom House, Transparency International and the Governance Matters project (see Chapter 15). Such an approach, increasingly favoured within mainstream political science and international relations, can yield valuable and counter-intuitive findings, but is of course heavily dependent on the availability of data that are reliable, valid, and appropriate (for an excellent account of these issues, see Landman 2003).

In arriving at propositions to be explored, or even tested statistically, studies draw on existing studies and middle-range theorizing. Some, however, establish their own central propositions more systematically and deductively, building on the precepts of rational choice theory. This is an approach that takes as its primary unit of analysis the individual actor who is presumed to make rational choices on the basis of self-interest. Within the framework of the 'new institutionalism' the focus is on the way in which institutional incentives and opportunities influence the individual's strategic calculations. As discussed further in Chapter 3, this approach has recently been very evident in work on constitutional and electoral systems design in new democracies.

The dominant assumption in the 'mainstream' comparative strategies and methods of analysis explored so far is that it is appropriate to apply them in contexts differing from those in which they first evolved. This is in many ways an attractive argument that emphasizes what is common and continuous in human experience—in contrast to those that point to possibly unbridgeable cultural differences, as is said to be the case in forms of 'Orientalism' discussed below. Nonetheless, there is a danger, unless these approaches are used sensitively, that aspects of politics in developing countries will be wrongly assumed or misinterpreted. For a long time comparative political analysts have been warned to beware of concept-stretching and to ensure that the concepts they use actually do 'travel'. We have seen the dangers of inadvertently projecting assumptions from a Western to a developing country setting in the elaboration of Almond's

structural-functional model. More recently, doubts have been raised about the relevance of rational choice theory, for instance in contexts in which cultural values weigh heavily; indeed, the notion of rational choice itself could be seen as the product of a specific US social science culture.

Here we can consider the contribution of alternative approaches that focus more centrally on issues of meaning and thus potentially suffer less from problems of cultural imposition or misinterpretation—constructivism and **discourse theory**. Constructivism or the application of constructivist epistemology—the idea that central concepts like 'power' or 'ethnicity' through which we organize our understanding are themselves 'socially constructed'—has been at the heart of a major challenge to traditional thinking in the field of international relations. Within comparative politics it is less a case of explicit confrontation and more one of reasonably amicable coexistence and a de facto division of labour. Thus constructivism is used particularly in analyses of the construction of political identities, for instance ethno-political identity (see Chapter 7).

Post-structural or 'discourse' approaches go much further than constructivism, in questioning the very epistemological foundations of knowledge, including political science. Within the study of politics, the ideas of Michel Foucault (1926–84) have been especially influential. He understood political processes, institutions, and indeed 'subjects' (actors) to be constructed through dominant 'discourses', understood not simply as language and ideas but also as the practices embodying them. A central concern of discourse theorists then has been to trace the governing rules (archaeology) and originating historical practices (genealogy) of such discourses. Whilst rigorous applications of this approach can be found for instance in Norval's (1996) analysis of apartheid ideology in South Africa, more typically its concepts and arguments have been drawn on selectively (as in some of the chapters in Manor 1991). As with constructivism, in practice within political studies, discourse-related approaches tend to be applied to particular issues, notably the constitution of political identities, including social movements, the articulation of hegemonic ideologies, and the construction of social or political antagonisms.

Key points

- Politics in developing countries is generally studied using 'mainstream' political science comparative strategies and methods, although these may not always be appropriate or sensitively applied.

- Constructivist and post-structural approaches run less risk of misrepresentation but have a limited range of applications.

Critical Perspectives

As the field of developing country politics has become more fragmented and complex, with no clearly dominant narrative in the way that the 'modernization' narrative dominated before, so it has become more difficult to identify a main line of critique. Within the broad compass of globalization theory, the debates between the liberal-modernizers and radical-socialists certainly persist, as we can see for instance in disagreements over the criteria for democratic consolidation or deepening (see Chapter 14), or for **good governance** (Chapter 15). At the same time alternative critical perspectives have emerged, although these are directed less at politics as commonly understood and more at social science understandings of development and non-'Western' societies. I shall consider here two in particular, both of which have tended to be associated, although by no means inevitably so, with post-structural modes of argument. Neither, it must be emphasized, originates within political studies or has had a major impact on the way in which politics in the developing world is studied. But each raises serious issues for those engaged in this field.

First is the critique associated with the notion of **Orientalism**. In his influential book, published in 1978, Edward Said wrote about the lens of 'Orientalism' through which many Western scholars have interpreted Asian and Middle Eastern societies, in imperial times. This discourse, which tended to 'essentialize' such societies, rendering them as exotic and 'Other', could also be seen as instrumental to the political aims of the imperialist powers (although it was not confined to them, as demonstrated in Marx's account of the 'Asiatic' mode of production). Although Said was primarily writing from a historical and cultural viewpoint, subsequently he argued that Orientalist discourse was being revived in the post-cold war context, and especially after September 11, to help to justify US policy in the Middle East. Huntington's (1996a) **clash of civilizations** thesis (see Chapter 7) could seem to bear out this perception.

Said's work is said to have inspired a broader movement of 'post-colonial studies'. Specifically in India it stimulated the emergence of 'subaltern studies', the original rationale of which was to rewrite India's colonial history from the standpoint of the oppressed, subaltern classes (for a fuller discussion of these developments, see Chapter 2). At the same time it generated much criticism. Halliday (1993), for instance, claims first that Said insufficiently acknowledged earlier formulators of this critique, and second that the notion of Orientalism has itself been too static, and overgeneralized.

Second is the critique that has emerged in different forms of the assumptions of development theory and the development 'industry', referred to as post-development theory. This entails a criticism of development as discourse. A forerunner, as we have seen, was Claude Ake with his indictment of development as ideology. Another influential exponent, who more explicitly situates himself within the parameters of discourse theory, is Arturo Escobar (1995). Escobar, who incidentally acknowledges a debt to Said, suggests that whatever kind of development is advocated, whether capitalist or 'alternative', there is still the assumption that developing countries have to be made to change, which helps to rationalize continuing intervention of outside interests, experts, perspectives, and so forth. Ferguson (1997) has also written about external intervention in Lesotho, drawing a contrast between the repeated 'failure' of development projects and the significance of their apparently unintentional political side-effects (see Box 1.4). Again such arguments have generated much counter-criticism, not least that 'development' is not just an elite preoccupation but also an almost universal aspiration.

Both these kinds of critique—of Orientalist thinking and of developmentalism—have implications for the way we think about politics in developing countries. It is probably fair to say they are stronger on pointing out problematic assumptions in mainstream literature than in offering satisfactory alternative approaches. Nonetheless, considering that these potential critiques have been around for well over ten years, their impact in this field has so far been quite limited.

Box 1.4 The Development Industry in Lesotho

Lesotho is a small landlocked country in southern Africa with a population of around 1.3 m. Ferguson (1997) lists 72 international agencies and non- and quasi-governmental organizations operating in Lesotho, and notes that in 1979 it received some $64 m in official development assistance.

" What is this massive internationalist intervention, aimed at a country that surely does not appear to be of especially great economic or strategic importance?... Again and again development projects in Lesotho are launched, and again and again they fail: but no matter how many times this happens there always seems to be someone ready to try again with yet another project. In the pages that follow, I will try to show... how outcomes that at first appear as mere "side-effects" of an unsuccessful attempt to engineer an economic transformation become legible in another perspective as unintended yet instrumental elements in a resultant constellation that has the effect of expanding the exercise of a particular sort of state power while simultaneously exerting a powerful depoliticizing effect.

"" (Ferguson 1997: 7–21 *passim*)

Key points

- In addition to continuing arguments between liberal and socialist-inspired camps, new critiques of conventional forms of social science have emerged drawing on discourse theory.

- In particular, the critique of Orientalism and post-development arguments are relevant for studying politics in developing countries, although their impact has been limited.

The dominant paradigms in the past, associated with modernization theory and dependency theory, were valuable to the extent that, by suggesting the importance of particular factors or relationships, they helped to generate debate; also, they encouraged political analysis and generalization beyond the particularities of individual country case studies. But at the same time, they were overgeneralized, excessively influenced by Western ideological assumptions and agendas, whether 'bourgeois' or 'radical', and Western historical experience, and based on inadequate knowledge and understanding of the developing world itself. They created, as Cammack, Pool, and Tordoff (1993: 3) phrased it, 'a problem of premature and excessive theorization'.

Over time our knowledge of the developing world has grown and with it inevitably our awareness of its diversity and complexity. Moreover, that developing world itself has become increasingly differentiated. Especially in the context of globalization theory, this greater recognition of diversity has called into question the coherence of the developing world as a geographic — and political — category. These developments have coincided with a tendency for political science to rein in its theoretical aspirations, focusing on 'middle range' rather than grand theory. Post-structural thinking has also diminished the appeal of grand interpretative narratives.

Presently, then, whilst globalization theory continues to provide an implicit backdrop to much political analysis, the field of politics in the developing world has become less obviously coherent. However, it is possible to perceive an implicit agenda of inquiry, focusing around democracy or governance, development and conflict and — still — strongly influenced by Western interests and perspectives. At the same time radical, critical perspectives persist. In addition to a continuing Marxist-inspired materialist critique can be found alternative critiques, some of them emanating from 'indigenous' sources, that seek to problematize the whole enterprise of 'Western' attempts to understand and influence politics in developing countries. For many of us, this may be a step too far but we should by now recognize the need to proceed with all caution and humility.

1. What were the main shortcomings of political development theory as a way of understanding politics in the developing world?

2. In what ways does globalization theory draw on modernization theory and dependency theory?

3. What are the implications of globalization theory both for the character of politics in the developing world and the way in which it should be studied?

4. Which theoretical approaches to politics in the developing world shed most light on the relative autonomy of politics and the state?

5. Is the study of politics in the developing world currently in 'disarray'?

6. Do we need a distinct theoretical framework for analysing politics in the developing world?

7. In what ways is Said's critique of 'Orientalism' relevant to the understanding of politics in developing countries?

8. To what extent do mainstream approaches to the analysis of politics in 'developing countries' embody or impose an ideology of development?

9. Discuss, with examples, the extent to which the concepts and assumptions of political development theory still influence the way in which we understand politics in the developing world.

10. Critically assess the pros and cons of employing rational choice approaches in analysing politics in developing countries.

→ **Further reading**

■ Berger, M. (ed.) (2004), 'After the Third World?', special issue of *Third World Quarterly*, 25/1. Collection of articles that reflect upon the historical significance and contemporary relevance of the notion of a 'third world'.

■ Cammack, P. (1997), *Capitalism and Democracy in the Third World: The Doctrine for Political Development* (Leicester: Leicester University Press). Well-argued, critical reflection, from a left-wing perspective, upon 'mainstream' accounts of the political development literature.

■ Hagopian, F. (2000), 'Political Development Revisited', *Comparative Political Studies*, 33/6 and 7: 880–911. Retrospective overview of political development thinking.

■ Higgott, R. A. (1983), *Political Development Theory* (London/Canberra: Croom-Helm). Account of the development and persistence of political development thinking.

■ Manor, J. (ed.) (1991), *Rethinking Third World Politics* (London: Longman). Collection of essays, some using post-structuralist concepts or approaches, seeking to go beyond old theoretical perspectives.

■ Moore, M. (2000), 'Political Underdevelopment', Paper presented to Tenth Anniversary of the Institute of Development Studies Conference, 7–8 September, available at www.ids.ac.uk/ids/govern. Attempt to rework the notion of political development, focusing on state legitimacy.

■ Randall, V. and Theobald, R. (1998), *Political Change and Underdevelopment: A Critical Introduction to Third World Politics*, 2nd edn (London: Macmillan). Provides an account of theories and debates concerning politics in the developing world, from political development to globalization.

■ Said, E. (1995, originally published in 1978), *Orientalism* (Harmondsworth: Penguin). Influential critique of 'orientalist' approaches to history and culture.

■ Smith, B. C. (2008), *Understanding Third World Politics*, 3rd edn (Basingstoke: Palgrave). Useful, recently updated, overview of themes in the study of the politics of the developing world.

Web links

■ http://faculty.hope.edu/toppen/pol242/   Hope College course website providing materials on the scope and methods of political science.

■ http://justtheory.com/   Collaborative site allowing users a further opportunity to explore post-structuralist ideas.

Online Resource Centre

For additional material and resources, please visit the Online Resource Centre at:
www.oxfordtextbooks.co.uk/orc/burnell3e/

2

Colonialism and Post-Colonial Development

James Chiriyankandath

 Overview

The variety of states and societies found in the developing two-thirds of the world is reflected in their political diversity. The contemporary polities of the global South bear the imprint of the legacy of colonialism but are also marked both by their pre-colonial heritage and their different post-colonial experiences. This chapter traces these ingredients in the making of politics in the developing world. It argues that while the historically proximate experience of colonialism has had a significant impact on post-colonial political development, attention to the *longue durée*, and to political agency after independence, produce a more rounded and nuanced perspective on the varied politics found across the developing world. The different ways in which post-independence politicians reacted and adapted to—and were constrained by—the past legacies and present situations of their countries helped to determine the shape of the new polities.

Introduction: The Post-Colonial World

It is hard to imagine how just sixty years ago the world was dominated by mainly European empires. By 1921, 84 per cent of the earth had been colonized since the sixteenth century and, there were as many as 168 colonies (Go 2003: 17). Although, by the mid 1960s, most were, at least formally, independent, subsequent decades showed how much the spectre of colonization still loomed over the post-colonial world. While the varied history of **post-colonial states** illustrates the importance of their pre-colonial past, as well as of factors such as geography, geopolitics, and political agency, Hall (1996: 246, 253) points out that the fact that countries are not 'post-colonial' in the same way does not mean that they are not 'post-colonial'—colonization 'refigured the terrain' everywhere. At the very least, the concept of the post-colonial offers a point of entry for studying the differences between formerly colonial societies (Hoogvelt 1997: xv).

Whatever the varied reality of their present condition, their colonial background is still used to identify the contemporary states of the developing world with a pre-modern, traditional, backward past—the antithesis of the 'modern' post-imperial West (Slater 2004: 61–2). In this way, a colonial cast of mind persists, one that geopolitical power relations (North–South, West–non-West) make it very hard to shake off. One important result is the remarkable resilience of racialized discourse in the West when it comes to discussing issues such as migration and development, albeit one that shifted from being expressed in biological terms during the heyday of colonialism to being voiced in a socio-cultural idiom in the wake of decolonization (Duffield 2006; see also Wallerstein 2003: 124–48).

It is to this reality that the rise of post-colonial theory, especially in the field of cultural studies, sought to draw attention. Influenced by post-modernist and **post-structuralist** perceptions, it was born out of disillusionment with the failure of the Third World to, in Frantz Fanon's words, start a new history and 'set afoot a new man' (1967: 255). Going beyond a temporal understanding of post-colonialism, post-colonial theory sought to analyse its cultural aftermath: the 'cultures, discourses and critiques that lie *beyond*, but remain clearly influenced by colonialism' (McEwan 2009: 17).

Colonialism was the obvious place to start explaining why political independence had not resulted in the emancipation for which people like Fanon, a black psychiatrist from the French Caribbean who devoted himself to the Algerian struggle for independence, yearned. The problem appeared to be that the emancipatory project, belying the hope expressed by Fanon, had been fatally undermined by its 'imperial genealogy' (Cooper 2005: 25). However, while a number of political scientists, historians, and anthropologists (Crawford Young, Mahmood Mamdani, Bernard Cohn, and Nicholas Dirks among them) sought to analyse the lasting impact of colonialism on the colonized, much post-colonial theory has followed Edward Said's seminal work on **Orientalism** (1993; 1995) in focusing attention more on imperial intent than colonial consequence (for example, Viswanathan 1990). That the colonial past might be of great significance in determining the future of post-colonial states was recognized even as decolonization proceeded, although then it was adherents of what they saw as the imperial mission who were more inclined to do so. Margery Perham, colonial historian of British Africa, remarked in 1961:

> our vanishing empire has left behind it a large heritage of history which is loaded with bequests good, bad and indifferent. This neither they [the critics of colonialism] nor we can easily discard.
>
> (Perham 1963: 18)

Thirty years later, the interest aroused by post-colonial theorists served to refocus attention on the nature of the colonial legacy. Birmingham, writing of post-colonial Africa, highlights lasting geographical, financial, and cultural legacies: the remarkable persistence of colonial borders, trade and currency links (especially in the ex-French colonies), and the way in which 'the minds of many Africans continued to work on colonial assumptions' (1995: 6–8). Mayall and Payne, dealing with the 'Commonwealth Third World', suggested that the more durable legacies of the British Empire may have been its military and statist characteristics rather than ideologies such as **liberalism** and nationalism (1991: 3–5). It is also argued that direct British rule led to more successful development (Lange 2009), and that the reason why former British colonies may have fared better was the role of Christian Protestant missions and the autonomy they enjoyed in relation to the colonial state (Woodberry 2004).

That the impact of colonialism has been transformative rather than transitory is now widely accepted. Half a century or more after their independence, developing countries still live with colonialism (Sharkey 2003: 141; Dirks 2004: 1) (see Box 2.1). However, while some like the Kenyan academic and human rights campaigner Makau Mutua maintain that 'colonialism has been the single most important variable in determining the future of Africa' (2008: 34), others see colonialism's impact as more indirect—a conditioning agency rather than a determinant factor (Hyden 2006: 26).

Despite the differences in formation and practice between the European colonial powers, it is argued that the phenomenon of colonialism is united to a large extent by its legacies (Dirks 2004: 2). Yet differences in the trajectories of post-colonial development matter and require explanation. One way of attempting to do so that has been gaining currency is **path dependence**, an idea borrowed from economics. This emphasizes the importance of history—of choices made and those not—and the difficulties of changing a course once set. Yet, as we shall see, other factors also matter—geopolitical and strategic considerations and political agency.

Box 2.1 Colonizing the Mind

How to come to terms with the survival of not just institutional forms (administrative, legal, educational, military, religious) and languages (English, French, Portuguese, Spanish, Dutch) but the mentality bequeathed in part by the colonial heritage has been a preoccupation of Third World intellectuals. Some, like the Kenyan writer Ngũgĩ wa Thiong'o, sought a resolution to the dilemma by abandoning the colonial language (English) to write in their native tongue, in Ngũgĩ's case, Gĩkũyũ (Ngũgĩ 1986). However, mentality is shaped by much more than just the language used, and Partha Chatterjee and Ramachandra Guha have noted nationalism's role in embedding colonialist historiography into Indian understandings of India (Chatterjee 1986; Guha 1989), European history serving as a kind of *metahistory* (Chakrabarty 2003) that relegated the people of the developing world to being 'perpetual consumers of modernity' (Chatterjee 1993: 5). When it came to defining state forms and political structures, Indian nationalist and post-independence leaders, 'coloured by the ideas and institutions of Western colonialism' (Jalal 1995: 11), preferred the familiar structures of the British Raj. Although no African or Asian state went to the extent of the founders of the Brazilian republic, who in 1889 adapted the motto of Auguste Comte, the nineteenth-century French Positivist philosopher, in adding the words 'order and progress' to their flag, the post-Christian myth of modernity (Gray 2003: 103) certainly found many devotees across the developing world.

Key points

- Politics in developing countries are influenced by their pre-colonial heritage and colonial and post-colonial experiences.

- Virtually all developing countries are in some sense post-colonial, although not necessarily in the same ways. Post-colonial theory seeks to examine the continuing impact that colonialism has on post-colonial development.

- The impact of colonialism was transformative rather than transitory. As well as reshaping economic and political forms, it also changed the way people, especially the educated, came to see the world.

- Path dependence is a concept borrowed from economics that emphasizes the importance of history in shaping choices for states and societies.

It is plausibly argued that among the best predictors of the resilience of post-colonial states is whether the societies they contain possess a significant pre-colonial experience of statehood (Clapham 2000: 9). From this perspective, it is instructive to consider the political map of the pre-colonial world. Eighteenth-century Asia was dominated by states that included some of the world's largest empires (Ottoman Turkey, Safavid Iran, Mughal India, and Manchu China) with only sparsely populated Central Asia and the interior of the Arabian peninsula occupied by nomadic pastoral societies. In contrast, prior to the sixteenth-century Spanish and Portuguese conquest, the Americas were largely inhabited by dispersed hunter-gatherer, fishing, and farming communities. The important exceptions were the Inca empire on the western seaboard of South America and in Central America the Aztec empire, a number of smaller kingdoms, and Mayan city-states. Before being overwhelmed in the nineteenth-century European **scramble for Africa**, more than two-thirds of the African continent was also occupied by non-state societies with kingdoms and other state formations found only along its Arabized Mediterranean coast and scattered across more densely populated pockets south of the Sahara.

In the Americas colonization by European settlers resulted in the creation of some twenty independent settler states in the century following the US Declaration of Independence in 1776, making America 'post-colonial' before some European colonial powers like Germany, Italy, and Belgium had even become states, let alone acquired colonies (McEwan 2009: 51). In the 1900s Australia and New Zealand also became self-governing British dominions. The post-colonial experience of the USA, Canada, Australia, and New Zealand is thus quite distinct from that of Asian and African states, while Latin American states are distinguished by the varying admixture of European and indigenous native American elements in their social make-up. In recent years Latin American political leaders, especially those of, at least partly, non-European descent, such as Hugo Chávez in Venezuela (president from 1999) and Evo Morales in Bolivia (president from 2006), have sought to emphasize the latter, still visible in syncretic political, religious, and social practice. In Africa and Asia, European settlement was not a significant feature of colonization except for isolated instances such as French Algeria, the 'white' highlands of Kenya, and, most importantly, South Africa, where the white supremacist **apartheid** state was only displaced in 1994 (Chapter 20b).

Box 2.2 Africa's Geography and the Concept of Extraversion

The history of Africa has been profoundly influenced by its geography. Clapham describes the bases for states in pre-colonial sub-Saharan Africa as 'peculiarly feeble' with the few relatively densely populated pockets creating a very discontinuous pattern of state formation across the vast continent (2000: 5). It is this historical geography that the French political scientist Jean-François Bayart has in mind when elaborating the concept of extraversion to explain the politics of post-colonial Africa. He argues that the relatively weak development of its productive forces and its internal social struggles have, through history, combined to make political actors in Africa disposed to mobilize resources from their relationship with the external environment (1993: 21–2). The collaboration of African rulers in the transatlantic slave trade that resulted in the transportation of perhaps 11 million Africans to the Americas between the sixteenth and nineteenth centuries was the most notorious aspect of this. Afterwards, colonialism and its legacy only served to emphasize the operation of the logic of extraversion, reinforcing a strong indigenous tendency to favour trade and commerce over manufacture (Chabal 2009: 117).

Pre-colonial Africa featured a variety of polities, among which were the city-states (e.g. Kano) and empire-states (e.g. Songhai, Ghana, Mali, Asante) of the west (Mazrui 1986: 272–3), as well as conquest states, such as that of the Zulus in the south, emerging in the period preceding European colonial rule. African scholars (e.g. Mazrui 1986: 273; Mamdani 1996: 40) have stressed the discontinuity between the pre- and post-colonial state, Mahmood Mamdani blaming, in particular, the deliberate colonial generalization of the conquest state and the administrative chieftainship as the basic modes of African rulership that were to serve as the template for their practice of **indirect rule** (see below). The colonial rulers disregarded differences between societies and the restraints sometimes placed by tradition upon rulers. For instance, among the Akan of southern Ghana, the king (Asantehene) was chosen by a group of 'kingmakers' from among a number of candidates from a royal matrilineage and could be removed if deemed to have breached his oaths of office (Crook 2005: 1). In contrast, societies in northern Ghana had kings who ruled in a much more authoritarian manner, or had chiefs imposed by the British of a kind that did not previously exist. Basil Davidson, in contrasting the achievements of Meiji Japan with the Asante state, argues that colonialism prevented the potential for the natural maturing of pre-colonial African institutions (1992), but this is unconvincing given the continent's relative economic backwardness and the deeply rooted historical factors that gave rise to the logic of **extraversion** (see Box 2.2). Reinforced by its relative isolation, nineteenth-century Japan was a nation-state in being—'Meiji political nationalism [creating] the modern Japanese nation on the basis of aristocratic (*samurai*) culture and its ethnic state' (Smith 1991: 105). There were hardly any pre-colonial nation-states in sub-Saharan Africa—although there might be a case for suggesting that Buganda in East Africa, what is now southern Uganda, was one (Green 2005)—an important reason why most African countries remain preoccupied by state formation rather than state consolidation (Hyden 2006: 70).

Pre-colonial Asia represented a considerable contrast to sub-Saharan Africa in being dominated by states, albeit diverse in size, depth, and durability. Indeed, the Mughal empire that flourished in India between the sixteenth and eighteenth centuries dwarfed its European counterparts in extent, population, and wealth, as did the Ming and, subsequently, Manchu, empires in China and the Ottoman and Safavid empires to the west. Only in the Philippines did the establishment of Spanish dominion in the sixteenth century largely succeed in erasing the pre-colonial past from history (the country has the dubious distinction of being the only post-colonial state that bears the name of a colonial ruler, Philip II of Spain). In terms of prior state tradition there is no gainsaying the antiquity of those in the rest of Asia. Yet, at first glance, the lineage of the post-colonial states of Asia too seems to owe far more to their immediate colonial predecessors than their historic traditions.

There are a number of reasons for this. Perhaps most important are the obvious institutional, and more subtly influential ideological, legacies of colonialism, both of which appear more tangible despite the efforts to trace a pre-colonial ideological lineage, not least by nationalist leaders like India's Jawaharlal Nehru (1961). Typically, descriptions of post-colonial institutions *begin* with the colonial past. For instance, an account of the Indian parliament by its then Secretary-General (chief administrative officer) devoted barely two unconvincing pages to the pre-colonial period, almost wholly focused on ancient India—the two millennia prior to the advent of British rule were thought to merit less than a sentence (Kashyap 1989: 1–3)! While between one and two centuries of British dominion over the subcontinent may have left only a slight imprint on aspects of the everyday lives of many people, especially in the more rural and remote areas, it was long enough, and the nature of the contrast stark enough, to alter the context of government and politics fundamentally.

Anthropologists have been better at capturing this alteration than political historians or political scientists (Cohn 1996; Dirks 2001). Bernard Cohn notes that while 'Europeans of the seventeenth century lived in a world of signs and correspondences . . . Indians lived in a world of substances' (1996: 18). His phrase captures a profound shift in how people first constituted and then transmitted, perceived, and interpreted authority and social relations. In the mentality of government, the malleability and pliability afforded by 'substance' gave way to the unyielding notional rigour of scientific classification—the intention being to set rigid boundaries so as to control variety and difference. As Cohn put it, the 'command of language' was paired with the 'language of command' (1996: 16). While this did not erase the legacy of the pre-colonial, it certainly transformed it. How it did so is what we shall now consider in examining patterns of colonial rule.

Key points

- Varying patterns of state formation in pre-colonial Africa, Asia, the Americas, and Australasia influenced both the kind of colonization they experienced and post-colonial development.

- The post-colonial experience of areas that were the focus of European settlement is quite distinct from that of Asia and Africa. However, in Latin America indigenous American influences are still perceptible.

- It has been argued that the geography and demography of Africa has had a significant influence in the persistent weakness of states, as reflected in Bayart's theory of extraversion.

- However, even in Asia, where the pre-colonial era was one dominated by state societies, the colonial state appears to have had a profound effect on the development of politics and government.

Colonial Patterns

The era of European colonialism overseas was proclaimed in 1493, a year after Christopher Columbus's 'discovery' of America, when Pope Alexander VI apportioned newly discovered non-Christian lands between the two main Catholic maritime powers of the day, Spain and Portugal. Over the next four-and-a-half centuries, the scope of European settlement and dominion expanded to cover the whole of the Americas and much of South and South East Asia, Oceania (including Australia and New Zealand), Africa, and the Arab Middle East. Typically beginning with small coastal, generally commercial enclaves, they subsequently expanded to cover the hinterland as conquest followed trade. The different periods in which regions were colonized by a number of European states (Spain and Portugal being followed by Holland, England, and France in the course of the sixteenth and seventeenth centuries, and by Belgium, Germany, and Italy in the nineteenth century) gave rise to a varied pattern of colonialism. The emergence of the United States (Hawaii, Cuba, Puerto Rico, Guam, and the Philippines) and Japan (Taiwan, Korea, Manchuria) as overseas colonial powers in the late nineteenth and early twentieth centuries added to the variety.

Although their respective colonialisms expressed their distinctive experience of statehood, colonial powers also borrowed and learned from each other, by the early twentieth century perceiving themselves as being engaged in a common progressive endeavour of developing 'scientific colonialism' (Young 1998: 105). While the pattern varied, it is therefore possible to discern certain common features across the colonial world. Referring to Michel Foucault's characterization of power as 'capillary', the African historian Frederick Cooper argues that power in most colonial contexts was actually 'arterial' — 'strong near the nodal points of colonial authority, less able to impose its discursive grid elsewhere' (2005: 49). This was, in part, because, as a number of writers put it, the colonial intent was to 'rule on the cheap' (Sharkey 2003: 122; Cooper 2005: 157). On the eve of its transfer from the brutally exploitative personal rule of King Leopold II to the Belgian state in 1908, the Congo Free State had only 1,238 European military and civilian officers covering over 900,000 square miles (Young 1994: 107). In British India, the centrepiece of Britain's colonial empire, the entire European population in 1921 amounted to just 156,500 (or 0.06 per cent) out of a total of over 250 million (Brown 1985: 95). The colonial state was therefore coercive and **extractive**, yet thin, with local collaborators, especially those recognized as 'traditional' rulers, forming an indispensable element. Such a state also made the exercise of symbolic, as well as punitive, power very important. The routine British use of aircraft to both awe and bomb into submission rebellious Arab tribes in Iraq in the 1920s was an innovative case in point.

Until relatively late in their history, colonial states had a poor record of investment with barely a tenth of total British overseas investment in the Victorian era going to the non-white colonies (Chibber 2005). Davis (2001: 311) damningly notes that India recorded no increase in its per capita income in 190 years of British rule, with the colonial regime operating a policy of deliberate neglect when it came to development (Tomlinson 1993: 217). Lord Lugard, the Indian-born first governor-general of Nigeria credited with introducing the policy of indirect rule to British Africa, admitted that 'European brains, capital, and energy have not been, and never will be, expended in developing the resources of Africa from motives of pure philanthropy' (1965: 617). The fact was that the philanthropic element was not readily evident. The widespread consequence of cheap colonialism was uneven development and wide disparities between small, more or less Westernized elites and the rest (Dirks 2004: 15). In addition, the movement of labour between colonies to work in the plantation sector in particular introduced new social and economic divisions. In the course of the nineteenth and early twentieth centuries, hundreds of thousands of Indians, mainly indentured labourers, were transported to British colonies in the Caribbean, as well as to Burma, Ceylon, Malaya, Fiji, South Africa, Kenya, and Mauritius — a factor that contributed to ethnic political tensions in all these territories after they became independent.

Leftwich (see Chapter 12) reviews the chief characteristics of the colonial state. The focus below is more upon its cultural and ideological impact. For colonial powers such as Britain and France, a central paradox of their rule was that its survival depended on *failing* to fulfil the universal promise of their liberal state ideology. For instance, the **rule of law** in British India was necessarily despotic in that the rulers could not be held to account by those they governed but only by their imperial masters in London. In the French colonies the concept of assimilation (that is, to ultimately make colonial subjects French) was never officially jettisoned, although by the 1920s it was obvious that the language of assimilation was merely the 'rhetoric of colonial benevolence' (Dirks 2004: 14). It could scarcely be otherwise since 'if the colonized . . . is found to be exactly the same . . . the colonizer is left with no argument for his supremacy' (McEwan 2009: 67). Under such circumstances it was logical that the post-eighteenth-century European Enlightenment discourse of rights should become translated into the language of liberation for the Western-educated colonized elite (Young 1994: 228).

A feature of colonial rule that was to have far-reaching consequences for the post-colonial world was what Nicholas Dirks has described as a 'cultural project of control', one that 'objectified' the colonized and reconstructed and transformed their cultural forms through the development of a colonial system of knowledge that outlived decolonization (Foreword to Cohn 1996: ix–xv; also Dirks 2004: 1). It was an approach that reified social, cultural, and linguistic differences, causing the colonial state to be described as an 'ethnographic state' (Dirks 2001). Yet while imperial anthropologists such as Herbert Risley, census commissioner and later Home Secretary in British India in the 1900s, helped to furnish 'a library of ethnicity, its shelves lined with tribal monographs' (Young 1994: 233), what colonial regimes generally did was adapt and develop pre-colonial differences and processes of identification rather than create them where none previously existed.

In India the British rulers certainly learned from the practices of their Mughal, Hindu, and Sikh predecessors in categorizing their Indian subjects, the novelty lying in their systematic method, modern 'scientific' techniques, and the scale on which they sought to enumerate and classify castes, tribes, and religions (Bayly 1999). The effect, as in Africa (Chabal 2009: 33), was to make the consciousness and instrumentalization of such group identities far more pervasive and politically potent. The creation of separate representation and electorates in the representative and elected bodies that were introduced from the 1900s on (Chiriyankandath 1992) also served to institutionalize these identities, making them less fluid than they had been. While such categorization may have initially had as its primary purpose making intelligible, and encompassing, an alien public sphere (Gilmartin 2003), it also proved useful in deploying divide-and-rule tactics against emergent anti-colonial nationalism. In the Indian case, the eventual outcome was the partition of the subcontinent in 1947 with the creation of Muslim Pakistan, and a post-independence politics in which such group identities remain of central significance (see Chapter 21a).

The colonial investment in emphasizing the traditional character of the colonized 'others' produced another of the peculiar paradoxes of colonialism—the civilizing colonizer's nostalgia for, in the words of the British imperial writer Rudyard Kipling, 'the real native—not the hybrid, University-trained mule—[who] is as timid as a colt' (1987: 183). Yet deprecating the 'inauthentic' hybrid did not prevent colonial regimes from

often favouring politically useful pre-colonial elites in imparting Western education, thereby creating a monocultural elite that created a nationalism in their own image; in more extreme cases such as Pakistan and Sudan, this proved impossible to sustain in the multicultural context of the post-colonial state (Alavi 1988; Sharkey 2003). However, internalizing the colonial representation of them as the 'other' caused Asians and Africans to stress their 'dedicated' non-Western identities (Sen 2006: 102), ironically making the identities shaped under colonialism the force for decolonization (Dirks 2004: 30). Anti-colonial nationalists sought to distinguish between a material 'outer' masculine domain of economy, statecraft, science and technology in which they acknowledged the superiority of Western modernity, and a spiritual and cultural 'inner' feminine domain of language, religion, and family—the 'private essences of identity' (Young 1994: 275)—the distinctness of which had to be preserved (Chatterjee 1993: 6–9).

Despite overarching commonalities, there were important differences between colonies (see Box 2.3). While the British colonial state left behind an entrenched legacy of autocratic government in both India and Africa, in India this was tempered by nearly three decades of a widening measure of partly representative quasi-constitutional self-government at the provincial level, as well as a superior administration (the Indian Civil Service) that was nearly half Indian when independence came (Chandra et al. 1999: 18). Although anti-democratic tendencies persisted in post-independence India (and, for reasons considered later, much more obviously in Pakistan) (Jalal 1995), the contrast with the rapid breakdown of post-colonial constitutional government in Britain's erstwhile African colonies was striking.

From the outset of the establishment of colonial rule, the weak demographics that underpinned what Bayart calls the politics of extraversion meant that the primary focus of colonial extraction in Africa was labour rather than land revenue as in the much more densely populated Indian subcontinent (Young 1994: 273). From their relatively late inception, mainly in the late nineteenth century, the European colonial states in Africa relied heavily on the institution of various forms of forced and tributary labour. Although its most brutal manifestations, as in King Leopold II's Congo Free State, largely disappeared after the First World War, the practice survived well into the first half of the twentieth century. The colonial economics of sub-Saharan Africa resulted in either the absence of — or a much weaker — indigenous capitalist class, with Africans effectively excluded from all but petty trade in most regions (Tordoff 1997: 42; Hyden 2006: 46–47). European companies and immigrant Asian merchants dominated larger-scale economic activity with African integration in the global economy mainly taking the form of cash crop farming, especially in French and British West Africa, and labouring in diamond, gold, copper, bauxite, and other mines, particularly in central and southern Africa. These features, together with the relatively brief span (sixty to eighty years) of colonial rule across much of the continent, had the consequence that both the colonial state in Africa and indigenous political and economic forces were more weakly developed than in India, the colonial powers having not modernized society enough (Hyden 2006: 232).

Colonies have been described as 'underfunded and overextended laboratories of modernity' (Prakash 1999: 13). They were laboratories within which the subjects of the experiments proved unwilling to live. Through specific ideologies such as Gandhian nationalism in India, Negritude, Pan-Africanism and African socialism in sub-Saharan Africa, Arabism in the Arab Middle East, and varieties of nationalism influenced by pre-colonial Muslim identity across the Islamic world and Buddhism in South East Asia, the anti-colonial nationalism of the Western-educated elite succeeded in mobilizing a mass following. Yet while this evocation of what Chatterjee termed the 'inner domain' proved effective as an anti-colonial tool, colonialism left a more material legacy in the institutions of state (bureaucratic, judicial, and educational systems, police and military) and entrenched patterns of trade and exchange (for example, the French franc zone and the British sterling area in Africa). It also bequeathed ideologies exported from the West — nationalism itself, liberalism, and socialism — as well as global languages of power (English, French, and, to a lesser extent, Spanish and Portuguese). The rest of this chapter describes how this polyglot legacy has served post-colonial states and societies.

Box 2.3 Colonial Mutations of the Modern State

Colonialism in Africa created mutations of the modern state. Among the ways in which this has been theorized is in terms of a 'gatekeeper' (Cooper 2002) or, from a different perspective, 'bifurcated' (Mamdani 1996) state. Unlike the night-watchman state favoured by libertarians (Nozick 1974), the role of the colonial gatekeeper state was not to serve its inhabitants but to control the intersection of the colony and the outside world, collecting and distributing the resources that that control brought. However, while such a state was conceived as weak in terms of its social and cultural penetration, the same could not be said of the bifurcated colonial state. Seen as the prototype for the apartheid regime in South Africa Mamdani (1996: 29) describes it as the outcome of the simultaneous operation of two different modes of dominion: a racially discriminatory direct rule, based on the exclusion of most,

if not all, natives from civil rights, in urban centres; and a method of indirect rule resting upon the institution of customary tribal authority that produced a system of 'decentralized despotism' in the rural hinterland. The latter generally involved the conflation of a variety of forms of pre-colonial authority into one essentially monarchical, patriarchal, and authoritarian model (1996: 39) that was also territorially demarcated. Such an approach had the effect of disassociating power from authority in a way that subsequently came to pose a formidable challenge to post-colonial African rulers seeking to establish their legitimacy (Chabal 2009: 41). Elements of this model could be discerned in colonial practices outside Africa, most notably in the colonial search for — or creation of — a more authentically native aristocracy to enlist as subordinate collaborators.

Post-Colonial Development

In contrast to the drawn-out history of colonization, the tide of decolonization came in fast across Asia, the Middle East, Africa, the Caribbean, and the Pacific. Beginning in Asia, the Middle East, and North Africa in the decade after the Second World War, it covered most of sub-Saharan Africa within a few years of Ghana (formerly the British Gold Coast) becoming the first independent black African state in 1957, and by 1980 had taken in much of the rest of the erstwhile European colonial empire in the Caribbean, the Persian Gulf and South Arabia, and the Pacific. This rapid transformation was in part the outcome of geopolitical factors: the perceptible weakening of European power following the two world wars, and the emergence of the United States and the Soviet Union, each competing to win over anti-colonial nationalists to their respective camps in the cold war, as the pivots of the post-war bipolar world. However, it was increasing pressure from anti-colonial nationalism, inspired in part by Indian independence in 1947, that forced the pace of change.

But how much change did decolonization bring? The passionate desire of anti-colonial idealists such as Fanon not to imitate Europe (1967: 252) starkly contrasted with the imperial paternalism of colonial officials such as Phillip Mitchell, the British Governor of Kenya, who could say as late as 1945 that faced with 'the choice of remaining a savage or of adapting our civilisation, culture, religion and language, [the African] is doing the latter as fast as he can' (quoted in Cooper 2002: 73). The post-colonial reality belied both Mitchell's belief and Fanon's hope. Colonialism, by globalizing the European template of an international system constituted of sovereign nation-states, determined that the primary object of anti-colonial nationalism would be the transformation of colonies into independent nation-states within a system that bore the deep impress of the erstwhile colonizers. Despite seeking to assert their political and cultural autonomy, anti-colonialists demanding independence had little choice but to operate within this system, since it was the only one that was also imaginable to their rulers (Cooper 2003: 67). This was the dynamic that helped to ensure that while, for instance, pan-African and pan-Arab dreams remained unrealized, Muslim insecurities in British India resulted in partition and the creation of Pakistan as a separate 'Muslim' nation-state.

The new states faced the unprecedented challenge of fashioning 'a peculiarly *modern* form of statehood', modelled not on earlier, more basic, forms of the state but on the elaborate modern Western state that had been developed over centuries (Clapham 2000: 6–7). They were also inhibited by the fact that the conditions in which power was generally transferred were far from optimal. Even though, in the majority of cases, independence was not accompanied or preceded by war or violence, it was marred by the hurried transfer of administrative responsibilities, belated and unsustainable political compromises, economic dependence, and largely untested legislatures and governments. In noting how colonialism fatefully structured political choices along regional and ethnic lines in Britain's most populous African territory, Nigeria, Sam Nolutshungu observed that the political systems of post-colonial societies 'carried . . . in their genes—the heritage of the colonialism that designed them, authoritarian in its day, but also, invariably, in its retreat, a champion of elitist and paternalist notions of democracy' (1991: 100). In Nigeria, the system quickly, and tragically, gave way—successive military coups in 1966, six years after independence, being followed by a three-year civil war that claimed between 1 million and 3 million lives.

Whether states achieved independence via a negotiated constitutional transition or a war of liberation did not appear to make much difference to the lasting influence of the colonial legacy. Certainly in Africa the trajectory of development of the minority of post-colonial states that were the outcome of armed struggle (Algeria, the ex-Portuguese colonies of Guinea-Bissau, Angola, and Mozambique, as well as Zimbabwe, Namibia, and Eritrea) showed much in common with that of their neighbours (Young 1998: 107). Although peaceful transfers of power may have assisted what Crawford Young calls the inertial forces favouring the retention of colonial legal and bureaucratic legacies (2004: 29), the troubled post-independence histories of the liberated colonies demonstrates that it was not possible to remove the long shadow cast by the colonial past through struggle. In fact, the bitterness of the struggle itself seems to have, in some cases (Algeria, Angola, Mozambique), contributed

to subsequent civil war. Being accepted as legitimate by its population was a major preoccupation for post-colonial states. Their colonial predecessors had demanded obedience, not consent, and been content with commanding fear rather than affection. This presented a formidable challenge, given the generally multi-ethnic and multi-religious character of most post-colonial states, and often, especially in Africa and the Middle East, the absence of a pre-colonial state tradition. While the legacy of anti-colonial nationalism was helpful, especially where, as in India, it encompassed decades of struggle and mass engagement, this plural context meant that the concept of development was particularly attractive to nationalist leaders pursuing popular acclaim and concerned with getting their publics to shake off habits of disobedience to the colonial state institutions they had inherited. Even in India, one of the main nationalist criticisms of British rule was that, having brought the gift of science, they were stunting India's growth and arresting her progress (Nehru 1942: 433–49; 1961: 508). A developmental ideology thus became central to the self-definition of the post-colonial state (Chatterjee 1993: 203)—in 1945, Jawaharlal Nehru, soon to become independent India's first prime minister, felt that 'planned development under a free national government would completely change the face of India within a few years' (1961: 504).

In Africa, the predilection on the part of post-colonial leaders to embrace the cause of development was strongly influenced by the late British and French colonial interest in ushering in a **developmental state**. A belated attempt to justify colonialism as it found itself under challenge, the shift from a primarily exploitative and preservationist colonialism to one that claimed to actively champion and invest in progress and development did not save the colonial state (see Box 2.4). Indeed, Cooper (2002: 66) suggests that, in Africa, it was the lead the British and French took in this shift that ensured that it was their empires that first started giving way as the changes introduced stimulated growing demands for self-government. The developmentalist authoritarianism subsequently pursued by their post-colonial successors also failed to secure their regimes. The successful military coup in Ghana in 1966 against President Kwame Nkrumah epitomized this failure (inheriting the economically interventionist and centralizing late colonial state in the Gold Coast, Nkrumah had assumed dictatorial powers and pursued a succession of wasteful and ill-planned projects aimed at transforming Ghana into an industrialized state).

Box 2.4 Ingredients for Post-Colonial Success: East Asia and Botswana

Despite lingering until the 1990s, developmentalist authoritarianism in Africa proved a dead end. Whereas in East Asian states like South Korea and Taiwan, both Japanese colonies in the first half of the twentieth century, it was credited with producing an economic miracle, post-colonial Africa was very different. It lacked the societal cohesion, state tradition, and cold war geopolitical significance of the East Asian states, as well as the peculiar legacy of state-led capitalist development left by a colonial power that was close both geographically and culturally. In this connection, it is noteworthy that Botswana, despite inheriting a 'colonial state not worth the name' and long serving as a labour reserve for the South African mining industry (Samatar 1999: 95), represented a rare African success story, recording average annual growth of over 6 per cent even in 1985–95, a decade in which most other African states recorded negative growth (World Bank 1997: 214–15). While very different in other respects, Botswana benefited, like Korea and Taiwan, from an ethnically homogenous society with a cohesive dominant class and a purposeful leadership under the country's first president, Seretse Khama, also the hereditary chief of the Ngwato, the biggest *morafe* (nation) in the country. Khama's administration built public development institutions that operated effectively on a commercial basis (the Botswana Meat Commission and the Botswana Development Corporation), avoiding the rampant corruption and autocratic tendencies that disfigured post-colonial Africa.

In most of Africa, the patterns of post-colonial government that developed in the 1960s and 1970s traced their lineage to colonial forms: 'Africanised but . . . still impervious, greedy and coercive' (Chabal 2009: 90). However, there were important differences that caused the post-colonial state to be seen as 'an albatross, a yoke . . . round the neck of Africa' (Mutua 2008: 2). Mamdani's 'bifurcated' colonial state mutated into two types. In the majority of cases, conservative post-colonial decentralized despotisms were not really transformed by the reintroduction of multi-party systems in many countries in the 1990s (for example, Kenya under President Daniel arap Moi in the 1990s). A minority turned into radical centralized despotisms in which local authority was dismantled without central government being democratized (for example, Uganda in the first decade after Yoweri Museveni's National Resistance Movement took control in 1985).

Alternatively, Cooper's **gatekeeper state** in its post-colonial form, lacking its predecessors' external coercive capacity or financial resources, was left dependent on either the former colonial power or one of the main protagonists in the cold war—the USA, the USSR, or, in a few cases, Communist China. This was perhaps most obvious in the Francophone states in West and Central Africa, most of which belonged to the *Communauté française d'Afrique* (French Community of Africa) and had their currencies pegged to the French franc (and, after 1999, the euro). Into the early twenty-first century, France continued to be an important source of economic aid. Often maintaining a long-standing military presence, she intervened militarily to prop up post-colonial rulers in several ex-French colonies. To a lesser extent, Britain played a similar role in countries such as Sierra Leone, intervening to put an end to the civil war there in 2000–02. Political independence, by placing the resources of the 'gate' in local hands rather than involving a change in the nature of the state, simply intensified the struggle for the gate, making the beleaguered new gatekeepers, usually ethnically defined, dependent on external agencies for international recognition and aid (Cooper 2002: 200).

These trajectories of dependent political development can be interpreted in different ways. Some see it as basically an adaptation of the inherited Western colonial template of **modernization** as Eurocentric development and progress, albeit inflected locally through a continuing process of hybridization (Ahluwalia 2001: 67–71). Others, a minority, reject the extraneous nature of the post-colonial state. Bayart, for instance, suggests that what is negatively described in terms of 'tribalism' or 'instability' in Africa reflects the local appropriation of alien institutions (1993: 265). He evokes the image of a rhizome—a continuously growing underground stem constantly generating both shoots and roots—to explain the dynamic linkage of African societies to institutions of the post-colonial state (1993: 220–1). However, these links can be viewed more critically as reflecting the emergence of a form of clientelism that while drawing upon pre-colonial customary patrimonial relations between rulers and ruled is more instrumentalist and unaccountable (Chabal 2009: 95).

Bayart's notion has the value of conceiving of the post-colonial as part of a historical continuum (the *longue durée*), but in doing so it risks underplaying the impact of colonialism. Bayart's rhizome concept avoids the link between political regimes in post-colonial states and the **globalization** of capitalism that European colonialism did so much to bring about. From a Marxist perspective, there was no gainsaying that 'two-thirds of the world's people do not have liberal states because of the structure of the capitalist world-economy, which makes it impossible for them to have such regimes' (Wallerstein 2003: 164).

The European export of the idea of the mono-cultural nation-state left most post-colonial states with the dilemma of how to reconcile this with ethnically and religiously plural societies. Chatterjee

identifies this 'surrender to the old forms of the modern state' as the source of 'postcolonial misery' (1993: 11). In some countries, such as Iraq, created under a British League of Nations mandate in 1921 and formally independent by 1932, the shallow foundations of colonial rule necessitated recourse to particularly high levels of violence, setting a pattern for post-colonial government that has persisted (Dodge 2003: 157–71).

As in Africa, colonialism in South Asia left in its wake visions of society and polity that were distorted. Some outside observers have suggested that India owes its comparatively stable post-independence political and economic development to its 'relative immunity from western ideologies' (Gray 2003: 18), but this is an argument that is hard to sustain. More to the point perhaps are three kinds of ingredient that were more evident in the post-colonial Indian mix than, say, in Africa. First, in the realm of cultural politics there ran a deep vein of the non- (if not pre-) modern. Gandhi tapped into this in developing the 'saintly' idiom of Indian politics (Morris-Jones 1987: 60), and the metaphor of the sanctified and patriarchal extended family has been described as one of the most important elements in the culture of Indian nationalism (Chakrabarty 2003: 71). Second, the phenomenon of **caste** associated with Hinduism, while rendered less fluid, more regulated, and institutionalized under colonialism, gave to India a particularly encompassing yet supple resource in adapting colonial institutions (Rudolph and Rudolph 1967). Third, there was the important role played by political agency, in this case the Congress Party that had spearheaded the campaign for independence. Already over sixty years old at independence, Congress under the leadership of Nehru reinforced India's liberal democratic institutional framework by accommodating not only the dominant classes but also a variety of caste, religious, linguistic, and regional identities, both through the party and in the structures of government (Adeney and Wyatt 2004: 9–11).

In contrast, lacking in these ingredients, India's subcontinental neighbours, Pakistan and Sri Lanka, proved far less successful, both in sustaining stable constitutional government and preventing civil war. While India experienced localized civil wars, these outbreaks were insulated and, ultimately, defused (in this respect, Kashmir, a bone of contention between India and Pakistan since independence, remains the exception). However, as the 'formal' democracy of the British Dominion of Ceylon (as it was until 1972) was displaced by the more brash and intolerant 'social' democracy of the Republic of Sri Lanka (Wickramasinghe 2006: 160), the island state witnessed a descent into decades of civil war between the Sinhala Buddhist majority and the minority Tamils. In contrast, although the 'democratization' of Indian democracy through the politicization of previously oppressed and marginalized lower castes and other peripheral groups (Yadav 1996) confronted the state in India with formidable challenges, its post-colonial **institutions** coped. The partition of the subcontinent, by removing roughly two-thirds of the Muslim population, might have made the issue of state and national identity in India less problematic. Even so it is because the post-colonial state in India transcended, in some measure, the colonial logic of divide and rule that it has been better at digesting ethnic and religious plurality. Despite the recent political salience of Hindu chauvinism, it is still possible to conceive of Indian culture as 'constructed around the proliferation of differences' (Ghosh 2002: 250).

Key points

- In contrast to colonization, decolonization occurred apace and 25 years after World War II was largely achieved.
- Colonies became nation-states despite the form being ill-suited to most post-colonial societies.
- Development was prominent as a legitimizing motif for late colonialism and became central to the self-definition of its post-colonial successors, albeit often degenerating into unsuccessful developmentalist authoritarianism.
- While the development record of many post-colonial states was disillusioning, a few registered conspicuous success due to history, geopolitical situation, and political agency.

Conclusion: The Colonial Legacy

As the tide of decolonization was reaching its peak, both the departing colonizers and the anti-colonial nationalists anticipating freedom were disposed to strike a positive note. The colonial historian Margery Perham held, in 1961, that 'Britain on the whole was the most humane and considerate of modern colonial nations and did most to prepare her subjects for self-government' (1963: 99). As power was handed over by the last British Governor of the Gold Coast, Kwame Nkrumah, Ghana's first leader, declared confidently: 'We have won independence and founded a modern state' (James 1977: 153). Yet less than a decade later, on the eve of losing power, Nkrumah's summed up his misgivings about the reality of independence in a book entitled *Neo-Colonialism*: 'The essence of neo-colonialism is that the State which is subject to it is, in theory, independent and has all the outward trappings of international sovereignty. In reality its economic system and thus its political policy is directed from outside' (Nkrumah 1965: ix). A quarter of a century later, one international relations theorist coined the phrase 'quasi-states' to describe the majority of post-colonial states (Jackson 1990).

More recently, there has been a resurgence of interest in the West in the idea of a **liberal imperialism**, if not the actual restoration of formal empire, as a solution to the continuing political and economic crisis that many post-colonial states, especially in Africa and the Middle East, appear to face (Ferguson 2004; Cooper 2004; Lal 2004). Echoing earlier justifications for colonial rule, these adherents of a revival of paternalist imperialism share a sense of civilizational superiority, and a common blind spot for the logic of domination and **exploitation** that underpinned European colonialism. This logic had also been apparent in the behaviour of the United States, the first post-colonial imperial power, towards native, African, and Hispanic Americans in extending its domain across North America in the course of the nineteenth century, and then in the Philippines, Latin America, and the Caribbean in the years following the Spanish–American War of 1898

(Slater 2006: 15, 44–53). Attributable to a 'geopolitical amnesia' engendered by imperial—and post-imperial—culture in the West (Slater 2006: 148), the renewed fascination with liberal imperialism is more a reflection of post-cold war Anglo-American hubris than a legacy of the historical experience of colonialism.

While virtually the entire developing world experienced colonialism, the experience differed from place to place, and this is reflected in the varried legacy (see Box 2.5). To begin with, the settler and slave societies of post-colonial Latin America and the Caribbean present a contrast to Africa and Asia. For example, in the Caribbean the private hierarchies of exploitation that underpinned slavery, and the subsequent drawn-out history of slave emancipation and struggle for political rights, helped the state structures, closely modelled on the British parliamentary system, to gain acceptance as autochthonous (Sutton 1991: 110).

Box 2.5 Assessing the Colonial Legacy

In 2007 the National Science Foundation in the United States endowed a three-year-long project to collect global historical data on the relationship between forms of colonialism, development, and democracy. With respect to development these aimed to assess the evidence for commonly held notions, notably that British colonialism led to greater development; continuity of borders, or the existence of a core region, allowed a more successful transition from colonialism and better development; directly ruled settler colonies exhibited the strongest developmental performance (and indirectly ruled non-settler ones the least); and areas with well-established property rights enjoyed greater development. In relation to democracy the project set out to investigate conjectures such as that British rule encouraged democratic development; that directly ruled colonies were more likely to later develop democracy because of the destruction of, often undemocratic, traditional power-holders; or that European settlement contributed to democratic development (Gerring and Mahoney 2007). The data from the project is expected to be available by 2011.

In the African case, the patchiness of pre-colonial state traditions, and the relative brevity and 'thinness' of colonial rule, generally resulted in post-colonial states incapable of achieving the ambitions of nationalist leaders and the expectations of their peoples. By the end of the twentieth century, a large part of the colonial state legacy in many African countries had been effaced by institutional decay

(Young 1998: 116), eroding 'the explanatory power of the post-colonial label' (Young 2004: 49). What also needs to be reckoned is the legacy of the anti- and post-colonial movements in Africa. The characteristics of these responses to colonialism militated against a transition to multiparty democratic politics, instead leading to a personalization of politics (Hyden 2006: 48, 232).

This is not to negate the continuing historical significance of the colonial and, indeed, pre-colonial past. For instance, contrasting the former Belgian Congo with regions that possessed effective states before colonialism, such as the south of Uganda (Buganda) and Ghana (Asante) and northern Ethiopia, the latter have proved better able to survive phases of bad government (Clapham 2000: 9). Although the model of the nation-state has proven a burdensome legacy for contemporary Africa, the consequences of **state collapse** in Somalia, Liberia, Sierra Leone, and Congo in the 1990s and 2000s showed the high human cost exacted by its absence. The lesson seemed to be that, in a world of states, vulnerable regions and their inhabitants are left dangerously exposed by state collapse. Although some (Clapham 2000) argue that societies might conceivably be able to function without states, it is difficult to foresee them being tolerated for long in the globalized world of states, and the unresolved question for many African countries remains how to fashion a sustainable state (Cooper 2002: 186).

Historical differences reflected in institutional weakness may have compounded the crisis faced by the post-colonial state in Africa, but in Asia too the colonial legacy presented post-colonial states with their greatest challenges, especially in grappling with issues of political identity. The problem in countries such as Sri Lanka was that the concept of multiculturalism introduced by the British colonial rulers stressed the fragmentary nature of society (Wickramasinghe 2006: 13). By doing so, it left the post-colonial state with its composite identity particularly vulnerable to being torn apart by incompatible visions of the nation.

The colonial legacy has been likened to a poisoned pill (Chibber 2005: 11). Reviewing the mixed record of post-colonial development, it is hard not to agree, the health of the poisoned post-colonial state being determined by its condition (history and geopolitical situation) and the skill of the doctor (the role played by political agency).

? **Questions**

1. Is 'post-colonial' the best way of describing countries that became independent after the Second World War?

2. How far did colonialism efface pre-colonial patterns of development?

3. How much does the colonial legacy still affect how people in the global 'South' and 'North' see each other?

4. How far can the diversity of post-colonial states be explained by their colonial past?

5. How did the 'bifurcated' colonial state influence political development following independence?

6. Is the idea of development fatally compromised by its association with the colonial past?

7. How far do the politics and international relations of the contemporary world reflect the colonial past?

→ **Further reading**

■ Chatterjee, P. (1993), *The Nation and Its Fragments: Colonial and Postcolonial Histories* (Princeton, NJ: Princeton University Press). An insightful examination of the impact of colonialism on the nationalist imagination in Asia and Africa by a leading Indian political theorist.

■ Chiriyankandath, J. (1992), '"Democracy" Under the Raj: Elections and Separate Representation in British India', *Journal of Commonwealth and Comparative Politics*, 30/1: 39–63. Shows how the British introduction of communal forms of political representation helped to shape the post-colonial politics of the Indian subcontinent.

■ Cooper, F. (2002), *Africa Since 1940: The Past of the Present* (Cambridge: Cambridge University Press). Considers the post-colonial development of Africa from a historical perspective with particular reference to the concept of the 'gatekeeper' state.

■ Hall, S. (1996), 'When Was "The Post-Colonial"? Thinking at the Limit', in I. Chambers and L. Carti (eds.), *The Post-Colonial Question: Common Skies, Divided Horizons* (London: Routledge), 242–60. A thoughtful exploration of the term 'post-colonial'.

■ Hyden, G. (2006), *African Politics in Comparative Perspective* (Cambridge: Cambridge University Press). A review of the development of post-colonial Africa.

■ Slater, D. (2006), *Geopolitics and the Post-Colonial: Rethinking North–South Relations* (Oxford: Blackwell). A political geographer's perspective on the post-colonial world, which devotes special attention to Latin America.

■ Young, C. (1994), *The African Colonial State in Comparative Perspective* (New Haven, CT: Yale University Press). Wide-ranging comparative study of the colonial state by a political scientist.

■ —— (2004), 'The End of the Post-Colonial State in Africa? Reflections on Changing African Political Dynamics', *African Affairs*, 103: 23–49. Young's reconsideration of the condition of the post-colonial African state.

:// Web links

■ http://bostonreview.net/BR30.1/chibber.html   Chibber, V. (2005), 'The Good Empire: Should We Pick Up Where the British Left Off?', *Boston Review*, 30/1. An Indian political sociologist's damning critique of Niall Ferguson's (2004) *Colossus: The Rise and Fall of the American Empire* (London: Allen Lane), and of the poor scholarship that lies behind the early twenty-first-century idea of a new liberal imperialism.

■ http://hdr.undp.org/fr/rapports/mondial/rmdh2004/documents/HDR2004_Nicholas_Dirks.pdf Nicholas Dirks (2004), 'Colonial and Postcolonial Histories: Comparative Reflections on the Legacies of Empire', Global Background Paper for United Nations Development Programme, Human Development Report, *Cultural Liberty in Today's Diverse World*. A historical anthropologist, specializing in South Asia, considers the colonial legacy.

■ www.nsf.gov/awardsearch/showAward.do?AwardNumber=0648292 'Colonialism and Its Legacies: A Comprehensive Historical Dataset'—outline of a project funded by the National Science Foundation (USA).

 ## Online Resource Centre

For additional material and resources, please visit the Online Resource Centre at:
www.oxfordtextbooks.co.uk/orc/burnell3e/

Institutional Perspectives

Lise Rakner and Vicky Randall

 Chapter contents

- Introduction
- New Institutionalism Applied to the Developing World
- The Theoretical Underpinnings of Institutionalism
- Institutional Applications
- Conclusion: Institutionalism and the Developing World

 Overview

This chapter focuses on the role of institutions and how institutionalism is increasingly applied in analysis of politics in the developing world. It presents central theoretical concepts and approaches helping us to understand institutional origins and change, and further explores the interrelationship between formal and informal institutions through three case studies. By way of conclusion, the chapter discusses the merits of the new institutionalism as a tool of analysis for developing countries.

Introduction

A key question for advocates of political and economic development is why, in some cases, efficient institutions emerge under the authority of development-oriented governments, whereas in other cases, government intervention produces inefficient institutions that hamper socially just resource allocation and development. Chapter 1 provided an overview of changing analytic approaches in the study of politics in developing countries.

In this chapter we focus more specifically on one approach—institutionalism. A notable feature of the literature relating to politics in the developing world since the 1980s has been the centrality assigned to institutions. This 'new institutionalism', which actually includes many different scholarly traditions, holds that institutions explain political outcomes and may provide a solution to political and economic problems across nations. At the same time as considering institutionalism as an approach, this chapter will also discuss the character of political institutions in developing countries, thereby anticipating chapters in Part 3 of this book that focus on political processes and the state. We begin by considering the increasing popularity of institutionalism within analyses of politics in developing countries. We then discuss the theoretical underpinnings of 'new institutionalism' before presenting three case studies that focus on the interrelationship of formal and informal institutions in developing countries. In a final section we assess the appropriateness of institutionalist analyses in developing countries.

New institutionalism and the study of the developing world

Institutionalism has always been a prominent approach in mainstream political science. Accounts generally suggest that in the early years there was an emphasis on historical and legal aspects of political institutions and on constitutions. The 'behavioural' revolution from the 1950s and subsequently the development of rational choice analysis entailed a reaction against this kind of institutionalism in favour of approaches that focused on the individual, conceived as a broadly autonomous actor. Obviously this did not mean the study of institutions ceased but it was not until the 1980s that the

beginnings of a counter-revolution in political science was discernible, famously launched by March and Olsen (1984) as the 'new institutionalism'.

'Old' and 'new' institutionalism

This new institutionalism had much in common with the earlier variant. It also took a number of different forms, as we shall see. Nonetheless these shared some important and novel features (as discussed for instance in Peters 2005; Lowndes 2010). In particular, comparing old and new forms of institutionalism, one can trace the following shifts. First, institutions were no longer implicitly identified with organizational structures; instead the focus of analysis moved towards rules and even norms. Second, where the focus had originally been on formal institutions, there was now at least as great an interest in informal institutions. In addition, the new institutionalism was more explicitly theoretical than the old institutionalism had been and more interested in processes of institutional change. The new institutionalism then emerged within 'mainstream' political science from the 1980s and in its different guises has become increasingly prevalent, leading to the claim 'we are all institutionalists now' (Pierson and Skocpol, cited by March and Olsen 2006: 5). As part of this trend, it has also been increasingly applied in the analysis of politics in developing countries.

New Institutionalism Applied to the Developing World

The growing application of the new institutionalism in analysis of the politics of developing countries is partly explicable in terms of more general developments in political science, together with the declining sense that developing countries need

their own specialized analytic frameworks. The new emphasis in the scholarly literature also coincided with a shift in the policies of the international financial institutions toward the developing world toward the late 1980s. During the 1970s and 1980s major international organizations like the World Bank de-emphasized the role of state institutions in terms of forging development in the South. Inspired by neoclassical economic analyses, the international financial institutions argued that a particular feature of the least developed nations was corrupt and inefficient state institutions and they encouraged a reduced role for the state. However, recognizing that the 'Washington consensus' had neglected the need for appropriate institutional design for achieving development, the World Bank in the 1990s began to actively promote the role of institutions to protect property rights and contract and to encourage civil society and good governance (World Bank 1994). Key in the new development scholarship and the policies of the multilateral institutions was the interest in institutions and how institutional practices could be built and nurtured to secure accountability in new and fragile democracies in the developing world.

This (new) institutionalism is everywhere apparent in the study of politics in developing countries. It arises in numerous thematic contexts and across regions, for instance in studies of democratization in Latin America (Helmke and Levitsky 2006), in accounts of parliaments in Asia, and in relation to African politics (Posner 2005; Lindberg 2006). To assess its implications for studying politics in developing countries, we need now to consider more systematically the theoretical foundations and complications of the new institutionalism.

Key points

- In mainstream political science, 'new institutionalism' has emerged from the 1980s.

- Compared with old institutionalism, new institutionalism focuses less on organizational structures and more on rules and norms; it is more explicitly theoretical, and interested in processes of change.

- The application of the new institutionalism to developing countries is partly a consequence of the recognition that the 'Washington consensus' neglected the role of appropriately designed institutions for achieving developmental goals.

The Theoretical Underpinnings of Institutionalism

The premise of the new institutionalism is that 'institutions matter' and that, to quote Peters (2005: 155), 'scholars can achieve greater analytic leverage by beginning with institutions rather than individuals'. It implies the importance of collective action, not just what people do as individuals. Or in terms of another influential dichotomy, it indicates the significance of structures as well as, or interacting with, individual agency.

Three kinds of institutionalism

But beyond this, and before we can explore more fundamental questions such as what, in this context, is to be understood by an 'institution', we have to recognize that what is called the new institutionalism actually embraces several different approaches. In an influential article, Hall and Taylor (1996) identified three main forms—historical, sociological, and rational choice. Although many other candidates have emerged and Peters (2005) claimed to have found seven types, for present purposes it is helpful to review the main differences between these original three.

Sociological institutionalism

Sociological institutionalism is also referred to as 'cultural' or 'normative' institutionalism. As its name implies this perspective has been heavily influenced by a tradition in sociology going right back to Durkheim and Weber, who were concerned with the ways in which collective institutions establish forms of social control over individual action. It also draws on the sociological study of organizations, particularly the work of Philip Selznick (1948). March and Olsen (1984; 1989), in some ways the founding fathers of the new institutionalism, are generally seen as falling into this category of sociological institutionalism. Like other new institutionalists, they do not equate institutions with formal organizations. Rather they define an institution as 'a relatively enduring collection of rules and organized practices' (March and Olsen 2006: 5) Sociological institutionalists tend to stress the role of norms and values in constituting institutions and in socializing individuals into conforming behaviour through what March and Olsen term a 'logic of appropriateness' (2006: 7). By the same token they tend to see individual preferences as shaped by the institutions within which they become embedded rather than arising exogenously. They stress the importance of these intermediary institutions in shaping and reshaping individual actions and thus collective outcomes. Civil society is one frequently researched institutional setting, as in Putnam's highly influential empirical analysis of the causes and consequences of civic traditions in modern Italy (1993). Finally, and in contrast with rational choice perspectives to be considered next, sociological institutionalism emphasizes that actors within an institution will be constrained and obligated by the norms and rules of the institution; people are considered to engage in satisfying behaviours within social groups and organizations (Granovetter 1985).

Rational choice institutionalism

Although the 'new institutionalism' can be understood as a reaction against what was seen as the extreme methodological individualism of behavioural and rational choice approaches, this form of institutionalism comes from within the rational choice perspective itself. (Many rational choice exponents would argue that the new institutionalism

was in any case misrepresenting their approach and attacking a 'straw man'.)

This strand has been strongly influenced by developments in economics. Within economics, the dominant research tradition has long centred on the neoclassical paradigm involving idealized free agents interacting in an idealized free market. Institutional analysis within economics has reacted against this by showing how collective action can be institutionally embodied and thereby shape and constrain individual choice. New institutionalism within economics is represented most prominently by the Nobel laureate Douglass North (1990), whose ideas have been extensively taken up in political science.

A key premise of rational choice institutionalist approaches in political science is that, for the purposes of analysing major social and political phenomena, individual behaviour can be regarded as rational. For rational choice institutionalists, institutions represent rules and incentives that constrain and enable individual action. The rationality concept in economics on which the rational choice approach draws is based on utility maximization — in other words, a behavioural pattern that links means to ends. Unlike some other forms of institutionalism that regard institutions as the primary unit of analysis, the rational choice approach focuses on individual rational behaviour and analyses its relationship with institutions. The emphasis on the concept of equilibrium may illustrate this: when decisive players prefer to play according to a different set of rules, the rules are not in equilibrium and the formal institutions become fragile (Shepsle 2006). Significantly, within this perspective, the fundamental principles of political behaviour are the same across different political systems despite seemingly different configurations of institutions and political phenomena. Rational actors respond to institutional contexts in identical ways regardless of strategic position, and institutions emerge and persist because of the value and benefits of their functions for the actors who cooperate voluntarily. Contrary to 'the logic of appropriateness' of sociological institutionalism, rational choice institutionalism considers actors to behave according to a 'logic of consequentiality': rules reflect the explicit intent and powers of individual actors. To act in conformity with rules that constrain conduct is to base behaviour on rational calculation and contracts and to be motivated by incentives

and personal advantage (Brennan and Buchanan 1985). One of the first analysts to apply the rational choice perspective to the study of institutions in developing countries is Robert Bates, whose work has generated huge interest amongst both scholars and policymakers (see Box 3.1).

> **Box 3.1** Robert Bates on the Rationality of African Peasants
>
> Writing against the interpretations prevailing at the time, in the mid-1970s Bates' work on African agricultural policies adopted methodological individualism, emphasizing economic reasoning and choice. He criticized the cultural interpretations that were dominant within development studies at the time and argued that instead of explaining the behaviour of African farmers in terms of tradition it was more fruitfully viewed as a result of choice, made under institutional constraints. Analysing the institutional origins of Kenyan agricultural institutions, he pointed to the importance of special interests and large agents to explain why it was rational for agricultural producers to
>
> pay the cost of political organizing in agricultural cooperatives. In addition to helping to counteract ethnocentric stereotypes depicting African peasants as 'backward', a major contribution of Bates' rational approach has been his contribution to applying a theoretical agenda to new empirical grounds. Bates' *Markets and States in Tropical Africa: The Political Basis of Agricultural Policy* (1981) and *Beyond the Miracle of the Market: The Political Economy of Agrarian Development in Kenya* (1989) generated important theoretical and empirical debates that have influenced the scholarship on political and institutional development in sub-Saharan Africa.

Historical institutionalism

The third strand to be introduced, although possibly the first to emerge, is historical institutionalism. An early statement of its approach can be found in Thelen and Steinmo (1992). Historical institutionalism is not a unified intellectual enterprise and some scholars within this tradition, relying on quantitative approaches, treat history as the outcome of rational and purposeful behaviour based on the idea of equilibrium. Other, more qualitatively oriented, scholars reject the idea of rationality and instead emphasize the idea that randomness and accidents matter in political and social outcomes. Historical institutionalism views institutions as the formal and informal procedures, routines, norms, and conventions embedded in the organizational structure of the polity or political economy. Institutions range from the rules of a constitutional order or the standard operating procedures of a bureaucracy to the conventions governing trade union behaviour or

bank–firm relations (Hall and Taylor 1996: 6–7). What differentiates historical institutionalism from the two other strands is really the emphasis on historical context. At its simplest, the historical institutionalist argument is that the choices made as an institution (or policy) is being formed, and the commitments the institution comes to embody as a consequence, will continue to shape its subsequent development. The term used to encapsulate this process is '**path dependence**' (Pierson 2000). Path dependence analysis includes the notion of critical junctures—or a critical moment in history with lasting consequences for subsequent political and economic developments (Thelen 2004). Dramatic historical moments, such as independence from a colonial power, may create new institutions and substantially change power resources of various groups in society. A central aspect of historical institutionalism is that sequences matter: outcomes depend upon the timing of external factors (such as inter-state competition or economic crisis) in relation to particular institutional configurations (Skocpol 1979).

What is an institution and how does it affect individual behaviour?

Given the central role of institutions in the new institutionalism, a crucial question to be asked is what we should understand an institution to be. Within 'classical' institutionalism, institutions were frequently identified with organizations or formal structures. Within new institutionalism — and although in practice there is still much interest in organizations — an institution is more typically understood as a 'stable, recurring pattern of behaviour' (Goodin 1996: 22), or as defined by North, 'the rules of the game in society, or, more formally, the humanly devised constraints that shape human interaction' (1990: 3). Thus in an institutionalized setting, behaviour is more stable and predictable. Beyond this, however, we have seen that different forms of institutionalism understand institutions differently. Sociological institutionalists tend to see them as embodying norms or culturally transmitted values. Adherents of rational-choice thinking see them more as the delimiting context within which rational, self-interested individuals make their choices.

By the same token there are different understandings of the process through which institutions affect individual behaviour. Exponents of the sociological approach suggest that individuals are socialized into the cultural norms of the institution. Rational choice institutionalists see the institution as limiting and guiding individual decisions through regulation and incentivization; individuals accept these constraints in exchange for the benefits and information that membership can bring. In practice these two accounts may not be incompatible. As we will see when turning to assess various institutional applications to explain political and economic developments, arguably, the various forms of institutionalism offer complementary explanations.

How do institutions emerge and change?

Institutions, although stable, are not eternal. Interestingly, the questions of the nature and manner of impact of institutions have received much more attention than questions about their origins and dynamics. Answers to the question of how institutions arise have been various, and often vague and unsatisfactory. Goodin (1996) suggests there are three main ways in which institutions could have come about — by accident, through a process of evolution, or intentionally — and in practice any actual instance of institutional change will almost certainly involve a combination of these three elements. However, in practice, sociological institutionalists have tended to depict institutions as emerging out of their social context and often as embodying dominant social values. Deriving from this perspective, the important notion of 'political institutionalization' as a process has been widely taken up, for instance in the study of political parties (Randall and Svåsand 2002). On the other hand, rational choice institutionalists have been criticized for having an implicitly functional approach — they are influenced by new institutional economics that sees institutions as a purposive reflection of the preferences and expectations of actors. From this perspective, institutions are consciously designed by individuals to reduce transaction costs and increase efficiency. If institutions work badly, that is in an inefficient manner, it is primarily because narrowly established groups with power benefit from maintaining the status quo of existing rules.

Rather more thought has been addressed to the connected question of how institutions change. What drives change and how do institutions respond to pressures for change? One issue here is how far the pressures for change come from outside the institution — in other words, whether changes are exogenous. Generally the assumption has tended to support this view but some more recent research points to a more complicated process in which external pressures or opportunities combine with the effects of internal dynamics and opportunism of 'institutional entrepreneurs' (Lowndes 2010). A related question then is whether the process of change is incremental or punctuated by more revolutionary episodes. In particular we have seen that historical institutionalists emphasize the role of path dependence. They tend accordingly to stress continuity and incremental change. But they have also introduced notions such as 'punctuated equilibria' and 'critical junctures' to indicate that more dramatic change occurs when the force for change becomes irresistible. Both historical and sociological institutionalists also recognize that institutions may respond to changing circumstances in ways that are in some sense 'dysfunctional' for the institutions concerned.

Theories of institutional design

Especially amongst rational choice-influenced institutionalists, there has been much theoretical interest in **intentional institutional design**, or how institutions can be designed *ab initio* or modified in order to achieve particular desired ends. A major area for this kind of work is the design and critique of electoral systems, but its scope is far wider, including for instance the design of constitutions, bureaucratic reform, and systems of party regulation. Of course the possibilities of institutional design have long been recognized not least by authoritarian regimes such as Pinochet's Chile discussed in the case study below. Not surprisingly this kind of analysis has also been taken up eagerly by those engaged in promotion of democracy, good governance see chapters 14 and 15), and reconstruction in post-conflict societies (see Chapter 13).

Interest is growing in the possibilities of engineering party systems. It is appropriate to talk about engineering where the party system is still inchoate but, in cases in which party systems are already relatively established, it is better to talk about modifying the system through forms of regulation. Reilly and Nordlund (2008) relate how a virtual consensus has emerged concerning the key role played by political parties in successful democratic consolidation. At the same time empirical research has demonstrated time and again the shortcomings of actual parties and party systems in emerging democracies. In that situation, interest has grown in finding ways to shape or modify the development of party systems. One way that has in fact been adopted in a succession of developing countries is to adopt a national system of party regulation. This is often aimed at encouraging the formation of national parties and involves specifying for instance that parties must field candidates in a certain proportion of constituencies. There is also interest in using the electoral system to modify the party system. Thus in Turkey parties must win at least 10 per cent of the national vote before they can be represented in the national legislature. Or, in fragmented or polarized party systems, electoral systems can be used to try to encourage greater cooperation between the parties.

Whilst, however, many political scientists, as well as multilateral agencies and national governments, have taken up such schemes enthusiastically, others remain more sceptical. We have seen that the rational choice assumption is that the principles governing political behaviour are broadly similar whatever the regional or cultural context. But others are more wary about the consequences of applying 'lessons' from one political context to another very different one. Whilst acknowledging that sometimes there is no option but to create or engineer new institutions, Bastian and Luckham (2003) caution against the risks of unintended consequences. Pierson (2000) underlines the difficulties posed for such initiatives by institutional inertia or 'stickiness'. It is also important to consider the political context in which such engineering is attempted — who is supporting it, whose vested interests may it in fact promote, and whose may suffer? In other words, what is the hidden political agenda? A related question is how well new institutions designed with external assistance function alongside already deeply embedded informal institutions.

The relationship between formal and informal institutions

It has long been recognized that alongside more formal rules or norms governing institutions there exist less formal ones. But it is only quite recently that there has been a more systematic attempt to think through this distinction and its consequences for institutional analysis. This attempt in turn has been particularly inspired by the challenge of applying new institutionalist approaches to politics in developing countries. Chapter 1 of this book discusses the 'modernization revisionism' that emerged in reaction to some of the cruder depictions in modernization theory of the relationship between tradition and modernity. Rather than expecting modernization to eliminate tradition, it was more realistic to recognize the persistence and reworking of tradition in new symbiotic forms with modernity. The present interest in informal institutions to some extent echoes that argument and examines some of the same kind of phenomena, especially forms of patron–client relationship that work in and through formal political institutions. However, informal institutions cannot simply be equated with tradition or culture; they are both less and more than this. Helmke and Levitsky (2006: 5) suggest the following definition of informal institutions: 'socially shared rules, usually unwritten, that are created, communicated and enforced outside officially sanctioned channels'.

Formal institutions involve defined organizational patterns, rules, and procedures that govern the behaviour of groups and individuals. In general, sociological institutionalism regards formal and informal institutions to be interlinked. Political scientists and economics tend to privilege formal institutions. But an exclusive emphasis on formal institutions risks omitting the fact that, in all political systems, formal rules interact in a variety of ways with informal institutions to mediate how the former shape political behaviour and outcomes.

Informal institutions interact with formal political institutions in highly significant ways. In many cases, informal political institutions—like political clientelism, corruption, the 'big man' syndrome, customary law—undermine the formally specified political rules, but in a few cases, the working of formal political institutions can actually be facilitated by a set of informal rules and conventions. Specifically in the context of democratization, Helmke and Levitsky (2006) build on the initial analysis of Lauth (2000) to suggest four different possible kinds of interaction (see Table 3.1). As the name suggests, *competing* informal institutions compete with and subvert weak formal institutions, a very common occurrence in new democracies. *Substitutive* informal institutions share goals with, and take the place of, weak formal institutions. *Accommodative* informal institutions have divergent goals and values from formal institutions but do not ultimately undermine them. In a *complementary* relationship, informal institutions are compatible with and may actually reinforce formal institutions. Indeed an important new insight emerging from the works of authors like Helmke and Levitsky is that, in emerging democracies, informal institutions can have a positive effect on governance, especially in presidential systems with multi-party or fragmented party systems, and increase the likelihood of governability (Helmke and Levitsky 2006: 11). In their edited volume this typology is illustrated by a range of issues in Latin American countries: electoral politics; party organization and finance; the rule of law; and the impact of clientelism on democracy.

Table 3.1 A Typology of Relationships between Informal and Formal Institutions

Outcomes/ effectiveness	Effective formal institutions	Ineffective formal institutions
Convergent	Complementary	Substitutive
Divergent	Accommodating	Competitive

Source: Helmke and Levitsky 2006

Key points

- An institution is a stable, recurring pattern of behaviour, often referred to as 'the rules of the game'.
- Informal institutions are socially shared rules, usually unwritten, that are created, communicated, and enforced outside officially sanctioned channels.
- Although categorization varies, the main strands of new institutionalism within political science are often referred to as historical, sociological, and rational choice institutionalism.
- Institutions come about by accident, through a process of evolution, or intentionally—or in a combination of these three ways.

Institutional Applications

Above, we have seen that scholars working within different institutionalist traditions emphasize various aspects of institutional origins and change. Variation relates to the weight given to actors vis-à-vis the structural context of institutions, the emphasis placed on history, and whether the focus of analysis is primarily on formal 'rules of the game' or on informal unwritten norms, regulations, and codes. An important feature of the application of the new institutionalism to developing countries has been a special emphasis on the role of informal institutions and their interaction with formal institutions. This emphasis on the interactions between formal institutional structures and informal practices offers important insights into why some formal institutional arrangements 'stick' and guide political actors' behaviour, why in some instances formal institutions change because they do not serve the interest of the elites, and under what circumstances informal norms and practices simply render formal written constitutions irrelevant.

Moving now to illustrate how institutional perspectives have been applied to the study of contemporary politics in the developing world, we highlight analyses that have addressed the interaction between formal and informal institutions. We begin by discussing Chile's electoral institution set-up since the return to democracy. A set of informal institutions has contributed to lessen the problems posed by Chile's formal electoral institutions of strong presidential powers and majoritarian parliamentary elections. We then turn to illustrate how informal institutions emerge as an attempt by social actors to adapt to empirical realities, which in turn lead to formal institutional change. The gradual institutional change in China from informal acceptance of capitalist firms to the final constitutional change that removed the ban on capitalism illustrates how formal institutional change may take place in the absence of 'big crises' through an informal adaptation leading to formal institutional change. Shifting our focus to the democratic developments in sub-Saharan Africa since the late 1980s, we introduce a literature that has emphasized how informal institutions linked to clientelism, neopatrimonialism, and 'one-man rule' have competed with and rendered formal democratic institutions ineffective. However, recent literature also detects an incipient trend towards stronger formal institutions.

Accommodating formal rules: The case of Chile's electoral institutions

Chile returned to democracy in 1990 with a weak congress and strong presidential powers, as embodied in the 1980 Constitution under Pinochet. At the centre of the preceding military government's project of social transformation was an attempt to reduce the number of political parties through electoral engineering and the adoption of a majoritarian two-member district parliamentary electoral system (known as a binominal system). This institutional 'heritage' of a presidential system, weak legislature and a majoritarian electoral system in principle creates major challenges and disincentives for cooperation and coalition formation (Mainwaring and Scully 1995). But, since the democratic transition, Chile has followed a stable pattern of two-coalition competition with an alliance on the left (the *Concertación*) and an alliance on the right (*Alianza por Chile*). Rather than reducing the number of political parties, the electoral system has encouraged relatively stable coalition formation. Instead of deadlock and instability as scholars would predict, Chile has experienced stable coalition governments marked by extensive consensus-building among political elites. One of the most striking elements of Chilean politics since the return to democracy in 1990 (and up until the most recent general election in 2009) is the stability of the coalition government *Concertación*, representing a broad alliance of four major parties. This stability contrasts with the coalition fluidity characterizing Chile's pre-Pinochet democratic experience. According to Siavelis, a complex set of informal institutions has contributed to lessen the problems posed by Chile's inflexible formal electoral institutions and helped to moderate the actions of presidents with formal powers to act in an authoritarian manner (2006: 34).

The role of the Cuoteo *(quota)*

Under the first post-authoritarian government in Chile, elites made an informal pact to counteract the negative characteristics of the constitutional powers vested in the presidency and the exclusionary characteristics of the electoral system. This pact has been referred to as the *cuoteo*, which translates into 'quota'. The informal quota system refers to the distribution of executive-appointed positions based on party affiliation and the quota of parliamentary candidates allotted each party within the government alliance. These informal institutions have been crucial to the maintenance of the government coalition and the legislative success of presidents and by implication, the stability of democracy in Chile since 1990 (Siavelis 2006: 40).

Managing coalition governments: The role of the partido transversal

The model of Chilean coalition governments in the past, and in particular during the years of Salvador Allende's Popular Unity Government (1970–73), was a situation of different parties negotiating to maximize their own gains at the expense of attention to collective problems. Another informal institution that has been critical to governing and the success of the *Concertación* coalition post-1990 is the informal group of leaders that held crucial roles in the first democratic government who refer to themselves as the leaders of the coalition government. Known as *partido transversal*, an informal, yet well-organized, cadre of party elites whose loyalty lies equally with the coalition as with their individual parties form a network between themselves, the parties, and the coalition government. Their object is to control the potentially damaging consequences of co-party government, in which each party might otherwise seek to maximize its own utility or advantage (Siavelis 2006: 47). The members, centred on the presidency and holding key ministerial positions, facilitate cross-party communication among actors in different branches of government, which helps to build consensus among the parties in the government coalition.

Democracia de los acuerdos:
Securing agreements

Multiparty presidentialism creates many negative incentives for coalition formation and the building of legislative majorities. In the case of post-authoritarian Chile this was made more complicated by strong political elites fearing the electoral powers of the *Concertación*. To overcome this threat to legislative success, presidents post-1990 have consistently engaged in a pattern of informal negotiations that has become known as *democracia de los acuerdos*, or democracy through consensus. These negotiations have been carried out with congressional opposition and powerful social groups outside parliament. Since the 1990s, presidents have routinely consulted with legislators of the government and opposition to reinforce coalition unity and ensure that the budget and other important bills are acceptable to the coalition partners.

Two member district elections and coalition strategies

Chile's binomial legislative electoral system ensures that all districts elect two representatives to Congress. Each list on the ballot may therefore include up to two candidates. The lists are open and voters indicate a preference for one of the candidates within their preferred list. Seats are allocated by the D'Hondt method, which means that the first placed list in a district can win both seats only if it more than doubles the total vote of the second-placed list; if not, each of the top two lists wins one seat each. Combined with the multi-party system, Chiles electoral system, known as the M=2 system, brings complexity for candidates, parties, and coalition leaders. Because of the high threshold for two-seat victories, most lists may expect one defeat in each district. Carey and Siavelis (2006) argue that the *Concertación* coalition has responded to the challenges imposed by the M=2 formula by creating and sustaining an informal institution for

ensuring strong candidates who incur risk on behalf of the coalition against the vagaries of the electoral marketplace. This is done through rewarding good losing candidates with appointed government positions. This 'insurance system' may be considered as a complementary institution in Helmke and Levitsky's model as it serves to compensate for dilemmas posed by formal institutions that run the risk of undermining cooperation.

The Chilean example shows that when formal institutions are strong, and the costs of changing institutions are high, accommodating informal institutions may emerge when political actors face difficulties in terms of operating within formal institutions. The case of Chile's electoral institutions shows how informal institutions may contribute to political stability and governability and the endurance of democratic electoral institutions.

Informal institutions and formal institutional change: The legalization of capitalism in China

We have seen that rational choice approaches see institutional change as emerging from outside the institution and therefore exogenous to the institutional models. For historical institutionalists revolutions, economic crises, wars, natural disasters, and foreign occupation provide clearly identifiable 'junctures' of institutional change. But history shows that major institutional change can occur also through 'normal periods'. How can we explain major institutional changes that occur in the absence of external shocks, domestic crises, or societal demands? Recent works have emphasized both the interaction between structures and agents and the role of adaptive informal institutions when explaining institutional change.

Tsai's (2006) analysis of the legalization of capitalism in China borrows perspectives from sociological, historical, and rational choice institutionalism to explain major institutional change in the absence of crises or social mobilization. China has so far shown no signs of making a transition to liberal democracy but has experienced significant institutional changes relating to the development of the private sector. In 1977, China did not keep statistics on private firms, because they were illegal, but by 2005, 29.3 million private businesses were registered employing 200 million people and accounting for nearly 50 per cent of GDP. In a complete reversal of its founding principles, the Chinese Communist Party now welcomes capitalists as party members and the Constitution of the People's Republic of China (PRC) was amended in 2004 to include protection of private property rights. China's private sector development since the late 1970s includes three interlinked processes: (1) the legalization of private enterprise; (2) the admission of Chinese capitalists into the Chinese Communist Party; and, finally, (3) the amendment of the state Constitution to promote the private economy.

The legalization of private enterprise: The red hat phenomenon

In China, 'wearing a red hat' refers to the practice of registering a business as a collective enterprise when in reality it is privately owned, or paying a state-owned enterprise for the use of its name in running a private business. Until 1988, China's private sector technically consisted only of individual households (*getihu*) with fewer than eight employees. In reality many of the collective enterprises were larger private businesses wearing red hats. By the time when private enterprises were officially permitted, an estimated 500,000 businesses were already there in a red hat disguise. Red hat enterprises emerged as an adaptive informal institution during the first decade of economic reform, when private enterprises with more than eight employees were not legally permitted.

Allowing red hat capitalists as members of the Chinese Communist Party

Chinese Communist Party (CCP) members were not allowed to operate businesses, but during the late 1980s it became apparent that many party members were active in the non-state sector. For many years the uneasy coexistence between China's official socialist ideology and the reality of private sector development accounted for the simultaneous growth of business owners among party members and the under-reporting of party members in official surveys of private entrepreneurs. In 1987, at the 13th National CCP Congress, Premier Zhao Ziyang announced that cooperative, individual, and private sectors of the economy in urban and rural areas should be encouraged to expand. The practice of wearing a red hat illustrates how an informal institution contributed to an institutional conversion of a formal regulation. On the CCP's 80th anniversary, 1 July 2001, the general secretary gave a landmark speech widely interpreted as inviting private entrepreneurs to join the party. Thus, within a relatively short time, the party line shifted from banning capitalists to welcoming them.

Changing the Constitution to legalize capitalism

Gradually, the informal coping strategies that both state and non-state actors had reproduced in their daily interaction took on a new institutional reality, challenging national leaders to adapt existing formal institutions to accommodate the widespread informal practices. In 2004 the protection of private property was brought into the Constitution of the PRC in the following manner: 'The state protects the lawful rights and interests of the private sector of the economy, including individual and private businesses. The state encourages, supports and guides the development of the private sector and exercises supervision and administration of the sector according to law' (cited in Tsai 2006: 23).

Tsai's analysis of private entrepreneurs in the CCP and the constitutional changes that made capitalism legal in China in the late 1990s builds upon notions of sequencing and conversion in historical institutionalism (Thelen 2004; Pierson 2000). The analysis concludes that, even in non-democratic settings in which formal institutions may be imposed in a top-down fashion every day, actors may appropriate formal institutions to serve their own ends. This is most likely to occur when there is a gap between the original intentions of formal institutions and the perceived needs of local actors. The analysis illustrates how informal practices paved the way for legalization of the private sector, which attracted the participation of party members in entrepreneurial activities. The rise of 'red capitalists' in turn paved that way for the formal incorporation of capitalists into the CCP, which enabled reform-oriented elites to justify revisions of the PRC Constitution that recognize the existence and contribution of the private economy. The analysis of institutional change in China is based in historical institutionalism. But the analysis also builds on insights from rational choice and sociological institutionalism by emphasizing that actors and structures intervene and that informal institutions emerge and take on a reality that corrects the problems of formal institutions and eventually pave the way for institutional change.

Institutional perspectives and Africa: Are formal rules beginning to matter?

The role of informality has been particularly marked in analyses of politics in sub-Saharan African countries and new institutionalist perspectives have illuminated our understanding of African politics. They have demonstrated the continuing salience and impact of informal institutions, especially those associated with neo-patrimonialism. Most recently however, they have also been associated with a new and cautious optimism that perhaps formal institutions, or rules of the game, really are beginning to matter as well.

Neo-patrimonialism in African politics

One classic neo-patrimonial account is Bratton and van de Walle's (1997) analysis of democratic transitions in Africa from the early 1990s (see Box 3.2). Situating themselves firmly in the 'new institutionalist' school, they pose the question how far these apparent transitions really constitute a turning point in African political development. They

note areas of change but also strong elements of continuity, for instance, the de facto persistence, despite ostensibly competitive elections, of traditional leaders and the old political elite. And they suggest that transition has not in general strengthened political institutions—by which they mean political parties, legislatures, and electoral institutions. Instead they show how the operation of such formal democratic political institutions has been affected by the persistence of largely informal institutions associated with the preceding neo-patrimonial regimes.

Chabal and Daloz, authors of another influential study, *Africa Works* (1999), similarly affirm the importance of informal institutions and processes. They suggest that the ongoing economic crisis in Africa is contributing to a growing trend towards the informalization of politics. They find only a superficial resemblance between African political institutions and those in the West: 'In reality it is the patrimonial and infra-institutional ways in which power is legitimated which continue to be most politically significant.'

> **Box 3.2** Neo-Patrimonialism Defined
>
> " In neo-patrimonial regimes, the chief executive maintains authority through personal patronage rather than through ideology or law .... Relationships of loyalty and dependence pervade a formal political and administrative system and leaders occupy bureaucratic office less to perform public service than to acquire personal wealth and status. The distinction between private and public interests is deliberately blurred. The essence of neo-patrimonialism is the award by public officials of personal favours, both within the state (notably public sector jobs) and in society (for instance, licences, contracts, and projects). In return for material rewards, clients mobilize political supporters and refer all decisions upwards as a mark of deference to patrons.
>
> " (Bratton and van de Walle 1994: 458)

Formal rules and presidential politics

This perception of African politics in which informal, neo-patrimonial institutions pervade and largely undermine formal institutions remains widespread and indeed largely appropriate. But in this case study we want also to bring attention to the emergence of a new theme in the literature, one that suggests that formal political institutions in Africa are beginning to affect the behaviour of political and economic elites. Posner and Young (2007: 126) reflecting on some recent trends in African presidential politics, conclude that 'The formal rules of the game are beginning to matter'. They note the increasing importance of elections—by 2000–08, 98 per cent of presidential elections were contested (although even then incumbent presidents were re-elected more than 85 per cent of the time). They also note that since 1990 more than 36 African countries have adopted new constitutions, most of which do not permit a third presidential term. It is encouraging that no incumbent president has tried to get rid of the constitution altogether and nine out of 18 agreed to step down after two terms. The remaining nine sought to change the constitution: three failed—Chiluba in Zambia, Muluzi in Malawi and Obasanjo in Nigeria—although six, including Nujoma of Namibia and Museveni of Uganda, succeeded. Posner and Young (2007) accept that the role of external pressures in modifying presidential behaviour should not be underestimated. Nonetheless, they find grounds for 'cautious optimism' in what appears to be the unwillingness of presidents to openly defy growing public support for contested presidential elections and presidential term limits. As a footnote to this argument it is worth mentioning the recent (February 2010) military coup in Niger, which is being blamed on the president's successful referendum extending his term of office. This could be seen as a further encouraging sign, although the fact of military intervention in itself is less reassuring.

Other formal institutions: Courts and anti-corruption commissions

This kind of argument has been echoed in other institutional contexts. Suberu (2008) looks at the role of Nigeria's Supreme Court. He notes the widely held view that Western-style institutions like courts are simply facades for neo-patrimonial rule but he argues that 'the neo-patrimonial framework of such analysis often trivializes the recent significant recent advances towards democratization, liberalization and institutionalization of power in Africa' (Suberu 2008: 458). This neo-patrimonial interpretation might have been appropriate for the Supreme Court before 1999, but since the transition in that year from military to civilian rule, the Court has emerged as 'a prominent and independent adjudicator of intergovernmental disputes'. He demonstrates this through an analysis of all 15 major intergovernmental disputes, concerning central government and Nigeria's 36 state governments, from 1999 to 2007. Beyond establishing the Supreme Court's increasing independence and integrity, he also points to the contributory role of two other institutions, the National Judicial Council and the Federal Judicial Service Commission which, under the 1999 Constitution, helped to ensure that members of the Supreme Court have been recruited on the combined basis of seniority and merit (see also Chapter 21b).

Lawson (2009) focuses on the issue of anti-corruption reform, comparing the achievements in this respect of Kenya's Anti-Corruption Commission with Nigeria's Economic and Financial Crimes Commission. She points to the way in which earlier studies tended to emphasize how incumbent elites used anti-corruption campaigns to target their political enemies. Lawson does not deny this aspect of anti-corruption initiatives but argues that a more subtle analysis is needed. In Kenya's case, she found that the Anti-Corruption Commission was indeed sidelined, but in the Nigerian case, the Commission had a degree of success. More generally she suggests that factors such as timing and 'unintended consequences' of reform can make a difference. If an anti-corruption clean-up following an election was too obviously targeted at the previous incumbents this could alienate public support. In addition those heading up the new organizations could, as appeared to happen in Nigeria, seek to assert their independence from the new political leaders by adhering to and implementing their formal organizational mandate.

The formal–informal institutional interrelations in the developing world

The case studies have illustrated the variety of national and thematic contexts in which the interrelationship of formal and informal institutions has increasingly been explored. Whilst the traditional assumption might be that informal institutions would tend to vitiate and compete with formal institutions of democracy and governance, the cases have shown a more varied and complex picture. In Chile, with strong formal democratic institutions, informal practices have helped to sustain

viable democracy; in China, informal institutional adaptation contributed to the process by which private enterprise was formally accepted and institutionalized. In Africa, where regimes have long been seen as quintessentially neo-patrimonial, with informal power relations subverting weak formal representative and administrative institutions, there may be signs that formal institutions are beginning to matter.

Key points

- The case of Chile illustrates how informal power-sharing institutions may allow elites to achieve their goals within an inflexible formal institutional context.

- The case of China shows that *adaptive* informal institutions may facilitate formal institutional change.

- The case of sub-Saharan Africa illustrates the salience of neo-patrimonial politics and *competing* informal and formal institutions but also offers examples of formal institutions beginning to shape the behaviour of political and economic elites.

Conclusion: Institutionalism and the Developing World

The new institutionalism that now pervades mainstream political analysis represents a welcome reaction to the reductionism of earlier individual actor-based approaches. Whilst it takes different guises, all institutionalist approaches include in their analyses a focus upon both formal and informal rules, organizations, and procedures. Moreover these different strands can be regarded as complementary (Goodin 1996). Although the new institutionalism

has been criticized for internal ambiguities, and for inadequately engaging with questions of the origins of institutions and how institutions change, this is part of an ongoing dialogue in which such shortcomings are being addressed.

The new institutionalism is increasingly applied in analysis of politics in the developing world. We have seen that this partly reflects the new institutional emphasis of development economics as purveyed by international bodies like the World Bank. Sound, effective governance institutions are seen as a prerequisite of development. This raises the question of how far the new institutionalism is an appropriate tool of analysis for developing countries. Actors and institutions engaged in promotion of good governance and sound institutions for development have turned to institutional analyses in search for tools for designing institutions that may achieve desired goals. But the question of intentional institutional design raises a number of critical questions. Can institutional designs 'travel' from different political settings? What are the potential unintended consequences of creating new formal institutions in political contexts in which the informal institutions may not be accommodating the stated aims of the formal institutions designed?

Arguably, institutional analyses have tended to ignore the uneasy relationship between formal institutions designed with external assistance and deeply embedded local informal institutions. Remmer (1997: 50), emphasizing the fragility and constrained character of institutions in developing countries, argues that the new institutionalism, with its emphasis on domestic issues, has ignored the overwhelming importance of international actors and institutions for the developing world as well as domestic economic constraints. She finds it ironic that new institutionalism places politicians and bureaucrats at the centre of analysis at a time when the activities, resources, and relative weight of the state are being reduced through processes of privatization, globalization, and the emphasis on civil society.

Some writers go further in questioning whether an institutional emphasis is really illuminating. Sangmpan (2007: 201) maintains that 'empirical evidence reveals that outcomes in developing countries consistently defy institutions as explanation and prescription'. He wants to distinguish three aspects of political systems—politics, institutions, and the state—and argues that in developing

countries it is what he calls society-rooted politics that imprints and even determines the other two aspects. Sangmpan's conception of politics is avowedly 'sociological', referring to interests within society that compete for property, goods, services, values, and political power. His argument is that an institutional approach marginalizes such factors. Although Sangmpan directs his criticism against the new institutionalism and its application to developing countries he maintains that this new institutionalism, like the old institutionalism, tends to focus on formal institutions. We have argued however that one of the great virtues of the new institutionalism has been its interest in informal institutions and their interaction with the formal sphere, which Sangmpam deliberately chooses to ignore. Even so his notion of society-rooted politics is broader than anything typically connoted by informal institutions and to that extent he may be right to argue that the new institutionalism runs the risk of exaggerating the significance of institutions as opposed to fundamental political interests and conflict.

In conclusion, the new institutionalism offers an exciting tool of analysis if used with sensitivity to context and without hegemonic claims to be the only proper approach to politics in developing countries. An important feature of the application of the new institutionalism to developing countries has been a special emphasis on the role of informal institutions and their interaction with formal institutions. This emphasis on the interactions between formal institutional structures and informal practices offers important insights into why some formal institutional arrangements 'stick' and guide political actors behaviour, why in some instances formal institutions change because they do not serve the interest of the elites, and under what circumstances informal norms and practices simply render formal written constitutions irrelevant. Our case studies demonstrated some of the productive ways in which this kind of analysis has been used.

1. What explains the new emphasis on institutional analyses applied to the developing world?

2. Discuss the following quote by Peters (2005) in the context of developing countries: 'Scholars can achieve greater analytic leverage by beginning with institutions rather than individuals.'

3. Compare the sociological, historical, and rational choice institutionalist approaches to understanding institutional change.

4. Discuss how a cultural and a rational choice approach may interpret traditional agrarian economies differently.

5. What are the potential pitfalls and unintended consequences of designing institutions with external assistance in a developing country setting?

6. Discuss the case study of China. Could an actor-centred approach (rational choice) have provided a different interpretation of the legalization and legitimation of capitalism?

7. With reference to Table 3.1, provide empirical examples of formal–informal institutional relations that are complementary, accommodating, substitutive, and competitive.

8. How persuasive do you find the argument of Posner and Young that, in Africa, 'formal rules of the game are beginning to matter'?

→ Further reading

■ Goodin, R. (1996), *The Theory of Institutional Design* (Cambridge: Cambridge University Press). A comprehensive review of major theoretical approaches to institutional design and change.

■ Hall, P. A. and Taylor, R. C. R. (1996), 'Political Science and the Three New Institutionalisms', *Political Studies*, 44/5: 936–57. A useful overview of the central debates between institutionalist approaches.

■ Helmke, G. and Levitsky, S. (eds) (2006), *Informal Institutions and Democracy: Lessons from Latin America* (Baltimore, MD: The Johns Hopkins University Press). A valuable framework for analysing formal and informal institutional relations with detailed case studies from Latin America.

■ Lowndes, V. (2010), 'The Institutionalist Approach', in D. Marsh and G. Stoker (eds), *Theory and Methods in Political Science*, 3rd edn (Basingstoke: Palgrave). An excellent overview.

■ March, J. and Olsen, J. P. (1989), *Rediscovering Institutions: The Organizational Basis of Politics* (New York: Free Press). A central text within new institutionalism.

■ Peters, G. (2005), *Institutional Theory in Political Science: The New Institutionalism*, 2nd edn (London: Continuum). A thoughtful and thorough overview.

■ Powell, B. J. (2000), *Elections as Instruments of Democracy: Majoritarian and Proportional Visions* (New Haven, CT: Yale University Press). A central text discussing key aspects of democratic institutional design.

■ Thelen, K. and Steinmo, S. (1992), *Structuring Politics: Historical Institutionalism in Comparative Analysis* (New York: Cambridge University Press). A key introduction to historical institutionalism.

LISE RAKNER AND VICKY RANDALL

 Web links

- www.isnie.org/   International Society for New Institutional Economics
- http://plato.stanford.edu/entries/social-institutions/   Social Institutions
- http://globalresearch.ca/   Centre for Research on Globalization (CRG)
- www.cgdev.org/section/topics/ifi   Center for Global Development
- http://genderindex.org/   Social Institutions and Gender Index

 Online Resource Centre

For additional material and resources, please visit the Online Resource Centre at:
www.oxfordtextbooks.co.uk/orc/burnell3e/

The Developing World in the Global Economy

4

Stephen Hobden

✳ Overview

This chapter and the following interlinked one provide an overview of the international context in which politics in the developing world operates. In this chapter the focus is on the global economy. Over the past fifty years there has been a general increase in global economic integration, often described as **globalization**. The chapter focuses on three key features of the global economy—trade, foreign direct investment, and financial flows—discussing their significance for the developing world. As the first decade of the twenty-first century comes to an end, the character of the global economy is marked by two distinguishing features: the most profound economic dislocation for eighty years; and the gradual erosion of the economic dominance of the 'North' (specifically Europe and North America).

Introduction: Trends in the Global Economy

For the purposes of this chapter, the term 'global economy' is understood as all international economic transactions that occur across national borders: trade; financial flows; and foreign direct investment (commonly known as FDI). Many observers claim to see evidence of increasing global

STEPHEN HOBDEN

economic integration, a feature usually associated with globalization. However, the meaning of the concept of globalization is a subject of much debate, and, in particular, there is considerable disagreement over the precise implications for economic well-being in the developing world of increased economic integration (see Box 4.1).

A major component of the emergence of a global economy has been the growth in the value of trade. For many writers, the economic growth of the West is largely explained by its involvement in an international trading system, leading to the view that 'free trade' is inherently beneficial. Yet, despite the developing world's increasing inclusion in the global economy, few of the benefits from trade appear to have reached the large proportion (1.4 billion people, or one in four of the human population) of the globe's population who live in absolute poverty (less than US$1.25 per day). Indeed, although the developing world increased its share of world manufacturing output from a mere 5 per cent in the early 1950s to close to 25 per cent by the end of the century, much of this was accounted for by only a handful of countries, which include China, Brazil, South Korea, and Taiwan (Dicken 2003: 37). The same is true of the increase in merchandise exports, where again China and Hong Kong dwarf other exporting countries such as Mexico, Singapore, and Taiwan. The arguments that lead many to suggest that there are enormous benefits to be gained from joining the world economy need to be balanced against a consideration of the reasons why developing countries are not always able to exploit the potential gains from trade.

Box 4.1 Globalization

Globalization is a term much used in contemporary social sciences. Some suggest that it 'might justifiably be claimed to be the defining feature of human society at the start of the twenty-first century' (Beynon and Dunkerley 2000: 3). However, it is a deeply problematic term because there is no accepted definition, and little agreement about how to measure the process or even whether the term provides a useful way of assessing contemporary global developments (Hirst et al. 2009).

O'Brien and Williams define globalization as 'an uneven process whereby the barriers of time and space are reduced, new social relations between distant people are fostered and new centres of authority are created' (2007: 133).

When we turn to the developing world the key argument is about whether globalization increases or decreases levels of poverty. As with the discussion over definition and measurement, there is little agreement over the impact. Here are two rather divergent views:

> Globalization has been a force for higher growth and prosperity for most, especially for those in the bottom half of the world's population.
> (Bhalla 2002: 11)

> Globalization speeds up the economy magnifying the chasm between [rich and poor]. Both at home and abroad, the extremes of wealth and deprivation have become so great that the stability of the global system is threatened.
> (Isaak 2005: xxi)

How are such divergent views possible? One reason is that that there is no agreement as to what constitutes poverty. Should poverty be measured in absolute or relative terms? The most widely used absolute measure of poverty is the World Bank's figure for the number of people living on little more than a dollar a day. Measures of relative poverty compare the proportion of global wealth enjoyed by the richest people in the world compared to the poorest. Although the figures are disputed, most absolute measures suggest that poverty is declining (there are fewer people living on less than a dollar a day), whilst relative measures suggest that poverty is increasing (the gap between the richest and poorest is getting wider). Attitudes towards globalization may depend on the way in which poverty is measured. The picture is complicated when the situation within countries is also considered. The population of China living on the country's eastern edge has benefited much more from the country's recent rapid growth compared to the large rural population living on the western side.

Globalization is best understood as a multifaceted process that affects different countries and different social groups within countries differently. Most observers would agree that levels of inequality have increased, both nationally and internationally, while levels of absolute poverty, when examined globally, have decreased.

There is evidence of trade between different social groups for as long as written records have existed, and it has provided much of the motivation for global exploration. By the end of the nineteenth century, much of Asia and Africa had been included in the European empires, and trade between the colonial powers and their subject states provided the bulk of trade between what came to be called 'First' and 'Third' Worlds. The colonies provided guaranteed sources of essential raw materials, and also markets for manufactured goods from the metropolitan centres. One historian of empire notes that 'Britain prospered . . . by manufacturing articles for sale abroad, which her customers paid for in raw materials and food' (Porter 1996: 4). An international division of labour developed in which European powers exported manufactured goods to the colonies and imported the materials needed to make these goods (McMichael 2008: 31–42). One way of imagining this process is to think of the international trading system as a number of segments, each segment comprising the colonial power and its colonies. A considerable amount of trade took place within the segment, and to have an empire was seen as essential for the economic well-being of the core.

Standing outside this segmented economic system was the United States, which in the early twentieth century was becoming a significant source of global production. Successive US administrations sought a larger role in the international economy, which would require the breaking up of the European imperial systems of trade. At the outbreak of the Second World War, planners in the United States started to think about what the post-war economic and political order might look like. The fruits of this planning emerged in a document known as the Atlantic Charter, signed by President Roosevelt and Britain's Prime Minister Churchill in 1941. At the core of the Charter was a commitment to the end of empire and the creation of an open world economy.

Despite the resistance of the European powers, decolonization gradually occurred following the end of the Second World War. However, as a result of the cold war, a world economy segmented by the European colonies was replaced by a world economy divided between, on the one hand, the USA, its allies and client states, and, on the other, the Soviet Union, its allies and client states. These systems resembled in many ways the imperial systems that had preceded them, in the sense that the cores provided manufactured goods whilst developing countries were major sources of raw materials.

One major attempt to overcome this reliance on the export of raw materials was the development of a policy of **import-substituting industrialization** (ISI). The promotion of local manufacturing was seen to have several advantages. It would employ local labour and thereby reduce unemployment, and allow production of manufactured goods at prices lower than available on international markets. Producing locally would reduce imports, potentially allow some of the production to be exported, and promote the introduction of new technology. To allow local industries to develop without competition, tariffs were imposed on imports.

ISI is generally regarded as having been a failure for the developing world. In general, it did not promote the stated objectives, but resulted in rather inefficient government-owned industries that were unable to compete internationally. The reason for this is generally cited as being a reluctance to move towards reducing the tariff walls so that the industries are forced to compete internationally. Particularly in Latin America, pressure was put on governments to maintain subsidies and high levels of protection underpinning the industries. A further problem was that, in many developing countries, the market was not large enough to reap economies of large-scale production. Finally, ISI did not even break the reliance on imports: instead of relying on imported manufactured goods, the countries became reliant on the import of machine tools, spare parts, and specialized knowledge. Although ISI is normally now depicted in negative terms, it should be remembered that much of European and US industrialization occurred behind tariff walls, and that the success of the newly industrializing countries of East Asia depended to varying degrees on this approach (see Box 4.2).

Box 4.2 The Newly Industrializing Countries (NICs) of South-East Asia and Export-Led Industrialization

The so-called NICs include Taiwan, South Korea, Hong Kong, and Singapore, with perhaps a second wave including Malaysia, Indonesia, and the whole of the People's Republic of China. The NICs have seen a remarkable turnaround in their economic fortunes, developing from being very poor, largely agricultural economies in the wake of the Second World War to industrialized countries, some with average incomes comparable to those of the developed world. Free trade advocates have cited the NICs with varying justification as models for how to develop an economy.

The economic success of the NICs has many possible explanations, for example, their exceptionally favourable geopolitical location during the cold war period and even the cultural attributes of the people. But to most economists a major reason is their adoption of policies of export-led industrialization. This can be contrasted with the policies of import substitution industrialization. The policy of the NICs has been to direct industrialization to fulfil the demands of world markets, and gradually to expose their industries to world competition through lowering tariff barriers. They have been prepared to switch production in order to maintain their position of comparative advantage—starting with textiles, then moving into mass-production items such as toys, and then into more high-tech goods. The NICs in particular have been successful in specializing in areas of production that have become unprofitable in the more developed world.

Economists who wish to promote free trade have seen the NICs as a good model because of their willingness to trade in the global economy, and their readiness to reduce tariff barriers over time. Furthermore, the NICs have succeeded in exploiting their comparative advantage. However, the position is more complicated. It is true that the NICs have reduced tariffs over time so that their industries are now more exposed to international competition. But they have been prepared to use tariffs to protect their industries in the early stages while they were becoming established. This is known as 'infant industry protection', and was used as an argument for the protection of industry in Europe during the nineteenth and early twentieth centuries. A further point that is often overlooked is the important role that the state played in developing industry in the NICs (see Chapter 22b on the South Korean example). The state-maintained subsidies and investment as a way of developing parts of the economy were perceived to have the greatest potential or were strategic in some sense. As with infant industry protection, this suggests that the history of the NICs is more complicated and perhaps more difficult to replicate than is suggested by free market proponents.

Despite an increasing level of contact between the capitalist and communist systems, it was not until the collapse of Communist Party rule in the Soviet Union that it is possible to start talking of a global economy—one, exclusively capitalist, system.

While trade has been a feature of human societies dating back thousands of years, there are two other features of economic activity, also associated with the term 'globalization', but which have gained greater significance over recent decades. The first of these is foreign direct investment. This refers to the practice of firms, usually described as transnational corporations (TNCs) locating production and marketing facilities in other countries. The level of this foreign direct investment has increased massively over recent years, and concerns have been raised about whether the activities of TNCs have assisted or undermined economic development. A further recent development has been the enormous financial flows occurring in the global economy. While foreign direct investment can be seen as a relatively long-term form of investment, financial flows are primarily short-term. They refer to the buying and selling of currencies and stocks and shares in local economies. While FDI refers to investments like buildings and machinery, and therefore takes some time to create, vast amounts of money in the financial system can be moved by the pressing of a computer button. Concerns have therefore been raised as to whether rapid financial movements can be destabilizing to developing world economies—although it should also be noted that economies in the developed world are not immune to the turbulence caused by rapid and speculative financial flows.

As the first decade of the twentieth-first century draws to a close, two important features of the global economic system have become apparent. First, there has been a major dislocation in the economic system, with implications for both developed and developing countries. Second, some commentators are pointing to a shift in economic power from Europe and North America to Asia. At the forefront of this shift have been the economies of China and India (sometimes linked together as 'Chindia'), both of which have been enjoying substantial growth rates—resumed very quickly after the worldwide economic slowdown in 2008–09. This shift of economic power may signal profound changes in the character of international relations, an issue that will be developed in the following chapter.

Key points

- The global economy can be considered as comprising three main activities that occur across national borders: trade; investment; and financial movements. There is a long history of trade between different societies, although large-scale FDI and financial flows are a relatively more recent feature of global economic activity.

- During the period of European colonialism, the major pattern of trade was for the colonies to export raw materials, while the metropolitan cores exported manufactured goods. These structures of trade have persisted into the post-colonial period.

- Following the end of the cold war, it is possible to talk about the emergence of a global economy—a single, capitalist system. Two contemporary features mark the global economy: a significant slowdown in economic activity and a shift in economic power to Asia.

Trade

Patterns of global trade

During the second half of the twentieth century, the rate of growth of trade far outstripped that of production. Between 1950 and the close of the twentieth century, world trade increased almost twenty times while production increased only sixfold (Dicken 2003: 35). Yet this growth has not been at a constant rate, and has been subject to considerable fluctuation. During the 1950s, levels of trade grew extremely rapidly as the world, and in particular Western Europe, recovered from the Second World War. In contrast, the rate of growth was much slower during the 1970s as the international economy contracted in the wake of large oil price rises.

World trade is relatively concentrated. Table 4.1 shows the breakdown between different regions of the world and their contributions to merchandise and trade in services. The developed world is responsible for the vast bulk of exports in merchandise and services, although the rapidly increasing contribution of China to merchandise exports suggests that the character of the global economy is undergoing a profound transformation. Manufactured goods make up approximately 75 per cent of merchandise trade, and one of the striking developments is the increasing amount of manufactured goods flowing from the developing world. Despite the large increases in the proportion of manufactured goods coming from some countries in the developing world, many maintain their traditional role of providing raw materials and agricultural products. Many countries in sub-Saharan African

rely on just one primary product for over 50 per cent of their exports (Harrison 2004: 219).

The promotion of free trade

The relative prosperity of the developed world during the latter half of the twentieth century is linked by many economists to the rapid rise of global trade. The idea that unimpeded trade will lead to a material benefit to developing countries is a core idea of the **neo-liberal** agenda, and is expressed in what became known as the **Washington consensus**. The neo-liberal agenda derives from classical liberal economics. The 'consensus' denotes the primacy of related ideas in the World Bank and the International Monetary Fund (IMF), both based in Washington (see Chapter 5). These ideas have proved to be very powerful. Policies based on the theory of **comparative advantage**, implemented by international organizations, have dramatically affected the lives of millions of people around the globe (for a clear discussion of the theory of comparative advantage, see Dunn and Mutti 2004: ch. 2).

Table 4.1 Relative Shares in Global Exports by Region and for Selected Countries, 2007

	Merchandise (%)		Services (%)	
Developed world	58		72	
Germany		*10*		*6*
USA		*8*		*14*
Japan		*5*		*4*
CIS & SE Europe	4		3	
Developing world	38		25	
Africa		3		2.5
S. Africa		*0.5*		*0.4*
Asia (excluding Japan)		29		20
China		*7*		*4*
Latin America (incl. Caribbean)		5		3
Brazil		*1*		*0.7*
Mexico		*12*		*0.5*

Note: CIS refers to Commonwealth of Independent States
Source: United Nations Conference on Trade and Development (UNCTAD) 2008a: Tables 1.1.1 and 5.1.1

The package of measures associated with the neo-liberal agenda comprises both national and international elements. At the national level, free trade policies fall into two main areas: the promotion of a more efficient use of labour, and the reduction of the role of the state in the economy. At the international level, policies are advocated that aim to remove hindrances to trade and to promote the inflow of FDI. Tariffs on imports or exports are seen as a major impediment to trade. Tariffs are a form of taxation that are levied on the value of goods that are entering or leaving a country. They can be both a form of revenue and a way of protecting domestic industries. For free trade advocates, tariffs are seen as acting to undermine the potential gains to be derived from comparative advantage. Therefore it is argued that removal or reduction of trade tariffs will promote trade and lead to a more efficient use of resources, as domestic industries are exposed to international competition. Free traders have also argued in favour of allowing currencies to float freely rather than being managed by governments. As part of free trade regimes, countries have been persuaded to allow their currencies to float freely. This often means devaluation of the currency, making domestic production more competitive internationally, while increasing the cost of imports. Many developing countries also placed considerable restrictions on the permitted levels and forms of international investment in their economy. Restrictions on the parts of the economy in which foreign investment is allowed, higher levels of taxation for international firms, and limits on the expropriation of capital have all been typical in the past, especially before the 1980s. However, free market policies argue that there should be no discrimination against foreign capital wishing to invest in the country, and that any barriers to investment should be removed. Box 4.2 discusses the **newly (or new) industrialized (or industrializing) countries** (NICs) of South-East Asia, often seen as examples of the successful implementation of free trade policies.

Limits on comparative advantage for developing countries

The examples of the Asian NICs suggest that in certain circumstances free market policies can contribute to rapid economic growth. Why have other developing countries not been able to replicate this success? Why has the enormous growth in international trade not resulted in a wider distribution of the fruits of that trade, as the theory of comparative advantage would suggest? And why have some parts of the developing world barely participated at all in the growth of world merchandise trade—Africa's share of such trade is now less than its contribution of over 5 per cent in 1980, and the developing countries of the Americas have remained static at just under 6 per cent (UNCTAD 2008a)? Critics of the neo-liberal agenda suggest that in some ways much of the developing world is disadvantaged in the global economy compared to more developed countries.

Following decolonization the same basic pattern whereby the developing areas under colonialism were primarily providers of raw materials and markets for manufactured goods has largely persisted, with some notable exceptions (see Weiss 2002). For many non-Asian developing countries, over 70 per cent of exports still comprise primary products. For many sub-Saharan African countries, the figure is over 80 per cent (UNCTAD 2009a). This can be a problem for developing countries because of the failure of the prices of primary commodities to keep pace with manufactured goods (known as the declining terms of trade). Also primary commodities have historically been liable to confront very large fluctuations in prices, coffee being a particular example (see Box 4.3).

Between 1997 and 2001, the United Nations Conference on Trade and Development (UNCTAD) combined price index of all commodities in US$ fell by 53 per cent in real terms—that is, primary commodities lost more than half their purchasing power relative to manufactures (UNCTAD

2003: 19). Movements like this make it harder to predict what revenues will be derived from exports in any particular year. Agricultural products are particularly prone to large price fluctuations. Years when there is a glut in production can lead to price falls, while crop failures can lead to massive price increases. Agricultural production can also be hit by changes in fashion in the developed world. One exception to this pattern for primary commodities has been oil (Box 4.4).

Box 4.3 Coffee

Coffee is a commodity that illustrates clearly the problems that can confront the producer of raw materials, especially agricultural products. With the exception of oil, it is the commodity that earns the most for developing countries. An estimated 125 million people in the developing world depend on coffee production for their livelihoods. Yet it is an item the price of which fluctuates wildly, and in recent years has shown a dramatic fall in price.

Coffee basics: Most coffee is grown on small independent farms, in contrast to, for example, bananas, which are frequently grown on large plantations. It takes three years from planting a coffee bush until it produces the first beans.

Coffee prices: Over the past 25 years, international coffee prices declined rapidly. After frost destroyed much of the coffee harvest in Brazil in March 1977, coffee reached a peak price of $3,000 a tonne, from $500 per tonne in 1975. Subsequently, it declined rapidly to a price of around $350 per tonne.

Coffee problems: Three main problems confront the producers.

- *Price fluctuations*: The price hike of 1977 demonstrates what can happen when a harvest fails. The fall in output (or even a fear of a fall in output) from one region can send the price rocketing. For a short while the production of the commodity can be extremely profitable, and this of course can prompt new producers to switch to growing the product, in the (mistaken) belief that the price will remain high.

- *Oversupply*: The price of coffee on the international market fell dramatically because too much was being grown. Global overproduction has been exacerbated by a World Bank programme to introduce coffee production into Vietnam, which has risen rapidly to account for 10 per cent of global production.

- *Structure of the industry*: Although the large fluctuations in price and the oversupply of raw commodities are not unique to coffee, the industry's structure adds special problems. The millions of small farmers, with very limited power, face a very small number of producers with enormous power to dominate the final retailing of the product. In between there are numerous levels of wholesalers and other intermediaries. Coffee beans can change hands more than 150 times between farmer and supermarket shelf, and each time they change hands a smaller proportion of the final price reaches the grower. Thus while the coffee growers earned $10–$12 billion of the $30 billion global retail market for coffee in the early 1990s, by 2004 they were forecast to earn just $5.5 billion from a market now worth $70 billion.

Can fair trade provide an answer? Much has been made of the increasing share of the coffee market that sells under the label of Fair Trade. Fair trade coffee aims to benefit growers by dealing directly with farmers, eliminating layers in the supply chain. Farmers are guaranteed a floor price that at least covers the costs of production. Additionally, a bonus is always paid above international prices should they rise above the floor. The premium is earmarked for development projects agreed with the producers. Clearly fair trade is advantageous for those producers fortunate to be included. However, although fairly traded coffee as a proportion of the total is increasing, the figure is still very low, benefiting only thousands of farmers out of the millions involved in coffee production.

(UNCTAD 2003: 24–5)

Many developing countries have also been hampered in their attempts to participate more fully in the global economy by a continuing and chronic shortage of capital. Investment is significant for trade, particularly in the modern world economy, because it is only possible to compete in the most profitable areas with the most up-to-date equipment. Where equipment is outmoded, or the technology outdated, it becomes harder to manufacture goods, or even to extract raw materials or grow crops that can compete on the global market. Patterns of direct foreign investment are discussed in the next section.

Box 4.4 Organization of the Petroleum Exporting Countries (OPEC)

In terms of commodity exports, oil represents a special case. Nevertheless, it highlights further the difficulties that commodity exporters face.

Oil basics: Amongst oil's many uses are: as a source of energy for domestic and industrial electricity; to power transportation systems; as a lubricant; as the raw material for plastics. It has become central to the way of life of the developed world, but ultimately is a limited resource.

OPEC was founded in 1960 by a number of oil-producing countries in the developing world in an attempt to increase export revenues. In the 1950s, world oil consumption was growing rapidly. But oil prices fell throughout the decade. However, between 1970 and 1973 OPEC succeeded in doubling oil prices, through negotiation with Northern governments. Then, between October 1973 and January 1974, OPEC was able to further quadruple oil prices, by reaching an agreement between the members to restrict supply. In the 1970s, OPEC's success in increasing oil prices seemed to be a signal to developing countries that others too could get a better price for their commodity exports. But was oil a special case?

Accounting for OPEC's success: OPEC is an example of an export quota commodity agreement. Its members have been able to manipulate the price by regulating the supply. But this is not easy, especially as not all major producers are members.

On the supply side, export quota commodity agreements tend to be fragile because there is always a temptation for producers to defect. When prices rise through joint action to limit supply, there is always a risk that some member(s) will exploit the situation by increasing their supply to take advantage of the higher price. At times this has been a problem for OPEC and would be a much bigger issue where the number of producers is larger, like millions of coffee growers. Moreover, oil is not perishable, and to leave it in the ground does not affect its quality, unlike agricultural goods, which cannot be stored indefinitely.

On the demand side, there are ways of reducing its use (seeking other non-OPEC-controlled sources; using increased insulation; using coal, nuclear power, or synthetic substitutes; or reducing energy use generally), but these take time to introduce. Oil is still an essential item even if the requirements of climate mitigation recommend using less. And although oil as a proportion of total energy use has declined since the 1970s (in 1973 oil supplied 46.1 per cent of the world's energy requirements, compared to 34.4 per cent in 2006), this decline has to be seen in the light of an overall increase in demand for oil, particularly from rapidly growing economies such as China and India.

Since 2003 oil prices have been rising rapidly, reaching a peak in the summer of 2008. This has been the result partially of events in Afghanistan and Iraq, and partially of an increased demand for oil. For many oil-importing countries in the developing world this has resulted in a worsening in their economic position. Compared to developed countries, developing countries use more than twice as much oil to produce one unit of economic output. However, for oil-producing countries the increased oil price has provided increased export earnings and government reveneue. Some argue that this allows authoritarian governments in oil-producing countries to entrench their positions, contrary to a global shift towards democracy (Friedman 2006), whereas Youngs (2009) takes a more sceptical view.

(BP 2009; International Energy Agency 2008)

A further problem that developing countries confront is that of protectionism. Perhaps the simplest is the implementation of a trade tariff, the application of a tax on imports. A large element of the Common Agricultural Policy (CAP) of the European Union involves the use of tariffs to protect

STEPHEN HOBDEN

farmers from certain agricultural products from outside Europe. One effect of these tariffs is that countries within the European Union produce more than 45 per cent of the world's agricultural exports (WTO 2008: Table II.13). Another form of protectionism is the use of subsidies; so, for example, cotton farmers in the USA receive large subsidies on their production, to the disadvantage of African producers like Egypt. Furthermore, there are non-tariff barriers, such as quotas, whereby only specified quantities of a product can be imported, and other restrictions such as safety requirements, environmental, or labour standards that must be adhered to and which might be judged unreasonable (see Chapter 17). This whole area has been described as the **new protectionism** because governments have sought to defend domestic industries, while at the same time honouring commitments to lower trade tariffs as part of international agreements.

It has been estimated that developing countries are losing US$1,000 billion each year from protectionist measures in industrialized countries (O'Brien and Williams 2007: 144). Tariff barriers are far higher in developed countries than in the rest of the world. At the same time, the richest countries in the world have increased their subsidies to their agricultural industries, making it harder for developing countries to compete.

Key points

- Since 1945 there have been massive increases in the levels of international trade.
- Although there are some exceptions, many countries in the developing world do not appear to have benefited greatly, and the proportion of the world's exports provided by Africa and Latin America has declined.
- Although the theory of comparative advantage suggests that all countries would benefit from participation in trading, the 'gains from trade' are not shared equally for various reasons.

Foreign Direct Investment

The theory of comparative advantage suggests that a country should specialize in those goods that it can produce relatively more cheaply. One area in which the developing world has a distinct economic advantage is in labour costs. Throughout the developing world it is cheaper to employ workers than in developed economies.

It would therefore seem logical for companies from the developed world to relocate production from those economies in which labour costs are high to those in which such costs are lower. For some companies the employment of female workers has been particularly attractive (see Box 4.5).

Box 4.5 Women in the Global Economy

In 2008, of the 3 billion people in paid employment worldwide 1.2 billion were women. Of these 1.2 billion, only 18 per cent were employed in industry (compared to 26.6 per cent of men). Women are consistently over-represented in the agricultural sector, especially in Asia and Africa, and a larger proportion of women are employed in the service sector. Women tend to be subject to more insecure employment, and have less choice in terms of sector of employment and working conditions. Wage inequality between men and women is a worldwide phenomenon. In most countries women can expect to earn 70–90 per cent of their male counterparts' pay, and, in some parts of Asia and Latin America, even lower proportions (ILO 2009).

One issue that has been particularly relevant to the role of women in the global economy has been the employment of women in export processing zones in developing countries. Export processing zones have been set up by governments to encourage inward investment by foreign companies, manufacturing products like electronics, toys, and clothes. The factories are often described as sweat shops because of the poor conditions for workers. Women are disproportionately represented (although in some countries this trend may be slowing) (Braunstein 2006), because they are deemed more suitable, that is to say passive and prepared to accept low wages and no job security as well as being nimble-fingered and amenable to training (Elson and Pearson 1981).

With improvements in transportation and communications associated with globalization it has become easier for companies to set up production facilities in different parts of the world. O'Brien and Williams define FDI as 'investment made outside the home country of the investing company in which control over the resources transferred remains with the investor' (2007: 176). In other words, a key feature of FDI is that production will be directed by (and presumably organized to benefit) a corporation from outside the territory in which the investment is made. One of the aims of much recent policy promoted by the World Bank and IMF has been to encourage governments in the developing world to promote inwards investment—for example by reducing taxation levels, and removing controls on capital flows. However, there has been much debate about the extent to which investment by TNCs benefits the host economies, with accusations that they use their size to extract inordinate benefits (see Box 4.6). This is an area of much controversy, and it is better to look at the actions of individual TNCs in different countries rather than necessarily drawing general conclusions.

There is a considerable amount of data on the levels of FDI, and one of the features of this activity is that it fluctuates on a year-by-year basis. Levels of FDI dropped off quite considerably following the terrorist attacks on the World Trade Center in New York in 2001, although they now appear to be increasing again. Tables 4.2 and 4.3 present data taken from statistics compiled by the United Nations Conference on Trade and Development. From these tables a few general observations can be derived.

Box 4.6 Advantages and Disadvantages of Foreign Direct Investment

Advocates of FDI argue that TNCs:

- *introduce additional resources*. In particular they bring capital, a resource of which many developing countries are particularly short. Furthermore, they bring technology, financial resources, managerial expertise, and access to foreign markets.

- *increase tax revenues*. TNCs will contribute to government revenues by paying local taxes.

- *increase efficiency*. By providing links to the global economy, TNCs introduce competition into the local economy, thus encouraging more efficient local production.

- *improve the balance of payments*. TNCs improve the balance of payments by producing local goods that previously had been imported, and producing goods for export.

While critics suggest that TNCs:

- *bring little in the way of new technology*. Most of the activities carried out by TNCs primarily involve assembly of parts produced elsewhere, and involve very little in the way of high technology.

- *contribute little to the local economy*. TNCs, through a process known as 'transfer pricing', are able to ensure that they pay their taxes on profits in countries with low tax regimes (usually in the developed world). Furthermore, critics argue, TNCs drive local firms out of business using unfair competitive practices.

• *worsen the balance of payments*. TNCs can have a negative impact on the balance of payments through the need to import machinery, spare parts, and payments to the parent company.

• *adversely affect the local culture*. By introducing global brands, TNCs can undermine the market for locally produced goods and tastes.

• *have a negative effect on the political system*. As TNCs are so large and powerful, and have a large impact on a small economy, they are able to extract concessions from governments by threatening to withdraw their facilities, or through bribery and corruption.

Table 4.2 Foreign Direct Investment Inflows by Region (US$ billion)

Region	1989–94		2000		2007	
	Annual average	% of total	Total	% of total	Total	% of total
World	200.2		1,270.8		1,833.3	
Developed world	137.1	68	1,005.2	79	1,247.6	68
Developing world	59.6	30	240.2	19	499.7	27
Central and Eastern Europe	3.4	2	25.4	2	85.9	5
Africa	3.9	2	8.2	0.6	52.9	3
Latin America and the Caribbean	17.5	9	86.2	7	67.5	7
Asia	37.7	19	143.8	11	319.3	17

Source: United Nations Conference on Trade and Development (UNCTAD) 2001: Table B1; 2008b: Table B1

Table 4.3 Top Ten Recipients of Foreign Direct Investment in the Developing World, 2000 and 2004

Country	2000 US$ billions	% of developing world total	Country	2004 US$ billions	% of developing world total
Hong Kong, China	64.5	27	China	83.5	17
China	40.8	17	Hong Kong, China	59.9	12
Brazil	33.5	14	Brazil	34.6	7
Mexico	13.2	6	Mexico	24.7	5
Argentina	11.2	5	Saudi Arabia	24.3	5
South Korea	10.2	4	Singapore	24.1	5
Bermuda	6.6	3	India	22.9	5
Singapore	6.4	3	Turkey	22.1	4
Malaysia	5.5	2	Chile	14.5	3
Taiwan	4.9	2	United Arab Emirates	13.3	3

Source: United Nations Conference on Trade and Development (UNCTAD) 2001: Table B1; 2008b: Table B1

- Levels of FDI have risen considerably since the early 1990s. In the year 2007, levels of FDI were nearly ten times higher than the average for 1989–2004, although it should be noted that this figure is expected to decline due to the 2008–10 world economic crisis.

- The bulk of FDI is made by companies from the developed world investing in other developed countries (for example, Japanese car plants in Britain). However, the figures for 2007 suggest that the proportion of investment flowing to the developing world is increasing. It should also be noted that developing world TNCs have now started to emerge as some of the largest companies in the world.

- Although the proportion of FDI flowing to the developing world is increasing, it is very concentrated. Just ten countries absorb 65 per cent of FDI directed to the developing world. In 2007, China was the largest recipient, and the combined figures for China and Hong Kong account for nearly 30 per cent of developing world FDI, albeit less than in previous years. The relative proportion of FDI flowing into Africa is increasing, and in 2007 stood at just over 10 per cent of all developing world inward investment.

Key points

- FDI is a major component of global financial flows.

- Although the bulk of investment occurs in developed countries, a small number of developing countries receive a significant, and increasing, proportion of the global total.

- There is considerable debate over the costs and benefits of FDI for developing countries.

Financial Flows

Trade and FDI are the more visible aspects of the global economy, yet in numerical terms they are dwarfed by the movements of money through the world's foreign exchanges. World merchandise trade amounts to approximately US$ 14 trillion per year (WTO 2008: Table I.6). This is the equivalent of just over four days' trading on the world's money markets (BIS 2007: 1). The sheer size of these financial flows compared to the volume of global production suggests that a large component of these transactions is speculative (see Scholte 2005: 166). The operation of financial markets and the rapid flows of what is described as 'hot' money are often perceived as having an adverse effect on local economies, especially those in the developing world, and have been the subject of considerable criticism (see Box 4.7).

These financial flows comprise two main elements. First, quite simply the buying and selling of money. Some of these transactions are related to trade and investment. For example, if a company in Britain were to want to purchase goods from Ghana, it would first need to purchase Ghanaian *cedi* in order to pay the supplier. However, much of the activity on the global currency markets could be more closely equated to gambling. Since the 1980s, many of world's major currencies have been free-floating. In other words, governments have allowed the value of the currency to be largely dictated by the sentiments of the market. Some investors have made, and continue to make, large fortunes simply based on the buying of currencies that they anticipate will go up in value and selling those that they expect will become worth less. These financial movements can have implications for even the largest of economies: in 1992 Britain was forced out of the European Exchange Rate Mechanism following large-scale selling of sterling.

Box 4.7 Susan Strange on the Irrationality of Financial Markets

❝ Mad . . . is exactly how financial markets have behaved in recent years. They have been erratically manic at one moment, unreasonably depressive at others. The crises that have hit them have been unpredicted and, to most observers surprising. Their behaviour has very seriously damaged others. Their condition calls urgently for treatment of some kind. ❞ (Strange 1998: 2)

A second feature of global financial flows is investment in the stock markets of other countries, usually described as 'portfolio investment', or indirect foreign investment. FDI usually involves the construction of factories and offices and the purchase of machinery. If the owner wishes to move production to another country these need to be disposed of or transferred, possibly a time-consuming activity. Holders of portfolio investment do not have a direct link to the bricks and mortar of the company concerned. They can sell their holdings of shares in overseas territories at the press of a computer button. This buying and selling of shares can take the pattern of a herd instinct. Certain countries or regions become very popular, meaning that large numbers of shares are bought, leading to stock market booms. At other times the same regions suddenly become unpopular — large numbers of shares are sold, leading to stock market crashes. These sudden changes of sentiment often have very little to do with the underlying economic stability or potential of the countries concerned. However, as with the buying and selling of currencies, for the insightful (or lucky) investor there are fortunes to be made by 'buying cheap and selling dear'. Furthermore, the rapid movements of money into and

out of economies can be extremely destabilizing to the domestic economy.

During the late 1980s and early 1990s, many countries in the developing world were encouraged to open their economies to these kinds of financial flow. Financial liberalization involved removing restrictions on the buying and selling of the country's currency, and on the movements of capital in and out of the country. Such policies were adopted by many countries in Latin America, East Asia, and the former Soviet Union. For many analysts it is not a coincidence that these regions were afflicted by severe financial disruption during the 1990s. Examples are the Mexican *peso* crisis of 1994–95, the Brazilian crisis, Russia's *rouble* crisis of 1998, and a crisis in Argentina dating from 2000.

Perhaps the most famous of the financial crises of the 1990s was the one that swept through East Asia in 1997. There is much debate about the causes, and no simple explanation. However, one factor might be that these countries were simply the victims of their own success. As discussed in Box 4.2, East Asian countries were very successful at following export-led models of development. They also were enjoying very high levels of domestic saving and low inflation—a perfect conjunction for continued growth. However, following financial liberalization, the perceived profitability of the region led to a vast inflow of speculative investment that the countries' domestic financial institutions were not able to manage. A speculative boom was followed by a crash. Bankruptcies in South Korea and Thailand led to a rapid withdrawal of funds from the entire region. The outcome was reductions in the rate of growth and in GDP per head, the second taking several years to recover. Analyses by the World Bank and IMF now suggest that the pace of financial liberalization was the problem. It is also worth pointing out that India and China, two of the fastest-growing economies in the world, have not implemented equivalent levels of financial liberalization, and were only indirectly affected by the crisis that swept through the region.

Key points

- A major component of the global economy is the movements of money involved in the buying and selling of currencies and stocks and shares in local economies.
- The rapid movement of capital associated with these markets can be extremely disruptive to local economies.

- In the 1990s, a number of countries in the developing world adopted financial liberalization policies, removing restrictions on the flows of international capital into and out of their economies. Many of these countries were affected by subsequent financial crises.

The Global Economy in Crisis: Implications for the Developing World

Many commentators claim that the global economic crisis that has materialized since 2007 is the most serious economic disruption since the great depression of the 1920s and 1930s. Although the crisis originated in the developed world, particularly the US, it became a global crisis with particular implications for developing areas. Although the origins of the crisis may look complicated, in essence it appears to be an old-fashioned credit crisis, sparked by ill-advised mortgage lending in the US (the so-called 'sub-prime' market). This crisis spread to the banking sector more generally, resulting in an unwillingness by banks to make loans. As a result economic activity slumped in the world's most advanced economies. This had a ripple effect on the global economy. In 2009 global gross national product (the aggregated gross national products of all the world's economies) dropped for the first time since the Second World War. This downturn created some specific problems for developing regions.

First, there was the substantial drop in the rate of growth of world trade. According to the WTO the rate of growth in 2007 was 5.5 per cent, down from 8.5 per cent in 2006, with an expected further drop in 2009. As more developing countries become integrated into the world economy, and often rely on

exports to contribute substantially to GDP, this is significant. A further feature of the downturn has been a drop in the prices of primary commodities. As noted earlier many developing countries are heavily reliant on the export of raw materials and are vulnerable to fluctuations in commodity prices. According to the World Bank non-oil commodity prices declined by 38 per cent in the second half of 2008. There are some benefits from a drop in commodity prices. For oil-importing countries in the developing world the drop in the price of oil from its July 2008 peak provided some relief on the import side, but the price began climbing again in late 2009.

The loss of income from exporting has been compounded by a reduction in financial flows into developing countries. As noted above the level of FDI increased dramatically since the 1990s with a substantial proportion of investment taking place in developing countries. As the global recession takes hold this is expected to decline further. According to UNCTAD estimates, global levels of FDI are expected to decline by 50 per cent in 2009 affecting both the developed and developing world.

Two further sources of income for developing countries, remittances and international development aid, will be affected. Remittances are money transfers from workers in one country back to their families in their country of origin. For some countries, remittances (especially from the Gulf states to South Asian countries) can contribute significantly to GDP, and for many families in the developing world remittances from a family member working abroad can make a sizeable addition to the household income. In previous economic crises, rich country governments have cut their aid budgets (UNCTAD, 2009b) and this seems likely to happen again, as they spend heavily on bolstering domestic economic activity.

Countries in the developing world are therefore likely to be hit by multiple reductions to their economic well-being—loss of income from exporting possibilities, reduced commodity prices, cuts in FDI, remittances and aid. Many developing countries (in Africa especially) are more likely to be affected by the economic downturn: most do not have the financial resources to substitute increased public spending for reduced capital and income streams from abroad. However, this goes beyond the purely economic realm. The global economic crisis is likely to result in increased numbers living in absolute poverty, throwing into reverse recent modest reductions in the numbers. According to the UN Standing Committee on Nutrition, the numbers living in extreme poverty have increased by 130–155 million in 2005–08, with a further increase of 53 million expected in 2009 (UNSCN, 2009). The World Bank estimates that an between 200,000 to 400,000 *additional* children will die due to poverty related illnesses as a direct consequence of the global recession.

Key points

- Since 2007 the global economy has entered a period of considerable instability. A credit crisis in the world's most developed economies has expanded outwards towards all sectors and regions of the global economy.

- Developing countries have been particularly susceptible to the downturn as a result of the slowdown in the rate of global trade, and reductions in investment, remittances and aid.

Conclusion

Since 1945, the global economy has seen not only massive increases in the levels of world trade, but also an enormous growth in the prosperity of the developed world. With the emergence of a single global economy since 1990, these processes have accelerated. For most analysts these two features are closely linked. Yet the benefits of greater engagement in the global economy do not appear to have been obtained by the poorest countries. Why, in an era of a global economy and neo-liberal policies, are some countries poorer than they were a decade or even much longer ago?

A free market analysis would suggest that there are still too many blockages to the free movement of investment and goods. Poorer countries have undermined their own prospects of development by working against the market. A second position maintains that greater engagement is potentially beneficial, but because developing countries are behind the developed world in terms of industrialization, reforms to the global economy are required. A more radical position would argue that the global economic system entrenches inequality between the richest parts of the world and the poorest. For the past twenty years, the free market philosophy has dominated development policy (see Chapter 16). But although many developing countries have followed neo-liberal prescriptions, they still face protectionist measures imposed in the developed world. This makes it more difficult to persuade them to proceed faster or in a more comprehensive fashion. Protectionist measures in the developed world have caused WTO talks on further trade liberalization to stall.

The reasons for the disparity of wealth in the global economy will be disputed indefinitely. For the foreseeable future developing countries will have to make their way within a global capitalist environment. The operation of global markets has the potential to generate enormous wealth as well as the capability to exploit the most vulnerable. The governments of developing countries have the awesome task of trying to minimize the negative impacts of global capitalism, while attracting the potential benefits for their populations. Economic crisis makes this task even more difficult. China's rise (see Chapter 23b) displays the possibilities for developing countries in a global economy. Indeed, its rapid economic expansion is a contributory factor in decreases in global absolute poverty. Yet China has not played, so far, by the globalization 'handbook'—its participation in the global economy is by its own rules. Thus far this seems to have been to its benefit, although consequences flowing from its accession to the WTO in December 2001 are now causing some resentment. Meanwhile, governments of the developed world also confront a challenge: to resolve the contradiction of promoting free trade as a solution for the developing world while maintaining protectionism at home. Until they resolve this it would appear that the global economy operates largely in the interests of the rich and powerful and against some of the poorest and least influential parts of the world.

? Questions

1. What impacts has globalization had on the developing world?

2. Who benefits from the 'gains from trade'?

3. Do the costs of direct foreign investment outweigh the benefits for developing countries?

4. What problems do developing counties confront in dealing with global financial flows?

5. Assess the impacts of the global financial crisis of 2008–09 on developing countries.

→ Further reading

■ Dicken, P. (2007), *Global Shift: Mapping the Changing Contours of the World Economy*, 5th edn (London: Sage). Clear overview of the emergence of a global economy, with good sections on the newly industrializing countries.

■ Mandle, J. R. (2003), *Globalization and the Poor* (Cambridge: Cambridge University Press). A good overview of arguments for and against economic globalization.

■ O'Brien, R. and Williams, M. (2007), *Global Political Economy: Evolution and Dynamics*, 2nd edn (Basingstoke: Palgrave Macmillan). Clear discussion of the development of the global economy and key contemporary issues in international political economy.

■ Scholte, J. A. (2005), *Globalization: A Critical Introduction*, 2nd edn (Basingstoke: Palgrave). A superb discussion of the subject and associated literature.

■ Todaro, M. and Smith, S. (2009), *Economic Development*, 10th edn (Harlow: Pearson). Regularly revised and updated, contains excellent chapters on the role of developing countries in the global economy and on theories of trade.

■ Valdez, S. (2007), *An Introduction to Global Financial Markets*, 5th edn (Basingstoke: Palgrave). Effective introduction to the murky world of global finance.

■ Van Marrewijk, C. (2002), *International Trade and the World Economy* (Oxford: Oxford University Press). Excellent introduction to theories of trade and investment in the global economy.

:// Web links

■ **www.cato.org/trade-immigration** The site of the Cato Institute ('individual liberty, free markets, and peace'), a Washington DC-based non-profit public policy research foundation committed to the principles of limited government and free markets, including free trade.

■ **www.twnside.org.sg/trade.htm** Third World Network page on trade issues; provides research critical of current global economic policies.

■ **www.unctad.org** United Nations Conference on Trade and Development, containing voluminous data on trade and investment, and reports on the latest developments in the global economy.

■ **www.oxfam.org** The site of the non-governmental organization Oxfam (UK), containing many of its reports on trade and protectionism.

■ **www.undp.org** United Nations Development Programme—the United Nations body that focuses on development issues and produces annually a Human Development Report.

Online Resource Centre

For additional material and resources, please visit the Online Resource Centre at:
www.oxfordtextbooks.co.uk/orc/burnell3e/

The Developing World in International Politics

Stephen Hobden

Chapter contents

Overview

The previous chapter examined the role of the developing world in the global economy. In this chapter, the emphasis changes to the role of the developing world in international politics. International relations as a discipline has traditionally overlooked the significance of the developing world in global politics. The chapter opens with an examination of the reasons for this and goes on to discuss why such an oversight is lamentable. The chapter will then look at the position of the developing world through the large structural changes that have occurred in the international system since 1945: the cold war; the post-cold war world; and the emerging multipolar world, in which China is anticipated to return to the centre of international politics.

Introduction: International Relations and the Developing World

The developing world has been 'on the periphery' of the study or discipline of international relations (IR) (Thomas and Wilkin 2004). The discipline has primarily been concerned with relations between the great (or super) powers. Although perhaps understandable, this focus is deeply problematic. First, it has meant that at least four-fifths of the global population was excluded as a subject of study. Second, it overlooks the central role played by developing countries as actors in international politics, and as sites of confrontation and competition. This has reflected a North American and European perspective on the world. It fails to acknowledge that while, during the cold war, there was a 'long peace' in Europe, many parts of the developing world were deeply mired in violent conflict, in which the superpowers were frequently involved. The rivalry between the superpowers was played out in a way that was far from 'cold', fuelling **proxy wars**, for instance in southern Africa and Central America. Third, it overlooks fundamental changes to the international system: the dissolution of the European empires; and the rise of China.

The focus on the superpowers may reflect a deeper problem with the discipline. That is quite simply that traditional IR theory does not have the tools to understand the developing world. The traditional world view of IR is one in which the state is the key actor, and is the guarantor of the 'good life' for its citizens. States operate in a situation of 'anarchy', in which they all have equal sovereignty, and must all in the final instance be liable for their own self-defence. Within the confines of the state there is order and hierarchy, while outside of the state is characterized by unregulated disorder. From the perspective of the developing world this world view may make little sense. The state, rather than being the guarantor of the 'good life', has frequently been a major threat to the well-being of the individual. Many developing countries have been governed at some time or another by military regimes, which have targeted sections of the society for repression. The states of Latin America have, by and large, lived at peace with each other since the 1930s, but regimes in virtually every country in the region have committed major human rights violations. The anarchy has been on the inside rather than the outside. Furthermore, the state, rather than being the key actor, has had to compete with numerous other powerful actors, such as **warlords**, guerrilla groups, and drug cartels, which in some places appear to threaten its very existence. More recently, when developing countries acquiesced in **structural adjustment programmes** (SAPs), external actors have had more power over the running of the society than the state itself. At the same time as domestic politics in the developing world perspective can be viewed as disordered, the external world appears to be more hierarchical, with the most powerful states determining the fates of the less powerful. Sovereignty, the right of states to govern within their own territory without external interference, a fundamental tenet of the Charter of the United Nations, has been breached many times since 1945 (see Dickson 1997: ch. 1; Neuman 1998: 2–12).

While traditional approaches have tended to focus on those states with the most power, there have always been perspectives that attempted to incorporate an analysis of the developing world. Marxist approaches, in particular dependency and world-systems schools, have stressed the importance of a global economic system in which the developing world has played a key role as the supplier of cheap labour and raw materials, and as a market for surplus production. More recently, post-colonial theorists (heavily influenced by post-structuralist approaches) have focused on questions of identity during and after the colonial period (see Chapter 2).

Key points

- The discipline of international relations has tended to focus on the role of the great (or super) powers.
- This focus has ignored the vast proportion of the global population, and the key role that the developing world has played in the global politics of the cold war and post-cold war periods.

The cold war

The term 'cold war' refers to the period of confrontation between the United States and the former Soviet Union between 1945 and 1990. The international system during this time is often described as bipolar, meaning two superpowers, although the now obsolete notion of a 'Third World' is also closely linked to this period. This term is derived from a perceived tripartite division of the world:

- a 'First World'—the United States, and its allies;
- a 'Second World'—the Soviet Union, and Eastern Europe;
- a 'Third World' comprising the rest—the newly decolonized countries of Asia and Africa, and the countries of Latin America, most of which had gained their independence at the start of the nineteenth century.

This was a ridiculous oversimplification, although the ideological and strategic conflict played out between the superpowers certainly had a major impact felt by most countries of the Third World. This conflict took a variety of forms. There were cases of direct military intervention by the superpowers, such as the USA in Vietnam, and the Soviet Union in Afghanistan. There were many examples of indirect intervention using either the carrot of aid policy, or the stick of sanctions, or the threat of the withdrawal of aid. There was also the use of proxy fighting forces to avoid direct intervention. Examples here include the funding by the USA of the Mujahidin to challenge the Soviet Union in Afghanistan, and the use of the Cuban army to support leftist governments in southern Africa.

Once both superpowers had access to nuclear weapons, any direct confrontation would have been, in the terminology of the time, MAD—mutually assured destruction. However, a history of the cold war is incomplete without a consideration of how the superpower competition was conducted in the developing world. A range of interests underpinned the superpowers' policies towards the developing world. For both there were security issues, both had trading concerns, and for both there were ideological issues that related to their views of themselves as nations. These different interests played out in different ways at different times.

In the beginning of the cold war (1945–55), the US government's main interest in the developing areas was in supporting the calls for decolonization, in line with its world view that a decolonized world would be more in its own interests. This was coupled, however, with a concern that newly independent countries should not fall under Soviet influence. Therefore there was a tension between the USA's support for decolonization, and its wish to maintain international stability. Additionally, with the triumph of Mao's revolutionary army in China, and North Korea's invasion of the South of the country, there was fear that communist influence was spreading in East Asia. The Soviet Union was barely engaged at this time. Stalin, now in physical decline, did not try to exploit Lenin's theory that the developing world was a weak link for the capitalist system, and had done little to support the Communist Party in China.

From the late 1950s and through the 1960s, both superpowers increased their activities in the developing world. The USA was particularly active in its own 'back yard', supporting the overthrow of democratically elected President Arbenz in Guatemala (1954), and attempting to overthrow Castro in Cuba (1961 onwards). Throughout this period it also became increasingly involved in the war between North and South Vietnam. Following the death of Stalin, the Soviet Union gave more attention to the newly independent countries, seeking to draw them under its influence. However, it lacked the power projection to protect potential satellite states. For example, in 1960 Prime Minister Lumumba of the Congo sought military aid to counter secessionists in his newly independent country, but the Soviet Union was not able to respond and the country soon came under the rule of Joseph Mobutu, who looked to the West. Likewise, in the autumn of 1962 the Soviet Union withdrew the missiles that it had placed on Cuba rather than risk a direct military confrontation with the United States.

As the USA became increasingly drawn into the Vietnam quagmire through the 1960s, confidence about its role in the world declined, and anti-US sentiment grew. The Soviet Union was now getting closer to strategic parity with the USA and was able to project its power with greater confidence. It gave direct support to revolutionary movements in Vietnam, Ethiopia, and Angola, and as a result gained strategic bases in Africa and Asia. It also supported revolutionary movements in Central America, giving it influence very close to the United States. This growing confidence led it to launch a major military intervention in Afghanistan in late 1979 to support a friendly regime on its southern border.

The global situation changed dramatically in the following decade. It was now the Soviet Union that was mired in a foreign war, and the USA under President Reagan exploited the situation. The USA sought 'rollback'—reversing Soviet gains of the 1970s, and under the 'Reagan doctrine' support was given to anti-communist guerrillas. In Afghanistan the USA supported the Mujahidin, in Nicaragua the 'Contras', and in Angola, UNITA (National Union for Total Independence of Angola). As the decade drew on, the cold war moved to a close. Mikhail Gorbachev's 'new thinking' as leader of the Soviet Union sought a new relationship with the West and a Soviet withdrawal from Afghanistan. The impact of the Afghan war on the Soviet Union was at least comparable to that of the Vietnam War on the USA. Although not the sole cause of the collapse of the Soviet Union, within two years of the withdrawal from Afghanistan, Communist Party rule had ended. At the same time, material support for former satellite states, even Cuba, also ended.

The cold war was a time of great upheaval for the developing world. In the period immediately after the Second World War, most of it was still under colonial control. By the end of the cold war it was mostly independent. This wave of decolonization was accompanied by an international conflict between the two superpowers, fought over and in developing countries. For their governments it meant making a choice to align with one superpower or the other. This pressure provoked the creation of the Non-Aligned Movement in 1961—a collection of states that claimed to reject both superpowers, although in reality most states (Cuba for example) were aligned with one or other superpower.

The existence of two competing superpowers did mean that a choice existed for developing countries. Many countries were courted by both sides, with rival offers of financial and economic aid. For some the possibility existed to switch allegiances (or at least to threaten to switch). Egypt in the early 1970s changed its alignment from the Soviet Union to the United States, becoming one of the largest recipients of aid. The cold war provided these countries with at least an option between two superpowers with two ideologies concerning the operation of social and economic systems, and the goals and modalities of development (see Allison and Williams 1990; Halliday 1989; Merrill 1994; Westad 2005).

The United Nations

An important actor during this period was the United Nations (UN). The UN was created during the latter part of the Second World War as an organization the key role of which was the maintenance of international peace and security. Although most would argue that the UN has been singularly unsuccessful in this aspect, it has played a significant role in a number of other aspects. In addition to its security remit, the Charter of the organization also commits its members to cooperation on economic and development issues, and these have had a number of implications for developing countries. In this development sphere (or the 'other UN') the organization can perhaps claim the largest area of success (see Box 5.1). Furthermore the organization had an inbuilt predisposition towards decolonization. Charter signatories with responsibilities for non-self-governing territories (in other words, colonies) committed 'to develop self-government, to take due account of the political aspirations of the peoples, and to assist them in the progressive development of their free political institutions' (UN Charter Article 73.B). As discussed in Box 5.2, the UN played a key role in the process of decolonization, and in turn the character of the organization was transformed.

Box 5.1 United Nations' Achievements in Development

The UN has been involved in development issues in a number of ways:

- as an information source, with experts in economics, agriculture, and industrial development;

- direct assistance in emergency situations;

- the creation of regional organizations to address the particular problems of specific areas, for example the Economic Commission for Asia and the Far East;

- specific development responsibilities of UN agencies, for example the UNDP and the UNHCR (High Commissioner for Refugees);

- numerous resolutions in the General Assembly related to development issues;

- a series of 'development decades', intended to keep issues such as global inequality on the agenda.

The UN can point to a number of areas of success:

- life expectancy globally has increased;

- child mortality rates for under-5s have decreased;

- immunization levels have improved, as has access to primary health facilities, availability of clean water, and literacy levels;

- an achievement that can be directly attributed to a UN agency is the eradication of smallpox, coordinated by the World Health Organization.

That the organization retains such goals is demonstrated by the Millennium Declaration adopted in September 2000. This pledged the member states to work towards ambitious goals including halving the proportion of the world's population living on less than US1 a day, and ensuring that all the world's children receive a primary education (see Chapter 16).

Box 5.2 United Nations and Decolonization

The end of the European empires is one of the most significant developments of the last century. The oversight of this process is perhaps one of the UN's greatest achievements. The notion of self-determination is at the core of the Charter, articulated in Article 1(2) and repeated in Article 55. Furthermore, a pledge to develop self-government in non-self-governing territories (a euphemism for colonies) is made in Article 73.

In the immediate aftermath of the Second World War a small number of countries became independent. For example, India gained independence from Britain in 1947. The first move of newly independent countries was to take up a seat in the UN General Assembly as a mark of sovereignty and independence. The newly independent states were critical of the continuation of empire, and the General Assembly became the main forum in which calls for decolonization were voiced. By 1960, there were sufficient members to allow the passing of Resolution 1514, which condemned the continuation of colonialism. In the 1960s, several African states became independent and further resolutions were passed calling for colonialism to be eradicated.

The UN also acted in a very practical way to smooth the process of decolonization. The withdrawal of colonial powers from territories was seldom a straightforward affair, frequently leaving civil strife and disastrous levels of underdevelopment. The UN was frequently drawn into such situations, as peacekeeper and as provider of essential services. With the withdrawal of the British from India, massive unrest broke out between the Hindu and Muslim populations of India and the newly created state of Pakistan. There was massive loss of life and displacement of population. The UN Security Council voted to send an observer group to monitor the situation in the hope that an outside group might calm the situation. UNMOGIP (United Nations Military Observer Group in India and Pakistan) was created in 1949 to patrol the border area in Kashmir. It remains in place today.

Decolonization also transformed the organization itself. There were 51 original members in 1945, and the USA and the West in general had a built-in majority in the General Assembly. By 1960 (when Resolution 1514 was passed) the situation had changed dramatically—to 100 members, of whom 66 were from the developing world, including 46 from Africa and Asia. By this point, the General Assembly was supporting the position adapted adopted by the United States in around half of all votes taken. By 1980, more than half of the UN consisted of non-founder members, which had not been sovereign states in 1945. Their loyalty to a US-dominated world order was low and the vast majority of the votes in the Assembly were against the US position and in support of the Soviet Union. As a result, the General Assembly became the forum for issues that were a priority for the developing world.

Key points

- During the cold war the superpowers intervened in the developing world in a variety of different ways.

- The superpowers were motivated by a variety of different interests: military security; trade; and ideology. The significance of these interests varied over time and location.

- The cold war was a source of instability for many countries in the developing world. However, in a world in which neutrality from the global struggle was difficult, there was a choice of ideology and model of development.

- A key feature of the cold war period was the dissolution of virtually all of the European colonies. The United Nations was a key actor in this process, and was itself transformed as a result.

North–South Relations in the 'Unipolar Moment'

The end of the cold war in the late 1980s was greeted with optimism. The United States emerged as the 'winner' of the contest, and appeared to enjoy an unassailable position in terms of economic, military, and political power. Some argued however, that this dominant position (or unipolarity) might be short-lived (see Krauthammer 1991). How would the remaining superpower employ that considerable power, and what would be the implications for the developing world? The father and son presidencies of George H. W. Bush (1989–93) and George W. Bush (2001–09) demonstrate very different visions of what came to be called the 'new world order'

In a 1991 speech, US President George H. W. Bush spoke of a new world order that would be 'an historic period of cooperation . . . an era in which the nations of the world, East and West, North and South, can prosper and live in harmony' (quoted in Acharya 1999: 84). In the early 1990s, there was a sense that a new form of global cooperation could result in solving many of the world's problems. For many in the developed world this sense of peace and well-being was enhanced by a prolonged economic boom through much of the 1990s.

For developing countries too, there were reasons to be optimistic. The cold war had been a cause of instability, and its end promised greater peace and stability. Accompanying the end of the forty-year superpower conflict a number of regional conflicts were also resolved—particularly in southern Africa (Mozambique, Namibia, and, temporarily, in Angola) and Central America (Nicaragua and El Salvador). A new spirit of cooperation in the United Nations Security Council enabled that organization to become more active in conflict resolution. The UN achieved notable successes in Namibia, El Salvador, and Cambodia. It authorized an international military response to Iraq's invasion of Kuwait in 1990. Furthermore, a number of corrupt regimes that had been supported by one side or the other were replaced by democratic governments. There was much talk of a 'peace dividend' and considerable reductions in arms spending, which could be funnelled towards development projects. At the Millennial UN General Assembly ambitious commitments were made by the member states to reverse global poverty. Also, the prospect of a truly global economy appeared to promise more extensive trading links with the hope of generating greater wealth.

Such developments did indeed suggest that the world had reached the 'end of history' as claimed by Francis Fukuyama in 1992. There were indications, however, that this view might be optimistic. A UN-sponsored intervention in Somalia resulted in a humiliating withdrawal following the killing of 18 US soldiers. In 1994, the global community looked the other way while **genocide** occurred in Rwanda. A more sombre account of post-cold war international relations was provided by Samuel Huntington's view that the cold war would be replaced by a **clash of civilizations** (see Box 5.3). The terrorist attacks on the USA in 2001 (9/11) appeared to confirm this gloomy prognosis, and the euphoria of the immediate post-cold war period was replaced by a 'global melancholy' (Halliday 2002: 214). The prospects for developing countries started to look less promising. While the end of the cold war did provide greater stability in some areas, there has been greater instability in other regions. Afghanistan, for example, has been in a constant state of upheaval, and the Democratic Republic of Congo descended into chaos, with its neighbouring countries intervening on opposing sides.

With the election of George W. Bush, concerns started to surface about how the USA would use its position as the only superpower. The unipolar era of cooperation appeared to transform into one in which 'cooperation' would be very much on the terms, and in the interests of the dominant power. In the aftermath of 9/11 the US government declared its willingness to act unilaterally and preemptively to further its national security interests, and the invasion of Iraq in 2003 occurred without the clear support of the United Nations Security Council (see Box 5.4). With the inauguration of a new US president in January 2009, there are signs of at least a new tone in terms of relations between the US and the rest of the world. What has been most striking has been President Obama's attempts to forge a new relationship with the Muslim world (especially the 'Cairo' speech in June 2009). It is too early to say whether his administration will constitute a significant break from that of his predecessor.

Box 5.3 'End of History' or 'Clash of Civilizations'?

With the end of the cold war, and the emergence of the United States as the dominant world power, two accounts of international politics made a crossover from the academic arena to the wider policy and media arenas. Both had implications for North–South relations. In 1989 Francis Fukuyama published a much-discussed article in which he speculated whether, with the demise of the Soviet Union as an ideological and military threat to the United States, the human race had reached the end of history.

> " The triumph of the West, of the Western *idea* is evident first of all in the total exhaustion of viable systematic alternatives to Western liberalism. What we might be witnessing is not just the end of the Cold War, or the passing of a particular period of post-war history, but the end of history as such: that is the end of mankind's ideological evolution and the universalisation of Western liberal democracy as the final form of human government. The vast bulk of the Third World remains very much mired in history and will be a terrain of conflict for many years to come, but large scale conflict must involve large states still caught in the grip of history, and they are what appear to be passing from the scene.
>
> " (Fukuyama 1992, first written 1989, emphasis in original)

Fukuyama's was essentially an optimistic liberal account. The global future was liberal democracy. Crucially, as conflict between democratic states was unlikely (the so-called democratic peace theory), the future prospect was for a more peaceful world.

A different view was offered by Samuel Huntington in an equally famous article, published in 1993. Rather than having reached the end of history, where conflict over the best form of social organization was over, Huntington argued that there were real differences at a civilizational level that would in the future lead to conflict.

> " The fundamental source of conflict in this new world will not be primarily ideological or primarily economic. The great divisions among humankind and the dominating source of conflict will be cultural. Nation states will remain the most powerful actors in world affairs, but the principal conflicts of global politics will occur between nations and groups of different civilizations. The clash of civilizations will dominate global politics. The fault lines between civilizations will be the battle lines of the future.
>
> " (Huntington 1993)

This more pessimistic, realist-influenced view of global politics suggests that the future will be dominated by conflict between the developed and the developing world, although primarily divided by civilization.

Box 5.4 US President George W. Bush, 9/11, and the 'War on Terror'

There has been much discussion about whether the administration of George W. Bush, the attacks of 11 September 2001, and the subsequent 'war on terror' marked a distinct turning point in US foreign policy. Two aspects of the Bush administration policy looked particularly important. First, the US appeared more prepared to act unilaterally, and to be openly hostile to global organizations and commitments. Before 9/11 the Bush administration had signalled that it would withdraw from the Kyoto Agreement, which the previous Clinton administration had been involved in negotiating. Following 9/11 the invasions of both Afghanistan and Iraq occurred without a Security Council mandate. The invasion of Iraq occurred after an attempt to get UN authorization had been blocked in the Security Council. This leads on to

a second area in which a major change is claimed to have occurred—the so-called 'Bush Doctrine'. Under the Bush Doctrine, the US claimed a right to intervene in other countries not only to *prevent* an imminent threat of attack on the US, but also to *pre-empt* such a threat from emerging. According to the September 2002 National Security Strategy of the USA:

> " For centuries, international law has recognized that nations need not suffer an attack before they can lawfully take action to defend themselves against forces that present an imminent danger of attack ... We must adapt the concept of imminent threat to the capabilities of today's adversaries ... The

United States has long maintained the option of preemptive actions to counter a sufficient threat to our national security . . . To *forestall* or prevent such hostile attacks by our adversaries, the United States will, if necessary, act preemptively.

(White House 2002, emphasis added)

The presidential letter accompanying the Strategy document puts the point more directly:

As a matter of common sense and self-defense, America will act against such emerging threats before they are fully formed.

(White House 2002)

These two developments would appear to be of particular concern to countries of the developing world. International organizations and international law provide some measure of protection for the weak against the strong. By distancing itself from such arrangements, the US government indicated that it was not prepared to be constrained by international commitments. Likewise, the claimed right to intervene in countries solely on the basis that a threat to US security *may emerge* is open to abuse.

However, did foreign policy under the Bush administration change dramatically? Although it played a central role in the creation of much of the current international architecture, the US has always had vacillating relations with international organizations. Relations with the United Nations have been uneasy since the General Assembly became dominated by countries from the developing world following decolonization. Relations were particularly difficult during the Reagan era, when the US fell into serious financial arrears. Furthermore, the US has displayed a consistent pattern of intervention in countries of the developing world, during and after the cold war. In the immediate aftermath of the cold war, the US invaded Panama (during the presidency of George W. H. Bush)—a country that could hardly be considered a threat to US security. The most distinctive feature of US foreign policy during the George W. Bush presidency was perhaps the readiness of policymakers to be explicit about the rationale of foreign policy (Slater 2004: 190).

The global picture for developing countries during the period of US dominance was therefore mixed. Some states benefited from a greater stability, while for many global citizens the end of the cold war has meant greater instability. The post-cold war boom of the 1990s also offered increased possibilities for more countries to participate in the global economy. However, the demise of the Soviet Union removed an option of choice. There was now one global economy, and one system—capitalism—and the costs of defaulting from this system became higher. The option of playing one superpower off against the other no longer existed, and hence the room for manoeuvre was reduced (see Fawcett and Sayigh 1999; Halliday 2002; Mesbahi 1994; Swatuck and Shaw 1994).

Key points

- The end of the cold war left the United States in an apparently unchallengeable position, with implications for the developing world.

- A post-cold war peace dividend has failed to appear for the developing world. Although some areas experienced greater stability, many have not. Increasing fears regarding the deployment of US power also became apparent, especially during the presidency of George W. Bush.

All Change? The Developing World in the 'Chinese Century'

The changing structure of the international system

Since 1945 the international system has experienced three major structural changes. Thus far we have discussed decolonization, and the end of the cold war, which resulted in a (short) period of US pre-eminence. This section assesses the third transformation, which is currently underway and may prove to be the most significant of all. The most prominent feature is the rapid economic development of China. (See Box 5.5 for a discussion of some views on the implications of China's rise and also Chapter 23b.)

Box 5.5 The End of the Western World?

The traditional accounts of the modern world have tended to depict the European example both as somehow exceptional and a model for the rest of the world. Europe and North America have been the dominant powers for the last 200 years. However, developments in the writing of world history (see Frank 1998, Hobson 2004) suggest that this was something of an exception, and that for the vast majority of recorded history the East has been the leading power in economic, scientific, military, and political terms. Furthermore the rapid growth of China's economy leads some to argues that the brief period of Western/North American domination is drawing to a close. But what does the rise of China mean for international relations?

Is it *the end of the Western world?*

In his provocatively entitled *When China Rules the World* Martin Jacques (2009, ch. 11) argues not only that China is likely to become the dominant power internationally, but that it will also provide a very different model of society and development from that which the West has promoted.

Does it mean that *conflict is inevitable?*

For realist writers power transitions (i.e., when one hegemonic power is challenged by another) rarely occur without conflict. China's rise and the US's apparent decline indicate that such a power transition is occurring, and is unlikely to happen peaceably. A stark account of such a view is offered by John Mearsheimer (2005): 'China cannot rise peacefully, and if it continues its dramatic economic growth over the next few decades, the United States and China are likely to engage in an intense security competition with considerable potential for war.

Yet, according to Hu Jintao (Chinese President), China seeks to *unswervingly follow the path to peaceful development.* In his report to the 17th Congress of the Chinese Communist Party he stated: 'Whatever changes take place in the international situation, the Chinese government and people will always hold high the banner of peace, development and cooperation, pursue an independent foreign policy of peace, safeguard China's interests in terms of sovereignty, security and development, and uphold its foreign policy purposes of maintaining world peace and promoting common development.'

While China's economic development is breathtaking, it shouldn't blind us to developments in other parts of the world (particularly India and Brazil), and the appearance of a new grouping of economically dynamic countries. These have been described by Parag Khanna (2009) as the 'second world' (not to be confused with the communist Second World of the cold war). Khanna argues that the countries of this second world are crucial to understanding developments in international politics. He notes that 'the second world shapes the global order as much as the superpowers do' (Khanna 2009: x). While for Khanna China is both part of the 'second' world, and one of three competing empires (together with the US and EU), another formulation has been to group it with Brazil, Russia, India as the BRICs (or sometimes BRICS, which includes South Africa).

The BRICs are seen by some analysts as a rival grouping to Western-based organizations such as the G8, and a challenge to Western domination in organizations such as the World Trade Organization, International Monetary Fund, and World Bank. The basis for much of the discussion of the BRICs was a report produced by the accounting firm Goldman Sachs, entitled *Dreaming With BRICS:*

The Path to 2050 (Wilson and Purushothaman 2003). The startling conclusion to this report was that by 2050 the BRICs' combined GDP would be larger than that of the current six largest economies (US, Japan, Germany, Britain, France, and Italy). While some of the underlying assumptions of the report may be questionable (pessimism about growth rates in the current largest economies; over-optimism regarding the growth prospects of the newly emerging economies), the report does indicate that even if the comparative growth rates for the BRICS are less than expected, major changes can be expected in the global architecture, which could have enormous implications for all global actors, and especially developing countries (see Box 5.6).

Box 5.6 The BRICs are Coming!

The term 'BRICs' to designate Brazil, Russia, India, and China was coined by the Goldman Sachs economist Jim O'Neill in 2001. It has since that time entered popular discussions of global international economic affairs to indicate the growing economic powers of a small number of countries, with large populations that are experiencing comparatively rapid rates of growth, which are anticipated to continue into the future. Currently the combined contribution of the BRICs amounts to 15 per cent of global gross domestic product. Not only are these countries seen as economic challengers to the current core economies, they are seen as representing a distinct set of interests, possibly at odds with the present dominant powers.

Without disputing the current exceptional growth rates of these countries, the view that the BRICs constitute a coherent bloc is questionable. First, their economies are radically different—Brazil and Russia's prime connection to the global economy is dependent on the export of raw materials, China on assembled manufactured goods, India largely on services. Second, they have radically different political systems: India and Brazil are fully functioning, and lively democracies, Russia a quasi-democratic authoritarian state, while China is a one-party state. Furthermore China has not always had the most peaceable relations with Russia and India. Despite these differences in June 2009 the BRICs held their first formal summit meeting. The leaders from the four countries issued a closing statement calling for a greater voice for developing countries in the international financial institutions, and a more diversified international monetary system.

Implications for the developing world

It would appear therefore that significant changes are occurring to the structure of the international system that will affect actors. A particular feature is the coming to prominence of large countries that would previously have been considered as developing (especially Brazil, China,

and India)—this indicates that truly revolutionary change may be occurring in the international system. This section examines some of the possible implications for the developing world (see also Chapter 23b).

China's reach

China, according to one Chinese government official, is 'all over Africa' (cited in Large 2008).

A striking impact of China's economic rise is the extent to which its influence is being exerted over regions formerly within the European and North American spheres of influence. This may offer benefits to many developing countries, but also comes with potential risks. This has been particularly marked over areas of Africa. Rising commodity prices during the early years of the twenty-first century are often connected to China's enormous demand for raw materials (Johnson and Blas 2009). China has become a major trading partner with a number of African countries, and also a major aid donor. The significance of this growing relationship between China and the continent of Africa was demonstrated when China held a November 2006 summit in Beijing attended by representatives from more than fifty African countries. A range of trade investment and aid proposals were announced. A major feature of this growing influence has been a 'no strings attached' basis to trading and aid relations. China has been prepared to enter into friendly relations with countries considered to be pariah states by European and North American countries. For example, China has received considerable levels of criticism for its relations with Sudan, a significant source of oil for the Chinese economy. While China has provided a ready market for many of Africa's exports, it has done little to alter the composition of those exports. This has led to fears that the neo-colonial relations with the West might be being reproduced, albeit with a different power. Former South African president Thabo Mbeki warned about the possible unequal relationship between African countries and China: 'China cannot just come here and dig for raw materials and then go away and sell us manufactured goods' (cited in Alden 2007: 120). Despite these potential fears, China has been able to expand its contacts with African countries, prompting fears in North America and Europe that it may become the dominant power on the continent. There are also indications of the growing influence of China in Latin America, a traditional site of US hegemony (Roett and Paz 2008).

Increased North–South conflict

The emergence of competing centres of power in the international system, and in particular the alternative development and political model offered by China, has reintroduced the possibility of choice of alliances for developing countries. There is some evidence that this increased range of possibilities has prompted developing countries to be more prepared to challenge the dominance of Europe and the United States in international financial institutions. A key example of this is the breakdown by 2008 of the Doha round of trade agreements in the World Trade Organization. Developing countries in a variety of coalitions blocked discussions of a range of issues of interest to the United States and Europe, pending progress helpful to their agricultural exports. Hurrell and Narlikar (2006) provide a detailed account of the possible contours of future North–South confrontation.

The return of bipolarity

The discussion of the cold war earlier indicated that while there was peace in Europe, the conflict between the superpowers was very far from 'cold' in the developing world, with a range of interventions through Asia, Africa, and Latin America. One possibility of the end of the unipolar moment, and the appearance of China as a possible second polar power is the return of great power confrontation and action along the lines that were evident during the cold war. Some writers in the US have already indicated their concerns about increased Chinese influence in Africa (see Campbell 2008) and growing links with Latin America. A direct military confrontation between China and the US, would be, as in the cold war, MAD, but this does not exclude the possibility of their rivalry again being played out in military form in the developing world.

Regional integration

The overlap between the international economy and international politics is also found in the attempts of developing countries to pursue policies of regional integration. Regionalism emerged as a separate strategy with a first wave in the 1960s, but that had run its course by the early 1970s, and a second wave or 'new' regionalism in the 1990s. The prime aim of the first wave of regionalism was to increase the size of the market for locally produced manufactures. Regional blocks were also thought to potentially increase negotiating power in international organizations. One of the features of the first wave of regional organizations, such as the Caribbean Common Market (established 1973), was the attempt to implement a high level of political control over production, so that decisions about the siting of industrial production were supposed to be made at a regional level. The idea was that by sharing out industrial production, the benefits from economies of scale could be maximized. This proved to be both politically and economically unviable. The first wave of regionalism foundered when the required degree of political cooperation and coordination failed to materialize. The maintenance of high tariffs once again resulted in inefficient industries, unable to compete internationally. Weak transport and other infrastructural links also played a part.

By the mid-1970s, many of the first wave of regional organizations were moribund in all but name. However in the 1990s, a 'new' regionalism emerged, inspired by the European Union. These organizations adopted a much larger free market agenda, without the political baggage associated with the first wave. Some formerly dormant organizations, such as the Central American Common Market, have been revitalized, and other new groups have emerged, such as MERCOSUR—the common market of the Southern cone, in South America (see Box 5.7). The aim of these organizations has been to promote inter-regional trade through the lowering of internal tariffs, without ambitious attempts at controlling the economic diversification of the countries involved.

Box 5.7 A Profile of MERCOSUR, the Common Market of the South

The origins of MERCOSUR date back to 1985 when Presidents Raúl Alfonsín of Argentina and José Sarney of Brazil agreed an 'Argentina–Brazil Integration and Economics Cooperation Program'. MERCOSUR itself came into existence in 1991 comprising Argentina, Brazil, Uruguay, and Paraguay. Bolivia (since 1997), Chile (since 1996), Colombia (since 2004), Ecuador (since 2004), Peru (since 2003), and Venezuela (since 2004) are associate members, which means that they can enter trade agreements with the member states, but remain outside of the institutional mechanisms of the organization. Venezuela has applied for full membership of the organization, and its application has been agreed and ratified by the governments of Argentina and Uruguay, but is currently stalled in the ratification processes in Brazil and Paraguay.

The stated aims of the organization are to increase the free movement of goods, capital, services, and peoples amongst the member states, with the possibility of the introduction of a common currency being considered. As an inter-governmental organization it is often compared to the EU, and is one of the most developed regional trade agreements in the developing world in institutional terms. In terms of area, it is four times the size of the EU, and has a population of 250 million people. The economic activity of MERCOSUR comprises more than three-quarters of that on the South American continent.

While, in relation to previous attempts at regional integration, MERCOSUR could be assessed as a success, it has not been without problems. Deepening of integration, in particular a move towards a full customs union, has been delayed by the economic storms that have swept the continent, in particular Argentina's financial and economic collapse in 2001. There have also been trade disputes between Brazil and Argentina over car production, and between Uruguay and Argentina over the construction of pulp mills on the Uruguay–Argentine border. Furthermore, the two smaller members, Paraguay and Uruguay have complained that they only enjoy re-stricted market access to the economies of the two larger members.

On the international stage, MERCOSUR has come into conflict with the United States over the possibility of cre-ating a Free Trade Area of the Americas (FTAA). While in principle, all countries in Latin America seek to be part of the FTAA, disputes have concerned both the nature of the agreement and the process of its creation. The mem-bers MERCOSUR, and in particular Brazil, have sought to counter what is regarded as a neo-liberal agenda implicit in the agreement. Furthermore, they have en-couraged the countries to negotiate as a bloc, rather than as individual states, which has increased the continent's bargaining power related to the United States. The failure to agree an FTAA in many ways parallels the collapse of the Doha round of the WTO—the issues, in particular rich country farm subsidies, were similar; Brazil played a key role in both.

Carranza 2004; BBC 2008

In some ways this can be seen as a reaction to the impacts of globalization. As a way of protecting their economies from the pressures of the global economic market, countries in different parts of the world have joined together to form regional blocks. However, in some ways, the 'new region-alism' can be viewed as a way of increasing the speed of globalization even further. The aim of the old regionalism was to erect *external* barriers to protect domestic production. The aim of the new regionalism is to *reduce* internal barriers to trade as a means of promoting trade within the region (Payne 2004: 16–17).

Nuclear proliferation

A further area in which there appears to be a change in relations between North and South is with re-gard to nuclear weapons, and their proliferation. In 2009 there were eight known nuclear weapons states: the United States; Britain; France; China; Is-rael; India; Pakistan; and North Korea. At the start of the twenty-first century there are fears that the non-proliferation regime is breaking down and that more states will be drawn into developing nuclear weapons, as a form of defence both against their neighbours, and against a perceived threat from a unilateralist superpower.

Central to limiting the spread of nuclear weapons has been the non-proliferation treaty (NPT), which came into force in 1970. In essence the NPT sought to limit the spread of nuclear weapons technology, and push for disarmament (or at least a reduc-tion in the numbers of nuclear weapons), while allowing non-nuclear states to develop nuclear en-ergy under international supervision. Implicit in the treaty was an agreement between nuclear and non-nuclear states: the nuclear states would move towards disarmament, and the non-nuclear states would not attempt to develop, or obtain the tech-nology. With the exception of North Korea, it could be argued that the treaty has 'worked' in the sense that, as far as we know, no other signatory has ob-tained nuclear weapons. India, Pakistan, and Israel have never been signatories. North Korea was a signatory, but announced its withdrawal from the treaty in 2003. The Islamic Republic of Iran is now considered to provide the most serious challenge to the non-proliferation regime. Yet it is very un-clear whether Iran is seeking nuclear weapons, or merely developing a nuclear energy capacity (for an excellent discussion, see Lodgaard 2007).

Since the attacks on the United States on 11 September 2001, the issue of non-proliferation has become entwined with the 'war on terror'. The concern has been that (given that the attacks in-dicated the organizational ability, and murderous intent of non-state actors) nuclear materials might be obtained by groups planning such attacks. This became part of the motivation for the 2003 attack on Iraq, and the enormous international pressure currently being placed on Iran.

Key points

- The structure of international politics is again in a period of transformation, with a (relatively) declining United States confronting a resurgent China, plus a group of 'second world' countries enjoying rapid economic growth and enhanced international influence. This is affecting, and will continue to affect, the developing world in a number of ways.

- In particular China has emerged as a major alternate source of influence, trade, aid, and investment. A

- bipolar world may result in a return to confrontation in the developing world between the US and China.

- Regionalism has increased significantly, with regional blocks being perceived as a possible source of confrontation between North and South.

- The nuclear non-proliferation regime appears to be under strain, with Iran a current focus of concern (see Online Resource Centre case study).

Conclusion

The notion of a 'Third World' was primarily a construction of the cold war. As the conflict drew to an end, increasing diversity between regions, based on divergent rates of economic growth and competition between countries for the supposed fruits of globalization, has eroded the perception of shared interests that underlay earlier groupings, such as the Non-Aligned Movement. Regional groupings are now tending to replace specific Third World organizations. The increasing economic power and confidence to act on a global stage displayed by countries such as India, and especially China, indicate the major changes that are occurring in the international system. The implications for all actors in the international system are enormous. While it may not be the end of the 'Western world', the 200-year period in which Europe and North America have been dominant appears to be drawing to a close, with a multipolar and culturally plural world replacing Western dominance.

The central argument of this chapter has been that countries in the developing world have had, and continue to have, a major impact on international relations. Through the various permutations (bipolar, unipolar, multipolar) that have constituted the international system, the countries of the

developing world have consistently played a significant role in international relations — as sources and sites of conflict, and as challengers to the existing political and economic order. Part of this contribution has come through the form of international organizations, such as the Non-Aligned Movement. The diversity of patterns of development now means that organizations claiming to represent all less-developed countries are unlikely to be effective. The new drive to regionalism offers an alternative forum and possibilities of exerting greater influence in negotiations with the developed world. The emergence of a global economy also offers immediate advantages to some. Where capital is more mobile, developing countries can exploit their advantage as sites of low wage production. Countries in which there are high educational standards are particularly likely to be able to gain from this. For example, India has been particularly successful in attracting jobs in the information technology and call centre sectors. India, Brazil, and China are all regional superpowers, able to exert their influence internationally. In due course the first two might gain more formal institutional recognition in the UN Security Council if that body is reshaped. The emergence of what has been described as a global civil society offers additional possibilities. Neo-liberalism is under attack from some quarters in the developed world, as the anti-globalization movement has demonstrated. There are increasing avenues for the development of transborder and supraterritorial alliances between the peoples of the North and South.

The character of the global system remains unsettled following the end of the cold war. But the situation of the majority of the world's population who reside in the developing world should become a more central area of study for those who seek to comprehend international processes.

? Questions

1. Assess the reasons for the failure of international relations theorists to incorporate the developing world in their analyses.

2. What roles did the developing world play in the cold war conflict between the Soviet Union and the United States?

3. Evaluate the impacts on the developing world of the changes in structure of the international system since 1945.

4. Why did Fukuyama argue that the world had reached the 'end of history'? How did Huntington's 'clash of civilizations' thesis challenge this view?

5. Does China's rise signal the 'end of the Western world'?

6. To what extent will relations between the 'North' and 'South' become more confrontational in the twenty-first century?

7. Why has regionalism become such a prominent feature of international relations?

→ Further reading

■ Duffield, M. (2001), *Global Governance and the New Wars: The Merging of Development and Security* (London: Zed). Analyses the position of the developing world in the emerging world (dis?)order.

■ Jacques, M. (2009), *When China Rules the World: The Rise of the Middle Kingdom and the End of the Western World* (London: Allen Lane). Excellent study of China's rise and its implications for the international system.

■ Jawara, F. and Kwa, A. (2004), *Behind the Scenes at the WTO: The Real World of International Trade Negotiations* (London: Verso). Accessible account of the WTO, detailing negotiating practices of the member states.

■ Payne, A. (2005), *The Global Politics of Unequal Development* (Basingstoke: Palgrave). Superb discussion of issues of development and underdevelopment from a New Political Economy perspective.

■ Slater, D. (2004), *Geopolitics and the Postcolonial: Rethinking North–South Relations* (Oxford: Blackwell). Outstanding overview of approaches to thinking about North–South relations, influenced by post-colonial and post-structuralist approaches.

■ Westad, O. A. (2005), *The Global Cold War: Third World Interventions and the Making of Our Times* (Cambridge: Cambridge University Press). Recent account of the cold war focusing on the key role played by the developing world, and the implications for contemporary international relations.

 Web links

■ www.twnside.org.sg/econ_1.htm   Third World Network reports on international organizations.

■ www.un.org   Official site provides overview of the organization and workings of the United Nations.

■ www.imf.org   Official site provides details of role of the International Monetary Fund.

■ www.worldbank.org   Official site provides complete overview of the operation of the World Bank Group.

■ www.wto.org   Overview of history, purpose, and working of the World Trade Organization.

■ www.jubilee2000.uk.org   Successor organization to the Jubilee 2000 campaign against 'Third World debt', it provides a wealth of information on debt-related issues.

■ www.worldbank.org/hipc   The World Bank Group's site for the heavily indebted poor countries initiative, containing much useful statistical and other information.

■ www2.goldmansachs.com/ideas/brics/book/99-dreaming.pdf   Contains D. Wilson and R. Purusho-thaman's 2003 report *Dreaming with BRICS: The Path to 2050*.

■ http://news.bbc.co.uk/1/hi/programmes/documentary_archive/4287124.stm   Links to podcasts on 'The Changing Face of Global Power'.

Online Resource Centre

For additional material and resources, please visit the Online Resource Centre at:
www.oxfordtextbooks.co.uk/orc/burnell3e/

PART 2
Society and State

In Part 2, we introduce the social and cultural aspects of developing countries within which their politics are embedded, and which are so central to understanding political behaviour.

The part has two main aims. The *first* is to indicate the great diversity of social structure found in the developing world and in countries individually; the variety in terms of religious, ethnic, and other identities; and the divisions to which these features together with gender- and economically based inequalities give rise. In contemporary social science, civil society also ranks very high as both a constituent feature and determining influence upon politics; that too can vary widely in practice. The role played by social movements and 'people power' too is gaining in recognition.

The *second* aim is to show the political significance of these complex social contexts and diverse forms of social and political organization and how problematic they can be for political management. They pose challenges as well as opportunities for the institutional arrangements centred on the state, in some cases expressly demanding political solutions outside of and alternative to the conventional mechanisms and processes of the state. The contents of this part thus set the scene for the investigation in Part 3 of how developing world states have responded to the many internal and external demands on them and to their transformation in recent decades. So, for instance, societal features introduced in Part 2 can help to explain tendencies towards state collapse and the pressures to engage in political liberalization and democratization as well as the forces resisting those agendas.

The illustrative material included in Part 2 is drawn widely from around the developing world. By comparison, case studies of individual countries selected to illustrate specific themes can be found in Part 5. For example, tendencies towards social fragmentation and political disintegration in developing countries, and conversely steps to nation-building are revisited in Chapter 20 in relation to Iraq and South Africa respectively. This choice of countries illustrates the multiplicity of social as well as economic and political challenges that can be present during attempts at post-conflict reconstruction. It also shows how easy it is to oversimplify the consequences of diversity for political unity, especially when set against a background of rapid change from more authoritarian and less inclusive forms of political rule to governing arrangements that resemble more closely Western-style liberal democracy (as in Indonesia). Readers are encouraged to study the introduction to Part 5 and consult the relevant case studies in that section when reading the chapters in Part 2.

Inequality

Jenny Pearce

Chapter contents

Overview

Inequality is at the heart of discussions on the political economy of development, whether amongst development economists, sociologists, political geographers, or political scientists. Debates, for instance, focus on the trade-off between growth and inequality, the different bases of inequality, on whether equality should be a goal for human development, and whether we should be concerned with equality of opportunity or of outcome. Following an introduction, the first section of this chapter charts the conceptual waters of thinking about equality, providing illustrations of social inequalities and their impact on politics in the developing world. The second section explores the debates around the politics and economics of inequality in the developing world during the cold war and in the neo-liberal decade that followed its ending. A measure of government responsibility around ensuring equality of opportunity, if not equality of outcome, gained broad acceptance during the polarized years of the cold war, although this was interpreted in very different ways in practice. However, market liberalization of the 1980s and 1990s sidelined or excluded equality as a goal of development. The third section explores how inequality came back on the agenda at the beginning of the twenty-first century, as evidence mounted of growing income inequality within and between developing countries, and between them and the developed world. This debate gained greater resonance with the rise of a handful of emergent economies, each with high or growing levels of inequality. The notion of a trade-off between growth and equality was revisited. The debate was no longer confined, however, to income inequality. It is acknowledged even in the mainstream that entrenched social and economic inequalities can constrain the poverty reduction impact of growth. The fourth section returns to the conceptual field and contemporary discussion on inequality. The idea of the 'equality of man' as an ontological assumption has been challenged by the recognition that human beings are born with different attributes and capacities, as well as into diverse belief systems and groupings, and the resulting divergences in needs might require policies that compensate the disadvantaged—in other words, unequal treatment. However, equality of human worth, whatever the differences between people, must be essential to such thinking. Translating this into political institutions and economic policy is still very limited in practice, however, but will surely require energetic political participation through civil society (see Chapter 10) and various forms of 'people power' (see Chapter 11), as well as formal politics, by those presently disadvantaged.

Introduction

The issue of inequality was raised by development economists soon after 'development' emerged as a field of policy and study. Harvard economist Simon Kuznets (1955) put forward his 'inverted-U hypothesis', arguing that relative income inequality increases in the early stages of economic development and does not improve until countries reach middle-income levels. If economic growth leads to increased inequality in this way, it could take many years to eradicate poverty in the so-called 'developing' countries. In the post-war years, the inequality and development debate remained framed in terms of income and wealth disparities, and the struggle for a model of development premised on economic equality was intense.

An implicit post-war consensus emerged in the industrialized world that government has a responsibility to address inequalities. This was disturbed in the 1980s when the rise of the paradigm of market liberalism posed a serious theoretical and practical challenge to redistributive theories of justice. Concern with income inequality as a goal of development policy declined. In its 1990 *World Development Report* (1990: 47) the World Bank

charted the effect on poverty of economic growth in 11 countries, concluding 'in the low-income countries inequality consistently improves (contrary to the Kuznets' hypothesis), and there is no case in which the effect of growth is offset by changes in inequality . . . In short growth reduces poverty.' This signalled a major shift in mainstream thinking about the relationship between inequality, poverty, and development. Pro-poor growth rather than the impact of growth on distribution became the core goal of development.

Paradoxically, the conceptual debate on inequality remained lively. The collapse of universalizing social theory has resulted in an unprecedented uncovering of differential life experiences throughout societies all around the world, which has favoured new thinking on social stratification dynamics. The cultural dimensions of inequality were exposed, while recognition of human differences suggested that the 'equality of man' is not necessarily the best foundation for egalitarian theory. In its 2001 *World Development Report*, the World Bank acknowledged that 'high initial inequality' reduces the poverty impact of a given rate of growth, and that there may even be circumstances in which addressing asset inequality can enhance economic efficiency and benefit growth. It also recognized that gender inequalities have a particularly negative impact on economic growth as well as poverty reduction, and that interventions in the market can aid poverty eradication amongst such socially disadvantaged groups as indigenous peoples and certain castes and tribes. In 2005–06, both the World Bank and the United Nations Development Programme produced annual development reports dedicated to the themes of equity and inequality. As some developing countries began to overtake the developed world in rates of economic growth, but manifested high rates of inequality, the debate around inequality was once again at the heart of the political economy of development.

The building of appropriate new social, political, and economic arrangements and institutions at the global and national levels remains, however, a distant goal. Improving individual advantages through aggregative growth approaches is still considered preferable on efficiency grounds to redistributive policies aimed at reducing the inequalities in the

distribution of advantages. Inequalities in income, assets, access to services, and political power continue to generate a politics of contestation, led sometimes by social movements seeking social justice and sometimes by politicians as a means of building political power. These extra-institutional challenges suggest that the inequality that has been confronted least is that of political power and its impact on all the other forms. Who, on what grounds and through what process, is to determine the developmental goals a society and indeed all of humankind sets for itself when initial inequalities become so embedded over time that they are not recognized as such? Inequality not only impedes access to the fruits of development, it also limits access to decision-making and the exercise of full citizenship. But which inequalities should be addressed first? Is political equality a precondition for economic equality or vice versa? Do we sufficiently understand how horizontal differences in terms of group identity become 'institutionalized categorical inequalities' (Tilly 1999) if we want to eliminate them from our social and political arrangements?

Key points

- Post-war acceptance that economic development can enhance inequality and that governments have some responsibility to redress this was challenged in the post-cold war by the rise of neo-liberalism.

- Major development institutions acknowledged that high existing inequality can retard poverty reduction. However, translating this insight into policies has been very limited.

- Inequality within the emergent economies has added a new dimension to the debate at the beginning of the second millennium.

- Recognition of human differences challenges the idea of 'equality of man'.

- Inequality impacts on the exercise of citizenship and ultimately who determines the goals of development within and between nations. What, then, is the relationship between political and economic equality?

Charting the Conceptual Waters

The importance that we attach to the issue of inequality is rooted in some fundamental questions of

political philosophy and shifting values and norms. Do societies think that equality is a legitimate aspiration? And if so, how is it to be achieved? Over the past two centuries or more these questions have been discussed repeatedly. During this period there was a 'steady erosion in the legitimacy accorded to social inequality . . . for students of social stratification, this . . . is perhaps the most important feature of the nineteenth and twentieth centuries' (Béteille 1969: 366). However, by the end of the twentieth century the pursuit of greater social and economic equality had become increasingly discredited; such concepts as 'social exclusion' and 'pro-poor growth' gained ground. The poor became 'targets' of anti-poverty programmes. Traditional leftist concerns about distribution and 'exploitation' were abandoned. At the same time, interest has grown in human diversity, in terms of identity and culture and their relationship with equality — a development that Fraser (1997) calls a shift from the 'politics of redistribution' to the 'politics of recognition'. Such a shift appeared to imply abandonment or at least weakening of the idea of economic equality in favour of more robust mechanisms for ensuring political equality. But does equality of civil and political rights compensate for, or even work in the context of, social and economic inequalities?

Ontological equality and equality of outcome

The relative material prosperity achieved by American colonizers by the eighteenth century demonstrated that poverty was not inevitable. However, it was the French Revolution of 1789 that brought equality and the 'social question' to world attention. It showed not only that traditional social stratifications were not divinely sanctioned but that they could be challenged by the people acting collectively as citizens with equal rights.

The idea that men are born equal had emerged as a philosophical challenge to the prevailing assumption that social stratification was a result of natural differences of rank between individuals. The Greeks had built the *polis* on that assumption, and equality only existed in that realm; it was an attribute gained

through citizenship not birth. Rousseau (*Discourse on Inequality*, 1755) began his investigation into inequality by assuming instead the equality of men in a pre-social original state of nature — an assumption of **ontological equality**. In the course of the eighteenth century, the idea that men are equal rather than unequal by nature took hold with powerful political and intellectual consequences. But it inevitably led to the question: what are the origins therefore of inequality? Rousseau's answer is usually summed up as 'private property', starting a debate that has raged ever since. Those who came to see private property as a social evil emphasized the need for society to promote **equality of outcome** despite individual human differences. Karl Marx made equality of outcome the central tenet of his vision of the good society.

For Marx, writing in 1845–46, inequality had its origins in the division of labour as well as private property. It is the former that 'implies the possibility, nay the fact that intellectual and material activity — enjoyment and labour, production and consumption — devolve on different individuals'. And with the division of labour comes the question of distribution and 'indeed the *unequal* distribution, both quantitative and qualitative, of labour and its products, hence property, the nucleus, the first form of which lies in the family, where wife and children are the slaves of the husband' (Marx 1970: 52). Capitalism is the most advanced system of labour division yet, in which the capitalist class owes its wealth to its exploitation of another class with only its labour to sell. Marx not only places this unequal relationship to the means of production at the heart of his class analysis of history, but the emphasis on exploitation indicates that such inequality between classes is unjust, and this has been a very influential argument for nationalist as well as socialist movements.

Marxist thinking tapped into deeply felt injustices at the popular level. For some, largely pre-industrial, developing societies, Marxist ideas appealed to the desire to retain some of the primitive communal forms of equality that persisted in agrarian societies and to restrain the differentiating process that comes with socio-economic change. Much Third World sociology in the post-war years was an effort to clarify its distinct forms of class composition and social inequality, and the relationship between class formation and development. A particularly vibrant debate concerned the analytical categories for exploring relationships between the developed and underdeveloped worlds. Could one nation exploit another? Gunder Frank (1971) powerfully argued that it could and traced the history of **underdevelopment** from 'core' to 'periphery'. He was criticized by others who claimed that he saw feudalism and capitalism only in terms of market exchange, not in Marx's true sense of relations to production and class exploitation. The ideas of **unequal exchange** and dependency would nevertheless provide one of the most important frameworks for understanding inequalities between countries in the North and the South in the early post-war decades.

Differentiating inequalities: Class, status, and power

Max Weber, writing early in the twentieth century, provided a more differentiated categorization than Marx. He argued that social divisions and the distribution of power they convey encompass a range of non-economic as well as economic determinants. In addition to class stratifications that emerge out of a person's relationship to the market, there is **status**—a quality of social honour or a lack of it, which is mainly conditioned as well as expressed through a specific style of life. A status group can be closed ('status by descent') or it can be open.

Weber's understanding of the distinctiveness of status groups was particularly helpful for those wishing to understand social differentiations in situations in which market transactions were fairly simple and class formation limited. He also observed, however, that technological advances and economic transformation threaten stratification by status and will push the class situation further into the foreground.

In terms of the developing world, Weber was able to draw into the picture the forms of social stratification that Marxists have often found particularly difficult to explain, such as caste and tribe and the distinctions between them. Caste, Weber argued for instance, belonged to the 'closed status group', in which status distinctions are guaranteed not just by conventions and laws but also by rituals, such as stigmatizing any contact between lower and higher castes through religious acts of purification. He explored the complexity of the **Hindu caste system** in India in some detail, seeking to explain its relationship to economic change and its 'elasticity' and hence survival in the face of the logic of labour demands in the modern economy.

The nature of these traditional relationships and the impact of processes of economic change are particularly significant for an understanding of social divisions in the developing world. Systems of 'inherited inequality' such as those based on descent, lineage, and kinship have persisted in many parts of the developing world. Anthropologists have long studied the lineage and kinship stratifications of indigenous populations. For example, Sahlins (in Béteille 1969: 239), who studied kinship in Polynesia in the 1950s, referred to 'a graduated series of different degrees of stratification'. He distinguished between stratified and egalitarian societies, and implied that ranking processes emerge in all human societies, but they vary a great deal in terms of ranking criteria and how far they formally sanction social inequality (see Box 6.1). This is why writers like Béteille (1969) have emphasized the values and norms that underpin social inequality or its qualitative dimensions. It has often been assumed that ranking on the basis of the hereditary principle will disappear with the process of economic development, and that industrialization will overcome the differentials associated with traditional and agrarian societies. The persistence of caste in India, where status is determined by birth and legitimized by religio-cultural belief, questions that assumption. In modern India caste and class intersect in particularly complex ways, creating a potent and enduring source of social, economic, and political inequality.

Box 6.1 Béteille on Inequality

Béteille (1969: 365) points out that the sanctioning of social inequality has taken place on very distinct grounds often legitimized by religious systems that paradoxically and simultaneously contain messages of equality. In the United States, commitment to the equality of man was a strong feature of cultural values and political ideals, although for many years black people were denied the vote and were evidently not treated as equals by the dominant white population. Most societies have denied, and many still deny, women formal as well as informal social, economic, and political equality.

But across the developing world even where 'closed status group' systems such as caste do not exist, kinship and ethnic group identity have been the basis of stratified as well as segmented forms of social differentiation. Ethnic coexistences have become the source of ethnically based stratifications at various points in history. Pre-colonial conquests, colonialism, and post-colonial political mobilization have all played a critical role in privileging some ethnic groups over others and usually for some political as well as economic gain. As market economies expanded, so some ethnic groups were in a more privileged position than others to take advantage of opportunities. In this context, the debate about whether emerging stratifications are derived from market positioning, or from the logic of capital and its search for exploitable labour, or from ethnic identity per se has been particularly protracted. Thus, relationship to production is a source of inequality but not the only source of social differentiation. When class and status, economic and social power all coincide, however, one of the most powerful sources of inequality is created with capacity to perpetuate itself through the generations.

The political consequences of inequality

One means by which inequality perpetuates itself is through the political system that develops around it. Unequal societies, no matter what the source of inequality, generate differential means of influencing political processes. This is true at all levels from micro to macro, and in traditional as well as more 'modern' development contexts. That means power and powerlessness emerge out of inequality and create the source for recycling it. As societies undergo transitions from more traditional to 'modern' economies, traditional power structures and ways of exercising power have often adapted to changing social conditions so that they survived more or less intact or persisted in new but recognizable forms. As the idea of political contestation (if not modern democracy) began to take root in the developing world, it frequently did so in contexts in which political and economic power was already tightly meshed. The 'delivery' of the political support of a dependent rural population to particular leaders and interests quickly became the norm. Such practices were then adapted to urban contexts, where the rapid growth of cities without adequate services or employment gave brokerage power to individuals with access to elites and decision-makers. **Clientelism** and **patronage** networks emerged throughout the developing world, creating vertical links to tie the poor to political power structures through favours granted in return for support. Such networks reflect differentials in power and income and act as obstacles to independent political action and democratization, further entrenching the pre-existing structures of inequality. More than this, the relationships between dominated and dominant create internalized feelings of humiliation that have a lasting impact on generations of poor people, (Scheper-Hughes 1992).

In Latin America, where inequalities across class, gender, and ethnic lines are so deeply entrenched, it is not surprising that centuries of humiliation can only be overcome when the denigrated group gain dignity through building a positive identity around themselves. At the same time, this can serve to mobilize politically the previously dispossessed. This is clear, for instance, in the case of those indigenous people of Guatemala who towards the end of the twentieth century began to see themselves as 'Mayans' as a way of re-valuing themselves and their differences from the non-indigenous elites who have dominated and oppressed them historically (Box 6.2).

Equality strategies and equality theories

The French Revolution placed equality on the political agenda, but some later argued that it succeeded only in abolishing the arbitrary privileges and restrictions imposed by the old regimes. In the mid-twentieth century, Tawney (1952: 106) made such a case, claiming that it resulted in the view that 'the inequalities of industrial society were to be esteemed, for they were the expression of individual achievement or failure to achieve'. He argued, that opportunities to rise were only one side of the

picture and appealed for measures (for example, progressive taxation, trade union rights) that would ensure that society actively aimed at 'eliminating such inequalities as have their source, not in individual differences, but in its own organization' (Tawney 1952: 57).

Over the next five decades, equality as a goal was hotly debated in the advanced industrial countries. It was agreed that governments had some responsibility to pursue strategies of greater equality, although there was less agreement on strategy. Yet by the 1960s social scientists on both sides of the Atlantic questioned whether their societies were becoming more equal despite the welfare state, estate duties, and higher taxation (in the UK), and equal opportunity measures (USA). This raised important questions about the relationship between equality strategies and social justice theories. John Rawls, in his influential *Theory of Justice*, proposed that: 'All social values—liberty and opportunity, income and wealth and the bases of self-respect—are to be distributed equally unless an unequal distribution of any, or all, of these values is to everyone's advantage.' (1971: 62).

Key points

- Both Rousseau and the French Revolution challenged assumptions that inequality was natural or divinely sanctioned; a good society should be dedicated to overcoming these ills.

- Weber's notions of status and honour, derived from non-economic as well as economic determinants, assisted understanding of social stratification in the developing world.

- Social stratifications have exclusionary political consequences; clientelism and patronage are ways in which political brokers have used inequality to build a power base amongst the poorest.

- Rawls sought to find a new basis for an agreed standard of social justice and equality, but still left open the possibility of inequality once such a standard was met.

The Politics and Economics of Inequality in Developing Countries: The Cold War and its Aftermath

In the twentieth century, the discussion around the relative weight to be accorded to equality as a goal in human development was intense and conflictive. During the cold war, the polarization amongst its protagonists played out intensely in the developing world. Political movements emerged with equality as their stated goal, and occasionally became governments. Huge controversies surrounded the efforts to put that goal into practice. This section discusses the controversies and the eventual demise of these efforts as neo-liberal economics challenged the very foundations of the argument for equality.

Equality as a political and moral goal

Moral and political arguments for an equitable model of economic development found concrete expression in a number of experiments that spanned the post-war decades, such as the model of socialism that followed the 1959 revolution in Cuba, the 1967 Arusha declaration and *Ujamaa* (*kiswahili* for community-hood) Socialism of Nyerere's government in Tanzania, and the Chilean Road to Socialism of Salvador Allende between 1970 and 1973. These experiments went further than economic egalitarianism. They were also about new forms of political participation and how to address the impact of economic inequality on political decision-making. They encountered hostility from Western governments opposed to non-capitalist paths to development. Cuba and Allende's Chile faced attempts at destabilization from the United States in their pursuit of more egalitarian development. Tanzania, one of the most heavily aided countries, found its strategy of self-reliance and equality extremely difficult to combine with growth and development.

Measuring inequality

The inequality question in development is partly about moral and political arguments, but it is also partly about the facts and how to measure them. Development economists in the Bretton Woods institutions (World Bank; International Monetary Fund) and universities were concerned with measurement and the potential trade-off between economic growth and inequality that Kuznets had highlighted. Their objective was to understand the contribution that factors of production such as land, labour, and capital make to output, and not who gets what and why. Inequality mattered if it impacted negatively on growth and development. Quantitative surveys during these decades broadly tended to confirm Kuznets's findings but they did not show a fixed relationship in all cases. However, the argument that inequality was impeding development appeared to have been partially accepted when, in the mid-1970s, the World Bank embarked on a new strategy of 'redistribution with growth'. At the same time, arguments that a New International Economic Order should address the inequalities between nations were also topical.

Income distribution measurement is by no means straightforward. Unreliable data, choices over the best unit of measurement (individuals or households), the timescale of measurement, and the definition of income itself, which given the high level of informal and unregistered earnings is particularly problematic in developing countries, all represent significant problems.

The most frequently used approaches to measurement are the Lorenz curve and the **Gini coefficient**. The Lorenz curve, named after the American statistician Lorenz, who developed it in 1905, uses a vertical axis (percentage of income earned) and horizontal axis (percentage of the population earning that income); the greater the bow of the curve, the larger the degree of inequality. The Gini coefficient, named after the Italian statistician who created it in 1912, uses areas of the Lorenz curve and is the ratio of the area between the line of equality and the Lorenz curve, and the total area under the line of equality. It offers an aggregate measure of inequality between 0 (perfect equality) and 1 (perfect inequality). The Gini coefficient for countries with highly unequal income distribution tends to lie between 0.50 and 0.70.

Following Kuznets's challenge, many studies in the 1960s and 1970s examined the impact of economic growth on income distribution and vice versa. Large-scale, cross-country surveys were undertaken. Some confirmed the trend towards rising inequality in the less developed countries, although they varied in terms of whether the trend was weak or strong. Evidence was clearly not uniform across countries. Chenery et al. (1974) argued that ultimately the evidence and judgements cannot be separated from 'social and ethical postulates'. In other words, the patterns of growth and distribution reflected political priorities and values in particular countries. He discussed three models: growth-oriented patterns, illustrated by Brazil and Mexico, including an equity-oriented, low-growth variant, illustrated by Sri Lanka; rapid growth with equity, illustrated by Taiwan, Republic of Korea, and Singapore; and an average pattern illustrated by India, the Philippines, Turkey, and Colombia, where patterns of growth and distribution follow the average relations of the Kuznets curve.

Structuralist and non-structuralist approaches to inequality

A great many qualitative, but empirically based, studies tried to identify the causes of income inequality, and some examined its consequences. A division arose between structuralists and non-structuralists. The former emphasized the impact on income inequality of such factors as historically unequal landownership patterns and social structures that excluded people on such bases as caste, race, sex, or religion. The concentration of physical and financial capital as well as land in the hands of small elites enabled them to buy access to educational opportunity and control an ever greater proportion of national product. The consequences of this unequal distribution included malnutrition, poor housing, and little or no education for the majority, resulting in low levels of productivity. In contrast the argument was made that a redistribution of income would increase production by increasing the consumption and hence the health and productivity of the poor.

Non-structuralists countered that inequality was the logical (some would say inevitable) outcome of economic growth. The apparent increase in inequality during the early stages of development is because development does not start at the same time in all parts of the economy. Growth in a poor, underdeveloped country will always raise some people's income before others—notably those where the growth is first located, for instance in urban rather than rural areas. Shifts in a country's structure of production will inevitably create inequalities between those engaged in agriculture compared to those in new, more highly remunerated industries. The non-structuralists argued that these inequalities would not necessarily result in absolute impoverishment but only a relative decline in income of the poorest. The argument that the poor would see their living standards rise through economic growth even though their relative share of income might not would gain ground in the 1980s.

However, in the 1970s, even the President of the World Bank, Robert MacNamara, was forced to admit that despite a decade of unprecedented increase in the gross national product of the developing countries, the poorest segments of their population had received relatively little benefit. Policies aimed primarily at accelerating economic growth in most developing countries had benefited at most the upper 40 per cent of the population.

Equality questioned

By the 1980s, support for the idea that reducing inequality is a task of government eroded in the Anglo-American world especially and in the international institutions it influenced. The global economic recession that followed the 1973 oil shocks had resulted in a shift from Keynesian policies of demand management and welfare-oriented state interventions, to monetarism, which cuts public expenditure on welfare and prioritizes investment and profitability. Toye (1987: 71) called this a counter-revolution in development thinking, referring specifically to the thinking of P. T. Bauer. Bauer had argued that some individuals are better off than others because of different aptitudes and personal advantages. Measures to counteract economic differences, 'the pursuit of the holy grail of economic equality', he argued, 'would exchange the promised reduction or removal of differences in income and wealth for much greater actual inequality of power between rulers and subjects. There is an underlying contradiction in egalitarianism in open societies' (Bauer 1981: 8).

Bauer attacked the political consequences of an increasingly coercive and bureaucratic state pursuing egalitarian goals. Many developing world egalitarian states had indeed shown that these dangers were real. Even where such states had consciously sought to avoid such tendencies, for example Nyerere's Tanzania (1962–85) and the Sandinistas' Nicaragua (1979–90), they could not entirely avoid state-heavy political structures that concentrated power in new elites, such as the 'bureaucratic bourgeoisie' of the former and the party *caudillos* of the latter. Bauer also maintained that promotion of economic equality and the alleviation of poverty are distinct and often conflicting goals, and that to make the rich poorer does not make the poor richer.

These and related ideas informed the broad trend in thinking away from government regulation and intervention in markets for any purpose, including social justice. The argument against Kuznets that in any case inequality had no inevitable consequences for poverty gathered support in the 1980s, boosted by the publication of several time-series studies showing that income inequality does not in any case change much over time, so economic growth must reduce poverty to some extent. The pattern of overall distribution of goods in society now seemed less important than individual well-being and freedom to pursue private interests in the marketplace. These arguments paved the way for market liberalization, which was expected to reduce poverty through growth. It was followed by emphasis on political liberalization and governance aimed at enhancing the institutional framework for growth and poverty reduction. It was not long, however, before confidence in neo-liberal-driven development policies was under challenge. One reason was the growing evidence that market liberalism was generating increased inequality within developing countries as well as income disparities at the global level.

Key points

- From the 1960s, egalitarian thinking influenced several policy experiments in developing countries, but most ran into difficulties.

- Measurement of inequality became an important field of study, whilst structuralists and non-structuralists debated the relationship between inequality and the economy.

- From the 1970s, as agreement grew that economic modernization was not benefiting the poor, international development policies focused on raising their living standards but without radical redistribution.

- In the 1980s, priority shifted to market-driven growth and new arguments claimed economic growth benefited the poor.

The construction of a World Income Inequality Database by the United Nations University–World Institute for Development Economics Research produced more reliable time-series data on income inequality and led to a research project into the relationship between income inequality and poverty reduction. On the basis of these data, Cornia and Court (2001) concluded that worsening inequality was due less to the traditional causes such as landownership patterns and urban bias or the impact of new technologies on skilled and unskilled wages, although all these remain significant. The new causes include most notably macro-economic stabilization, labour market and financial deregulation, and excessively liberal economic policies. Inequality returned as a major issue for those involved in development thinking.

Statistical evidence portrayed a stark picture of the extent of income inequality in the first decade of the new millennium, particularly in Latin America and Africa. The Gini coefficient for sub-Saharan Africa is 72.2 and for Latin America it is 57.1, compared to 52.0 for East Asia, 42.8 for Central and Eastern Europe and Commonwealth of Independent States, 36.8 for the high-income OECD countries, and 33.4 for South Asia (UNDP 2005: 55). Countries with high income inequality, it was argued, require much higher rates of growth for poverty reduction than those with lower inequality (Ravallion 2001). Ravallion (2005) went on to question other assumptions of the previous decade; for instance, that absolute poverty in terms of income is the overriding issue in poor countries and that only economic growth can reduce it. He raised the issue of initial inequality and how it might affect the poverty reduction effects of growth. 'Making growth more pro-poor', he argued (Ravallion 2005:15) 'requires a combination of more growth, a more pro-poor pattern of growth and success in reducing the antecedent inequalities that limit the prospects for poor people to share in the opportunities unleashed in a growing economy'.

In this debate, the experiences of emerging economies (those making the main contribution to global GDP from the developing world) provided new evidence. China, India, Brazil, Mexico, Russia, and South Africa are such emerging economic powers, in which rapid growth has taken place in the last two or three decades. China's exponential growth since 1980 brought rapid poverty reduction, and some have used it to reaffirm the case that growth and poverty reduction do go together. Inequality has also grown over time, but not continuously and with geographical differences and different dynamics across the economic sectors. The Gini index rose from 28 per cent in 1981 to 39 per cent in 2001, with adjustments for the higher cost of living index in urban areas (Ravallion 2005:17). Ravallion concludes that it was growth in the primary sector, notably agriculture, which could do more to reduce poverty *and* inequality than that in manufacturing or services, within both urban and rural areas and between them (Ravallion 2005:21). This was due to the fact that levels of poverty were so high when China began its economic reforms in the early 1980s that inequality was not a significant issue. However, these effects are diminishing, and inequality is now rising in ways that are affecting poverty reduction, in a context in which the meaning of 'poverty' is also shifting.

India, argues Ravallion, has shown a similar trend. Economic growth did reduce poverty, but the poverty impact of rapid growth in the 1990s has been reduced by rising inequality. In India also, growth in mean rural incomes has been particularly effective against poverty, but in India this is limited by the unequal distribution of agricultural land compared to China. Geographic and sectoral imbalances have also contributed to the rise in inequality in India. The overall conclusion that Ravallion reaches is that ultimately *inequality is bad for the poor*. He has shifted the debate from the big argument based on aggregate data of a trade-off between growth and equity, and argued that some redistributive polices may well be necessary for growth to benefit the poor. Even a distribution-neutral growth process can leave many poor people behind, particularly in high-inequality countries. Moderate redistributive policies have been 'sanctioned' and even praised by the international community, such as that of the left-wing Brazilian government of President Lula, who channelled extra income to poor families on condition that their children are in education.

The World Bank has accepted (at least conceptually, although evidence of policy change on the ground is much weaker) that institutions must be made to work better for the poor. This requires, however, a political system in which such institutions do not only serve the most powerful/resourceful parts of the population that tend to benefit the most from growth. The World Bank also recognized how inequality impacts on the distribution of power as well as the quality of institutions (see Box 6.3). However, all the emerging powers, despite poverty reduction, share the challenge of rising inequality to different extents. Although only one measure of inequality, the Gini Index, remains high for all of them, between a high of 57.0 for Brazil to a relatively low 36.8 for India.

Gradually, the debate on inequality has moved beyond income inequality, to explore the relationship between social and political inequalities, and economic inequalities, and between all of these and poverty and development. This renewed mainstream interest in inequality and its relationship to development is reflected in the 2005 and 2006 development reports of the UNDP and World Bank respectively, which were devoted to inequality (UNDP) and equity (World Bank). These reports explore the deep effects of income inequality on wider life chances of people in developing countries, including staying alive. The UNDP (2005: 57) points out that, in Bolivia and Peru, infant death rates are four to five times higher for the children of the poorest 20 per cent of the population than for the children of the richest 20 per cent. However, what is most interesting about these reports is that they go well beyond income inequality in their understanding of the relationship between inequality and development, a trend that has unfolded over the past decades, led by the discussion on gender inequality. The impact of inequalities in race and ethnicity as well as gender have begun to be analysed. Brazil, for instance, reveals a large discrepancy in income inequality between population groups based on skin colour. Brazil has the second largest population of African descent in the world after Nigeria (almost half of all Brazilians are of African descent). Yet in 2005, about 33 per cent of Afro-Brazilians lived in poor households whose incomes were below 50 per cent of the median income of the country compared to 14 per cent of whites falling into this group (Gradin 2009). Similarly in South Africa, where income inequality has risen in the post-apartheid years, measured by a Gini Coefficient that went from 0.64 in 1995 to 0.69 in 2005, it is the inequality between black African and white people that continues to drive overall inequality, although there is evidence of growing inequality also amongst black Africans.

Economic and political inequalities have been created around human differences and embedded over time in structured social relationships. The next section explores the way in which conceptual tools have evolved to help to understand these links further, but suggests we are far from understanding how to address them either in institutional arrangements or social relationships.

Box 6.3 The World Bank on Inequalities of Power and the Quality of Institutions

❝ How do societies develop equitable non-market institutions? First, there must be sufficient political equality—equality in access to the political system and in the distribution of political power, political rights and influence. Poor institutions will emerge and persist in societies when power is concentrated in the hands of a narrow group or an elite . . . . Because the distribution of power, through its impact on institutions, helps to determine the distribution of income, the possibility of vicious and virtuous circles is clear. A society with greater equality of control over assets and incomes will tend to have a more equal distribution of political power. It will therefore tend to have institutions that generate equality of opportunity for the broad mass of citizens. ❞ (World Bank 2006: 108)

Key points

- With increasing evidence that market liberalization was fuelling growing inequalities within and between nations, mainstream economists are reassessing conventional assumptions about growth, distribution, and poverty reduction.

- Inequality is back on the mainstream agenda and recognized as an obstacle to poverty reduction in development.
- But now not only income inequality, but also a range of social and political differences are seen as the problem.

Inequality and Human Diversity

Various egalitarian theories have identified at least three different kinds of socio-economic injustice: exploitation; **economic marginalization**; and **deprivation**. In Fraser's words (1997: 13), exploitation means 'having the fruits of one's labour appropriated for the benefit of others', economic marginalization is 'being confined to undesirable or poorly paid work', and deprivation is 'being denied an adequate material standard of living'. She contrasts these approaches with those that emphasize cultural or symbolic injustice, rooted in social patterns of representation, interpretation, and communication. The dilemma that interests Fraser is that while the claim for redistribution calls for the abolition of economic arrangements that underpin group specificity, such as the gender division of labour, recognition claims call attention to the specificity of a group and the affirmation of its value as a group. How can a society's social and political arrangements embrace both imperatives together? In the developing world, such questions have considerable salience for ethnic as well as gender stratifications and debate has intensified with the growth of conflict and violence in the name of identity differences.

Progress has been made in terms of the abandonment of the single axis of difference such as woman or class, and the acknowledgement of the differences between women, for example, and the interaction among race, gender, and class identities. But how are the multiple connections between identities and social position linked to the question of equality in terms of the practical design of human social arrangements? And without some rethinking of those arrangements, are not certain people doomed to political as well as social exclusion? Recently, the impact of horizontal inequalities between cultural and religious groups and between geographical regions has been explored as a source of violence and conflict in the developing world (Stewart 2008).

Sen, in *Inequality Re-examined* (1992), offers one of the most sophisticated efforts to address the relationship between human diversity and equality. It has been particularly influential in development studies, refocusing attention away from income to human capabilities—a shift that can be followed in the evolution of the United Nations Development Programme's annual *Human Development Reports* (Box 6.4). Sen is less interested in equality as such than in the question, 'equality of what?'. His thinking is heavily influenced by Rawls, but he has gone beyond Rawls' emphasis on the *means* of freedom, to the **extents of freedom**, meaning the capabilities or freedom to achieve whatever functionings an individual happens to value.

The logic of Sen's argument is based on the assumption of human diversity. Equality claims must come to terms with this fundamental empirical fact, as there are times when equal consideration for all may demand unequal treatment in favour of the disadvantaged. Indeed, because we are diverse in our personal qualities, such as age, gender, talents, proneness to illnesses, physical abilities, as well as in our external circumstances like material assets, social backgrounds, and environmental circumstances, insistence on egalitarianism in one field may imply rejecting it in another. Disadvantage is itself diverse. Moreover, disadvantage is not just about consumption of resources. Our capabilities to achieve whatever we value do not ultimately depend on income but on all the physical and social characteristics that make us what we are. Substantial inequalities in well-being and freedom can, given our variable needs and disparate personal and social circumstances, result directly from an equal distribution of incomes. As Sen notes, some countries with higher per capita incomes enjoy lower life expectancies. The Indian state of Kerala has one of the lower real per capita incomes in India but the highest life expectancy, lower infant mortality, and higher general literacy—particularly female literacy. This is true even if the average gross national product is adjusted for distributional inequality; Kerala remains, even with this statistical adjustment, one of the poorer Indian states. The explanation lies in the history of public policy, most notably education, health services, and food distribution, which reaches the rural as well as urban population (Sen 1992: 128).

Box 6.4 Human Development Index

The UNDP's annual *Human Development Reports* contain a range of indices that try to take into account non-income measures of development and enable us to view the performance of a country in terms of both growth and freedoms. The best known is the Human Development Index, which incorporates data for human longevity and educational attainment as well as material living standards. Comparing countries by their place in the Human Development Index produces a very different picture from a rank that is based on the Gini coefficient alone. For example, Chile and Guatemala have a comparable level of inequality measured by the Gini coefficient that is very high. But in human development terms, Chile easily qualifies among the top 50 countries (high human development) whereas Guatemala is in the middle of the medium human development range, placed many countries below Chile. The contrast between, for instance, South Korea and Rwanda is even greater. Similar in terms of the Gini coefficient (where both appear significantly more equal than, say, the United States or UK) in human development, Rwanda features among the least developed countries anywhere while South Korea features in the top 30 countries of the world.

So it is now possible to appreciate the diversity of inequalities and to take a wider view of the social and political arrangements that should be aspired to. However, we are still left with some very intractable problems, such as how, given their relative powerlessness, the politically and economically marginalized can transform the social, political, and economic arrangements that marginalize them? Some market liberals may have recognized that embedded social inequalities negatively impact on development and the need for equal political representation and citizenship rights, and a very, very few have started to discuss whether a small amount of targeted income redistribution might be less negative to growth than conventionally assumed.

However, the challenge of addressing inequality goes much deeper. Anne Phillips (1999), for example, argues that political inequality cannot be addressed without addressing economic inequality. Disparities between rich and poor impede recognition of equal human worth. Political equality assumes equal worth as well as equal access to political influence: 'The problem for democracy is not just how to equalize people's political resources but how to establish their equal human worth; the problem with economic inequality is not just that it constrains the exercise of political rights but that it shapes (and damages) perceptions of fellow citizens' (Phillips 1999: 83).

When, in its 2001 *World Development Report*, the World Bank acknowledged that social discrimination can have economic effects that will undermine efforts at pro-poor growth, it advocated making 'public spending pro-poor', recognizing that this would encounter political resistance: 'Governments face important political issues in redistributing public spending to support asset accumulation by poor people. With finer targeting, public funds may in principle reach more poor people. But such targeting may lack political support from powerful groups that may lose out. Hence the importance of building pro-poor   coalitions' (World Bank 2001: 82) (for more on the policy issues, see Chapter 16). While

political liberalization has opened up some new political spaces for participation, these have often been filled by self-appointed allies of the poor, such as non-governmental organizations. These organizations can at least advocate policies that might equalize the playing field politically and/or economically. Collective action remains another means by which the disadvantaged make their voice heard, and **social movements** have proliferated in the developing world (see Chapter 11). Such movements see struggles in terms of rights and entitlements and challenge the mainstream thinking that the poor are a 'target group' for policies, which ultimately maintain the division between 'rich' and 'poor'. Political leaders can also emerge to mobilize the poor on grounds of class and ethnic exclusion, such as Hugo Chávez in Venezuela and Evo Morales in Bolivia. However, whereas in India the space for such movements remains relatively open, in China it does not. The next decades will reveal how growth and inequality impact on social and political movements in these two distinct contexts.

We may have progressed in understanding the many forms inequality takes and the need for nuanced policy responses, but the politics of inequality remains highly contentious. Inequality is a motor for political action of all kinds in the developing world, sometimes with productive outcomes, but sometimes with violent and even anti-democratic ones. Horizontal inequalities around religious and ethnic identities, particularly when they are reinforced by economic inequality, have in some contexts generated extreme violence and even civil war. This suggests that the struggle for political systems in which all individuals and social groups can participate and feel represented in decision-making cannot be divorced from the struggle for egalitarian economic systems. It is the latter that guarantees the recognition of equal human worth despite the multiple differences of belief, identity, and allegiance, and ensures that political equality is meaningful.

Key points

- New awareness of social and cultural diversity has increased the complexities of the inequality issue and encouraged a focus on recognition as well as redistribution.

- Sen argues that policies need to recognize that people are diverse in their disadvantages and advantages, while the UNDP has introduced new measures to estimate non-income aspects of inequality.

- Inequality is a source of contentious politics in the developing world, which can be positive in the case of self-empowering social movements but can also be negative, polarizing, and potentially violent.

- The struggle for political equality could enhance the representation of excluded or marginal groups, but political equality includes recognition of equal human worth, a recognition undermined by economic inequalities.

Conclusion

The conceptual waters of the inequality debate have ebbed and flowed since the eighteenth century, with ontological equality challenged by the end of the twentieth century by the idea of equality based on human diversity. Sen has advanced on Tawney's vision of the 'largest possible measure of equality of environment', to the multiple environments that must be tailored to the capability enhancements of a diverse humanity. However, humankind is a long way from constructing the new social, political, and economic arrangements that would enable inequalities to be addressed in the multiple 'spaces' in which they appear. Equality practice has foundered on the power at the global, national, community, and family levels that protects embedded inequalities and allows some people to exploit, marginalize, and deprive others of a full life. In turn, inequality impacts on the political system, limiting participation of poor and discriminated people and hence the possibilities of prioritizing the search for new solutions that might truly enhance the life chances of all.

The prevailing development discourse has shifted since the 1990s but still has a long way to go before inequality is given full weight in the measurement and understanding of economic development. Economic policy continues to prioritize efficiency over equity and to assume that there is a tension between the two. The idea that the success of economic management should be assessed in terms of increasing social cohesion and lessening social disparities rather than growth and efficiency, has only recently begun to receive serious attention. In the meantime, according to the *Human Development Report 2002* (UNDP 2002), the level of worldwide inequality is 'grotesque'—the world's richest 1 per cent of people being reckoned to receive as much income as the poorest 57 per cent, and the combined income of the world's richest 5 per cent being 14 times that of the poorest 5 per cent. In turn, the way in which economic inequalities impact on recognition of equal human worth has now begun to generate debates on a new economics of egalitarianism that eliminates the 'rich–poor' divide.

? Questions

1. Is inequality unjust?

2. Does it matter if the evidence shows that economic growth increases inequality but nevertheless raises absolute living standards amongst the poor?

3. To what extent should the state address the question of inequality as well as poverty in its development strategies?

4. Assess the evidence that there is a relationship between neo-liberal globalization and increasing inequality between and within nations.

5. Can cultural and social inequality be tackled by addressing income inequality?

6. How has the experience of growth and inequality in the 'emerging powers' influenced the debate on inequality and development?

7. Compare the inequality impact of the approaches to development and growth of either Brazil and India, or India and China.

8. Discuss the impact of horizontal inequalities across cultural and religious groups on development and conflict.

9. To what extent does Sen's approach to inequality, human diversity, and capabilities satisfy a feminist critique of social inequality?

10. Is political equality meaningful without economic equality?

→ Further reading

■ Bauer, P. T. (1981), *Equality, the Third World and Economic Delusion* (London: Methuen). A major source of the neo-liberal questioning of the goal of pursuing equality in development.

■ Béteille, A. (ed.) (1969), *Social Inequality* (Harmondsworth: Penguin). A good set of conceptual and anthropological essays on social inequalities that still merits reading.

■ Chenery, H. et al. (1974), *Redistribution with Growth* (New York: Oxford University Press). Had a major impact on World Bank and other institutions involved in development policy in the 1970s.

■ Fraser, N. (1997), *Justice Interruptus, Critical Reflections on the 'Postsocialist' Condition* (London: Routledge). A very useful discussion on the relationship between the redistributionist and recognitionist emphases within inequality thinking.

■ Gottshalk, R. and Justino, P. (eds) (2006), *Overcoming Inequality in Latin America: Issues and Challenges for the Twenty-first Century* (London: Routledge). A useful collection of essays on one of the unequal regions of the global South.

■ Gradín, C. (2009), 'Why Is Poverty So High Among Afro-Brazilians? A Decomposition Analysis of the Racial Poverty Gap', *Journal of Development Studies*, 45/19, 1426–52. A useful attempt to understand the differential poverty levels between whites and blacks in Brazil.

■ Kuznets, S. (1955), 'Economic Growth and Income Inequality', *American Economic Review*, 45: 1–28. An important benchmark study on the relationship between inequality and development.

■ Phillips, A. (1999), *Which Equalities Matter?* (Cambridge: Polity Press). A very lucid discussion of the relationship between political and economic equality.

■ Ravallion, M. (2001), 'Growth, Inequality and Poverty: Looking Beyond Averages', *World Development*, 29/11: 1803–15. A good discussion of the relationship between growth, distribution, and poverty.

■ —— (2005), 'Inequality is Bad for the Poor', *World Bank Policy Research Working Paper 3677*, August available at. www.worldbank.org This background paper to the 2006 World Development Report on Equity and Development puts forward the arguments for bringing the issue of inequality back into development debates, with useful sections on China and India.

■ Rawls, J. (1971), A *Theory of Justice* (Oxford: Oxford University Press). A very influential contribution to the political philosophy of inequality.

■ Sen, A. (1992), *Inequality Re-examined* (Oxford: Oxford University Press). Includes good discussions of both the state of welfare economics measurement and the relations between aggregative and distributional considerations and economic efficiency.

■ Stewart, F. (ed.) (2008), *Horizontal Inequalities and Conflict: Understanding Group Violence in Multiethnic Societies* (Basingstoke: Palgrave Macmillan).

■ Tawney, R. H. (1952), *Inequality* (London: Allen and Unwin). A classic essay on inequality that challenges the notion that equality of opportunity is a sufficient approach to the question.

 Web links

■ www.worldbank.org/poverty/inequal   The World Bank Group site on the concept of inequality and its links to poverty and to socio-economic performance, and pro-poor growth specifically.

■ www.wider.unu.edu/   Contains United Nations University–World Institute for Development Economics Research Database on world income inequality.

■ http://ucatlas.ucsc.edu   The University of California, Santa Cruz Atlas of Global Inequality, includes downloadable maps and graphics.

■ www.undp.org   Site of the United Nations Human Development Programme contains links to its annual Human Development Report.

 Online Resource Centre

For additional material and resources, please visit the Online Resource Centre at:
www.oxfordtextbooks.co.uk/orc/burnell3e/

7

Ethnopolitics and Nationalism

James R. Scarritt

  Overview

This chapter stresses the significance of both: (1) differences among ethnic, ethnopolitical, and **national identities**; and (2) different types of relations among groups having these identities in countries of the developing world. **Ethnic identities** are constructed and reconstructed over time, and some but not all are politicized. Specific processes for construction and politicization and their variations across countries are discussed. National identities in the developing world, which are inherently political, vary in strength as well as the degree to which they are civic, multi-ethnic/multicultural, or ethnic, and the chapter explains these variations. Both types of identity have been strongly influenced by European colonialism. Both types interact variously with group morphology, group advantages and disadvantages, organizations, institutions, mobilization and state response histories, and international influence. Based on such interactions ethnopolitical groups engage in conflict, competition, and cooperation with one another and the state in different countries and at different points in time. Different interaction patterns are explored. Since national identities are relatively weak in many developing countries while sub-national ethnopolitical identities and groups are often stronger, developing states more or less successfully engage in a variety of **nation-building** activities; the chapter describes these activities and explains their degree of success in the current era of **electoral democracy**, **globalization**, and the 'war on terror'.

Introduction

Defining ethnicity and nationalism in ways that are uncontroversial is probably an impossible task. Yet these are vitally important topics in the politics of the developing world, affecting and affected by the other social and economic cleavages and characteristics discussed in this book, the nature of the state and its degree of democratization, and policies for economic development and human rights protection. Boldly stated, a reasonably strong sense of civic or multi-ethnic nationalism and interactions among politicized ethnic groups based primarily on cooperation and institutionalized competition rather than on conflict tend to moderate economic and religious cleavages, strengthen civil society, and enhance state-building, democratization, economic development, and the provision of human rights. Although these generalizations are only tendencies rather than universal relationships, and reverse causal effects of other cleavages, civil society, state-building, democratization, economic development, and human rights on ethnopolitics and nationalism are also important, these relationships leave no doubt about the vital importance of ethnicity and nationalism.

Rather than dwell on controversies about the definition of ethnicity and nationalism, this chapter assumes that: (1) they are different and only sometimes closely related; (2) both are socially constructed identities (as discussed in Abdelal et al. 2009) that are subject to change in interaction with group morphology, group advantage or disadvantage, political organizations and institutional rules, mobilization histories, and international influences; and (3) ethnicity is only politicized in some cases, but nationalism has an inherent political component. The discussion thus begins with the construction and politicization of ethnic identities, or—in other words—the construction of ethnic and ethnopolitical identities, and then turns to the construction of a variety of nationalist identities. The next section deals with the conflictual, competitive, and cooperative interactions of groups based on these identities with one another and with states, while the final section before the conclusion deals with states' efforts to mould these interactions in ways that enhance the legitimacy of state-based nations and their support from various groups.

The Construction and Politicization of Ethnic Identities

Ethnic identities are constructed when some people self-consciously distinguish themselves from others on the basis of perceived common descent (perhaps mythical), shared culture (including values, norms, goals, beliefs, and language), or—most commonly—both. There is thus a wide variety in the specific contents of these identities even within a single country, to say nothing of across the countries of the developing world. Actual commonalities of language, a broader culture, or a common line of descent are often but not always central to ethnic identities. In spite of this wide variety in specific content, the common characteristics of these identities are sufficient to separate them clearly from other identities and to justify generalizing broadly about them (Eriksen 1993: 10–12; Gurr 2000: 3–5; Horowitz 1985: 51–64). Religious identities are the closest ones to ethnicity but, as discussed in Chapter 8, it is useful to separate them.

Many but not all ethnic identities are politicized or, as Chandra and Wilkinson (2008: 523–6) put it, activated in politics. This distinction is obviously very important for the analysis of the role of ethnicity in politics in the developing world and elsewhere. **Ethnopolitical identities** are those ethnic identities that have been politicized. This term deliberately emphasizes the interactive causal significance of the ethnic and political components of these identities in their formation, continuing mobilization, and interaction with concrete organizations, institutional rules, and international influences (Gurr 2000: 5–8; Mozaffar, Scarritt, and Galaich 2003: 382–3). There is much debate about the relative strength of each component of ethnopolitical identities, with a majority of recent analysts giving predominance to the political. But their relative strength, as well as the specific form of their interaction, may vary across ethnicities or countries and over time, so what is crucial is to emphasize their interaction and examine it empirically in different cases. Young (2001: 176) suggests that the political component is more important in Africa than in Eurasia. That ethnopolitical identities are constructed through the processes just discussed, and thus change over time, does not mean that they are not often held with deep emotional intensity. They are constructed through a variety of interactions between leaders and masses in which everyone's rational calculations are structured by their existing values, norms, and identities.

With very few exceptions, the countries of the developing world experienced European colonialism, which played a crucial role in the construction of ethnic identities and an even more crucial role in their politicization and organization into ethnopolitical groups. But the timing of colonial rule, the European powers involved, and the specific policies that affected ethnic identities varied sharply between Latin America and the Caribbean on the one hand, and Asia, the Middle East, North Africa, and sub-Saharan Africa on the other, and to a lesser extent among and within the latter areas.

The Spanish and Portuguese colonized virtually all of Latin America and much of the Caribbean from the sixteenth century until the first quarter of the nineteenth century. They brought in large numbers of settlers from their own countries and other European countries, and it was the Creoles — the American-born descendents of these settlers (Anderson 1991: 47; Young 1976: 84) — who seized power from the decaying colonial empires at the time of independence. In many of these countries they were outnumbered by indigenous Indians alone, or (as in Brazil) in combination with imported African slaves, although extensive intermarriage created intermediate groups of people, many of whom adopted Creole identities. European or Creole, mixed-race or Mestizo, Indian and African ethnopolitical identities developed over the following decades, roughly in that order. The increasing strength of Indian identities as disadvantaged minorities — more focused on individual 'tribes' than on multi-tribal Indian populations in specific countries — has been the primary change in the landscape of ethnopolitical identities in recent decades. Ethnopolitical mobilization and the globalization of information have played crucial roles in strengthening these identities, as discussed below. British and French colonialism in the Caribbean began slightly later, and the British held on to their colonies until the end of the Second World War. Descendants of former slaves from Africa are the overwhelming majority of the population in most of these countries. However, those countries with substantial East Indian populations are deeply divided in terms of ethnopolitical identities.

English, French, Dutch, and Spanish/American colonialism in South and South-East Asia occurred somewhat later, beginning as early as the sixteenth century in the Philippines and as late as the late nineteenth century in Indochina, and lasting until after the Second World War. Very few permanent European settlers were brought in, although Chinese and Indian settlers were brought into some South-East Asian countries. A core pre-colonial ethnic identity existed in many but not all Asian colonies, and was usually reinforced and given increased political significance by colonial rule. Burma is a clear example of this pattern. But minority ethnic identities within or outside the core were recognized and also politicized, especially by the British. Minority identities were strengthened in the process of resistance to the colonial reinforcement of the core identity. The two largest Asian colonies — British India and Dutch Indonesia — and a few others were amalgamations of a vast array of ethnic identities without a single dominant core. The British politicized these multiple identities more intensively and intentionally (through granting limited political autonomy to indigenous princely states) than the Dutch did, but the latter's classification of customary law zones constructed and politicized the ethnicity of their residents (Young 1994: 270), and amalgamation of groups into a common state inevitably had a politicizing effect. Post-independence politics have intensified group politicization in both countries, reinforced by international support for some disadvantaged minorities.

English, French, Belgian, and Portuguese colonialism in sub-Saharan Africa occurred much later, not really penetrating the subcontinent beyond a few coastal areas, the Portuguese-influenced Kongo Kingdom (most of which is now in Angola) and areas of European settlement in South Africa until the 1880s. Colonial rulers' reliance on local agents to cope with the dilemma of maintaining control at low cost encouraged these agents to differentiate their groups from those not so privileged by colonial authority, either by recombining and redefining existing objective markers of ethnicity or by accentuating previously minor group differences. Colonial rulers' creation of administrative units to secure additional economies in the cost of governance incorporated culturally disparate groups within single administrative units or separated culturally similar groups into separate units.

At independence, therefore, sub-Saharan African countries inherited a distinctive **ethnic morphology** (the form and structure of groups) with three defining features: (1) marked differences in group size, such that very few ethnopolitical groups comprise an outright majority in a country, although some comprise a large plurality; (2) considerable variety and complexity in ethnic markers combined with limited cultural differences among groups; and (3) the territorial concentration of some ethnic groups that facilitates their construction as cohesive units for collective political action. These three features have combined with the accommodation by post-colonial regimes of instrumental ('pork-barrel') ethnopolitical demands to foster *communal contention* as the typical pattern of political interactions in which ethnopolitical groups serve as cost-effective strategic resources for organizing political competition for power and resources. Communal contention discourages political entrepreneurs from exaggerating cultural differences among groups and encourages them instead to maintain strong group and coexisting sub-group identities that are strategically sustained by their ability to access the state and secure valued goods and services for their followers (Mozaffar, Scarritt, and Galaich 2003: 382–3).

In sub-Saharan Africa, construction of *ethnopolitical* groups occurred through organized group mobilization (primarily in ethnic associations or cliques of leaders within the same party, the bureaucracy, or the military), articulation of grievances by leaders claiming to speak for a group rather than a party, participation in collective action or (violent or non-violent) conflict with other groups or the state and being subjected to state violence, encapsulation within or domination of an officially designated administrative unit, occupying a disproportionate number of high positions in the bureaucracy or the military, controlling disproportionate socio-economic resources, or forming or joining an ethnic or multi-ethnic political party (Mozaffar, Scarritt, and Galaich 2003: 383).

French and British colonialism came to North Africa with the French occupation of Algeria in 1830 — fifty years before neighbouring Morocco and Tunisia — and the British occupation of Aden in 1839. The presence of numerous French settlers in Algeria who campaigned to incorporate the colony permanently into France was eventually a major force in politicizing Algerian and regional (Maghreb) Arab identity. Colonial rule by the same European powers came to the Asian Middle East the latest of all regions (the end of the First World War in which the Ottoman Empire—the former colonial power in most of this region—was defeated), and lasted less than thirty years. Ottoman rule was assimilative rather than alien, but it was more interventionist and integrative than previous localized rulers, and thus stimulated Arab nationalism within its territories, especially in its waning years. Post-independence interventionist states continued this process, as did the conflict surrounding the arrival of large numbers of European Jews in Palestine before and after the founding of Israel in 1948. Other Arab countries have had few European settlers. Thus the construction and politicization of Arab as the dominant ethnopolitical identity in the entire bi-continental region was a long process in which European colonialism played a more limited role than in other regions (Young 1976: 373–427). Apart from the Kurds of Iran, Iraq, and Turkey, whose identity was politicized primarily in the twentieth century, and Berber speakers in western North Africa, the main lines of division are religious. The Western powers have been seen as opposed to the emergence of a transnational Arab identity, and not only with respect to Palestine. This opposition has been a powerful politicizing force.

Key points

- Ethnic identities are constructed and then are often politicized to become ethnopolitical.
- The ethnic and political components of ethnopolitical identities are both important, but their relative importance varies among groups, countries, and regions.
- Most ethnopolitical (politically relevant ethnic) identities in the developing world were constructed during the colonial period, but some have been modified by post-independence politics.
- Differences among regions of the developing world in the timing of colonialism, the policies of the major colonial powers, and the presence of European settlers significantly affected the construction of ethnopolitical identities.

Varieties of Nationalism in the Developing World

National identities are inherently political, emphasizing the autonomy and unity of the nation as an actual or potential political unit (Hutchinson and Smith 1994: 4–5). They can be broadly characterized as civic, multi-ethnic and multicultural, ethnonational, or a combination of these types (Croucher 2003: 3–5; Eriksen 1993: 118–20; Scarritt and Mozaffar 2003). Civic national identities involve unity among citizens of an autonomous state. Whatever social cleavages may divide these citizens are irrelevant; their common citizenship unites them. The only cultural uniformity that is demanded is commitment to the existence of the nation and its political institutional norms and values. Ethnonational identities define the nation in ethnic terms, attaining unity through the merger of ethnic and national identities, and demand autonomy for ethnic nations. Multi-ethnic/multicultural national identities define the nation in terms of several ethnic identities that are united by or nested within citizenship and political interaction in an autonomous state, while often excluding other ethnic identities.

They differ from **civic nationalism** in accepting the legitimacy and political utility of ethnopolitical identities, as long as they do not undermine national unity. This difference is not sufficiently recognized in the literature on nationalism. Very few national identities in the developing world are purely civic, but a substantial majority of them contain civic or multi-ethnic aspects, so that they do not identify the nation with a single ethnic group. Consequently, there is an ongoing tension between the ethnic, multi-ethnic, and civic aspects of these identities in their interaction with group advantages and disadvantages, concrete organizations, institutional rules, and international influences.

Since nationalism is a constructed identity, the significant variations in the specific nature of nations in the developing world are not surprising. Colonialism played an even greater role in the construction of national identities than it did in the construction of ethnopolitical identities. The boundaries of the vast majority of developing states were determined by colonial rulers, and the varieties of nationalism are products of the interaction between the states that rule within these boundaries and the morphology of ethnopolitical identities, the tactics of ethnopolitical groups, and the presence of alternative identities within the same boundaries, which is discussed in the next section of this chapter: 'The normative model of the contemporary polity calls for the coincidence of nation and state' (Young 1976: 70). States attempt to create national identities that are coextensive with their boundaries, and the constituent ethnopolitical groups support or oppose these identities. Disadvantaged minority groups are especially likely to oppose **ethnonational identities**, and groups that are politically dominant demographic majorities are likely to oppose civic or **multi-ethnic national identities**, but other patterns of support and opposition also occur. National identities are still being constructed, and this process is more advanced in some regions of the developing world than in others. But only in a very few developing countries have national identities become banal—accepted as a matter of course and constantly reinforced by popular culture—as these

identities are in most developed countries (Billig 1995). Thus nationalism in every country—one nation in a world of nations—develops in relation to nationalism in all other countries, but especially in relation to nationalism in neighbouring countries and to the strong nationalism of the former colonial powers including the United States, which is all the more galling to the developing world because it is banal. It is impossible to specify exactly the number of nations or potential nations in the developing world, but if one includes every state and every ethnopolitical identity that engenders an ethnonationalist movement, there are probably several hundred.

Latin American states are former colonial administrative units: 'The first century of independent life saw the gradual transformation of what began primarily as the territorial heirs to colonial administrative divisions into nation-states' (Young 1976: 85). These countries officially pursue civic nationalism but until the late twentieth century this was actually a cover for Creole assimilationist ethnonationalism. Since the awakening of indigenous and/or African ethnopolitical identities in most countries, there has been a struggle by these groups to redefine national identity in more multi-ethnic/multicultural terms. Because of Creole elite resistance, the outcome of this struggle is very much in doubt. Civic and ethnic nationalism tend to merge in racially homogeneous Caribbean countries, but civic national identities are much weaker and ethnonational ones much stronger in countries such as Trinidad and Guyana with significant East Indian populations.

Nationalism in Asian countries having politicized ethnic cores has tended to be ethnonationalism focused on these cores, and thus is often rejected by members of non-core cultural groups who advocate civic or multi-ethnic nationalism or desire secession. As discussed in the next section, this can lead to violent conflict over the definition of the nation. In substantially different ways, multi-ethnic India and Indonesia constructed relatively strong multi-ethnic/multicultural national identities during the struggle for independence and the first decades of post-colonial rule. In India, the multiplicity of types of ethnic identity and the integrating force of the multi-ethnic and nationalist Congress Party facilitated the emergence of a multi-ethnic national identity, while the adoption of a lingua franca developed through trade as the national language did the same for Indonesia. These multi-ethnic national identities have weakened substantially in recent decades, as discussed in the following section and in Chapter 20a on Indonesia. The role of religion in weakening these identities is discussed in Chapter 8.

Sub-Saharan Africa is the region in which multi-ethnic nationalism is most commonly found, although ethnonationalism is by no means absent there. The predominance of ethnopolitical cleavages, their complex multilevel morphology described above, the absence of large cultural differences in most African countries (in contrast to the multi-ethnic/multicultural societies of Asia, Latin America, and the Caribbean) except those divided by religion, and the politics of communal contention (mentioned above) combine to produce multi-ethnic national identities that most effectively integrate national and ethnopolitical identities in this context. The presence of substantial numbers of foreign Africans in the presently or formerly wealthier African countries helps to solidify the multi-ethnic national identities that exclude them but include all ethnic groups comprised primarily of citizens. It should be noted that these identities are emerging rather than fully formed, and that they mitigate rather than eliminate ethnopolitical conflict. A minority of African societies are deeply divided, and thus torn by conflicts about national identity. That small cultural differences do not always eliminate such conflict is amply illustrated by Rwanda and Burundi, which can be called culturally homogeneous because the pre-colonial Tutsi conquerors adopted the culture of the conquered Hutu, but in which colonial policies and post-independence political competition have created violent, deeply divided societies.

In the Middle East and North Africa the national identities of states with colonially (Ottoman or European) created boundaries compete with the transnational Arab nationalism—the primary competitor in the middle decades of the twentieth century, transnational Islamist identities (see Chapter 8); a primary competitor today, transnational non-Arab identities—Berber in Algeria and Morocco and Kurdish in Iran, Iraq, and Turkey, and small sub-national identities. Consequently, these national state identities are probably the weakest in the developing world.

Key points

- National identities are inherently political.
- National identities can be ethnonational, multi-ethnic/multicultural, and civic in varying degrees.
- Most national identities in the developing world were constructed during the colonial period, but some have been modified by post-independence politics.
- Differences among regions and countries of the developing world in the morphology of ethnopolitical identities, the tactics of ethnopolitical groups, the policies of the major colonial powers and post-independence states, and the presence of alternative identities significantly affected the construction of national identities

Ethnopolitics in Multi-Ethnic and Deeply Divided Societies

Ethnopolitical morphology

The discussion of the construction of ethnopolitical and national identities in various regions of the developing world has revealed that the morphology of ethnopolitical groups varies greatly among the developing countries. Borrowing from Young (1976: 95–7), it is possible to specify five patterns of ethnopolitical morphology: (1) homogeneous societies such as Korea, Lesotho, and Haiti; (2) societies with a single clearly dominant group, numerically and socially, and minorities such as Algeria, Burma, and Nicaragua; (3) bipolar or deeply divided societies such as Burundi, Guyana, Rwanda, and Sri Lanka; (4) multi-polar societies, divided primarily on a single dimension, with no dominant groups, such as many sub-Saharan African countries; and (5) societies with a multiplicity of cultures, with more than one dimension of differentiation, such as India and Indonesia. Countries having the last two patterns and those having the second pattern in which the minorities do not cohere (a substantial majority of societies in that pattern at most points in time) can be called multi-ethnic societies.

Another approach to comparing ethnopolitical morphologies is to develop an index of fractionalization or fragmentation for each country. To do this, one must first specify all of the ethnic or ethnopolitical groups that exist in each country of the developing world because of past construction processes. Fearon (2003) has recently attempted to do this; Scarritt and Mozaffar (1999) have attempted to do it for Africa; and Gurr and his associates in the Minorities at Risk (MAR) project (Gurr 1993, 2000) have attempted to specify a narrower list of groups 'at risk'. These authors have different definitions of politically relevant ethnic groups; it may be the case that different groups have been politicized for different purposes, including economic

policymaking (Fearon), electoral politics (Scarritt and Mozaffar), and political protest and rebellion (Gurr 1993; 2000); construction and politicization are ongoing processes. But it is nevertheless useful to examine these efforts to specify groups, as is done in Table 7.1, in order to get an idea of the very large number of them and to show that the regions are ranked in the same order in the three data sets in terms of the number of groups specified: sub-Saharan Africa first; Asia second; Latin America and the Caribbean third; and the Middle East and North Africa last.

Table 7.1 Numbers of Ethnopolitical Groups in the Developing World

Region	Fearon	Scarritt/ Mozaffar	Gurr
Latin America–Caribbean	84		32
Asia	108		59
Sub-Saharan Africa	351	382	67
Middle East–N. Africa	70		28
Total	613		186

Table 7.2 Ethnic Fractionalization in the Developing World

Region	Average	Range	% of countries with majority group
Latin America–Caribbean	0.41	0.743–0.095	78
Asia	0.44	1.00–0.002	78
Sub-Saharan Africa	0.71	0.953–0.180	28
Middle East–N. Africa	0.45	0.780–0.039	84

Only Fearon's data allow comparison of countries and regions in terms of fractionalization, which varies in his scale between 0 (homogeneous) and 1 (totally fragmented). These data (Fearon 2003: 204, 209, 215–19), summarized in Table 7.2, show that, within the developing world, the average level of ethnic fractionalization is lowest in Latin America–Caribbean, slightly higher in Asia and the Middle East–North Africa, and much higher in sub-Saharan Africa. The range of countries in terms of fragmentation is greatest in Asia, almost as great in sub-Saharan Africa, and less in the other two regions. Finally, the percentage of countries in which the largest group comprises the majority of the population is only 28 per cent in sub-Saharan Africa and between 78 per cent and 84 per cent in the other three regions. Thirty African countries (70 per cent of the total) have fragmentation scores above 0.7, while only four Asian countries (including the two largest ones, India and Indonesia), three Middle Eastern countries, and one Latin American country have scores this high. Fearon's data thus support the conclusion that most African countries are far more fragmented than most countries in other regions.

Other relevant aspects of ethnopolitical morphology are geographic concentration, the extent of cultural differences among groups, and the presence of ethnic groups that have not been explicitly politicized as described above. Available data indicate that ethnopolitical groups in sub-Saharan Africa tend to be the most geographically concentrated and to have the smallest cultural differences, and that there are more ethnic groups that have not been politicized there than in other regions of the developing world (Fearon 2003: 211–14; Gurr 1993: 344–51; Scarritt and Mozaffar 2003: 9–10).

Collective action and interaction

These different ethnopolitical morphologies interact with group advantage or disadvantage, political organizations and institutional rules, mobilization and state response histories, and international influences in causing different types of collective action by ethnopolitical groups and different types of interaction among them or with the state. Human agents who are rational within their belief and normative frameworks carry out these processes enabled and constrained by social structures (Gurr 2000: 65–95; Mozaffar 1995; Mozaffar, Scarritt, and Galaich 2003: 380–2, 385–7; Scarritt and Mozaffar 2003: 12–16). Ethnopolitical interactions cannot be fully explained without taking all of these factors and their interactions into account; the following presentation is organized factor by factor but incorporates interactions among factors into the discussion of each one. Group advantage or disadvantage can be economic, political, or cultural, or any combination of these forms. Crucial political organizations include various civilian state agencies, the military and police, political parties, and interest associations that are not ethnically based. Some are more institutionalized than others. Institutional rules can be broadly categorized as democratic, transitional, or autocratic (Gurr 2000: 154). Rules about the formation and control of ethnopolitical associations and the conduct of elections are of special importance. Group collective action and state responses have historical patterns that have varied in violence and intensity in different countries of the developing world, although these patterns are more firmly established in some countries than in others. These patterns are of course subject to change, but they have self-perpetuating qualities that resist change unless the forces supporting it are sufficient to overcome them. Finally, although ethnopolitics is primarily internal to states, it is significantly influenced by several aspects of globalization, diffusion, and contagion among identical or similar groups across state boundaries, and external political and material support.

Interaction among groups and between them and the state can be categorized as cooperative, competitive, or conflictual. The boundaries among these three types of collective interaction are by no means perfectly clear, and a given action by a group or the state may involve any two or all three types vis-à-vis various targets. The relative importance of these interaction patterns nevertheless provides a very useful way of comparing ethnopolitics in the countries of the developing world. As illustrated in Box 7.1, the literature on ethnopolitics there (Gurr 1993, 2000; Horowitz 1985; Young 1976) emphasizes the complex causation of conflict involving some degree of violence, and to a lesser extent competition, but a greater emphasis on the latter and the inclusion of cooperation are necessary for a more balanced treatment. To highlight this point, it is useful to separate—within the discussion of each factor and its interactions with others—the explanation of cooperation, institutionalized competition, and peaceful protest from the explanation of conflict and non-institutionalized competition.

Cooperation and institutionalized competition among ethnopolitical groups and states in the developing world do not get much attention in the global media, yet they occur with great frequency and have significant consequences. They are substantially greater in frequency and consequences than conflict is in many countries, although they often coexist with conflict (involving the same or other groups). Peaceful protest attracts more media attention. It is not institutionalized but is more properly seen as competition rather than conflict, although it is easy for such protest to turn violent and thus become conflictual through the actions of the protesters or the authorities (usually the police). This is one reason why the boundaries between cooperation and competition and between competition and conflict are often difficult to draw. On the other hand, conflict in the forms of violent protest, rebellion, and repression, as well as its almost indistinguishable

cousin non-institutionalized violent competition, get a great deal of attention from global media (and scholars); they are 'newsworthy'. The consequences of such conflict can indeed be horrific, but this is not always the case, and the media's view of ethnopolitical conflict as prevalent in most developing countries is distorted.

Ethnopolitical morphology and types of ethnopolitical interaction

Cooperation, institutionalized competition, and peaceful protest, aspects of the politics of communal contention, are much more frequent and consequential in multi-ethnic than in deeply divided societies, although they are not limited to the former type. The impossibility of majority support for the regime (which is important even for autocratic regimes) in the absence of such cooperation in the former type of society, and the tendency towards the mutual fears and hopes of ethnonationalist winner-takes-all politics among both groups in the latter type of society, account for this difference. Small cultural differences and the presence of non-politicized groups (impossible in deeply divided societies) facilitate cooperation, while geographic concentration (less likely in deeply divided societies) has more ambivalent effects. Conflict and non-institutionalized violent competition are more likely to occur in deeply divided than in multi-ethnic societies, although they are not limited to the former type. The reasons for this are the inverse of those for the greater significance of cooperation in the latter type of society. Organizations such as political parties and the military tend strongly to be arenas of conflict in deeply divided societies (Horowitz 1985: 291–525). But within each type of society, other factors account for substantial differences in cooperation, competition, and conflict.

Box 7.1 Two Conceptions of the Causes of Ethnopolitical Conflict

Horowitz: 'An adequate theory of ethnic conflict should be able to explain both elite and mass behavior. Such a theory should also provide an explanation for the passionate, symbolic, and apprehensive aspects of ethnic conflict. Group entitlement, conceived as a joint function of comparative worth and legitimacy, does this—it explains why the followers follow, accounts for the intensity of group reactions, even to modest stimuli, and clarifies the otherwise mysterious quest for public signs of group status.'

(Horowitz 1985: 226)

Gurr: 'The motivations at the heart of ethnopolitics are assumed to be a mix of grievance, sentiment, solidarity, ambition, and calculation. It is simplistic to argue that one kind of motivation is primary and others subsidiary. Ethnopolitical protest and rebellion are consequences of complex interactions among collective experience, normative commitments, contention for power, and strategic assessments about how best to promote individual and collective interests.'

(Gurr 2000: 66)

Group advantages and disadvantages and types of ethnopolitical interaction

Cooperation is easier the smaller the advantages or disadvantages of different groups. Advantages or disadvantages can be economic, political, or cultural, and can be due to discrimination in either state policies or well-established social structures, or to more accidental factors such as regional differences in resource endowments. Disadvantages that are seen as caused by discrimination in state policies make cooperation especially difficult (Gurr 1993: 34–60; 2000: 105–32), but disadvantages caused by social structural discrimination and not counteracted by state policies also hinder it. Since many groups in most countries of the developing world have advantages or disadvantages caused by discrimination (as described below), ethnopolitical cooperation and the reduction of discrimination through state policies tend to go together.

Conflict is more likely to occur the greater the advantages or disadvantages of different groups, especially if these advantages or disadvantages are seen as due to discrimination in state policies. Horowitz (1985: 32) indicates that 'virtually all ranked systems of ethnic relations [in which class and ethnicity coincide] are in a state of rapid transition or of increasing coercion by the superordinate

group to avert change'. Almost 90 per cent of the 186 groups in the developing world that were included in the MAR survey in the mid-1990s because they were judged to be at risk of being involved in violent conflict experienced one or more forms of discrimination, and most of the rest were at risk because of advantages gained from such discrimination. Over two-thirds of these groups experienced economic discrimination, and 40 per cent experienced high levels of such discrimination. Within the developing world economic discrimination is greatest in Latin America and the Caribbean (where indigenous peoples are subject to severe discrimination of all types), followed by the Middle East and North Africa, Asia, and sub-Saharan Africa in that order. Political discrimination is even more prevalent in the developing world. Over 80 per cent of the 186 groups experienced political discrimination in the 1990s and over half experienced high levels of such discrimination. This form of discrimination is also greatest in Latin America and the Caribbean and least in sub-Saharan Africa, but Asia ranks a close second in this case. Finally, cultural discrimination is less frequent, with small majorities of groups experiencing it in Latin America and the Middle East, a large minority of groups in Asia (mainly 'hill tribes'), and only a few groups in sub-Saharan Africa. Unlike the other forms of discrimination, a majority of groups that experience cultural discrimination experience it at low or medium levels. These forms of discrimination were highly correlated with group disadvantages (Gurr 2000: 105–27).

Organizations, institutional rules, and types of ethnopolitical interaction

Cooperation among ethnopolitical groups occurs primarily within the political organizations listed above, operating with more or less firmly institutionalized rules. Institutional differences are probably the most important factor in explaining cooperation in such organizations. Cooperation requires a relatively high degree of institutionalization of the organizations within which it occurs, although it is impossible to specify the required level exactly. Democratic institutions, particularly if they are strong (highly institutionalized), promote cooperation, are the primary basis of institutionalized competition, and allow — and in some ways encourage — relatively peaceful protest. Institutional rules providing relatively unrestricted freedom for group activities are crucial for both institutionalized competition and peaceful protest. Not surprisingly, the MAR data demonstrate the greater use of peaceful protest and less ethnopolitical conflict in democratic countries and, perhaps more surprisingly, in transitional countries in the developing world as well.

In multi-ethnic societies, political parties contesting democratic elections need multi-ethnic support to win unless one group constitutes a majority of the population or is close enough that a nonproportional electoral system can give them control of a majority of seats in the legislature (Scarritt and Mozaffar 2003: 1). But even in the latter cases, democratic institutions value inter-ethnic cooperation (and thus multi-ethnic parties) more than autocratic institutions do. Multi-ethnic parties predominate in sub-Saharan Africa, and are found in a number of countries in other regions of the developing world. There is considerable debate about whether proportional representation or

first-past-the-post electoral institutions are more likely to promote cooperation in multi-ethnic parties. The influence of such electoral institutions is probably outweighed by other factors. Horowitz (1985: 291–440) has analysed the ways in which ethnic parties, the support for which comes overwhelmingly from a single ethnopolitical group, enhance conflict in deeply divided societies by unreservedly pursuing the interests of that group and failing to form stable majority coalitions.

Conflict and non-institutionalized violent competition occur within and among the organizations in which cooperation occurs (Horowitz 1985: 291–525), but more frequently occur outside formal organizations in the forms of violent protest, armed rebellion, and state repression varying from restrictions on civil and political liberties through conventional policing to genocide. Conflict has been most violent in deeply divided societies, when groups are severely disadvantaged by multiple forms of discrimination, and under weak autocratic institutions. In the MAR data violent rebellion between 1985 and 1998 had a mean annual magnitude in autocracies that was two-and-a-half times that in new democracies. Rebellion in transitional regimes was much closer to the level in new democracies. Partial or failed transitions in the developing world tend to increase protest but decrease rebellion (Gurr 2000: 151–63). The data show that, in part, democratization decreases conflict by decreasing discrimination (Gurr 2000: 163–77). Thus, while the institutional instability engendered by democratization can increase ethnopolitical conflict, as Snyder (2000) suggests, this is not its most common effect, at least beyond the transition period.

Mobilization, state response, and types of ethnopolitical interaction

Ethnopolitical identity construction and ethnopolitical group mobilization are closely related processes that tend to occur together over time. As discussed above, mobilization of ethnic associations is part of the politicization of ethnic identities, which then leads to ethnopolitical mobilization through political parties. Thus ethnopolitical mobilization has a history going back to the colonial period in most countries of the developing world. Since independence, such mobilization has been most intense and most violent in deeply divided societies, when groups are severely disadvantaged by multiple forms of discrimination, under weak autocratic institutions, and in the presence of international political and material support for or against mobilization. It has been least intense and most peaceful in highly multi-ethnic societies, when few or no groups are severely disadvantaged by any form of discrimination, under strong democratic institutions, and in the absence of international political and material support. The longer a specific pattern of mobilization occurs, the more likely it is to be self-perpetuating unless changed deliberately by powerful actors. It is very difficult to change a primarily conflictual pattern of collective interaction into a primarily cooperative pattern or vice versa, and somewhat difficult to institutionalize un-institutionalized competition or change violent protest into peaceful protest.

The tendency for patterns of mobilization to be self-perpetuating is reinforced by state repression of a pattern of mobilization or the absence of such repression. Not surprisingly, the more intense and violent the mobilization, the more severe the repression. In the MAR data, repression varies from conventional policing to **genocide** (extermination of an ethnic group) and **politicide** (extermination of political enemies). Between 1955 and 1995 extensive ethnopolitical repression occurred in all areas of the developing world. It involved the largest number of groups in Asia and sub-Saharan Africa, but was least intense in Latin America and the Caribbean during the last decade of that period. Repression was far more likely to intensify violent mobilization than to stop it. Harff (2003: 66) found that genocide or politicide is most likely to occur or to be repeated after political upheaval in autocracies based on the support of advantaged minorities with

exclusionary ideologies. State response to peaceful protest, most common in democratic states, has often been to grant only a small proportion of the protesters' demands but not to engage in repression. This response has typically led to the continuation of peaceful protest.

International influences and types of ethnopolitical interaction

International influences have fostered both ethnopolitical cooperation and ethnopolitical conflict. Scholars have given some attention to the direct diffusion or indirect contagion of ethnopolitical conflicts across national borders through the presence of the same or closely related groups on both sides of the border. Much less attention has been paid to the diffusion of ethnopolitical cooperation, which is more difficult to study. But as democracy has been diffused to much of the developing world since the end of the cold war it is possible to argue that ethnopolitical cooperation and institutionalized electoral competition have often been diffused with it.

During the cold war, the superpowers and former colonial powers frequently gave material, political, and/or military support to parties to ethnopolitical conflict in the developing world. This was done to further the objectives of the powers giving aid, but it undoubtedly substantially exacerbated such conflict in a number of countries, including Afghanistan, Angola, Ethiopia, Guatemala, and Nicaragua. It is argued below that international intervention in ethnopolitical conflicts has been less self-interested since the end of the cold war, but the combination of the persistence of some degree of self-interest and lack of adequate information about the consequences of specific forms of intervention mean that political and/or material support can still have conflict-enhancing effects. French intervention in Rwanda in favour of the existing government (and thus of its followers who were bent on genocide) before and during the genocide of 1994 and increased Sunni–Shi'a conflict in

Iraq after the Anglo-American invasion are cases in point. Regional powers within the developing world have also supported parties to ethnopolitical conflict in their regions out of self-interest, which formerly included rewards from their cold war patrons. Finally, regional and international organizations—governmental and especially non-governmental—have struggled to resolve a number of ethnopolitical conflicts with consequences that have varied from success to exacerbating the conflict, but it appears that some of them are becoming more successful.

Globalization has stimulated ethnopolitical mobilization and probably terrorism as tools in ethnopolitical conflict, but it has also strengthened international norms of democratization, human rights, and non-discrimination. International norms now favour ethnopolitical cooperation, institutionalized competition, and the peaceful resolution of ethnopolitical conflicts to a greater extent than ever before. However, this may be changing with terrorism and Anglo-American reactions to it, as discussed below. Economic globalization has strengthened national identities in the developing world, while also weakening the capacity of most developing states to carry out nationalist policies that challenge multinational corporations or international financial institutions. Globalization of communications has provided new tools for constructing ethnopolitical groups as well as nations. But, as Billig (1995: 128–43) argues, global culture cannot serve as the primary basis of resistance to economic globalization because it is less banal than the cultures of the developed nations, which support such globalization.

Key points

- Ethnopolitical morphology takes a variety of forms in the countries of the developing world ranging from highly multi-ethnic to deeply divided and homogeneous.

- Interaction among ethnopolitical groups and between them and states involves a mixture of cooperation, competition, and conflict.

- Cooperative interactions are most easily achieved in multi-ethnic societies that have small group advantages and disadvantages, democracy based on relatively institutionalized multi-ethnic parties, a historical pattern of non-violent ethnopolitical mobilization and minimal repression of it, and international influences that support 'managed heterogeneity' rather than one side of ethnopolitical conflicts.

- Cooperation is possible when some of these conditions are absent.

The State and Nation-Building in the Developing World

Nationalism was relatively weak in most developing states at independence, and was essentially absent in those that lacked meaningful nationalist movements and won their independence through a combination of the spillover effect of nationalist movements in neighbouring countries and the colonial powers' desire to extricate themselves from their colonies: 'The initial "nation-building" ethos [in Africa] proposed to resolve the ethnic question by confining it to the private realm' (Young 2001: 174). Civic nationalism was asserted ideologically in spite of its empirical weakness. But authoritarian 'banishment of ethnicity from political assertion merely drove it underground' (Young 2001: 176), while rulers continued to make ethnopolitical calculations in appointments to high political positions and the placement of development projects. Many essentially similar histories of failed efforts to extinguish ethnopolitical identities and movements and either create civic nationalism by fiat or assimilate minorities into the core ethnonational identity by force are found in other regions of the developing world. Forced assimilation to ethnonationalism has had the more severe consequences; in deeply divided societies with long histories of ethnopolitical mobilization, especially those characterized by great group differences and external material and political support for one side or the other, it has usually led to extremely violent conflict.

Due in part to the desire to reduce the negative effects of economic globalization and the support received from international norms and the globalization of communications, there has been a shift in some developing states from these unsuccessful policies of trying to impose civic nationalism by fiat or majority ethnonational identities by force to accepting multi-ethnic/multicultural national identities as a viable compromise. As Sen points out (see Box 7.2), there is a substantial difference between state policies promoting rational multiculturalism and policies promoting plural monoculturalism. In the former, national identity is based on a freely chosen blend of diversity and commonality among interacting ethnic groups. In the latter, full diversity is enforced by isolated groups and national identity is based on a 'federation' of group identities. The shift to rational multiculturalism/multi-ethnicity has been easier in multi-ethnic societies than in societies with a single dominant group or deeply divided societies, but such national identities are potentially viable in all of these societies (Snyder 2000: 33). They tend to make state and nation mutually reinforcing; 'the persistence of states, however challenged or changed by globalization they may be, offers a partial explanation for the continuation of nationhood as a salient form of belonging' (Croucher 2003: 14). Immigration compels states to clarify and reinforce national boundaries; responses to terrorism have the same effect. 'Nationhood, then, continues to be a functional, familiar, and legitimate mechanism for belonging' (Croucher 2003: 16). The aspirations of stateless peoples to national states prove its value.

Gurr (2000: 195–211, 275–7) presents data to show that the number and severity of ethnopolitical conflicts have declined since the end of the cold war, reversing the upward trend of the preceding three decades. He attributes this change to the emergence of a 'regime of managed ethnic heterogeneity, shorthand for a bundle of conflict-mitigating doctrines and practices' (Gurr 2000: 277–8). This regime has both domestic components—essentially those described above as promoting ethnopolitical cooperation—and international components—international norms and changes in the behaviour of outside states and transnational organizations reflecting decreased self-interest and increased competence. It fosters multi-ethnic/multicultural nationalism. But Gurr (2000: 223–60) also acknowledges that some ethnopolitical groups are still at risk of being involved in future violent conflicts because they maintain the interaction patterns with other groups and states that have led to violent conflict in the past.

Box 7.2 Sen's Definitions of Types of Multiculturalism

Plural monoculturalism: Values the diversity of existing cultures for itself and makes the nation a federation of isolated cultures.

Reason-based multiculturalism: Focuses on the freedom of reasoning and decision-making, and celebrates cultural diversity among interacting groups to the extent that it is as freely chosen as possible by the persons involved, and makes the nation truly multicultural.

(Sen 2006: 150–60)

The United States, an important player in this international regime, moved back to self-interest and interventionism under the Bush administration, although the Obama administration has reversed this trend slightly. The consequences of this change for national identities are uncertain. As mentioned above Iraqi national identity was weakened rather than strengthened by the Anglo-American invasion (see Chapter 20c), and the same can be said even more emphatically for national identity in Afghanistan. Terrorists tend to promote transnational identities. On the other hand, national identities have probably been strengthened in countries such as Venezuela and Bolivia, in which elected leaders have both reached out to indigenous groups and defied US pressures. It is far too soon to declare the demise of ethnopolitical conflict, exclusionary ethnonationalism, or their exacerbation through foreign intervention and terrorism.

Key points

- Many states of the developing world have attempted to suppress ethnopolitical identities and conflicts by declaring civic nationalism by fiat or assimilating minorities into their core ethnonational identity by force, but more are now accepting multi-ethnic national identities as a viable compromise.

- National identities in the developing world, usually based on existing states, continue to be viable in the era of globalization, and offer a basis for resisting the negative effects of economic globalization.

- The number and severity of ethnopolitical conflicts have declined since the end of the cold war because of the emergence of a 'regime of managed ethnic heterogeneity', but some violent conflicts persist.

Conclusion

In conclusion, we can briefly summarize the major themes of this chapter. Ethnopolitical and national identities are different, although both are socially constructed and thus change over time. The pattern of ethnopolitical identities (the ethnopolitical morphology) within countries involves the number and relative size of groups, their geographic concentration and degree of cultural differences, and varies from deeply divided to highly multi-ethnic. National identities are civic, multi-ethnic, or ethnonational. Collective action by ethnopolitical groups and cooperative, competitive, and conflictual interactions among them and with states are influenced by the interaction of ethnopolitical morphology, group advantages and disadvantages, political organizations and institutional rules, mobilization and state response histories, and international influences. Cooperative interactions are most easily achieved in multi-ethnic societies that have small group advantages and disadvantages, democracy based on relatively institutionalized multi-ethnic parties, a historical pattern of non-violent ethnopolitical mobilization and minimal repression of it, and international influences that support 'managed heterogeneity' rather than one side of ethnopolitical conflicts. These interactions, in turn, tend to promote nation-building through multi-ethnic/multicultural nationalism. There is evidence of a shift in this direction in some countries of the developing world, but conflictual interactions and failures of nation-building still occur all too frequently.

(?) Questions

1. If ethnopolitical and national identities are constructed and thus can change, why do they not change more frequently and rapidly?

2. What are the major types of national identity and how different are they?

3. How many ethnopolitical groups and nations are there in the developing world?

4. Does the nature of ethnopolitical and/or national identities determine whether democracy can be effective in the developing world?

5. If the amount of violent ethnopolitical conflict has declined in the developing world as a whole, why is such conflict still so strong in some countries?

6. What are the effects of globalization and foreign intervention on national identities in the developing world?

7. What are the effects of policies of plural monoculturalism and reason-based multiculturalism (as defined by Sen) on different types of national identity?

(→) Further reading

■ Eriksen, T. H. (1993), *Ethnicity and Nationalism: Anthropological Perspectives* (London: Pluto Press). Presents an anthropological perspective on ethnicity, identity, ethnic relations, nationalism, and relations between states and ethnic minorities.

■ Fearon, J. D. (2003), 'Ethnic Structure and Cultural Diversity around the World: A Cross-National Data Set on Ethnic Groups', *Journal of Economic Growth*, 8: 191–218. Describes a global data set under construction on ethnic and linguistic/cultural groups and compares it to other data sets; highlights the difficulties encountered in specifying ethnic groups cross-nationally.

■ Gurr, T. R. (1993), *Minorities at Risk: A Global View of Ethnopolitical Conflicts* (Washington DC: United States Institute of Peace Press). The first book based on the Minorities at Risk project. It identifies communal groups at risk and analyses forms of risk, group grievances, group mobilization, group protest and rebellion, and the resolution of group conflicts; it includes chapters on the Middle East and Africa.

■ ——(2000), *Peoples Versus States: Minorities at Risk in the New Century* (Washington DC: United States Institute of Peace Press). The second book from the same project analyses the same topics as its predecessor plus the role of democracy and the risk of future ethnic violence; it includes a number of illustrative sketches from the developing world.

■ Horowitz, D. L. (1985), *Ethnic Groups in Conflict* (Berkeley, CA: University of California Press). Presents a definition of ethnicity and a theory of ethnic conflict among unranked groups derived primarily from social psychology; discusses the roles of political parties and the military in ethnic conflict and strategies for its resolution; emphasizes deeply divided societies in South-East and South Asia, Africa, and the Caribbean.

■ Hutchinson, J. and Smith, A. D. (eds) (1994), *Nationalism* (Oxford: Oxford University Press). A very comprehensive reader that includes selections from classic works on the definition of nationalism, theories of nationalism, nationalism in the developing world, and the effects of trends in the international system on nationalism.

■ Sen, A. (2006), *Identity and Violence: The Illusion of Destiny* (New York: W. W. Norton). Argues that all people have multiple identities, and that movements that restrict relevant identities to ethnic or national ones only promote violence.

■ Young, C. (1976), *The Politics of Cultural Pluralism* (Madison, WI: University of Wisconsin Press). Discusses cultural pluralism, identities, the state, nationalism, and cultural mobilization in Africa, the Arab world, Asia, and Latin America; includes comparative case studies from these regions.

 ## Web links

■ http://webhost.bridgew.edu/smozaffar   The website for the Scarritt/Mozaffar data set on African ethnopolitical group fragmentation and concentration.

■ www.minoritiesatrisk.com   The website of Minorities at Risk project, covering 285 politically active ethnic groups coded on approximately 1,000 variables. Qualitative assessments of every group's risk are included.

■ www.stanford.edu/~jfearon   Go to egreousrepdata.zip for Fearon's data, which is summarized in this chapter in Tables 7.1 and 7.2.

 ## Online Resource Centre

For additional material and resources, please visit the Online Resource Centre at:
www.oxfordtextbooks.co.uk/orc/burnell3e/

8

Religion

Jeff Haynes

 Overview

Recent decades have seen widespread involvement of religion in politics, especially, but not exclusively, in parts of the developing world. This chapter, examining the relationship between religion and politics, is structured as follows. First, the concept of religion is defined and its contemporary political and social salience in many developing countries is emphasized. Second, the chapter examines the notion of religious fundamentalism, not least because it is often associated with religious competition and conflict. Third, a survey of extant religious competition and conflict in the developing world is presented, with brief examples drawn from Christianity, Islam, Hinduism, and Buddhism. Fourth, the chapter considers the extent to which, after 11 September 2001—that is, the epochal day on which the USA was attacked by al-Qaeda terrorists, resulting in the loss of around 3,000 lives—the world has changed in terms of the political salience of religion. We examine the importance of both domestic and external factors in conflicts characterized by religious concerns in the developing world.

Introduction

Open a 'quality'—that is, a 'broadsheet'—newspaper on almost any day of the week and turn to the foreign news pages. You might be struck by the number of news items with religious and political dimensions (religio-politics). For example, a recurring theme is widespread Islamic militancy or 'fundamentalism', particularly in the Arab Middle East. It sometimes seems that the entire region is polarized between Jews and Muslims—both over the status of holy sites claimed by the two sides and the political and economic position of the mostly Muslim Palestinians.

However, it is not only international relations that are informed by Islamic militancy. For example, for a decade from the early 1990s Algeria endured a decade of civil war between Islamic 'fundamentalist' (or, as I prefer, for reasons to be noted later, Islamist) rebels and the state. The roots of this conflict went back to a contested election and, more generally, highlight the often problematic political relationship between religious and secular actors in the Middle East. In December 1991 Algeria held legislative elections that most independent observers characterized as amongst the freest ever held in the Middle East. The following January, however, Algeria's armed forces seized power to prevent what was likely to be a decisive victory in the elections by an Islamist party, the Front Islamique du Salut (FIS). The assumption was that if the FIS were to achieve power it would then erode Algeria's newly refreshed democratic institutions. In London *The Economist* posed the question, 'What is the point of an experiment in democracy if the first people it delivers to power are intent on dismantling it?' (2 January 1992). The answer might well be: 'This is the popular will, it must be respected—whatever the outcome.' Instead, Algeria's military leaders imposed their preference. The FIS was summarily banned, thousands of its supporters were incarcerated, and between 150,000 and 200,000 Algerians died in the subsequent civil war. Even now, nearly

twenty years after the initial outburst of violence, Algeria still endures intermittent attacks from Islamist rebels, unhappy about the nature of the political system in the country.

It is worth noting at this point that there is no obvious reason why **political Islam** cannot compete for power democratically. Political Islam refers to a political movement with often diverse characteristics that at various times has included elements of many other political movements, while simultaneously adapting the religious views of Islamic fundamentalism or Islamism. In both the Palestinian authority and Iraq in recent years, as well as in Turkey, Islamists have gained power either alone (Hamas in the Palestinian authority and the Justice and Development Party, or AKP, in Turkey) or as part of a ruling coalition (Iraq). In none of these cases were Islamists unwilling to play by the democratic rules of the game.

Elsewhere in the developing world, Islamists are also politically active. For example, in Africa, Nigeria is increasingly polarized politically between Muslim and Christian forces, fragmented Somalia may eventually have an Islamist government, while Sudan has also experienced a long-running civil war between Muslims and non-Muslims. In these cases Islamists have not sought to use the ballot box to achieve power, but then again that particular option has not been available as a result of constitutional restrictions or constraints or wider political factors.

Not only Islamists pursue political goals related to religion. In officially secular India, a growth in militant Hinduism was highlighted by, but not confined to, the Babri Masjid mosque incident at Ayodhya in 1992, instrumental in transforming the country's political landscape. This mosque, according to militant Hindus, was built on the birthplace of the Hindu god of war, Rama. As long ago as 1950, the mosque was closed down by the Indian government, for militant Hindus wanted to build a Hindu temple there. Since then, Hindu militants or 'fundamentalists', whose primary political organization is the Bharatiya Janata Party (BJP), have grown to political prominence. From 1996 to mid-2004, the BJP was the dominant party in three ruling coalitions.

On the other hand, religion can significantly contribute to political and social stability, for example, in the way in which the Roman Catholic Church was a leading player in the turn to democracy in Latin America in the 1980s and 1990s.

> **Key points**
>
> - The last three decades have seen widespread involvement of religion in politics, especially in many countries in the developing world.
> - Several religious traditions have experienced increased political involvement.
> - Religion and democracy do not always seem compatible, although religious actors have contributed to democratization.

Religion and Politics

Before proceeding, it is necessary to define 'religion'. In this chapter, religion has two analytically distinct, yet related meanings. In a *spiritual* sense, religion pertains in three ways to models of social and individual behaviour that help believers to organize their everyday lives. First, it is to do with the idea of *transcendence*—that is, it relates to supernatural realities. Second, it is concerned with *sacredness*—that is, a system of language and practice that organizes the world in terms of what is deemed holy. Third, it refers to *ultimacy*—it relates people to the ultimate conditions of existence.

In another, *material*, sense, religious beliefs can motivate individuals and groups to act in pursuit of social or political goals. Very few—if any—religious groups have an *absolute* lack of concern for at least *some* social and political issues. Consequently, religion can be 'a mobiliser of masses, a controller of mass action . . . an excuse for repression [or] an ideological basis for dissent' (Calvert and Calvert 2001: 140). In many countries, religion remains an important source of basic value orientations; this may have social and/or political connotations.

One final point concerns the relationship between religion and ethnicity. As Chapter 7 demonstrates, religion is one of the bases for ethnic identity. For instance in India, Sikh ethnic identity has been defined largely in terms of adherence to a common religion. It could seem then that ethnicity is the overarching concept and religious identification is one sub-type. However, there are situations in which people sharing a single religion are divided by ethnicity, as for example in Pakistan where people share a common Islamic faith but are ethnically divided on the basis of region and language. Moreover appeals to religion often seek to transcend particular local or ethnic identities in the name of a supposedly universal ideal. It is wisest, therefore, to see ethnicity and religion as terms the potential meaning and content of which overlap but remain distinct.

An American commentator, George Weigel, claims there is an '**unsecularization** of the world'—that is, a global religious revitalization (quoted in Huntington 1993: 26). This is manifested in a global resurgence of religious ideas and social movements, not confined to one faith or only to poor, developing countries. This unexpected development can be explained in various ways. No simple, clear-cut reason or single theoretical explanation covers all the cases. Yet the widespread emergence of religious actors with overtly social or political goals is often linked to **modernization**—that is, the prolonged period of historically unprecedented, diverse, massive change, characterized by urbanization, industrialization, and abrupt technological developments that people around the world have experienced in recent times. Modernization is said not only to have undermined traditional value systems but also to have allocated opportunities—both within and between countries—in highly unequal ways. This has led many people to feel both disorientated and troubled and, as a result, some at least (re)turn to religion for solace and comfort. In doing so, they seek a new or renewed sense of identity, something to give their lives greater meaning and purpose.

A second, although linked, explanation for apparent religious resurgence moves away from the specific impact of modernization to point to a more generalized 'atmosphere of crisis'. A key factor is said to be widespread popular disillusion with the abilities of secular state leaders to direct their socioeconomic polities so that people generally benefit. Such disappointment can then feed into perceptions that these leaders hold power illegitimately—a sense bolstered when leaders resort to political oppression. Adding to the sense of crisis is widespread popular belief that society's traditional morals and values are being seriously undermined, not least by the corrosive effects of globalization, Westernization, and **secularization**—the reduction in influence or even withdrawal of religion from the public realm. These circumstances are said to provide a fertile milieu for many people's 'return' to religion.

This suggests that the influence of religion will not be seen 'only' in relation to personal and social issues. Commentators have additionally pointed to *political* effects of the 'return of religion' where, in many developing countries, highly politicized religious groups, institutions, and movements have emerged—or adopted a higher profile—in recent years. Such actors are found in many different faiths and sects and what they have in common is a desire to change domestic, and in some cases international, arrangements, so as to (re)instate religion as a central societal and political influence. They adopt a variety of tactics to achieve their goals. Some

actors confine themselves to the realm of legitimate political protest, seeking reform or change via the ballot box; others resort to violence and terror to pursue their objectives.

Other explanations are offered for what is widely seen as a global religious revival and revitalization, but some commentators suggest that, in the developing world, there is not a religious resurgence per se; rather, political religion is simply more visible—largely as a consequence of the global communications revolution. In other words, religion is not a novel political actor, so much as a stubbornly persistent one. For Smith (1990: 34), 'what has changed in the present situation . . . is mainly the growing awareness of [global manifestations of political religion] by the Western world, and the perception that they might be related to our interests'. This makes the recent trends just the latest manifestation of *cyclical* religious activity, made more highly visible (and to many alarming) by advances in communications technology and availability. In short, globalization is a multifaceted process of change, universally affecting states, local communities, and individuals. Religions are not exempted from its influence and, as a result, like other social agents, they participate in and are affected by globalization. Academic discussions of religion and globalization often highlight trends towards cultural pluralism as a result of globalization, examining how various religions respond (Haynes 2007). Some believers react 'positively', accepting or even endorsing pluralism, including some Christian ecumenical movements. Others emphasize more inter-religious differences, sometimes confronting non-believers in attempts to preserve their particular values from being eroded by globalization. So-called fundamentalist Christian, Muslim, and Jewish movements are well-known examples.

But they are not necessarily *sui generis*. In the developing world, various religious traditions—for example, Hinduism, Buddhism, and Islam—all experienced periods of pronounced political activity in the first half of the twentieth century in what were then mostly colonized countries. In the 1920s and the 1930s, religion was frequently used in the service of anti-colonial nationalism, and was a major facet of emerging national identity in opposition to alien rule (see Haynes 1996: 55–6). For example, in various Muslim countries, such as Algeria, Egypt, and Indonesia, Islamic consciousness was the defining ideology of nationalist movements. In 1947, immediately after the Second World War, Pakistan was founded as a Muslim state, religiously and culturally distinct from India, which was 80 per cent Hindu. A decade later, Buddhism was politically important, inter alia, in Burma, Sri Lanka, and Vietnam. Later, in the 1960s in Latin America, both **Christian democracy**—the application of Christian precepts to politics—and **liberation theology**—a radical ideology using Christianity as the basis of a demand for greater socio-economic justice for the poor—were politically consequential. More recently and in diverse countries including Iran, the United States, and Nicaragua, religion (re)appeared as an important political actor. Religious actors became skilled at using the media to spread their political messages (Tarrow 1998: 115).

In sum, political religion is nearly always in opposition to the status quo; in the developing world this has been the case since at least the early years of the twentieth century, a time of widespread external colonial control. Current manifestations of political religion can be located in this historical continuum and context, to stress *continuity* rather than *change*.

Key points

- Religion has spiritual, material, and in some cases political, aspects.

- Religion played an important political role in many developing countries during the last years of colonialism.

- Patchy modernization and/or a more generalized 'atmosphere of crisis' are said to underpin religious resurgence.

- It is often claimed that there is a near-global religious revival but globalization may simply be rendering religion in politics more visible.

Religious Fundamentalism

Many religious actors with political goals are routinely labelled 'fundamentalists'. **Religious fundamentalism** has been described as a 'distinctively modern twentieth-century movement' albeit with 'historical antecedents' (Woodhead and Heelas 2000: 32). The label, 'religious fundamentalism' has been widely employed since the 1970s, especially by the mass media, to describe and account for numerous, apparently diverse, religious and political developments around the globe. The term's genesis is in a group of socially conservative evangelicals inside the mainstream Protestant denominations in the United States. There, in the early twentieth century, such people first applied the designation 'religious fundamentalist' to themselves. Now,

however, as a generic term, it is widely applied to groups outside the corpus of Christianity, notably Hindu and Islamic entities.

What fundamentalist doctrines generally have in common is that their character and impact are located within a nexus of moral and social issues revolving, in many cases, around state–society interactions. In some cases, the initial defensiveness of beleaguered religious groups later developed into a political offensive that sought to alter the prevailing social and political realities of state–society relations. Religious fundamentalists often accused their rulers of performing inadequately and/or corruptly; with the exception of Buddhist and Hindu fundamentalists, they criticized contemporary developments in the light of religious texts, such as the Bible or the Koran.

The significance of this from a political perspective is that religious fundamentalism can, and often does, supply an already restive group with a ready-made manifesto for social change: fundamentalist activists use suitable religious texts both to challenge secular rulers and to propose a programme for radical political and social reform. Under these circumstances, it can be relatively easy for fundamentalist leaders to gain the support of people who feel particularly aggrieved that, in various important ways, society's development is not proceeding according to God's will and/or the community's interests.

Contemporary examples of religious fundamentalism are often said to be rooted in the failed promise and impact of modernization, such as apparently declining morals. To many fundamentalists the current era is one in which God is in danger of being superseded by a gospel of technical progress accompanying sweeping socio-economic changes. The pace of change strongly challenges traditional habits, beliefs, and cultures. In an increasingly materialist world, individual worth often seems to be measured according to standards of wealth and status, while religion is ignored or belittled.

But some argue that, in fact, religious fundamentalism is a meaningless term, erroneously employed 'by western liberals to refer to a broad spectrum of religious phenomena which have little in common except for the fact that they are alarming to liberals!' (Woodhead and Heelas 2000: 32). Critics contend that the range of so-called fundamentalist groups is so wide — for example, resurgent Islam in Iran and Latin American Pentecostalism — that the term has no meaning and, moreover, is insulting to many people described as fundamentalists. Such groups actually differ markedly among themselves: some aspire to influence or even control the public and political arena; others actively work to disengage from social and political issues. As a consequence, Hallencreutz and Westerlund (1996: 4) argue the:

broad use of the term has become increasingly irrelevant. In sum, viewed as a derogatory concept, tied to Western stereotypes and Christian presuppositions, the casual use of the term easily causes misunderstandings and prevents the understanding of the dynamics and characteristics of different religious groups with explicit *political* objectives.

(my emphasis)

In contrast, those accepting the analytical relevance of the term do so because they perceive contemporary movements of religious resurgence — albeit encompassing different religious traditions — as having features in common that denote a shared concern with fundamentalism. In general, fundamentalist doctrines share the following: (a) a strong desire to return to what are believed to be a faith's fundamentals; (b) forceful rejection of Western-style secular modernity; (c) 'an oppositional minority group-identity maintained in an exclusivist and militant manner' (Woodhead and Heelas 2000: 32); (d) rejection of secularization, and a demand to retrieve the public realm as a place of moral and religious purity; and (e) perception that patriarchal and hierarchical ordering of relations between the sexes is both morally and religiously appropriate.

Drawing on data from a large variety of fundamentalist movements, Marty and Appleby (1993: 3) define religious fundamentalism as a 'set of strategies, by which beleaguered believers attempt to preserve their distinctive identity as a people or group' in response to a real or imagined attack from those who, it appears, want to draw the religious believers into 'syncretistic, areligious, or irreligious cultural milieu[s]'. Such defensiveness may develop into a political offensive aiming to alter prevailing socio-political realities.

Religious fundamentalists then share a fear that their religiously orientated way of life is under threat from unwelcome alien influences, especially secular-orientated governments. As a result, they often seek to reform, even re-traditionalize, society in accordance with their religious tenets. They are willing in some cases to fight governments if the latter's jurisdiction appears to be encompassing areas they believe are integral to social reform—education, gender relations and employment, and social morality. Fundamentalists may also attack those they see as 'nominal' or 'backsliding' co-religionists and members of opposing religions.

Drawing on the example of contemporary Christian fundamentalists in the United States, many analysts who employ the term fundamentalism also suggest that it is only properly applicable to Christianity and other Abrahamic religions of the 'book': Islam and Judaism. This is because, like fundamentalist Christians, Muslim, and Jewish fundamentalists take as their defining dogma what is believed to be the inerrancy of God's own words set out in holy books like the Bible. It is suggested that because neither Hinduism nor Buddhism have central tenets of political, social, and moral import conveniently accessible in holy books, it is not logically possible for there to be Hindu or Buddhist fundamentalism. However, in recent years a popular fundamentalist movement within Hinduism has emerged in pursuit of demonstrably political goals. Such a group is not defined by its absolutist insistence upon the veracity of God's revealed will, but instead by a desire to recapture elements of national identity that are perceived as being lost, either by dint of cultural dilution or mixing, or by perceived deviations from the religious philosophy and/or teaching (Ram-Prasad 1993: 288).

Key points

- All major religious traditions have fundamentalist variants.
- Fundamentalist doctrines are concerned with moral, social, and sometimes political, issues.
- Fundamentalist concerns may supply an already restive group with a manifesto for social and political change.
- Fundamentalists fear their way of life is under threat from secular forces.

Religious Fundamentalism and Politics in the Developing World

This section considers three kinds of religious fundamentalism, most prominent in the developing world—Islamic, Christian, and Hindu—focusing on their main socio-political characteristics.

Islamic fundamentalism

Like Christianity, Islam is by no means monolithic but has taken many different forms, one important distinction being between the Sunni and Shi'a traditions (see Box 8.1). From the mid-2000s, clashes between these two communities in Iraq and Pakistan have been only the latest tragic reminder of the endurance of these divisions. Both these main branches however have given rise to fundamentalist movements.

A defining character of religious fundamentalism is that it is always socially but not necessarily politically conservative. Thus some Islamic fundamentalist (Islamist) groups seek to overthrow the existing socio-economic and political order by various means, including violence or terrorism, incremental reform of existing political regimes, or winning elections through the mobilization of a political party. Islamists take as their defining dogma what are believed to be God's words written in their holy book, the Koran. In other words, singular scriptural revelations are central to Islamic fundamentalist beliefs.

Box 8.1 Theological Differences between Sunnis and Shi'i

More than four-fifths of all Muslims are Sunni, the largest sect of Islam. Less than 20 per cent of Muslims are Shi'a, although in some countries, such as Iran, they are in the majority. Differences between Sunni and Shi'a sects of Islam are not that extensive. Both emphasize the importance of five key beliefs—or pillars—of Islam (profession of faith in the one God and in Muhammad as his Prophet; pray five times a day; donate alms to the poor; fast during the month of Ramadan; undertake pilgrimage (*hajj*) to Mecca), read the same holy book—the Koran—and regard each other as Muslims. Differences between them centre on two issues: how each attaches meaning to the history of Muhammad's family; how each regards their religious leaders.

Sunni and Shi'a sects divided nearly 1,400 years ago, soon after Muhammad's death in 632. Ali, his son-in-law, received support as the figure who henceforward would lead the struggle to spread Islam. ('Shi'a' is an abbreviation of 'Shiat Ali', or the people of Ali.) But not all Muslims believed that Ali should play this leading role, although most did believe that he was a holy man. Shi'a believed Ali was the first Imam, a direct descendant of Muhammad and messenger of God. Twelve Imams lived before the lineage came to an end over 1,000 years ago. Within Shi'a Islam, each of the 12 has sub-sects who worship them.

Sunnis do not attach any special power to the Imam, and overall have a somewhat less structured hierarchy of religious leaders, called caliphs. They are important advisers and community leaders who teach Islam; they are not infallible or chosen by God.

Modern Islamic resurgence dates from the 1920–40 period, when growing numbers of countries in the Middle East were demanding—and in some cases receiving—national self-determination. The main point of contention was how far these predominantly Muslim states should employ the tenets of *Sharia*—that is, Muslim religious—law in their legal systems. This example of a desire to Islamicize polities had its precedents in the Muslim world in anti-imperialist and anti-pagan movements (*jihads*), periodically erupting from the late nineteenth century, especially in parts of West Africa and East Asia (see Haynes 1993). In these regions, conflict between tradition and modernization and between Islam and Christianity was often acute.

In the early stages of Islam, nearly 1,400 years ago, religious critics of the status quo periodically emerged in opposition to what they perceived as unjust rule. Contemporary Islamists are only the most recent example of such a phenomenon, often characterizing themselves as the 'just' involved in a 'holy war' against the 'unjust'. This dichotomy between just and unjust in the promotion of social change parallels the tension in the West between state and civil society: both juxtapose mutually exclusive concepts whereby a strengthening of one necessarily implies a weakening of the other. The implication is that the unjust inhabit the state while the just look in from the outside, aching to reform the corrupt political system. The Islamic 'just' strive to achieve their goal, which is a form of direct democracy under the auspices of *Sharia* law, in which the ruler uses his wisdom to settle disputes brought before him by his loyal subjects. The Islamic concept of *shura* (consultation) by no means necessarily implies popular sovereignty, which is with God alone; 'rather it is a means of obtaining unanimity from the community of believers, which allows for no legitimate minority position' (Dorr 1993: 151–2).

The goal of the just is an Islam-based society. Currently, in many Muslim countries, Islamist groups believe themselves to be the appropriate vehicle to achieve this goal. For them, Western-style liberal democracy is fatally flawed and compromised, a concept relevant only to secular, Western(ized) societies that appear unacceptably decadent. As a young Algerian graduate of the Islamic Science Institute of Algiers averred in the early 1990s: 'The modern world is going through a major moral crisis which can be very confusing to young people. Just look at what is happening in Russia. Personally I have found many of the answers and solutions in Islam' (cited in Ibrahim 1992).

The global Muslim community, the *umma*, is a good example of a transnational civil society (the Roman Catholic Church, with its institutional support for democratization in the 1990s, is another), containing the seeds of both domination and dissent. Shared beliefs, relating especially to culture and identity link Muslims. For this reason it is unsurprising that international manifestations of Islamic resurgence appeared after the humbling defeat of Arab Muslims by Israeli Jews in the six-day war of June 1967. Since then a combination of bad government, growing unemployment, and generalized social crisis in the Muslim world has produced Islamist movements. When possible, as in the Persian Gulf, rulers have been content to live on the 'rents' accrued from their control of oil exports with little done to reduce unemployment and under-employment, develop more representative polities, or plan successfully for the future. In short, there has been a skewed modernization; urbanization and the creation of a centralized state proceeded at the same time as many people became increasingly dissatisfied with the way in which their rulers rule.

Christian fundamentalism

Africa has experienced the spread of **evangelical Christianity**. Evangelical Christianity usually refers to conservative, nearly always Protestant, Christian religious practices and traditions, which emphasize evangelism, a personal experience of conversion, faith rooted in the Bible, and a belief in the relevance of Christian faith to cultural issues. Some commentators suggest this spread is linked to the influence of American fundamentalist Christian churches (Gifford 2004). Sponsored by American television evangelists and their local allies, thousands of conservative, mainly foreign, Protestant evangelical crusaders have promoted American-style conservative Christianity in Africa since the 1980s.

Norms, beliefs, and morals favourable to American interests were in turn disseminated as a fundamental aspect of the religious message (Freston 2004). African converts to US conservative evangelical churches have been said to be victims of manipulation by the latest manifestation of neo-colonialism. The objective was not, however, to spirit away Africa's material resources, but rather to deflect popular political mobilization away from seeking structural change of the society and the economy, in order to serve either American strategic interests and/or financial objectives of US transnational corporations (Pieterse 1992: 10–11).

Others contend that foreign Christian proselytization in Africa resulted *not* in imposition of an alien doctrine but instead in the indigenization of Christianity (Ter Haar and Busutill 2005; Freston 2004: 1–2). During the colonial era European-style Christianity tried unsuccessfully to appropriate the richness of local people's imagination and beliefs, in order better to convert and to dominate. But the outcome was different to what was anticipated: African independent churches emerged.

Some such churches have been described as fundamentalist. Nigeria is a useful example to highlight because of the significance of this issue to the country's political and economic developments. Since the 1970s there have been growing signs of tension between Islamists and the state in Nigeria. This has paralleled increasing hostility between Muslim and Christian communities leading to the emergence of an organization representing fundamentalist Christians whose main purpose is to comment on both religious and political issues. The Pentecostal Fellowship of Nigeria (PFN) is an influential voice in the inter-denominational Christian Association of Nigeria that claims to represent the interests of the country's Christians at both federal and national levels. The PFN was formerly an avowedly apolitical organization. It re-evaluated its traditional stance of indifference to political issues in the mid-1980s because of its fear of creeping Islamicization. Some influential figures in the PFN, including the late Benson Idahosa, founder of the international Church of God Mission, have warned of religious war in Nigeria—if tensions between Muslims and Christians are not diminished.

Somewhat ironically, religious tensions were exacerbated in northern Nigeria from the 1990s in part because of the aggressive proselytizing of missionaries of several of the fundamentalist churches, including Idahosa's, which led to some conversions in the predominantly Muslim north. In that region, where socio-cultural norms make Islam an integral facet of many people's lives, conversion to Christianity was facilitated by a modern variant of the colonial missionaries' 'gospel of prosperity' argument. During colonial times, Christianity was seen to bring medicine, education, and wealth to the country, so it was quite sensible for those who wished to share these benefits to follow the Christian faith. 'Muslims in power know that they have nothing to offer the country,' claimed Idahosa (Elliot 1993), alluding to the three decades of 'Muslim rule' from the 1960s that saw living standards of most Nigerians plummet, despite the country enjoying massive oil wealth.

In Nigeria, the Christian fundamentalist churches consider themselves involved in a three-way conflict, not only with Muslims, but also with mainstream Christians. They accuse the latter of being apostates who have abandoned the fundamentals of the Christian faith, while their leaders have set themselves up as individuals whose power challenges that of God. In short, all people of whatever religious faith outside the community of Christian fundamentalists are beyond the pale of true believers and can only be saved from hell if they convert.

The growth of fundamentalist churches in Nigeria has probably been encouraged by the country's deteriorating socio-economic conditions over the last thirty years (see Chapter 21b). The volatility of the religious environment mirrors the unpredictability of the political arena: the battle for power between various ethnic groups, and between civilian politicians and military figures, corresponds to the fight for 'theological space' between traditional and arriviste religions. Interlinked economic, social, and spiritual crises help to spread fears of the end of the world and an accompanying, increasingly desperate, striving for salvation. Emergent preachers can capitalize on these fears and a common desire for stability, and community. Traditionally, politics, business, and religion have been the three areas of endeavour from which individuals may expect financial reward; politics in Nigeria has long been the domain of a homogeneous (northern-military) elite. Business success requires capital, contacts, and luck, all generally in short supply, while religious success may only require a charismatic personality with the ability to attract disciples and followers. The supporters, as a sign of their faith, are often willing to pay for the costs of running a church and the considerable expenses incurred by its leader.

With economic decline from the 1980s and increasing social disorder, the hierarchies of the mainline Christian churches conspicuously failed to speak up for ordinary people, or even to criticize the inept political system. The fundamentalist churches offered, in contrast, a sense of solidarity between co-religionists, a code of behaviour, moral values, and, above all, a sense of stability in a world profoundly disrupted. The Christian revival involved a movement away from the crassly materialist ways of the established churches and an attempt to reconstruct a new type of socially responsive organization, stressing a fundamentalist return to the tenets of the Bible.

In sum, the growth of fundamentalist Christian communities in Nigeria is linked to the country's socio-economic deterioration. Like fundamentalist churches elsewhere in Africa, those in Nigeria have offered their followers the possibility of joining a new Christian community—in which solidarity between individuals is a function of religious belief. At the same time, Nigeria's Christian fundamentalists' political concerns reflect their fear of a growth in Islamist groups in the country.

Hindu fundamentalism

The roots of Hindu fundamentalism are said to lie both in the desire of some Hindu nationalists in India to privilege their culture over others and in the perception that 'Hindu' India is surrounded and threatened by Islamic resurgence — notably in Pakistan (where the Kashmir issue focuses such concerns), Iran, and Afghanistan. We should note, however, that Hindu nationalism is not a new development. Mahatma Gandhi, the leading Indian nationalist and a committed Hindu, was assassinated by a Hindu extremist in 1948 for the 'crime' of appearing to condone the creation of a new homeland — Pakistan — for India's Muslims. Subsequently, Prime Minister Indira Gandhi played to such sentiments in the early 1980s, in her confrontation with Sikh militants. From that time also simmering Hindu fundamentalist suspicion of India's largest religious minority — the Muslims, comprising about 14 per cent of the population, around 150 million people — has been reflected and fostered by a growing 'family' (*parivar*) of organizations embodying the Hindu chauvinist doctrine of *Hindutva*, and reached a kind of apotheosis in the violent destruction in 1992 of a historic mosque at Ayodhya in Uttar Pradesh. Since then, the BJP has grown out of this movement, becoming an important political player; by May 2004 it had led the ruling NDA (National Democratic Alliance) coalition government for six years, although ousted from power in that year's general election by the secular Congress Party, the dominant party in the subsequent ruling coalition. Further elections, in May 2009, cemented the Congress Party's hold on power, although it remains possible that the BJP will regain power at some stage. The BJP was the second largest party in the *Lok Sabha* (India's parliament) in late 2010.

> ### Key points
>
> - Many Islamic fundamentalists in the developing world seek to change political arrangements by a variety of methods.
> - Christian fundamentalists in Nigeria fear Islamicization.
> - Hindu fundamentalists feel under threat from Muslims, both within India and without.

Religion and the State

These examples of religious fundamentalisms in the developing world point more generally to the importance of **state–church relations** — that is, the interactions in a country between the state and the leading religious organization(s). A major difficulty in trying to survey existing church–state relations in the developing world is that the very concept of *church* reflects a somewhat parochial Anglo-American standpoint with most relevance to Western Christian traditions.

Extending the question of church–state relations to non-Christian and developing world contexts necessitates some preliminary conceptual clarifications — not least because the very idea of a prevailing state–church dichotomy is culture-bound (Box 8.2). *Church* is a Christian institution, while the modern understanding of *state* is deeply rooted in the post-Reformation European political experience. Overloaded with Western cultural history, these two concepts cannot easily be translated into non-Christian terminologies. Some religions — for example, Hinduism — have no ecclesiastical structure at all. Consequently, there *cannot* be a clerical challenge to India's secular state comparable to that of Buddhist monks in parts of South-East Asia or of *mullahs* in Iran. However, political parties and movements energized by religious notions—such as Hinduism and Sikhism—have great political importance in contemporary India. Within the developing world, only in Latin America is it per-

tinent to speak of church–state relations along the lines of the European model. This is because of the historical dominance in the region of the Roman Catholic Church and the creation of European-style states in the early nineteenth century.

Box 8.2 Religion, Nationalism, and Identity

What is the relationship between religion and nationalism? The first point is that nationalism is a source of identity for many people in the developing world. Many identities are based on shared values, beliefs, or concerns that not only include religion but can also extend to ethnicity, nationality, culture, and political ideologies (Gopin 2000; 2005). This does not imply that such expressions of identity are necessarily monolithic entities—because in fact *everyone's* self-conception is a unique combination of various identities that can include, but are not limited to, community, religion, ethnicity, nationalism, gender,

class, and family. Their relative importance and compatibility will differ at various times and circumstances. For example, race and religion are important sources of identity in some societies, while in others political ideologies and nationalism are judged to be of more significance. In short, both individual and collective senses of identity are socially constructed from a number of available traits and experiences, all of which are subject to interpretation. People *choose* their history and ancestry and, as a result, can *create*, as much as *discover*, differences from others (Gopin 2000; Malek 2004).

The differences between Christian conceptions of state and church and those of other world religions are well illustrated by reference to Islam. In the Muslim tradition, mosque is not church. The closest Islamic approximation to 'state'—*dawla*—means, conceptually, either a ruler's dynasty or his administration (only with the specific proviso of *church* as generic concept for 'moral community', *priest* for 'custodians of the sacred law', and *state* for 'political community' is it appropriate to use these concepts in Islamic and other non-Christian contexts). On the theological level, the command–obedience nexus that constitutes the Islamic definition of authority is not demarcated by conceptual categories of religion and politics. Life as a physical reality is an expression of divine will and authority (*qudrah*). There is no validity in separating the matters of piety from those of the polity; both are divinely ordained. Yet, although both religious and political authorities are legitimated Islamically, they invariably constitute two independent social

institutions. They do, however, regularly interact with each other. In sum, there is a variety of church–state relations in the contemporary world (see Box 8.3). Note, however, that the typology is not exhaustive but instead identifies common arrangements.

In the *confessional* church–state relationship, ecclesiastical authority is pre-eminent over secular power. A dominant religion—Islam in the countries in Box 8.3—seeks to shape the world according to its leadership's interpretations of God's plan for humankind. However, confessional states are rare in the early twenty-first century. One of the most consistent effects of secularization is to separate religious and secular power almost—but not quite—regardless of the religion or type of political system. However, as events in Saudi Arabia after the country's creation in 1932, in Iran since the 1978–79 Islamic revolution, and in Sudan and Afghanistan from the 1980s indicate, several Muslim countries have sought to build confessional polities.

Box 8.3 A Typology of Church–State Relations

Confessional	'Generally religious'	Established faith	Liberal secular	Marxist secular
Iran, Saudi Arabia, Sudan, Afghanistan (under the Taliban, 1996–2001)	Indonesia, USA	England, Denmark, Norway	Netherlands, Turkey, India, Ghana	China, Albania (until 1991), Russia (until 1991), North Korea

---

Because of Islam's pivotal role, the overthrow of the Shah of Iran in 1979 was one of the most spectacular political upheavals of recent times. Because of space limitations, however, this chapter contains relatively little on the important topic of religion and politics in that country. (Interested readers may, however, consult the Online Resource Centre where they will find a commentary on the issue of religion and politics in Iran.) The Shah's regime was not a shaky monarchy but a powerful centralized autocratic state possessing a strong and feared security service (SAVAK) and an apparently loyal and cohesive officer corps. Unlike earlier revolutions in other Muslim countries, such as Egypt, Iraq, Syria, and Libya, Iran's was not a revolution from above, but one with massive popular support and participation. The forces that overthrew the Shah came from all urban social classes, Iran's different nationalities and ideologically varying political parties and movements. Nevertheless, when an Islamic Republic was eventually declared, the outcome of the revolutionary process was a clerical, authoritarian regime. In these events the *ulama* or Muslim clerics, who adhere like the bulk of Iran's Muslims to the Shia tradition, played a central role. Organized in and by the Islamic Republican Party, they came to power, established an Islamic constitution and dominated the post-revolutionary institutions.

Alongside the confessional states such as Iran there are the 'generally religious' states, like the USA and Indonesia. They are guided by religious beliefs in general, but are not tied to any specific religious tradition. Both the USA and Indonesia have a belief in God as one of the bases on which the nation should be built. In Indonesia, under

General Suharto (1965–98), such a belief formed one of the five pillars of the state ideology, *Pancasila*. This position is very similar to the notion of 'civil religion' in the USA. However, whereas the generally religious policy of religion in Indonesia is an official policy, civil religion in the USA is not formally recognized.

Then there are countries that have an officially established faith but are also socially highly secular, of which the Scandinavian countries and England are examples. Over time the voices of the established churches in public policy issues have generally become increasingly marginal.

Next, and frequently encountered in the modern era, the *liberal secular* model encapsulates the notion of secular power holding sway over religion, with detachment and separation between church and state. Here, the state may try to use religion for its own ends, to 'legitimate political rule and to sanctify economic oppression and the given system' of social stratification (Casanova 1994: 49). Secularization policies are widely pursued as a means of national integration in post-colonial multi-religious states, like India. It is worth noting, however, that the concept of secularism is not necessarily straightforward. For example, Hindu critics of India's religiously 'neutral' Constitution contend that it is not neutral but rather privileges India's religious minorities, including Muslims, Sikhs, and Christians.

In the liberal secular model, no religion is given official predominance. In fact, in vigorously modernizing countries such as India and post-Ottoman Turkey, state policies of modernization were expected to lead—inevitably—to a high degree of secularization; hence, their constitutions are neutral towards religion. But things turned out differently: in recent years, democratization and secularization have worked at cross-purposes. Increasing participation in the political arena has drawn in new social forces in India, religious Hindus, Sikhs, and Muslims—who, in demanding greater formal recognition of their religions by the state, have been responsible for making religion a central issue in contemporary politics. In Turkey, the accession to power of the Justice and Development Party (AKP) in 2002—claiming to be the party of the poor and the alienated—suggests that even when secularization is pursued with great determination over a long period—in Turkey's case for eighty years—there is still no certainty that, for important constituencies, the socio-political appeal of religion will wither. Indeed, the AKP, which does not call itself an 'Islamic' party yet has some Muslim characteristics and credentials, achieved a landslide victory in the 2007 elections, which underlined its wide appeal in Turkey.

Finally, there is the category of *Marxist secular* states. Before the overthrow of communism in 1989–90, Eastern Europe contained anti-religious polities in which religion was stifled by the state. Most Marxist regimes were less hard-line than Enver Hoxha's Albania—where religion was 'abolished'—but religion was typically permitted to exist only as the private concern of the individual. This constituted a kind of promise that the authorities would respect the people's religious faith and practice—as long as it remained behind closed doors.

Skeletal religious organizations were, however, allowed to exist—but only so the state could use them for purposes of social control. They were reduced to liturgical institutions, with no other task than the holding of divine services. Numbers of permitted places of worship were greatly reduced.

Paradoxically, however, even the most strident and prolonged Marxist anti-religion campaigns failed to secularize societies. The pivotal role of the Christian churches in the democratic openings in Eastern Europe and non-Marxist Latin America in the 1980s and 1990s, and the contemporary revival of Islam in some of the formerly communist Central Asian countries, indicate that popular religiosity has retained immense social importance. But we should not take it for granted that Marxist, 'anti-religion' states are only of historical interest. For example, the government of China—home to more than a billion people—launched a fierce, continuing, campaign in the mid-1990s to 'teach atheism to Tibetan Buddhists'. This was necessary, the Chinese government argued, to enable Tibetans to 'break free of the bewitchment' of religion.

In sum, none of the various models of church–state relations has been permanently able to resolve the tension between religion and the secular world. The chief manifestation of this tension in recent times is the desire of many religious organizations not to allow the state to sideline them as—almost everywhere—increasingly secularized states seek to intervene ever deeper into social life.

Key points

- 'Church' is a concept that derives from Christianity and may have little relevance in other religious settings.
- There are various relationships between church and state in the developing world.

- States often seek to secularize their societies, to the dismay of religious actors.
- No model of church–state relations has been permanently able to resolve tensions between the religious and the secular world.

So far, we have been concerned primarily with the domestic interaction of religion and politics within developing countries. However, no survey of the issue can legitimately ignore the impact of the terrorist events of 11 September 2001 (9/11) on issues of religion and politics in general and those of the Muslim world and the West, in particular.

Prior to the eighteenth century and the formation and development of the international state system, religion was the key ideology that stimulated conflict between social groups. However, following the Peace of Westphalia in 1648 and the consequent development of centralized states, religion took a back seat as an organizing ideology at the international level. As already noted, it was not until the Iranian revolution of 1978–79 that religion resumed a significant political role. Ten years later in 1989, the cold war came to an end. Since then, international politics has been characterized by four significant changes:

- change from a bipolar (USA, Soviet Union) to an arguably unipolar (USA) structure of power;
- culture replacing ideology as a chief source of identity, leading to changes in extant affiliations and antagonisms in world affairs;
- according to some commentators, a worldwide religious resurgence, excepting Western Europe;
- change in the nature of international conflict, with fewer inter-state wars. Of the 110 major conflicts during the 1990s—that is, those involving more than 1,000 fatalities each—only seven were inter-state wars, while 103 were civil wars. Of the latter, over 70 per cent are classified as communal wars—that is, wars among ethnic and other national groups, with religion very often playing an important part.

Western Europe, including Britain, is characterized by both religious privatization and secularization. In contrast, over half of all US citizens claim to attend regular religious, mostly Christian, services.

Moreover, eight words are juxtaposed—'In God We Trust' and the 'United States of America'—on all US currency, both coins and notes.

The issue of what role religion should play there was sharpened by the arguments of the US academic, Samuel Huntington (1993; revised and expanded version, 1996a), in his now (in)famous **clash of civilizations** thesis. Huntington's key argument is that, following the end of the cold war, future international conflicts are increasingly likely to be along cultural fault lines. Now, he suggests, new rivalries are most important, notably between the (Christian) 'West' and the (mostly Muslim, mostly Arab) 'East'. In short, the core of Huntington's argument is that in the post-cold war era the 'Christian', democratic West is likely to find itself in conflict with radical Islam (Islamic fundamentalism), a global anti-Western political movement said to be aiming for fundamental changes to the political order. Another influential US commentator, Francis Fukuyama (1992: 236), argued that Islamic fundamentalism is the antithesis of Western liberalism, with 'more than superficial resemblance to European fascism'.

Critics of such arguments argue that although many radical Islamist movements and political parties would not classify themselves as liberal democratic, we cannot assume this necessarily implies that such actors are willing to engage in violent conduct, including terrorism, to pursue their aims. The 9/11 atrocities in the USA—as well as the Bali and Kenya terrorist incidents that followed—appear to have been carried out by a shadowy transnational terrorist group—al-Qaeda. However, it is by no means clear that most 'ordinary' Muslim men and women support either its goals or its violent methods.

It is also important to see the struggle in the Islamic world of groups like al-Qaeda as directed against their own rulers as well as the West. Since the beginning of Islam in the seventh century,

Muslim critics of the status quo have periodically emerged to oppose what they perceive as unjust rule. Current Islamists, including, arguably, bin Laden and al-Qaeda, are contemporary examples, who portray themselves as the 'just' involved in struggle against 'unjust', 'anti-religious' rulers and their allies. Bin Laden's key goal is said to be the creation of a pan-Islamic state to revive the glories of the Ottoman caliphate that collapsed after the First World War. Bin Laden and his followers certainly oppose Western interpretations of democracy, in which sovereignty resides with the people, because it is seen as a system that negates God's own sovereignty. Finally, it is suggested that Western support for so-called 'un-Islamic' rulers in, for example French support for the military junta in Algeria and US support for Saudi Arabia's allegedly unpopular rulers, led some radical Islamist groups to target the West.

But it would be wrong to attribute the rise of Islamist groups to bin Laden. Instead, we might look to the failure of state-sponsored modernization as a key explanation. Contemporary Islamist resurgence is argued to be a vehicle for popular disillusion with many governments in the Muslim world, which have failed to achieve what they promised—both developmentally and politically—since independence from colonial rule. In addition, existing communitarian structures have been confronted by state power that apparently seeks to destroy and replace them with the idea of a national (increasingly secularized) citizenry. Thus the widespread Islamic awakening can be seen in relation to its *domestic* capacity to oppose what are perceived as oppressive states: 'It is primarily in civil society that one sees Islam at work' (Coulon 1983: 49). The point is that this domestic response does not necessarily translate into a wider Muslim threat to *global* order.

The issue of Islam in international relations was given additional focus at the April 2009 Durban Review Conference, the official name of the 2009 United Nations World Conference Against Racism. The aim of the conference was to review implementation of the Declaration and Programme of Action from the 2001 World Conference against Racism, Racial Discrimination, Xenophobia and Related Intolerance. Many Western countries boycotted the conference fearing it would be used by some Muslim countries, such as Iran and Saudi Arabia, to promote anti-Semitism, laws against blasphemy (seen as contrary to key principles of free speech), and attacks against Western countries for alleged racism and intolerance, but without mentioning such problems in the developing world. Such fears were given credence by a speech from the Iranian president, Mahmoud Ahmadinejad, who used the opportunity to attack Israel and accuse the West of using the European Holocaust as a 'pretext' for aggression against Palestinians. His speech polarized opinion among his audience, with European Union delegates leaving the conference room, while a number of the remaining delegates applauded him.

Key points

- Religion now plays a central role in international politics.
- Most Islamic critics of the status quo see their own governments as the main cause of political and developmental failures.

- 9/11 is sometimes said to provide evidence of an emerging 'civilizational' clash between Christianity and Islam, but most Muslims were probably appalled by these and related terrorist acts.

The last thirty years have seen much involvement of religion in politics. A serious new threat to world order, some claim, now emanates from Islamic fundamentalism, with 9/11 as the key example. However, such fears do not appear to have very strong foundations. In the case of Islamic fundamentalism (Islamism), various domestically orientated groups threaten the incumbency of their own rulers rather than the security of the global order. In short, there is very little—if anything—in the spectre of an 'Islamic' threat per se to global order.

Globally, the recent political impact of religion falls into two—not necessarily mutually exclusive—categories. First, if the mass of the people are not especially religious—as in many Western countries—then religious actors tend to be politically marginal. However, in many developing countries, most people are already religious believers. Unsuccessful attempts by many political leaders to modernize their countries have often led to responses from various religious actors. Often, religion serves to focus and coordinate opposition, especially—but not exclusively—that of the poor and ethnic minorities. Religion is often well placed to benefit from a societal backlash against the perceived malign effects of modernization. In particular, various religious fundamentalist leaders have sought support from ordinary people by addressing certain crucial issues. These include the perceived decline in public and private morality and the insecurities of life, the result of an undependable market in which, it is argued, greed and luck appear as effective as work and rational choice.

And what of the future? If the issues and concerns that have helped stimulate what some see as 'a return to religion'—including socio-political and economic upheavals, patchy modernization, increasing encroachment of the state upon religion's terrain—continue (and there is no reason to suppose they will not), then it seems highly likely that religion's political role will continue to be significant in many parts of the developing world. This will partly reflect the onward march of secularization in many countries and regions, linked to the spread of globalization—which no doubt will be resisted by religious leaders and their followers, with varying degrees of success. For this reason it would be very unwise to neglect religion in analyses of contemporary politics in the developing world.

? Questions

1. What are the characteristics of religious resurgence in the developing world and how are they important politically?

2. What do religious fundamentalists have in common? Illustrate your answer with examples from *two* developing countries.

3. Why does India, a constitutionally secular country, have an important religious party, in the form of the BJP?

4. Now, more than eight years after September 11, is it fair to say that religious issues dominate the international relations of the developing world?

JEFF HAYNES

5. Are modernization and secularization the same thing?

6. Does underdevelopment in the developing world increase the significance of religio-political actors or undermine them?

 Further reading

■ Flanagan, S. (2009), *For the Love of God: NGOs and Religious Identity in a Violent World* (West Hartford, CT: Kumarian Press). The book examines the ways in which history and religious identity influence faith-based organizations in Lebanon, Sri Lanka, and Bosnia Herzegovina and finds that they often reinforce rather than transcend schisms found in the larger society.

■ Gifford, P. (2004), *Ghana's New Christianity: Pentecostalism in a Globalising African Economy* (London: Hurst). Comprehensive account of the economic and political significance of the changing religious emphasis on a belief in success and wealth, in Greater Accra, Ghana.

■ Haynes, J. (1998), *Religion in Global Politics* (Harlow: Longman). A survey of religio-political developments around the world.

■ —— (2007), *Introduction to Religion and International Relations* (Harlow: Pearson Education). A survey of how international relations is affected by religious global resurgence.

■ Huntington, S. P. (1996a), *The Clash of Civilizations* (New York: Simon and Schuster). Articulates the thesis that the world is poised to enter an era of 'civilizational clashes'.

■ Mainuddin, R. (ed.) (2002), *Religion and Politics in the Developing World: Explosive Interactions* (Aldershot: Ashgate). Examines a number of key religio-political interactions in the developing world.

■ Volpi, F. (2003), *Islam and Democracy: The Failure of Dialogue in Algeria* (London: Pluto). A well-researched account of the failure of religious and political actors to arrive at a modus vivendi.

■ Westerlund, D. (ed.) (1996), *Questioning the Secular State: The Worldwide Resurgence of Religion in Politics* (London: Hurst). Series of predominantly developing country, national case studies examining the attitudes of 'fundamentalist' groups to the state and state policies.

■ Woodhead, L. and Heelas, P. (eds) (2000), *Religion in Modern Times* (Oxford: Blackwell). A very useful survey of the contemporary position of religion.

 Web links

■ www.uga.edu/islam/   Islam and Islamic Studies resources.

■ www.calvin.edu/henry/   The Paul B. Henry Institute for the Study of Christianity and Politics at Calvin College, USA.

■ www.csmonitor.com/   *The Christian Science Monitor*. This is a useful source of material on many aspects of religious politics, including in the developing world. It does not have a Christian bias in its coverage.

■ www.vanderbilt.edu/csrc/politics.html   Center for the Study of Religion and Culture at Vanderbilt University, USA.

■ www.assr.nl/   Details of a research programme on 'Religion, Politics and Identity' at the Amsterdam School of Social Research.

■ www.archive.org/details/iraq_911   A collection of archive video footage and films relating to the 11 September 2001 terrorist attacks against the World Trade Center and Pentagon.

 Online Resource Centre

For additional material and resources, please visit the Online Resource Centre at:
www.oxfordtextbooks.co.uk/orc/burnell3e/

9

Women and Gender

Kathleen Staudt

 Chapter contents

- Introduction: Historical Perspectives
- Women's Policy Interests
- Policy Injustices
- Women's Political Activism: Movements, Non-Governmental Organizations, and Decision-Makers
- More Global Dimensions
- Conclusion

 Overview

Nearly all nations in the world could be considered still 'developing' or not yet developed if judged against full democratic standards both of women's representation in decision-making positions and of responsiveness to women's policy interests. Only a few exceptions exist, most notably Scandinavia, but even there countries became more inclusive and responsive to women only in recent decades, a result of women's organized strength (including in unions), progressive public policies since the 1930s, and especially open and democratic political structures. This chapter draws attention to the widespread reality that women have little voice in established politics, and that their 'interests' are muted, given the existence of overwhelming male privilege and preference in the policymaking and policy implementation processes. Here and there women's activism has produced some change in policies, altering power relations between men and women.

The chapter first examines key ways in which men's privileges became institutionalized in the state, political institutions, and governments during history. In so doing, it will not only incorporate the language of gender that leads to an examination of social structures that 'construct' male and female differently in different nations, regions, and historical eras, but also the political institutions that shape women's and men's lives. While the term 'gender' is contested and does not translate well into all languages, it facilitates emphasis on the larger social structure, including relations between men and women, and away from biology as the essential determinant of behaviour. The chapter then considers women's work, paid and unpaid, and women's reproductive capabilities in order to outline typical obstacles that women face in different places and why gendered 'stakes' have been maintained or changed in the policy status quo. It moves on to examine women as voters, activists, and decision-makers in different nations and the effects of their actions on policy responsiveness. Finally, more global and local perspectives are introduced as being essential to moving towards gender-fair politics and policies.

Introduction: Historical Perspectives

In geographic spaces around which national boundaries are drawn, relatively stable institutional structures and decision-making patterns have emerged that reflect values and ideologies, including beliefs about men and women. This structure is known as the state, and it is different from the regional units of government also known as states, provinces, or districts, such as the State of Coahuila in Mexico, Western Province of Kenya, or the State of Texas in the United States. From the outset of the modern state in Europe, men, not people generally, crafted the skeletal structure of the state during an era when men spoke for most women and children in both societies and families, as fathers, husbands, and brothers and when institutions absorbed gender assumptions and practices like these. While wealth, position, and authority concentrated power among the few, virtually all men exercised formal power and authority in 'their' households. Power is relational: the relatively more and less powerful can shift the balance through force, knowledge, and resistance, among other things, opening opportunities for women to exercise power. Men were the first to benefit from rights to hold office and to vote. These rights and opportunities themselves augmented the social construction of gender in ways that associated men with the public sphere of politics and paid labour, and women with the private sphere of family and household.

Patriarchy—the ideology and institutions of male rule, male privilege, and female subordin-ation—exists in most societies to different degrees. It is embedded in all states, made 'normal' and routine in laws and public policies that often change only incrementally over time. By the twentieth century, state policies and laws institutionalized male privilege and transplanted the tools, ideology, and machinery of privilege from one nation to another, and throughout colonial empires in nearly global breadth. This gender baggage constructed men as family breadwinners, legally and financially responsible for land and households, and attendant policies benefited men through education, training, and employment. For Latin America and the Caribbean, colonial masters included Spain, Portugal, the Netherlands, Britain, and France. For Africa, the masters included Britain, Belgium, France, Germany, Italy, and Spain. For Asia from west to east and south, the masters included France, the United States, Britain, and the Netherlands. Nations like China and Japan, despite alternative and historically deeper indigenous patriarchal sources in those states, also exhibited male dominance in and benefit from the public sphere.

Consider a recent example from South Africa. High-level political leader (and now President) Jacob Zuma raped a young woman, used Zulu masculine culture as the justification, and was judged not guilty at the trial in 2006. The case roused people to reflect on misogyny, and organized women pushed Parliament (and its large critical mass of female parliamentarians) to pass stronger sexual assault laws.

Male privilege and gender social constructions have enduring legacies for women's quality of life and opportunity. Life itself may be in question (see Box 9.1).

Box 9.1 Are '100 Million Women Missing'?

Using demographic data for Asia, some regions of which showed highly imbalanced gender ratios for regions with strong patriarchal traditions, economist Amartya Sen found that 100 million women were 'missing' in existing demographic ratios. What he meant was that gender ratios, usually displaying relative balance (slightly over or under) 100:100, exhibited skews as disparate as 88 females to 100 males. In northern India and elsewhere, girl infants and children are ignored so badly that some die needlessly for lack of food, amounting to the waste of enormous numbers of female lives. Patriarchal traditions like these developed long before colonialism. Many indigenous societies vested control over economic resources and political voice in men rather than women or both. Deep patriarchal traditions, both indigenous and 'modern', are legacies that people will have difficulty shedding.

(Sen 1990)

Forty years ago, scholars and activists focused on 'women,' making them visible in research and action. Back then, the term 'gender' was buried in sociology and linguistics, but by the 1980s, it offered the opportunity to conceptualize the social construction and consciousness that shape the lives and relationships of women and men from global to national and local levels. A focus on gender also permits one to problematize men and masculinities, whether hegemonic or hyper-masculinity in institutions and behaviour, including war, peace, and security studies (Staudt et al. 2009: 4). In this and other chapters, readers should use a 'gender lens' to ask questions about public policies and power relations such as: Why? How? What consequences for whom? And readers should examine other social constructions, ranging from ethnicity/race and class to nationality and sexuality among others.

Key points

- Laws, public policies, and decisions about how to implement public policies are deeply and historically embedded in states, with their concentrated political authority in government that affects the whole of society.

- Men captured and controlled these political institutions in ways that disempowered women and muted their policy interests.

- In the developing world, this patriarchal state model both emerged from indigenous practices and/or was spread through colonialism.

- One may focus on both (or either) 'women' and 'gender,' offering different lenses for research and action.

Women's Policy Interests

Women and men have stakes in any and all public policies, from education to health, safety, and employment. Policies articulate official decisions on issues that have been perceived as public, rather than private matters; and governments raise money—through taxes, tariffs, and fees—and spend that money (documented in budgets) in ways that resemble official policies. However, policy implementation is crucial, for much policy is merely rhetoric, lacking budgetary resources, staff, and commitments to put policy decisions into practice.

From private problems to public policies

The social construction of gender has given men and women different stakes in policies, for the ways in which policies are formulated, finalized, implemented, and evaluated have usually meant that women's and men's 'interests' were benefited and burdened in distinctive ways. **Women's (or gender) policy interests**, then, refer to stakes in issues over which governments exercise decision-making, spending, or withholding money for implementation. The identification of shared stakes is complex, given the differences that exist among women based on ethnicity, class, age, geography, and other factors. People contest whether policies should be neutral to gender or take into account gender specifics, such as realities over who—men or women—care for infants after birth. In other words, questions can be raised about whether public policies should be neutral to gender (for example parental leave from paid employment obligations after birth, rather than just maternal leave) or should recognize gender difference, whether constructed through social norms or reduced to biological factors, such as reproductive organs. And if difference is recognized, will that reinforce and sustain gender difference?

Often extraordinary efforts are required to bring issues and problems deemed part of a 'private' sphere onto the public policy agenda (Box 9.2). A key example is found in sexual assault and domestic violence, which primarily burdens women.

Box 9.2 A 'Private Problem' is Made Public

Only in the last three decades have most governments treated violence against women as a public, rather than a private, problem. Historically, in many cultures worldwide, women moved from the patriarchal control of the father to the husband, reinforced in legal systems. Control often authorized physical punishment, short of death. Assault from strangers merited more accountability than assault from intimate partners. In many countries, radical feminists spread awareness in the late 1960s to put violence against women on the public agenda, later joining forces with liberal feminists to change laws and law enforcement. The study of changing masculinities explores abusive behaviour and the conditions under which such behaviour changes.

Weldon (2002) compared 36 countries in various regions and different levels of development with respect to factors that led to seven progressive policy responses. She examined cultures, which are notoriously difficult to generalize about, women politicians, women's offices in the bureaucracy, and social movements and non-governmental organizations (NGOs) to find that the last two are the most significant factors. Public policies to diminish violence against women are a recent innovation for most countries. Governments with better records than most on the issues include Costa Rica in the developing world and Canada.

Police agencies in many countries are dominated by men who work in a militaristic organizational culture that has historically been unresponsive to women. In some countries, special women's police stations have been established, with Brazil as one of the pioneers. India is the largest country to have established staffed police stations in this way. The stations produce mixed results: more crimes are reported, but serial battering and raping persist.

Women and wage inequalities

Until the latter part of the twentieth century, it was legal to pay women lower wages and salaries than men. International organizations, sparked by scholarship and transnational NGOs, established equality norms and standards that sometimes shaped national policy if and when activists used this leverage. While the United Nations-affiliated International Labour Organization produced conventions that established principles (such as 'Equal Pay for Equal Work')—agreed to in tripartite negotiations among government, business, and labour—national governments enforced these principles only to the extent that internal political forces and laws supported such measures. For women who laboured for income in the **informal economy**, laws and regulations had no impact on earnings.

Women work in many kinds of occupation, from paid to unpaid. But virtually everywhere, women earn less than men in paid employment. The United Nations Development Programme (UNDP) annual *Human Development Report* shows no countries without gender wage gaps, even the Scandinavian countries. But wage gaps range in degree, with some countries that govern by rule of law instituting laws that require equal pay for equal work or equal employment opportunity. Where rights-based approaches prevail, individuals may require access to expensive and time-consuming legal services.

Box 9.3 Latin American Wage Struggles

Labour unions have been slow to organize women workers. Historically, men organized men, viewed as the family breadwinners, to obtain 'family wages' that could support women and children. In many countries, the percentage of economically active people organized into unions diminished by the close of the twentieth century. Informal workers are rarely organized despite their labour burdens: they work outside regulations on minimum wage, social security benefits, and maximum hours.

In most Latin American countries, the most common paid job for women has been domestic labour: working as servants in other people's households. Live-in maids are notoriously exploited, with employers calling upon them for far more than a 40- or 50-hour working week. And their pay supplements may consist of discarded clothing and leftover food. Employer–employee relationships take on feudal overtones, and women may be labelled *muchachas* (girls) well beyond the age of adulthood. Chaney and Castro (1989) document the struggles of domestic workers to organize themselves in cities like Bogotá, Colombia, and Mexico City. They show that although organized *trabajadoras domésticas* agree on wage rates and hourly commitments, organizing domestic workers is very challenging, given the competition for work and desperation that characterizes many who seek earnings.

Because women generally form at least a third to a half of the labour force, the unequal pay adds up to considerable value or profit that is extracted from, but does not benefit women. Worldwide, labour unions are the collective means by which workers use the power of numbers to threaten work stoppage, strike, and/or negotiate with generally more powerful employers, whether nationals or foreigners. A minority of workers belongs to such organizations; and genuinely independent unions, able to negotiate on national and transnational bases, are rare. Moreover, lower wages, discriminatory job entry, and/or high unemployment levels leave many women dependent upon men (see Box 9.3).

With the rise of the global economy, much attention has focused on the recruitment of young women into export-processing factories such as garment and electronics manufacturing. Compared with work as maids or street vendors, the factory jobs have fixed hours and pay the legally minimum (although artificially low) wages. However, the jobs are often unsafe and insecure, involving minuscule wages compared with profits earned or executives' salaries. In Mexico, workers' minimum wages are less than US$4 daily, compared with US$1 daily or less in parts of Asia (or 10–30 times those values in many developed countries, or 50–100 times those values for management executives) (Staudt and Coronado 2002; the annual UNDP *Human Development Reports*).

Unpaid labour in households

Women also invest considerable unpaid labour in households, from food cultivation and preparation to caring for family members, especially children. In subsistence economies, which characterize many parts of the developing world in Asia and Africa, female labour time in unpaid labour to grow food, process it, cook and feed, and provide water for families usually exceeds male labour time in unpaid labour.

Managing households is a time-consuming activity in most societies, considering the child-rearing and emotional care that is generally thought necessary to hold families together. Women are primarily care-givers in families. In societies lacking running water and basic technology, tasks that seem manageable in the developed world become onerous physical and time constraints. For example, carrying water from rivers or collecting firewood from forests surrounding villages can consume an inordinate number of hours each day. Or pounding dried grains to make flour for cooking can take hours of arduous labour.

Reproductive choices

State policies and local customs mean that many women lack the abilities to make decisions about their bodies and voluntary motherhood. Although, historically, women relied on indigenous knowledge and practices related to birth, most states until the last few decades have been **pro-natalist** (that is, encouraging multiple births and restricting contraception and abortion). As primary care-givers, multiple births consumed much female time and energy. As **overpopulation** became a global issue with United Nations conferences beginning in 1972 (Stockholm) and cheap contraception technology widespread, more governments began to legitimate and to disseminate advice and the means of contraceptive use. Total fertility rates (average numbers of births per woman) have dropped, with impoverished countries like Niger, Uganda, and Afghanistan reporting rates of six–seven births per woman in contrast to developed country figures of one–three births per woman (UNDP 2009). However, the population policy agenda has often appeared to prioritize government planners' desires to slow population growth, rather than enhance women's choices over healthy and voluntary motherhood, wherein women themselves decide on the timing and spacing of pregnancy, or even if they choose to become mothers. Exploration of the connections between user-friendly women's health and development emerged in the United Nations International Conference on Population and Development in Cairo in 1994, at which many international NGOs participated. Approximately half a million women die annually giving birth, yet restrictions are still in place for contraception, emergency contraception, and abortion. Women resort to informal providers, resulting also in complications and even death. A backlash to women's voluntary motherhood is occurring worldwide.

Key points

- Women may have different policy interests from men, requiring policies that recognize gender rather than being gender neutral.
- Many issues affecting women are defined as 'private' and it is a struggle to get them onto the public agenda.
- International organizations and NGOs establish rights-based, equality, and other norms that activists

sometimes use as leverage within their own countries and communities.
- Women workers are regularly paid less than men and the value of women's unpaid domestic and agricultural labour is insufficiently recognized.
- Women generally lack autonomy over reproductive choices.

Policy Injustices

How and why could these unequal gender patterns prevail for so long? The answers involve a confluence of education, discrimination, state inaction, economic inequalities, embedded male privilege, and women's muted political voices. The most privileged people rarely organize to dismantle privilege, so organized constituencies and political parties rarely advocated gender equality until women acquired voices, rights, economic strength, networks, and organizations to promote change. This section looks first at educational inequalities, then voting rights, and finally the growing women's movements.

Mass education arrived only in the twentieth century in most countries, but usually boys had preferential access and wider opportunities for education that prepared the privileged among them for technical, management, legal, business, health, and other professional occupations. Even in the twenty-first century, girls are the majority of illiterates in South Asian and some African countries, although equal access to primary and secondary education now exists in many Latin American countries. Adult literacy rates continue to display huge gender gaps, concentrated in the band of deep patriarchy (West Asia and North Africa) and in the impoverished countries of

Africa and South-East Asia (UNDP 2009). Many of those countries contain desperately impoverished majorities. However, poverty and opportunity are structured to produce different outcomes for men and women, the essence of a gendered approach.

Who is responsible for the massive historical disinvestment in girls' education, parents or governments? In nations without social security and state-provided welfare or poverty alleviation programmes, parents have typically relied on grown children to support them in old age. Marital and customary settlement patterns tended to result in girl children joining their future husbands' families upon marital age, but with boy children remaining near home, and therefore expected to support their parents. Yet, historically, governments did little to alter inequalities.

In the late twentieth century, states like Bangladesh, Pakistan, and Nepal offered incentives, such as free uniforms, subsidized fees, and books, to parents with girl children in school attendance. These incentives, sometimes funded through international assistance, reduce the costs of female education to parents. However, even under such conditions of equal access, girls' and boys' experiences may be quite different, for subtle but accumulating cues are communicated to both boys and girls that men are and should be the leaders, household breadwinners, and decision-makers.

Box 9.4 Access to Credit via Women-Friendly Approaches

Women often resort to self-employment, usually as part of the informal economy, in income-generating strategies outside the state regulatory apparatus. Outside the state, women's group members save money and rotate total amounts to individuals. These are called *mabati* groups in Kenya and *tandas* in Mexico. Many NGOs model themselves on the Grameen Bank in Bangladesh, started by Mohammed Yunus. The Bank channels credit to micro-entrepreneurs, either as individuals or in groups, and peer responsibility provides the guarantee for loans. The approach has flaws, but many view the model as an advance from the male-to-male credit approach that still dominates banking throughout the world.

Even when girls and boys complete primary and secondary school in relatively equal proportions, gender patterns diverge in higher education, especially in coursework that results in marketable employment and political careers. In most societies, leaders emerge from professional, business, and economic careers, providing money to fund political careers and organizations. Men are channelled into these occupations, thereby accumulating wealth and contacts that translate into political recruitment opportunities. 'Money talks' in many countries, despite attempts to create democratic machinery and voting rights that seemingly foster equality (see Box 9.4).

On voting rights, when foreign powers controlled large parts of the developing world during the eras of imperialism and colonialism, few inhabitants exercised political voices except those appointed to or co-opted in the colonial state. After the Second World War and the general movement towards independence, women participated in nationalist movements, but often did so primarily as budding nationalists, not advocates of women's interests. Yet the voting franchise was often granted to all adults—women and men—once independence came, in countries that instituted elections. The countries in which women currently still lack the right to vote include Brunei and the United Arab Emirates.

Finally there is growth in women's movements that began to challenge policies mainly in the latter quarter of the twentieth century, legitimized with the global organizing around the United Nations-sponsored International Women's Year of 1975, which turned into an International Women's Decade, followed up with global conferences in 1980 (Copenhagen), 1985 (Nairobi), and 1995 (Beijing). These conferences fostered the development of more networking, from global to regional, and local, and gender visibility at other UN meetings. Naturally, women's movements experienced resistance to change from those with stakes in perpetuating the status quo and the privileges they enjoyed.

Women's movements rose hand in hand with the emergence of diverse **feminist** philosophies, which at a generic level focus on inequalities and injustices between men and women, especially in the areas of income, political voice, and violence (Staudt 1998: 18–31). Ironically, many women's movements do not use feminist labels, so as to avoid the appearance of replicating or accepting philosophies developed elsewhere rather than customizing issues within their own communities and nations. Feminist approaches are wide-ranging, preceded with adjectives that provide distinctive ways in which to problematize and address injustices: 'liberal', 'socialist', 'radical', 'black', 'maternal', 'conservative', and others. But by the late twentieth century, feminists converged in their efforts to deal with typical widespread injustices like, for instance, domestic abuse and sexual violence. For example, liberal feminists who had worked within given political-economic systems to change the laws found common ground with radical feminists, who are suspicious of the state. They combined forces to demand stronger laws regarding rape, policy implementation over police training to enforce domestic violence laws, and resources for battered women's shelters and counselling services for abusers.

Not everyone agrees that political power is the key to generating greater equality. Some focus on strengthening women's ability to earn and control income and other assets. If women had greater economic resources, or resources comparable to men, then they could either make individual choices to benefit themselves or organize collectively to press governments to change. After all, public policy often changes in response to constituencies with money. But it is only public policies that have the capacity to make systemic change, involving large numbers of people.

Key points

- In women's everyday lives, from unpaid and paid work to reproductive activities, the political framework has devalued women's experiences and increased their dependency on men.
- Gradually, once private issues within the household have entered the public policy agenda, women have made gains that increase their value and autonomy.
- The explanations for past policy disadvantage are numerous, herein focused on (still linger-

ing) educational inequalities, economic inequalities, and delays in women's exercise of their political voices. Those causes for policy disadvantage invite specific solutions: women's increasing economic and political power will enhance their ability to gain responsive and accountable government that serves their interests and needs.

Women's Political Activism: Movements, Non-Governmental Organizations, and Decision-Makers

Women's political activism has gradually increased at the local, regional, national, and transnational levels, both in government and non-government organizations. Still, however, the power that women exercise collectively is far less than men, and few countries exhibit gender-balanced decision-making. Men continue to monopolize politics, and much of that monopolization contributes to sustaining male privileges in the status quo. During transitions to democracy, women's civil rights

usually increase, but not necessarily their economic and social rights, according to a ten-country study, unless women's interests resonate with the political climate, government, and party in power (Waylen 2007). Thus, it is important to consider the political context, as Waylen (2007), Krook (2009), and other comparative political scientists do in their studies. Cynical observers recognize that some political parties hostile to feminism and/or gender equality select women as 'decorations' to mobilize voting support (such as in US Vice Presidential candidate, Sarah Palin, in 2008 or Mexican law enforcement officials in the anti-femicide struggles of the last decade).

In preparation for the United Nations-sponsored women's conference in Beijing in 1995, the UNDP *Human Development Report* produced a special publication on gender (1995). One of its chapters focused specifically on women in political decision-making positions and politics. That represents a baseline from which to examine change in women's participation, over ten years later.

Political structure matters

In the 1995 UNDP report, the concept of a 'participation pyramid' was introduced and graphed. It illustrated how men's monopolization was stronger at the pinnacle of the pyramid, for chief executives, and how this steep pyramid broadened only slightly in descent from the top, to cabinet members, elected representatives of the legislature, and finally to eligible voters, the bottom of the pyramid that exhibited greater gender balance. In some parts of the world, namely western Asia, no women serve in cabinets. Often there is only a token female presence in cabinet, serving in posts with limited resources, staff, and authority. Yet there are differences among countries, based on their political structures. Even democracies come in different forms, and questions have often been raised about which form is the more gender-friendly (see Box 9.5).

Chief executives in government consist primarily of presidents and prime ministers, illustrating two variations in democracy: presidential and parliamentary (although hybrid systems also exist). Presidential forms of government, most common in the western hemisphere, have three separate branches (executive, legislative, judicial) that, ideally, are equal and check one another's power. The president is elected separately from legislators in what is often a bicameral congress of a lower and upper house. The president appoints cabinet members from various walks of life: interest groups; campaign supporters; loyal friends; experts; and/or academics. These appointees are not elected, but are indirectly accountable to the people. Presidential systems, as is evident, are fragmented, consuming a great deal of time for decision-making. Their officials are elected for fixed terms, lending stability to the system but also less responsiveness. Yet presidential systems also offer many decision points at which to advocate or resist policy change, including policy that concerns women especially.

Parliamentary forms of government, most common in European and former European colonies in Asia and Africa, fuse the executive and legislature in the form of a chief executive called prime minister. The prime minister is elected to Parliament, and rises to executive leadership as a result of leadership in the majority political party or party coalition. Cabinet ministers come from the majority party or a coalition of parties, and are thus elected officials. As is evident, parliamentary systems concentrate power, thus making the decision-making process potentially more efficient and more responsive to the people because new elections can be called if, on important measures before Parliament, a majority vote does not prevail (that is, a 'vote of no confidence').

Box 9.5 Imagine Femistan! (An Exercise for Readers)

A new country has emerged, after twenty years of mostly non-violent struggle amid economic chaos. Both men and women actively participated in the struggle for democracy. Fifty people will be appointed to design democratic political institutions at a Constitutional Convention. Use your knowledge and imagination after reading this whole chapter to outline gender-fair political institutions that address formerly 'private' problems that have entered the public policy agenda.

Women in decision-making positions

Few women have risen to become a chief executive in democratic governments. In the 1995 *Human Development Report*, only twenty had ever achieved the position, about equal numbers of presidents and prime ministers. In the early twenty-first century, only a handful more women have been added; the Philippines, Sri Lanka, and Bangladesh are the only countries to have elected two different women as chief executives. In recent years, women have ascended to head of state in several key countries: first-ever President on the African continent, Ellen Johnson Sirleaf in post-war Liberia; socialist-feminist President Michele Bachelet in Chile (until her term ended in 2010); President Pratibha Patil in India; and President Cristina Fernández de Kirchner in Argentina. The German Chancellor, Angela Merkel, was re-elected to a second term in 2009.

Women are beginning to be selected or appointed for cabinet positions in larger numbers than two decades past. For the 1995 report, women held 7 per cent of cabinet posts, and in two out of every five governments, men monopolized all the cabinet posts. Often, however, women's portfolios involved 'women's affairs', 'family affairs', or peripheral bureaucracies not central to core government missions and budgets. Now the annual UNDP Human Development Reports routinely report on the percentage of women among cabinet members.

Moving to legislatures, the 1995 *Human Development Report* calculated an average of 10 per cent women's participation, illustrating men's near-monopolization of legislative politics. The average figures had actually decreased, from 13 per cent in the late 1980s when women's participation was slightly inflated until the demise of the former Soviet Union and authoritarian Eastern European countries.

Women's representation varied by world region a decade ago. Asian, European, and Latin American figures surpassed world averages, while African, Pacific, and Arab countries were well below world averages. But the differences were not dramatic. Since 1995, women's participation in legislatures has risen slightly, to 18.5 per cent in 2009. The Inter-Parliamentary Union compiles data on parliaments for many countries. Scandinavian countries and the Netherlands are always at the top, exhibiting critical masses of women, at a third or more of the representatives, with the UK ranked #58 (19.5 per cent) and the US, #71 (16.9 per cent). Of course, one-third never constitutes a majority—the proportion usually required for voting bills into laws! Updated lists are easily available for readers who wish to consult each and every country (www.ipu.org; see Table 9.1).

Table 9.1 Women in National Parliaments: IPU Regional Figures

	Single or Lower House (%)	Upper House (%)	Both (%)
Nordic countries	40		
Americas	22.4	19.9	22
Europe (excluding Nordic)	19.2	19.4	19.3
Sub-Saharan Africa	18.3	21	18.6
Asia	18.5	16.7	18.4
Pacific	13	32.6	15.2
Arab States	9.7	7	9.1

Source: Inter-Parliamentary Union: www.ipu.org/wmne/world.htm [accessed 22 Oct 2009]

The regional patterns outlined for a decade ago still persist. That is, among developing countries, the Latin American region retains the highest level of female participation, with African, Asian Pacific, and Arab countries following in that order (IPU 2009). The highest levels in Latin American are found in Cuba (43.2 per cent) and Costa Rica (36.8 per cent). Post-war Rwanda sets the world record, with 56.3 per cent in its lower house, and second on the African continent is South Africa at 44.5 per cent. In Asia, the highest levels are in South-East Asia (Vietnam, 25.8 per cent). In several Pacific, Arab, and/or Middle Eastern countries, there are no women elected to the legislature. Alas, no quantitative data exist on the percentage of feminists — women and men — in legislative bodies.

Why the variation? The answers lie in constitutions and political party rules about the structure of electoral systems and quotas for under-represented people like women. Proportional representation electoral systems produce higher percentages of women in politics than do single-member systems.

Female quotas: A solution for inequality and injustice?

In more than a hundred countries, governments and political parties have adopted three special measures — reserved seats, party, and legislative quotas — to increase women's representation but not necessarily to improve gendered outcomes (Krook 2009: 4, 6). In 1992, India passed a law that required women to hold one-third of all local council (*panchayats)* seats, although a similar law was not passed at the national level. This introduced nearly a million women into public decision-making positions, theoretically a stepping-stone into other political offices (Rai 2003). Yet in 2009, India falls well below the international median in national representation rates for women: 10.7 per cent in the lower house and 9.5 per cent in the upper house. Feminist scholarly critics point to the problem of 'essentialism', in female quota systems, built on body-based assumptions for political and policy

difference leading to different policy outcomes that offer more equality and justice. As stressed throughout this chapter, attention to race/ethnicity, class, and belief systems is also important. Commitment to gender and social justice is related to more than the female or male bodies of politicians, bureaucrats, and leaders.

Do women in the legislature expand the policy agenda and address gender inequalities? This is a perennial question in research on women in politics. Women often follow different pathways into the political process, such as through non-government organizations with possible commitments to women's policy interests. As a result, they may even bring a new way of interacting with colleagues and constituents. Once in office, women's party loyalties, ideologies, and constituencies influence their legislative behaviour. Elected and appointed women may come from markedly different and privileged income backgrounds than the majority of (poor) people. And women may belong to political parties that operate under ideologies that ignore 'private' injustices. Conservative politicians cut public spending programmes from which poor women may benefit. Yet women have sometimes coalesced across party lines to vote for women's policy interests. This happens periodically in Mexico around anti-violence laws. And in Rwanda, with the world's greatest gender balance, women worked to pass laws to address gender-based violence. Yet consider the South Africa rape case cited earlier, which occurred despite the near gender balance in that country's Parliament. Neither women nor men are of single minds on ideologies and policies.

Non-governmental organizations

The crucial ingredient for bringing about more gender-just policies and better accountability lies with the political engagement of NGOs and social movements with women (and men) representatives. NGOs come in many different forms, active at the local, regional, national, transnational, and international levels. Some NGOs are registered with the United Nations or with government (the latter seeking to qualify for tax-exempt status), known as non-profit organizations or *asociaciones civiles* in parts of the Spanish-speaking world. Others are looser informal networks or coalitions, including movements that may avoid registration (particularly with undemocratic governments). In these circles, consultants create organizations, but tend to operate more like a business. Just as governments need to be accountable to their citizens and residents, so must NGOs become more accountable than many of them actually are.

In many countries, NGOs work with political parties, legislatures, political executives, and bureaucracies to press for more responsive policies and resources. They push for goals like equal employment opportunities, non-sexist education, better health care, loans for micro-businesses, and laws to prevent violence against women, among many other areas. It is NGOs that give life and energy to democracies and the women (and men) who are elected and appointed to office.

Tools for policy change

Women are gradually increasing their share of power in public affairs, in NGOs and governments. Women's participation expands public policy agendas to include women's policy interests. What tools exist to ensure that policies are implemented?

Once public officials adopt new policies, some resistance can be expected in the policy implementation process of government bureaucracies. The last quarter-century has pioneered the use of several tools to overcome that resistance, including more academic research and the innovative policy tools associated with gender **mainstreaming**, such as establishing women's 'machinery' in government and introducing gendered budget-making (BRIDGE 2003). The popularity of the term gender among international agencies has prompted some feminist scholarly critics to challenge the co-optation potential in this technical approach. They see the possibility of 'disappearing' women and gender altogether once status quo leaders declare that mainstreaming has been accomplished.

Although policymaking is an inherently political process, in which power is brought to bear on policy adoption, the idealized policymaking process involves the application of research findings to policy deliberation and adoption. There is now a considerable body of findings concerning various developmental, education, and health policies relevant to women and gender. This research has been spurred on by the rise of policy, programme, and project evaluation (see Box 9.6).

Box 9.6 Evaluation Research as an Accountability Tool

Evaluation research typically asks: What outcomes occurred as a result of the programme intervention or policy changes? Who benefited and who was burdened? How well were programme and policy goals accomplished? What lessons can be learned for future change? Evaluation research of this type has lent itself well to addressing inequalities, whether by gender, ethnicity, class, and/or geographic regions.

Other innovations have moved beyond just policy rhetoric that promises greater equality and more responsive governance towards initiating real action in government bureaucracies as they interact with people. The first such innovation involved the creation of what the United Nations initially referred to as **women's policy machinery**, or units within government such as women's bureaux, commissions of women, ministries of women, and women's desks. Within ten years, virtually all governments hosted some women's machinery, but many had minimal staff and low budgets. Optimally, they allow government 'insiders' to work with 'outsider' feminist organizations. But many are separate sideline units, unable to 'mainstream' gender in all government efforts, even those without obvious women's policy interests or those based on women's special needs (Staudt 1997; Goetz 1997; Rai 2003; Waylen 2007). The effectiveness of mainstreaming strategies depends on good leadership, adequate resources, strong incentives for change, outside constituency strength, and strategic locations within governments that resonate with feminist change.

Budgetary decision-making is at the very heart of the political process, and some countries have pioneered methods to dissect budgets by gender and make the process more transparent in this way, and to involve more women and their organizations. The phrase 'gender audits' has also been used to analyse spending, and it resonates well with the technical accountability tools deemed necessary to exercise oversight on government.

Key points

- Women are gaining power both in official positions and in relation to government through social movements and NGOs.

- Political structure and government resonance with feminist agendas matter: democratic systems that are parliamentary, with political parties with female quotas that gain seats through proportional representation that implement goals for more critical masses of women, have higher rates of women representatives than presidential systems, although fewer decisional access points.

- However, once in office, bureaucratic or elected, women decision-makers will respond to women's interests and needs only if committed to justice in a political party that does the same and where accountable to relevant NGOs.

- Tools are available to nudge the more resistant bureaucracies include mainstreaming strategies, budgets, and audits, but civil society 'outsiders' must exercise constant vigilance about co-optation.

More Global Dimensions

This chapter has focused primarily on nations, but it cannot close without noting the growing global inequalities in which nations are fixed. Even as developed countries exhibit average annual per capita incomes of many thousands of dollars, there are numerous countries in which per capita income is equivalent to only a few hundred dollars (US$1–2 per day). As the annual UNDP *Human Development Report* documents in grim continuity, the world's richest 10 per cent of people receive as much income as the poorest 50 per cent. Women in developing countries are burdened by this grave inequality and poverty.

International conferences, many of them held under the auspices of the United Nations, have provided space for women to articulate their interests. These meetings range from those that focus specifically on women, such as the women's conferences of 1975, 1985, and 1995 (mentioned earlier), and those that focus on public policies in which women have stakes, such as the environment, population, and others. Typically, official delegations meet and, at the same time, parallel meetings of international or national NGOs also take place. Transnational networks and bonds are formed, and resolutions are passed. While the United Nations exerts little authority over sovereign countries (save peacekeeping missions), the passage of resolutions provides leverage for local and national organizations to press their governments for accountability and change. Legal instruments, such as the UN Convention on the Elimination of All Forms of Discrimination against Women (CEDAW), also provide leverage for change. War and civil conflicts take their tolls on all people, but women often bear disproportionate burdens on themselves and their children in refugee and humanitarian crises. Women face special forms of terror, such as sexual assault and torture in civil war.

Key points

- Analysts must think outside the box of nation-states to understand the global politics of over-prosperous women (and men) versus desperate women (and men) struggling for basic amenities.

- Gender balance within the nation-state obscures those politics.
- Global inequalities and local forces structure women's everyday lives and gender relations.

Conclusion

Women and their policy interests have been marginalized as a result of historic state structures and political institutions that privilege men and their voices in the decision-making process. Over the last century, women have gradually increased their participation in politics as voters, decision-makers, and members of non-government organizations. Public policy agendas have widened, taking into account discrimination and gendered inequalities. Progressive policies have yet to be fully implemented, but various bureaucratic tools and NGO oversight increase the prospects for implementation and accountability. Women are gaining ground in most nation-states, thus altering power relations between men and women. The meagre pace of change in most countries, however, may mean that at least our great grandchildren will be among the first to experience a gender-balanced polity in most of the developing (and developed) nation-states.

? Questions

1. Does the state 'matter' in sustaining female subordination or moving society toward gender equality?

2. Discuss key turning points in history, political institutional development, and transitions to democracy that open political space for women's voices and for advocating their issues in government.

3. Under what conditions do 'private' or 'personal' issues become politicized as public policy issues? Use examples associated with violence against women.

4. Do women share identical policy interests?

5. Compare the contribution of economic and political power in facilitating gender equality.

6. What role does reproductive choice have in gender equality?

7. Will poverty alleviation policies automatically address gender inequalities? Make reference to education and literacy in the response.

8. Discuss three features of the political structure that open or close spaces for women's voices, individually and collectively.

9. Compare parliamentary and presidential governance institutions in terms of prospects for women's participation in strategic decision-making.

10. Do women in the legislature expand the policy agenda and address gender inequalities?

11. Design a debate around the merits of female quotas in a particular country.

12. Develop an evaluation plan for the education system in a particular country.

13. Consider the analysis of women versus gender. Provide some examples of how a 'gender lens' might stimulate new questions and avenues of research or action.

14. Analyse the trade-offs between prioritizing an agenda of greater global equality among nations versus an agenda that focuses on gender equality within nations.

Further reading

■ Basu, A. (ed.) (1995), *The Challenge of Local Feminisms: Women's Movements in Global Perspective* (Boulder, CO: Westview Press). A collection of chapters on grass-roots women's movements in Asia, Africa, and Latin America, most of them authored by women from those areas.

■ —— (ed.) (2010) *Women's Movements in the Global Era: The Power of Local Feminisms* (Boulder, CO: Westview Press). An updated collection (from 1995) containing new country chapters and theoretically expanded chapters connecting the global to the local.

■ BRIDGE Development–Gender (2003), *Gender and Budgets* (Brighton: Institute of Development Studies, University of Sussex). Offers valuable concepts for application to real problems in government and organizations.

■ Goetz, A. M. (ed.) (1997), *Getting Institutions Right for Women in Development* (London: Zed). About transforming and tinkering with institutional machinery to make it more accountable to women and gender equality.

■ Jahan, R. (1995), *The Elusive Agenda: Mainstreaming Women in Development* (London: Zed). A comparison of two multilateral organizations (World Bank and UNDP) and two relatively progressive bilateral technical assistance institutions (NORAD-Norway and CIDA-Canada).

■ Jaquette, J. S. and Summerfield, G. (eds) (2006), *Women and Gender Equity in Development Theory and Practice: Institutions, Resources, and Mobilization* (Durham/London: Duke University Press). Compares recent analyses on the women in development and gender and development approaches.

■ Krook, M. L. (2009) *Quotas for Women in Politics: Gender and Candidate Selection Reform Worldwide* (New York: Oxford University Press). This is the latest, perhaps definitive, quota study revealing the variety of techniques and outcomes.

■ Seager, J. (2009) *Penguin Atlas of Women in the World*, 4th edn (New York: Penguin Press). This is the latest version of eye-catching maps and graphics about women and gender inequality.

■ Sen, A (1990), 'More Than 100 Million Women Are Missing', *The New York Review of Books* (20 December 1990, online edition), available at www.nybooks.com/articles/archives/1990/dec/20/more-than-100-million-women-are-missing/

■ Staudt, K., Payan, T., and Kruszewski, Z. A. (eds) (2009), *Human Rights along the US–Mexico Border: Gendered Violence and Insecurity* (Tucson: University of Arizona Press). Scholars from Mexico and the US broaden the national security versus human security debates in a focus on everyday violence, migration, and activism.

■ Stromquist, N. P. (ed.) (1998), *Women in the Third World: An Encyclopedia of Contemporary Issues* (New York/London: Garland Publishing). A 683-page reference work with geographic, functional, and international sections, divided into 70-plus chapters and selections.

■ Waylen, G. (2007), *Engendering Transitions: Women's Mobilization, Institutions, and Gender Outcomes*. (Oxford: Oxford University Press). This ten-country study examines the conditions under which women's civil rights expand during transitions to democracy.

:// Web links

■ www.bridge.ids.ac.uk/ BRIDGE Development–Gender, Institute of Development Studies, University of Sussex 'cutting-edge' packs on trade, migration, citizenship, participation, and many more issues.

■ www.wedo.org Women's Environment and Development Organization.

■ www.wluml.org Women Living Under Muslim Laws.

■ www.awid.org Association for Women's Rights in Development (English, Spanish, French).

■ www.globalfundforwomen.org (English, Spanish, French, Portuguese, Arabic).

■ www.ipu.org Inter-Parliamentary Union.

■ www.unifem.org United Nations Development Fund for Women (UNIFEM).

■ www.worldbank.org/gender World Bank Gender Home Page.

■ www.undp.org/women/ United Nations Development Programme (UNDP) Women's Empowerment home page.

■ www.un.org/womenwatch United Nations gateway on women's advancement and empowerment.

■ www.un.org/womenwatch/daw United Nations Division for the Advancement of Women.

■ www.sewa.org Self-Employed Women's Association (SEWA), India.

■ www.vday.org Provides organizing ideas, including drama performances of *Vagina Monologues*, a play by Eve Ensler, performed in thousands of cities worldwide (in mid-February, 'V-Day') to raise funds to stop violence against women.

■ www.womensenews.org A website and source of daily news about women.

■ http://libarts.wsu.edu/polisci/rngs Research Network on Gender Politics and the State (RNGS).

■ **www.who.int/gender/en/** World Health Organization's Department of Gender, Women, and Health.

■ **www.womenlobby.org** European Women's Lobby, over 4,000 NGOs.

■ **www.amnesty.org** Amnesty International, with a global campaign to stop violence against women.

 Online Resource Centre

For additional material and resources, please visit the Online Resource Centre at:
www.oxfordtextbooks.co.uk/orc/burnell3e/

Civil Society

Marina Ottaway

＊ Overview

The expression 'civil society' has metamorphosed during the 1990s from a relatively obscure concept familiar mostly to scholars of Marxism into a mainstream term freely used by social science analysts in general and by practitioners in the international assistance field specifically. Several factors contributed to these developments. First, there was growing interest by the United States and many European countries in promoting democracy abroad during the 1990s. The demise of the Soviet Union and the Eastern European communist regimes triggered a wave of more or less successful democratic transitions further afield, where regimes formerly influenced by the Soviet model and often by the Soviet government struggled to transform themselves into something both more acceptable to their populations and less anachronistic internationally. This wave of political transformations provided an opportunity for the industrialized democracies to actively promote the spread of political systems similar to their own. As international actors devised **democracy promotion** strategies, they focused much effort on promoting citizen participation and activism—what quickly came to be known as a vibrant civil society.

Another factor was the changes taking place in the established democracies themselves. Many organizations of what used to be called broadly 'the left', inspired by socialist or social democratic ideals of socio-economic equity and justice, were replaced by newer groups whose concept of justice extended beyond the traditional concerns of socialist parties and labour movements. They embraced a broad array of causes such as environmental protection and sustainability, opposition to globalization, and protection of gay rights. The old left was rooted above all in political parties and labour unions. The new activists were organized in smaller non-governmental organizations, often loosely tied in broad networks that saw themselves as the embodiment of a mobilized civil society.

Disenchantment with the performance of state institutions was an additional factor, as political leaders made concerted efforts to narrow the functions of government and enlarge the spheres of the private and non-profit sectors. At the same time, the corruption and inefficiency of many developing countries' governments prompted international development agencies to rethink the assumption that development required state intervention. As a result, they sought ways to bypass governments and implement some development projects and programmes through non-governmental organizations.

Needless to say, the popularization of the concept of civil society has led to a blurring of its meaning. It has also led to a blurring of its political connotations: a greater role for civil society is now extolled by conservatives, liberals, and radicals alike as a crucial component of political and even economic reform. Analysts of different persuasions do not agree about which organizations should be considered part of civil society and which should not, but they all agree that civil society is a good thing.

Introduction: Defining Civil Society

Defining the meaning of **civil society** is difficult because the term is laden with theoretical assumptions, unsolved problems, and value judgements. According to Hegel's oft-cited but ultimately unsatisfactory definition (in his *Philosophy of Right*, 1821), civil society comprises the realm of organizations that lie between the family at one extreme and the state at the other. While superficially clear and logical the definition generates a lot of conceptual confusion and some political booby traps. The result is that very few scholars, and virtually no practitioners of democracy promotion, now accept such a broad definition in practice, even if they cite it.

Intellectual conundrums

The definition is clear on one point: civil society is not the whole society, the entire web of social institutions and relations, but only one part of it. The problem is how to define that part with any degree of precision. Citing the realm of voluntary associations between the family and the state does not provide sufficient clarification. Three problems deserve special attention: (1) distinguishing organizations that are truly voluntary from those that are not; (2) determining whether all voluntary organizations between the family and the state deserve to be considered civil; and (3) determining whether there is a conceptual difference between civil society and political society, as some argue, or whether this is a distinction with little analytical value, which has gained currency for reasons of political expediency.

The concept of voluntary association contains ambiguities, particularly when applied to the less formal organizations that constituted civil society in the past and are still important in the developing world. According to definitions that stress civil societies' voluntary character, a civil society group is a formally constituted association of which individuals become members as part of a completely free choice—a club, for example, is undoubtedly a voluntary association. The family is not, because membership in it is not chosen. But there is a grey area of groups in which membership is not formally compulsory, but is not completely a matter of free choice, either. Religious associations offer one example. Very often people are born into a church or another type of religious association by virtue of having been born in a family, and inertia explains continued membership; in other cases, membership in a religious group is a truly voluntary choice. Similarly, people are born members of a clan, tribe, or ethnic group, but membership in an organization that claims to represent that group is a political choice made voluntarily and deliberately by some but by no means all members of that particular group. South Africa provides a telling example of how membership in an ethnic group can be an accident of birth or a voluntary decision to join a group. In the early 1990s, at a time of intense fighting between the supporters of Inkatha, a political party with a Zulu nationalist agenda, and other black South Africans, ethnic Zulus who did not support the party and its agenda referred to Inkatha supporters, but not to themselves, as Zulus.

The ambiguities even extend to organizations that appear at first sight to be clearly voluntary, such as political parties. In the early twentieth century many Europeans were born as members of social democratic parties, figuratively, because of their families' allegiances, or even literally, being delivered by 'midwives' paid by the party as a service to their members. Membership was voluntary in that anybody could stop paying dues and quit the party, but, for many, membership became part of an identity acquired at birth. A contemporary example of this phenomenon is offered by the Sudan, where major religious brotherhoods, into which people are born when families belong, have formed political parties to which adherence is equally automatic.

Another common problem in determining whether an association is voluntary arises in relation to ruling political parties and the mass organizations they control. Membership in the party or mass organization is rarely compulsory, but the absence of membership has negative consequences and many are forced to join. One of the difficult tasks faced by the United States as the occupying power in Iraq in 2003 was to distinguish between committed members of the Ba'th Party, who were part of the defunct regime of Saddam Hussein, and those who had joined in order to keep their jobs so as not to attract undue attention to themselves.

A second thorny problem in determining the boundaries of civil society is ideological in nature, hinging on the interpretation of the word 'civil', which can mean both 'relating to citizens or the general public' and 'civilized'. The expansive definition of civil society as comprising all voluntary associations between family and state is based on the first meaning. For many, this is an unacceptable approach because it combines in one category, for example, human rights groups and terrorist organizations. In practice, the word civil society is almost invariably used to denote organizations that share certain positive, 'civil' values. But there is no consensus on that point. During the 1980s, Scandinavian countries considered the organizations fighting apartheid in South Africa as 'civil' and provided support. The United States defined them as terrorist organizations and refused to help; Nelson Mandela, the much acclaimed first president of post-apartheid South Africa, was once considered a terrorist by the United States. Many liberals or radicals have no problem accepting labour unions as organizations of civil society, but are often reluctant to see a federation of employers in the same light.

Another controversial issue influenced by political and policy consideration is whether it is valid to draw a distinction between civil and political society. Those who defend the distinction, first made by Gramsci (in 1929–35 in *Prison Notebooks*), admit that both civil society and political society play a political role and seek to influence policy decisions. But the political role of civil society is indirect: civil society groups do not aspire to control the government and exercise power, but see their role as that of influencing policies in the public interest. Political society organizations—essentially, political parties—want to control the government. A corollary of this view is that the civil society is virtuously dedicated to giving citizens a voice, while political society is power-hungry, self-interested, and considerably less virtuous. A second corollary is that international agencies seeking to promote democracy can and should provide assistance to civil society organizations; supporting political society, which aspires to power and thus is partisan by definition, would be morally questionable and could also represent unjustifiable interference in the domestic politics of another country.

The distinction between civil and political society has theoretical justification. Its usefulness, however, is scant, because most civil society organizations are, overtly or covertly, more partisan and political than they claim to be. True, there are organizations of civil society that act purely as pressure or advocacy groups and have no intention of contesting public office. But civil society activists are often close to specific political parties, and many move freely between civil society organizations and parties. Furthermore, many political parties, including some in power, set up organizations of civil society in an attempt to capture some of the assistance that is available only to civil society organizations.

Examples of the blurring of the lines between political and civil organizations exist in most countries, although more pronounced in some than in others. Civil society organizations may be pushed into close alliance with political parties by government repression. Many non-governmental organizations (NGOs) in Zimbabwe, for example, developed during the 1990s as bona fide, non-partisan civil society organizations lobbying for improved human rights, constitutional reform, better legal services for the poor, and a variety of similar causes. As the government turned increasingly repressive, violating laws and human rights principles in order to stay in power, civil society organizations increasingly became part of the political opposition. Formally organized NGOs operating at the national level are particularly likely to become politicized when confronted by a repressive regime. But less formal, local groups, sometimes referred to as community-based organizations (CBOs), rarely become openly political. CBOs are usually concerned about local level development and welfare issues, focusing on service delivery or simply self-help.

Politics and expediency

The abstract problems of how to define civil society remain a source of debate among academics, but in the meantime, civil society is being defined in practice by the policies of bilateral and multilateral aid agencies, by the governments of countries receiving democracy assistance, and by civil society organizations themselves.

Bilateral and multilateral international aid organizations define the boundaries of civil society when they decide which organizations are eligible for assistance under democracy promotion programmes or should be consulted in the preparation of an assistance strategy. This definition is based on a mixture of political considerations and administrative requirements. The major political requirement is that such organizations focus their activities either on civic education or advocacy for democratic reform. Civic education programmes, particularly common in countries in the early stages of political transition, seek to convey the basic meaning of democracy as well as to teach about the political and institutional mechanisms of democratic systems. In its more sophisticated, advanced form, civic education is also training for political activism: citizens are encouraged to scrutinize the action of politicians, to lobby them to enact reforms, and to hold them accountable by voting them out of office. Advocacy organizations that attract international support focus on human rights, women's rights, legal reform, judicial reform, and, occasionally, environmental sustainability. To be part of civil society thus means to belong to one of these types of organization.

The aid agencies' definition of civil society is further narrowed by their administrative requirements. The groups must be organized in a formal way because donors cannot provide support for an organization that is not registered in some way, that does not have a name and address, or that cannot be audited. Informal networks or vaguely organized civic movements may play an important part in a society or a democratic transition, but they do not meet donors' needs and only some foreign funders will provide support for them on an exceptional basis. For example, during the apartheid era in South Africa, a few donors, mostly Scandinavian countries, agreed to provide assistance to informal organizations affiliated to the African National Congress. Such willingness to deal with informal organizations is exceptional, however. For practical reasons, donors also prefer to deal with organizations that speak, literally and figuratively, the same language.

As a result, the donors' civil society is an entity very different either from the society at large or from civil society as the realm of voluntary organizations between the family and the state. The term 'civil society' as used, and financed, by the international aid agencies refers to 'a very narrow set of organizations: professionalized NGOs dedicated to advocacy or civic education work on public interest issues directly relating to democratization, such as election monitoring, voter education, governmental transparency and political and civil rights in general' (Ottaway and Carothers 2000: 11).

Direct funding of civil society is not the only way in which international assistance agencies support that society. NGO influence is strengthened by the requirement, under which many agencies now operate, that they consult with local civil society in implementing a wide variety of development and democracy aid programmes. The World Bank has such civil society requirements and many bilateral agencies also hold wide consultations. In practice, many of the groups so contacted are the same organizations the assistance agencies helped set up or fund in the first place—the ones that they know and which are capable of sending representatives to meetings.

The governments of countries that are recipients of democracy assistance also try to shape the definition of civil society by imposing registration requirements, which are sometimes very strict and used to prevent the formation of antagonistic organizations. Many also try to limit the access to donor funding to only some categories of organization or to prevent it outright. Some international agencies are willing to circumvent such regulations and provide funding covertly; others are more anxious not to antagonize the government.

Civil society activists have also played a very important part in determining which organizations are recognized as part of civil society. Transnational networks of NGOs, usually led by the better-funded groups of the industrialized countries, have been particularly influential here. For example, they successfully pressed the United Nations to accept their presence at international meetings; the World Bank agreed to undertake re-evaluations of some of its practices, particularly lending for the construction of dams, and to consult with the NGO sector before reaching decisions on certain issues. And, in the early 2000s, oil companies in Chad were required to pay royalties into specially controlled funds where they were administered under strict controls with the participation of civil society organizations (the requirement was rescinded by Parliament in December 2005). These examples are counterbalanced by more numerous examples where the militancy of transnational civil society networks has failed to earn them recognition as rightful participants.

Traditional and Modern Civil Society

It is common for donors to bemoan the weakness, or even the absence, of civil society in countries in which they try to promote democracy. This concern has spurred governments of industrialized countries, as well as international NGOs and private foundations, to launch an array of civil society assistance programmes to strengthen what is invariably referred to as a 'fledgling' civil society. In many instances, even after years of effort, donors express concern about the slow progress of civil society development and its continuing need for support (see Box 10.1). Paradoxically, in the countries in which civil society is deemed at its weakest, for example in war-torn African countries, the population relies for survival on civil society networks that go well beyond the family and reveal a high degree of sophistication and organization. One of the problems faced by countries undergoing political upheaval is that some civil society networks quickly establish themselves in major fields of economic activity and even within parts of the government. The criminalization of the state that has been witnessed in **failing states** in West and Central Africa is the result of the disparity between the power of civil society organizations and that of a duly constituted government and administrative structure.

These considerations point to the need to put the discussion of civil society in a broader perspective. Following the current use of the term,

the discussion so far has dwelt on 'modern' civil society—that is, the part of civil society organized into formal, professionalized NGOs typical of the late twentieth century. But in all countries, including the industrialized ones, there is another civil society—'traditional society'. This society is organized more informally, often through networks rather than formally structured organizations, and often following patterns that existed in earlier times.

Traditional forms of civil society exist in most countries today, but particularly so in countries in which the state is weak. Organizations that are traditional in form do not necessarily perform only traditional roles. On the contrary, they grow in new directions in response to contemporary needs and requirements. West African Sufi organizations such as the Mourides are ancient, but when they establish control over the wholesale rice trade in Senegal, or set up mechanisms to help members of the brotherhood emigrate to the United States and find jobs there, they are performing definitely non-traditional functions in response to new challenges.

Modern and traditional civil society stand in inverse relation to each other. In countries in which the state is strong, traditional civil society is weak and modern civil society is strong. If the state is weak, so is modern civil society but traditional civil society is strong (Migdal 1988). This explains the paradox outlined above: in countries in the throes of a difficult, state-weakening transition, citizens rely on civil society networks in many aspects of their lives even as donors bemoan the weakness of civil society.

Box 10.1 Poppy Growers and the Afghan State

Poppy cultivation for heroin production has become the most important economic activity in Afghanistan since the overthrow of the Taliban in 2001. In 2006, an estimated 2.9 million farmers, or 12.6 per cent of the population, grew poppies. During this time, poppy growers could obtain production loans from illegal organizations controlling the illicit trade, but farmers growing legal crops could not obtain loans through government banks or extension services. Poppy cultivation generated over US$3 billion in revenue in 2006 while the government could only generate about $300 million in custom and tax revenue, and foreign assistance only brought the country's total budget to $600 million.

Traditional civil society

Organizations of civil society have taken a great variety of forms traditionally, from the very informal to the highly structured. Loosely structured but culturally sanctioned mechanisms for swapping labour and joining efforts in the performance of large collective tasks exist in all societies, as do more structured mechanisms — for example, the rotating credit associations that exist, under different names, almost everywhere (Box 10.2). Compared to modern ones, traditional civil society organizations were less specialized and formal.

They were extremely unlikely to have full-time organizers and certainly not offices. Even in industrial countries, the professionalization of civil society, hence its separation from the society at large, is a recent phenomenon. When Alexis de Tocqueville visited the United States in the first half of the nineteenth century and wrote *Democracy in America* (published in two volumes, in 1835 and 1840), he was struck by the American propensity to form intermediate associations in the pursuit of a wide range of interests and projects; he was looking at loosely structured, ad hoc groups, not at formal organizations with professional staffs.

Modern civil society, defined as a set of NGOs, has clear boundaries that separate it from the family and indeed from the rest of society as well as from the state. The expression 'members of civil society' refers to a rather small number of people who belong, and very often work for, such NGOs, not to all citizens. **Traditional civil society** has no such clear boundaries, but fades into the larger society at one extreme and non-state forms of political authority on the other. In non-state societies, governance was an extension of the overall social organization, not the activity of specialized institutions.

The blurring of the lines between the society at large, more organized associations within it, and political authority is not completely a thing of the past, but can reappear in extreme situations of **state collapse**, as in Somalia (see Box 10.3).

Traditional civil society performed important economic activities that today are considered to be the responsibility of state authority. For example, long-distance trade was once organized and carried out through private, civil society networks that extended over long distances. States took over much of the responsibility for protecting trade routes and otherwise making large-scale economic activity more feasible. In places where the state has collapsed or is severely weakened, civil society is again taking on some of those functions. This has been the case in the Democratic Republic of the Congo (formerly Zaire) since at least the 1980s, for example.

Box 10.2 From Rotating Credit Associations to Micro-Credit

Rotating credit associations exist in all countries and provide loans, usually small, to people who do not have access to or do not trust banks. Members of such associations pay a small fee to the association every week, and every week one of the members, in turn, receives the entire amount. Women use such credit associations to capitalize small businesses, pay school fees, or finance a celebration. Shoeshine boys in Addis Ababa use the system to cover the costs of a can of polish or a new brush.

The modern, formal variant of the rotating credit association is micro-credit. The Grameen Bank in Bangladesh pioneered the idea. The bank grants small loans to clients, predominantly women who cannot offer collateral and thus cannot obtain loans from a normal commercial bank. Repayment of the loan is ensured by a group of guarantors, who are not entitled to receive loans themselves until the original borrower has repaid his or her loan. The idea has been replicated widely across the world. The founder of the Grameen Bank, Muhammad Yunus, was awarded the Nobel Peace Prize in 2006 for his pioneering work on micro-credit.

Box 10.3 Islamic Courts in Somalia

In the power vacuum created by the Somali state's collapse and the failure of the United States and the United Nations to secure an agreement among warring clans and warlords, clan elders and ad hoc organizations tried to provide order and structure. Among these organizations were the Islamic courts, which sought to impose order and administer justice on the basis of a strict interpretation of *sharia*. First appearing in the early 1990s, these courts slowly organized into a Union of Islamic Courts. By 2006, the Islamic courts were well armed and competing with an official but powerless government, which had emerged from negotiations backed by the international community, for control over the country.

Traditional civil society and the state in the contemporary world

Some traditional forms of civil society exist even in the industrialized countries and they pose no problem. On the contrary, they contribute to the reservoir of what Putnam (1993) calls **social capital**. When traditional forms of civil society grow very strong as a result of the weakness or total collapse of the state, however, they can become highly problematic. Traditional civil society in the contemporary world is both indispensable and dangerous. Where the state is incapable, it can help people to survive and maintain a semblance of normal life under very difficult conditions. But in the absence of a strong state, civil society networks can also turn into a source of power and domination for an oligarchy, become estranged from the broader society, and thus prevent the rebuilding of the state and the introduction of democratic forms of governance (Migdal 1988: 24–41).

The benign side of the reappearance of traditional civil society is apparent every day in countries in which government is unable to perform functions expected of a modern state. The government cannot fund schools for all children, and civil society responds by setting up alternative schools. (This also happens in some industrialized countries: the Charter School movement in the United States is a civil society response to the failure of many urban public school systems.) State collapse forces banks to close, and civil society responds by setting up informal systems that may not be officially recognized or formally registered. Noteworthy particularly in the Arab world (the *hawala* system), they move money rapidly and efficiently across continents and into remote villages. The formal economy cannot provide jobs for everybody, and civil society develops an informal sector that provides the livelihood of the majority of the population.

Another traditional civil society mechanism that becomes more prominent in weak states is **clientelism**. Instead of coming together in an organization to solve the problem they face collectively, people who cannot get what they need through formal state institutions, be it medical care and schooling, or justice through a corrupt court system, may turn to a powerful and rich individual for help. This person, the patron, will help them to get their children into school, to obtain the ration card necessary to receive subsidized food, and to make sure their unlicensed small business will not be closed down by the police. The recipient of this largesse, the client, will repay the patron by giving his or her allegiance, voting for the patron if elections are held, or otherwise providing political support. **Patron–client relations** provide poor, powerless people with a useful form of access to power. However, they do so to the detriment of the development of modern institutions and forms of collective action that may lead to a long-term power redistribution (Nelson 1979).

There is also a much more malignant side to the reappearance of traditional civil society, because it can further undermine the failed state institutions for which it is trying to compensate. During the transition from apartheid in South Africa, a weakened government lost its capacity to enforce the laws that kept peddlers away from the business district of Johannesburg. Informal sector businesses took over the sidewalks, to the benefit of the people who were trying to make a living by selling vegetables and braiding hair on the street. But the informal marketplace also became the territory of criminal gangs, legitimate businesses were driven out, and the once thriving business district became a 'no-go' area.

And parts of the civil society that flourish because of the absence of the state may be hostile to efforts to revive it. The trading networks that form in war-ravaged countries respond to a need, but they can also become profitable organizations that resist the efforts of the new, stronger government to revive institutions. Vigilante groups, such as those that operate in many parts of Nigeria, are a civil society response to insecurity. But they tend to turn into criminal organizations that end up by preying on those they were supposed to defend. In extreme cases, the re-emergence of traditional civil society is a threat to the continued existence of the state or can challenge its reconstruction, as in Somalia today where the clans, warlords, and Islamic courts resist any transfer of power to the state.

The tension between traditional civil society and the state is also evident in the cultural domain. Traditionally, civil society has always been a major vehicle through which culture has been transmitted. In many countries public education has deliberately sought to create a new culture, different from that transmitted by civil society and in many ways alien to it. A central part of the new public education was the effort to create a new national identity, different and often hostile to the local identities transmitted by traditional civil society. Public education historically was part of a struggle between state and traditional civil society. Thus in Turkey under Kemal Ataturk the state tried to impose secular values on a traditional society that upheld Islamic ones. This cultural conflict between states and traditional civil society continues today even in the most industrialized, democratic societies — it is evident for instance in the disputes in France over the right of Muslim girls to wear a headscarf in school. In societies in which the state is weaker, or less determined to influence the culture, the battle is often won by civil society — the re-Islamization of culture in Egypt after decades of secular public education is a striking example (Wickham 2002).

Key points

- Traditional forms of civil society exist in all countries, but they do not necessarily perform traditional functions.
- When the state is weak, traditional civil society tends to be strong.

- Traditional forms of civil society help to alleviate certain problems created by the weakness of the state, but they can also prevent the strengthening of the state.

The Modern State and Civil Society as a Specialized Entity

The rise of civil society as an entity separate from the broader society and from the state is part of an overall process of specialization that has affected all social and political institutions, particularly in the later part of the twentieth century. This specialization of functions has been accompanied by a formalization of the organizations that discharge those functions.

The phenomenon of specialization and formalization is visible everywhere. Governments are spawning increasing numbers of agencies and bureaux in order to perform a growing number of intricate functions. Although more evident in industrialized than in developing countries, a trend towards specialization exists in the developing countries too, driven in part by similar factors: economic change and urbanization. The multiplication of government functions is made necessary by the increasing complexity of the economy and the requirements of more urban societies. The change in lifestyles resulting from industrialization creates the need for new social institutions while reducing the importance of others. In developing countries these trends are also driven by the example of the industrialized countries and by the direct pressure exercised by international development agencies that seek to reproduce familiar forms of organization.

Such pressure is entirely understandable and probably useful in some cases, but it can also create distortions. For example, the insistence by international financial institutions such as the International Monetary Fund and the World Bank that aid-recipient countries set up special anti-corruption agencies could prove beneficial, at least if the agencies were to work efficiently. However, the creation of specialized organizations in this way can lead to development of a civil society sector that is poorly suited to the prevailing conditions and financially unsustainable. It may undermine forms of civil society organizations that are more in line with the resources and needs of the developing countries (Ottaway and Chung 1999).

Contemporary civil society: Myths and realities

In order to address the problem of whether the emergence of a specialized civil society in developing countries is a positive phenomenon or a distortion created by international development agencies, it is necessary to consider the main functions that civil society organizations perform in the contemporary world. This section focuses on three major functions of civil society and asks whether the new, specialized, and professionalized civil society can perform them in developing countries. The first and vaguest of these functions is the generation of social capital; the second, somewhat more specific, function is the representation of the interests and demands of the population; and the third, quite concrete, function is the provision of goods and, above all, services for the population. The specialization of civil society alters the way in which civil society performs these functions in all countries, but raises particularly serious problems in developing countries.

Take first the widely held view that civil society organizations generate social capital, a concept first set forth by Putnam (1993) in a study of regional government in Italy, as an explanation of why the same institutions functioned differently in the north and south of the country. He observed that the inhabitants of the northern region shared a civic culture rooted in earlier experiences with self-government and sustained over the centuries by a rich associational life. These attitudes constituted the social capital that determined the way in which people viewed government and related to its institutions. This social capital was scarce in the southern regions, which had both a different historical experience and a dearth of associational life.

It is open to question to what extent the more specialized civil society organizations of today, with their professional staffs and narrow focuses, generate social capital. Professional, specialized organizations tend to have small or even non-existent membership and thus they do not reach many people. Even if they do, they engage them only on very specific issues. They probably do not inculcate in their members the attitudes of trust and cooperation that constitute social capital. Putnam argues that professional NGOs, even if devoted to democratic causes, contribute less to the social capital that supports democracy than seemingly irrelevant associations such as bowling leagues or the charitable and social clubs once widespread in American towns. He even sees in the decreasing popularity

of these organizations a harbinger of the decline of American democracy.

Putnam's concern about the capacity of specialized and professionalized NGOs to generate social capital may be exaggerated in the case of the United States. There, many types of voluntary association thrive and NGOs are numerous, extremely varied in their ideological and policy positions, and draw support widely, thereby contributing to pluralism. But in developing countries, many NGOs have small memberships, focus on a narrow range of issues and are highly dependent on foreign governments or international NGOs. Their contribution to social capital is highly questionable, particularly when compared to the social capital generated by more traditional social institutions (Box 10.4). Such traditional institutions also teach values and attitudes, but not necessarily those extolled by Putnam as necessary for democracy. They may include, for example, extremely negative views of other ethnic or religious groups, deep distrust of all strangers, or demeaning attitudes towards women. The fact that the content of this social capital is different and may be contrary to democratic values does not alter the fact that it is deeply embedded in social relations and not easily erased, particularly by professional NGOs with weak social roots.

The second of the three functions attributed to civil society—the representational function—raises the question of whether or how far such groups can actually represent the society vis-à-vis the government. The simple answer is that specialized civil society organizations do not represent society as a whole in any country. But in developing countries and within non-democratic international institutions, civil society organizations do broaden the range of interests that are expressed. Yet they do so in a lopsided way that favours groups with the capacity to organize and to access resources, even if their ideas are not widely held.

In well-established democracies, the problem of representation is solved by the existence of elected officials, freely chosen by the voters to represent their interests. Organizations of civil society are simply one among many types of organized interest group that put pressure on the elected officials to adopt the policies they favour. Professional NGOs are numerous and hold a variety of conflicting positions, as already stated, and compete for influence with a lot of other groups including paid lobbies; thus, they cannot advance a credible claim to represent the interests and the will of the entire population.

Box 10.4 The Conundrum of Islamic Charities

Since alms-giving (*zakat*) is one of the five pillars of Islam, Muslim countries have extensive webs of Islamic charitable organizations. Islamist movements and political parties have built on this charitable tradition to reach out to the population, providing educational and health services while spreading their religious and political message. Islamist movements, in other words, build on the social capital of Muslim societies. This creates a conundrum for liberal democracy advocates in Muslim countries and their Western supporters: social capital favours Islamist organizations while liberal organizations struggle to put down roots outside intellectual circles.

But in many developing countries representative institutions are often weak and elections fall short of being free and fair; as a result, civil society organizations may more credibly claim to represent voiceless citizens. Civil society organizations also have a degree of credibility when they claim to speak for unrepresented constituencies in international institutions, which are designed to represent states, but provide no formal channels through which popular demands can be expressed. Because lack of popular representation is a real problem in many developing countries and in international organizations, NGOs' claims that they voice the voiceless have won a degree of acceptance in recent years, and even gained them a place at the table in many policy discussions.

The issue whether NGOs should be consulted despite their lack of representativity remains highly controversial, and unlikely to be resolved soon. As long as countries do not have truly democratic institutions, the voice of NGOs adds an element of pluralism to the political system, and the distortions created by this imperfect form of representation may be an acceptable price for such a broadening of the political process. On the other hand, there is an element of risk in mandatory consultations with organizations that are not representative and above all not accountable to the people in whose name they claim to speak.

The third function performed by modern, professional civil society organizations is the provision of goods and services to the population. Many voluntary organizations provide a wide range of assistance—from the very basic, survival-oriented food distribution or provision of emergency shelter to the funding of research on rare diseases or the formation of support groups for people facing an almost infinite variety of problems. In this field, too, there are considerable differences between the importance of this civil society in industrial and less developed countries, as well as in the issues raised by the existence of these organizations. On the one hand, these civil society organizations are much more numerous, better organized, and more capable in the industrialized countries. In developing countries they are usually highly dependent on external funding and very often find themselves in a subordinate position to the more affluent international NGOs that can access with greater ease money from rich countries and international organizations.

On the other hand, professional NGOs delivering goods and services often have a more important role in developing countries compared to richer counterparts in the industrialized West. In the poorest countries, for example, the assistance provided by NGOs is the main form of assistance available to the population, while in the richer countries NGOs supplement rather than replace the safety net provided by the government. This gives the foreign organizations that provide the funding for activities in developing countries a role that is often more important than that of the government. In extreme cases, the imbalance between the capacity of a developing country's government and that of the foreign and domestic NGOs operating there becomes dramatic and can hollow out the role of the government. To illustrate, in Afghanistan between January 2002 and March 2003, foreign donors channelled US$296 million in assistance through the Afghan government and US$446 million through international NGOs (see Box 10.5).

Box 10.5 The Danger of International Civil Society

The policy of donors funding two civil services—the government bureaucracy at an average wage of $50 per month and a parallel bureaucracy of their own at $500 per month—draws talented people out of government in the short term and fundamentally undermines the creation of a sustainable state in the medium to long term.

(Ashraf Ghani, Governor of the Bank for the Islamic State of Afghanistan, speaking to World Bank Governors, 3 October 2004)

Key points

- Professionalized and specialized civil society organizations generate little social capital.
- Specialized civil society organizations are not truly representative, but they broaden the range of interests expressed in the political process.
- Professional organizations can play a crucial role in the provision of services.

Civil Society and the State in the Developing World

Relations between state and civil society, both in its traditional and modern forms, are quite complex in the developing world, more so than in industrial countries. Political systems are undergoing change in many countries, some states are still consolidating or conversely are on the verge of failure, modern civil society is a recent construct, and traditional forms of civil society are still making adaptations to a changed social and political environment. As a result, relations between state and civil society are in flux. In consolidated democracies, the relationship is more stable and thus more predictable.

Civil society organizations relate to state institutions and officials in one of three different ways: they ignore them and try to avoid their control; they oppose them and work for their replacement; or they seek to influence their policies. The pattern of avoidance is most often found in countries in which the state is incapable of delivering services or other public goods. Civil society organizations give up on the state and seek to provide essential public goods on their own. Some of these activities are benign: for example the organization of alternative self-help schools for children neglected by the public system. Others are quite problematic: for example, in countries in which the police force is incapable of ensuring a minimum of security for citizens, vigilante groups sometimes degenerate into protection rackets or become predatory. The organizations of civil society that flourish in the space left by a failing state are unregistered and unlicensed, often illegal. In terms of structures, they thus fall into the category of traditional civil society, although the functions they perform are a response to contemporary problems created by state collapse and/or political repression.

When the state is capable of performing its functions, but the government is repressive and unresponsive, civil society organizations are more likely to take an antagonistic position. Some civil society organizations that take on an opposition role are simply fronts for political parties, deliberately set up to circumvent donors' rules against funding political organizations. As mentioned earlier, in some countries civil society organizations have strong party links. In others, civil society organizations turn into opposition groups after trying to influence the government and discovering they cannot do so. The example from Zimbabwe cited above illustrates this point very well. Organizations that see themselves as guardians of universal principles—human rights organizations for example—are particularly likely to turn antagonistic when the government continues to violate those principles. Civil society groups that oppose the government can be organized as professional NGOs or along less formal lines as broad social movements or loosely structured networks. Such a broad, loosely structured alliance of hundreds of small local organizations or 'civics' formed in South Africa during the 1980s. The existence of this many-headed and elusive hydra was crucial in convincing the apartheid regime that peace could not be restored by repressive measures and that a political solution was necessary.

Finally, the relationship of civil society to state and government can be a cooperative one. This is the ideal promoted by democratization programmes. There are various forms of cooperation. Civil society organizations, which possess a degree of expertise in their specialized area, lobby the government to promote specific policy reforms and even provide the government with the expertise to implement the reforms, like helping to write legislation. Women's organizations, which are not usually seen as particularly threatening by governments although they may antagonize conservative social forces, are adept at this advocacy role. For example, they helped to craft legislation in Uganda that expanded landownership rights for women, as well as a new divorce law more favourable to women in Egypt.

Another form of cooperation between government and civil society is found when the government contracts out the delivery of services to non-profit NGOs. This is rarer in developing countries than in Europe because it requires strong governments, capable of establishing a regulatory framework and providing supervision, and strong civil society organizations capable of delivering complex services. The existence of a weak government on one side and strong international NGOs, often backed by large amounts of foreign money, gives rise to the common complaint that in such conditions international NGOs de facto make policy, further weakening the government and undermining its capacity.

The relationship between state and civil society in developing countries is rarely an easy one. This explains why many governments see civil society organizations as dangerous enemies to be tightly controlled. In democratic countries, setting up and registering an NGO is an easy process and regulations aim above all at preventing abuse of tax-exempt status or the misuse of donations. By contrast, in many developing countries NGOs are subject to complicated regulations aimed at suppressing groups that aspire to an advocacy role, instead of merely dispensing charity. An important issue that emerged in the 1990s in some countries is whether organizations of civil society should be allowed to receive foreign funding. Most governments welcome foreign funding of charitable organizations—for example, groups that provide assistance to AIDS orphans in Africa. Foreign funding of advocacy organizations, on the other hand, is very controversial.

Key points

- When the state is repressive, civil society organizations are usually antagonistic to it.
- When the state is weak and incapable of delivering services, civil society organizations seek to ignore the state and avoid its control, rather than to press for reforms.
- When the state is strong and civil society organizations are well developed, relations tend to be cooperative and constructive.

Civil Society and Democratization

The rapid transformation of the term civil society from an obscure concept known to a few scholars to one that finds its place in all discussions of political transformation is due to the rapid spread of democracy assistance initiatives that followed the end of the cold war. However, by the end of the 1990s it was clear that many so-called democratic transitions had led at best to the formation of semi-authoritarian regimes rather than democratic ones (Ottaway 2003). Furthermore, the reform process was losing momentum almost everywhere (Diamond 1996). Nevertheless, democracy promotion abroad remains on the political agenda of most industrial democracies. And leaders in the developing world, including many with no democratic credentials and no visible intention of acquiring them, embraced the rhetoric of democracy.

The concept of civil society became an important part of all discussions of democratization for reasons grounded to some extent in theory—as discussed earlier—and to a larger extent in pragmatism. In order to provide democracy assistance, aid agencies had to break down the abstract idea of democracy into concrete component parts that could be supported with limited amounts of aid. Civil society was such a component, and a particularly attractive one. Developing civil society meant promoting government by the people and for the people. And when civil society was defined as a narrow set of professional NGOs, it was also an entity to which assistance could be easily provided.

NGOs are easy to organize and cheap to fund; small grants go a long way. Professional NGOs were also a new type of association in many countries. Without roots in the traditional civil society and the culture of their countries and highly dependent on outside funding, professional NGOs were easy to train and influence to conform to the funders' concept of what civil society should do. With donor support, NGOs multiplied rapidly in all regions of the world, displaying remarkably similar characteristics. This made the aid agencies' job of supporting civil society easier. It also raised the question of whether these organizations were truly addressing the specific challenges of democratization in their countries.

Many studies of the donor-assisted civil society have reached the conclusion that pro-democracy NGOs tend to be quite isolated from the society at large. For instance this was a nearly unanimous conclusion of the contributors to *Funding Virtue* (Ottaway and Carothers 2000), with the only exception being two experts on the Philippines, where the growth of civil society was an indigenous process that owed much less to foreign assistance. This suggests that donor support is an important contributor to the isolation of civil society organizations. Many professional NGOs have small or no membership. They are often exclusively urban organizations with little reach in the countryside—only the best organized are able to extend their reach through networks of less formal community-based organizations (CBOs). Exchanges (often called 'networking') among the NGOs from different countries provide an opportunity for organizations to discuss their problems and learn from each other, but they also contribute to creating a special international NGO world the inhabitants of which talk to each other more easily than they do to their compatriots. These observations do not call into question the genuine commitment of many NGO leaders to democracy, human rights, or other causes. They do call into question, however, the capacity of these so-called organizations of civil society to influence their societies.

Democracy NGOs have other problems worth mentioning briefly. One is the opportunism that exists in the NGO world alongside genuine commitment—when assistance is available, setting up an NGO can simply be a way of making a living. **Corruption** also exists in the NGO world, which is unsurprising in view of its very rapid growth. And many, as mentioned earlier, become partisan organizations affiliated with political parties. These problems are tangible, but also inevitable to some extent and not particularly worrisome unless they are extremely widespread. They are simply part of the inevitable imperfection of the real world.

What is more worrisome is whether the growth of a small professional civil society actually contributes to democratization and whether the attention lavished on these organizations has led to the neglect of organizational forms that might have greater popular appeal and greater outreach within the population. Democracy promoters recognize the weakness of the NGOs they support and they equate it with the weakness of civil society. And yet, in many of the countries in which the organizations officially designated as civil society are weakest, for example in many war-torn African countries, informal civil society organizations have proven very resilient in trying to address the most severe difficulties created by state collapse. In their search for a society that is civil by their definition and assistable in terms of its formal characteristics, aid providers may have marginalized groups with a proven record of effectiveness.

Arab countries, with their contrast between a vast Islamic civil society and their struggling official civil society, illustrate the problem particularly well. In Egypt the world of Islamic civil society is large and multifaceted. It includes charitable groups, organizations that provide free-of-charge medical services the state has stopped delivering, organizations that offer some educational opportunities for students under-served by failing public schools, and groups that provide textbooks for university students who cannot afford them. It also includes organizations with political goals that do not satisfy the principles of liberal democracy, and terrorist groups that can only be defined as uncivil.

This Islamic civil society is well rooted in the society at large. Even organizations that are by no means traditional, but represent a contemporary and, from a religious point of view, aberrant response to contemporary problems, can cast themselves as part of a well-established tradition. They are certainly better rooted in the society than the modern, professional, pro-democracy NGOs favoured by donors. But the new donors' civil society espouses the values of liberal democracy, while the more traditional Islamic civil society is at best ambiguous on this point. In the end, neither an isolated **modern civil society** nor a well-rooted Islamic one are good vehicles for democratic transformation.

Key points

- The difference between traditional organizations well rooted in the society, relatively close to the population, but not necessarily democratic or official and the civil society recognized by international democracy promoters may be starker in the Muslim world than elsewhere at this time, but is found in all parts of the developing world.

- Democracy requires a large, active, democratically oriented civil society, but what is found in most countries is a bifurcated situation: an official civil society—small, democratic but essentially elitist; and a less formal, traditional civil society—large, popular, well-rooted but of dubious democratic credentials.

- How to combine the democratic commitment of the former to the popular roots and outreach of the other is a major conundrum for democratization.

Conclusion

The chapter started with an acknowledgement of the ambiguity of the concept of civil society and of its lack of definitional clarity. It ends on the same note, but with a normative addendum. Not only is the concept of civil society an imprecise, ambiguous one, but it must also be accepted as such. The more strictly the concept is defined, the less it helps us to understand how people come together voluntarily to address problems that they cannot solve as individuals and that the state cannot or does not want to help solve for them.

It is of course possible to narrow down the definition closely. This is what the international development agencies do all the time when they pick the organizations to support on the basis of the civility of their goals and the adequacy of their organizational structures. But what is gained in terms of clarity is lost in terms of the understanding of the society. First, the narrow definition loses sight of the many ways in which people in any society organize themselves to pursue their interests and satisfy their needs. It may reduce the effectiveness of any outside intervention, by focusing attention on groups that may be quite marginal to the society but happen to appear all-important to aid agencies. Second, a definition that separates a democratic, virtuous civil society acting in the public interest from a non-democratic, uncivil one, selfishly promoting narrow interests is more normative than analytical. The idea of the common good and the public interest obfuscate the reality that all societies are made up of groups with different and often conflicting interests, and that all groups are equally part of the society, whether their goals conform to a specific idea of civility or not.

In conclusion, despite the caveat expressed at the outset, from an analytical point of view we need to accept that we cannot do better than accept that civil society comprises the entire realm of voluntary associations between the family and the state. It is a vast and complex realm. Voluntary associations take many different forms, ranging from small, informal self-help groups and ad hoc committees with narrow goals to large, professional, and bureaucratic organizations with large budgets. In developing countries, civil society organizations perform a wide range of functions. At one extreme, there are narrowly focused groups that seek, for example, to provide support for AIDS orphans in a community or to raise money to improve the track that connects a village to the nearest highway. At the other, there are organizations tied into transnational networks with goals such as changing the World Bank's outlook on the construction of dams or delivering humanitarian assistance to populations in need. Many voluntary associations in developing countries try to provide services the state is unable to deliver. Others form to help citizens to resist pressure from predatory governments.

Organizations citizens develop voluntarily are not always 'civil' in the normative sense of the word. The realm of civil society comprises organizations that promote human rights and vigilante groups that prey on the people they are supposed to protect. While it is tempting to narrow the definition of civil society to organizations with commendable goals, this is not helpful. If we want to understand how people come together to defend their interests or pursue their goals, we need to accept the diversity, the complexity, and in many cases the flaws of the associational realm that has become known as civil society.

? Questions

1. Compare different definitions of civil society and explain which one(s) you find most useful.

2. Where does the boundary between civil society and political society lie?

3. How can traditional forms of civil society persist in modern states, and what benefits and drawbacks do they offer to politics and development?

4. Should we be concerned about the potential negative repercussions of an empowered civil society for a weak state?

5. How far, and in what sense, can civil society organizations represent the population?

6. Is the development of a modern civil society sector a precondition or conversely an inevitable effect of democratization?

7. Should Western NGOs try to strengthen modern civil society groups in the developing world and, if so, how can they do this without putting their legitimacy at risk?

→ Further reading

■ Edwards, M. (2009), *Civil Society* (Cambridge: Polity Press). Updated version of the original 2004 edition, dwelling mostly on the practice rather than the theory of civil society. Addressing the recent challenges from persistent oppressive regimes and developments in the economic market.

■ Florini, A. M. (ed.) (2000), *The Third Force: The Rise of Transnational Civil Society* (Washington DC: Carnegie Endowment for International Peace). Case studies of the role of transnational networks of civil society including the global anti-corruption movement, human rights movement, organizations for democracy, and against dam-building, and for environmental sustainability.

■ Hann, C. and Dunn, E. (eds) (1996), *Civil Society: Challenging Western Models* (New York: Routledge). A critical account.

■ Kasfir, N. (ed.) (1998), *Civil Society and Democracy in Africa* (London: Frank Cass). A critical view of conventional Western attitudes towards civil society in Africa.

■ Nelson, J. (1979), *Access to Power: Politics and the Urban Poor in Developing Nations* (Princeton, NJ: Princeton University Press). A wide-ranging empirical assessment of political participation by the urban poor in many developing countries, which downplays their revolutionary potential.

■ Ottaway, M. and Carothers, T. (eds) (2000), *Funding Virtue: Civil Society Aid and Democracy Promotion* (Washington DC: Carnegie Endowment for International Peace). A critical examination of civil society aid drawing on cases in Africa, Asia, the Middle East, and Latin America.

■ Ottaway, M. and Chung, T. (1999), 'Debating Democracy Assistance: Toward a New Paradigm', *Journal of Democracy*, 10/4: 99–113. A cautious view of international 'democracy assistance' to civil society and to elections and parties too.

■ Putnam, R. (1993), *Making Democracy Work: Civic Traditions in Modern Italy* (Princeton, NJ: Princeton University Press). A seminal work on social capital.

■ Wickham, C. R. (2002), *Mobilizing Islam: Religion, Activism, and Political Change in Egypt* (New York: Columbia University Press). A highly acclaimed analysis of the role of cultural identity, political economy, mobilization, and organization in political Islam in Egypt.

:// Web links

■ www.ids.ac.uk/ids/ The site of the civil society and governance research project at the Institute of Development Studies, University of Sussex, which examines the interplay of civil society and governments in 22 countries. Funded by the Ford Foundation.

■ www.carnegieendowment.org/publications/index.cfm *Middle Eastern Democracy: Is Civil Society the Answer?* by Amy Hawthorne. A critical examination of the question.

■ http://business.un.org/en Links to the ways in which the United Nations system works 'in partnership' with civil society on issues of global concern.

■ www.un.org/en/civilsociety/index.shtml/ The United Nations and Civil Society site explains the different ways in which the United Nations interacts with and promotes the development of civil society.

■ www.civilsocietyinstitute.org The Civil Society Institute is an advocacy group 'committed to improving society with breakthrough thinking and creative action'.

■ www.lse.ac.uk/collections/CCS The Centre for Civil Society at the London School of Economics is 'a leading, international organisation for research, analysis, debate and learning about civil society'.

■ www.imf.org/external/np/exr/cs/eng/index.asp The International Monetary Fund's Civil Society Newsletter provides regularly updated information on the IMF's collaborative efforts with civil society groups around the world.

■ www.imf.org/external/np/exr/cs/index.aspx   The International Monetary Fund's Civil Society website.

■ www.grameen-info.org   The website of Grameen Bank Organization, including articles about microcredit by its founder Muhammad Yunus.

 Online Resource Centre

For additional material and resources, please visit the Online Resource Centre at:
www.oxfordtextbooks.co.uk/orc/burnell3e/

11

People Power and Alternative Politics

Kurt Schock

 Chapter contents

 Overview

In the developing world over the last few decades 'people power' movements emerged to challenge the 'authoritarian logic' of undemocratic regimes as well as the dominant 'development logic' promoted by the governments of developed countries, international economic institutions, and multinational corporations. The chapter looks at people power movements that challenged political authoritarianism in the Philippines and Myanmar, and people power movements that challenge development policies in India, Thailand, and Brazil. It explains how these social movements mobilize people and generate pressure for social change. For pragmatic or principled reasons, people power movements incorporate methods of non-violent action in struggles against governments, large landowners, and corporations. Drawing on environmentalist, sustainable development (see Chapter 17), and/or human rights (see Chapter 18) discourses, they promote democratization and alternative visions of development.

In many parts of the developing world, grass-roots movements have emerged as a political force to be reckoned with. People excluded from politics are increasingly engaging in organized collective action to defend their livelihoods, promote a more equitable distribution of land and resources, challenge state and corporate-driven development policies, and advance democratization.

From the 1980s onward, citizens in numerous authoritarian regimes mobilized campaigns of non-violent resistance to challenge the entrenched political elite and promote democratization (Schock 2005). Marginalized peoples suffering from negative consequences of the 'development project' and the **globalization** project of **neo-liberalism** (McMichael 2008) struggle against deforestation, over-fishing, industrial and export agriculture, large dam projects, and increasing land inequal-

ity. Furthermore, resistance is being mobilized against neo-liberal economic policies and the 'new enclosures' (Harvey 2003; Shiva 2005), such as the privatization of public utilities and resources, and an intellectual property rights regime that contributes to the **privatization** and **commodification** of resources and traditional knowledge of peasants and indigenous peoples.

Much resistance takes the form of **people power movements** that attempt to transform the politics, economics, and social relations of developing countries. Traditional strategies such as participating in institutional politics or seizing state power through violence are increasingly being discarded for a social movements approach that mobilizes people through loose networks, engages in non-violent direct actions, and promotes democratization and **sustainable development** (see Box 11.1).

Box 11.1 Ten Principles of Sustainable Societies

New democracy—Democracy is not limited to periodic elections; officials are held accountable and there is greater popular participation in decision-making.

Subsidiarity—The authority of more distant levels of administration is subordinate to the authority of more local levels; whatever decisions and activities that can be undertaken locally should be.

Ecological sustainability—Rates of resource exploitation do not exceed rates of regeneration; rates of resource consumption do not exceed rates of renewable replacement; rates of pollution do not exceed rates of harmless absorption.

Common heritage—Prohibition on the privatization and commodification of common resources, such as water, land, air, forests, fisheries, culture and knowledge, and basic public services.

Diversity—Resistance to homogenization and the promotion of diversity in cultural, economic, and biological spheres.

Human rights—Assurance of economic, social, and cultural rights, as well as civil and political rights.

Jobs, livelihood, employment—Assurance of the right to work, free choice of employment, just and favourable working conditions, protection against unemployment, and the right to form and join labour unions.

---

[1] This chapter draws upon the author's research, which was partially funded by the United States Institute of Peace. The opinions, findings, and conclusions are those of the author and do not necessarily reflect the views of the United States Institute of Peace.

Food security and safety—Local self-reliance in food production and the assurance of healthy and safe foods.

Equity—Greater equality between developed and developing countries, between the rich and the poor within countries, and between women and men.

The precautionary principle—If an action, policy, product, or technology might cause severe or irreversible harm to the public or the environment, in the absence of a scientific consensus that harm would not ensue, the burden of proof falls on those who would introduce it.

(Cavanagh and Mander 2004: 77–104)

Social Movements and People Power

Social movements are collective, organized, and sustained efforts to promote social change that occur partially or entirely outside conventional politics. Their participants are often drawn from marginalized segments of society that are excluded from decision-making processes. Thus, they must engage in extra-institutional methods of political action to exert political influence. These methods may be violent, non-violent, or a combination of the two. Box 11.2 provides examples of methods of non-violent action.

Box 11.2 Examples of Methods of Non-Violent Action

- *Protest and persuasion*
- Protest demonstrations
- Marches
- Political rallies
- Public speeches
- Declarations
- Displaying symbols
- Vigils

- *Social non-cooperation*
- Offering sanctuary
- General strikes
- Social boycotts
- Social ostracism
- Student strikes

- *Disruptive intervention*
- Land occupations
- Encampments
- Sit-ins
- Pickets
- Non-violent obstructions
- Paralysing transportation
- Non-violent sabotage

- *Political non-cooperation*
- Civil disobedience
- Publication of banned newspapers
- Refusal to participate in the military
- Refusal to obey government orders

- *Economic non-cooperation*
- Economic boycotts
- Labour strikes
- Labour slowdowns
- Refusal to pay debts or taxes

- *Creative intervention*
- Alternative money schemes
- Parallel institutions
- Constructive programmes
- Alternative markets

(Sharp 1973)

Although the twentieth century was characterized by extreme violence of many kinds, methods of non-violent action were increasingly used in struggles against oppression and injustice. Non-violent resistance was transformed from a largely ad hoc strategy based on either moral or religious principles, or a lack of violent alternatives, to a conscious, deliberate, and reflective strategy of social change. There was a shift from informal and unorganized non-violent struggle to formal and organized non-violent struggle as expressed through mass-based social movements. By the end of the twentieth century, non-violent action had become a modular and global method for challenging oppression and injustice (Ackerman and DuVall 2000; Schock 2006).

People power movements rely primarily on methods of non-violent action. They are composed of diverse networks of people united by an oppositional consciousness rather than a distinct ideology, and there is a tendency towards decentralized and democratic organizational structures and a diffuse leadership. Their power inheres in their ability to mobilize large numbers of people to participate in various forms of protest, non-cooperation, and disruption, as well as to implement **constructive programmes** that are autonomous from state-dominated political relations or corporate-dominated market relations.

Key points

- People suffering from negative consequences of authoritarianism and development policies are increasingly engaging in collective action and participating in social movements to defend livelihoods, promote a more equitable distribution of land and resources, challenge state and corporate-driven development policies, and promote democratization.

- Non-violent methods have been increasingly used to challenge the direct violence of authoritarianism and the structural violence of development policies.

- People power movements represent an alternative strategy for promoting social change to both conventional politics and violence.

People Power Movements and Democratization

People power movements have contributed to democratization in some parts of the developing world, including South America (Bolivia, Brazil, Uruguay, Chile, and Peru), the Caribbean (Haiti), Africa (Sudan, Benin, South Africa, Mali, Madagascar, and Nigeria), Asia (Philippines, South Korea, Taiwan, Bangladesh, Nepal, Thailand, Mongolia, and Indonesia), the Middle East (Lebanon), and the former Soviet Union (Georgia, Ukraine, and Kyrgyzstan). In some of these countries democracy took root; others subsequently experienced de-democratization and a slide back to overt authoritarianism. Comparable pro-democracy movements in other places failed to promote democratization. Movements in El Salvador, Niger, Palestine, Pakistan, Myanmar, Tibet, and China were brutally crushed. Below, two pro-democracy people power movements are discussed: a successful one (the Philippines) and an unsuccessful one (Myanmar).

The Philippines: The people power movement of 1986

President Ferdinand Marcos' declaration of martial law in 1972 marked the beginning of a personalistic dictatorship. Marcos claimed it was necessary to counter threats of communist insurgency and to implement land reform. He eliminated political opposition, consolidated his control over the state, and enriched his personal wealth.

Although the ultimate basis of Marcos' power was the military, he relied on legalistic arguments, and incorporated referenda and plebiscites as mechanisms for building regime legitimacy. These procedures were characterized by intimidation and fraud and ultimately failed to provide legitimacy. Moreover, his plundering of national wealth and repression of dissent alienated large segments of society.

The emergence of the people power movement dates from the assassination of Benigno Aquino in 1983. Aquino, a long-time political opponent of Marcos, was murdered upon his return to the Philippines from exile. Approximately 2 million people gathered for Aquino's funeral procession, which took on the trappings of an anti-Marcos demonstration. Afterwards many people shifted from passive acceptance of the Marcos regime to active opposition; social movement organizations mobilized protest demonstrations, strikes, and campaigns of civil disobedience. By 1985 it was apparent that Marcos had lost legitimacy of a broad segment of society.

In response to the rising protests, Marcos called for snap elections, confident in his ability to intimidate the seemingly unorganized opposition and manipulate the election results. Benigno Aquino's widow, Corazon Aquino, headed the opposition, a loose coalition of pro-democracy groups with little in common beside their desire to oust Marcos and their adherence to the strategy of non-violent resistance.

Shortly after the election 35 government election workers, responsible for the computerized tabulation of votes, protested election fraud. Corazon

Aquino responded by leading a rally of approximately 2 million people, proclaiming victory for her and 'the people', and launching a civil disobedience campaign. On 22 February, Defence Minister Juan Ponce Enrile led two battalions of soldiers in a mutiny, barricading two major military camps just outside Manila. General Fidel Ramos joined him and they announced their support for Aquino. Shortly thereafter, Manila Archbishop Jaime Cardinal Sin condemned the election as fraudulent, declared that the regime had lost its moral authority to govern, and urged people to non-violently resist. The appeal mobilized hundreds of thousands of pro-democracy sympathizers. Marcos ordered the military to respond, but the troops retreated in the face of a mass of unarmed civilians. These dramatic events sparked a nationwide defection among the military. On 26 February, Corazon Aquino was sworn in as president and Marcos was escorted out of the country by the US military. The people power movement succeeded. It prevented a violent clash between the divided segments of the armed forces, forced Marcos from office, and promoted democratization.

Myanmar: The 8–8–88 pro-democracy movement

Myanmar has been ruled by a military dictatorship since 1962, when General Ne Win assumed power in a coup against the democratic regime of U Nu. The alleged justification for the military takeover included a perceived turning away from the state's founding socialist principles, U Nu's policy of establishing Buddhism as the state religion, and his negotiations with leaders of non-Burman states for greater autonomy, inviting attempts to exercise their constitutional right to secede. Upon declaring martial law, Ne Win expanded the role of the military in the polity and economy. The Burma Socialist Programme Party (BSPP) was formed as a means of mass mobilization and political indoctrination. All other political parties were banned and potential political rivals were eliminated. The result has been gross inefficiency, rampant corruption, and economic decline.

Overt protest against the regime in the 1980s was minimal until 1988, when students at a university in Rangoon protested against the killing of students by police. Students from other universities soon joined in daily protests that took an explicit anti-government, pro-democracy stance. Hundreds of students marched from university campuses to the centre of Rangoon. They gathered supporters along the way and the protest grew into the thousands. The police and army again met the demonstrators with violence. Scores of protestors and bystanders were killed and thousands were arrested. The government shut down the universities and the movement temporarily collapsed. But by mid-June students once again took to the streets, joined by Buddhist monks, workers, and the unemployed. Again they were met by violence, a new curfew was imposed, and the universities were closed again.

The government announced the BSPP would hold an extraordinary congress, at which Ne Win stepped down from his position of president and chairman of the BSPP and proposed a referendum to gauge public support for a multi-party system. The proposal for the referendum was rejected by the BSPP congress, touching off a new and intensified round of protest.

On 8 August 1988 (8–8–88) a broad-based general strike was held, in protest against the military regime. The festive atmosphere in Rangoon was broken that night when the military massacred up to 3,000 people. Demonstrations outside Rangoon were also brutally suppressed. On 12 August it was announced that Sein Lwin, a widely despised commander of riot police who had been appointed President and BSPP chairman, would be succeeded by Dr Maung Maung, the highest ranking civilian in the party and a 'moderate' in the military regime. Demonstrations resumed as tens of thousands of people rejected Maung Maung's nomination, demanding an end to one-party rule.

Martial law was unexpectedly lifted and the military withdrew from the cities. On 23 and 24 August

1988, an estimated 1 million people participated in protest demonstrations in Rangoon. As many as 500,000 people gathered to hear Aung San Suu Kyi, the daughter of one of Myanmar's independence heroes, General Aung San, give her first public speech. She emerged as the leading voice of the pro-democracy opposition. But in early September the Philippine-style people power movement was brutally suppressed. Military agents provocateurs engaged in arson, looting, violence, and other destabilizing activities apparently in an effort to legitimize the military's restoration of order. A group of generals organized by Ne Win and led by General Saw Maung announced the formation of the State Law and Order Restoration Committee (SLORC) and re-took power. Once again martial law was imposed and the army returned to the cities, brutally repressing all opposition and executing alleged dissident organizers. In need of food and money, the striking workers returned to work. The movement failed as sustained collective action ceased and the regime reorganized and consolidated power.

Similar to Marcos' tactics in the Philippines, SLORC scheduled elections for the National Assembly in May 1990 in an effort to increase its legitimacy. To the regime's surprise, the most outspoken opposition—the National League for Democracy (NLD)—won a clear majority of the vote. The goal of the NLD, led by Aung San Suu Kyi, was to form a federalist democratic system with full respect for human rights. SLORC refused to honour the elections. Thus, after more than two years, the people power movement, although successful in forcing the government to hold multi-party elections, was ultimately unsuccessful in toppling the military regime.

Divergent outcomes

What accounts for the divergent outcomes of the two pro-democracy people power movements? Characteristics of the movements themselves as well as the political context each played a role (Schock

1999; 2005). In the Philippines, two broad-based organizations emerged to coordinate the unarmed struggle against Marcos, namely Bayan (*Bagong Alyansang Makabayan*) and the United Democratic Opposition (UNIDO). Bayan acted as an umbrella organization, coordinating the activities of a diverse array of progressive organizations promoting the interests of women, peasants, and workers. UNIDO, representing the traditional political elite opposition and its middle-class followers, acted as both a political party and a social movement organization, engaging in both non-violent action and electoral activity. Both strands of the anti-Marcos challenge implemented varied non-violent actions and responded innovatively to government repression. General strikes, civil disobedience, and the rejection of the official election results undermined the state's power and legitimacy. These actions, along with the growing armed communist insurgency in the countryside, promoted capital flight, contributed to regime defection, and led the US government to sever ties to Marcos and throw its weight behind Corazon Aquino.

In Myanmar, during the short but intense period of organizing and protest prior to the military crackdown in September 1988, protest demonstrations and general strikes directly undermined the regime to the point of virtual collapse. However, there was no umbrella organization to coordinate the diverse strands of resistance or to organize a parallel government. The NLD emerged only after the state had suppressed the movement, channelling opposition activity into tightly controlled electoral campaigning for the 1990 elections. In contrast to the movement in the Philippines, which continued to implement methods of non-cooperation in addition to participating electorally, the challenge in Myanmar, which at first used various non-violent tactics, was primarily limited to electoral campaigning after the military crackdown. Unlike the Philippines, where the movement challenged the regime's refusal to honour the election results, the demobilization of the Burmese movement foreclosed this option. Moreover, the leverage generated by the challenge in Myanmar was also constrained by Myanmar's international isolation, where no foreign government could pressure the government to step aside.

A more recent people power movement emerged again in Myanmar in September 2007. This movement, led by Buddhist monks, was also brutally repressed by the military regime. Once again, aspects of the political context influenced the outcome: no splits emerged within the military regime, and the two countries with some economic leverage over Myanmar, China and India, refused to pressure the regime for reform or support the pro-democracy movement (Fink 2009).

Key points

- From the 1980s onward, a wave of people power movements contributed to democratization throughout the developing world.

- The people power movement in the Philippines in 1986 ousted Ferdinand Marcos and contributed to democratization, but in Myanmar, the 8–8–88 people power movement and the attempted Saffron Revolution in 2007 were suppressed by the military regime.

- Variations in the outcomes of pro-democracy movements are a function of characteristics of the movement (such as organization, leadership, and strategy) and the broader political context (such as coherence of the military and political elite and the international response).

While many of the people power movements that contributed to democratization from the early 1980s onwards were largely urban-based and aimed at toppling a regime, increasingly, throughout the developing world, rural-based people power movements are struggling against the structural violence of the 'development logic'. Mobilizing segments of society most adversely affected, such as indigenous peoples, small farmers, landless rural workers — and in some cases, urban slum-dwellers — they challenge social structures and economic relations advanced by capitalist modernization that frustrate their basic needs. These movements have taken up a host of interrelated issues, including, but not limited to: opposing large centralized development projects (for example, dams); opposing agricultural policies that favour industrial and export agriculture; opposing the privatization of infrastructures (for example, water and utilities) and the commodification of local knowledge and resources; protecting natural resources and the environment (for example, fisheries and forests); promoting a more equitable distribution of resources (for example, land); protecting indigenous cultures and societies; and advancing human rights and participatory democracy. Movements addressing these issues — when linked transnationally — can be considered part of an emerging grass-roots global justice movement that promotes an alternative politics of development.

People power movements that use various methods of non-violent action to promote grass-roots democracy, the redistribution of land and resources, and sustainable development include Ekta Parishad, a Gandhian organization in India that promotes the access of marginalized people to livelihood resources, the Assembly of the Poor, a grass-roots movement in Thailand that opposes large dam projects and promotes community control over land and resources, and the Landless Rural Workers Movement (MST), an agrarian reform movement in Brazil that promotes the redistribution of agricultural land and food sovereignty.

India: Ekta Parishad[2]

A variety of social movements in India address issues related to the control over and access to land and natural resources, including movements concerned with biopiracy, deforestation, dam building, indigenous people's rights, land reform, and agricultural policy. Ekta Parishad (Unity Forum), a Gandhian land rights organization founded in 1990, struggles to prevent land alienation and to promote the access of marginalized people to livelihood natural resources. Its members are drawn from the most disadvantaged segments of society, such as lower-**caste** farmers and rural workers and *adivasis*. *Adivasis* are indigenous tribal peoples in India who traditionally inhabit forestland.

Ekta Parishad is concerned with a number of issues. One problem is that although various land reform acts were enacted at the state level, such as land ceiling Acts that limit the amount of land that individuals can own, in many cases the Acts were never properly implemented. Thus land inequality remains high. Another problem is that although many large landowners donated land to the government for redistribution to the landless in the Bhoodan movement (led by the Gandhian Vinoba Bhave) in the 1950s, much of the land was never redistributed, due to the corruption of government officials. A third problem concerns neo-liberal policies implemented by the government over the last two decades, which have contributed to the indebtedness of small farmers and the concentration of landholdings. Fourth, many small farmers never received official land titles from the government,

---

[2] This section is based on Ramagundam (2001) and the author's field research in India.

even though they, or their families, have been working on the land for years or even for generations. Without land titles, they are easily evicted by powerful landowners or government officials. A fifth problem is the eviction of *adivasis* from the forests, due to timber extraction, mining operations, dam projects, and the creation of tiger reserves. Generally speaking, powerful individuals, groups, and corporations, use a combination of cunning, corruption, intimidation, and violence to alienate people from the land. Those alienated from the land are typically under-compensated, if compensated at all.

Ekta Parishad attempts to organize, mobilize, and build solidarity among marginalized groups, generate public awareness about land-related problems, and put pressure on the government to address these problems. A major method is the *yatra*, an extended journey through the countryside that may last in duration from a few weeks to many months. It draws on the Hindu tradition of spiritual pilgrimages, and is used as a political method to draw attention to injustices and to generate pressure against the government. Well-known *yatras* include Mohandas Gandhi's Salt March in 1930, as part of a campaign of civil disobedience against the British, and Vinoba Bhave's travels throughout the countryside during the Bhoodan movement for land reform in the 1950s.

Since 1999, Ekta Parishad has undertaken numerous major state-wide *yatras* and smaller *yatras* focused in a few districts. Prior to commencing a *yatra*, Ekta Parishad releases a 'Declaration of Satyagraha' that proclaims the intent and purpose of the campaign, arguing that conventional politics has been ineffective and large-scale mobilizations and acts of civil disobedience are now necessary.

Campaign success has been uneven, the most successful being in Madhya Pradesh where Ekta Parishad was founded and where it is the strongest. The Madhya Pradesh *yatra* in 1999 and 2000 resulted in the distribution of over 150,000 land plots

to landless rural workers, numerous land titles were given to people who had been working on their land for years, and the eviction of tribal people from the forests was stopped, at least temporarily.

In 2007, Ekta Parishad organized a *Janadesh*, or 'Peoples Verdict' *satyagraha*, the largest Gandhian mass mobilization since the struggle for national liberation. From 2 October to 28 October 2007, approximately 25,000 landless people, mostly *dalits* and *adivasis*—along with their supporters—marched 350 kilometres along the national highway from Gwalior, Madhya Pradesh to New Delhi. Political rallies and press conferences were held along the way and the campaign received national and international media attention.

Upon reaching New Delhi, the landless set up an encampment and Ekta Parishad threatened to march to the Parliament building and engage in a sit-in and fast for an indefinite period until their demands were met. The government conceded their demands and established a National Land Reform Committee, headed by the Rural Development Minister with half the members selected by Ekta Parishad. The committee is responsible for drawing up a new National Land Policy and empowered to direct state governments to enact appropriate land reform legislation. Thus the *Janadesh* campaign succeeded in raising the public's awareness about land-related problems and conflicts, forced the government to publicly acknowledge the legitimacy of the issues and concerns of the landless, and put land reform on the national agenda.

Ekta Parishad is significant, because it is organizing, empowering, and promoting the rights and citizenship of some of the most marginalized people in Indian society. It is also significant because it is part of a larger movement in India to revitalize the radical Gandhian tradition of open defiance against injustice, the implementation of constructive programmes, and Gandhi's vision of revolutionary social change in an effort to transform society.

Thailand: The Assembly of the Poor[3]

The Assembly of the Poor (*Samatcha khon chon*) is composed of various groups adversely affected by development policies implemented by the Thai state to promote industrialization, export-oriented agriculture, and commercial forestry. A substantial proportion come from the hundreds of thousands of rural and forest-dwelling people who have been adversely affected by the construction of large-scale dams, which have caused the loss of fisheries and the flooding of land upon which people depend for their livelihoods. The government has often failed to adequately compensate displaced people for their losses.

The Assembly of the Poor, officially founded in 1995, grew out of pre-existing small farmer and villagers' organizations and also includes urban slum-dwellers, many of whom were forced off the land. The Assembly is not a centralized organization, but rather a horizontal network of grass-roots organizations and supporting **non-governmental organizations** (NGOs), which retain autonomy and independence. The Assembly was established to enable villagers' organizations from around the country to come together in a forum to exchange information and resources, and to increase their bargaining power.

The Assembly initially attempted to redress grievances through conventional politics, but the government ignored their efforts. Subsequently the movement turned to non-violent methods such as marches, rallies, protest demonstrations, and civil disobedience. They realized that mass protest was the only way in which to create the power they needed to bring decision-makers to the negotiating table on a more equal footing.

The most powerful method developed by the Assembly of the Poor is the encampment, a makeshift 'rural village' set-up in the streets of Bangkok, wherein activists live for the duration of the campaign. The encampment is located near the Government House, which houses the offices of the prime minister and other government officials. Political rallies and meetings are held on a daily basis, and marches through the streets are sometimes undertaken.

The first major encampment was in 1996, in which up to 12,000 activists participated. The Assembly of the Poor successfully obtained agreements in principle from the government to compensate their members for the expropriation of their land and loss of livelihood. It was vigilant in following up the implementation stages with committees and government agencies. Government procrastination sparked a second, larger encampment to pressure the government to honour its earlier promises. The Assembly mobilized up to 25,000 people from 35 provinces, putting pressure on the government to compensate people for their losses, promote more sustainable forms of development, and democratize the policymaking process.

The second encampment was the most sustained and well-organized mass protest ever mounted in Bangkok. Its success depended on the protestors' ability to maintain non-violent discipline. In doing so, it mobilized pressure against the government without raising the anxiety of the public beyond a critical threshold or justifying a violent response by the government. The government finally agreed to implement the agreements that it had previously made. The Assembly of the Poor won unprecedented concessions including compensation to almost 7,000 families for loss of land and livelihood due to dam construction, the cancellation of one dam project and the review of five others, three resolutions ending summary evictions of villagers from forest land, and the admission in principle that long-settled groups should be allowed to remain on forest land. Moreover, a Bill was initiated in Parliament that would recognize community rights to forest management.

The government of Prime Minister Chavalit Yongchaiyudh guaranteed to address all of the grievances in the Assembly's petition. However,

---

[3] This section is based on Missingham (2003) and Baker (2003).

when the government of Prime Minister Chuan Leekpai assumed office in November 1997, it refused to honour previous agreements. During the more authoritarian rule of Chuan, the Assembly adopted the strategy of coordinated but geographically scattered protests at strategic sites of conflict throughout the country, rather than staging major political events in Bangkok. However, once the hard-line Chuan was replaced by Thaksin Shinawatra as prime minister in February 2001, the Assembly again pressed the national government for reform through concentrated large-scale mobilizations.

The Assembly of the Poor is significant because it represents the first major reassertion of the rural political voice in Thailand since the suppression of the Peasant's Federation in the 1980s. It differs from earlier rural political groups, due to its decentralized network style of organization, its diffuse leadership, and its ability to address local and national issues. Moreover, the movement avoids co-optation by not seeking links to political parties or state power.

While its success has varied in part due to the political context, the Assembly of the Poor has been successful in putting the issue of sustainable development on the national agenda. It works to transform social relations of power to enable communities the freedom to manage local resources and to compel the state to guarantee local community rights over the use of land and resources.

Brazil: The Landless Rural Workers' Movement (MST)[4]

Brazil has one of the highest levels of land inequality in the world, a legacy of Portuguese colonization and the continued political influence of the land-owning elite. The 1964 Land Statute Act and the 1988 Brazilian Constitution specify that the government has the responsibility to redistribute land that is not being productively used, but no serious land reform programme has been implemented. In fact,

a progressive government that was considering land reform was removed by a US government-backed military coup in 1964.

From the 1970s onward, the number of landless people and unemployed rural workers increased due to the building of several hydroelectric dams, the expansion of large industrial farms for export agriculture, and the implementation of policies favouring large-scale farming and contributing to the indebtedness of small farmers. Disillusioned peasants began taking over unproductively used land through unarmed land occupations. Further land occupations were subsequently organized by the Landless Rural Workers' Movement, or the MST (*Movimento dos Trabalhadores Rurais Sem Terra*), a social movement organization that was officially founded in 1984. The MST originated in Brazil's southern-most states, Rio Grande do Sul, Santa Catarina, and Paraná, growing out of a network of progressive members of the Catholic Church who practised **liberation theology** and Marxist activists concerned with rural violence and inequality.

The land occupation became the major weapon for putting pressure on the government to redistribute land. It is a highly organized and disciplined method of non-violent direct action involving substantial planning and preparation. Before a land occupation occurs, MST activists identify parcels of land that are not in productive use and suitable for sustaining an agricultural settlement. Next, the MST mobilizes landless people who are interested in obtaining land. Ideally, this is facilitated by a sympathetic member of the local community such as a priest or a union leader, but alternatively MST activists go door-to-door attempting to recruit people. Numerous meetings occur in churches or schoolrooms where MST activists explain what the movement is about, why it struggles for land, and how land might be attained through land occupations.

An occupation occurs when a group of families—perhaps anywhere from 30 to 300, depending on the size of the land to be occupied—occupy land. Entire families participate in the occupations,

---

[4] This section is based on Branford and Rana (2002), Wright and Wolford (2003), and the author's field research in Brazil.

bringing with them items like materials to construct temporary housing, cooking equipment, basic agricultural tools, and non-perishable food staples. Once the land is occupied, the families must be self-sufficient since the police sometimes set up roadblocks to prevent further incomers.

Sometimes land occupations are met with violence by landowners or police. If this occurs, the policy of the MST is to retreat and organize another land occupation at a different location.

Once the land is occupied the MST commences legal proceedings to have the land officially expropriated by the government. If the land is expropriated, then the MST organizes a permanent agricultural settlement.

The MST views non-violent action as a pragmatic means and their comparative advantage against the monopoly on violence held by landowners and the state. Violent struggle would decrease their support from the public and progressive segments of the Catholic Church, which is important for their success.

Since the mid 1980s, the MST has carried out over 230,000 land occupations. It has successfully put agrarian reform on the national agenda and brought about the redistribution of 20 million acres of agricultural land to over 350,000 families.

The MST is significant because is has forged a strategy of land reform that does not depend on revolutionary violence or on state-imposed market-led reform. Moreover it has been able to successfully challenge the entrenched power of the land-owning elite, and promoted the rights of landless people who have historically been marginalized in Brazilian society.

Key points

- Examples of people power movements that challenge development policies and promote grass-roots democracy and sustainable development include Ekta Parishad in India, the Assembly of the Poor in Thailand, and the Landless Rural Workers Movement (MST) in Brazil.

- People power movements organize, empower, and give political voice to some of the poorest and most marginalized segments of society.
- Non-violent resistance implemented by the movements ranges from the principled non-violence of Ekta Parishad to the pragmatic non-violence of the MST.

Politics of Alternative Development

The development policies implemented by many developing countries over the past half-century have prioritized constructing large dams, promoting industrial farming and export-oriented agriculture, and extracting timber and minerals. These policies have contributed to the displacement of people, the privatization of communal land and resources, increasing levels of land inequality, and environmental degradation. They have threatened the material bases of small farmers, landless rural workers, and indigenous peoples. In response, social movements with strong critiques of the dominant models of development have mobilized and pursued goals consistent with environmentalism, sustainable development, and grass-roots democracy. Social movements, like those discussed above, not only resist destructive policies. They also challenge entrenched systems of inequality and traditional rural social relations such as authoritarianism, violence, and patriarchy, with traditional caste relations in India and traditional patron–client in both Thailand and Brazil being good examples. All three organizations promote gender equality and empower people to take a stand against corruption, violence, and traditional deference to authority.

These social movement organizations, and others like them, have adopted organizational forms and politics that represent a distinct break from the past. They have broken from old ideological camps and deliberately eschewed the conventional political party and lobby group format for a networked social movement approach. They reject the goals of becoming political parties or seizing state power. Instead they attempt to transcend institutional politics by emphasizing grass-roots participatory democracy, decentralization, and organizational autonomy from political parties and the state. They organize marginalized people to increase their power to influence the state through extra-institutional methods of protest, non-cooperation, and disruption. Just as importantly they stress the empowerment of poor people and their collective capacity to address the problems they experience.

In addition non-violent strategies provide a sharp contrast to guerrilla insurgencies and traditional anti-imperialist movements that used violence to capture state power. They also contrast with the violence that has characterized enclosures, colonization, the expropriation of land and resources by states and corporations, and violent repression against people protesting elite imposed development policies.

In order to break vicious cycles of violence, these struggles have responded creatively. Their methods of non-violent action have been used to mobilize people, draw attention to significant social problems, and generate pressure against their opponents. Direct actions have been taken to rectify problems that governments have failed to address. Rather than challenging the state on its own terms, the people use methods with which they have a comparative advantage, through mass-based non-violent resistance.

Significantly, there is an increasing tendency toward using non-violent resistance in struggles over land, resources, and development policies, even among struggles that were originally violent, such as the Zapatista rebellion in the Chiapas state of Mexico. The Zapatista Army of National Liberation (*Ejército Zapatista de Liberación Nacional*, EZLN) emerged in 1994 in opposition to the North American Free Trade Agreement (NAFTA) that opened the Mexican economy to North American enterprises. Its struggle is framed as an indigenous struggle against imperialism. It promotes the autonomy of the indigenous people in Chiapas, their right to use and benefit from the resources in their region, and their right to exercise communal control of land, something that was outlawed by the NAFTA agreement. After 1994 the Zapatistas increasingly turned to non-violent action to promote their cause, although, paradoxically, they continue to be armed.

Non-violent resistance may be the most promising strategy for addressing problems associated with enclosures, commodification, and privatization, and for transforming the dominant development model. In contrast, throughout Africa and Asia violent movements for national liberation, for example, have typically resulted in authoritarian regimes that then used state power to exploit resources and labour.

Non-violent strategies have a number of strengths: (1) their means are consistent with their ends; (2) they allow maximum popular participation; (3) they are more likely to win over opponents and third parties; (4) they lead to more lasting change, because they mobilize a larger portion of the population in a participatory fashion than violence or official channels; and (5) their struggles usually result in fewer casualties (Martin 2001; 2006).

Nevertheless, a problem with pro-democracy movements in particular is that while they unite a diverse opposition to challenge the authoritarian regime, once a transition occurs, there tends to be conflict and fragmentation among the previously united opposition. In the Philippines, for example, after the successful people power movement, members of the traditional elite regained political prominence while the more progressive segments of the movement were marginalized (Mendoza 2009). Moreover, the process of democratization may be deflected into moves to establish limited democracy and a neo-liberal economy, under the influence of the US government and international financial institutions seeking to prevent genuinely popular democracy from taking root (Robinson 1996). Other problems with promoting social change through social movements include the inadequate resources available to poor people, the difficulty of aggregating diverse groups into a coordinated movement, maintaining social mobilization and the capacity to disrupt over extended periods, the co-option of movement leaders by ruling elites, the formal institutionalization of the movement and consequent loss of vitality, and, of course, the vulnerability to state or paramilitary repression.

The global justice movement

While people power movements that challenge the dominant development paradigm are part of a long tradition of resistance, they also differ from earlier struggles. In the current era of globalization, these diverse struggles, which in previous times would have been isolated from each other, are increasingly part of an emerging broader **global justice movement**. New transnational solidarities and organizational networks have developed and an increasingly globalized discourse of human rights, environmentalism, and sustainable development provide new ways of expressing and legitimizing their claims (Box 11.3 provides examples).

Box 11.3 Nodes in the Global Network of Resistance to Dominant Development Policies

Focus on the Global South 'combines policy research, advocacy, activism and grassroots capacity building in order to generate critical analysis and encourage debates on national and international policies related to corporate-led globalisation, neo-liberalism and militarisation'.

FoodFirst Information and Action Network 'analyzes and documents concrete cases of violations of the right to food. We raise awareness on the right to food among social movements, non-governmental organisations and governmental bodies. We respond to requests from victim groups whose right to food is threatened or has been violated and mobilise support'.

Global Exchange is 'a membership-based international human rights organization dedicated to promoting social, economic and environmental justice around the world'.

International Forum on Globalization is 'a North–South research and educational institution composed of leading activists, economists, scholars, and researchers providing analysis and critiques on the cultural, social, political, and environmental impacts of economic globalization'.

International Rivers' 'mission is to protect rivers and defend the rights of communities that depend on them. We oppose destructive dams and the development model they advance, and encourage better ways of meeting people's needs for water, energy and protection from damaging floods'.

Third World Network's 'mission is to bring about a greater articulation of the needs and rights of peoples in the Third World, a fair distribution of world resources, and forms of development which are ecologically sustainable and fulfill human needs'.

Via Campesina aims to 'develop solidarity and unity among small farmer organizations in order to promote gender parity and social justice in fair economic relations; the preservation of land, water, seeds and other natural resources; food sovereignty; sustainable agricultural production based on small and medium-sized producers'.

Note: Quotations are from respective websites.

Transnational NGOs as well as the social forums that have emerged over the past decade, most notably the World Social Forum, provide mechanisms for activists and concerned citizens from many countries to attempt to share their experiences and analyses, define their commonalities, and build collective strength and solidarity. In the past, the isolation of local struggles from each other as well as from concerned citizens in other countries contributed to their defeat. These constraints are beginning to lessen due to a fusion between local and global activism and the emergence of a global civil society. The barriers of time and space, which isolate people, are becoming increasingly less formidable and the social mobilization of marginalized groups and their connection with other like-minded people in other parts of the world is increasing.

People negatively affected by policies of international economic institutions such as the World Bank, the International Monetary Fund, and World Trade Organization are increasingly mobilizing to influence these institutions. As a result, World Bank projects, for example, now include environmental assessments, attention to gender issues in development, and considerations of core labour standards (O'Brien et al. 2000). Nevertheless, while the global justice movement shares some common goals serious divisions exist. Some segments are simply trying to reform the most serious abuses of development policies but others reject entirely the conventional ideas of development and seek a radical alternative. Moreover some serious criticisms have been levelled against the global justice movement, such as the domination of northern agendas and the issue of too little accountability.

Key points

- In addition to development policies, many people power movements address problems concerning patriarchy, corruption, violence, and traditional deference to authority.

- Increasingly, local social movement organizations concerned with development issues are networked with each other and with a transnational global justice movement.

- Non-violent action has been shown to be effective in promoting beneficial social change.

- Problems with a social movements approach to social change include the difficulty of aggregating diverse and resource challenged groups into a coordinated movement, maintaining mobilization over extended periods, co-option and institutionalization of the movement, and the vulnerability of challenges to state and paramilitary repression.

Conclusion

From the 1980s onward, a wave of people power movements challenged authoritarian regimes throughout the developing world. Many movements contributed to human rights and democratization. Less dramatically, but perhaps more importantly, people power movements have also emerged throughout the developing world to challenge the dominant development logic and neo-liberal economic policies. Drawing on human rights, environmentalism, and sustainable development discourses, these movements are increasingly becoming linked through transnational networks.

One way of looking at people power movements that challenge the dominant model of development is that they are simply part of a long, but ultimately futile, resistance—in other words, anachronistic movements against the inevitable process of capitalist modernization. However, there are reasons to believe that the dominant development logic, which has transformed the world, has inherent contradictions that humanity must confront sooner rather than later. What is novel about the current global situation is that there are ever fewer isolated areas for those alienated from the land to migrate to, many cities are no longer able to absorb people evicted from land in the countryside, and environmental degradation has become a major social problem. So, another way of looking at these struggles is that they are the crucibles in which alternative, more sustainable and democratic forms of development are being nurtured, forged, or re-created. Rather than futile actions against the inexorable march to development, they are seed beds for the emergence of alternative development paradigms. They emphasize the use of land and resources to promote the welfare of local communities rather than for the profit of distant corporations or government officials, and emphasize using natural resources in a sustainable manner. Significantly, rather than engaging in conventional politics or taking up arms against the state, people power movements have relied on non-violent resistance, which has been effective in promoting beneficial social change as well as attenuating vicious cycles of violence.

? **Questions**

1. What are social movements? What is 'people power'? What is non-violent resistance? How do these differ from conventional or institutional politics? How do these differ from violent resistance?

2. Why have some aggrieved groups turned away from both conventional politics and violent resistance to the 'alternative' politics of social movement networks and non-violent resistance to promote social change?

3. What methods of non-violent action have been implemented by social movement organizations to promote democratization, land reform, and sustainable development?

4. How do the models of development envisioned by people power movements differ from those promoted by states, corporations, and international economic institutions?

5. Are the encampments in Bangkok organized by the Assembly of the Poor justified? Are MST activists in Brazil justified in trespassing and occupying privately owned land?

6. Whose interests are served by conventional development policies? By neo-liberal economic policies?

7. What opportunities and constraints does globalization pose for social movements and transnational activism?

8. What barriers inhibit North–South dialogue and cooperation among activists and social movements?

→ **Further reading**

■ Ecologist, The (1993), *Whose Common Future? Reclaiming the Commons* (Philadelphia, PA: New Society Publishers). A critical overview of the history of enclosures. Justifies and discusses strategies for reclaiming the commons.

■ Harvey, D. (2003), *The New Imperialism* (Oxford: Oxford University Press). Examines the current mode of capitalist expropriation—accumulation by dispossession, and potential strategies of resistance.

■ Khagram, S. (2004), *Dams and Development: Transnational Struggles for Water and Power* (Ithaca, NY: Cornell University Press). Examines resistance to large dam projects and challenges to the dominant development paradigm.

■ McMichael, P. (2008), *Development and Social Change: A Global Perspective*, 4th edn (Thousand Oaks, CA: Pine Forge Press). Explains how development was institutionalized as an international project in the post-colonial era and how the project of development is being revised by neo-liberal globalization and contested by social movements.

■ Martin, B. (2001), *Non-violence versus Capitalism* (London: War Resisters' International). Assesses the role and potential of non-violent resistance in challenging capitalist economic relations and developing alternatives.

■ O'Brien, R., Goetz, A. M., Scholte, J. A., and Williams, M. (2000), *Contesting Global Governance: Multilateral Economic Institutions and Global Social Movements* (New York/Cambridge: Cambridge University Press). Examines the impact of environmental, labour, and women's movements on multilateral economic institutions and development regimes.

■ Rossett, P. M., Patel, R., and Courville, M. (eds) (2006), *Promised Land: Competing Visions of Agrarian Reform* (Oakland, CA: Food First Books). A critique of market-led agrarian reform. Examines popular struggles for agrarian reform and food sovereignty.

■ Schock, K. (2005), *Unarmed Insurrections: People Power Movements in Nondemocracies* (Minneapolis, MN/London: University of Minnesota Press). Examines several people power movements that mobilized to promote democratization in the late twentieth century.

■ Shiva, V. (2005), *Earth Democracy: Justice, Sustainability, and Peace* (Cambridge, MA: South End Press). Examines the history of enclosures of the commons, and discusses alternative ways of organizing economy and society.

■ —— (2008), *Soil Not Oil: Environmental Justice in an Age of Climate Crisis* (Cambridge, MA: South End Press). A critical examination of three interrelated crises of climate, energy, and food. Promotes subsidiarity approaches to overcome the crises.

:// Web links

■ www.ektaparishad.com *Ekta Parishad*, Bhopal, India; contains information about the history and activities of India's Ekta Parishad (Unity Forum).

■ www.mst.org.br *Movimento dos Trabalhadores Rurais Sem Terra*, São Paulo, Brazil; contains information about the history and activities of Brazil's MST.

■ www.internationalrivers.org International Rivers, Berkeley, United States; this organization opposes destructive dams and the model of development that they advance. Works with environmental and human rights movements around the world.

■ www.forumsocialmundial.org.br *Fórum Social Mundial*, São Paulo, Brazil; website for the World Social Forum, an annual event in which members of social movements and NGOs meet to discuss alternative forms of politics and development and strategies of resistance.

■ **www.focusweb.org** Focus on the Global South, Bangkok, Thailand; a NGO that engages in policy research, advocacy, activism, and grass-roots capacity-building for promoting alternative development models. Contains research reports and position papers.

 Online Resource Centre

For additional material and resources, please visit the Online Resource Centre at:
www.oxfordtextbooks.co.uk/orc/burnell3e/

PART 3
State and Society

The heading of Part 3 reverses the order of the two terms contained in the previous part to signify that Part 3 focuses chiefly on the institutions of state and their importance to society. In politics, institutions matter. The state is not merely one among many political institutions but historically has been the pre-eminent focus of attention. In the modern world, under the impact of rapid social, economic, technological, and other changes taking place at the global, regional, and sub-state levels, the exact nature, role, and significance of the state are continually evolving. Undoubtedly, the term 'governance' has taken a hold in recent development discourse, and in globalization theory too, to convey a wider set of governing arrangements than those that are controlled by states either individually or collectively. Nevertheless it would be no less foolish to suggest the end of the state is nigh and to dissolve its analysis into a soup of exogenous actors and currents—domestic or international—than it is to ignore how those actors and currents set limits on and provide options for what government can do.

This part has two main aims. The *first* is to explore the idea of the state in a developing world context and how, if at all, it differs from the state in more developed countries. Among other things this must involve some reference to past history. Can one framework accommodate all the varieties of state formation? And what is most distinctive about the politics of countries characterized by endemic violent conflict or trying to emerge from state failure?

The *second* aim is to show how the governance capabilities of states and even more so the kind of political regime—the relationship between the institutions of government and society—have become a major focus for political inquiry. In at least some developing countries there have been significant changes in the last few decades. This part is essential for enabling us to address important questions about how far the state in the developing world can be held responsible for addressing (or failing to address) fundamental developmental issues. And for determining whether it is equipped to resolve issues including those affecting the economy, welfare, the environment, and human rights. For instance what is the relationship between democracy or democratization and development? Is there a specific sequence in which these must arise? And how are governance and policy convergence connected to globalization?

While Part 3 ranges over these issues, the more detailed policy matters that are bound up with them will comprise the substance of Part 4—which is best consulted after or alongside the material in Part 3. The illustrations in Part 3 are widely drawn from around the developing world. By comparison case studies of countries selected to illustrate specific issues and themes can be found in Part 5. For example, while Chapter 20 includes a case study of post-Saddam Iraq, Chapter 21 shows how Pakistan, Nigeria, and Mexico offer contrasting trajectories of political regime transformation. Readers are encouraged to read the introduction to Part 5 and consult the relevant case studies alongside the chapters in Part 3. In addition, for more extended discussion of the contribution that party politics specifically makes to politics in developing countries, readers should visit the Online Resource Centre, where there is a specially written comparative examination of the role of political parties by Vicky Randall.

Theorizing the State

Adrian Leftwich

Overview

Explanation of successful and failed states in the developing world requires an understanding of the provenance, characteristics, and functions of the modern state as it evolved in what is now the developed world. This chapter first explores the nature of institutions and, in particular, the modern state as a set of political institutions of rule, geared to the organization and continuous management of economic development. Second, it analyses the emergence and features of the state in what is now the developed world; third, it investigates the transportation of the modern state to the now developing world and the consequences of that. The central argument is that the characteristics of any state, anywhere, are largely defined by its evolving relations with the economy and society that it reflects and both represents and dominates, in its historical, regional, and international context. The chapter argues that political processes in many developing countries are moving towards the establishment of state institutions of rule that may provide more stability and effectiveness for economic development and greater participation for citizens in decision-making processes. But the process is very difficult, slow, and uneven.

Introduction: Political Institutions and the Modern State

Human societies cannot endure, prosper, or—especially—develop without broadly agreed and appropriate rules and conventions governing the conduct of social, economic, and political affairs, and about how human and other resources are to be used and distributed. Such sets of rules are what political scientists mean by **institutions** (see Chapter 3). Essentially, institutions direct and constrain human interaction. All societies have them; they must. The different institutional spheres often overlap (and sometimes conflict to produce undesired outcomes), and include social institutions (governing social interaction and behaviour), economic institutions (the customs, rules, and procedures governing economic behaviour, ranging from silent barter to rules governing stock-market behaviour)—and political institutions (governing relations of power and authority).

The *forms of rule* expressed in different political systems, or *polities*, have varied widely. For instance, some polities initially involved only very basic forms of localized village headship or leadership; others, perhaps starting with such local and limited forms of rule and power, subsequently evolved at different speeds into steeper and more extensive hierarchies of centralized control and power over an increasing territorial space. The emergence of centralized polities (which some theorists refer to as early states) sometimes expanded over wide areas to encompass other societies so that they came to constitute what have been called 'centralized bureaucratic empires'.

However, the immense range of historical political systems that have given institutional expression to the different forms and distributions of power has shrunk dramatically since the sixteenth century when one type of polity emerged in Europe and came to be the dominant political form of the contemporary world: *the state*, or, more accurately, the *modern state*. Although it varies in its forms, the characteristics of the modern state need to be distinguished from earlier polities, or 'non-modern' states, such as ancient city-states, feudal states, pre-modern, early modern, or absolutist states, or even 'princely states'.

The emergence of the modern state in Europe was a largely endogenous process, occurring within the geography and history of particular regions in the course of conflict, competition, and, especially, consolidation among them. To illustrate, in late fifteenth-century Europe there were some 500 independent political units, but by 1900 this had shrunk to about 25. And from within this history of European state formation, there developed, from the fifteenth century, outward thrusts of discovery, conquest, and control, loosely called imperialism and colonialism. These imperial processes carved out new 'countries' (in most cases that had not existed beforehand), they established new institutions of rule in the form of the colonial state (which either suppressed or used and sometimes transformed existing institutions of rulership), and drew such countries (or parts of them) into different kinds of largely subordinate economic relations with the metropolitan countries of the increasingly dominant 'West'.

Key points

- The emergence of specialist political institutions and organizations represents the differentiation of political systems or polities from other institutional spheres.

- The most recent and dominant form has been the modern state the origins of which were primarily European.
- This form was carried outwards by European imperialism and colonialism, and imposed on diverse societies, or adopted and adapted by them. The external provenance of the state in many developing countries has been a critical factor in shaping and influencing their particular forms and the politics associated with them.

The Modern State

Traditional polities

The modern state was the product of slow evolution from prior political systems, or polities, but by the nineteenth century its central features were clear. The German sociologist Max Weber (1964) theorized those features of the 'modern' state that distinguished it from prior 'traditional' institutions of rule, or systems of authority. These earlier forms, he suggested, like the 'patrimonial' form of authority as he called it, were characterized by two overriding features.

First, there is the absence of any sharp distinction between the *rulers* and the *institutions of rule*. This was typical of the absolutist rule of some European monarchs well into the eighteenth century as well as elsewhere in East Asia and Middle America. For instance, Louis XIV, the king of France in the mid-seventeenth century, made the point with great effect when he is alleged to have said to the *parlement* of Paris in April 1655, *'L'État c'est moi'* (I am the state).

The second defining feature of traditional forms of rule was the relative absence of open, meritocratic entry, autonomy, independence, and security of tenure for the officials who surrounded the rulers. Unlike officials in the ideal-typical bureaucracy of the modern state, they were essentially the personal staff of the ruler, often paid by him or her, and with the more or less explicit requirement of personal loyalty to him or her rather than to the state or its constitution.

Defining the modern state

Many characteristics and functions distinguish the modern state. But it was the development of institutions of rule and governing that were formally separated from not just the rulers and the officials who ran them, on the one hand, and the citizenry, on the other hand, that was central in the shift from what Weber called 'traditional' forms of rule and authority, including patrimonial polities, to the modern state. The modern state consists of a set of **public institutions** and other public organizations that together define and implement the legitimate and hegemonic control, use and distribution of power over a given sovereign territory and people. This definition identifies all the key elements of the modern state.

Public institutions: The institutions of the modern state are all 'public' and include the constitutional arrangements, laws, regulations, and other formal conventions that stipulate how formal power is achieved, used and controlled and which provide for the legal framework within which social, economic, and political life carries on.

Public organizations: Where institutions are best understood as rules, laws, and constitutions, the *organizations* of the state are those agencies of rule and implementation, including 'the government', the legislature, the courts, civil service, army and police, plus any state-owned agencies.

All of these institutions and organizations in the modern state are formally differentiated from other institutions (especially private and non-state institutions) and individuals, and also from the incumbents of the offices and the citizens or subjects over whom they exercise authority.

Sovereignty and hegemony: The institutions of the modern state and its laws have authority over a particular demarcated geographical area and apply in theory to everyone within its territory.

Formal monopoly of violence: The modern state has a monopoly of the legitimate use of violence and it is, or should be, the dominant agency of rule and law, whether democratic or not, in principle superordinate over all others. In practice, in the course of their history, most modern states have struggled at times to achieve that dominance (Bates 2001). And some, until very recently, have continued to do so. An example is the Peruvian state's battle to subdue the *Sendero Luminoso* guerrilla movement, which exercised considerable power over parts of the country in the 1970s and 1980s.

Impartial bureaucracy: The bureaucracy is (theoretically) impersonal, impartial, and neutral and does not make law. But in practice, policymaking is much more complex, and, increasingly, specialist bureaucratic input into policymaking is the norm. Nonetheless, the central characteristic that distinguishes the modern state from prior forms of rule is the principle, at least, of *relative* independence and autonomy of the public service from both the elected political elites and parties and also from the public. Moreover, the offices of state officials, whether constitutional monarchs, presidents, ministers, legislators, judges, police, or civil servants belong to the state, not to them personally. It is a fundamental assumption of the modern state that these public offices and powers should not be used for *private* gain by their incumbents (what would normally be called **corruption**). Occupancy of such offices should entail no powers of private **patronage**

nor be used for the support of any particular private client base (**clientelism**), whether personal, regional, ethnic, or economic.

These characteristics are of course ideal-typical. No state in the modern world has been, or can be, found that fulfils them to perfection. And while many theorists may agree on this limited set of characteristics of the modern state, the most contentious issues of debate and interpretation in political science revolve around questions such as: is the modern state 'neutral'? Can it be? Do classes dominate its policy output and, if so, which ones? Does the state have its own interests? What should its role in economy and society be? How far should the state intervene in the 'private' life of its subjects or should it be limited or constrained in what it does by constitutionally defined bills of rights?

Modern states differ with respect to many other variables, for example: their *historical traditions* (some have longer continuous traditions of centralized rule than others, as in England, Russia, or Japan); their *structural properties* (for example whether unitary, as in France and Korea, or federal, as in the USA, India and Nigeria, and hence how state power is distributed regionally); whether they are formally *democratic or not* and for how long; their *electoral systems* and/or *consultative patterns* (and how these influence state power and policymaking); and the nature and extent of their *legitimacy* in the perception of their subjects.

The modern state: Imperatives, functions, and challenges

As the modern state consolidated and proliferated through the nineteenth and twentieth centuries, more countries began to adopt its broad template as their system of rule. For example, many Latin American countries adopted and adapted from France and (to a lesser extent) the United States in shaping their constitutions (rules of the political game) as they gained independence from Spain and Portugal between 1811 and 1900.

But the really central point is that the modern state emerged in the course of the 'great transformation' from agrarian to industrial societies (mainly in Europe) and in the consequential requirements for appropriate institutional and regulatory frameworks and functions to facilitate and extend this. It was both product and agent of that transformation. Indeed it is essential to understand that the fundamental defining role and function of the modern state has been to promote, organize, protect, and sustain this economic and social transformation to industrialism—and beyond into the 'post-industrial' era. In the nineteenth and twentieth centuries, the histories of the now industrial powers, and more recent modern history of the contemporary developing world, shows that successful and effective modern states and successful economies go hand in hand, as do 'failed' states and failed economies. This process of state formation was of course intensified through the competitive economic, military, and other forms of nationalism that it promoted, and by the turbulent sociopolitical changes associated with the economic transformation. And by the early twentieth century four critical issues had come to confront the modern state: defence against external attack and internal security; the promotion and protection of the economy; democratization; and the associated demand for state provision of welfare. The manner in which each state dealt with them acted to define its character and its relations with the society it claimed both to represent and to manage.

First, with regard to defence, the period 1850–1939 saw an intensification of what has been called **despotic power**—that is, the power to control and suppress—as opposed to **infrastructural power**—the power to penetrate and transform society (Mann 1986: 169–70; Weiss and Hobson 1995; Scott 1998). But, second, as indicated above, national economic development also was central to the emergence and defence of the modern state, and was closely associated with the competitive nationalisms of the nineteenth century. Thus successful modern economic growth and successful modern states with influence that extends beyond their borders have been inextricably linked. And there is nothing that sums this up better than the slogan 'National Wealth, Military Strength' (often translated as 'rich country, strong army') adopted by the new post-Meiji elites in Japan after 1870.

In pursuit of these goals, most of today's leading industrial economies used state-directed industrial, trade, and technological policies (Chang 2002: 58 and *passim*) to get ahead, to stay ahead (as in the case of Britain), or to catch up as Germany, Japan, and the United States began to do in the nineteenth century. Three broad strategies, or models, were used (although each contained a variety of distinctive forms). The first was the Anglo-American and Western European model, which involved the state ensuring four prime conditions for the promotion of private, market-driven growth, as argued by Douglas C. North (1990): securing property rights; establishing a fair and efficient judicial system; setting out an open and understood system of rules and regulations; and facilitating market entry and functioning, although at times state action has gone much further than this as in the Depression years in the USA and in post-war reconstruction in Europe. The second model has been the Soviet model, of forced-march top-down industrialization, pioneered from the 1920s and involving pervasive state ownership, control, and management of the economy, and the mobilization by the state, not the market, of resources (including human ones) in pursuit of transformative objectives. The third model is essentially the East Asian model of the **developmental state**, pioneered in Japan after 1870, and especially after the 1920s, which has been replicated in some other countries like Korea and Taiwan (Leftwich 1995). This involved a much closer symbiosis between state and private sector (see Chapter 22b) and has sometimes been called 'managed capitalism' or 'governing the market'.

Modern states in the developing world have sought to adopt modified versions of the three different strategies outlined above in their pursuit of economic growth through industrialization. Crucially, however, successful intervention along any of the strategic paths has only occurred where the appropriate political coalitions and distributions of power underpinning the state have allowed rather than hindered growth-promoting institutions and strategies. This has been one of the key differences between the older 'modern states' and the new 'modern states' of the developing world.

With regard to the challenges of democratization and redistribution, Huntington (1991) identified three great 'waves' of democratization (between 1828 and 1926, between 1943 and 1962, and from 1974 to the present). In each, dominant state elites (almost always male-dominated) responded to democratic pressures in different ways, hence shaping the character of the polity, depending on whether and to what extent they saw their interests being threatened by such demands. Where

democratic progress continued—as in the extension of the suffrage to women—the associated deepening and extension of civil society had the effect of redistributing some political power through the forms of electoral, bargaining, and consultative processes. Moreover, the growth of powerful and increasingly well-organized labour movements in particular meant that few states in the developed world could ignore the demand for redistributive programmes, for example through taxation policy, welfare provision (health, old age, and education for instance), and wage-level agreements. In consequence, those societies managed effectively by modern states are mainly characterized by levels of income inequality far less extreme than in many parts of the developing world (see Chapter 6).

Key points

- Modern states are the public political institutions and organizations of rule that are in principle differentiated and distinct from both the rulers and the ruled.

- The modern state emerged, evolved, consolidated, and was borrowed as the set of centralized institutions and organizations of rule the central function of which was to manage national transitions from agrarian to industrial society, and to sustain economic growth.

- Historically, the modern state has been characterized typically by its public institutions and organizations, its sovereignty and hegemony, its formal monopoly of legitimate coercion (violence), and its theoretically impartial bureaucracy.

- Although different states adopted different strategies, successful economic growth and stable states have without exception been inextricably linked.

- In promoting economic growth and development, modern states have had to provide defence and ensure law and order, respond to demands for a more inclusive set of civic and democratic rights, and manage some redistribution of resources through tax and welfare arrangements.

- The broad strategy adopted in the pursuit of economic growth has depended crucially on the character of the political forces and coalitions underpinning state power, which in turn has influenced the achievement of developmental goals.

The State in the Developing World: Provenance and Forms

Most of the conditions and capabilities associated with the state's emergence in the now developed world have been largely absent in the developing world. In short, the formation of modern states in colonial and post-colonial contexts was not geared to the development of institutions and organizations of rule directed at promoting economic growth or transformative development, as occurred in Europe and elsewhere, whether on a capitalist, socialist, or mixed-economy basis. Moreover, most of the challenges that those earlier states had to meet—especially those of democratic pressures and redistributive and welfare demands—have thus far exceeded the capability of many of the newer states. And, crucially, apart from some very important exceptions, this is explained by the quite diverse political forces and coalitions formed during or after the colonial era and which set up, inherited, adapted, or battled for control of the institutions of the modern state. Simply stated, these political forces, representing varying kinds of socio-economic elites and interests, seldom had the interest, the will, or the power to establish or encourage growth-promoting institutions in accordance with any of the three models sketched above. This is why so many states in the contemporary developing world have been associated with weak or uneven developmental performances. But before proceeding further, two important introductory points should be made.

First, the problems facing these states are, in principle, no different from those that faced states and societies in the developed world, although they may differ in timing and context. These problems have been (and remain) essentially those of how to establish and sustain the institutions of rule that promote economic development, within or outside democratic polities, whether state-led or market-led, in the face of increasing pressures for democratization and redistribution, in a globalizing political economy.

Second, the kinds of modern state institution in post-colonial developing countries varied widely and were everywhere shaped by the interaction of four main factors: the nature of the pre-colonial polities; the economic purposes of colonial rule; the characteristics of the colonial state institutions and the socio-political groups that dominated

them; and the manner of incorporation of pre-colonial political processes and institutions in the systems of colonial and post-colonial rule. Accordingly, the contemporary developing world is at least as diverse as were those societies in which the modern state emerged. Nevertheless there are some major, common underlying themes too.

The modern state in the developing world: Provenance

While the modern state in the now developed world grew largely through complex *internal* political processes in the course of the great transformations from agrarian to industrial societies, most states in the developing world owe their existence (and indeed their very borders) to the geographical definitions and institutional impositions of the colonial era. With few exceptions, the provenance of states in the developing world has largely been *external*, and few of them developed endogenously from prior local polities and systems of rule. In Asia, the exceptions include China, Korea, Japan, and Thailand where some continuity can be traced back to prior local (absolutist, monarchical, and imperial) systems and institutions of centralized rule, as in Egypt and Ethiopia in the case of Africa. In Latin America, the main pre-colonial political institutions, especially the great centralized tribute-extracting empires of the Aztecs (Mexico) and the Incas (Peru), were extinguished by the Spanish conquest from the early sixteenth century, although cultural legacies remain even today.

Although the patterns of colonial state institutions varied widely across time and space (Young 1994: 244–81), they everywhere left very important influences on the politics and state structures after independence. Everywhere, and almost without exception, the project of colonial rule and control was undertaken initially for the benefit of the metropolitan countries or their particular interests.

Colonial states: Imposed borders and the institutional patterns of rule

External design and imposition of 'national' boundaries

Perhaps the most far-reaching influence and impact has been the external shaping of geographical boundaries and institutional structures, the most dramatic illustration being the **scramble for Africa**, which produced the national boundaries of Africa today (see Box 12.1). Of course there were no 'countries' with formally defined 'national' boundaries before this in Africa: political boundaries were often vague and porous. What there were, however, was a wide range of 'multiple, overlapping and alternative collective identities' (Berman 1998: 310) expressed in an equally wide range of institutional political arrangements. Such was the artificiality of the new, imposed boundaries that some 44 per cent of those still existing today are straight lines (Herbst 2000: 75), representing lines drawn cartographically on open maps. There was almost no indigenous definition of geographical boundaries, nor were any major 'national' movements, or 'nationalist' sentiments, involved in establishing the boundaries of modern African nation-states. The Latin American experience was not much different, where the new states were carved from the huge vice royalties of the colonial system of rule in the course of the struggles for independence in the nineteenth century. Led largely by the conservative *criollos* (colonial-born Spaniards or Portuguese, as in Brazil), the new states in consequence expressed political and socio-economic relations that even today reflect deep and profound inequalities between a small (and very rich) elite and a large (and very poor) mass, illustrated particularly well by Brazil (a former Portuguese possession), now one of the most unequal societies in the world.

In Asia, a similar pattern occurred and the Indian subcontinent provides the best example, where British rule brought diverse ethnic and religious communities, often tense with communal rivalries, not to mention over 500 princely states, together in colonial India. But at independence, the country was divided between India and Pakistan, with East Pakistan (later to become independent as Bangladesh) being separated by a great chunk of India from West Pakistan. Indonesia emerged from Dutch rule as an improbable 'nation-state' of about 13,000 islands stretching for about 3,500 miles from west to east, containing diverse linguistic, cultural, and religious communities (see map in Chapter 20a). Cambodia, Korea, Thailand, Myanmar, and, to some extent, Malaysia have been notable exceptions to this pattern, each reflecting closer lineages with some historical polity.

Box 12.1 The Colonial Impact in Africa

In Africa, large tracts of land were claimed by European powers as their possessions, either as colonies or protectorates or, as in the case of King Leopold of Belgium, as private property in the form of the Congo Free State. The distribution arising out of the powers' scramble for Africa was formally recognized by their representatives at the Congress of Berlin, 1884–85. In all of this Britain, France, Germany, and Portugal paid no regard to the enormous differences among the different African societies that ranged from small-scale self-governing hunting and gathering bands to large, hierarchical political systems, as in the empires of Mali, Ghana, and Songhay in West Africa. Peoples with diverse cultures, religions, languages, and political systems who had previously lived alongside one another, sometimes peacefully and sometimes in violent conflict, but without formal boundaries, were now pulled together into entirely artificially created 'nation' states.

Extractive rather than developmental purposes of rule

The purpose of imperial rule was not developmental in the manner of the emerging modern states of Europe. On the contrary, all the major colonial powers (and often the early private companies that acted for them) saw the extraction of riches, raw materials, and taxes as their primary objective.

External design and imposition of the institutions of rule

In trying to understand the problems and failures of many states in the developing world it is fundamental to recognize that these extractive purposes shaped the kind of institutions of rule, which in turn formed the foundations for the states after independence. In so far as the institutions of colonial rule can be termed 'colonial *states*' (Young 1994), they were essentially states of extraction, and not aimed at promoting, and organizing national economic development. With the exception of Japanese rule in Korea (Kohli 2004), no colonial institutions of rule bore any resemblance to any of the three models sketched above. In short, throughout the colonial world, and until well into the twentieth century, the institutions of colonial rule and control were authoritarian, elitist, and geared to maintaining high levels of extraction for the benefit of the metropolitan powers (Box 12.2).

Box 12.2 The Extractive Nature of Imperial Rule

The Spanish conquistador and conqueror of Mexico, Hernando Cortés, in the sixteenth century, is reputed to have said 'I came to get gold, not to till the soil, like a peasant'. In the Caribbean, plantations exploiting unfree labour (first, indentured servants and then almost entirely slaves) were established for the production and export of cotton, tobacco, and especially sugar. In Indonesia, the 'culture system' of the Dutch, first under the Dutch East India Company and then through formal colonial rule, required Indonesians to deliver set amounts of spices to the authorities. Likewise, the ruthless requirements of King Leopold's Free State in the Congo demanded that rubber and ivory be collected, on pain of often cruel punishment of villagers (amputation of hands or feet was not unknown). Elsewhere throughout colonial Africa raw materials such as palm oil, beeswax, wild rubber, cocoa, and, later, tea, plus diamonds, gold, and copper flowed back to Europe.

Intensities and paradoxes of colonial institutions

The institutions of colonial rule displayed something of a paradox. At the centre, power was generally held very firmly, 'despotic' power that is: the capacity to deploy force and coercion (Mann 1986: 169–70) in order to suppress and control. Challenges to colonial rule were usually put down with sometimes spectacular brutality, commonly with the assistance of locally recruited indigenous police and soldiers. The real locus of despotic power was largely confined to areas of economic or strategic importance—such as the cities, mines, plantations, or ports.

Yet there was seldom much infrastructural power (Mann 1986: 169–70)—that is, the capacity to penetrate, administratively, the length and breadth of the country and to use that capacity to facilitate programmes of economic change and development (Migdal 1988). For example, large areas of non-urban Latin America, in the Amazon and the Andes and especially in the huge rural hinterlands of countries like Mexico, Brazil, and Argentina, although formally under Spanish or Portuguese colonial rule, remained far beyond effective control of the centre and were run in effect by the *patrons* and *hacendados* of the great estates and the emerging *caudillos*, the local strongmen (see *caudillismo*). The same was true for much of sub-Saharan Africa and large parts of South-East Asia. This lack of infrastructural power should not be at all surprising, given that the central purpose of European colonial rule was extractive, not developmental or transformative, and much of colonial rule was done on a very limited budget and a minimal administrative presence. But this dearth of infrastructural power of the colonial state created a legacy that still characterizes many new, modern states in the post-colonial world, while despotic power—protecting the new elites that took over after independence—remained pronounced in urban centres.

Because of weak infrastructural power, all colonial regimes came to depend on local-level 'bosses', 'big men', brokers, or oligarchs, some of whom derived their power originally from their traditional positions (such as the *caciques* of Latin America and—the sometimes artificially created—'headmen' or 'chiefs' in colonial Africa). The net overall effect of this was generally to constrain the emergence of effective modern states capable of establishing national institutions and organizations of rule for the promotion of national economic development. Indeed, the weakness of its infrastructural penetration required the central organizations of the state always to bargain and deal with the local brokers—often later institutionalized in federal political systems after independence, as in India and Nigeria and Brazil—thereby establishing complex, reciprocal networks of political influence and patronage in and around the institutions of the state, and hence imposing serious constraints on their capacity and autonomy (Barton 1997: 49; Kohli, 2004). This is illustrated in Parry's description of the legacy of colonial rule in Latin America:

> This is *caudillismo* or *caciquismo*: the organisation of political life by local 'bosses' whose power and influence derives from personal ascendancy, family or regional association. In most countries the concentration of formal authority at the centre, the weakness of lawfully constituted provincial and local authority, leave wide scope for the activities of such people. The real effectiveness of central government may depend upon the nature of the bargain which it can strike with those who wield local influence and power; while the prestige of the *cacique* (local boss) may be enhanced by the 'pull' which he can exert in the capital.
>
> (Parry 1966: 371–2)

Patron–client relations and the politics of the new states

This particular 'organization of political life' was the context within which patterns of patronage and **patron–client relations** became so pervasive in the post-colonial world, frustrating the emergence and consolidation of the institutions of the

modern state. Patron–client relations have typified human polities, before the modern state, almost everywhere. As discussed in Chapter 3 of this book, the basic characteristic of the institution of patron–client relations is of an unequal power relation between patrons ('big men' in African terminology) who are powerful, rich, and high in status, on the one hand, and clients ('small boys' in African terminology) who lack power, wealth, or status, on the other hand. The patron–client relationship is reciprocal but uneven in that the patron has control of, or access to, resources and opportunities that he (it is usually a male) can provide for the client in return for deference, support, loyalty, and (in the context of post-independence electoral politics) votes. Patrons have an interest in maintaining their client base by being good 'big men'—that is, by delivering the goods—while clients (depending on the particular pattern of the relationship) may have some freedom to move from one patron to another from whom they might expect a better deal.

Clearly the rules defining the institution of patronage are entirely at odds with the rules underpinning the modern state, and bear a striking resemblance to the pre-state European institutions of patrimonial rule, discussed by Weber. But as societies in the colonial world achieved independence from metropolitan powers, and as attempts were made to build modern states, the principles and practices of patronage quickly established themselves in the interstices of the new institutions of rule, from top to bottom, thereby weakening state capacity and undermining its autonomy. Thus in Latin America, even under the 'bureaucratic-authoritarian regimes' of the 1960s and 1970s, whether on the left or the right politically, the regimes were constrained by the immense regional and local power of the old bosses, oligarchies, and political elites, in country and town, who could contain if not derail reform even under the toughest of military regimes, as in Brazil after 1965. And in Africa, where patrimonialism pre-dated the colonial impact and where, at independence, the commercial, capitalist, or landed classes were small and weak, it was almost inevitable that the resources of the state would be the target that competing groups would seek to capture, in order to feed and fuel their patronage links to 'friends and followers', whether of a regional, kin, or ethnic character. It was little different in much of South and South-East Asia during and after the colonial period.

Only in those few cases in which revolutionary political movements seized state power and largely crushed prior elites and dominant classes, as in Cuba and (North) Vietnam, has the power of patronage been contained, although it has sometimes reappeared. Other exceptional cases, in which electorally or militarily dominant elites have taken over and pursued national economic growth for purposes of national defence—the classic recipe for state formation and consolidation—include the developmental states of South Korea, Taiwan, and Singapore (see below).

Key points

- Most contemporary states in the developing world had their borders and main institutions imposed from without.

- Most colonial states were marked by the paradox of having strong 'despotic' (coercive) power and weak 'infrastructural' or transformative capacities.

- Many countries in the developing world achieved independence in circumstances in which powerful economic and political forces in society exerted considerable regional and local influence and hence constrained dramatically the emergence of centralized, autonomous, and effective modern states.

- In the post-colonial era, these institutions of patronage merged with the formal institutions of the modern state, commonly transforming it so that it has been unable to perform the central function of the modern state—namely, the encouragement, promotion, and maintenance of economic growth.

- Many of the characteristics of pre-modern politics and 'patrimonial' polities were entrenched within the institutions of the modern state, leading to their characterization as neo-patrimonial states.

The State in the Developing World: Characteristics, Features, and Types

State characteristics in the developing world

Public institutions

One of the central characteristics of the modern state is that its institutions and organizations of rule are, or should be, essentially 'public', not owned or treated as their private domain by their incumbents. But one of the greatest problems in establishing modern states in the developing world has been to liberate public institutions and organizations from the private control of political leaders or from their 'capture' by special interests (Hellman, Jones, and Kaufmann 2000). The combined effects of patrimonial rule and patronage have been to distort the neutrality of public institutions and erode the independence of public organizations—whether they are policymaking bodies, courts, bureaucracies, armies, or other state-owned agencies. The net effect has often been the informal privatization of public organizations in so far as they have been used to advance the private interests and clients of (usually) long-standing civilian or military leaders who have become heads of state. Essentially, this private use of public office and resources is the core definition of corruption. Certain heads of state — for instance Presidents Marcos and Suharto in the Philippines and Indonesia, Presidents Mobutu and Kenyatta of Zaire and Kenya, and Presidents Batista, Duvalier, and Somoza of Cuba, Haiti, and Nicaragua — might quite easily have repeated the view of Louis XIV that *'L'État c'est moi'* (I am the state). One of the key institutional instruments of the modern state in the developed world for protecting the public institutions (such as the civil service) has been the establishment of bodies such as independent civil service commissions, responsible for appointing, managing, and disciplining civil servants, thereby establishing clear differentiation from the political leadership and protecting bureaucrats from political interference. It has been profoundly difficult to establish and sustain the independence of such bodies in many developing countries.

Sovereignty, hegemony, and the monopoly of violence

Many states in the developing world have had great difficulty in establishing their hegemony and maintaining sovereignty within their borders. This is not only because of the power of local, private, or regional 'bosses' or 'influentials', but because the legitimacy of the state has been commonly challenged by various groups (ethnic, religious, cultural, or regional), which do not wish to be part of it, or by political opponents who refuse (for good or bad reasons) to accept the incumbent regime. Also, secessionist, irredentist, and civil wars have plagued the modern states of the developing world from Peru to the Philippines and from Angola to Afghanistan.

The earlier generation of modern states also faced these nation-building challenges. For instance, state education policy in nineteenth-century France had as one of its prime concerns the building of a sense of national identity and unity. Indeed such issues persist to this day, as demonstrated in Basque separatism in Spain and Quebecois nationalism in Canada. However, such challenges have arguably been much more severe in the developing world. While the present chapter has not identified nation-building as itself one of the core imperatives of the modern state, it must nonetheless be recognized that failure to achieve some degree of national, or multinational, integration, and cohesion will jeopardize the state-building project. In effect it is in Africa that the greatest incidence of conflicts of this kind and the adverse consequences are to be found. But there are many examples from elsewhere, such as Sri Lanka's long-running conflict between the Ceylonese majority in the south and the Tamil minority in the north. Moreover, Indonesia struggled for many years to hold on to East Timor. Guerrilla movements, both urban and rural, have challenged the hegemony and legitimacy of a number of Latin American states since the 1960s. Many states in the developing world cannot claim a formal monopoly of violence, a characteristic that marks them off sharply from most states in the developed world although not all of those have in recent years been free from all violent internal conflict, as Northern Ireland and Spain illustrate. In some societies, the collapse of the centre and the proliferation of non-state sources of violence and hence civil conflict have produced a series of failed or **collapsed states** (Rotberg 2004), as in Somalia, Afghanistan, and Cambodia at various points in their recent history.

Elsewhere, there are states characterized by what scholars such as Ross (1999) referred to as the 'resource curse'. This refers to states sometimes described as **rentier states** in which a major part of state revenues are derived from such sources as taxes (hence rents) on companies involved in the extraction of some valuable natural resource, such as oil (classically) or diamonds or copper. It is argued that at least two consequences may flow from this dependence on resource revenues. First, it undermines democracy or democratization by reducing the state's need to be accountable to its citizens. Secondly, as occurred in Sierra Leone, the presence of such resources (diamonds) can fuel intense conflict between groups determined to control the trade or the state in order to capture the rents, which further weakens and sometimes simply destroys the central power and authority of an already weak post-colonial state.

Thus, weakened from within by internal conflict and held down by low rates of economic growth, many states in the developing world have found it difficult to maintain sovereignty. Poor countries, especially, find it harder to maintain their sovereign independence in the international arena than rich countries. Economic strength not only provides for defensive (or offensive) military capacity but also reduces dependency and increases bargaining capacity in relations with public institutions such as the World Bank, the International Monetary Fund, foreign governments, and with sources of private investment and finance. In particular, where foreign aid inflows form a significant part of government expenditure, de facto sovereignty is seriously reduced as aid donors come to apply increasingly stringent conditions. As a percentage of central government expenditures, aid contributions have been very high in some less developed countries but less in countries with lower aid-dependency overall. The latter countries have been better able to maintain a grip on their own policymaking, although this has not meant that they have escaped entirely high levels of debt, another element that impacts on sovereignty.

Impartial bureaucracies

The pervasive legacy of patron–client relations, the culture of patrimonialism within the state, the absence of democratic accountability (even in its limited electoral form), low levels of economic growth, the power — and wealth — of special private interests through 'state capture', limited and often aid-dependent state budgets, low pay, high levels of state involvement in the economy, and hence much opportunity for discretionary bureaucratic decisions, have all contributed to the undermining of bureaucratic impartiality in many developing countries. Moreover, bureaucratic continuity in much of Latin America has been constrained by the politics of the appointive bureaucracy, a system whereby incoming governments are able to dismiss (often many thousands of) bureaucrats (especially senior ones) and appoint their 'own' men and women (Schneider 1999: 292–4). Corruption, too, erodes state capacity to pursue coherent and consistent policies of economic growth, undermines development, and institutionalizes unfairness. By discouraging political elites from taking the tough decisions that development requires and by disabling the bureaucratic institutions of the state from carrying out effective implementation, the consequences for development can be severe. The difficulties in achieving appropriate forms of land reform in many developing countries offer a prime example, of which President Bhutto's failed attempts at land reform in Pakistan in the 1970s provides an excellent case study (Herring 1979).

Effective and developmental states

Despite this generally bleak picture of state characteristics in the developing world there has also been a small group of *effective states* that must be mentioned. Chile, for instance, is generally perceived as having enjoyed an effective state for long periods of its history. Such states—whether democratic or not, and pursuing a wide range of economic policies—have usually been successful in promoting growth, reducing poverty, and enhancing overall welfare, even where their civil and human rights has not necessarily been good (although in some, like Chile today compared to President Pinochet's rule, it has improved greatly in the last 15 years with deepening democratization). Described more generally as 'developmental states' (Woo-Cumings 1999), these states have taken both democratic and non-democratic forms, as well as pursuing both formally socialist and non-socialist paths. While most examples have been concentrated in East or South-East Asia (such as South Korea, Taiwan, Singapore, Malaysia, China, and Vietnam), there are some non-Asian examples including Botswana, Mauritius, and perhaps Cuba. But in all cases, whether officially capitalist or socialist, democratic or non-democratic, the effectiveness of these states has been driven by political dynamics that have concentrated sufficient power, autonomy, capacity, and—sometimes—accountability at the centre to

ensure the successful achievement of their developmental goals (see Box 12.3).

Box 12.3 Types of State in the Developing World

In addition to the conventional classifications of states as democratic or authoritarian, federal or unitary, presidential or parliamentary, it is useful to think in terms of an additional and qualifying list of categories into which states in the developing world may be classified at different periods of their history: bureaucratic-authoritarian states; patrimonial states; developmental states; rentier states; weak, failed, and collapsed states. None of these display the characteristics of the ideal-typical 'Weberian' state of the West, although with the third wave of democratization (see Chapter 14) things have begun to change.

Key points

- States in developing countries vary greatly but, in many, institutional and political legacies blur the boundaries between public institutions and private interests.

- Establishing organizations to monitor and control these boundaries have been difficult where there is no political will or capacity to do so.

- Many states in the developing world have found it difficult to maintain hegemony within their own territory, to protect their sovereignty and achieve a monopoly of violence.

- Impartial bureaucracies are less common in the developing than in the developed world.

- Patrimonialism and patronage, low levels of pay, and pervasive opportunities for discretionary behaviour all contribute to varying, but sometimes intense, patterns of corruption, thereby subverting the central purpose of the modern state: the promotion of economic growth and welfare.

- Both high levels of aid and rents from major extractive industries may undermine democratic processes.

The State in the Developing World: Facing the Challenges

The central function of the modern state has been to establish the institutional framework and organizational capacity for the promotion, management, and maintenance of economic transformation and growth, and especially the shift from agrarian to industrial society, and all the social and political complexities that this has entailed. The effective elimination of patronage, the de-institutionalization of corruption, the clear differentiation of private and public interests and institutions, and the establishment of relatively impartial bureaucracies have always and everywhere been both condition and consequence of national economic growth, managed directly or supervised indirectly by the organizations of the state. In the course of its evolution, the modern state has also had to respond to the challenges of democratization and the associated demands for redistributive welfare measures, and has done so more or less successfully in the more developed economies in the course of the twentieth century.

The same cannot be said of many parts of the developing world in which many states have not yet been able to organize or manage economic transitions on any of the three main models outlined earlier. Instead, where attempted, industrial capitalisms have been distorted by excessive state regulation, corruption, and the sorts of general weakness where social and economic classes would normally be expected to demand change. Elsewhere, revolutionary socialist, 'forced march', state-led, economic transformations and the state institutions of rule and management they have required—of the kind that occurred first in the Soviet Union after 1917 and then in China after 1949, where the political forces that backed it were strong—have generally failed too. And the extraordinary symbiotic marriage of state and market, typified by various forms of the developmental state that have promoted economic progress in countries as different as South Korea, Taiwan, Singapore, Malaysia, Thailand, Mauritius, Botswana, and most recently China and Vietnam (Leftwich 1995), has simply been impossible to replicate elsewhere. It is the particular constellation of social, economic, and political forces that explains the success of these states, and not whether they happen to be democracies or not. In all cases they illustrate the axiom that successful and effective modern states and successful economies go hand in hand.

Until the 1980s, few states in the developing world qualified as consolidated democracies. There were important exceptions—India, Jamaica, Venezuela, Costa Rica, Mauritius, and Botswana are but some, although many would question whether they all counted as *liberal* democracies (Burnell and Calvert 1999). This is because in much of the developing world, conflicts—of class, regional, religious, or ethnic groups—have been so sharp that achieving consensus about rules of the political game has proved to be impossible. Different groups tend to prefer rules that would protect or advance their own particular interests and limit or reduce the interests of others. Second, many, although not all, of the conflicts have been about distributional issues: land, jobs, income, welfare support. Where economic growth has been slow or negative, it has simply proved impossible (even if desired) to meet such demands. Elsewhere, especially in Africa, cycles of military coup and counter-coup (although declining but far from absent since the 1990s) have been symptomatic of rival factions—ethnic, political, religious, or regional—seeking to gain control of the state and hence its resources and opportunities, in order to feed their clientelistic chains. This again illustrates a central theme of the chapter. The modern state in the developed world has been compatible with democratic (at least electoral) politics only where it has ensured that economic growth could subsidize a steady (if slow and sometimes intermittent) increase in the broad welfare of the majority. The more the state has been able to do that, the more robust has been its legitimacy and the more consolidated has its democracy become.

> **Key points**
>
> - Most states in the developing world have experienced great difficulty in overcoming the challenges of economic growth, democratic claims, and re-distributional demands.
>
> - Many states in the developing world have been unable to establish the institutions and organizations of rule that would permit economic growth according to capitalist, socialist, or developmental state models.
>
> - In the absence of economic growth and in the presence of profound inequalities, states in the developing world have found it impossible to absorb and institutionalize democratic demands.
>
> - Many states in the developing world have found it impossible to deliver improved human welfare through re-distributional means.

Conclusion

Strong, stable, and effective states are inconceivable without strong economies. And strong economies are inconceivable without the institutional framework established by the state to enhance growth and welfare, whether capitalist or socialist. All examples of sustained economic growth and development have required effective states to make (and adjust and adapt) appropriate institutions and organizations of rule and to facilitate the coordination of the public with the private institutions. Market-oriented models would not have been successful in the West without pervasive state support in the form of investment in human and infrastructural capital, the raising of taxes, the regulation of commerce, the establishment of judicial and legal systems, and welfare provision—and much more. Top-down, state-led, Soviet-style, post-revolutionary industrialization, likewise, has also required appropriate institutions and organizations for success, as have the complex developmental states of East Asia. But in each and every case, behind the state and the institutions of development it has created or facilitated, has been a coalition of political and social forces willing and able to establish, maintain, and adapt those institutions. The problem, however, in many developing countries has been that the politics underpinning states in many developing countries have made them inept, disjointed, and divided agencies of economic growth and hence have done little to promote human welfare or the reduction in poverty.

With the collapse of the bipolar world, the processes of globalization have accelerated. If such processes do indeed stimulate capitalist growth, then political forces will also gather momentum and help to build modern states on the template of their European precursors. Instead of being the agents and beneficiaries of patronage and corruption, such forces will become the agents of their destruction and of the creation of both the public and private institutions of rule that promote economic growth. In short, they will become much more like the states of the developed world. For sure, this will not happen everywhere. Nor will it happen quickly or simultaneously. Nonetheless, such developments will bring into politics other popular social forces—sometimes based on the classical coordinates of class, sometimes ethnicity, sometimes religion, and increasingly gender. They will use the new democratic space to demand social and welfare reforms that will constitute new challenges for the state and, in the process, transform it, as in the case of gender inclusion and equality. How each will respond and adapt remains uncertain and will depend on the shifting coalitions of power and resistance that such politics will create. But what is certain is that the political science of the modern state in the developing world, and elsewhere, has not by any stretch of the imagination reached its terminus.

? Questions

1. Why are the institutions and organizations of the state so important for development?

2. In what ways, if any, has the largely external origin of many states in the developing world influenced their form and function?

3. To what extent did the different colonial economic institutions influence the character and capacity of the colonial and post-colonial states?

4. How would you distinguish between the rules that govern institutions of patronage and institutions of bureaucracy?

5. Good governance presupposes effective states. But can either be achieved without the political will and political processes to keep them in place?

6. What is the case for developmental states in an era of globalization?

7. Identify some of the different types of state found in the developing world, compare their distinguishing characteristics, and illustrate with examples.

Further reading

■ **Bates, R. H. (2008),** *When Things Fell Apart: State Failure in Late-Century Africa* **(Cambridge: Cambridge University Press).** This compact account charts and explains the causes and conditions of state failure in Africa.

■ **Fukuyama, F. (2004),** *State Building. Governance and World Order in the Twenty-First Century* **(London: Pantheon Books).** A concisely and elegantly written account of the complexities and dimensions of effective states and how they are built.

■ **Kohli, A. (2004),** *State-Directed Development: Political Power and Industrialization in the Global Periphery* **(Cambridge: Cambridge University Press).** An excellent comparative account of states and development in South Korea, Brazil, India, and Nigeria.

■ **Leftwich, A. (1995), 'Bringing Politics Back In: Towards a Model of the Developmental State',** *Journal of Development Studies,* **31/3: 400–27.** Outlines a model of the developmental state.

■ **———(ed.) (1996),** *Democracy and Development* **(Cambridge: Polity Press).** Essays exploring the relationship in theory and practice between democratic practices and developmental outcomes in a number of different countries.

■ **Migdal, J. S., Kohli, A., and Shue, V. (eds) (1994),** *State Power and Social Forces* **(Cambridge: Cambridge University Press).** Explores the relations between social and political forces and state power and capacity in a number of developing countries.

■ **Woo-Cumings, M. (ed.) (1999),** *The Developmental State* **(Ithaca, NY: Cornell University Press).** Explores the conditions and characteristics of developmental states.

■ **Young, C. (1994),** *The African Colonial State in Comparative Perspective* **(New Haven, CT: Yale University Press).** One of the finest accounts of the colonial state and its legacy, with insightful comparative observations.

Web links

■ **www.transparency.org/** Website of Transparency International, offering important and interesting information on global corruption plus the annual Corruption Perception Index for all countries. You can use this site to navigate to the annual Global Corruption Report.

■ **www.gsdrc.org/** Website of the Governance and Social Development Resource Centre at the University of Birmingham. It offers access to many papers, publications, and guidance concerning institutional aspects of states and governance in the developing world.

■ www.foreignpolicy.com/story/cms.php?story_id=3098 Website of the *Foreign Policy* journal's failed state index, with quantitative measures for state strength and weakness. Funded and published by the Carnegie Endowment for International Peace.

■ www.crisisstates.com/ Many publications and research projects on crisis states in the developing and transitional world, based at the London School of Economics and Political Science.

■ www.ids.ac.uk/gdr/cfs/ Work and publications of the Centre for the Future State, at the Institute of Development Studies, University of Sussex, which promotes research on how public authority can be strengthened and reconstituted to meet the challenges of the twenty-first century.

 Online Resource Centre

For additional material and resources, please visit the Online Resource Centre at:
www.oxfordtextbooks.co.uk/orc/burnell3e/

From Conflict to Peacebuilding

13

Astri Suhrke and Torunn Wimpelmann Chaudhary

Overview

This chapter examines patterns of organized, violent conflict in the developing world since the onset of decolonization. It also discusses shifts in how scholars and policy makers have understood such conflicts, and how these understandings have informed the international peacebuilding regime that developed in the 1990s.

Introduction: Decolonization and its Aftermath

In retrospect, it seems remarkable how few of the over a hundred transfers of authority associated with decolonization in Africa and Asia were violent. The transition from colonial rule to independence mostly took the form of widened political participation, enabling the colonial rulers to formally disengage yet retain some influence. In some cases, however, the transition was violent. A key variable was the willingness of the colonial power to leave peacefully, which in turn was heavily influenced by the nature of the colonial political economy. The existence of plantation economies with a sizable number of white settlers seemed to predispose the transition towards a violent resolution, as Aristide Zolberg writes, and as evident in Indochina, southern Africa, and Kenya—possibly because plantations are immobile property that is difficult to divide or transfer (Zolberg et al. 1989).

Plantation economy by itself was not a necessary condition however, as the long and perhaps extraordinarily violent war over Algeria's independence from France demonstrated. India was another exception, where decolonization entailed an extremely violent partition (see Chapter 2).

In Indochina and Southern Africa wars over decolonization were transformed almost seamlessly into continued wars that lasted for several decades, as we shall see below. In several other post-colonial countries, peace was fragile and punctured by renewed strife. While the new states were amalgams of populations separated by 'artificial' boundaries drawn by the colonial powers, the post-colonial elites mostly accepted these boundaries as given and very rarely went to war to dispute them. Rather, conflicts arose in relation to identity politics within the state, sometimes involving separatist demands, and in revolutionary struggles to capture the state and reshape the social order in line with socialist visions and **liberation theology**.

Conflicts related to ethnicity or 'identity politics' followed several patterns (see Chapter 7). Polities with 'ranked' or 'hierarchical' ethnic systems (Horowitz 1985), where distinctions between ethnic groups coincided with that of the ruler versus the ruled, appeared particularly fragile. The ex-Belgian colonies of Rwanda and Burundi experienced early and repeated ethnically directed violence between Hutu and Tutsi. In Rwanda the ruling Hutu majority attacked the Tutsi minority, while in Burundi the pattern was reversed. The violence started soon after independence and continued with some regularity in both countries until 1990, when an army of Tutsi in exile invaded Rwanda from neighbouring Uganda and sparked a civil war that culminated in the genocide of Tutsi in Rwanda in 1994. The colonial legacy that hardened and reified ethnic distinctions was partly to blame but so were the organization of politics, intensified competition over land, and the reinforcing effect of each cycle of violence in the creation of mutually exclusive and separate communities (Banégas 2008). Ethnically directed violence against minorities also occurred as part of state formation and nation-building policies, a

phenomenon known from European history as well. Thus, Uganda's President Idi Amin in 1972 forcibly expelled the country's Indian minority, a move that enabled him to seize the assets of a prosperous trading group and, perhaps more importantly, harness an African national identity as a source of legitimacy for his rule. In much of South-East Asia, Chinese trading minorities were vulnerable to nationalistic restrictions as well as mob violence when conflicts over the ethnic political order spilled into the street, as in Malaysia and Indonesia.

Communal conflict involving ethnic groups that were geographically separated generally placed the periphery in opposition to the centre over autonomy or separatist demands. While expressed in ethnic terms, secessionist conflicts typically reflect concurrent economic and political grievances or ambitions. Secessionist conflicts were common in early post-colonial Africa and Asia, for example the Outer Islands rebellion in Indonesia in 1957–58, the secession of the Katanga province from Congo in the early 1960s, and Biafra's quest for independence from Nigeria in the 1960s. In the Biafra conflict, the pictures of starving children in besieged rebel territory made a lasting imprint on Western images of the state of newly independent African countries.

However, the solid consensus among post-colonial governments against redrawing colonial boundaries ensured that very few secessionist struggles succeeded. Vested interests in the principle of sovereignty was one factor. There was also deep suspicion that ex-colonial powers were supporting would-be secessionist movements for economic gains and to demonstrate that the new governments were incapable of governing. The role of Belgian mining interests (*Union Minière*) in the secession of Katanga from Congo became a cause célèbre, causing a major civil war that sparked other secessionist off-shoots and threw Congo into a long period of political turmoil. When the Katanga crisis finally ended in 1963, the Organization of African Unity passed a resolution at its Cairo meeting in 1964 that explicitly called for 'respect for borders at the time of independence'. The only two exceptions were the separation of East Pakistan to become

Bangladesh in 1971, and Eritrea's separation from Ethiopia in 1991. Both were truly exceptional cases. East Pakistan was physically separated from the rest of the country by the northern part of India, and India openly supported separation. Eritrean rebel forces had wrestled control over the entire territory they claimed as a homeland by 1991, at a time when Ethiopia was internally weakened and internationally isolated. The secession appeared as a fait accompli to the international community, and easier to accept in so far as Eritrea's status as a separate entity had been recognized at an earlier point in its history.

Conflicts over the political and socio-economic order that pitted revolutionary social movements against the old elites appeared in some cases as a continuation of the independence struggle, as in southern Africa and Indochina. In Latin America, where decolonization had taken place in the early and mid-nineteenth century, struggles over the social order followed different trajectories. In Central America, agrarian protest developed into armed liberation fronts that in the 1970s and 1980s challenged the established landed oligarchy and their grip on the state. In South America in the same period, the armed forces seized power in Argentina, Brazil, Chile, and Uruguay to quell what they perceived as national security threats from leftist and communist forces, including urban guerrillas, the Tupamaros, in Uruguay. These conflicts became hardwired into the cold war, and will therefore be discussed under this heading.

Key points

- Post-colonial secessionist struggles occurred, but colonial borders mostly held.
- Independence struggles in South-East Asia and southern Africa were transformed into protracted cold war conflict with devastating effects on the local societies.

Social Order Conflicts and the Cold War

By definition conflicts over the social order have local roots. Above and beyond the particular local dimensions of the social order conflicts of the 1970s and 1980s, however, was a common element that gave added coherence and destructive intensity. The conflicts interacted with an especially severe phase of the cold war, and this had important consequences. Conflicts over social change became expressed in the dominant discourse of the time—revolutionary socialism versus liberal democracy—which linked them to the ideologized power struggle between the United States and the Soviet Union. Acting on the premise of a global competition, but recognizing that direct conflict between themselves would be mutually and totally destructive given their nuclear parity, the superpowers moved to competitive interventions in the periphery. Local conflicts in what was then the 'Third World' became wars by proxies, enabling local protagonists to receive military, economic, and political support.

In this logic, the United States supported military regimes in South America to crush actual or suspected leftist movements, and in Chile helped to overthrow the democratically elected government of Salvador Allende in 1973. Washington supported anti-communist rebels in Nicaragua (the *contras*) and provided military, economic, and political support to the governments of Guatemala (see Chapter 22a) and El Salvador to defeat the increasingly broad-based opposition to the oligarchy and the iniquitous and repressive social order it represented. The Soviet Union provided material support to the other side, in particular Cuba. As the lone communist outpost in the region, Cuba served as a funnel for general assistance to rebel movements on the left, while leaders like Fidel Castro and Che Guevara were sources of inspiration.

In Africa, a similar pattern developed. The South African apartheid regime and the still white-ruled Rhodesia actively helped to fight the US wars of proxy in Angola, Namibia, and Mozambique. On the other side, Cuba sent doctors, the Soviet Union provided massive economic and military aid, and sympathetic independent African governments extended sanctuary for fighters and refugees. The result was an intricate web of interaction between local, regional, and international actors and their respective interests, as illustrated in the case of Mozambique (see Box 13.1). It was a self-reinforcing dynamic that served to sustain violence on the local level and increase systemic hostility between the superpowers.

Box 13.1 The War in Mozambique

A socialist national liberation movement, FRELIMO had been in the vanguard of the long independence struggle against the Portuguese and formed the first independent government in 1975. Its policy of radical socialist change, however, alienated many traditional farmers, antagonized the Catholic Church, and sharpened divisions between the northern and the southern regions of the country. When the government also denounced apartheid and colonialism it alienated external forces as well. Neighbouring white-ruled Rhodesia sponsored a rebel force (RENAMO), received backing from the South African government and, in the background, the United States. The main reason for the US engagement was the active support given to the Mozambican government by the Soviet Union, which provided direct budget support and virtually all its military equipment. The war between the government and RENAMO forces lasted for 15 years, causing enormous death, destruction, and displacement, and a post-war population of *mutilados* who had been crippled, maimed, or tortured. The rebels had targeted the destruction of schools and health centres in order to undermine popular support for the government, leaving only a skeletal structure when the war ended.

Even a more indirect backdrop of large power rivalry could fuel local violence on an unprecedented scale, as demonstrated in the case of Indonesia in 1965. President Sukarno, who had led the independence struggle against the Dutch, had ruled with few serious challenges to his power for almost a decade, but by the early 1960s, two other main forces had emerged—the Communist Party of Indonesia (PKI) and the Army. The delicately balanced tripod collapsed in 1965 in a context of rising international tension between the United States and the main communist powers. China was accused of using the PKI as a fifth column and an instrument of global communist expansion, while the United States was increasing its military engagement in Vietnam to prevent the 'dominoes' from falling to communism throughout South-East Asia. Against this background, the Indonesian armed forces, provoked by an abortive coup rumoured to be linked to the PKI, set in a motion a massive operation to physically eliminate the PKI. At least half a million people were killed over a several months period, many in private vendettas that occurred in the wake of the purge. The next president, General Suharto, abrogated the previous foreign policy of non-alignment and Indonesia became a main recipient of US military aid as well as economic assistance from the International Monetary Fund (IMF) and the World Bank (see also Chapter 20a).

The most destructive of these local-cum-cold war dynamics occurred when the superpowers moved from supporting wars of proxy in the developing world to become a belligerent with their own troops on the ground. In Indochina, the United States became heir to the failed French attempt to prevent the Vietnamese from gaining independence after World War II. The French withdrew in 1954, leaving a country divided between a northern part ruled by the Vietnamese Communist Party, and a southern part ruled by a staunchly anti-communist, Catholic elite. To shore up the south, the US gradually increased its own troop commitments to fight what successive US governments and its close allies considered to be the forces of global communism, thus giving the war a world-historical significance as well as testing the status of the US as a superpower.

The Vietnam War also spilled over into Laos and Cambodia, in the latter case setting in motion a chain of events that produced the Khmer Rouge and its social revolution. Seeking to turn Cambodia back to 'year zero', the Khmer Rouge rule in Cambodia (1975–79) cost between 1 and 2 million lives (in a population of around 7 million) as people useless to the revolution were killed or succumbed to its rigors. The excesses were stopped by another military intervention (led by a rival Khmer faction supported by neighbouring Vietnam) but ignited a new civil war as the Khmer Rouge and other Khmer factions fought on from sanctuaries in neighbouring Thailand.

A mirror image of the disastrous Indochinese developments appeared in Afghanistan, where a local communist party (the People's Democratic Party of Afghanistan (PDPA) seized power in April 1978 and proceeded to launch a radical revolutionary program. The Afghan revolution violently eliminated its enemies, brooked no compromise with established landed elites and religious leaders, and sparked a counter-revolutionary movement of *mujahidin* ('holy warriors') who assembled across the border in Pakistan. By late 1979, the Soviet Communist Party, which had close 'fraternal relations' with the PDPA and long-time interest in securing its strategic and economic interests in Afghanistan, decided to send its own troops to impose greater order. The result, predictably, was an escalation of the war as the resistance movement gathered force, now very significantly helped by the United States, its allies, and China (which by this time was locked in a deep conflict with the Soviet Union). After a decade of fighting a losing war, the Soviet Union withdrew its forces in 1989, but peace did not come to Afghanistan. The resistance movement now split into warring factions, which started a civil war of their own in the early 1990s, the excesses of which enabled the Taliban to gain power as a force of order and justice.

Key points

- The cold war intensified conflicts over the social order in Africa, Asia, and Latin America, leading to 'proxy wars'.

- Conflicts involving the troops of one or the other superpower directly were most destructive, as in Indochina and Afghanistan.

The Nature of Conflicts in the Post-Cold War World

The end of the cold war gave decisive momentum to peace negotiations dealing with some of the most stubborn and difficult wars of proxy. Between 1991 and 1994, peace talks commenced or were concluded in Angola, Cambodia, El Salvador, Guatemala, and Mozambique; of these only the Angola accords collapsed. The peace settlements—based in all cases on compromises between the contending parties—signalled the end of the era of revolutionary struggles, and also the end of unfettered power of landed oligarchies and military dictatorships. With the collapse of the Soviet bloc and the consequent blow to the status of state socialism, liberal democracy and the market economy became dominant paradigms for social change and foreign assistance. Economic and political liberalization were also advocated by Western states and international organizations as a foundation for a more peaceful world. The idea of democracy as a cornerstone of peace was celebrated in triumphalist terms by Western policy-oriented scholars. In the words of a co-founder of the American *Journal of Democracy*:

> The experience of this century offers important lessons. Countries that govern themselves in a truly democratic fashion do not go to war with one another . . . [they] do not 'ethnically' cleanse their own populations . . . [they] do not sponsor terrorism . . . [they] do not build weapons of mass destruction to use on or to threaten one another . . . . [They] form more reliable, open and enduring trading partnerships . . . [they] are more environmentally responsible because they must answer to their own citizens

(Diamond, cited in Paris 2004: 35).

Both democratic theory and reality were more complex, however, and hopes that the 1990s would inaugurate a New World Order without wars were not vindicated. The number and overall severity of conflicts as measured by battle-related deaths decreased overall, but varied by region (Human Security Report Project 2005). The Americas remained relatively peaceful as measured by number of violent conflicts; there is a steady decline of even small wars in east and South-East Asia, and in central and south Asia the data show no clear trends. In sub-Saharan Africa, however, the numbers climb steeply. Civil war erupted in Liberia (1989) and Sierra Leone (1991), in both cases lasting for a decade or more. The Democratic Republic of the Congo (DRC) was the scene of almost continuous war from 1996 to 2003, followed by subsequent, smaller wars. In Angola, a temporary peace in 1992 collapsed, followed by low-level renewed war until 2002. In the Horn of Africa unrest continued.

What were the forces driving these conflicts? The surface manifestations seemed chaotic, with military factions mobilized along clan, tribal, or ethnic lines, fighting for no clear political agenda apart from capturing the state. In the DRC neighbouring states intervened in the fighting as well; at one time three states were supporting the government and three more were supporting the rebels. With the end of the globalized struggle between communism and capitalism, analysts struggled to understand the nature of these and other conflicts in the developing world. The explanations focused variously on ethnicity and tribalism, the structure of resources, state failure, poor governance, and rapid democratization. New analytical approaches to the study of conflict were generated as well (see Box 13.2). Some analysts argued that the wars of the 1990s were qualitatively different from previous wars, marked by extraordinary violence against civilians, the force of ethnicity and the internationalized structure of funding (Kaldor 1999). The claim of newness in relation to violence against civilians was decisively refuted (Kalyvas 2001), but other features were more novel.

Box 13.2 Studying the Processes of War

The study of the social and economic processes of war became more important, partly as an entry point to understand the post-war order. Some scholars focused on how wars were organized and financed, how illegal or shadow 'war economies' functioned and sustained themselves. One result was to question conventional and rigid distinctions between war and peace as discrete phenomena. Anthropologists and other social scientists studied war (and other forms of violence) as a social process, conditioned by and understandable only in its social, economic, and political contexts (Richards 2004). Rather than seeking to identify discrete causes of war (such as ethnicity, poverty, profit-seeking, or state failure), these studies examine the historical conditions that enabled and shaped conflicts in particular ways.

In this perspective, if there was something fundamentally new about the wars after the end of the cold war, it was linked to changes in the historical settings that shaped the way conflicts were fought. For instance, the need for new sources of funding gave rise to 'war economies' as rebel parties engaged in resource accumulation, which attracted 'conflict entrepreneurs' and often took on a logic of their own. Some governments raised militias in order to fight wars on the cheap. As the discipline and cohesion of national armies disintegrated, warfare decentralized, often intersecting with local conflict dynamics. Militias were mobilized with appeal to tribal and ethnic identities. Demobilized military personnel also found jobs as mercenaries in conflict elsewhere. Many former soldiers of the South African apartheid era army, for instance, went to work for private military companies in countries such as Sierra Leone and Angola.

'New wars'?

The Balkan wars, the Rwandan genocide, and the war in Somalia were at the forefront of international attention in the first half of the 1990s. The importance of ethnicity in the first two cases, and of a related social dimension (clan) in Somalia, served to revive the notion that ethnicity was a principal driver of conflict. All cases were of course more complex. In Somalia, for instance, the state—which equated with the patronage-based rule of President Siad Barre—had imploded when the cold war ended and Siad Barre lost his principal source of patronage from the superpowers, which previously had competed for a strategic foothold in the Horn of Africa. Absent the central state, a protracted, clan-based struggle for power ensued, with varying degrees of violence. In Afghanistan, the Soviet withdrawal and subsequent loss of financial support for Najibullah's government led to its gradual but definitive demise, opening the way for a civil war among the former resistance fighters that now divided largely along ethnic lines, most notably between Pashtun, Tajik, Uzbek, and Hazara.

The importance of natural resources as a source of conflict was highlighted in relation to the wars in Africa, where the availability of diamonds, timber, and rubber helped to finance warring factions. Taking the point much further, some analysts claimed that contemporary wars were largely driven by the search for profit; the real purpose of war was not to win, but to engage in profitable crime under the cover of warfare (see Box 13.3). The most elaborate and influential formulation of this claim was made by a World Bank/Oxford University economist, Paul Collier. Using statistical analysis, Collier argued that civil wars were driven by individual, economic 'greed', rather than by political and social collective grievances. Collier's economic model is derived from rational choice theory, in which the self-interested, cost–benefit calculating individual is the starting point for explaining social behaviour. In his model of war, the existence of primary resources suggests ready availability of lootable goods, which makes rebellion a profitable undertaking, and poverty reduces the opportunity cost of war. A large number of unemployed and uneducated young men provide a pool of likely soldier-entrepreneurs. The most important exit from the perpetual conflict that traps African countries, therefore, is rapid economic growth and diversification (Collier et al. 2003).

The 'conflict trap' model was a more specific version of the long-standing theme in Western liberal discourse to the effect that economic underdevelopment causes conflict. As such, it fed into the stock of policy-oriented knowledge that informed the peacebuilding interventions from the 1990s and onwards (see below). Other analysts were critical, however (Cramer 2006). There were concerns about assumptions and methods. A low level of education, for instance, might mean young males were ready to join a rebel army in order to make a living ('greed'), or angry young males joining to claim their social rights ('grievance'). The unstated but obvious policy implications of the model were decidedly conservative: if rebels are driven only by personal greed, by implication they have no claim to political legitimacy.

Analysts drawing on fieldwork from Africa drew different conclusions. Young, unemployed men were indeed readily mobilized for war, but not simply for reasons of profit. Rather, rebellion was a response to a crisis of the state, manifested in lack of employment and educational opportunities, and widespread corruption and malgovernance, which generated widespread discontent. The absence of recognizable ideological claims or organizational cohesion consequently did not mean that African rebel movements were apolitical (Keen 2005).

Box 13.3 Sierra Leone's 'Blood Diamonds'

In 1999, a Canadian non-governmental organization (NGO), Partnership Africa Canada, published a report on the ongoing war in Sierra Leone claiming that 'diamonds—small pieces of carbon with no great intrinsic value—have been the cause of widespread death, destruction and misery for almost a decade in the small West African country of Sierra Leone'. The levels of violence in Sierra Leone, the authors argued, could only have been sustained through diamond trafficking: 'The point of the war may not actually have been to win it, but to engage in profitable crime under the cover of warfare.' The report received worldwide attention and eventually led to a global certification system tracing the origin of diamonds, designed to stop diamonds mined by rebels from reaching the world market.

The focus on diamonds, however, risked reducing the war, and particularly the rebel movement Revolutionary United Front (RUF), to a simple greed for profit that obscured its political dimensions. In reality, the conflict was rooted in political exclusion and deteriorating living conditions, which had been a mobilizing factor for many rebel soldiers. The wartime diamond economy, moreover, did not represent a radical departure from peacetime practices in trade and production. A regional network of illicit trade and production in diamonds had existed for decades before the war. RUF and other factions tapped into and sometimes altered these structures, often entering into alliances with established traders, miners, and exporters. Many of the actors in Sierra Leone's diamond industry thus remained the same throughout war and peace.

Another serious limitation on the economic interpretation of the new conflicts in Africa was its strongly internalist perspective, which did not adequately reflect the changes in the international setting. While the end of cold war patronage forced both governments and rebels to find other means of financing their wars, the looting and trading of valuables were made possible by the international demand for diamonds, timber, and coltan, and big profits brought home by international traders. More generally, it is clear that the increasingly deregulated global economy in the post-cold war world, which has accelerated global trade, communications, and

financial transfers, has also enabled the emergence of networks for arms trade, money laundering, and drug trafficking that generate instability in the South. The developed world has been slow to recognize this, if at all; rather, the dominant reaction in the North has been to interpret instability as a symptom of underdevelopment. The arms race is a case in point. Cheap and light weapons, partly pilfered from ex-communist army stockpiles, are readily transported to conflicts spots in the South by a large, global network of arms traders. UN efforts to introduce international regulations on conventional arms trade have long been stymied by the main national arms suppliers, above all the United States, but the change of government in the US in 2009 opened a door. In October 2009, the UN General Assembly for the first timed resolved without opposition that its members would start negotiations on a 'strong and robust' Arms Trade Treaty. As a first step towards global, treaty-based restrictions on the supply of arms, the resolution signalled new constraints on international processes that fuel local violence.

An additional particular understanding of underdevelopment came to figure prominently in explanations for conflict and justification for interventions in the developing world—the concept of state failure.

State failure

The policy and academic discussion around 'state failure' forms a large web with many strands. Early formulations were built around the divergence between *de jure* and de facto status, as developed by Robert H. Jackson (1990) in his book on 'quasi-states'. Many countries in the developing world have *de jure* status—that is, they are formally recognized in the international systems as states—but lack de facto statehood—that is, the capacity to perform basic functions associated with the modern state, above all providing security and basic services for development—Jackson argued. As a result, these states were only 'quasi-states'. The concept soon gained currency in the Northern policy discourse as a diagnosis of severe development or security problems in the South. Around half of the countries of Africa appeared on one or more of the many

indexes of 'failed', 'fragile', or 'collapsed' states constructed by Northern think tanks and institutes. Somalia and the DRC often led the list; Afghanistan and Haiti were frequently cited as well. After the September 11 attacks on the United States, 'failed states' were linked to fears of terrorism as well. The UN Secretary-General, Kofi Annan, lent the weight of his office to the idea that failed states represented an international security threat. A major UN report issued in 2004 described a world of 'new and evolving threats . . . threats like nuclear terrorism, and State collapse from the witch's brew of poverty, disease and civil war' (United Nations 2004: 1).

The academic literature on the nature, causes, and consequences of 'failed states' is fragmented. In one school of thought, internal dynamics of state formation has produced a vacuum of authority; here comprehensive, sustained international assistance is necessary. An opposing perspective holds that the main causes of weak or 'failed' states are foreign intervention and pressures to conform to economic neo-liberalism, including structural adjustment that forces states to downsize, thereby losing power and legitimacy (Doornbos 2006). More generally, critics question the usefulness of the term on analytical and normative grounds. So-called failed states are quite diverse. While arguably 'failed', the Haitian state hardly represents a security threat to Western interests (see Box 13.4), although some political factions in Somalia arguably might. Internally, some countries with 'failed states' seem to manage relatively well for long periods, even Somalia (Menkhaus 2006–07). The term, moreover, has derogatory connotations and is overtly normative in its reference to a model, Western state.

Box 13.4 Haiti: Failed State, Failed by Whom?

Haiti has been a failed state since before the term was invented, demonstrated most clearly by its capacity for exercising despotic power but failure to marshal infrastructural power (see Chapter 12). The absence of effective public services of any kind—notably, security, health communication, water supply, and public

administration generally—was cruelly exposed by the severe earthquake in January 2010 that flattened much of the capital.

The lineages of this state go back to French colonialism based on slavery. A slave revolt in 1804 made Haiti the first black-led post-colonial state in 1804, but in 1915 the country was invaded by the US Marines and occupied for twenty years. A second phase of independence was marked by the ruthless dictatorship of Francois 'Papa Doc' Duvalier and his son, 'Baby Doc', whose thirty years' rule laid the foundation for another rebellion. In the late 1980s, Haiti's peasants, farmers, and urban poor mobilized around Father Jean-Bertrand Aristide and his liberation theology of social justice. On the other side were Haiti's tiny economic elite of reconstituted plantation owners, other landowners, and merchants, who had strong links to the army and established political and financial circles in the United States, France, and Canada. The struggle between these forces shaped the nature of the Haitian state from Aristide's first election as president in 1990 until he was forced out in 2004. International support for Aristide was premised on a restructuring of the patrimonial and bloated Duvalierist state through liberalization, restructuring, and downsizing. Viewing the state as an instrument for radical redistribution, Aristide failed to fully cooperate on economic policy. He also failed to transcend the despotic state of the Duvaliers, using violence to maintain his power and alienating the masses he once had mobilized (Dupuy 2007). In the end, he was defeated by the combined efforts of the Haitian elite, the US, and France, and involuntarily whisked out of the country on a US plane. Subsequent governments failed to reduce Haiti's desperate poverty and inequality—about 1 per cent of the population controls almost half of its wealth (Carillo 2007)—and some 9,000 UN peacekeepers struggled to maintain order amid pervasive crime and the presence of numerous violent gangs.

A more nuanced policy discourse gradually developed. By 2009, the OECD and major donor organizations were talking of 'states in fragile situations'. Noting that non-state actors such as traditional kinship structures and religious brotherhoods often performed many functions conventionally associated with the central state, aid agencies started to consider strategies that involved local private and customary structures. Analysts coined a new term to describe the mixed process: the 'hybridization' of the state (Boege et al. 2008).

Governance and democratization

The 'third wave' of democratization that occurred in the wake of the collapse of the Soviet Union and affected much of the developing world as well was premised on the notion that poor governance and lack of democratization is a major source of social conflict. The proposition underpinned Western support for democratization and became a pillar in the emerging international peacebuilding regime. It was validated in many parts of Latin America, where traditional oligarchies and military-led governments were replaced by democratically elected governments. In these cases, organized collective violence against or by the state became much less prevalent, although other forms of violence clearly did not. As a general proposition, however, the relationship between peace and democracy is not so clear-cut.

Statistical studies initially showed that non-democratic countries were much more likely than democratic ones to experience internal violence of almost all kinds, ranging from civil wars to political assassinations and terrorist bombings. Subsequent studies using similar statistical methods affirmed the point, but added a significant modification. Countries defined as autocratic are as stable as democracies when it comes to internal conflict. It is the countries in between, the 'anocracies' with both autocratic and democratic features, which are statistically most likely to experience internal violence (Hegre et al. 2001). The last finding challenges liberal theory. Even if democracies were stable and non-violent internally, the process of getting there, or being half-way there, would be associated with violence and instability. This pattern, of course, harmonized with the understanding of social change as necessarily a conflictual process, although the incidence of violence would vary.

Democratic transitions that establish new rules and practices in an already conflictual setting seemed particularly vulnerable to violence

(Sisk 2009). For instance, imminent democratization was an important factor in the conflict dynamic that led to the 1994 genocide in Rwanda. The Arusha peace agreement, which marked the end of the civil war between the Hutu and the Tutsi, laid down procedures for power-sharing in a transitional government, to be followed by general elections and a shift from a presidential to a parliamentary system. Hutu fears that the agreement would erode the near-monopoly on political power they had exercised since independence accelerated preparations for the physical elimination of the Tutsi, and the massacres started as soon as the agreement was signed. On a much smaller scale, but expressing a similar logic, was the devastating election violence in Kenya in 2007. In a polity organized around patron–client relationships that follow ethnic lines, the losers in a presidential election marked by fraud confronted the presumptive winners. Around 1,000 people were killed and up to half a million forced from their homes in the ensuing violence.

Key points

- The end of the cold war made space for the settlement of many protracted conflicts; notably in Cambodia, Guatemala, El Salvador, and Mozambique.
- New wars erupted, however, leading analysts to search for explanations in 'wars for profit' financed by natural resources, underdevelopment, state failure, and poor governance.
- Claims that these 'new wars' were qualitatively different from 'old wars' were disputed.

New Forces

The West versus militant Islam

The attacks on Washington and New York on 11 September 2001 triggered a globalized, US-led military offensive against militant Islamic movements and their supporters. Conducted mainly in the Middle East, South-West Asia, and the Horn of Africa, the 'war on terror' interacted with local conflicts to create increased tension, escalating violence, and, in some cases, major hostilities.

In Iraq, violent sectarian struggles erupted in the wake of the 2003 US invasion that brought down the rule of Saddam Hussein. In Afghanistan, the US intervention in late 2001 crushed the Taliban regime, which had imposed a harsh peace. By the time of the US intervention the Taliban controlled some 90 per cent of the countryside, although partly through 'franchise' to local leaders. The main Afghan opposition had regrouped in the north. This 'Northern Alliance' was the local partner in the US-led invasion and afterwards shared power with other Afghan factions in the new government installed in Kabul. Conflicts among the factions soon surfaced, however, partly on ethnic grounds. More serious was a revived insurgency led by the Taliban, who had regrouped in the mountainous border area between Afghanistan and Pakistan. By 2005, most of the south-eastern part of the country had become a war zone. The US and its allies continued to send more troops—estimated to reach 130,000 by mid-2010. The Taliban fought back, using 'asymmetrical warfare' such as suicide bombings and attacks on civilians to achieve its declared aim of driving out the 'infidel' invaders, defeating the government, and restoring Afghanistan as an Islamic emirate. The movement had sufficient support, both locally and from militant Islamists elsewhere, to seriously challenge the government and the international forces. The war escalated on the Pakistan side of the border as well. Prodded and aided by the United States, Pakistani military forces launched military offensives against militant Islamists in the large and traditionally autonomous border region. By early 2010, there had been no strategic breakthrough, only increasing hostilities.

Local conflicts elsewhere were also brought into the orbit of the 'war on terror'. The Philippine government received US assistance to help to defeat Muslim rebel movements that had been fighting for autonomy in the Muslim minority areas in the southern islands for a long time. In Somalia, the emergence of local Islamist bodies (the Islamic Courts Union) provoked an invasion of Ethiopian forces in December 2006, assisted by the United States. A new, 'moderate' Somali government was installed to help to deny Islamic militants the use of Somalia as a sanctuary. The government controlled little territory beyond the capital, however, while militant, undefeated factions of the Islamic Courts formed a new, hard-line movement (*Al-Shabaab*) to fight the government and its international supporters. In Yemen, the US government worked with the ruling head of state to defeat militant Islamists who opposed the government and reportedly had links with international terrorism and al-Qaeda. Overall, the pattern created a strong sense of déjà vu; except for the absence of a superpower on the other side, the process resembled the escalating conflict dynamic of the cold war.

Globalization

Economic globalization affects national development trajectories and hence the potential for conflict. In general, globalization of economic neoliberalism tends to sharpen inequalities within and among nations, but the relationships are typically subtle, indirect, and often unpredictable. In Asia, for instance, the financial crisis in 1997 produced populist leaders who appealed to peasants and

workers who were hard hit by the crisis. In Thailand, populism triggered protracted social conflict that turned violent. The story of the rise and fall of Prime Minister Thaksin Shinawatra, and of the conflictual forces his populism unleashed, illustrate the subtle ways in which a global financial crisis can reverberate locally.

Thaksin rode to power on the back of widespread discontent among peasants and the urban poor after the 1997 financial crisis. By the time the crisis hit, Thailand's open economy policy and invitation to foreign capital had produced significant shifts in the social structure. The middle class had developed. So had a substantial new urban 'class' working in the informal sector. The urban informal sector and farmers together represented some 65 per cent of the labour force, and a voting majority if they coalesced. When the financial crisis brought unemployment and agrarian debt, Thaksin rapidly reinvented himself from being a successful businessman to being an equally successful populist who addressed the grievances of farmers and the urban poor. Thaksin's ability to mobilize the masses for stunning election victories in 2001 and 2005 frightened the royalists and the growing middle class, however, and his corrupt business practices (also on a legendary scale) made him vulnerable. In 2006 he was unseated by a military coup, forced into exile, and his very considerable financial assets were frozen. The conflict between Thaksin and his opponents and their respective supporters now turned into street politics that had an ugly violent side. Masses of red-shirts (Thaksin's supporters) alternated with yellow-shirts (the colour associated with the King) to occupy the streets, block vital communication areas (including airports) and lay siege to government offices. Bombs exploded, guns were fired, and economic losses mounted. When the street battles appeared inconclusive, Thaksin fought for a political comeback by exploiting long-standing tension between Thailand and neighbouring Cambodia, bringing the two countries to the brink of war in November 2009.

A decade after the Asian financial crisis, its downstream effects in Thailand had become clear. The crisis had crystallized social tensions, moved politics out of the parliament and into the street, and created enduring uncertainty about the future

relationship between the main institutions of the country—above all the role of the monarchy—and hence national stability.

Key points

- International sources of conflict in the developing world have changed. The US-led global 'war on terror' interacted with local tension to create major instability in much of the Muslim world, particularly in Iraq, Afghanistan, Pakistan, and the Horn of Africa.

- Financial crises associated with economic globalization created instability and political havoc in several Asian countries.

Post-Conflict Peacebuilding

The end of the cold war opened up space for new forms of international activities. In the Western industrialized world, there was renewed interest in ending conflicts and building peace in the developing world, but also greater opportunities for military intervention regardless of motive (which ranged from humanitarian concerns to neo-imperial interests). A reinvigorated UN engaged itself early in 'peacebuilding' efforts to end wars that had been fuelled by the rivalry among the superpowers. The UN was actively involved in all the major peace negotiations that took place in the aftermath of the cold war. This way, the UN laid the foundation for what became into an international peacebuilding regime.

The then UN Secretary-General Boutros Boutros-Ghali had defined the agenda in a 1992 document called *The Agenda for Peace*. A long decade later, the international peacebuilding regime had expanded massively. The UN had by 2008 more than fifty active peace operations around the world, most of them multi-dimensional with a wide range of military, political, economic, and legal support functions. A UN Peacebuilding Commission had been established to closely direct and monitor

peacebuilding in select countries. Traditional development agencies had reshaped some of their activities as peacebuilding and launched programmes early in post-war transitions. Both the World Bank and the UNDP established special organizational units to deal with post-conflict or conflict-prevention programs.

'Peacebuilding' had by this time come to mean an increasingly standardized package of post-war aid, designed to provide security in the initial phase, to promote and monitor demilitarization of the ex-belligerent armies and factions, to assist refugees to return, to help to restart or kick-start the economy, to help to restore or reform political institutions and the holding of democratic elections, to promote the establishment of rule of law, and to strengthen institutions to establish and monitor human rights, sometimes including accountability mechanisms for war crimes and massive human rights violations perpetrated during the conflict. The package was developed by the major donors and aid agencies, the international financial institutions (the World Bank, the International Monetary Fund, the regional development banks), and the UN specialized agencies (especially UNDP, WFP, UNHCR) as well as the UN Secretariat. It was further streamlined by international organizations such as the OECD, which started harmonizing guidelines for aid from the rich, industrialized states to peacebuilding activities.

There was some flexibility in the peacebuilding system, including significant innovations towards a minimalist approach. In Nepal, for instance, the UN peace operation after the ten-year civil war between the state and the Maoists (1996–2006) was a small operation with a narrow mandate focused on monitoring the cantonment of the opposing armies before and during the scheduled parliamentary elections, assisting with the elections, and monitoring human rights. There were no armed peacekeepers, in deference to the Nepalese, who insisted on national ownership of the peace process, and the Indian government, which did not want UN peacekeepers in its immediate neighbourhood. The important function of monitoring the ex-belligerents was undertaken by a small number of international observers, spread thinly around the countryside and armed with only a UN insignia on their blue caps. As a confidence-building measure, small teams consisting of a Maoist, a government soldier, and a UN observer visited villages to visibly demonstrate that the war was over. The overall structure was innovative in the UN system, and effective and cost-efficient on the ground by helping to ensure that the critical period leading up to the elections was largely peaceful.

The peacebuilding regime was influenced by the literature that had developed on the causes of war in the 1990s. Broadly, it was assumed that if the causes of war were to be found in poorly functioning state institutions, economic stagnation and unemployment, lack of democracy, or ethnic polarization, then peacebuilding had to remedy these conditions by, first, helping to provide security and then assisting in creating strong, yet democratic political institutions, a modern national army, a justice sector reflecting the rule of law, rapid economic growth in a market economy, and privatization if the state had been a major economic actor. The urgency of comprehensive reconstruction of war-torn societies as a means to prevent further conflict was heightened by influential but weakly substantiated claims that half of all post-conflict societies tend to return to war within five years (Suhrke and Samset 2007).

How do we assess the impact on peace of this diverse and vast set of activities? Quantitative studies suggest that the post-conflict package tends to stabilize peace at least in the sense of preventing a relapse into full-scale war (Doyle and Sambanis 2006). Historical analysis of the capacity of the UN system to meet the enormous challenges of peacebuilding confirms that peace operations usually have stabilizing functions, but note problems of legitimacy and effectiveness (Berdal 2009). Case studies can be marshalled on either side of the balance sheet. Insider criticism from within the UN system recognizes that a greater sense of local ownership of the reconstruction and peacebuilding process must be achieved if peace is to be sustainable, as the UN Secretary-General's 2009 *Report on Peacebuilding* concludes. Outside critics stress that intrusive missions have counter-productive effects and that the 'liberal peace' paradigm, which currently frames peacebuilding as currently practised, is more likely to generate conflict than peace given the unsettled conditions of countries emerging from internal strife (Newman, Richmond, and Paris, 2009). A much more radical critique claims that the basic function of peacebuilding is to manage the effects of economic exclusion of the developing world that threaten Western interests in the form of refugee flows, transnational crime, epidemic diseases, and terrorism. As formulated by Mark Duffield (2001), peacebuilding in this perspective is a security intervention by the developed world to control and contain the global poor.

Key points

- After the end of the cold war, international peacebuilding became an increasingly standardized package, which included economic and political liberalization, administrative reform and institution-building, and the holding of elections.

- Critics argued that peacebuilding interventions are not tailored to local context, often generate instability, and fail to address underlying problems of global inequity.

Conclusion

This chapter has surveyed different phases of conflict in the developing world, starting with the independence struggle. The decolonization itself was a major driver of violence, although far from all transfers of power took a violent form. The decades of the cold war saw local conflict dynamics shaped in decisive ways by the ideological and political competition between the communist and the capitalist world, with devastating effects on local societies. Continued violence in developing countries in the post-cold war period raised new questions about the causes of these wars, including their relationship to natural resource exploitation, 'failed states' and poor governance. Yet also these wars were profoundly shaped by global political and economic developments, only more subtly. During the 1990s, novel international interventions in the form of 'peacebuilding' emerged as a concerted strategy to manage violence. The international peacebuilding regime was largely premised on the assumption that the main causes of conflict in the developing world were internal, in other words, a function of their underdevelopment. As this chapter has shown, however, the international setting of internal conflict is critically important, and an internalist perspective alone can therefore not be the basis for sound analysis and appropriate response.

 Questions

1. What were the most important factors determining whether colonized countries experienced a peaceful or violent transition to independence?

2. In what ways did the cold war impact on violent conflict in the developing world?

3. Was there a shift in the nature and patterns of conflict in the developing world after the end of the cold war, and if so, how can it be explained?

4. How can attention to economic factors add to the understanding of conflict?

5. What are the assumptions of peacebuilding interventions regarding how to reduce violence and consolidate peace?

6. What has been the significance of religion in violence that takes place in the context of the global 'war on terror'?

ASTRI SUHRKE AND TORUNN WIMPELMANN CHAUDHARY

Further reading

■ Cramer, C. (2006), *Civil War is Not a Stupid Thing: Accounting for Violence in Developing Countries* (London: Hurst & Co.). Critically examines the assumptions that violent conflict is inimical to development.

■ Kaldor, M. (1999), *New and Old Wars: Organised Violence in a Global Era* (Cambridge: Polity Press). Develops the controversial argument that wars after the cold war are fundamentally different from previous wars.

■ Paris, R. (2004), *At War's End* (New York: Cambridge University Press). Critically assesses the impact of economic and political liberalization on post-war peacebuilding.

■ Richards, P. (2004), *No Peace, No War: An Anthropology of Contemporary Armed Conflicts* (Oxford: James Currey). An anthropological perspective on the nature of conflict that considers the continuity in structures between a state of war and a state of peace.

■ Zolberg, A., et al. (1989), *Escape from Violence: Conflict and the Refugee Crisis in the Developing World* (New York: Oxford University Press). Examines the nature of conflict in the developing world before and during the cold war.

Web links

■ www.hrdgroup.org/humna-security-reports/human-security-report.aspx   Focusing on people rather than states, the Human Security Reports examine global and regional trends in armed conflict and other forms of organized violence.

■ www.un.org/peace/peacebuilding   For UN Peacebuilding Commission efforts to garner international support for nationally owned and led peacebuilding efforts.

Online Resource Centre

For additional material and resources, please visit the Online Resource Centre at:
www.oxfordtextbooks.co.uk/orc/burnell3e/

14

Democratization

Peter Burnell

Overview

The 1980s and early 1990s saw a wave of change embracing political liberalization and democratization in Latin America, Africa, and Asia. However, by the turn of the new millennium many doubts and reservations had begun to surface, and attention turned to the quality of democracy, democratic erosion, and authoritarian persistence. This chapter elucidates the idea of democratization, summarizes recent trends, and compares different understandings of democratic consolidation. Relations between democratization and development provide a central theme, not least because of worries that social and economic problems could undermine democratic progress. Some implications of globalization and international democracy promotion are also raised.

Introduction

Democracy is an essentially contested concept. The long history of theorizing about its meaning provides few certainties about what democratization means. Clearly democratization refers to a process of change; most writers conceive of it as a journey without end. Obviously it is not a new phenomenon. In a widely used metaphor, Huntington (1991) characterized the extension of democracy beginning around 1974 as the **third wave of democracy**, the two earlier waves (1828–1926; 1943–62) each being followed by a reverse wave. For some countries the experience has been attempted redemocratization following earlier democratic failure(s). Examples include Argentina's return to elected civilian rule in 1983 and Uruguay, which had military-controlled civilian government from 1973 to 1985. Ghana, now resembling a stable liberal democracy, made successive earlier attempts to re-establish elected civilian government following military rule in 1966–69, 1972–79, and 1981–92.

Regime Transformation, Democracy, and Democratization

Democratization is not a unilinear movement from political authoritarianism to democracy. The simple dichotomization of regime types is an oversimplification. There are different kinds of authoritarian regime: monarchy, as in some Gulf states; many examples of personal dictatorships, military-bureaucratic rule, and *de jure* one-party states, as in Tanzania and Zambia before the 1990s (see Brooker 2009). Authoritarian and semi-authoritarian regimes can enjoy a measure of legitimacy in the eyes of some citizens. They draw on such sources as religious beliefs, as in theocratic Iran and Saudi Arabia, nationalism and anti-imperialism (resounding strongly in China and Cuba for example). Also a conviction may exist that the status quo serves personal security and material well-being better than the likely political alternatives, which could mean social conflict and political instability. Invidious comparisons with political experiments elsewhere may strengthen the conviction. Turmoil in post-Saddam Iraq bolstered conservative instincts in neighbouring Jordon and Syria. Even so, a plausible claim is that no competing political ideology to democracy currently shows itself capable of achieving comparable acceptance throughout the world, even though some rivals have strong local or even regional roots, Islamist political beliefs for example. Ottaway (2009) argues that even socialism no longer presents a potent global ideological challenge, notwithstanding the persistence of other kinds of *political* challenge to democratization.

Similarly, authoritarian breakdown can produce a variety of possible outcomes: protracted civil war came to Angola and Mozambique following independence; 'warlordism' and the state's disintegration overtook Somalia in the 1990s; or the installation of a different kind of authoritarian regime or a diminished sub-type such as **competitive authoritarianism**, in which although formal democratic institutions may appear to exist they are regularly ignored or violated (Levitsky and Way 2002: 52). Robert Mugabe's Zimbabwe is an example. Regime transformation can lead to several distinct intermediate hybrid types, prefaced by labels like 'proto', 'semi', 'quasi', 'limited', 'partial', 'defective', 'low-intensity', and so on — all examples of what Collier and Levitsky (1997) called 'democracy with adjectives'. In large countries, and/or federal systems, democratic unevenness can occur across provinces or municipalities.

Democracy, from the Greek for 'rule by the people', has been called an inherently debatable and changeable idea. Yet ideas resembling the model of polyarchical democracy (**polyarchy**) advanced by the American political scientist Robert Dahl in the 1970s (see Box 14.1) have dominated much of the democratization discourse, at the expense of deliberative and emancipatory or more radical social ideas. Polyarchy centres on two main pillars: public contestation and the right to participate. Liberal democracy, which is akin to polyarchy, remains the most commonly cited yardstick for judging the progress of democratization, and is generally believed to avoid the **fallacy of electoralism**. Diamond (1996), a prominent contributor to the literature, usefully distinguished between liberal democracy, in which there is extensive provision for political and civic pluralism as well as for individual and group freedoms, and mere 'electoral democracy', in which civil freedoms are less prized and minority rights are insecure even if elections seem largely free and fair.

How do we know which countries are democracies? Many scholars consult Freedom House ratings of freedom. Freedom House (FH) is a US non-profit organization that conducts annual evaluations of political rights and civil liberties throughout the world. It defines democracy, at minimum, as a political system in which people choose their authoritative leaders freely from among competing groups and individuals who are not chosen by the government. Freedom is the chance to act spontaneously in a variety of fields outside the control of government and other centres of potential domination. Democracies are judged either free or partly free, as measured along a seven-point scale (1–2.5 = *free*; 3–5 = *partly free*; 5.5–7 = *not free*). Although the FH methodology has attracted criticism, the ratings are widely used for depicting global trends in democratization and making national and inter-temporal comparisons. They are convenient and accessible; alternatives like the Polity IV codings and the Ibrahim Index of African Governance are also instructive, but not flawless. For Diamond, Freedom House's 'free rating' is the best available indicator of liberal democracy.

> **Box 14.1** Dahl on Democracy
>
> Citizens must have unimpaired opportunities to formulate their preferences, signify them and have them weighted equally. This requires certain institutional guarantees: freedom to form and join organizations; freedom of expression; right to vote; eligibility for public office; right of leaders to compete for support; alternative sources of information; free and fair elections; institutions for making government policies depend on votes and other expressions of preference.
>
> (Dahl 1971)

Trends

The data indicate that, following a dramatic initial increase in democracies following the start of the 'third wave', the number of liberal democracies levelled off by the early 1990s. While some countries, Vietnam, and Libya for instance, were never caught up in the tide, several emerging democracies soon began to show signs of democratic backsliding or 'hollowing out'. FH data suggest that by 2008 many countries were seeing freedom erode even while remaining within the same category, such as 'partly free', The Gambia and Fiji for example.

Abstracting just the developing countries from FH's 2008 Global Survey reveals the following regional patterns.

- Africa including North Africa: Ten free countries; 25 partly free; 17 not free—22 countries were judged to meet the conditions for electoral democracy.

- Asia–Pacific (including China but exclusive of former Soviet Central Asian republics): Eleven free countries (including several small island states); 15 partly free; eight not free—14 countries were judged to meet the conditions for electoral democracy.

- Latin America and the Caribbean: Twenty-two free countries; ten partly free; one (Cuba) not free—32 countries were judged to meet the conditions for electoral democracy.

- Middle East (excluding Israel): none free; six partly free; six not free—no countries appeared to meet the conditions for electoral democracy.

Key points

- The dichotomy of authoritarian and democratic regimes ignores the variety of non/pre-democratic regime types and different possible outcomes of political transition.

- As an idea democratization is beholden to the fact that the very meaning of democracy itself is contested.

- Democratization's progress in the developing world has been uneven and now seems to have reached a plateau, exhibiting marked regional variations and some instances of decline.

Democratization as Process

Conceptual distinctions between political liberalization, democratic transition, and democratic consolidation are commonplace, but there is no necessary or inevitable sequence of events. As a prelude to 'political opening', authoritarian breakdown can happen in different ways—gradual or sudden, violent or peaceful—and may range from moderate to absolute. Political liberalization usually refers to a top-down process: political leaders aim to maintain power for themselves, reluctant to accept that institutionalized uncertainty over electoral outcomes should be the determining principle of who governs (and the possibility of alternation in office that implies). Liberalization advances political freedoms less than some civil liberties. In contrast democratization introduces arrangements for genuinely competitive elections. Liberalization can become stalled rather than lead on to democratization. Also, it can go into reverse. Conversely, largely free elections might be introduced without first establishing the rule of law, full executive accountability, and the flourishing civil society that are so important to democracy (see Chapter 10)—or what has been

called **democratization backwards**. This occasions what Zakaria (1997) called 'illiberal democracy', citing Iran and President Fujimori's Peru as examples. Liberalization and democratic opening can also happen simultaneously, where authoritarian collapse is sudden and complete, as in apartheid South Africa. Rulers who at first allow some liberalization without intending to embrace democracy may lose control of the momentum, overtaken by demands for full democratic opening. But in countries like Egypt limited political liberalization under President Mubarak has proven an effective strategy for preventing genuine democratization.

A related distinction made by some analysts is that democratization 'comes from below', and involves political, although not necessarily violent, struggle. This has some synergy with the idea of people power (see Chapter 11). However some of the earliest 'third wave' cases of redemocratization in Latin America were what have been called **pacted transitions**, negotiated by the political elites. So there is not just one but several different routes to democratic reform: evidence about which ones provide the most durable change is not clear-cut. Pro-democratic alliances that bridge different elements within the ruling elite and include civil society activists offer an optimum combination.

Democratic consolidation

Just as there can be political transition without transition to democracy so there can be democratic transition without democratic consolidation. Conversely democratic decline need not lead to full-blown autocracy. But how do we recognize democratic consolidation? Answers range from equating consolidation with longevity to democratic 'deepening' or qualitative improvements in such indicators as the rule of law, minority rights, and gender issues (see Chapter 9). Schedler (1998) recommended restricting consolidation to two 'negative' notions: avoiding democratic breakdown and avoiding democratic erosion. Put differently, democratic consolidation means an expectation of regime continuity—and nothing else. A minimal definition like this maximizes the number of developing countries qualifying for democratic consolidation. More demanding accounts that rest on democratic 'widening'—the incorporation of democratic principles in public *and* private spaces in economic and social arenas like the family—impose criteria that few countries satisfy. Somewhere in between lie accounts that draw heavily on the people's political attitudes and perceptions, an example being an Afrobarometer study (2009) of popular demands for and judgements about the supply of democracy in 20 African countries over 1999–2008. This found unconsolidated hybrid systems and one consolidating autocracy (Lesotho) but no consolidated democracies (defined as a sustained balance between popular demand and perceived supply at levels of 70 per cent and more). Botswana came closest. While the literature's concern with what makes for 'good democracy' (or, conversely, 'defective democracy') can look premature for developing countries in which the regime is still undergoing change, some developing world democracies

like South Africa compare favourably with OECD democracies in terms of female political representation—surely an important indicator of quality.

More significant for democratic consolidation than simple longevity may be the ability to withstand shocks—whether generated either at home or abroad, either directly such as in an attempted military coup or indirectly through dramatic deterioration in the economic climate. India's democracy, for example, shows great resilience in the face of terrorist provocations, whereas recurring conflict involving civilian elites, the military, and monarchy—much of it class-based—has repeatedly undermined democracy in Thailand. One thesis is that democratic deepening strengthens resilience. However, if a new democracy has yet to be put to the test can we know whether it is consolidated and that expectations of continuity are justified? And what counts as a sufficient test? For some African countries the growing food insecurity that will originate with global warming may well threaten political stability and democracy's survival in the coming years.

A more easily applied notion of consolidation is Huntington's (1991: 266–7) double turnover test. This requires that a party that took office after a democratic election should relinquish office after losing a comparable election without seeking to resist or overturn the result. This would exclude Botswana, where the Botswana Democratic Party has yet to lose an election since gaining independence (1966). A more persuasive view sees consolidation as being achieved once democracy has become the **only game in town**. This requires an appropriate attitudinal shift, not just a temporary behavioural accommodation. On that basis Venezuela, after 1958 one of Latin America's longest continuous democracies, failed the test in 2002, when the army briefly deposed the elected president, Hugo Chávez. Ironically President Chávez's return and accumulation of power in recent years make critics doubt Venezuela's democratic credentials now (in 2009 FH rated Venezuela only partly free, with a deteriorating trajectory). Chávez's populist and left-leaning pretensions that lambaste US imperialism may be one factor here, but more fundamentally institutional changes have lessened executive accountability. The February 2009 referendum's abolition of term limits for all elected offices is symptomatic.

Democrats regard **legitimacy** as one of democracy's most distinguished properties. For Diamond, democratic consolidation is legitimation. Legitimacy is like reinforcing glue: it helps democracy to survive shocks. Indeed, we could say a democracy truly consolidates when it ceases to rely on 'performance legitimacy' (acceptance grounded on meeting society's wants or needs), and achieves principled or 'intrinsic legitimacy'—grounded in acceptance of and respect for democracy's fundamental values, as well as adherence to the procedures that these inform: free and fair elections for instance. Intrinsic legitimacy shelters democracy against such failings as weak developmental performance—India's experience after independence. In a settled democracy discontent with the performance of government is exacted on the government, by peacefully removing it from office at the polls. So far public support for many of Africa's new democracies appears to have weathered economic hardship (Bratton, Mattes, and Gyimah-Boadi 2004). But in Latin America one view is that neither populist demagoguery nor the military pose the main threat to democracy now but rather a 'continuing mediocre performance—the inability of democratic governments to meet the most important needs and demands of their citizens' (Hakim 2003: 122). This becomes more potent when combined with popular perceptions of bad governance and massive corruption.

In conclusion, the conceptual baggage of democratic transition and consolidation may be too rigid a framework for analysing what in reality are multi-faceted, multi-dimensional and multi-directional processes of political change. In practice these may resemble variable geometry: some of democracy's ingredients could be moving in one direction (possibly at different speeds); others moving in the opposite direction (again at different speeds); and yet others standing still. For example a stable competitive party system may emerge even as civic activism decreases from the heights that successfully brought down an autocracy. A more appropriate assessment is offered by the idea of democratic audit elaborated for the International Institute for Democracy and Electoral Assistance (IDEA) by David Beetham and colleagues, in the *Handbook on Democracy Assessment* (2002; later revisions are incorporated in publications on assessing democracy's quality, posted on IDEA's website). It groups issues under: citizenship, law, and rights; representative and accountable government; civil society and popular participation; and international dimensions. The methodology is intended for universal use and application by the people of any country. So far assessments including El Salvador, Bangladesh, South Korea, Malawi, and Nepal have been published.

Key points

- A minority of developing countries are liberal democracies although many more approximate to electoral democracies.

- Democratic consolidation has been defined in different ways, with implications for which developing countries qualify. The quality of democracy is as important as its longevity.

- The idea of democracy assessment offers a potentially powerful tool of comparative analysis and self-assessment.

- We must not exaggerate democratization's usefulness as a lens through which to examine politics in the developing world: other political variables such as the strength of the state and quality of governance are very important.

Explaining how democratization occurs and why it takes particular forms generates considerable debate. Explanations of consolidation can be expected to diverge from democratic transition. Similarly, the reasons that illuminate stalled transition could differ from those that explain a democracy's collapse, which may connect to state failure, or authoritarian persistence through brutal oppression, as in Myanmar.

One approach to explaining different experiences with democratization emphasizes the impact of historical, political, and other legacies and **path dependence**. At its most elaborate, path dependence claims that the nature of the pre-existing regime and the mode used to change it influence the sequel and, ultimately, can determine a new democracy's chances of survival. This confirms why it is important to distinguish between types of authoritarian and semi-authoritarian regime as well as to establish if there were any previous, failed attempts to democratize. Like much theorizing about democratization, path dependence provides valuable insights more for some countries than for others (see Box 14.2). Failure to incorporate women on anything like equal terms in the power structures that emerge following civil conflict, even where they contributed significantly to the struggles for change is not untypical, but can often be explained by in-depth historical and sociological analysis.

One of the most durable ideas is that national unity 'must precede all the other phases of democratization' (Rustow 1970: 351). By national unity Rustow meant 'the vast majority of citizens . . . must have no doubt or mental reservation as to which political community they belong to' (ibid.). Some developing countries lack this simple condition. Indeed, transition to democracy may be cherished as a means to manage or resolve violent and endemic conflict between groups, but democracy's advance can itself occasion increased (violent) domestic conflict. Minorities harbouring fears of a majority tyranny may be stirred to demand national self-determination for themselves. Sri Lanka's history has been one of both democracy and long-running civil war between the Sinhalese and Tamil separatists in the north. The Tamils were defeated militarily in May 2009 but the prospects for liberal democracy in Sri Lanka, which Freedom House still calls a partly free electoral democracy in 2009, remain unclear.

Box 14.2 Rustow's Methodological Propositions

- The factors that keep a democracy stable may not be the ones that brought it into existence; explanations of democracy must distinguish between function and genesis.

- Not all causal links run from beliefs and attitudes to action; the flow can be in both directions.

- The genesis of democracy need not be geographically uniform; there may be many roads to democracy.

- The genesis of democracy need not be temporally uniform; different factors may become crucial during successive phases.

- Correlation is not the same as causation; a genetic theory must concentrate on the latter.

- Not all causal links run from social and economic to political factors; the flow can be in both directions.

- The genesis of democracy need not be socially uniform; even in the same place and time the attitudes that promote it may not be the same for politicians and citizens.

(Rustow 1970: 346)

More broadly, the literature explaining democratization can be distinguished into accounts emphasizing structure and accounts that dwell on agency. The first investigates the 'conditions' and even preconditions whereby democratic trends are facilitated or actively promoted, or frustrated. The second focuses on process, highlighting the role of actors, as well as recognizing the importance of institutions broadly defined (see Chapter 3). The impact of actors may be greater at key turning points, such as democratic transitions or their timing, than over the long haul. All things considered, democratization is perhaps best understood as a complex interaction that links structural constraints and opportunities to the shaping of contingent choice (Karl 1990). Waylen (2007) explores the distinctive politics of engineering democratic transition through the mobilization of women and related institutional design, drawing on Latin America and South Africa in particular.

Socio-economic conditions

Lipset's seminal article on the social requisites of democracy first published in 1959 (revisited in 1994) presents a powerful theory of the positive relationship between the persistence of stable democracy and socio-economic modernization. 'Requisites' are not *pre*requisites or *pre*conditions: shared prosperity does not have be established in advance, for democratic transition can occur amid poverty and economic backwardness. But the idea that material progress enhances the chances of extending democratic longevity continues to be strongly supported by developing world evidence. In contrast, where economic misfortune persists and especially where the burdens that women endure are compounded by the existence of many female-headed households, the drawbacks for democracy and its quality in poor societies are particularly evident.

Only relatively recently did social scientists begin to investigate seriously the possibility that development could be the dependent variable and treat democracy as the independent or 'causal' factor. The idea that certain sorts of freedoms, notably economic freedoms, are beneficial to wealth creation goes back a long way, to Adam Smith (1723–90). But for many years the view that developing countries face a cruel choice proved very persuasive. Either countries could do what was necessary to develop their economies, mainly by concentrating on saving and investing to expand the productive capital stock, or they could emulate the political systems of the West. The former requires government to take unpopular decisions, such as enforcing abstinence from current consumption. Authoritarian regimes that are well insulated from social pressures have an advantage. In contrast the structure of political incentives posed by competitive party politics appears biased towards raising popular expectations about immediate consumption and public welfare spending. Politicians running for office will promise 'jam today', at the expense of doing what is needful for 'jam tomorrow'. In the long run, economic decline beckons — the experience of Argentina for much of the second half of twentieth century, culminating in a spectacular financial crisis in December 2001.

The moral seemed to be that democracy is a luxury that poor countries can ill afford. Only after development has progressed beyond a certain threshold does sustainable democracy appear more viable. The term wealth theory of democracy captures the idea. The dramatic economic performance of East Asian tiger economies like Taiwan and South Korea (see Chapter 22b) in the cold war era followed by successful democratic transition subsequently appear to bear out the general theory. Critics, however, point to examples of developing world democracies like Mauritius (since independence, 1968) and Costa Rica (a democracy since 1899 with only brief interruptions in 1917 and 1948) that have a generally good record of economic and social development. East Asia's examples of an undeniably successful deployment of the authoritarian model, which are continued today by Vietnam and China (see Chapter 23b), perhaps are the real exceptions. Moreover, rising prosperity does not guarantee transition to democracy. In oil-rich **rentier states**, like those in the Gulf, the manipulation of rent-funded public spending by authoritarian regimes, able to avoid imposing heavy taxation, looks quite durable. But this 'resource curse' seems not to apply where democracy is already established, as Botswana, blessed with diamond revenues as well as income from cattle-raising, illustrates.

The significance of development for democratization

There is much statistical evidence that democracies can survive even in the poorest nations especially *if* they can generate development with widely distributed benefits while meeting certain other conditions (Przeworski et al. 1996). But what is it about modernization and development that is so significant for democratization? Is it primarily a matter of resources, or a case of transforming attitudes, values, and patterns of behaviour, or the changes in class structure that come with capitalist development in particular? Or does the connection have more to do with development's integration of society into global structures and norms? Different theories emerge from concentrating on different aspects.

- Democratic institutions are expensive and demand high organizational commitment and public involvement that affluent, well-educated societies can more easily provide. Technological and economic progress improves the physical infrastructure of political communication.

- Social modernization erodes old values that inculcate deference to traditional authority, and generates self-confidence; people come to see themselves more as citizens than subjects. This increases the constituencies for rational-legal authority. Pragmatic values sympathetic to the politics of compromise and consensus lying at the heart of the 'democratic way' supplant non-negotiable values like exclusive ethnic loyalties that divide society. Integration into the global economy also brings exposure to the liberal and democratic values already enjoyed elsewhere (demonstration effect).

- There is a well-known aphorism 'no bourgeois, no democracy'. Development breaks the exclusive power of feudal landlords. Capitalist development creates a plurality of potential centres of power and influence independent of the state. A property-owning middle class has a vested interest in checking the arbitrary use of executive power; it has the economic means and know-how to organize pressure for the redistribution of power. There is a caveat, however: economic growth can widen the economic inequalities that sustain inequalities of power. Middle-class elements will defend an illiberal or undemocratic regime if they believe it serves their interests, for instance by providing stability. Singapore, judged only partly free by Freedom House, is an example.

- Industrialization and urbanization help an organized working class to mobilize mass support to demand rights for ordinary people. Thus Rueschemeyer, Stephens, and Stephens (1992) disavow that democracy is created solely by the bourgeoisie, emphasizing instead the progressive role of the working class acting together with middle-class elements. The relevance of this insight grows as more developing countries in Asia and Latin America become prominent industrial manufacturers. In Brazil, for example, the political base of President Luiz da Silva lies in the labour movement. Elsewhere, in Africa organized labour is a major weakness, with the notable exception of South Africa where the ruling African National Congress is formally allied with the trade union movement, and in the Arab world it is usually tightly controlled by the state.

The ambivalent relationship of market economy and democratic polity

A frequent assumption is that the market constitutes a necessary but not sufficient condition of democracy: there have been authoritarian regimes with market economies (President Pinochet's Chile, for example) but no examples of non-market democracies. In reality the relationship is ambivalent. As Beetham (1997) explained, there are some negative effects associated with the virtues of the market; even its positive points must be qualified (Box 14.3). This issue can be reformulated in terms of the effects on democracy's quality. Thus for example for Rueschemeyer (2004: 89): 'To deepen democracy in the direction of greater

political equality requires systematic and strong policies promoting social and economic equality. The quality of democracy, then, depends on social democracy, on long-sustained policies of social protection and solidarity.' This is especially pertinent to countries like Brazil and South Africa that historically are among the most unequal of all societies, and even to India where a substantial middle class develops alongside a large number of extremely poor people.

Box 14.3 Positive and Negative Connections between Democracy and the Market

Positive connections

- The more extensive the state, the more difficult it is to subject to public accountability or societal control.

- The more that is at stake in elections, the greater is the incentive for participants to compromise the process, or reject the outcome. Market freedoms and political freedoms are mutually supportive: both require the rule of law, and in ensuring one ensures it for both.

- Sovereignty of consumer and voter both rest on the same anti-paternalist principle.

- Market economy is necessary for long-term economic growth, which assists durable democracy.

Negative connections

- Independence of the market from the state distances the economy from democratic control.

- Free market competition intensifies socio-economic inequalities, which produce political inequalities and compromise democratic institutions.

- Market dispositions undermine the integrity of the democratic public sphere: market choices prevail over political choices; the logic of private self-interest colonizes the public sphere.

(Beetham 1997)

Political culture

The perceived significance of political culture dates from Almond and Verba's *The Civic Culture: Political Attitudes and Democracy in Five Nations* (1965). **Political culture** embodies the attitudes, beliefs, and values that underlie a political system. For Almond and Verba 'civic culture' supports democracy. After years during which the concept came under fire, democratization scholars

now agree that sustainable democracy requires a special set of values such as tolerance, mutual respect, a willingness to trust in fellow citizens (**social capital**), not just acquaintance with democracy's procedures. Observers pore over the public attitude surveys such as Latinobarometer and Afrobarometer (2009); analysts dissect discrepancies between support for democracy and dissatisfaction with the institutions and political leadership (Doorenspleet 2009).

The principal constituents of a democratic political culture and relations among them and their requisites are all contested. For instance, it was once thought that the Protestant ethic made famous by the German sociologist Max Weber is more favourable to democracy than are Roman Catholicism and Confucianism, yet evidence from Latin America and Asia now refutes this. An especially topical debate is over whether it is the Muslim world not the Arab world that offers relatively inhospitable terrain for democracy, given the poor scores for political and civil liberties in the Middle East and the seeming incompatibility of ideas of popular sovereignty and the sovereign power of God. However, the large consolidating democracies of Turkey and Indonesia contradict any simple conclusion; different versions of Islam have different implications for democracy. But attitudes towards women's rights and female equality are quite critical here: the political advancement of women generally in Muslim countries seems especially difficult, but not impossible (see Chapter 9). Progress depends as much on overcoming culturally and historically embedded forms of disadvantage as on reforming the institutions of government such as introducing female quotas in legislative representation (Cornwall and Goetz 2005).

If something like civic culture is essential to democracy, is it a prerequisite or can it be allowed to develop later and, if so, what can make it happen? This not only raises the idea of civic education but also sparks other questions about whose culture is most important, particularly in democratization's early stages: the elite level or the mass? One argument is that the primary threat to new democracies comes from the people in power, especially 'old generation' politicians who assume democratic pretensions reluctantly but not from conviction, Kenya's President arap Moi being an example. Bermeo's (2003) argument drawing on Europe and the Americas in the 1960s and 1970s is that small elite coalitions, not the ordinary people, bear major responsibility for democratic failure.

This seems to be borne out by broader developing world experience, especially where high-level corruption and the jealous possession of power by a few (as in Zimbabwe), great institutional or class-based privilege (as with Guatemala's military and wealthy elite) persist unchanged.

Institutional crafting

Chapter 3 introduced institutional perspectives on politics in developing countries. Clearly institutional design can have significant consequences for the distribution of power generally and democracy's quality and sustainability specifically. Formal organizational changes may barely affect the way in which things actually work, if inherited **informal institutions** or patterns of behaviour like patron–clientelism look impervious to change (and prevent whatever economic benefits might otherwise flow from formal democratic transition, as Lewis 2009 argues with respect to Africa). Moreover, as Chapter 13 suggests, tensions between crafting democracy's institutional architecture on the one side and the larger imperatives of peacebuilding and state-(re)building or their requisites on other side can quickly surface in societies needing to escape internal violence (Burnell 2009). The recent troubled history of Iraq and ongoing turmoil in Afghanistan, where fraudulent voting in President Karzai's re-election in 2009 attracted strong international condemnation, are illustrative.

Two institutional concerns that have attracted special attention in new democracies are: first, the balance of power and mutual oversight among the executive, legislature, judiciary, and other constituents of a 'self-restraining state'; second, elections and party systems. A self-restraining state embraces multiple institutional mechanisms for making government accountable (see Schedler, Diamond, and Plattner 1999). Latin American experience implies that presidentialism is more likely to be unstable than parliamentary democracy when combined with vigorous multi-partyism, but recent thinking (Kapstein and Converse 2009) warns against such simple correlations, by re-emphasizing that what matters most is the effectiveness of strong institutional constraints on executive power.

O'Donnell (1994) proposed the category **delegative democracy**, much cited in a Latin American context. It rests on the premise that whoever wins election to the presidency behaves as if they are entitled to govern as they think fit—constrained only by the hard facts of existing power relations and constitutional limits, which they may attempt to have removed or relaxed. O'Donnell distinguished between vertical accountability, which makes government accountable to the ballot box and could even be extended to more direct forms of societal accountability, through the activities of civil society (see Chapters 10 and 11), and judicial power to enforce the rule of law—even, indeed especially against democratically elected governments. This last, horizontal accountability more generally, tends to be weak in delegative democracies and virtually non-existent in illiberal non-democracies.

Elections and parties

Although in some countries people power has been credited with bringing down discredited rulers,

President Ferdinand Marcos in the Philippines for example (Chapter 11), and a vibrant civil society is deemed essential to healthy democracy (Chapter 10), organized political parties remain indispensable too. A party system is defined by the number of parties and the relations between them, their relative size, and how much meaningful choice they present to the electorate. At minimum an effective party system furnishes government, and a competitive party system means there is some possibility of alternation in power.

In many emerging democracies the development of viable parties and the establishment of reasonably competitive party systems are proving to be challenging. In numerous African countries one party remains dominant, but there and elsewhere many parties serve as little more than vehicles for the personal ambitions of their leader, as in Nigeria. The parties are poorly anchored in society; they lack organizational strength and a sound financial footing other than through patronage from the state. Intra-party democracy is rare, and the equal participation of women unusual. These issues and wider political significance are elaborated in detail in Vicky Randall's study of political parties on the Online Resource Centre.

Key points

- Different dimensions and phases of democratic change require their own explanation.

- Economic development may be one of the best guarantors of durable democracy especially if the benefits are widely distributed, although the reasons are contested.

- The relationship of market-based or capitalist development to democratization is ambivalent.

- Institutional and cultural perspectives on democratization are complementary to more economistic explanations.

International Dimensions of Democratization

The end of the cold war and collapse of Soviet power help to explain the increase in agitation for political reform in the developing world from the late 1980s, although democracy's return to Latin

America was already well advanced. Now, however we see the growing economic and financial engagement of China (and India) with developing countries (see Chapter 23), and in international forums both China and Russia defend the principles of state sovereignty and non-interference in the internal politics of countries. These developments mean that growing attention should be paid to examining how domestic and international factors interact to affect politics inside developing countries.

External influences can work in many ways, such as by example, persuasion, and more direct involvement. The active engagement of prominent Western democracies in international democracy promotion is now well established, but the United Nations too has become a major actor—one that claims unique legitimacy—as in arranging practical support to the staging, monitoring, and observing of elections, especially valuable in new states and post-conflict situations. The United Nations Development Programme is a substantial funder of projects in democratic governance. In 2005 the UN launched a Democracy Fund, with India as a major sponsor, investing in civil society initiatives especially. By late 2009 the scope of UN involvement overall in democracy support was such that the Secretary-General issued a formal 'Guidance note on democracy'.

The influence exerted by developments in a region should not be ignored either. Several regional organizations have undertaken to encourage—and defend from domestic attack—democratic institutions, values, and practices in their member states. In Latin America the Organization of American States (OAS) sets out to uphold the Inter-American Democratic Charter (see Box 14.4). The African Union's (AU) New Partnership for Africa's Development (NEPAD) established the African Peer Review Mechanism (APRM), with a view to advancing both economic and democratic governance (Box 14.5). The OAS helped Venezuela to restore democracy after the 2002 military coup. Expectations of the AU's performance have yet to overcome the difficulty in bringing Zimbabwe's political malaise to a convincing end, where Mugabe's government has been hostile to the APRM.

Box 14.4 Key Issues for the Organization of American States

According to the Inter-American Democratic Charter of 2001: 'The peoples of the Americas have a right to democracy and their governments have an obligation to promote and defend it'. The Charter:

- reflects the political will and collective commitment of the Americas' democratic nations and defines what the OAS member countries agree are democracy's essential elements;

- responds directly to a mandate from the region's heads of state and government, who stated at the 2001 Summit of the Americas that the hemisphere needed to enhance its ability to strengthen democracy and respond when it is under threat;

- establishes procedures for when democracy has been ruptured, as in a coup, or is seriously altered and at risk;

- identifies how democracy can and should be strengthened and promoted in the hemisphere;

- under the terms of the Charter, OAS member states may seek advisory services or assistance from the OAS to strengthen their electoral institutions and processes.

(Extracts from Organization of American States, *Key OAS Issues*, 2005)

Box 14.5 NEPAD and Democracy

NEPAD's first stated *priority* is 'establishing the conditions for sustainable development by ensuring peace and security; democracy and good, political, economic and corporate governance; regional co-operation and integration; and capacity building'.

NEPAD's statement of *immediate desired outcomes*: 'Africa adopts and implements principles of democracy and good political economic governance, and the protection of human rights becomes further entrenched in every country.

'We undertake to work with renewed determination to enforce: the rule of law; the equality of all citizens before the law and the liberty of the individual; individual and collective freedoms, including the right to form and join political parties and trade unions, in conformity with the constitution; equality of opportunity for all; the inalienable right of the individual to participate by means of free, credible and democratic political processes in periodically electing their leaders for a fixed term of office;

and adherence to separation of powers, including the protection of the independence of the judiciary and of effective parliaments.

'Women have a central role to play in Africa's efforts at democracy, good governance and economic reconstruction.

'In support of democracy and the democratic process we will ensure that our respective national constitutions reflect the democratic ethos; promote political representation; enforce strict adherence to the position of the African Union on unconstitutional changes of government; strengthen and, where necessary, establish an appropriate electoral administration and oversight bodies in our respective countries and to provide the necessary resources and capacity to conduct elections which are free, fair and credible.'

(Extracts from *NEPAD in Brief* and *A Summary of NEPAD Action Plans: African Peer Review Mechanism*. For extracts on NEPAD on economic and corporate governance, see Box 15.2.)

Much of the attention paid to the international promotion of democracy, especially following the announcement of President George Bush's mission to advance freedom and democracy in the Middle East during his second term, has focused on the role of the West. Two approaches stand out: one attaches democratic, human rights, and governance **conditionalities** to offers of development aid and other concessions such as trade concessions; the other provides technical, financial, material, and symbolic support to democracy projects and programmes involving political parties, civil society, legislatures, and other institutions — namely **democracy assistance**. By and large democracy conditionalities have been found to be ineffective when faced by determined opposition. Even the more narrowly defined human rights conditions have failed to win concessions from autocrats like Myanmar's military. Democracy assistance, now worth over US$5 billion worldwide, has a mixed record. Although support to elections has long been considered insufficient, building durable capacity in civil society

too has often encountered difficulties (see Chapter 10): external involvement can easily compromise NGOs' independence, as has long been found in the world of international development cooperation too. A growing number of authoritarian and semi-authoritarian governments obstruct external assistance to pro-democracy groups and human rights campaigners; some, as in Sudan, have even denied access to assorted foreign humanitarian workers.

A third alternative, the coercive imposition of democracy is largely discredited. In fact the conflating of democracy promotion with **regime change** understood as ousting governments by force, as in Afghanistan (2001) and Iraq (2003), is believed to have harmed the cause of international democracy promotion. It gave authoritarian rulers a reason to stir nationalist sentiment and to utilize anti-imperialist rhetoric against even non-coercive democracy promotion from outside. A widely cited argument is that the density of a country's ties generally to the West, not Western leverage, is the most helpful to real and sustainable democratization

(Levitsky and Way 2005). But of course domestic determinants still remain uppermost. And the current mood is that the legitimacy and credibility of international involvement have lost ground. This state of affairs is probably linked to the loss of momentum that worldwide democratization per se has experienced, even if the connections between the state of democratization and the state of democracy promotion, and the direction of causal travel, are exceptionally difficult to establish (Burnell and Youngs 2009).

Democratization's significance for international development

The idea of a 'cruel choice' between democracy and development no longer carries much weight. Many authoritarian regimes—especially weak and fearful autocracies and some rentier states—have badly mismanaged their economic and financial affairs, not least because of inadequate accountability. In contrast party-based democracy can provide a more responsible approach where the parties judge that their electoral fortunes over the long run will be influenced by how they perform in office. Democratically elected governments can possess the legitimacy to take tough but necessary economic decisions. Accountability makes the gross abuse of public resources less likely: corruption surveys, like those from Transparency International, find that democracies generally are less corrupt, although significant variations exist across developing world democracies. To the extent that the sustained poverty reduction required for human development will happen only if poor people are empowered, the political rights and civil liberties that liberal democracy should bestow equally on all citizens looks more conducive compared to the concentration of power in just a few hands. A virtuous circle is possible: society exerts pressure for an expansion of social and economic opportunities, which then improve the prospects for stable democracy. That said, our understanding of democratization's benefits for economic growth and development urges caution,

and remains very imperfect (Williams et al. 2009). In particular, democratization appears to offer no surety for a progressive redistribution of wealth and incomes (Bermeo 2009a). Many reasons explain why and how democracy and poverty, especially absolute poverty, can coexist over long periods (see Box 14.6). Adherence to a market-based approach to development undoubtedly supplies one major contributory factor that is accentuated by globalization. Yet a shrewd insight claims that attempts to reduce economic inequality especially by populist leaders utilizing populist measures may come to threaten democracy's durability more than does inequality itself, especially if the measures actually damage the economic prospects of the poor in the long run (Bermeo 2009a:33).

Globalization, democracy, and democratization

Inconsistencies in the West's promotion of democracy and the spotlight placed on democratic development in developing countries may both look like sideshows in the presence of increased globalization and its effects.

Globalization can be understood as processes whereby many social relations become relatively delinked from territorial geography, so that human lives are increasingly played out in the world as a single place. Economic globalization is only a part, albeit a very important part. Globalization diminishes the value of conventional democratic models if it makes state-bound structures less tenable. This has been said to be particularly true in parts of the developing world in which weak or ineffective states and poor governance abound. In a globalizing world the human forces that most influence people's lives are increasingly transnational and supra-territorial; in contrast democracy is historically rooted in and remains confined to the borders of the national state. While globalization's impact on the state as distinct from democracy is explored in Chapter 15, some democratic implications are noted here.

First, powerful agencies of global governance are shrinking the space available for national political self-determination. These agencies are not themselves democratically accountable. They have the advantage of specialized technical knowledge of complex global issues that many small and poor countries can only envy. The value of democracy there is brought into question. The science of, and international negotiations on, climate change are illustrative.

Second, the political space in which self-rule remains an option is increasingly penetrated by various non-accountable external actors, establishing local branches or subsidiaries and forming domestic linkages and alliances that capture the policy processes. Transnational business provides many examples. Again, small and poor states with political and bureaucratic weaknesses are among the most vulnerable. The legitimacy enjoyed by a democratically elected government may even facilitate development policy initiatives that are demanded by international donors in return for their support (see Chapter 15). International democracy assistance has been said to make the world a safer place for capitalism, which critics believe

retards the genuine empowerment of ordinary people.

Third, economic globalization renders states, governments, and political regimes more vulnerable to weaknesses in the international financial system and to gyrations in world trade and capital flows, such as those dating from the collapse of 'sub-prime' housing loans in the United States, in 2007–08. According to the International Monetary Fund and World Bank's *Global Monitoring Report 2009: A Development Emergency* (2009) some of the poorest countries are hardest hit by these events precisely because they are now more connected with world trade than before, and yet, unlike Britain or the US, cannot borrow heavily abroad to fund unexpected financial deficits. For example, it was in mid-2009 that South Africa entered recession for the first time since 1992. The longer term effects on democratization, together with damage done to the very idea of democracy through association with crisis-prone market-led financial and economic models, can only be speculated. India's democracy, like China, weathered the storm and resumed impressive economic growth very quickly.

Box 14.6 Three Views on Democracy and Development

- Democracy is too conservative a system of power. It has a bias towards consensus and accommodation that cannot promote radical change in the system of wealth that is essential to establishing developmental momentum, especially in late developing societies. A truly developmental state needs more insulation from society than democracy allows (Leftwich 2002).

- Developing countries differ from the West in that democratic contestants do not have to compromise

with capitalists; instead they capture power for their own enrichment. This rent-seeking behaviour by politicians destroys the chances of development (Khan 2002).

- Powerlessness and poverty go together. Democratic models might empower the poor and serve development, such as by attacking the corruption that benefits only a few (Grugel 2002).

Adapted from 'Debate: Democracy and Development', in *New Political Economy*, 7/2 (2002)

There are also counter-arguments that suggest that globalization has some worthwhile benefits for democratization in the developing world.

First, the international spread of human rights and other democratic values is itself a part of globalization. This process is furthered by the increased opportunities for popular mobilization that come from revolutions in information technology, international communications, and transportation—highly visible signs of globalization. Globalization forces political openness, which threatens authoritarian regimes. Some developing countries now help to further the spread of values central to democracy, through membership of organizations like the OAS or subscribing to bodies like the UN Democracy Fund and International IDEA.

Second, if globalization can be made a more powerful force for economic progress and especially if development's benefits can be shared equitably, then the prospects for *stable* democracy increase.

Third, democracy is predicated on there being some measure of state capacity, if only to counter the many physical, economic and other challenges. States that are made stronger by the resources generated by globalization and improve the effectiveness of their governance can then respond more generously to society's demands. As meaningful choices become possible, voting for political leaders gains more point.

Fourth, there is the globalization of civil society, which offers vehicles for people to try to influence supranational institutions even where nationally rooted public structures like parliaments and political parties look obsolete. Global networks help local civic actors in their struggles to open up political space at home; local actors draw support from regional and global coalitions when endeavouring to stand up to powerful international institutions. The global justice movement (see Box 11.3) is an example; coalitions for action on climate change are another. Yet the democratic accountability of such civil society organizations is often questionable, and the unequal capacity to shape agendas—biased towards the Northern-based civic actors—is a matter for concern. Nevertheless, an increased role for global civil society features prominently in reflections on how a more democratic international order could emerge (for example, Scholte 2008).

Key points

- The jury is still out on the potency of democratization to bring about socio-economic conditions that could underpin new democracies.

- There are many different routes by which the international environment can influence democratization in developing countries: only some are supportive; some are unintentional; and their effects vary among countries.

- From a democratization perspective, globalization invites us to think not only about how to make the political space more democratic but how to restore power to the political as well.

- Globalization has undermined some authoritarian regimes but could pose longer-term threats to democracy.

Conclusion

Key issues at the heart of contemporary debates about democratization in developing countries include: what is democratization? How much progress has there been? Is a reverse wave under way? What explains democratic developments and the influences that determine both forwards and backwards movements? What are democratization's relationships to development? And how important is the international environment? This chapter has argued that democratization's meaning, like democracy itself, is contested. And while most developing countries have undergone political change over the last two decades or so, the number of new consolidated or stable liberal democracies is modest. In many countries competing analytical frameworks such as nation-building and state-building may offer greater insights into their current-day politics.

Attention has turned away from explaining democratic transition (transitology) and describing democratic consolidation (consolidology) and towards specifying a democracy's quality, identifying democracies' hazard rates (the probability that they will decay), and explaining authoritarian persistence. Regime typologies have been enriched by the proliferation of different forms of diminished authoritarianism (authoritarianism with adjectives) and diminished democracy. There is a chicken-and-egg conundrum of how to sort out democratization's apparent requisites from its possible consequences.

Thus it is important to establish how far both economic circumstances and external forces over which governments might have little control influence democratization's fortunes, and how much is determined by political choices (decisions and non-decisions) and institutional initiatives at home. In the long run, development appears to favour democracy, but there are reservations about the full effects of the market, and global capitalism in particular, especially where popular aspirations for human security and human development are thwarted. Although substantial economic inequality appears not to be a barrier to democratic durability, it can reduce democracy's quality.

A comprehensive assessment of the possibilities for democratic self-rule and progress to date must take account of the international relationships of developing countries and globalization, the policy significance of which is elaborated further in Chapter 15. And while closely connected with matters intrinsic to the classification of types of political regime, 'governance' embraces a larger set of political issues that have now come to the fore.

? Questions

1. Which developing countries have democratized most effectively and what explains their success?

2. How do concepts of democratic consolidation and democracy's quality help us to understand politics in developing countries?

3. Does the persistence of poverty explain why many developing countries have not made a transition to stable liberal democracy?

4. What are the chief alternatives to liberal democracy in a developing world context and what are the main political differences between them?

5. Should building democracy be a priority in conflict-prone societies in which the state is weak?

6. Can developing countries make globalization serve the purpose of building democracy?

7. Is the democratization literature gender-neutral or gender-blind, and if so how far do these features limit its usefulness?

8. What new challenges do democratic reformers face now that were less visible at the end of the end of the twentieth century?

■ Beetham, D., Bracking, S., Kearton, I., and Weir, S. (2002), *International IDEA Handbook on Democracy Assessment* (The Hague/London/New York: Kluwer Law International). A foundation guide to how to assess democratic achievement, which can be supplemented with more recent guidance from the International IDEA website.

■ Bermeo, N. (2009a), 'Does Electoral Democracy Boost Economic Equality?', *Journal of Democracy*, 20/4: 21–35. A compact survey of arguments and evidence pertaining to a relatively neglected but important issue.

■ Brooker, P. (2009), *Non-Democratic Regimes*, 2nd edn (Basingstoke: Palgrave Macmillan). The most accessible source on the state of the remaining non-democracies during and after the 'third wave' of democratization.

■ Burnell, P. and Youngs, R. (eds) (2009), *New Challenges to Democratization* (New York and Abingdon: Routledge). Assesses linkages between challenges to democratization and challenges to international democracy support.

■ Cornwall, A. and Goetz, A. M. (2005), 'Democratizing Democracy: Feminist Perspectives', *Democratization*, 12/5: 783–800. A critical review of the issues.

■ *Journal of Democracy*, 'The Quality of Democracy' (2004), 15/4, Special issue. On what is meant by the quality of democracy and its significance for evaluating 'good' or 'better' democracy'.

■ Leftwich, A. (2002), 'Democracy and Development', *New Political Economy*, 7/2: 269–81. Contending perspectives on relations between democracy and development.

■ Levitsky, S. and Way, L. (2005), 'International Linkage and Democratization', *Journal of Democracy*, 16/3: 20–34. Compares the effectiveness of international linkage and leverage.

■ Rustow, D. A. (1970), 'Transitions to Democracy', *Comparative Politics*, 2/3: 337–63. A seminal article on how democratic transitions come about.

■ Scholte, J. A. (2008), 'Reconstructing Contemporary Democracy', *Indiana Journal of Global Legal Studies*, 15/1: 305–51. Reconciling democracy and globalization.

■ Waylen, G. (2007), *Engendering Transitions: Women's Mobilization, Institutions and Gender Outcomes* (Oxford: Oxford University Press). A valuable corrective to the gender-blind approach of much democratization literature.

■ Williams, G., Duncan, A., Landell-Mills, P., and Unsworth, S. (2009), 'Politics and Growth', *Development Policy Review*, 27/1: 5–31. Surveys current understanding of the connections between political change and economic growth.

■ *Democratization* (edited in the UK) and the **Journal of Democracy** (edited in the US) are two well-known journals, the second publishing an annual digest of the latest Freedom House survey.

 Web links

■ www.freedomhouse.org The site of the US-based Freedom House; includes access to its annual comparative measures of freedom.

■ www.idea.int The site of the multi-member International Institute for Democracy and Electoral Assistance (Stockholm) and its democracy research and promotion activities.

■ **www.afrobarometer.org** The site for national public attitude surveys on democracy, markets, and civil society in Africa.

■ **www.consilium.europa.eu** Contains Council of the European Union 'Conclusions on democracy support in the EU's external relations'.

■ **www.latinobarometro.org** The site for national public attitude surveys in Latin America.

■ **www.ned.org** The site of the Washington-based, non-governmental, National Endowment for Democracy, which houses the International Forum for Democratic Studies.

■ **www.undp.org/governance** Presents the UNDP's work on democratic governance.

■ **www.oas.org** The site of the Organization of American States, containing statements on themes such as strengthening the democratic commitment and protecting human rights.

■ **www.nepad.org** The official site of the New Partnership for Africa's Development, including documents representing the AU's formal commitment to democratization among member states.

■ **www.un.org/democracyfund/** Includes the UN Secretary-General's 'Guidance Note' applying to all UN democracy promotion activities.

 Online Resource Centre

For additional material and resources, please visit the Online Resource Centre at:
www.oxfordtextbooks.co.uk/orc/burnell3e/

Governance and Aid Conditionality in a Globalizing World

Peter Burnell and Lise Rakner

15

Chapter contents

- Introduction
- Globalization and the State
- From Aid Conditionality to Selectivity
- Governance
- Conclusion

Overview

This chapter introduces debates about the implications of globalization for the state and public policy with a focus on aid and governance. Many poor indebted developing countries are linked to the global economy through aid transfers from developed nations (the European Union (EU) and bilateral donors) and the international financial institutions (for example, World Bank and International Monetary Fund (IMF)). Over the past three decades, many developing countries have been required to agree **conditionalities** concerning policy and institutional reform with these external actors. The chapter surveys the theory and practice of conditionality-based aid, as well as recent moves towards greater selectivity in lending. Several 'generations' of conditionality and the **process conditionality** connected with tackling poverty are introduced. The conditions set for lending to poor indebted nations are increasingly linked to demands about improved governance. As a result, **governance** and debates about **good governance** have become central to the development discourse and hence to aid policies and debates about conditionality and selectivity. The chapter discusses the problems associated with operationalizing the concept of governance at the state level and the growing importance that donors attach to assessing governance in aid recipient nations.

Introduction

Three major trends in the contemporary discourse on politics in the developing world are an increasing tendency to locate politics at the level of the country within the international context; an erosion of disciplinary boundaries between politics and development studies; a meshing of theoretically oriented and policy-relevant investigations. Evidence of all three trends can be found in the strongly related debates on **globalization**, governance, and the influence of globalization on governance through such mechanisms as international aid conditionality. The first section of this chapter dwells on globalization's implications for the state in developing countries. The second section traces the evolution of aid conditionality through to its recent connection with poverty reduction. The third section shows that notwithstanding the prominence achieved by 'good governance', especially in the development discourse, disagreement remains over how to make sense of the term and its significance both for politics and development. The proliferation of quantitative and qualitative assessments of the state of governance in developing countries developed by various international agencies and governments may provide new insights, but the large number of assessments and varied outcomes also underline the lack of consensus about the concept of governance.

Globalization and the State

Globalization occupies a vast literature. Its meaning, historical origins, significance for developing countries and desirability are all extensively debated. Baylis and Smith (2007) see globalization as a process that involves the widening, deepening, and speeding up and growing impact of worldwide interconnectedness. Economic globalization while not coterminous with globalization is certainly a major component.

Not all states are touched evenly or make equal contribution to this momentum. And in so far as globalization entails both costs and benefits, their nature and extent varies greatly within the developing world as between different countries and social groups. In terms of economic globalization, India and China have become major engines of international trade and investment (Chapter 4) and are reaping substantial economic gains, whereas other developing countries differ greatly among themselves in terms of their overall globalization. An individual country can even differ considerably as between its economic, political, and social globalization. (Box 15.1 illustrates with figures from the Centre for the Study of Globalisation and Regionalisation (CSGR) Globalization Index. Appendix 2 provides figures for this book's case-study countries and comparators for the US and UK, and explains how the index is constructed.) Poor and fragile states that depend on exporting commodities to distant markets may become even more vulnerable as a result of disadvantageous trade deals engineered by powerful lobbies in the OECD countries, or by downturns in the global economy and international financial crisis of the kind that broke in 2008. Indeed, in the past, private capital flight from Africa has contributed to the poverty of African countries and can be held responsible in part for their financial indebtedness to the Bretton Woods institutions and other aid donors. While Asia and Latin America increasingly are integrated to the global world economy through trade, foreign direct investments and other financial flows (Chapter 4),

Africa continues to remain on the margins and is primarily linked to the globalized world through commodity exports and aid transfers.

Box 15.1 Globalization Rankings and Scores from the Developing World for 2004

- Of all the world's regions sub-Saharan Africa is the least globalized *overall* but the Middle East and North Africa rank lower in terms of *economic* globalization. Nevertheless even sub-Saharan Africa's absolute measure of globalization has increased markedly.

- In terms of *globalization overall*, only three developing countries made the top 20: Singapore (top), Malaysia (14), and South Korea (20). In purely *economic* terms, developing countries occupied nine of the top 20 places, but in social globalization there was only one (Barbados, at 19). In *political globalization* China was fourth placed after France, the US, and Russia, with Egypt (8), India (13), Malaysia (15), Pakistan (16), Nigeria (18), and Jordan (19) also featuring in the top 20.

- Several developing countries are significantly higher in the rankings for political globalization than for economic globalization, for example Brazil (31 and 86 respectively), India (13 and 42), Nigeria (18 and 110), and South Africa (35 and 60), which in part may owe to their size.

(Lockwood and Redoano 2005)
Note: Additional data for countries in Part 5 of this book together with details of the CSGR index methodology can be found in Appendix 2.

But none of these differences fully captures the aspect of globalization that comprises the rise of a plurality of centres of governance—polycentrism and multilevel governance—existing at levels above and below the national state. Power and even authority appear to be relocating to a large and disparate group of supranational and trans-territorial institutions. The emergence of global sites of regulation and decision-making together with growing political interconnectedness between supra, sub, and non-state actors contribute to what Higgott and Ougaaard (2002: 1) call the 'globalization of political life'. The implications for the state and public policy merit investigation.

The impact of globalization on the state and public policy

Our understanding of what globalization means for the state has evolved from sweeping claims that sovereignty is seriously threatened to more complex, nuanced, and even ambiguous perspectives. These perspectives distinguish among different states and dwell on how states are being transformed in a variety of ways, as they address the challenges posed by globalization. They also look at how states to varying degrees shape and harness the opportunities that globalization provides. Beyond that, there are contrasting views.

For some analysts the triumph of economic **neo-liberalism** and the increasingly competitive scramble to attract international capital and retain global market share inevitably means that the state has less freedom to deviate from a narrow range of market-friendly economic policies. The political implication may be that in democracies, electorates face restricted scope to make meaningful choices between alternative programmes for economic management and welfare provision; socialism is no longer a viable option. To be credible political parties must occupy the centre ground, in a context in which the centre of gravity has itself moved to the right. However, other commentators claim the reality is less straightforward because of the difference that domestic political institutions and political agency still can make, such as through mediating the impact of external linkages and events. Weiss (2005: 346), who counters the 'myth' of the powerless state even goes so far as to argue that rather than a loss of state power there has been structural and political entwinement—a mutual reinforcement of contemporary global networks and the domestic structures of nation-states.

She argues that globalization is actually reinforcing and in some important respects augmenting the role of territorially based institutions, while at the same time the power distribution among different institutions of state and government departments is altered as a result.

As one part of this scenario professional technocrats in the government bureaucracy are being empowered vis-à-vis elected politicians, although politicians with technocratic qualifications like Liberia's President Ellen Johnson-Sirleaf, in 2005 Africa's first elected female head of state and a US-educated economist who formerly worked for the World Bank and Citibank, might claim to have an advantage. The executive too may gain in power relative both to the legislature and municipal institutions, owing to the growing importance of working with regional and global governance institutions, although in some large countries like India and Brazil international financial institutions and transnational corporations now do also deal directly with city and provincial administrations, circumventing the central government. In relation to poor, aid-recipient nations critics have argued that, within central government, the power of Finance Ministries and Central Banks increases relative to spending ministries, in consequence of having to agree terms and conditions of borrowing with external creditors and because aid donors have moved towards offering general budget support instead of emphasizing direct project and programme assistance.

Overall, then, Phillips (2005: 102) observes that while a 'mainstay of the globalization-state debate, in both orthodox and critical perspectives, is the contention that states are increasingly centralized, insulated and "technocratic", and accountable primarily to global market forces rather than national societies', this should not be applied absolutely or uniformly. Instead, what is called a transformationalist approach argues not just that states are undergoing variegated processes of adaptation and transformation but that the state may be critical to the 'authoring' and propulsion of globalization

(Phillips 2005: 95). And although the international political economy literature has tended to focus its attention mainly on the developed world and to say that the developing world has less freedom to adopt distinctive policy responses in the presence of globalization (Mosley 2005: 357; Phillips 2005: 107–8), the transformationalist approach does not apply to developed countries only. Thus for example Mosley (2005: 357), in her account of government autonomy and cross-national policy diversity, drew attention to the differences in social policy between Chile and Mexico, which she explained by referring to domestic political alliances, the organization of the poor, and competitiveness of the political party system. In Latin America also Kaufman and Segura-Ubiergo (2001) found that although globalization has had some negative social consequences by reducing social security transfers there has been increase in investment in health care and education too. Social spending as a whole has risen during the very period when Latin America was becoming more closely integrated into the global economy, and not just in countries with a left-leaning and populist government in power like Venezuela under President Chávez. The domestic politics of electoral competition and political participation are responsible, at least in part.

So, while for developing countries the state's role in economic governance is said to be 'about how to incorporate societal actors in order to gain the capacity to formulate and implement efficient economic policies' (Kjaer 2004: 148), the *type* of intervention by the state and the specific policies they pursue are no less significant than the actual amount of state intervention in markets that globalization allows or brings about (Phillips 2005: ch. 4). Even where strong convergence towards standard neo-liberal solutions does take place in the process of policy formation, intrinsically domestic features such as the **neo-patrimonialism** and **clientelism** found in much of Africa can then make an enormous difference to the way in which policies are actually implemented and to their eventual outcomes.

Key points

- There are notable differences in political, economic, and social globalization among developing countries.
- Asia and Latin America are integrated to the global world economy through trade and foreign direct investments but Africa continues to remain on the margins.
- Competing claims that pitch arguments about state transformation against notions that say the state is being eclipsed mean that globalization's

consequences for states in the developing world warrant more attention, especially analyses of how different features of globalization and the different aspects of economic globalization affect different states in different ways.

- The responses to globalization vary in accordance with domestic political circumstances; even policy convergence on a standard policy menu is not absolute or universal.

From Aid Conditionality to Selectivity

For many developing countries, especially those categorized as **heavily indebted poor countries** and many African countries especially, their relationship with the international donors (hereunder the Bretton Woods institutions, EU, and the major bilateral donors) is one feature of globalization that has special significance. For while the World Bank group and the IMF along with regional development banks, the European Union, and bilateral donors have been important sources of finance, the policy and institutional conditionalities associated with their assistance has proven to be controversial. High levels of aid dependence as found among many of the least developed countries mean the state and public policy are more exposed to external influence than is true of such large economies as India and Brazil. To illustrate, for a country like Malawi, where the international aid donors contribute approximately 40 per cent of the government's annual budget, the economic and political conditions attached to the aid disbursement may be expected to influence the government's policy-making.

Conditioning financial and development support spells out steps that the recipient must agree to take;

in theory, non-compliance jeopardizes the support. In terms of the actual conditions that have supplied the content of conditionality, at least three generations can be identified. Each successive generation has added to rather than supplanted its predecessors. The first phase, concentrated on economic and financial policy measures that reflected the so-called **Washington consensus**, was expressed in the structural and sectoral adjustment lending of the 1980s. The second generation beginning in the late 1980s introduced governance considerations, which some major bilateral donors supplemented with more explicitly political considerations embodying ideas of human rights and democratic political reform.

Around a decade later a new or third generation of conditionality began to gain prominence. This added social policy concerns in the form of poverty reduction strategies. It has also been called process conditionality, because it touches on how policy is arrived at and not just the policy content. Following an influential report for the World Bank (Dollar and Burnside 1998) in 1998 the idea and practice of **aid selectivity** has come to over-layer—although not eliminate—conditionality, as some major donors moved towards allocating their development assistance on a more discriminating basis.

Harrison (2001) then introduced the term 'post-conditionality', not with a view to suggesting that conditionality is finished but instead to characterize a new relationship emerging between donors and favoured aid recipients. Relying less heavily on conditionality this resorts to more subtle, yet more intrusive, ways of penetrating the policy process in the recipient states.

The nature of conditionality

Just as the idea of conditionality is open to different interpretations, so the parties to conditionality in the real world have their own perspectives on the nature of this relationship. Much of the debate originated during the era of economic conditionality. Harrison (2001) summed up three main alternatives as follows. One, contributed by scholars influenced by radical international political economy and endorsed by Third World nationalists, sees conditionality as a new form of imperialism. Emphasis is placed on an essentially political relationship of power: domination and subordination. Conditionality has often been described as coercive, but more revealing could be investigation of the precise circumstances whereby the lender's power to offer assistance turns into power *over* the would-be recipient. The coercive interpretation becomes more compelling where the recipient has no tolerable alternative but to agree to the conditions. It is more provocative where this situation has come about more as a result of structural global forces or foreign machinations outside of the developing country's control than due to bad governance and its own policy failings. **Cross-conditionality** adds an extra twist. This makes access to support from some sources, bilateral donors for instance, conditional on compliance with conditions laid down by other powerful donors such as the Bretton Woods institutions. These established formal cross-conditionality among themselves in the second half of the 1980s.

A second way of understanding conditionality sees it as a form of partnership, one that reflects liberal notions of globalization: it is benign involvement, not intervention. This approximates to the international financial institutions' use of the term policy dialogue, which presents relations with borrowers less in terms of financial or any other form of power and more a case of sharing of economic know-how and expertise. Reasoned persuasion lies at the heart of the relationship. Loans serve the purpose of helping a recipient government to buy time during which policy reforms can take effect and in the meantime issue 'side-payments' to groups who would otherwise oppose, and possibly thwart, the reform process. Once the 'winners' from policy reforms become strong enough to provide solid political foundations for the new policy regime, aid will have served its purpose and can be phased out. This type of aid has been likened to bridging the short-term bad news/long-term good news gap. Its success is premised on compliance with the policies and on the nature of the policies and their implementation offering sound economic solutions.

Harrison's (2001) third model conforms to rational choice and principal–agent models of the relationship between states and external institutions. The two sides interact in the manner of self-interested actors: their original interests do not coincide. This perspective resembles what Mosley, Harrigan, and Toye (1995) portrayed as exchange relationship in which bargaining takes place: on the one side, offers of finance may be portrayed as a bribe or inducement; on the other side are promises to enact policy and institutional reforms. The interaction has the character of a game; the relative bargaining power of the two sides will determine the final terms of the exchange. The balance can shift dramatically after the deal has been signed and money has changed hands, but donors responded by deciding to release financial support in stages (tranches), while closely monitoring compliance with the conditions in the meantime. However, sanctions for non-compliance that push a country to default on its debt and lose creditable status may not serve the interests of lenders, and this extreme measure tends to be a very last resort.

Insights couched in terms of imposition, persuasion, and purchase need not be mutually exclusive. At any one time each one might have relevance to a specific group of countries, whether highly debt-distressed countries on the one side or countries offering important geo-strategic advantages to the West on the other. And as a country's circumstances change so might the best choice of model for characterizing the relationship change too. For example Argentina's financial and economic collapse in 2001–02 led the government to default on part of its external debt. In 2003 the new leadership of President Kirchner pushed through large-scale debt restructuring on favourable terms and against IMF opposition. Subsequently it gained sufficient confidence from the return of economic progress to join with the government of Brazil in announcing that all outstanding debt to the IMF would be paid off by early 2006—a development greeted in the country as tantamount to restoring Argentina's sovereignty, its right to govern itself.

Economic conditionality's record

In practice the record of conditionality has been found to be generally ineffective, especially in respect of first-generation conditionalities. 'Slippage', the non-implementation of agreements reached with the World Bank, was common (Mosley, Harrigan, and Toye 1995). The IMF's experience was no better (Killick 1998).

The reasons range from the political weakness and inability of governments to take the necessary measures without incurring unacceptable political risk for themselves or to political stability more broadly, to administrative or technical reasons preventing policy reforms delivering the benefits claimed by the textbooks. Compliance has often been selective and applied in distorted ways to serve the interests of the ruling elites, the sale of state-owned assets at very favourable prices to leaders or their close allies being a typical example. More

fundamental economic critiques argue that the neo-liberal recommendations are in any case ill-adapted to the economic circumstances of developing countries, especially when their financial or economic problems originate in the international system (see Chapter 4)—the global downturn sparked by the financial crisis that began with the collapse of sub-prime lending to the US housing market in 2007–08 being a recent illustration. Also, the regressive social consequences of structural adjustment attracted much comment; indeed in the developing world the 1980s were dubbed a 'lost decade for poverty' largely because of the economic conditionalities. By the 1990s and precisely because economic conditionalities were deemed to have been unsuccessful—which in turn suggests a very limited ability to coerce—governance came to be identified as an integral part of the problem. More specifically, development studies recognized that conditionality does not produce what has come to be called 'ownership' of reforms; yet ownership is what delivers results, especially long after the aid relationship ends. As part of this realization improvements in governance came to be identified as a necessary part of the solution. This ushered in a second generation of conditionalities, and international development policy turned towards offering support for capacity-building in 'good governance'. But experiences with the first 'two generations' of conditionality-based aid suggest that conditionality had little effect in terms of shifting domestic policies. Furthermore, much of the conditionality-based aid that was transferred outside public channels and state agencies made many recipient countries less capable of managing their own development. Project management units designed to curb corruption (anti-corruption agencies) and enhance domestic revenue collection (autonomous revenue authorities) were often set up in parallel to government departments and talented people were pulled away from the civil service by offering better work conditions and services. In short, some of the conditionality-based aid to strengthen the governance capacity of poor developing countries became part of a vicious circle.

Aid selectivity

The weak performance of economic conditionality even where the policies were believed to be correct combined with the catalyst provided by a report for the World Bank titled *Assessing Aid: What Works, What Doesn't and Why* (1998), which encouraged donors to consider allocating aid on a more selective basis. Instead of using conditionality to try to leverage change, the new idea was to concentrate support on countries that had already shown a commitment to sound economic policies and the institutional conditions for development. Reform ceased to be the object of lending; instead, lending was predicated on a favourable environment. This turn towards aid selectivity has influenced the lending policies of the World Bank and bilateral donors such as the US and more particularly the Millennium Challenge Account set up by the Bush administration in 2004, and which outlined 16 indicators for judging country eligibility.

However, far from driving out conditionality selectivity has been viewed as just a more subtle approach—one that expects certain conditions to be met by developing country borrowers *ex ante* rather than reached *ex post*. Borrowers are induced into taking certain measures no different from those that formed the substance of previous conditionality, in the hope of gaining reward. Behaviour of this nature does not amount to accepting the logic of the reforms themselves, or ownership. More punitive even than the threat of penalties in the event of non-compliance with conditionalities, aid selectivity may run the risk of imposing sanctions on some countries in advance. Countries the need of which for international assistance may be among the most desperate, such as where the economy has been severely affected by civil conflict, but which are unable to meet the tests for eligibility began to find themselves excluded from the donors' shrinking lists of substantial aid partners. Support for improvements in governance, however, can offer a better alternative in as much as the state's capacity to meet the conditions for receiving selective economic assistance is advanced.

From policy conditionality to process conditionality

Whereas second generation conditionality comprises political and more especially governance conditionalities (discussed further below), the new millennium brought a new consensus in the **international community** holding that international development assistance cannot make development happen, it can at best reinforce the efforts of countries to mobilize their own resources to improve people's lives. The end of the 1990s saw the introduction of a third generation, one that coincides with the **Millennium Development Goals'** prioritization of poverty alleviation as a goal of international development cooperation. The OECD's 2005 *Paris Declaration on Aid Effectiveness* formalizes that aid is effective when aligned to the recipient countries policies and political systems. This 'new conditionality' has social concerns rather than objectives conceived more narrowly in terms of economics and government capabilities. The objective is not just tackling poverty but also influencing the policy- and decision-making process by which governments arrive at poverty reduction as a policy objective (Gould 2005). For this reason it has also been given the label 'process conditionality', at least in the form in which it has become enshrined in the Poverty Reduction Strategy Process (PRSP).

The essence of PRSP was adopted by the executive boards of the World Bank and IMF in 1999. Initially, governments seeking to benefit from debt relief under the **Heavily Indebted Poor Countries Initiative** (HIPC), and subsequently all low-income-country candidates for concessional lending, must institutionalize a process leading to a strategy to reduce poverty and then monitor and evaluate progress, based on consultation with representatives of civil society. By influencing the very process by which public resources come to be allocated there was an expectation that the inability of aid conditionality to generate local ownership of development policy would be overcome. Strategy papers have now been written for around seventy countries and in some case like Uganda and Tanzania they are now well into their second three-year cycle. Several criticisms have been levelled both at the conception and the way in which the PRSP has operated (Driscoll with Evans 2005; Lazarus 2008).

First, the requirement that governments adopt the PRSP approach in order to qualify for international assistance represents not the rejection of a failed policy of conditionality but rather a double version: one that applies both to policy substance and policy process. Second, the poverty dimension still sits within the familiar neo-liberal economic policy framework and does not signal a retreat from that framework. Donor insistence on orthodox monetary policy and fiscal discipline in return for advancing general budgetary support still constrain the possibilities for increasing public spending on health or education, especially when backed up by growing donor support for strengthening the instruments of *ex post* financial accountability. Extensive advice and training from organizations like the World Bank Institute, the United Nations Development Programme (UNDP) and bilateral development agencies is now being made available to national audit offices and to the public accounts committees of legislatures for the purpose of exercising fiscal oversight (see Stapenhurst et al. 2008).

Third, as with previous conditionalities PRSPs have been seen to encourage an element of game-playing: government elites have an incentive to adopt the process in order to qualify for assistance. But there may be no genuine commitment to either the process or policy substance; on the contrary, domestic political forces—most notably the government's own political priorities and the informal politics of neo-patrimonialism—are seen to influence the budgetary decisions and actual public spending disbursements, still (Lazarus 2008). Moreover evidence of policy 'ownership' by a bureaucratic elite does not necessarily mean ownership by the country as long as the grass roots of society, or at minimum the people's formally elected representatives in Parliament, are kept largely remote from the consultation process—as has been the case in many countries. Just as the **civil society** organizations that are consulted may not have very strong credentials to be fully representative or democratic, so it has been argued that only the participation of more broadly based constituencies inclusive of the poor will move development policy in a more sustained pro-poor direction. Bräutigam (2004) for example found that evidence including from Brazil, Chile, Mauritius, and Costa Rica suggests the political organization of the poor in the form of political parties together with greater legislative involvement in the formulation of development policy and the national budget is essential. Strengthening rather than undermining these institutions could be the way forward, especially where the legitimacy of civil society organizations as partners in governance is rendered questionable by their dependence on foreign donors for status and funds. While in very recent years donor interest in parliamentary strengthening has started to increase (see Hudson and Wren 2007), the modalities are still under review and resistance to the idea by government is a typical response.

Contrary to what is often assumed, recent experience shows that IMF and the World Bank (WB) have amended their conditionality practice by streamlining their conditions and by making fewer attempts to compel poor developing governments to do things they do not want to do. Bilateral donors and the EU, on the other hand, appear to have increased their conditionalities and are now more involved in the micro-management of country policies and in attempts to use disbursement decisions as levers to obtain policy changes. The increased conditionalities are related to the need for bilateral donors to 'safeguard' themselves as a defence against accusations from domestic public opinion worrying that public money is being wasted. While it is laudable that there is scrutiny of public resources, the question is whether increased conditionality serves the intended purpose, as so far conditionalities have proven to have limited influence in the absence of domestic political commitment—that is to say, strong 'ownership'.

Post-conditionality

'Post-conditionality' has affinities with both se-lectivity and process conditionality. It refers to a state of affairs inside the machinery of govern-ment in developing countries that makes heavy *ex post* conditionalities and threats of sanctions in the face of non-compliance seem superfluous, while still achieving great influence for the international donors.

According to the idea of post-conditionality donor involvement comes to be internalized in the state: in Harrison's words (2001: 669), donor power can then be conceptualized as 'part of the state itself', not a 'strong external force to the state'. A mutual but still unequal dependence takes hold. In poor countries like Tanzania for example the international financial institutions have invested so much capital and, just as important, credibility in achieving at least the appearance of a success story for their role that they cannot break off relations lightly. But far from encouraging the kind of 'slip-page' that Mosley, Harrigan, and Toye (1995) and Killick (1998) formerly documented in respect of conditionality, post-conditionality embeds inter-national donor recommendations for reform and perhaps even the rationales that underlie them in the very fabric of government. This is achieved by external involvement in shaping key institutions such as relations between central bank and the finance ministry and by influencing the thinking of the people who staff them. Many of the de-veloping world's senior finance officials have been educated in the West. However, there are excep-tions to post-conditionality, states like Vietnam that possess the residual strength of a nationalist ideology or Venezuela when oil revenues have been high, excusing the need for external financial sup-port; others have bargaining chips that come from the possession of strategic assets in international politics (Gould 2005). And once again, the way in which domestic forces, interests, and actors interact to determine the informal and not just the formal politics of government can make a difference, not just to the policy outputs but even more importantly

to the relevance of formal policy commitments and their outcomes.

Furthermore, there is no teleological inevitability to post-conditionality. Although Harrison claimed to see examples in Uganda and Tanzania it is not necessarily a permanent condition even there. And yet the idea of something like post-conditionality may come close to what the international financial institutions themselves hope to achieve through the provision of technical assistance rather than the overt manipulation of financial incentives or a more unambiguously coercive approach. And it is more in keeping with the changing global fi-nancial market that began to emerge at the outset of the twenty-first century, when a growing num-ber of developing economies like Argentina and Brazil began to feel less in need of the Bretton Woods institutions and more able to exploit alter-native sources of finance, such as direct inwards investment (Woods 2006). Significant oil exporting countries appeared to be arriving at an analogous position, as they reaped the financial harvest of high oil prices. At the same time, however, state autonomy—understood as the capacity to formu-late and implement policy preferences separately and differently—still remains questionable for the poorest countries. The international financial crisis and global economic slowdown of 2008–09 served to reinforce that message: indeed, because world leaders have turned to the Bretton Woods institu-tions for both short-term and long-term solutions the apparent decline in the power of these insti-tutions that had previously drawn some comment (see for example Woods 2006) may have been ar-rested and will now go into reverse. So, something like the essence of conditionality may still continue to be a 'central aspect of the donor–state relation-ship' (Harrison 2001: 668) for the most aid-reliant countries, and in other developing countries too so long as the international institutions are able to dominate the supply of knowledge about how to manage development and devise the new inter-national financial architecture. This point applies just as much to the theme of governance as to any other theme in development.

Key points

- For thirty years developing world recipients of aid have experienced the practice of attaching conditionalities to concessionary international support.

- Conditionality's significance for the political autonomy of countries depends on how we understand the concept and the specific circumstances of the states involved.

- The policy and institutional content of conditioned lending has diversified and multiplied over time, from economic to political and social conditions.

- Conditionalities do not substitute for policy ownership and cannot of themselves create ownership. Conditionality's perceived ineffectiveness has led to more selective approaches to lending, but analysts have argued that its essence continues even in the form of post-conditionality.

- The process conditionality associated with PRSPs has not conceded much power to the poor and for this reason may not offer an effective solution to poverty in the long term.

Governance

The starting point for the governance debate dates back to the 1980s and the observed deficit of politics in the development debates. But, while a consensus has emerged arguing that governance is important in its own right and as a means for achieving equitable and sustainable growth, there is still little clarity on what governance is, how it differs from democracy, how it relates to development processes, and what elements of the governance agenda are most conducive to development. According to Payne, the word governance 'is probably second only to globalization in use and abuse' (2005: 55). Governance as it has evolved may be understood as a fairly elaborate theory about how power is exercised and checked, whereas democracy is about how power is attained through electoral processes and participatory institutions. Governance has an economic dimension that usually refers to property rights, transparency of economic transactions, freedom of information, public sector management, and the rule of law. The political dimension of governance is usually taken to mean government legitimacy, human rights, rule of law, and government accountability.

Governance is not the same as government. Governance can take place in venues and at levels other than the formally constituted governing authorities of the state. Intergovernmental networks, transnational non-state actors, and state–society interactions more generally have all been loosely linked to ideas of governance. For example Higgott and Ougaard (2002) see the development of an international institutional architecture for global governance as part of a trend towards an 'emerging global polity', the World Trade Organization (see Chapter 4) being but one example.

Global governance, according to McGrew (in Higgott and Ougaard 2002: 208), refers to the process by which governments, inter-governmental bodies, non-governmental organizations, and transnational forces come together to establish global rules, norms, and standards, or to resolve specific trans-border problems, the global trade in illicit drugs for instance. Regional governance is exemplified most strikingly in the EU: nothing comparable exists in the developing world but regional institutions like the Organization of American States and the African Union do aspire to exert influence throughout their respective continents. Among the various rules, norms, and standards that have come to the fore in processes of dialogue and engagement between developing countries and institutions of global and regional governance are many that concern the quality of governance in countries' internal arrangements. Initially this was encapsulated in the good governance agenda of second-generation conditionality, led by the Word Bank at the end of the 1980s. Since then, governance, whether defined as a process or activity or both, has become a major *leitmotif* in the development discourse, having particular relevance for the climate for investment and effectiveness of international development cooperation. Ideas for improving governance and better governance have become central to aid donor–recipient relations, even though institutions of global governance like the IMF are themselves deficient in respect of at least some of the features now associated with good governance, transparency, and democratic accountability for instance (Higgott and Ougaard 2002; Stiglitz 2003; Woods 2006).

How does governance matter?

The majority of qualitative analyses looking at links between government and development find that improved governance has a significant and positive impact. The finding that good governance is associated with development success has been given as a rational for promoting a wide range of reforms from public financial management, property rights, political regimes, to public administration. But there are still many unanswered questions about the types of institution that work for development and which should be supported. Both China and Vietnam have a number of 'non-conducive' governance features linked to authoritarian governments, high levels of corruption, and insecure property rights. Yet, both states have achieved economic growth linked to reduced levels of poverty and improved public services in areas of education and health. Arguably, the governance debate tells us that institutions

matter but we know less about what types of institution matter the most. Perhaps it is necessary to distinguish the governance needs of poor and middle-income developing countries? Grindle (2007) argues for degrees of good governance or 'good-enough governance', finding that the list of required institutions for development is simply too costly to sustain for the poorest developing nations.

From good governance to governance indicators

Disappointing results for economic conditionality prompted the World Bank to identify poor governance in developing countries and weak governance rather than simply too much government as major problems. In the 1990s the Bretton Woods institutions wove good governance into the fabric of conditionality and then into criteria for aid selectivity.

Strong echoes began to surface from the developing world. For example in Africa a commitment to 'Democracy and Good Political Governance' and to 'Economic and Corporate Governance' was enshrined in the Action Plans of the New Partnership for Africa's Development (NEPAD) (see Box 15.2), an initiative backed by the Organisation of African Unity (now the African Union), that began work in 2002. A self-monitoring mechanism—African Peer Review Mechanism (APRM)—has been established to make progress in furthering better governance; around thirty countries are now members, and a handful of countries starting with Ghana have already undergone review. In 2005 the Commission for Africa containing a majority of political figures from Africa vested considerable hopes in these arrangements for improving governance, in its report *Our Common Interest* (2005) (see Box 15.3).

At the outset the World Bank, in its idea of good governance, focused on such qualities as transparency, fiscal accountability, and sound management of the public sector—in short, economic governance. Other actors including foreign ministries in the West and bilateral aid agencies quickly expanded the agenda towards political governance, bringing in issues of democracy and human rights in general and political pluralism and free and fair elections specifically. However even in the narrower definitions good governance touches on issues to do with the distribution of power in society and between state and society, and has consequences for relations with external actors like the international financial institutions. The World Bank soon came to embrace the rule of law, a capable judiciary, and freedom from corruption among its governance objectives and has devoted considerable support to help to build national capacities in these areas. In a telling phrase, Harrison said that the Bank's initiatives here have been 'as concerned with *constructing* the state as they have with *reforming* it' (Harrison 2005: 250), especially in the situation of weak and ineffective states. The earlier **Bretton Woods consensus** and related enthusiasm for structural economic adjustment that seemed to insist on rolling back the frontiers of the state should be assessed against this background.

Box 15.2 New Partnership for Africa's Development

The first of NEPAD's eight *principles* reads 'Good governance as a basic requirement for peace, security and sustainable economic development'. Listed second in NEPAD's *priorities* for *establishing the conditions for sustainable development* is 'democracy and good, political, economic and corporate governance'. 'Good' *economic and corporate governance* including transparency in financial management 'are essential pre-requisites for promoting economic growth and reducing poverty. Mindful of this, we have approved eight prioritized codes and standards for achieving good economic and corporate governance'.

'These codes and standards have been developed by a number of international organisations through consultative processes that involved the active participation of and endorsement by African countries. Thus the codes and standards are genuinely global as they were endorsed by experts from a vast spectrum of economies with different structural characteristics.'

(Extracts from *NEPAD In Brief* and *A Summary of NEPAD Action Plans. African Peer Review Mechanism*. For NEPAD statements on democracy and political governance, see Box 14.5.)

Box 15.3 Commission for Africa Report: *Our Common Interest*

'One thing underlies all the difficulties caused by the interactions of Africa's history over the past 40 years. It is the weakness of governance and the absence of an effective state. By governance we mean the inability of government and the public services to create the right economic, social and legal frameworks which will encourage economic growth and allow poor people to participate in it.' (p. 28)

'The issue of good governance and capacity-building is what we believe lies at the core of all of Africa's problems. Until that is in place Africa will be doomed to continue its economic stagnation.' (p. 29)

'There is more to governance than how the government conducts itself. It is about the whole realm in which the state operates, including areas like parliament, the judiciary, the media and all the other organisations of society which remain in place when government changes. Next it is about the policies of government. But it is also about whether a government has the staff and organisational systems to design its policies and the ability to implement them with the participation of its citizens.'

'It has another crucial dimension: how well the government answers to its people for its policies and actions, whether it is "accountable" to its citizens. Democracy of some kind is an absolute fundamental here.' (p. 33)

'Good governance is about much more than sound policies. Governments have to be able to put those policies into effect.' (p. 33)

(Commission for Africa 2005)

Solutions for improving governance must reflect a good understanding of why good governance is not always present. The scope for explanations is almost as wide as the study of politics in the developing world. They range from the legacy of colonial rule (see Chapters 2 and 12) to weaknesses in the domestic architecture of government, low democratic accountability in particular (see Chapter 14); other possibilities include the political culture, most notably **patron–clientelism** and the privileging of informal practice over formal rules-based behaviour in public office and political life more generally; and claims about the malign influence of 'metropolitan countries'. For example Moore (2004) highlighted the negative impact of **rentier states** on governance and 'political under-development', whereby state elites who can rely on support in the form of foreign aid or resource rents gained from imposing duties on commodity exports can ignore pressures from society. A more recent argument suggests that the misuse of such rents for personal gain can rebound and provoke society to demand greater accountability from their government (Youngs 2009). By forcing government to reduce public spending a significant contraction in available rents occasioned by a global economic downturn as in 2009 may sharpen the contradictions. However, even Moore (2004) falls short of arguing that in rentier states a better governance 'dividend' will inevitably follow if government has to become more dependent on taxing citizens. And any theory that tries to explain differences in governance with a view to offering solutions must be amenable to empirical tests, which in turn requires that indicators must be specified—ideally in a form that can be measured.

Governance indicators

Measuring the quality of governance can seem to turn into a largely technical exercise, but it can never be separated from discussion about what governance and good governance in particular ac-tually mean. Daniel Kaufmann and others at the World Bank Institute have pioneered the collection of data on indicators, and the findings exert influence on policy. For instance the US Millennium Challenge Account consults it before determining which low-income countries should be eligible for funds, as do the World Bank and other donors when deciding on programmes for capacity-building in governance.

Beginning in the late 1990s and periodically updated ever since, Kaufmann et al.'s studies titled *Governance Matters* proceed from a definition of governance as the traditions and institutions that determine how authority is exercised in a country. This includes the process by which governments are selected, held accountable, monitored, and replaced, and as well as the capacity to effectively formulate and implement sound policies, and the respect of citizens and the state for the institutions that govern economic and social interactions among them. Now covering 212 countries and territories and compiled from 35 data sources and 32 different organizations, the most recent findings are displayed in *Governance Matters VII: Governance Indicators for 1996–2007* (Kaufmann, Kray, and Mastruzzi, 2008). The data fall into six dimensions: voice and accountability; political stability and absence of violence/terrorism; government effectiveness; regulatory quality; rule of law; and control of corruption (see Box 15.4). The research overall confirms that good governance is correlated with better development and claims to find a large causal effect running from improved governance to better development outcomes *and not the other way around*. The findings also support beliefs that good governance significantly enhances the effectiveness of development assistance. While useful for cross-country and over-time comparisons, the methodology cannot say much about the specific institutional failures responsible for poor governance in particular settings, in which the in-depth study of individual countries must add more light.

Box 15.4 *Governance Matters VII: Some Leading Findings*

Good governance can be found at all income levels.

- Developing countries such as Chile, Botswana, Uruguay, Mauritius, and Costa Rica score higher on certain dimensions such as government effectiveness, rule of law, and control of corruption than do some developed countries such as Greece or Italy.

- Since 1998 substantial improvements have included Ghana, Indonesia, Liberia, and Peru for Voice and Accountability, and Rwanda, Algeria, Angola, and Sierra Leone for Political Stability and Absence of Violence/Terrorism, and South Korea, Rwanda, and Ethiopia for Government Effectiveness. Regulatory Quality in Iraq has improved, as has Control of Corruption in Tanzania.

- Since 1998 Zimbabwe, Côte d'Ivoire, and Thailand deteriorated in terms of Voice and Accountability and the first two declined in respect of most other governance dimensions as well. Government Effectiveness and Regulatory Quality both deteriorated in Bolivia, as has Rule of Law in Venzuela and Voice and Accountability in Iran.

- Change does not always proceed in parallel across dimensions, for example Nigeria has recorded improvement in Voice and Accountability but worsening of Political Stability and Violence.

- The quality of governance globally has not improved much over the past decade.

(Kaufmann, Kray, and Mastruzzi 2008)

The *Governance Matters* project is not the *only* source of information and analysis. For 2008–11 the UNDP's Governance Centre in Oslo has a Global Programme on Capacity Development for Democratic Governance Assessments and Measurements. This seeks to build on its existing Governance Indicators project—a project that set out to be more sensitive to human development and to raise the profile of pro-poor and gender-sensitive indicators in particular, in a more country-contextualized way than other leading studies of governance. From a UNDP perspective governance is the exercise of economic, political, and administrative authority to manage a country's affairs at all levels. Good governance really means democratic governance, which is considered valuable in its own right as well as a means to realising the MDGs. The UNDP's ideal is for governance assessments to be conducted in line with the democratic principles that they should set out to measure. UNDP-funded programmes for strengthening institutions of democratic accountability like parliaments and judiciaries along with support for decentralization and e-governance are present in around 130 countries. They help with developing nationally owned processes for assessing and monitoring democratic governance, which is considered a priority. This last ambition travels in the direction of recent research on a World Governance Assessment first trailed by Hyden, Court, and Mease (2004), for whom political notions of governance must be ascribed at least as much importance as economic notions.

Governance for Hyden, Court, and Mease (2004) refers to the formation and stewardship of the informal and formal rules that regulate the public realm, the arena in which the state and not simply economic and societal actors interact to make decisions. They see governance more as a matter of behavioural disposition than technical capacities. Crucially, the subjective opinions of 'local stakeholders' in the developing countries—experts from the government, civil servants, legislators, lawyers, representatives of media and civil society organizations including trade unions, religious groups, business people, and academics—must be consulted over defining what governance means and how it is measured. In fact increasing the relevance of governance assessments to national stakeholders in recipient countries is now emerging as a theme in international development cooperation, in the wake of the *Paris Declaration on Aid Effectiveness* (2005), which brought together views from both sides of the international aid relationship and gave emphasis to, among other things, the principle of ownership. In the meantime, some of the more notable findings reported from Hyden et al.'s (2004) study of 16 countries including three from Latin America, six from Asia, two from Africa, and one from the Middle East support the theory that successful democratization enhances the quality of governance while also showing that not every country with a high governance score is also very democratic. Just as significant, increase in autocracy was found not to bring improvement in governance quality.

Considerable scope remains to increase our understanding of governance and how it can be improved, and the impact of external actors specifically. Capacity-building projects have become popular with donors including the World Bank Group, but the record of achievement remains patchy if superior to trying to improve governance through conditionalities (second-generation conditionality). This could be because such investments do not tackle fundamental determinants of relations of power and influence lying deep in the political structures, culture, and society. For donors to become more directly and heavily involved in trying to change these, however, would place the maintenance of good relations with the governments at risk. Moreover, it invites criticism as an unacceptable intervention in the internal politics of countries that are constitutionally independent sovereign states.

Key points

- In the late 1980s the donor community started to actively campaign for the promotion of good governance in response to the fact that adjustment lending of the 1980s had been largely ineffective due to the governance environment.

- Consensus on the importance of governance conceals different perspectives on how to construct the meaning of 'good governance' for the purpose of studying its origins and significance for development.

- Over the past decade donor interest in governance has become progressively more intense and focussed. In relation to this, donors are also putting increasingly more efforts into producing qualitative and quantitative governance assessments.

- Global trends in governance overall show no great improvement but evidence from individual countries shows that it is possible to make significant improvements over fairly short periods.

- Identifying harmful consequences of bad governance is much easier than devising effective international strategies for ensuring good governance.

- Paying attention to governance in developing countries should not lose sight of the relevance of improving governance in powerful institutions of global governance and making those institutions properly accountable.

- Lessons suggests that international donor agencies should be careful in terms of making judgements on the basis of existing indices as well as about advocating specific reforms in developing countries.

Conclusion

Globalization is a multifaceted phenomenon that touches unevenly on different parts of the developing world. Nowhere does it make the state redundant. Conditionality as practised by the main international lenders of balance-of-payments support and development finance is a long-established but contentious feature of developing country participation in the global financial and economic system.

An enduring tension exists between conditionality-based lending and country ownership of donor-inspired recommendations. The devolution of conditionality through regional arrangements to monitor institutional and policy performance like the African Peer Review Mechanism has yet to prove its full worth.

Over the last two decades the contribution that governments can make to the more efficient and effective operation of economic markets has acquired growing recognition. In line with this the quality of governance in developing countries has come to be accepted as a crucial determinant of developmental performance. This is a significant expression of globalization understood as a political intellectual or ideological movement and not just a process of global economic integration.

Governance assessments are a current fascination especially for international aid donors still employing mechanisms of conditionality and investing in governance capacity-building for the purpose of furthering development. But caution is warranted over how far this equates to building democracy let alone empowerment for the poor majority. Reservations exist about what can be achieved by external efforts to improve governance and implement poverty reduction strategies, especially where the linkages with powerful transnational forces and supranational actors become increasingly strong but remote from democratic control. The lesson learnt about governance is that an essential condition for successful outcomes is that there is a domestic drive for development and that aid supports such a domestic drive. But, if the political environment is unfavourable to providing effective leadership, governance reforms will have limited effect. The problem is of course that this is actually the case in the majority of the poorest countries in the world today that now receive the bulk of development assistance. Both governance and conditionality in a globalizing world point towards what governments do and how they do it—that is, their policy responses to the challenges and opportunities of development: these are elaborated in Part 4.

? Questions

1. What challenges and opportunities does globalization present to the state in the developing world?

2. Compare and contrast the different generations of aid conditionality, 'post-conditionality' and the idea of aid selectivity.

3. Discuss why bilateral donors appear to increase the conditions attached to aid delivery, while the multilateral agencies have reduced the number of conditions attached to aid.

4. What influences determine whether aid conditionality is successful in achieving the intended outcomes?

5. Do ideas of governance make a valuable contribution to understanding politics in the developing world?

6. Discuss the merits of the 'good-enough government' argument. Can it be argued that some aspects of governance are more important that others?

7. How can the quality of governance be assessed?

8. Why is there such great variation in respect of 'good governance' experienced by different countries in the developing world?

9. Assess the statement made by the Commission for Africa in *Our Common Interest* that issues of good governance and capacity-building are at the core of all of Africa's problems.

PETER BURNELL AND LISE RAKNER

■ Baylis, J. and Smith, S. (eds) (2008), *The Globalization of World Politics*, 4th edn (Oxford: Oxford University Press). Authoritative and wide-ranging text that is periodically updated.

■ Chang, H.-J. (ed.) (2007), *Institutional Change and Economic Development* (London: Anthem Press).

■ Doornbos, M. (2006), *Global Forces and State Restructuring* (Houndmills: Palgrave Macmillan). Essays on issues relating to globalization, governance, and the state in developing countries.

■ Gould, J. (2005), *The New Conditionality: The Politics of Poverty Reduction Strategies* (London: Zed Press). A critical examination informed by a variety of case studies.

■ Grindle, M. (2007), 'Good Enough Governance Revisited', *Development Policy Review*, 25/5: 533–74.

■ Harrison, G. (2005), 'The World Bank, Governance and Theories of Political Action in Africa', *British Journal of Politics and International Relations*, 7/2: 240–60. A critical analysis of the World Bank's governance agenda and prospects for reform in Africa.

■ Hudson, A. and Wren, C. (2007), *Parliamentary Strengthening in Developing Countries: Final Report for DFID* (London: Overseas Development Institute). Reviews a topical theme.

■ Hyden, G., Court, J., and Mease, K. (2004), *Making Sense of Governance: Empirical Evidence from Sixteen Developing Countries* (Boulder, CO: Lynne Rienner). A comprehensive assessment informed by extensive evidence covering half the world's population.

■ Kaufmann, D., Kray, A., and Mastruzzi, M. (2008), *Governance Matters VII: Governance Indicators for 1996–2007* (Washington, DC: World Bank Policy Research Working Paper No. 4654).

■ Kjaer, M. (2004), *Governance* (Cambridge: Polity Press). A useful survey of the issues.

■ Lazarus, J. (2008), 'Participation in Poverty Reduction Strategy Papers: Reviewing the Past, Assessing the Present and Predicting the Future', *Third World Quarterly*, 29/6: 1205–21. Survey highlighting the influence of domestic politics on PRSP outcomes.

■ Lockwood, B. and Redoano, M. (2005), *The CSGR Globalisation Index*, available at www2.warwick.ac.uk /fac/soc/csgr/index A large data set on globalization.

■ Moore, M. (2004), 'Revenues, State Formation, and the Quality of Governance in Developing Countries', *International Political Science Review*, 25/3: 297–319. Explores the implications of fiscal sociology for governance in the developing world's rentier states.

■ Mosley, L. (2005), 'Globalization and the State: Still Room to Move?', *New Political Economy*, 10/3: 355–62. Assesses globalization's impact on developing world states.

■ Woods, N. (2006), *The Globalizers: The IMF, the World Bank and Their Borrowers* (Ithaca, NY: Cornell University Press). A critical account of the Bretton Woods institutions.

 Web links

■ www.worldbank.org/wbi/governance The World Bank Institute's site on governance and its activities in support of governance capacity-building.

■ www2.warwick.ac.uk/fac/soc/csgr The CSGR Globalization Index compiled by Ben Lockwood and Michela Redoano.

■ http://commissionforafrica.org/ The report of the Commission for Africa (2005), *Our Common Interest*.

■ www.nepad.org The official site of the New Partnership for Africa's Development (NEPAD).

■ **www.undp.org/oslocentre/**   Provides information on the UNDP's Global Programme on Democratic Governance Assessments.

■ **www.odi.org.uk/wga_governance/About_WGA.html**   Site for World Governance Assessment.

■ **www.oecd.org/**   Site includes *The Paris Declaration on Aid Effectiveness* (2005), a shared vision of aid relations by international donors and developing world partners, including the idea of ownership by partners.

 Online Resource Centre

For additional material and resources, please visit the Online Resource Centre at:
www.oxfordtextbooks.co.uk/orc/burnell3e/

PART 4
Policy Issues

In this part, several major policy domains in development are examined. The themes do not concern developing countries only; in all the developing regions they represent notable challenges to both state and non-state actors at the present time. Our concern is not with 'development' per se or as a universal concept, although the increasingly holistic way in which development tends to be understood these days inevitably has implications for the presentation here. Rather, this part again has two main aims.

First, it aims to show how states, like other major actors in the economy and society, are confronted by certain key issues in development and face seemingly inescapable challenges. States in particular have to entertain large decisions that involve political risks and impose considerable administrative burdens, concerning such matters as economic development, welfare, the environment, and human rights. However, as for instance Chapter 19 on Security amply illustrates, we cannot understand the precise nature of the issues simply by seeing them through the lens of concerned actors in the West. All of the policy issues must be viewed against the background of the local context in the developing countries. This can differ dramatically from one country and social group to another.

If the first aim is to explore the issues, a *second* aim is to show the different ways in which governments and non-governmental actors and international bodies too determine their response, by comparing different strategies and their likely consequences. Here, the relevance of international influences to the way in which policy agendas are formed and, often to policy implementation is undeniable but nevertheless should be examined critically. The object of Part 4 is to illuminate the policy process while necessarily being limited in how much detail it can convey about the policy substance. What choices really are open to developing countries, and just how much scope for exercising choice independently have they experienced to date? Does state action necessarily offer the most appropriate way forward? Does one size fit all, or does the evidence suggest that the political response can embody distinct national and sub-national frameworks for defining problems, devising solutions, and implementing a course of action? Readers are encouraged to read the introduction to Part 5 and to consult relevant case studies alongside the chapters in Part 4.

16

Development

Tony Addison

Overview

This chapter discusses development policy objectives, noting how these have changed over the years, with a more explicit focus on poverty reduction coming to the fore recently. It also examines the relationship between economic growth and poverty reduction. The chapter then discusses how to achieve economic growth and then moves on to the big question of the respective roles for the market mechanism and the state in allocating society's productive resources, before discussing the relationship between trade and development. The chapter then discusses how economic reform has been implemented, and the political difficulties that arise. It concludes that getting development policy right has the potential to lift millions out of poverty. The issue of how to achieve economic growth and development in an environmentally sustainable way—the idea of environmentally sustainable development—is introduced in Chapter 17.

Introduction

There are nearly 1.4 billion people living in extreme poverty today, defined as having less than US$1.25 per day on which to survive (see Table 16.1). This is a quarter of the population of the developing world.

The situation in sub-Saharan Africa is especially desperate: nearly half of the population is poor and poverty has increased over the last decade. Some 799 million people, or 17 per cent of the population in developing countries, are undernourished, and in sub-Saharan Africa one-third of the population is undernourished, the largest of any developing region, and a percentage that is rising (World Bank 2003: 6). Yet, set against this grim picture there has also been considerable progress, notably in East Asia where extreme poverty is a fraction of its level thirty years ago (see Table 16.1). Even in South Asia, which has the largest numbers of poor people of all the main regions, the percentage of people in poverty has fallen substantially over the last decade.

Looking at **economic growth**—(the rate of growth in gross domestic product (GDP) often presented on a per capita basis—many East Asian countries have grown at rates that are historically unprecedented. Whereas it took the United Kingdom—the world's first industrial nation—54 years to develop from a low per-capita income economy to a middle-income economy, it took Hong Kong, Singapore, and Taiwan (the 'tigers') only ten years to achieve middle-income status (estimates from Parente and Prescott 2000). China is presently growing at over 9 per cent a year, and India's growth has accelerated as well, and their demand for oil and other commodities has pushed up global commodity prices to the benefit of sub-Saharan Africa (which remains overwhelmingly dependent on commodity exports) as well as Latin America (where commodities still have a large export share). But while growth in sub-Saharan Africa has risen in recent years, Africa has performed very badly for much of the period since 1980 (with notable exceptions such as Botswana and Mauritius), and GDP per capita is lower than in 1960 in the Democratic Republic of the Congo, which has gone through years of war and turmoil. Latin America achieved steady if unspectacular growth in the period up to the late 1970s but then went into deep recession during the debt crisis of the 1980s (described by Latin Americans as the 'lost decade'). Latin America recovered in the 1990s, but then underwent another bout of turbulence (with a spectacular economic collapse in Argentina, which was the star reformer of the early to mid-1990s) before strong commodity earnings once again pushed up growth (especially in Brazil and Chile). Lastly, oil wealth raised living standards in the Middle East and North Africa but this region has, with only a few exceptions, largely failed to achieve economic diversification and provide employment for a growing and young population (see Table 16.2).

Table 16.1 Extreme Poverty, 1990–2005

	People living on less than $US1.25 a day (millions)			Share of people living on less than $US1.25 a day (%)		
	1981	1996	2005	1981	1996	2005
East Asia and Pacific	1071.5	622.3	316.2	77.7	36.0	16.8
of which China	835.1	442.8	207.7	84.0	36.4	15.9
Eastern Europe and Central Asia	7.1	21.8	17.3	1.7	4.6	3.7
Latin America and Caribbean	42.0	52.2	46.1	11.5	10.8	8.2
Middle East and North Africa	13.7	10.6	11.0	7.9	4.1	3.6
South Asia	548.3	594.4	595.6	59.4	47.1	40.3
of which India	420.5	441.8	455.8	59.8	46.6	41.6
Sub-Saharan Africa	213.7	355.0	390.6	53.7	58.7	50.9
Total	1896.2	1656.2	1376.7	51.8	34.4	25.2

Source: Chen and Ravallion 2008: 42, 44

Table 16.2 Economic Growth, 1980–2008 (average annual % growth)

	1980–90	1990–2000	2000–08
Low income	4.5	3.4	5.8
Middle income	2.9	3.4	6.4
Lower middle income	4.0	3.7	8.3
Upper middle income	1.7	3.1	4.6
Low and middle income	3.2	3.4	6.4
East Asia and Pacific	7.5	7.5	9.1
Europe and Central Asia	2.1	21.0	6.3
Latin America and the Caribbean	1.7	3.2	3.9
Middle East and North Africa	2.0	3.0	4.7
South Asia	5.6	5.5	7.4
Sub-Saharan Africa	1.6	2.6	5.2
High income	3.3	2.5	2.3

Sources: World Bank 2003: 188; 2009: 385

In sum, the developing world today presents a very mixed picture: very fast growth and poverty reduction in much of Asia; hesitant growth after long-term decline in sub-Saharan Africa combined with high poverty; growth after considerable economic volatility in Latin America; and disappointing performance in North Africa and the Middle East, despite often abundant natural resources. Growth fell over 2008–09 as the world entered its worst economic recession since the 1930s (see Chapter 4), although the larger 'emerging economies' (Brazil, China, and India) have done better in the crisis than the poorer and smaller economies (many of them in Africa). Climate change could reduce economic growth in countries that are vulnerable to flood or drought, thereby increasing poverty especially in regions that are already environmentally stressed. Therefore differences between developing countries could widen in future.

What role has development policy played in these different outcomes? What policies are most important for accelerating development? Is the development past a guide to the development future?

What lessons can we transfer across countries? As Nobel Laureate Robert Lucas says, 'the consequences for human welfare involved in questions like these are simply staggering. Once one starts to think about them, it is hard to think about anything else' (Lucas 1988). And thinking about development policy has changed over time. On some issues there is now considerable agreement about what needs to be done. But many issues remain deeply controversial, with starkly contrasting viewpoints.

Key points

- Nearly 1.4 billion people live in extreme poverty, about a quarter of the developing world's population.
- Poverty is falling in Asia, but remains high in sub-Saharan Africa and widespread in Latin America.
- Asia is growing fast, but sub-Saharan Africa has performed very badly and Latin America tends to boom and bust.

Much of today's debate is centred on poverty reduction as the primary objective for development policy (as can be seen when you look at the websites of the international agencies given at the end of this chapter). People differ as to how to define 'poverty': economists typically favour monetary measures, using data collected from household surveys of incomes and expenditures. If the household falls below a defined poverty line then it is classified as poor. However, not all countries have the data to define poverty in this way, so measures of the 'dollar a day' variety are often used to calculate the global and regional aggregates (this is now US$1.25 to reflect the rise in the cost of living in the period since the World Bank first introduced the 'dollar a day' measure twenty years ago).

Non-monetary measures of poverty are increasingly used—measures such as infant mortality, life expectancy, and literacy—and people vary in how well they are doing across these different dimensions. Some may have a rising income but remain illiterate, for example, and women often do worse than men, reflecting gender discrimination (in access to education and jobs, for example). People in chronic poverty suffer from multiple deprivations making it very difficult for them to ever escape, and poverty is passed down the generations; the children of the chronically poor generally remain poor when they become adults (Chronic Poverty Research Centre (CPRC) 2008). The **Millennium Development Goals** (MDGs), which were adopted by the world's leaders in the UN Millennium Declaration of September 2000 as guiding principles for the international development community (see Box 16.1), reflect the multi-dimensional view of poverty. The smaller, poorer, and conflict-affected countries (mostly in Africa) are unlikely, on present trends, to fully achieve all of the MDGs, but this is not to say that significant progress cannot still be made in areas such as child killers like malaria (in which there are major initiatives and funding). The larger and faster-growing economies such as Brazil (which has also stepped up its anti-poverty programmes) and China stand the best prospects for MDG success.

In the early days of development policy, during the era of decolonization from the late 1940s through to the 1960s, poverty reduction was often more implicit than explicit in development strategies. These tended to focus on raising GDP per capita (more loosely income per capita) by means of economic growth—it being assumed that poverty reduction would then follow, more or less, from growth. Early development thinkers emphasized raising output, in particular increasing overall labour productivity (output per person) by shifting labour from sectors in which its productivity is low to sectors in which it is high. This led to a concentration on industry (which was seen as the dynamic sector) while many policymakers saw smallholder (peasant) agriculture as hopelessly backward and unproductive (it could therefore release large amounts of labour for industry). Crudely put, industrialization and urbanization became synonymous with development in the minds of many policymakers from the 1940s to the 1960s. This was reinforced by what appeared, at the time, to be the successful example of the Soviet Union—a country that achieved large-scale industrialization from the 1930s onwards. Aid donors enthusiastically supported big infrastructure projects, especially when these benefited the commercial interests of their own countries.

Box 16.1 The Millennium Development Goals

Goal 1: Eradicate extreme poverty and hunger

Target 1: Halve, between 1990 and 2015, the proportion of people whose income is less than US$1 a day.

Target 2: Halve, between 1990 and 2015, the proportion of people who suffer from hunger.

Goal 2: Achieve universal primary education

Target 3: Ensure that, by 2015, children everywhere, boys and girls alike, will be able to complete a full course of primary schooling.

Goal 3: Promote gender equality and empower women

Target 4: Eliminate gender disparity in primary and secondary education, preferably by 2005 and in all levels of education no later than 2015.

Goal 4: Reduce child mortality

Target 5: Reduce by two-thirds, between 1990 and 2015, the under-five mortality rate.

Goal 5: Improve maternal health

Target 6: Reduce by three-quarters, between 1990 and 2015, the maternal mortality ratio.

Goal 6: Combat HIV/AIDS, malaria, and other diseases

Target 7: Have halted by 2015 and begun to reverse the spread of HIV/AIDS [human immunodeficiency virus/acquired immunodeficiency syndrome].

Target 8: Have halted by 2015 and begun to reverse the incidence of malaria and other major diseases.

Goal 7: Ensure environmental sustainability

Target 9: Integrate the principles of sustainable development into country policies and programmes and reverse the loss of environmental resources.

Target 10: Halve by 2015 the proportion of people without sustainable access to safe drinking water.

Target 11: Have achieved by 2020 a significant improvement in the lives of at least 100 million slum-dwellers.

Goal 8: Develop a global partnership for development

Target 12: Develop further an open, rule-based, predictable, non-discriminatory trading and financial system (includes a commitment to good governance, development, and poverty reduction—both nationally and internationally).

Target 13: Address the special needs of the least developed countries (includes tariffs- and quota-free access for exports, enhanced program of debt relief for and cancellation of official bilateral debt, and more generous official development assistance for countries committed to poverty reduction).

Target 14: Address the special needs of land-locked countries and small-island developing states (through the Program of Action for the Sustainable Development of Small Island Developing States and 22nd General Assembly Provisions).

Target 15: Deal comprehensively with the debt problems of developing countries through national and international measures in order to make debt sustainable in the long term.

Target 16: In cooperation with developing countries, develop and implement strategies for decent and productive work for youth.

Target 17: In cooperation with pharmaceutical companies, provide access to affordable essential drugs in developing countries.

Target 18: In cooperation with the private sector, make available the benefits of new technologies, especially information and communication technologies.

(UNDP 2003: 1–3)

Income per capita is an *average* measure of a country's living standard, and there can be a wide *variation* around this mean. This variation—the inequality of income—exhibits substantial differences across countries, reflecting differences in the distribution of wealth (land, other property, and financial wealth) and **human capital** (peoples' skills and capabilities, which are partly a product of their education, and which make them more productive). The differences in turn reflect country-specific histories of colonization, war, and policies. South Africa's extreme inequality in income and wealth is a legacy of apartheid and Latin America's high inequality reflects the dispossession of indigenous communities by Portuguese and Spanish colonial elites, for instance.

Some people worry about inequality more than others (see Chapter 6). Quite apart from the ethical dimension (do the rich deserve their wealth?) and social stability (will resentment against the rich lead to violence and undermine development?) and the implications for democratic development (see Chapter 14), high inequality makes economic growth less effective in reducing poverty. A Latin American landowner with millions of hectares will benefit much more from agricultural export growth than a smallholder eking out a living on just a few hectares. Put differently, high-inequality societies need to grow a lot faster to achieve the same amount of annual poverty reduction as low-inequality societies.

So, countries need to protect and build the assets of the poor, particularly their human capital as well as the **natural capital** such as the soils, forests, and fisheries on which their livelihoods depend. Providing primary education, basic health care, water, and sanitation will not only raise the **human development** of poor people but will also raise their productivity. This will help them to diversify their livelihoods in both self-employment (for example from dependence on subsistence agriculture and into cash crops and micro-enterprises) and wage-employment (the poor will earn more as skilled workers than as unskilled workers). Asset *redistribution* may also be necessary to build the assets of the poor. Often this applies particularly to land and its transfer from the rich to the rural poor. Asset redistribution is much more challenging politically, and large-scale redistributions tend to be associated with political revolutions. In these ways, economic growth will start to become more pro-poor, and each percentage point of growth will deliver more poverty reduction. This is not to say that all of the poor are in a position to benefit from growth; the chronically poor who suffer from multiple deprivations may be elderly or so sick that they are unemployable, and the illiterate are the least attractive to employers even in a growing economy. Many of the chronically poor live in remote regions far from the main economic centres, and even strong economic growth can

bypass them. For the chronically poor it is important to use the additional public revenues generated from growth (collected through the tax system) to finance more social protection (pensions, food assistance, as well as education and health provision targeted to their needs). State-building is therefore vital to achieving poverty reduction through public programmes.

Awareness of what holds poor people back came to the fore in the 1970s, in part because of disillusion with the outcomes of the first development decades. The high hopes of decolonization proved to be largely illusory in Africa, and poverty persisted in Latin America notwithstanding growth. This led to a radicalization of the development debate with **dependency theory** much in vogue. In addition, by the 1970s there was much more evidence from academic research on the determinants of poverty and how poverty responds to economic and social change. This led to a reconsideration of the earlier view that smallholder agriculture was un-dynamic, and a new emphasis on the talents of poor people as farmers and micro-entrepreneurs. Development professionals began to see new ways of helping the poor to build their livelihoods, and for the first time the knowledge of the poor themselves came to be valued. The World Bank, under its then president, Robert McNamara, began to move away from its traditional emphasis on lending to physical infrastructure and towards poverty reduction, particularly through agricultural development, the principal livelihood of the world's poor.

Note that a direct focus on poverty reduction has a sharper political dimension than a focus on growth in a development strategy. For a start, the poor may be poor because they have very little, if any, political voice. This is true of many of the rural poor in sub-Saharan Africa, for instance, and is evident in the way in which development strategies often ignored them or, perversely, taxed them (see Bates 1981). Politicians need to expend very little political capital when they talk about economic growth being 'like a tide that raises all boats'. But when it comes to spending public money, basic pro-poor services—especially those that serve the rural poor—are often left behind, after services that prioritize the needs of more vocal, and more effectively organized, non-poor groups (especially in urban political centres). A general bias against the rural areas and in favour of the urban areas (**urban bias**) was evident in much of post-independence Africa. Vocal and wealthy interests can effectively control the legislatures that determine the pattern of public spending and taxation (as in Central America) and the political power that accompanies wealth is another reason why many people worry about high inequality. When economic crisis strikes governments often let the burden of adjustment fall on the meagre services that actually benefit the poor. They protect presidential spending and make cuts in basic health care for example.

However, some governments do more for poor people than others, and there are substantial differences in outcomes for poverty and human development across countries at similar levels of per capita income . This can be seen if you consult the United Nations Development Programme's (UNDP) annual Human Development Report (available at www.undp.org). Vietnam is one such success story (Box 16.2). Moreover, within countries, different regions often spend very different amounts on pro-poor services, reflecting the operation of local political factors: for instance in India, the state of Kerala is an outstanding success.

Box 16.2 The Vietnam Success Story

Vietnam, a country of 84 million people that suffered a devastating war from the 1950s to the 1970s, is Asia's best-performing economy after China; it grew by 7.8 per cent in 2006. Vietnam is also one of the world's success stories in poverty reduction. Poverty has fallen from 58 per cent of the population in 1993 to under 20 per cent in 2004.

The key to this success has been the construction of a vigorous export economy, the creation of more opportunities for small enterprises, and investment in agriculture. Exports have expanded rapidly enabling the economy to diversify, with considerable foreign investment especially following a 2000 bilateral trade deal with the United States that opened up the latter's market to Vietnamese exports (thereby encouraging US multinationals such as Disney and Nike to establish factories employing Vietnam's cheap and abundant labour). This trend is set to accelerate with Vietnam's accession to the World Trade Organization (WTO) in 2007.

Following the end of the war in 1975 and the country's unification, the Hanoi government extended Marxist central planning with its heavy restrictions on private enterprise to the country's capitalist South (which had, along with its ally the United States, lost the war). The economy performed badly under this system, with hyperinflation and a sharp fall in living standards being the main results. Tentative reform began in the 1980s with a move from collectivized agriculture to a market-orientated smallholder system and gathered pace with the adoption of the *Doi*

Moi (new changes) strategy in 1986. Reform intensified in the early 1990s as financial pressures grew with the drying up of aid from the Soviet Union, Vietnam's old cold war ally. The government restored macro-economic stability, liberalized restrictions on small private enterprises, and sought out foreign investment. However, the government is far from relinquishing all control over the economy, and there are still many state-owned enterprises; these account for 40 per cent of GDP in what is officially called a 'socialist-orientated market economy' (also the case in China, which, like Vietnam, has pursued economic liberalization in the context of a one-party Marxist state).

Export manufacturing has led to more urban jobs, and urban poverty has fallen substantially. Vietnam has gone from a country of food shortages to become a leading exporter of rice and coffee, resulting in increased incomes and a diversification of livelihoods in rural areas. But poverty remains stubbornly high in less advantaged regions such as Vietnam's Central Highlands where many of Vietnam's ethnic minorities live. They constitute 15 per cent of the total population but 40 per cent of the poor. Vietnam's rapid economic growth is not therefore delivering enough benefits for these people, and they need better education and health care, and more investment in transport and communications infrastructure, to improve their market access.

Vietnam is a success, but its economic growth has come from a very low level of per capita income, reflecting the impact of the long war and the economic crisis of the immediate post-war years. Its government administration is very bureaucratic, corruption is a growing problem, and the Communist government's grip on power is threatened by the economy's opening-up and the accompanying increased flow of ideas and information from abroad. Vietnam therefore faces some tough challenges ahead in maintaining the momentum of its success.

Key points

- Poverty reduction has become a more explicit objective of development policy, and economic growth is now seen as more of a means to an end, rather than a final objective in itself.

- Growth is important to reducing poverty, but not all poor people benefit from growth, and the chronically poor often miss out.

- Effective states are necessary to achieve development objectives, particularly in providing pro-poor services and infrastructure.

Markets and States

Achieving growth is far from easy, especially in countries that are land-locked and distant from markets (Bolivia and Niger, for example), subject to tropical diseases (West Africa in particular), and with climates and terrain that make them vulnerable to floods and droughts (Bangladesh and Africa's Sahel zone). Some countries therefore start with more favourable prospects for growth than others. But the prospects for growth also very much depend upon the design of development strategy, and particularly on the state's role.

Most people agree that states have an important role to play in protecting property rights, enforcing contracts, and defending their citizens against external aggression. Economists have emphasized the importance of the first two of these in providing a favourable climate for investment and for reducing the **transaction costs** of market exchange, both of which facilitate growth.

However, beyond a core set of **public goods** such as law and order and defence, people start to disagree about how much economic and social infrastructure the state should provide (public versus private education and health care, for example). And people often have radically different views about how far (if at all) the state should intervene in market mechanisms to set prices, control quantities (to ration, for example), set standards, and regulate producers (or to act as a producer itself through public ownership). Much of the debate about development strategy can be reduced to differences in views about what is the appropriate level of state provision and whether the state should mostly leave the market alone, or intervene extensively.

These different viewpoints partly arise from different perspectives on how markets work. Much disagreement centres on how well market mechanisms yield poverty reduction — or, indeed, whether markets sometimes work against poor people, making them poorer. Market optimists favour light regulation to let the market deliver the economic growth that best reduces poverty. Market pessimists favour state intervention, arguing that market outcomes reflect power and that this is often unfavourable to the poor (monopolies rather than competition might prevail in unregulated markets for example).

But people differ over the appropriate role for the state because they also hold different views over what constitutes the 'ideal society'. Thus nearly everyone is agreed that an ideal society must achieve absolute poverty reduction, but some people also favour state action to reduce overall income inequality as well. Others are vehemently opposed to such egalitarian ideas, citing individual freedom, including the right to accumulate wealth (this is reflected in the traditional political debates of social democracy versus conservatism). Also controversial are the ability of market mechanisms to yield economic growth, and whether a higher (or lower) growth rate will result from state intervention in the market mechanism (and how different types of intervention increase or decrease the prospects for growth). Similarly, there is much debate on how far 'market-led' or 'state-led' development is supportive of democratization and domestic political stability, as well as national sovereignty.

Market optimists will favour a minimal state: one that provides protection for property rights together with public goods that the market either does not supply or under-supplies (defence is one example, transport infrastructure is another). In contrast, people who are pessimistic about the market's ability to deliver their ideal society will favour a more active state, but their conceptualization of what the state should do can show a very wide range. At one extreme is central planning (practised by the former Soviet Union) where, by society's productive factors are allocated according to a plan without reference to market prices, and under which state ownership of enterprises and property prevails (North Korea is one of the few examples left, and even it has partially liberalized the economy). The 'European model' is at the other end of the scale of active states: continental European states provide very high levels of public goods, regulate the market 'in the public interest', but otherwise encourage a very vigorous private sector (the Nordic countries being the most successful at implementing this model).

Views on state effectiveness have swung like a pendulum over the last fifty years. As countries came to independence, they built national planning apparatuses and wrote national plans. The Soviet Union's example was very influential in China, Cuba, and Vietnam and so was the state planning that even the capitalist economies introduced during the 1940s and many retained afterwards. However, by the late 1970s this confidence in the state's abilities was starting to erode as growth slowed down due to policy failure in many (but certainly not all) countries that pursued state-led development, together with the first (1974) and second (1979) oil price hikes, and the associated world recessions, which tested state capacities to breaking point.

The intellectual pendulum swung back (albeit with considerable resistance) towards the market mechanism in the 1980s and accelerated with the collapse of communism, and the start of the transition to market economies in Eastern Europe and the Soviet Union. This was reinforced by the International Monetary Fund (IMF) and the World Bank and their loan conditionality (often dubbed the **Washington consensus** on what constitutes good policy). Policy change was not always externally induced. India undertook significant economic liberalization in the early 1990s, reflecting domestic criticism of the long-standing strategy of planning and state ownership.

More recently a reaction against market liberalization and privatization has set in, and the intellectual pendulum has begun to swing back towards the state, owing to sharp increases in inequality, rising concern over liberalization's social effects, the mismanagement of privatization, and the role of the liberalized financial sector in creating the global recession of 2008–09. This is bound up in an intense debate about globalization and its effects (see Nayyar 2002). Latin America is experiencing especially intense criticism of liberalization, reflecting the very mixed outcome from reform programmes in the 1990s (see Box 16.3). Economists increasingly recognize the importance of **institutions** to making the market mechanism work well for development and poverty reduction. The World Bank has stepped back from its emphasis in the 1980s on the market alone and now gives more attention to institution-building, although its critics argue that Bank policy still fails to equip countries with the strategies that they need to cope with globalization.

Venezuela is an example of the political forces that are now playing out right across Latin America. Bolivia and Peru have similarly moved to extend state control over their mining and energy sectors (see Box 16.3). The commodity price boom is enabling governments to pay off their debts and the

improved credit rating of the region's sovereign borrowers is reducing the influence of the IMF and the World Bank upon which Latin America relied for financing in times of economic crisis. The influence of the Washington consensus on domestic policymaking is therefore falling. Whether this leads to better development outcomes depends upon how governments use their new revenues, whether they can reduce political polarization to get agreement on effective development strategies, and whether they can build better states capable of helping the poor.

Box 16.3 Venezuela: Reacting Against the Washington Consensus

Venezuela is the world's fifth largest oil producer. But nature's bounty has not delivered economic success: growth largely collapsed from 1980 to 2000. Inequality and poverty are both high: 48.5 per cent of Venezuelans were below the poverty line in 2000, and the richest 20 per cent of Venezuelans receive over half of all income.

Foreign oil companies began producing oil in the early twentieth century. The state increasingly intervened from the 1940s onwards as oil became the main source of government revenue (it now accounts for about half of total revenue) and the oil industry was fully nationalized in 1976. Global oil prices were driven up by the Organisation of Petroleum Exporting Countries (OPEC) (of which Venezuela was a founding member in 1960) and grand promises were made that within a few years Venezuela would be a developed country with no poverty. Between 1950 and 1980 Venezuela was one of Latin America's fastest growing economies. But the massive windfall eventually undermined the non-oil economy (a phenomenon often called 'Dutch disease' after the problems that the Netherlands faced in adjusting to an energy windfall). Venezuela became heavily indebted as it borrowed on the back of high oil prices in the late 1970s, thereby exposing itself to the price collapse that came in the 1980s. Severe problems in debt servicing resulted, growth collapsed and living standards fell precipitously, with the country going through a succession of unstable governments in the 1990s each with its own unsuccessful economic recovery plan.

The present president, Hugo Chávez, a former military officer who first took office in the 1998 elections, attracts strong opinions. Some see him as a heroic figure doing battle with the forces of global capitalism, a champion of Venezuela's national interests, and defender of the country's poor. Others see him as a demagogue intent on consolidating his personal power by changing the constitution and cracking down on media criticism after the 2007 presidential elections (which he won with a large majority). The president has become more radical in recent years, denouncing neo-liberalism and the Washington consensus (and he is also highly critical of the United States).

With a robust world economy (until 2008) and growing energy demand in China and India, oil prices are high once again and export earnings have filled the government coffers allowing it to massively expand public spending, including spending on programmes for the poor whose numbers appear to be falling. Political support for President Chávez is not surprisingly high among the poor.

President Chávez now proclaims the need for '21st century socialism' including the reversal of the privatization of Venezuela's telecommunications and electricity utilities so that public ownership of the economy's 'strategic sectors' is restored. This has frightened foreign investors who have invested large amounts in the country since the privatizations of the early 1990s. Chávez is also further extending state control over Venezuela's oil sector by negotiating new agreements with the oil multinationals to capture more of the revenue for the Venezuelan state.

Key points

- The economic role of the state is one of the central issues dividing opinion on development strategy.
- An early emphasis on state-led development was eventually challenged by a market-liberal view, leading to widespread economic liberalization.

- Despite the roll-back of the state, it still has many roles to play in providing public goods as well as in regulating markets in the public interest.

Trade Policy as an Instrument for Development

For market liberals, developing countries that follow their **comparative advantage** will reap higher living standards by trading as much as possible with the developed countries and with each other (see Chapter 4). Their export earnings can then finance imports of products in which they have a comparative *disadvantage*. The market-liberal story of trade is one of mutual gains from trade for both the developing and the developed worlds.

For market liberals comparative advantage also underpins their view of how trade contributes to economic growth, through **outward-oriented development**. Growth in developing countries' labour-intensive exports (their comparative advantage) will eventually bid up the price of labour (thereby contributing to poverty reduction) and encourage capital-for-labour substitution. The skill content of exports will also rise as educational investment builds human capital, allowing developing countries to start competitively producing what is presently made in the developed world. The state must assist this process through judicious public investment, in infrastructure for example, but it is the market that drives it.

In the early years, many policymakers felt that such outward-orientated development would not yield much growth. Instead, many saw the domestic market as the main growth driver, and they favoured inward-orientated development and import-substituting industrialization (see Chapter 4). Producers who would benefit from protected markets also lobbied for the policy and their influence increased over time as they used the **economic rents** associated with protection to fund sympathetic politicians and political parties, sometimes engaging in outright **corruption**. Critics of protection argue that **rent-seeking** comes to dominate the strategy, no matter how well-intentioned initially, and this view underpinned the World Bank's efforts to open up economies in the 1980s.

In practice the effects of lobbying and rent-seeking vary widely. They were at their worst in sub-Saharan Africa where weak states were easily captured by powerful rent-seekers, and where the smallness of domestic markets made import-substitution unviable without high tariffs and very tight import quotas (which encouraged massive evasion and smuggling). Criticism of India's 'license Raj' led to economic liberalization in the early 1990s but India's growth was respectable, if undramatic, prior to liberalization. And import-substitution achieved some 'learning by doing', facilitated by India's enormous domestic market, which gives domestic manufacturers larger economies of scale. South Korea's planning mechanism effectively contained rent-seeking and export subsidies offset the disincentive to export production inherent in import protection. Since South Korea is an outstanding development success, it is difficult to believe that it would have achieved even higher growth without import protection (see Chapter 22b).

The conduct of trade policy is also made more complex by the scale of protectionism that still exists in world trade despite the liberalization conducted under the General Agreement on Tariffs and Trade (GATT) and WTO auspices. Nowhere is this more apparent than in world agriculture. Rich countries pay large subsidies to their farmers, and restrict imports from developing countries (although some countries exporting to the European Union currently still get preferential access). This depresses the world prices of some major export earners for developing countries, notably cotton and sugar, thereby reducing the incomes of their farmers. Brazil has used the WTO to successfully challenge US protectionism, but the smaller and poorer countries lack the resources to defend their interests. They also find it difficult to access the markets of the larger developing countries such as India, which also protects its farmers from foreign competition (although the scale of this protection has been recently reduced). The developing countries do not always have common interests in world trade negotiations and they face powerful political bodies, such as the European Union, which are adept at protecting their interests. The doctrine of comparative advantage is therefore a useful guide to development policy but it offers only a start since world trade is far from being a completely free market. For this reason, many policymakers continue to favour a very interventionist policy when it comes to the role of trade in development, but much depends on the state's capacity to implement it successfully. This in turn raises issues of governance (see Chapter 15).

Key points

- Import-substitution works much better in countries with large domestic markets, and where policy encourages export production as well.
- While the failure of many countries to achieve growth through import protection increased support for outward-orientated development, this too requires a well-designed strategy, particularly in creating new skills to sell in the global marketplace.

Capital Flows and Economic Reform

The world economic shocks of the 1970s and 1980s were a major catalyst for reform. But changes in the level and composition of international capital flows — foreign aid, commercial bank lending, and foreign direct investment — to developing countries have also been influential in inducing reform.

In the 1970s the non-oil-producing developing countries encountered serious macro-economic trouble with the first (1974) and second (1979) oil price shocks when the Organization of Petroleum Exporting Countries (OPEC) quadrupled the world price of oil. During this time the IMF became very important in providing balance of payments support. Several of the oil exporters also borrowed heavily using their oil revenues as collateral (for example Nigeria, Mexico, and Venezuela) and they suffered macro-economic crisis when the world oil price fell during the 1980s. All this brought about the debt crisis (see Chapter 4). In Asia, Malaysia, Singapore, South Korea, and Taiwan escaped largely unscathed and indeed maintained high growth during the 1980s and into the 1990s, until the Asian financial crisis of 1997–98. And although by the early 1980s South Korea was as highly indebted as some Latin American countries, by then its strong export economy was able to generate the foreign exchange necessary to maintain debt service. This brought home an important lesson: countries neglect export markets at their peril. Chinese policymakers quickly learned this lesson and China now has a significant share of global manufacturing exports. Some analysts believe China's success poses a problem for smaller developing countries also seeking to grow by increasing their share of world markets for relatively low-cost manufactured goods.

Structural adjustment

With so many of its client countries in deep distress, the World Bank was compelled to move beyond its traditional project lending and in the 1980s it started to provide balance-of-payments support through **structural adjustment loans** (SALs). These carried such policy conditionalities as: currency devaluation (to stimulate the supply of exports); the conversion of import quotas into import tariffs to reduce rent-seeking (and then tariff reduction in order to place more competitive pressure on inefficient infant industries); the removal (liberalization) of market controls in agriculture (to provide more incentives for farmers); and the reform of public expenditures and taxation (to shift more spending towards development priorities and to mobilize more public revenues to finance spending). The IMF's policy conditionality also includes reducing the fiscal deficit to curb inflation (high inflation reduced export competitiveness and economic growth).

Although World Bank and IMF adjustment lending was intended to deal with the immediate macro-economic crises, it was also seen as a way of making poor economies more efficient and therefore more able to grow. For, according to the Washington consensus, that required a reduced role for the state in the productive sectors (hence the start of privatization in the 1980s) as well as reduced controls (liberalization) on the private sector. Irrespective of the merits or otherwise of reform, most countries had little alternative but to sign up to the conditionality, since private capital flows slowed dramatically with the onset of the debt crisis in the 1980s, and official development flows became one of the few sources of external finance. This was especially true for the low-income countries (see Chapter 15).

Yet market liberalization has had very mixed results. Take the market for food staples, for example. This market is vital, for it affects farmers, who produce a surplus to sell, farmers who produce too little themselves and must buy food, rural wage-labourers, and urban households. If the state withdraws (partially or wholly) from buying, storing, transporting, and selling food, then it has to be replaced by private entrepreneurs willing to undertake these tasks and bear the risks. But there is more profit to be made in supplying food to major urban centres than in marketing in remote and poor rural areas. Similarly, market liberalization in the manufacturing sector has had mixed effects. The rapid removal of import protection led to factory closures and the loss of jobs in many reforming countries. New jobs may eventually be created once export activities grow, but the necessary investment takes time. In the meantime, unemployment may rise sharply.

Not surprisingly, liberalization has many opponents and it is risky for governments, who often procrastinate (thereby deepening the severity of the economic crisis). Moreover, reform's effects are never clear-cut. Many people oppose reform (*ex ante*) fearing a loss, even if this is not the case (*ex post*). Conversely, some people may gain a lot (for example those producing exports) but the gains are not immediate. Sometimes a particular reform will benefit the majority of people but if each person's gain is small then they do not have much incentive to mobilize in support of reform, whereas the minority may stand to lose a lot and therefore has a much greater incentive to mobilize against reform. Reform can therefore stall even if, in aggregate, it benefits the majority. This is a good example of what Olson (2001) calls a collective action problem, which refers to the difficulties that arise in organizing a group of people to achieve a common objective.

Although it is highly controversial, liberalization is straightforward in its implementation because the state simply withdraws, partially or wholly, from the market. But some reforms require a strengthening of state capacity and better governance for their success. This is especially true of revenue and public expenditure reforms. The state's capacity to mobilize tax and customs revenues and to then spend these resources effectively on pro-poor services and development infrastructure requires a capable, well-motivated, and corruption-free government administration, at both central and local levels (the latter being especially important to improving local education and health, for example). However, the quality of civil services, together with their motivation, was in steep decline before reform began in many countries, especially in Africa where inflation eroded real wages in the public sector. Governments were therefore attempting to implement demanding changes with very limited institutional and human resources, and in some cases IMF fiscal-conditionality weakened state capacities further. Reform breakdown and policy reversals are common. Zambia, for example, has gone through many donor-supported adjustment programmes that largely failed to achieve progress, notwithstanding there being greater political commitment by the government to this in the 1990s than previously. There is also a fierce debate on whether economic reform contributed to the breakdown of states and societies in countries like Sierra Leone and Somalia (on conflict-prone societies, see Chapter 13).

So-called 'second-generation' economic reforms (privatization and financial reform, in particular) have been taking place since the 1990s in countries such as Ghana, Uganda, and Tanzania that began their first-generation reforms (devaluation and trade liberalization) in the 1980s. Implementation of second-generation reforms has often been problematic. For instance privatization has been non-transparent in many cases, thereby transferring valuable assets to the politically connected. Financial reform has been especially difficult. Asia's financial crisis and Africa's bank failures both highlight the need to build capacity for prudential supervision and regulation in central banks before major liberalization of financial controls. Tax reform and the construction of better systems of public expenditure management (both essential to not just more investment in development infrastructure but pro-poor services specifically) have stalled in many cases. All this illustrates the importance of building effective state capacities and improving governance (Chapter 15), to regulate the (financial) market in the public interest, and to achieve improvements in the public goods essential to a well-functioning market economy as well as poverty reduction.

Key points

- Economic reform is driven by the failure of past development strategies, policy conditionality attached to development aid, and the need to attract private capital.

- Market liberalization is much easier to achieve than making states effective, which is often a long haul.

- Reform may be opposed because it has large social costs, or because the losers from reform often have more incentive and find it easier to organize themselves politically than the winners.

Conclusion

There are issues on which there is considerable consensus and issues regarding which deep controversy remains. That development policy must have an explicit focus on poverty reduction is one of the main areas of consensus in today's development policy community. In contrast to the period up to the 1970s, when it was thought that economic growth would automatically deliver poverty reduction, it is now recognized that pro-poor policies are necessary to maximize growth's benefits for the poor. Moreover, it is widely agreed that poverty reduction does not just entail higher incomes, but also improving human development indicators: poverty is a multi-dimensional concept. This implies improving the delivery of pro-poor services, particularly in basic health care, safe water and sanitation, and primary education, with a particular emphasis on delivery to rural areas (which contain high levels of poverty) and to women (see Chapter 9). Relatedly, it is widely agreed that the formation of human capital through better health and education is not only good for poverty reduction, but also contributes to growth by enabling diversification into skill-intensive manufactures and services. In this way, poor economies can seek to benefit from globalization.

Compared with the early years of development there is now a greater recognition that the market is important to growth. This shift is somewhat grudging and reflects more the failure of state-led development in many (but certainly not all) countries rather than a large-scale intellectual conversion. Accompanying this has been a move away from heavy import protection and a greater awareness of the value of exporting. Yet, many of the poorer countries find it difficult to achieve export success, especially outside their traditional primary products. They are highly vocal critics of rich country protectionism, especially in agriculture. There is much less support for public ownership of factories and farms and a greater recognition of the private sector's strengths. However, there is much less consensus on whether utilities — power, water, transport infrastructure — should be in private or public ownership, although the fiscal crises of developing countries have driven many governments to privatize their state utilities nevertheless. Countries are now keener to attract private capital flows especially when they bring new technologies but private flows remain concentrated on relatively few countries, and smaller and poorer economies are less attractive to private capital. Finally, how to adapt to the impact of climate change will increasingly drive the development debate (see Chapter 17), leading to new demands on state capacity.

Getting development policy right has the potential to lift millions of people out of the misery of poverty. But making the right policy choices is not just a technical matter. It requires careful political judgement about how to promote economic and social change in ways that stand the most chance of success, in an environment that, as the global financial crisis and recession of 2008–09 and the demands imposed by climate change show, is becoming ever more complex.

? Questions

1. What are the main causes of East Asia's success in economic development? Can other countries adopt the East Asian model successfully?

2. How can poor people participate more fully in economic growth? How will their participation vary across developing regions?

3. If economic reform does yield significant benefits for growth and living standards as its proponents argue, then why is it often so difficult politically?

4. What should be the role for the state in economic development, and how might this differ across developing regions?

5. Why has Africa found it so difficult to achieve economic development and what can be done to improve Africa's performance in future?

6. How far should our ideas of development reflect political and social variables as distinct from economic variables?

7. Does economic development necessarily make the state stronger and the country more influential in world affairs? Give reasons for your answer.

8. What do you think a socialist model of or path to development looks like and is it plausible in the twenty-first century?

→ **Further reading**

■ Addison, T. (2003), 'Economics', in P. Burnell (ed.), *Democratization through the Looking Glass* (Manchester: Manchester University Press). Examines how democracy affects economic performance, and contrasts democracy to autocracy in its development effects.

■ —— and Brück, T. (eds) (2008), *Making Peace Work: The Challenges of Economic and Social Reconstruction* (Basingstoke: Palgrave Macmillan). Examines the political and economic tensions inherent in rebuilding societies from war.

■ Amsden, A. H. (2001), *The Rise of the 'Rest': Challenges to the West from Late-Industrializing Economies* (Oxford: Oxford University Press). A comprehensive discussion of the East Asian success, and the role of the state in guiding the growth process.

■ Chang, H.-J. (2002), *Kicking Away the Ladder: Development Strategy in Historical Perspective* (London: Anthem Press). Contrasts the historical experiences of today's developed countries, and challenges the conventional wisdom on how development institutions are created.

■ Chronic Poverty Research Centre (CPRC) (2008), *The Chronic Poverty Report 2008–09* (London: Chronic Poverty Research Centre). Discusses people who remain poor for much or all of their lives, and who benefit least from economic growth.

■ Collier, P. (2007), *The Bottom Billion: Why The Poorest Countries are Failing and What Can Be Done About It* (Oxford: Oxford University Press). An influential analysis of success and failure in development, including Africa.

■ Kanbur R. (2001), 'Economic Policy, Distribution and Poverty: The Nature of Disagreements', *World Development*, 29/6: 1083–94. A clear and balanced view of the contemporary poverty debate, and why people differ over growth's effects on poverty. Includes very useful comparisons between the differing viewpoints of the World Bank and non-governmental organizations on poverty.

■ Kirkpatrick, C., Clarke, R., and Polidano, C. (eds) (2002), *Handbook on Development Policy and Management* (Cheltenham: Edward Elgar). Provides summaries of the main economic and political issues in development policy, including further discussion of many of the topics of this chapter.

■ Nayyar, D. (ed.) (2002), *Governing Globalization: Issues and Institutions* (Oxford: Oxford University Press for Unu-Wider).

■ Rodrik, D. (2003), *In Search of Prosperity: Analytic Narratives on Economic Growth* (Princeton, NJ: Princeton University Press). A good place to start on the causes of the different development outcomes of countries, and the role of development strategy in determining success.

■ Wade, R. (1990), *Governing the Market: Economic Theory and the Role of Government in East Asian Industrialization* (Princeton, NJ: Princeton University Press, repr. 2003 with a new introduction by the author). An authoritative assessment of how East Asia achieved its economic success, which challenges the market-liberal view and emphasizes the role of the state.

■ **www.developmentgateway.org** An independent site that introduces the latest development research, with frequent updates of new research papers and breaking news in development.

■ **www.chronicpoverty.org** An international partnership of researchers and NGOs working on chronic poverty and its eradication in Africa, Asia, and Latin America.

■ **www.eldis.org** Very easy-to-use site, with downloadable research papers, reports, and many links to other sites. It has a very useful section on how to use the web for development research, and the issues facing web users in developing countries with slow band width.

■ **www.imf.org** The IMF posts reports on its member countries, and agreements with governments (such as 'Letters of Intent'), which spell out in detail economic reforms. The IMF's annual reports on the state of the world economy are also widely read.

■ **www.odi.org.uk** The website of the Overseas Development Institute (UK), an independent think tank on development issues. The ODI *Briefing Papers* provide authoritative insight into the latest development issues.

■ **www.undp.org** The website of the United Nations Development Programme (UNDP), which is leading the UN's work on the Millennium Development Goals. The UNDP's annual Human Development Report can also be viewed at this site.

■ **www.unrisd.org** The website of the United Nations Research Institute for Social Development (UN-RISD). UNRISD focuses on the social dimensions of development, as well as development's political aspects.

■ **www.wider.unu.edu** The website of the United Nations University's World Institute for Development Economics Research (UNU-WIDER). WIDER's Discussion Paper series offers a wide range of viewpoints on economic development issues, particularly in the areas of measuring poverty and the development effects of violent conflict.

■ **www.worldbank.org** The website of the World Bank offers an enormous range of country material, particularly on poverty reduction, as well as many of the statistics (such as the World Development Indicators) used by the development community.

■ **www.un.org/millenniumgoals** For progress towards the MDGs.

 Online Resource Centre

For additional material and resources, please visit the Online Resource Centre at:
www.oxfordtextbooks.co.uk/orc/burnell3e/

17

Environment

Peter Newell

 Overview

This chapter explores how developing countries are managing the relationship between the environment and development. Often considered a threat to their economic development and prospects for growth, environmental issues have nevertheless come to feature centrally on policy agendas throughout the developing world. Driven by donors, public concern, and vocal environmental movements, responses to these issues have taken a number of different forms as they compete for 'policy space' with other pressing development concerns and are subject to changing thinking about the effectiveness of policy tools to tackle environmental problems. This chapter explores these issues, connecting global agendas to national policy processes, explaining differences and similarities between how countries respond to these issues, and identifying patterns of continuity and change in the politics of environment in the developing world.

Introduction

From an issue on the periphery of the policy agendas of most developing country governments, the environment has assumed an important and rising status on the national political agendas of states in

Africa, Latin America, and Asia. This shift results from a combination of pressures from global institutions, donors, and active citizen movements, and has evolved alongside a growth in both scientific understanding of environmental problems and rising levels of public concern, often generated by environmental disasters. In particular regarding the issue of global warming, there is a growing recognition that development gains may be systematically reversed by extreme and unpredictable climate change, which impacts most directly on the world's poor whose livelihoods depend on agriculture, fishing, and other productive sectors particularly vulnerable to changes in rainfall and temperature.

Yet the status of the environment as an issue on developing country agendas often remains precarious. Environmental issues in many areas of the world are only loosely embedded within national policy processes, incoherently related to wider economic and social agendas and subject to displacement by issues that assume a greater priority for most countries. The theme of this chapter then is continuity and change. Most countries are operating in a radically different policy context, in which an increasingly globalized economy impacts more directly than ever before on the relationship between environment and development. Moreover, the institutions and structures of global environmental governance shape more strongly than ever before the nature of environmental policy within the developing world. At the same time, environmental issues have been grafted onto existing policy agendas, national priorities, and decision-making processes that, in many cases, are characterized by bureaucratic inertia, organized opposition to reform, and reluctance to realign priorities.

The chapter is organized into five main sections. The first two sections sketch the increasingly important global context for debates about environment and development and the links between them. Such links have been institutionalized through the growth of global bodies and areas of international environmental law produced through a series of United Nations (UN) negotiations. The third looks at policy processes at the national level: how these global agendas have been responded to and addressed by individual governments. This means tackling questions about what is unique about policy processes in developing countries and what extra challenges are associated with tackling environmental problems in these settings. The fourth section looks at the range of tools and strategies that developing countries have adopted in order to combat environmental degradation. This includes discussion about the shifting roles of governments, market actors such as businesses and **civil society** in natural resource use management and protection. The fifth section explores probable future directions of environmental politics in the developing world, pulling together these patterns of continuity and change.

Key points

- The environment has assumed an important and rising status on the national political agendas of states in Africa, Latin America, and Asia.

- Yet the status of the environment as an issue on developing country agendas is precarious. It is often displaced by issues that assume a greater priority for most countries.

- We can observe a process of continuity and change. Environmental challenges are handled within existing national policy frameworks, but globalization has changed the relationship between environment and development and among the actors charged with delivering sustainable development.

Global Context

In an unequal and fragmented international society, it is perhaps not surprising that is has been very difficult to construct a global consensus about which environmental issues are most urgent. It is often assumed that differences of opinion on this issue fall along North–South lines, where developed countries are more concerned with global problems such as climate change and ozone depletion and conservation issues such as whaling and forest protection, while developing countries attach greater priority to rural issues such as desertification and soil erosion and local environmental issues such as water pollution and air quality in cities. Even a cursory look at the politics of global negotiations on these issues suggests that these categorizations are at best only partially accurate.

First, we need to consider issues of causation and impact. Many of those people who contribute most to global environmental degradation are not those that will suffer its worst effects. While climate change will have global impacts, wealthier countries are better placed to adapt to its adverse consequences. While the Netherlands can build sea defences against sea-level rise, Bangladesh does not have the resources to protect itself against widespread flooding of low-lying agriculturally important areas. Likewise, while Australians can use sun lotions to protect themselves from harmful ultraviolet rays that are stronger as a result of ozone depletion, many rural Chileans will not be able to afford the luxury. Yet it is the developed world that contributes to global environmental problems to a proportionally much greater extent. For example, 80 per cent of the world's climate-changing carbon dioxide is produced by less that 25 per cent of the world's population. One country alone, the United States, which makes up just 4 per cent of the world's population, is responsible for 20 per cent of global emissions, while 136 developing countries together account for 24 per cent. We should also recall, however, that exposure to environmental harm and culpability for causing it is highly uneven and differentiated within countries in which inequalities along class, gender, and racial lines are often magnified and exacerbated by global environmental change.

Second, the economic importance of natural resources to a country's economic development is a significant determinant of its position on a particular environmental policy problem, making it difficult for developing countries to form common policy positions. Brazil has traditionally resisted calls to view the Amazonian rainforests as part of the common heritage of humankind because of their strategic importance to the country's economic development. Many other developing countries, however, have called for this principle of **global stewardship** to apply to a range of common pool resources such as Antarctica and the deep seabed, on the basis that if those resources are to be exploited, they should be for the benefit of all and not just those that are in a position to exploit them. Similarly, while the Alliance of Small Island States (AOSIS), threatened by sea-level rise associated with global climate change, has strongly advocated controls on greenhouse gas emissions, the Organisation of Petroleum Exporting Countries (OPEC) bloc, the economies of which are heavily dependent on the export of oil, have resisted such controls.

While some developing countries view environmental policy as an opportunity to secure additional aid and new forms of technology transfer, others feel threatened by agendas that appear to constrain their prospects for growth. The G77 bloc of least-developed countries — formed at the UN after a meeting of the United Nations Conference on Trade and Development (UNCTAD) in 1964, for the purpose of promoting the collective economic interest of Third World countries — has traditionally placed the responsibility for short-term action on climate change upon the North in the negotiations on the subject. But many Latin American and Asian countries now see opportunities to earn much-needed revenue from participating in projects under the Clean Development Mechanism set in train by the Kyoto Protocol concluded in 1997. Such projects entitle Northern countries to pay for emissions reductions in parts of the developing world where it is cheapest to do so. The rapid growth of industrial power-houses such as India, China, and Brazil has further fractured the unity of the G77 bloc. It is increasingly difficult, in light of their rising contribution to the problem of global warming, where for example China is now the single largest emitter of greenhouse gases (although not on a per capita basis), for these countries to refute the need for their own legally binding emissions reduction obligations. Countries such as the US have made their cooperation in further negotiations contingent on these countries accepting cuts in their own future emissions. Indeed the Bali Roadmap, negotiated in 2007, makes an explicit call for nationally appropriate mitigation actions from developing countries to be funded and supported by Annex 1 (most industrialized countries) parties to the Kyoto Protocol. At the Copenhagen climate change summit in December 2009, however, the US in particular suggested that proposals for up to US$100 billion annually for developing countries by 2020 to fund action on climate change adaptation and mitigation required assurances that countries are indeed enforcing and achieving their reductions. China attracted significant criticism in this regard for its reluctance to allow international oversight of its proposed emissions reduction actions, which it claimed amounted to an infringement of sovereignty.

Third, aside from areas in which core national economic interests may be at stake, global environmental institutions have played a key role in shaping the national environmental policy agendas of many developing countries. Box 17.1 summarizes the mandates and key activities of some of the more prominent global environmental institutions. It is their access to financial resources and the mandate they have to oversee the implementation of key global environmental accords that allows these bodies to play this role. As Box 17.1 shows, the Global Environment Facility (GEF) has responsibility for overseeing the transfer of aid and technology to developing countries in order to help meet their obligations under the Rio agreements, for example on climate change and biodiversity conservation. The provision of aid and technology to developing countries to meet these commitments recognizes that these countries require assistance in making a contribution to global efforts to tackle forms of environmental degradation to which most currently contribute very little. Concern was expressed at the time of the UN Conference on Environment and Development in Rio that aid for the implementation of these international environmental agreements should be 'additional' to that which developing countries receive for other development purposes. This concern continues today in relation to calls for 'new and additional' finance for climate change mitigation and adaptation.

Box 17.1 Key Global Environmental Institutions

United Nations Environment Programme

- Created following Stockholm conference on the Human Environment in 1972

- Initially conceived as clearing house of environmental data and research and to set up demonstration projects

- No statute or charter to describe its function and role

- Governing Council of 58 members elected by UN General Assembly on regional formula for four-year terms

- The council is mandated to promote cooperation on environmental issues and recommend appropriate policies

- Budget of only US$10.5 million a year from regular UN budget

- Depends on voluntary contributions from member countries for financing specific projects

- No structured system of dispute settlement

- Enforcement reliant on peer review and moral pressure

Commission on Sustainable Development

- Inter-governmental body; members selected from UN

- Composed of 53 members elected for three-year terms

- Meets annually

- Reports to ECOSOC (Economic and Social Council) of UN

- Purpose: to review progress at international, regional, and national levels in implementation of Rio ('Earth summit') agreements such as Agenda 21, the Rio Declaration, and the Forest Principles

- Means: provide policy guidance; promote dialogue; build partnerships with major groups

Global Environment Facility

- Key financing body for actions on climate change, biodiversity loss, ozone depletion, international waters, land degradation, persistent organic compounds (POPs); new and additional grant and concessional funding for incremental costs for global benefits

- Three implementing agencies: United Nations Environment Programme (UNEP); United Nations Development Programme (UNDP); World Bank

- World Bank administers facility on day-to-day basis and is trustee of the GEF trust fund

- Decisions made by consensus; where dispute, decisions made on double majority basis

Increasingly, however, these institutions and the conventions they seek to enforce have sought to facilitate the integration of environmental and developmental concerns rather than see them as competing issues. There has been a clear shift towards addressing development concerns that can be traced from the Stockholm Conference on the Human Environment in 1972 onwards (see Box 17.2). This prepared the ground for the famous Brundtland Report *Our Common Future* (1987)—which first coined the phrase **sustainable development**, defined as 'Development which meets the needs of the current generation without compromising the ability of future generations to meet their own needs'. The title of the Rio conference that followed five years later encapsulated the rhetorical integration of environmental and developmental objectives: the 'United Nations Conference on Environment and Development'. Ten years on, the language of sustainable development was placed

centrally in the naming of the follow-up to Rio, the 'World Summit on Sustainable Development' in Johannesburg in 2002.

Despite this rhetorical shift, many developing countries and activists have been critical of the way in which certain issues have been actively kept off the agenda of these summits. The Rio conference attracted criticism for not addressing issues such as debt, terms of trade, or the regulation of multinational companies, issues that some developing countries have sought to advance since the early 1970s, initially through the platform of the New International Economic Order. The US delegation to the conference fought hard to remove references to unsustainable levels of consumption in the Rio documents, and concerns were raised during the World Summit on Sustainable Development (WSSD) at attempts to thwart the negotiation of a new convention on corporate accountability.

Box 17.2 Chronology of Environment and Development on the International Agenda

1972: Stockholm Conference on the Human Environment

- Created UNEP
- Established key principles of responsible global environmental stewardship
- Set in train global scientific cooperation

1980: Brandt Commission

- North–South: A Programme for Survival
- Addressing North–South elements more clearly: trade; debt; energy; food

1987: World Commission on Environment and Development

- *Our Common Future* (Brundtland Report)
- Birth of a concept: sustainable development

1992: UNCED (United Nations Conference and Development)

- United Nations Framework Convention on Climate Change

- Convention on Biological Diversity
- Rio Declaration
- Statement of Forest Principles
- Agenda 21

2002: WSSD (Johannesburg)

- Agreement on water and sanitation (to halve the number of people without access to basic sanitation by 2015)
- Agreement on fisheries (plan to restore world's depleted stocks by 2015; create marine areas around the world by 2012)

2009: United Nations Climate Change Conference (Copenhagen)

- Produced an 'accord', but not a legally binding treaty, on reducing greenhouse gas emissions

Rather than viewing environmental issues as stand-alone concerns, it is becoming increasingly clear that it is necessary to 'mainstream' environmental concerns into the activities of leading development actors. While the World Bank continues to draw fire for the environmental impact of some of its lending operations, as far back as 1987 it set up an environmental department and now insists on detailed environmental impact assessments of all its lending programmes. Also, largely as a result of a vocal lobbying by environmental groups, the World Trade Organization (WTO) has created a Committee on Trade and Environment. This first met in 1995 to look at the relationship between environmental standards and trade liberalization, although notably and controversially not the environmental impacts of trade. The emphasis has, therefore, been on defining the legitimate circumstances in which environmental and human health concerns can be invoked as exceptions to the normal obligations countries assume through membership of the WTO, rather than the ecological cost of transporting greater volumes of goods across ever larger distances, for example. The question is whether environmental considerations should be allowed to drive decisions about which types of trade are desirable and necessary from the point of view of sustainable development, or whether all environmental measures that impact upon trade have to be compatible with WTO rules. For developing countries, one of the key concerns has been the growth in environmental standards that many fear will be used as barriers to trade and disguised forms of protectionism to protect Northern producers from competitive exports from the South. High-profile cases that have come before the WTO's Dispute Settlement Mechanism, such as the dolphin–tuna case, have reflected this fear. In this case, the US sought to ban yellow-fin tuna imports from Mexico on the grounds that the nets being used by the Mexican fishing industry to catch tuna fish were also killing dolphins.

This apparent integration of environmental issues into the policy practice of development actors has not just occurred at the inter-governmental level. One of the Millennium Development Goals agreed by the Development Assistance Committee

of the Organisation for Economic Co-operation and Development (OECD) is for all countries to have in place by the year 2005 a National Strategy for Sustainable Development (NSSD). Interestingly, country ownership is highlighted as a central component of an effective NSSD. Broad consultation to open up the debate and build consensus are seen as key for strategy formulation. This approach acknowledges that while sustainable development is a universal challenge, the practical response to it can only be defined nationally and locally according to different values and interests. An OECD report on the issue notes that a standardized blueprint approach should be avoided, and is at best irrelevant and at worst counter-productive (OECD 2001). Instead, working with existing approaches and institutional arrangements according to individual countries' needs, priorities, and available resources is preferable.

Key points

- There is now a wide range of global environmental agreements that developing countries have signed and are in the process of implementing.

- Although development issues have gained a higher profile in global environmental summits and agreements, there is still some concern that Northern countries continue to control the agenda.

- Countries' positions on these issues do not fall neatly along North–South lines, however, and key differences exist between developing countries on many high-profile global environmental issues.

- There has been a move towards mainstreaming environmental concerns into the lending practices of multilateral development agencies and into poverty reduction strategies.

Environment and Development: An Uneasy Relationship

The relationship between environment and development is not an easy one, and many conflicts are subsumed under the convenient banner of 'sustainable development', the aims of which it is difficult for anyone to refute. Many have, therefore, questioned its value as an analytical concept, when it can

be invoked so easily to justify 'business as usual' polluting activities. The term disguises conflicts over priorities between environment and development, gives few, if any, indications about which forms of development are sustainable, and is inevitably interpreted by different actors to mean different things. Fundamental conflicts over the causes and appropriate solutions to environmental degradation persist. These include the debate about the extent to which population growth is a cause of environmental degradation. Malthusian (after the eighteenth-century thinker the Reverend Thomas Malthus) analysis of resource degradation, popular in certain strands of 1970s environmental thinking (Ehrlich 1972), suggested that rapid increases in population were driving the planet towards ecological collapse. The influential 'limits of growth' report in 1972 of the Club of Rome suggested instead that unsustainable patterns of resource use would ultimately bring about ecological collapse because of the finite nature of the natural resource base upon which we all depend. Many developing countries and more radical environmental groups target over-consumption and affluence in Western societies, rather than population, as the key cause of the global environmental crisis.

Given this lack of consensus on the causes of environmental degradation, it is unsurprising that consensus eludes attempts to find appropriate solutions. Old conflicts in development over aid, trade, debt, and the role of technology get replayed through discussions about how to combat environmental degradation. Those believing that poverty leads people to use resources unsustainably have looked to ideas such as debt-for-nature swaps as a way out of this cycle. These swaps provide debt relief in exchange for commitments to preserve areas of forest. Critiques of the effects of aid and technology transfer on developing countries also get rehearsed in environmental debates. For example, it is alleged that technologies that are transferred as part of global environmental agreements are often out of date and rather serve as a subsidy to Northern producers of technologies for which markets no longer exist. In environmental terms, it is also argued that technology is no substitute for tough action aimed at reducing unsustainable patterns of production and consumption, and that developed countries often prefer to transfer technologies to developing countries rather than take measures to address the source of environmental degradation in their own countries.

This then is the global historical and contemporary context that shapes the ways in which developing countries have been tackling environmental issues at the national level. The next section looks in more detail at the commonalities and differences in the ways in which developing countries have responded to these global environmental agendas while grappling with their own unique environmental problems and development needs.

Key points

- The term 'sustainable development' disguises key conflicts over priorities between environment and development.

- There is no consensus on the social causes of environmental degradation and the importance that should be attached to population growth in the South as opposed to unsustainable consumption in the North.

- Fundamental disagreements arise concerning the role of aid, trade, and technology as appropriate solutions to environmental problems.

Policy Processes

Political diversity

It is impossible to make generalizations about environmental policy that would apply across the entire developing world. Although nearly all developing countries are involved in global negotiations on the issues raised above, the processes by which they translate those commitments into workable policies at the national level are very different. First, there is the issue of power. There is clearly a difference between a country like China or India, with significant scope for independent action and power to assert their interests in global forums, and smaller and less powerful countries such as Uruguay or Zambia. This difference relates in part to the resources that can be committed to participating in global processes, which can be highly time- and resource-intensive. Environmental negotiations often take place in Bonn, Geneva, or New York and to participate effectively in them requires a large delegation with access to scientific and legal expertise. Developing countries are often only able to send at most one or two government representatives to these negotiations, which are often run with parallel meetings that a small delegation cannot attend. But it is also about power. At critical moments, such as in the final hours of the Copenhagen climate change summit in December 2009, it was larger developing countries such as Brazil, South Africa, India, and China that were invited to participate in a closed meeting to advance progress in the talks. They were the actors whose cooperation and support was most required.

But the degree of power that a country wields in global economic terms and the extent to which it is aid-dependent also affects its exposure to pressure to take environmental action. Countries such as Mali and Ethiopia are highly dependent on aid. In Mali's case, the overwhelming majority of that aid comes from its former colonizer, France. Research programmes and policy priorities are, therefore, strongly affected by such bilateral financial ties. Countries such as Brazil, on the other hand, have a larger degree of discretion in determining policy positions and they can draw on greater economic weight in trade and industrial terms to advance their preferences on environmental issues.

Second, but related, are issues of capacity for the enforcement of policy. Many countries, such as India, have some of the most impressive legislative Acts on environmental issues in the world.

But lack of resources, training, and corruption of local pollution control officials often conspire to delay implementation. Sometimes the nature of the problem and the size of the country are the key constraints. For example, regulating the cultivation and trade in genetically modified (GM) seeds is almost impossible in a country the size of China and many instances of illegal growing of non-authorized seeds have been reported. Managing the trans-border movement of GM seeds, as is required by the Cartagena Protocol on Biosafety (Secretariat of the Convention on Biological Diversity 2000), presents many problems for developing countries, where seed markets are often poorly regulated and even basic equipment with which to test shipments of seeds across borders is unavailable. Where countries have a strong economic and developmental incentive to ensure active compliance, extra steps may be taken. Kenya is keen to be seen as an attractive tourist location for wildlife safaris. Because tourism provides a large source of revenue, officials have gone to controversial lengths to tackle the problem of illegal poaching of elephants and rhinos for their ivory and horns. These include shooting poachers and banning tribal groups from culling animals for food, even on their own ancestral lands.

Third, the degree of importance that will be attached to environmental concerns, at the expense of broader development goals, will reflect the nature of democratic politics in the country. The strength of environmental groups in a country, pushing for new policy and acting as informal 'watchdogs' of compliance with environmental regulations will be determined by the degree of democratic space that exists within the country. Countries such as India and Mexico have strong traditions of active civil society engagement in environmental policy. India, for instance, hosts such globally recognized non-governmental organizations (NGOs) as the Centre for Science and Environment and its more research-oriented counterpart, TERI (The Energy and Resources Institute), which are active in global policy debates as well as domestic agenda-setting. In Singapore and China, by contrast, the avenues for policy engagement are few and tightly restricted. The scope and effectiveness of environmental policy will also be shaped by the extent to which the interests of leading industries are affected by proposed interventions. Where policy directly impinges on the interests of a particularly powerful industry, policy reform is often stalled or environmental concerns are kept off the agenda altogether. The close ties between logging companies and state officials that often have personal commercial stakes in the companies is an often-cited reason for the lack of progress to reverse unsustainable logging in South-East Asia (Dauvergne 1997).

The way in which governments formulate and implement policy also reflects a broad diversity of styles of environmental policymaking. Each country has a unique history when it comes to its approach to regulation, the organization of its bureaucracy, and the extent to which public participation in policy is encouraged and enabled. The Chinese government is able to act decisively and in a 'command and control' fashion to sanction industries failing to comply with pollution control regulations. In India, the Supreme Court has played a decisive role in moving environmental policy forward, often in controversial circumstances, setting strict and sometimes unrealistic targets for the phasing out of non-CNG (compressed natural gas) vehicles in Delhi, for example, or instructing the eviction of thousands of small industries from the outskirts of Delhi because of the pollution their activities were generating. Other countries have a more reactive policy style, influenced by popular politics. In Argentina, the government had consistently failed to take action to protect a forest in the north of the country until football legend Maradona joined Greenpeace's campaign to protect the forest, prompting immediate government action.

Approaches to environmental policy also reflect the different ways in which knowledge, especially scientific knowledge, informs policy. Scientific knowledge does not provide a neutral and value-free guide to which environmental problems are the most serious or how they should be addressed. It is employed strategically by government officials to support their position within the bureaucracy, but can also change political practice and priorities by highlighting some areas of concern while ignoring others. The power of expert communities in this regard explains why developing countries have sought greater representation of Southern-based scientists in international environmental bodies providing advice to policymakers, such as the Cartagena Protocol on Biosafety's 'roster of experts'.

Given these factors, there is sometimes also a mismatch between the expectations contained in multilateral environmental agreements about the way in which commitments should be implemented and the realities of what is possible in many developing country settings. There is the problem of capacity whereby the resources and skills to oversee micro-level implementation of environmental regulations emanating from central government to meet global commitments are often lacking. In addition, many agreements, including the Cartagena Protocol on Biosafety, specify the process by which national environmental frameworks should be designed, for example to involve active public consultation and participation. Yet many are poorly placed to meaningfully set up elaborate participatory processes for deliberative and inclusive decision-making across a wide range of issues, involving a cross-section of their societies. Democratic values are weakly embedded in many societies, and publics in many places remain sceptical of interaction with official bodies such that good global intentions may not translate well into local practice.

Common challenges

Despite these differences in the policy positions and policy styles that developing countries have adopted, it is worth highlighting some common challenges that nearly all developing, and of course many developed, countries face in the design and execution of environmental policy. First, there is the scale of resources required to tackle environmental problems. Undertaking scientific research and monitoring the enforcement of pollution control places large resource demands on developing countries in particular. International environmental agreements create new demands of governments for more regulation, more monitoring, and an efficient and effective bureaucracy to oversee these, often across multiple levels of governance right down to the local level. Despite the availability of global funds to support some of these activities (see Box 17.1), it remains difficult even for larger developing countries to meet these expectations.

Second, in spite of the efforts of active environmental movements within developing countries, as well as globally, it remains the case that political constituencies with a strong preference for more effective environmental policy are often very weak. The issue is not only that the beneficiaries of environmental policies are not present in policy debates (future generations) or not adequately represented (indigenous peoples for example), but that political parties with strong commitments to environmental issues are not well developed in most parts of Asia, Africa, and Latin America. Conversely, the presence in Europe of Green parties has served to keep environmental issues on the agendas of the main parties.

Where social movements have taken up environmental issues, they often touch on deeply sensitive issues—for example access to resources such as forests and water or of land reform—bringing them into conflict with state elites. *Campesino* (peasant-based) movements in Latin America often incorporate environmental issues into broader campaigning platforms for land redistribution and greater levels of compensation for the appropriation of natural resources (Newell 2007). Movements for environmental justice that oppose the location of often hazardous and highly polluting industries in poorer communities often frustrate the development ambitions of policy elites. The ability of movements to use environmental issues to advance broader political agendas serves to entrench the suspicion that many governments have of environmental agendas. Occasionally, however, governments see in environmental issues an opportunity to gain political capital on an issue of national concern. The Argentine government is locked in conflict with neighbouring Uruguay over pulp mills set up there, which it is alleged are contaminating the Uruguay river that the two countries share. Argentina even initiated proceedings at the International Court of Justice in The Hague over the issue after large popular protest.

Third, we have to recognize the global economic pressures that all countries face, but which developing countries face more acutely. Crushing debt burdens and the conditions attached to **structural adjustment programmes** often create incentives for economic activities that are highly destructive of the environment. Export-led growth patterns, which often require intensive use of land with heavy applications of chemical fertilizers, and the creation of export-processing zones the aim of which is to attract foreign capital to areas in which labour is cheap and environmental standards are lower, are indicative of this. Deteriorating terms of trade for timber, minerals, and agricultural produce also drive developing country economies, dependent on single commodities, to exploit that resource unsustainably. In the aftermath of the financial crisis in South-East Asia in the late 1990s, for example, timber producers increased exports to unsustainable levels to compensate for the losses they incurred from depreciating national currencies.

The broader issue is what has been termed the 'race to the bottom' in environmental standards as developing countries compete to lower environmental regulations in order to attract increasingly mobile investors. The evidence for this is mixed. Some argue that increased patterns of trade interdependence have the effect of raising standards as developing country exporters seek access to lucrative Western markets that require higher environmental standards (Vogel 1997). However, there are many examples of regulatory reforms not being introduced or not implemented for fear of deterring investors. For example, in response to pressure from soybean exporters in the US, the Chinese government delayed plans to introduce a series of biosafety measures that exporters considered overly restrictive. In other cases, lack of environmental regulation has been used as a comparative advantage to attract environmentally hazardous production of substances such as toxic wastes and asbestos that have been banned in the North. The desperation of many developing countries to attract investment on any terms clearly, therefore, both affects their ability to prioritize action on the environment and in certain situations will lead them to lower standards in order to attract mobile capital.

It is also the case that many developing countries have abundant natural resources that make them key locations for extractive industries. For years activists have berated the mining industry for its environmental pollution, human rights violations, and displacement of indigenous peoples. The oil industry too has been accused of double standards when it operates in developing countries. The activities of firms such as Shell in Nigeria's Niger Delta and Texaco in Ecuador have attracted global attention as a result of activist exposure and high-profile legal actions against the companies.

By way of response, many firms have developed corporate social responsibility programmes to defend and promote their reputations and present themselves as a force for good. It is now commonplace for larger companies to claim that their companies adopt the principles of sustainable development in their investment decision-making. Among globally connected industry associations in the developing world, such as the Makati Business Club in the Philippines or the Confederation of Indian Industry, this discourse is being picked up as Southern-based multinationals and state-owned firms come under pressure to improve their own social and environmental performance. However, it remains the case that many of the drivers of corporate environmental responsibility, including government incentives, civil society watchdogs, and consumer and investor pressure are currently underdeveloped in many parts of the developing world. Firms within countries with strong trading ties to overseas markets in which compliance with tougher environmental regulations is expected will have higher standards than many firms in parts of sub-Saharan Africa, for example, which are more isolated from such global pressures.

Fourth, the underdevelopment of the scientific expertise that underpins environmental policy is a characteristic common to many developing countries. While there are many international scientific research programmes on environmental issues and many international environmental agreements have panels, or rosters, of experts associated with their activities, the representation of scientists from developing countries is often low. There have been initiatives from UNEP to try and address this problem by ensuring, for example, that a percentage of scientists on such bodies are from developing countries. But the problem endures, and the implication is that the agendas of Northern researchers and their policy networks attract greater attention and resources than issues and concerns that are more pertinent to the developing world. This criticism has been levelled at the work of GEF, for instance, for being more responsive to the agendas of Northern donors upon which it is dependent for funding than to the recipients of its capacity-building measures in the South. The World Bank (2000: 14) has also conceded that its' 'preference for big loans can easily distract regulators from confronting their communities' most critical pollution problems'.

Key points

- Despite facing similar international pressures to integrate environmental issues into development policy, the willingness and ability of developing countries to address environmental challenges is highly uneven.

- There are some important differences in priorities, power and policy autonomy, resources and capacity, policy styles, and the role of environmental and business groups in policy formulation and implementation across the developing world.

- There are, however, many common challenges that developing countries face when it comes to environmental policy: weaknesses in enforcement capacity; economic vulnerability, which means trade and aid leverage can be used to change policy; and an underdeveloped knowledge base from which to develop environmental policy.

New Policy Instruments for Environmental Protection

We have already noted the different policy styles that developing countries around the world have employed in the design and implementation of environmental policy. It is also the case, however, that they have been affected by shifts in prevailing thinking about the most efficient and effective way to provide environmental goods, particularly an increased emphasis on the use of market-based mechanisms. This is not to suggest strong **developmental states** are not able to intervene forcibly to close down polluting industry, or to overlook the important role of legal systems in driving environmental policy reform and in protecting the rights of citizens against their own government. Courts have been a key site for poorer groups to seek compensation for socially and environmentally destructive investments that have undermined their livelihoods. They have provided a venue to draw attention to grievances that have not been recognized elsewhere. Where successful, legal cases can uphold key rights to environmental information, to have environmental impact assessments undertaken in advance of large industrial projects, or to contest the forced displacement that is associated with infrastructural projects such as dams. In Nigeria numerous cases have been brought against oil companies by communities seeking compensation for damage to land caused by oil spillages from company pipelines in the Niger Delta. Companies exploiting lower health and environmental standards in developing countries, providing their workers with less protection than counterparts in the North, have ended up paying large out-of-court settlements to victims of industrial hazards. More positively and proactively, poorer groups have also been able to use legal remedies to realize their rights to key resources such as water, which is a constitutional right in South Africa (Box 17.3), or to access forests (Newell and Wheeler 2006).

Relying on legal remedies to tackle environmental problems is often inadequate, however. Often people resort to the law only after the pollution has occurred. There are also limits to how poorer groups can use the law to their benefit. Poorer communities frequently lack the financial resources to bring a case. They lack the 'legal literacy' necessary to understand their rights under the law and how they can be realized. These problems of access are often compounded by long backlogs of cases, and distrust in the independence of the legal system. There are many legal barriers to successfully demonstrating cause and effect between a polluting activity and evidence of damage to human health or the environment particularly when poorer groups are exposed to such a range of hazards in their day-to day-lives.

State-based environmental regulation, in general, however, has been subject to sustained criticism from key development actors such as the World Bank on the grounds that it is excessively inflexible, inefficient, and often ineffective at delivering the change in behaviour that it intends. Increasingly, the preference is for the use of the market as a tool for incentivizing positive action and deterring polluting activities. Examples of pollution charging in China, Colombia, and the Philippines show that pollution from factories has been successfully reduced when steep, regular payments for emissions have been enforced. Market tools such as labelling have also been accepted in many developing countries, as a means by which to assure global buyers of the environmentally responsible way in which the product has been produced as well as to facilitate consumer choice. For example certification has been used in the forestry sector by the popular FSC scheme (Forestry Stewardship Council), until recently based in Oaxaca, Mexico. The World Bank, UNDP, and many regional development banks are also now active in setting up carbon markets throughout the developing world, as a way of accessing carbon finance and bringing down their contribution to climate change.

Box 17.3 The Right to Water in South Africa

- South Africa is the only country that recognizes the human right to water at the constitutional and policy level through its Free Basic Water policy.

- The Water Services Act of 1997 provides for a basic level of water for those that cannot pay. People are entitled to 25 free litres of water per day for personal and domestic use.

- There is, nevertheless, uneven access to water. Problems of capacity of local authorities to deliver on the commitment and financial constraints have led to undersupply and people being cut off. This has led some people to get water from unprotected sources; leading to health problems.

- The government is also under immense pressure to introduce user fees and cost recovery in line with market-based approaches to water provision.

- Many people are also unaware of their constitutional right to water and therefore when their rights are violated.

- Although some legal cases have secured interim relief from disconnections by invoking the right to water, the onus on proving inability to pay rests with the water user and depends on their access to legal representation.

(Mehta 2006)

Another general trend in environmental policy that is catching on in the developing world is the adoption of voluntary measures by industry. Codes of conduct among leading companies are now commonplace in the North and many of those firms investing overseas are insisting that their suppliers and partners adopt them. The trend forms part of the rejection of the alleged inefficiencies and ineffectiveness of central government 'command and control' policy measures noted above. But it also reflects the preference of firms to set their own standards appropriate to their own circumstances in a way that avoids or pre-empts state intervention. In the environmental context, environmental management systems such as ISO 14001 created by the International Organization for Standardization (ISO) are increasingly popular. While traditionally such standards have tended only to apply to larger firms that can afford the compliance costs and those seeking access to developed country markets, small and medium-sized enterprises are increasingly seeking ISO certification in order to serve as subcontractors for ISO-certified enterprises.

There are also sector-specific programmes such as 'Responsible Care' in the case of the chemical industry, which set up a programme to deflect criticism away from its track record in the US. It has also been adopted in countries like Mexico and Brazil. Garcia-Johnson (2000) describes this as 'exporting environmentalism'. It is clear then that global market pressures from buyers and consumers increasingly exercise as significant an influence on environmental policy practice in many parts of the developing world as the international agreements to which governments sign up.

As a reaction to the limitations of market-based and voluntary mechanisms, there has also been a growth in what has been termed **civil regulation** (Newell 2001): civil-society-based forms of business regulation. The increasing use of such tools as shareholder activism and boycotts, and the growth of watchdog groups such as OilWatch based in Nigeria, are illustrative of the trend. New forms of engagement in constructing codes of conduct and building partnerships between business and civil society also come under the umbrella of civil regulation. Concern has been expressed that many of these tools are only available to well-resourced groups with good access to the media and in societies with strong traditions of free speech. But there does seem to be evidence of these strategies being employed on an increasing scale in most parts of the global South. Strategies of resistance and exposure of corporate wrongdoing date from colonial times, but there has also been a notable proliferation in groups across the entire spectrum, ranging from confrontation to collaboration. Many of these groups are also increasingly

globally well connected. This means that companies engaging in environmentally controversial activities in the developing world can also expect to face shareholder resolutions and embarrassing media publicity in their home countries. The Canadian company Tiomin, for example, has faced considerable pressure from activists in Canada over its mining operations on Kenya's coast, working with local NGOs such as CoastWatch.

It is unclear at this stage what the net effect of these forms of civil regulation will be on the environmental performance of investors in developing countries. The hope is that groups with the expertise and capabilities to plug gaps and weaknesses in systems of government pollution control and monitoring can play an important complementary role as informal regulators. O'Rourke's study of community-based regulation in Vietnam shows how this has been possible when 'the energies and actions of average community members and the responses of front-line environmental agencies' have been brought together (2004: xvii). Their very presence may encourage firms to respect the environmental standards of the countries in which they operate to a greater degree than if they were not there, and so help to dissuade companies from adopting double standards when they operate in developing countries. The extent to which groups will be allowed to perform this role will depend on the strength of civil society in a given setting and the extent to which its activities are tolerated or encouraged by the state. Issues of whom the groups represent and to whom they are accountable will also have to be faced if they are to be seen as legitimate actors in environmental policy. It will be important that such groups do not deter much-needed investment, but instead seek to attract investors that are more socially and environmentally responsible, and therefore more likely to bring long-term development gains to countries.

Key points

- Many countries continue to use central government controlled 'command and control' environmental policy measures.

- Despite their limitations, poorer groups have sought to use legal remedies to claim rights to resources, contest planning processes, and seek compensation for loss of livelihood.

- There has been a shift, however, in thinking about how best to tackle environmental pollution towards the use of market instruments and voluntary approaches and away from state-based approaches.

- Many companies in developing countries are seeking certification for their products in order to get access to Northern markets.

- In recent years there has been a trend towards informal industry regulation by civil society groups. The long-term impact of this form of civil-society-based regulation will vary by country and the extent to which such groups are able to address issues of their own accountability and representation.

Futures

Attempting to predict the likely future of environmental policy in the developing or developed world with any degree of accuracy and precision is a fruitless endeavour. It is, however, possible to identify certain patterns of continuity and change. We have seen how many developing countries face common challenges in terms of how to reconcile pressing development needs with longer-term environmental goals. Countries have inevitably responded in different ways that reflect, among other things, their political systems, the nature of their economies, and the level of civil society engagement. But we have seen similar problems of enforcement at the national level, constraints that arise from economic relationships of trade, aid, and debt, and conflicts between global, often Northern-determined, environmental priorities and more pressing issues at the local level.

Through global processes of negotiation, increasingly integrated supply chains, and globally interdependent trading patterns, we have seen how pressures come to be exerted on developing countries to design and implement environmental policies in ways that reflect the priorities of others.

Shifts in thinking about environmental policy and what makes it more effective and efficient are transmitted through donor lending and the global reach of transnational companies. These are the sorts of pressures that bring about conformity and harmonization in environmental politics in the developing world.

But there is much that is subject to change, such is the fragile and often ephemeral status of environmental issues on the policy agendas of countries the world over. The status of such issues is as vulnerable to the state of the world economy as it is to the health of the planet. Despite calls in the North for a 'green new deal' (increased public investment in new jobs and green technology in the wake of the financial crisis in 2008), government spending on environmental programmes notoriously goes down in times of recession as other issues assume a higher profile. The links between security and the environment continue to attract increasing attention. Resources such as oil and water are often both a cause and a manifestation of geo-political conflicts, in the Middle East for example, while the way in which drought has exacerbated the conflict in Darfur has led some to call it the world's first 'climate war'. Priorities shift according to global events as much as they reflect changes in domestic politics following changes of government. A re-alignment of donor priorities in the wake of these shifts may have a significant impact on resource allocations for environmental projects, or the extent to which some regions of the developing world come to be favoured over others on the basis of their strategic value to Western interests. Nevertheless, with or without donor support, developing countries face many environmental challenges of their own, including water pollution and urban air quality. It is often the human impact of these problems that attracts attention and acts as the driver for change. The increasingly high human cost of environmental degradation exacts an economic price: costs to health systems increase; levels of disease increase; and an unhealthy workforce is an unproductive workforce. Despite increasing acknowledgement of the human and developmental case for tackling environmental degradation, stark trade-offs between environmentally damaging

investment and no investment at all continue to force governments to put profit before the needs of their own people or the planet. Global economic pressures from highly mobile companies and global economic institutions further load the dice towards investment and exports over the imperatives of sustainable development.

Sometimes, of course, environmental problems draw attention to themselves, and demand action from governments. Floods in Mozambique, droughts in Ethiopia, tsunamis in South-East Asia, the intensity of which will increase as our climate changes, prompt short-term emergency measures. Rarely, however, do they initiate deeper reflection about the causes of the crisis. Nevertheless, the increased incidence of such human-induced yet seemingly 'natural' events may, more than any other single factor, serve to focus the world's attention on the environmental consequences of current patterns of development. They may come to act as a catalyst to more far-reaching action aimed at combating environmental degradation.

Conclusion

Developing countries face a range of often contradictory pressures from international institutions, market actors, and civil society regarding how to reconcile environmental protection with broader development goals. How they handle these challenges will be a function of many domestic political factors. This pattern of change will continue as national events shift priorities and the context in which environmental policy is made is continually altered by change in the global political economy. Access to diminishing supplies of resources such

as oil and conflicts over water, exacerbated by climate change, will link environmental issues ever more closely to questions of national and international security. A key driver of policy responses will continue to be environmental disasters that focus public attention on the impacts of particular types of development. The challenge is to harness this concern towards longer-term change aimed at tackling the causes of environmental degradation rather than merely to address some of the consequences.

Questions

1. Why has the relationship between environment and development been so uneasy?

2. Is the environment still primarily a 'Northern' issue?

3. Does the concept of sustainable development have any practical or analytical value?

4. Is it still meaningful to refer to the global South in international environmental negotiations?

5. How can environmental issues be integrated within national development strategies?

6. Is poverty a cause or a result of environmental degradation?

7. Can globalization contribute to greening the global economy and, if so, how would this benefit developing countries?

8. Discuss the relationship between environment and national and international security.

9. How far does climate change force us to rethink conventional models of development?

10. Under what circumstances might environment and development challenges be reconciled more effectively in the future?

11. Which institutional reforms could improve the international community's ability to effectively address environmental problems, and how far would they threaten the sovereignty of developing countries?

Further reading

■ Adams, W. M. (2008), *Green Development: Environment and Sustainability in the Third World*, 2nd edn (London: Routledge). Provides a detailed history of the concept of sustainable development and the different ways in which it has been interpreted and applied in the mainstream and by its critics.

■ Barry, J. and Frankland, E. G. (2002), *International Encyclopedia of Environmental Politics* (London/New York: Routledge). This encyclopaedia provides short summaries and guides to further reading on key issues from 'African environmental issues' to 'Water pollution' and just about everything in between.

■ Bryant, R. L. and Bailey, S. (1997), *Third World Political Ecology* (London: Routledge). Provides a useful actor-based introduction to the key forces shaping environmental politics in the developing world from business and multilateral institutions to NGOs and the role of the state.

■ Elliott, L. (1998), *The Global Politics of the Environment* (London: Macmillan). Wide-ranging textbook that covers not only the global environmental agenda, but also issues of trade, debt, and aid, which bring together environmental and development agendas.

■ Keeley, J. and Scoones, I. (2003), *Understanding Environmental Policy Processes: Cases from Africa* (London: Earthscan). Drawing on research in Ethiopia, Mali, and Zimbabwe, this book examines the links between knowledge, power, and politics in understanding how environmental issues come to be framed and the consequences of this for how they are acted upon.

■ Newell, P. and Wheeler, J. (eds) (2006), *Rights, Resources and the Politics of Accountability* (London: Zed Books). Drawing on cases of struggles over resources such as water and oil as well as for livelihood rights such as health, housing, and work, in countries as diverse as Bangladesh, Nigeria, and the US, this book provides an analysis of how poorer groups mobilize to claim resources from state and private actors.

■ Peets, R. and Watts, M. (eds) (2004), *Liberation Ecologies: Environment, Development and Social Movements* (London: Routledge). Explores the theoretical implications of the relationship between development, social movements, and the environment in the South. Draws this out through case studies on a range of environmental issues from countries including China, India, Zimbabwe, Ecuador, and Gambia.

:// Web links

■ www.steps-centre.org Institute of Development Studies and Science Policy Research Unit, University of Sussex, UK. This research centre on social, technological, and environmental pathways to sustainability produces research on a range of environmental and development issues. The IDS site also provides access to the Eldis gateway from where searches for information and studies on particular environmental issues in specific developing countries can be undertaken.

■ www.iied.org International Institute for Environment and Development, London, UK. This contains details on latest research and publications produced by the institute on a range of environment and development issues.

■ www.iisd.org The International Institute for Sustainable Development, Winnipeg, Canada. Among other useful databanks, this site gives access to the Earth Negotiations Bulletin, which provides updates on all the leading international environmental negotiations.

■ www.cseindia.org Centre for Science and Environment, Delhi, India. Contains reports and details of campaigns on key environmental challenges facing India, although maintains a global focus too.

■ www.twnside.org.sg Third World Network, Kuala Lumpur, Malaysia. Contains position papers, reports, and information updates from the network's members on issues such as trade, biotechnology, and climate change.

■ http://practicalaction.org/home Practical Action, UK (formerly known as Intermediate Technology and Development Group). Contains details on the organization, its project and research work, and reports and publications on a range of environment and development issues.

■ www.acts.or.ke African Centre for Technology Studies, Nairobi, Kenya. Provides useful studies, resources, and news items on issues such as agriculture and food security, climate change, and biotechnology.

■ www.unep.org United Nations Environment Programme, Nairobi, Kenya. A mine of information about global environmental issues and the negotiations aimed at tackling them.

■ www.worldbank.org Contains the World Bank's *World Development Report 2010: Development and Climate Change*.

@ Online Resource Centre

For additional material and resources, please visit the Online Resource Centre at:
www.oxfordtextbooks.co.uk/orc/burnell3e/

18

Human Rights

Michael Freeman

 Overview

The language of **human rights** is a pervasive feature of contemporary international politics, but it is not well understood. This chapter offers an analysis of the concept, a brief account of its history and a description of the **international human rights regime**. It proceeds to examine two persistent problems that arise in applying the concept to developing countries: the relations between human rights and development; and the relations between the claim that the concept is universally valid and the realities of cultural difference around the world. The idea of human rights derives from historical problems of the West. It is necessary to consider its applicability to the problems of developing countries in a world constituted by great inequalities of political power and wealth.

Introduction

The concept of human rights derives primarily from the United Nations Charter, which was adopted in 1945 immediately after the Second World War. The preamble to the Charter declares that the United

Nations (UN) was determined to 'reaffirm faith in fundamental human rights, in the dignity and worth of the human person, in the equal rights of men and women, and of nations large and small'. In 1948, the General Assembly of the UN adopted the Universal Declaration of Human Rights, which sets out a list of human rights 'as a common standard of achievement for all peoples'. The list includes such civil and political rights as those to freedom from slavery, torture, arbitrary arrest, and detention, freedom of religion, expression, and association, and a number of economic and social rights, such as the rights to education and an adequate standard of living. These rights were intended to protect everyone from tyrannical governments like that of Nazi Germany, and from the economic misery that was thought to have facilitated the rise of fascism.

Although the countries of Latin America, Asia, and Africa formed the majority of those that produced the Declaration, many of the world's people lived at that time under colonial rule, and were thus excluded from this process. The concept of human rights was derived from a Western philosophical tradition, and was shaped mainly by European historical experience. Colonialism was itself condemned for its human rights violations, and, when worldwide decolonization brought many new states to the UN, the post-colonial states accepted human rights in principle, although their priorities differed from those of the West, emphasizing self-determination, development, economic and social rather than civil and political rights, and anti-racism.

Disagreements about which human rights should be legally binding led to the adoption of two UN human rights covenants in 1966: the International Covenant on Civil and Political Rights; and the International Covenant on Economic, Social and Cultural Rights. The UN's World Conference on Human Rights, held in Vienna in 1993, declared all human rights to be 'indivisible and interdependent'. Now, each covenant has been ratified by more than 80 per cent of the UN's member states.

The UN has adopted several more specialized conventions (see Box 18.1). There are also regional human rights conventions, although these do not cover the whole world, especially the Middle East and Asia. The European Convention on Human Rights was adopted in 1950; the American Convention on Human Rights in 1969; and the African Charter on Human and Peoples' Rights in 1981.

Box 18.1 Universal and Regional Human Rights Regimes

Universal Declaration of Human Rights 1948

European Convention on Human Rights 1950

International Covenant on Civil and Political Rights 1966

International Covenant on Economic, Social and Cultural Rights 1966

International Convention on the Elimination of Racial Discrimination 1966

American Convention on Human Rights 1969

Convention on the Elimination of Discrimination against Women 1979

African Charter on Human and Peoples' Rights 1981

Convention against Torture 1984

Convention on the Rights of the Child 1989

International Convention on the Protection of Migrant Workers 1990

Many developing countries have poor human rights records. There are internal and external explanations of this. The internal explanations include poverty, ethnic tensions, and authoritarian government. Some of the internal problems of developing countries are legacies of colonialism. The external explanations include support for dictatorships by the great powers, especially during the cold war, and the global economic system, which many believe is biased against developing countries, and thereby hinders their capacity to develop the institutions necessary to protect human rights. Since the end of the cold war, and the discrediting of the Soviet, state socialist model of development, **neo-liberalism**—the ideology of free markets—has dominated global economics. Whether neo-liberalism promotes respect for, or violation of human rights is highly controversial. The Universal Declaration's conception of human rights, however, presupposed effective states, and neo-liberalism tends to weaken states, and especially their capacity to protect social and economic rights, such as those to health, education, and freedom from poverty. The harmful effects of such policies disproportionately affect women and children. Recently, following criticism of neo-liberalism from many quarters, international economic policies have been modified, at least in theory, to address the problems of global poverty.

Developing countries have been vulnerable both to military coups and to ethnic conflict. Both are attributable to legacies of colonialism, and both lead to serious human rights violations. While the dominant human rights discourse is highly *legalistic*, and emphasizes legal solutions to human rights problems, social scientists have recently revived the concept of **civil society** (see Chapter 10) as a barrier to tyranny. Developing countries vary considerably in the strength of their civil societies, but some observers see civil society as the best hope both for development and the improvement of human rights protection. Human rights seem to require a balance between effective states and strong civil societies, which is difficult to achieve when resources are scarce.

In 1979 the authoritarian, Westernizing regime of the Shah was overthrown in Iran, and an Islamic republic established. This stimulated challenges to dominant conceptions of human rights from the perspectives of Islam and other non-Western cultures. In the mid-1990s government representatives and intellectuals from the economically successful countries of South-East and East Asia argued that human rights should be reinterpreted according to 'Asian values' in their societies. The critique of human rights from the standpoint of cultural diversity was thereby added to, and sometimes confused with, the critique from the standpoint of economic inequality. Following the financial crisis of 1997, talk of 'Asian values' diminished. Debates about Islam and human rights, however, increased, and became more intense after the terrorist attacks on the USA on 11 September 2001.

Key points

- The concept of human rights, promoted by the UN after the Second World War to combat dictatorship, was embodied in the UN Charter (1945) and the Universal Declaration of Human Rights (1948).

- At that time people living under colonial rule were excluded from participating in the concept's elaboration; thereafter new, post-colonial states accepted human rights in principle, but prioritized development-related rights.

- In the decades after 1948 the UN developed a large body of international human rights law.

- Many developing countries have poor human rights records for a combination of internal and external reasons and many have also challenged dominant interpretations of human rights by appealing to their own cultural traditions.

The Concept of Human Rights

MICHAEL FREEMAN

Human rights are rights of a special kind. The concept of 'rights' is derived from that of 'right'. Right is distinguished from wrong, and all societies have standards of right and wrong. 'Right' is sometimes called 'objective', because it refers to a supposedly objective standard. Many people would say that the prohibition of murder is objectively right. Rights are sometimes called 'subjective' because they 'belong' to individuals or groups who are the 'subjects' of rights. Thus subjective rights are **entitlements**, and differ from objective concepts such as 'right' by emphasizing the just claims of the rights-holder. The idea of subjective rights is often said to be distinctively Western and relatively modern.

Human rights are commonly defined as the rights that everyone has simply because they are human. Philosophically, this is problematic, because it is not clear why anyone has rights because they are human. A theory of rights is needed to justify this belief. Legally, it is also problematic, because some human rights are denied to some humans: for example, the right to liberty is denied to those who have committed serious crimes. Politically, human rights are those rights that have generally been recognized by governments. The Universal Declaration provides us with an authoritative list of human rights, but it is difficult to distinguish precisely between human rights, other rights, and other social values. It may, however, be important to do so, because people increasingly claim as their human rights what may not be human rights, or may not be rights at all, but social benefits or merely what people happen to want.

The two 1966 Covenants distinguish between two categories of human rights: civil and political rights, on the one hand, and economic, social, and cultural rights, on the other. Western governments tend to prioritize the first type, and developing countries the second. The distinction itself is, however, controversial: the right to property, for example, is often regarded as a civil rather than an economic right, which seems absurd. The Vienna Declaration (1993) sought to overcome the distinction by proclaiming that all human rights are 'indivisible'. This idea has become increasingly influential as the United Nations, its member governments, and international institutions, such as the World Bank, have come to recognize that neglect of human rights is at least sometimes a barrier to development. It is now also often said that there are three generations of rights: the two types already mentioned constitute the first and second generations, while there is a third generation, consisting of 'solidarity' rights, such as the right to development. These distinctions are also controversial, both because the reference to generations misrepresents the history of human rights, and because the meaning and value of third-generation human rights are questionable.

A brief history

Some say that the concept of human rights is ancient, and found in all or most of the world's cultures. This claim usually confuses subjective rights with objective right. Notions such as justice or human dignity are found in many cultures. The idea of individual, subjective rights is more unusual and, consequently, more controversial.

Some scholars have argued that individual rights cannot be found before the late Middle Ages, and did not become politically important until the seventeenth century in England. The concept of *citizens' rights* is, however, found in ancient Greek and Roman thought. The modern concept of human rights derives from that of natural rights, which was developed in Europe in the late Middle Ages, and featured prominently in the political struggles of seventeenth-century England. Natural rights were derived from natural law, and were known by reason. This idea burst onto the stage of world politics with the American and French revolutions in the late eighteenth century. In the nineteenth century it fell out of favour, because it was thought to be unscientific and subversive of social order. The concept of human rights evokes that of natural rights, but differs in at least two important ways: first, it does without the controversial philosophy of natural law; second, it sees rights as social rather than natural.

Contemporary conceptions

The dominant conception of human rights today derives from its origins in Western **liberalism**, the philosophy that gives priority to individual freedom. Human rights are the rights of individuals, and the individualism of the concept (its isolation of the human individual and the special value placed on that individual) is often said to be alien to non-Western cultures. It is not certain, however, that all human rights are individual rights. Both the 1966 Covenants recognize that *peoples* have the right to self-determination. The right to development may be an individual or a collective right, or both. Western countries have a strongly individualistic conception of human rights, whereas developing countries have a more collectivistic conception.

Key points

- Human rights are rights of a special kind, not simply entitlements but the rights everyone has because they are human or those generally recognized as such by governments or international law.
- Distinctions between civil and political rights, on the one hand, and economic, social, and cultural rights, on the other hand, and among three generations of human rights, can be criticized on theoretical grounds.

- Human, as opposed to citizens', rights are modern, deriving from the late mediaeval idea of natural rights, which fell out of favour after the French Revolution but was revived by the UN as the concept of human rights.
- The dominant conception of human rights is controversial in developing countries because it is thought to express the Western philosophy of individualism.

Human Rights Regimes

A **regime** is a set of rules and practices that regulate the conduct of actors in a specified field. Human rights regimes exist at international, regional, and national levels.

The UN system

The international human rights regime consists of a large body of international law and a complex set of institutions to implement it. Chief among these institutions was the UN Commission on Human Rights, established 1945–47. Its members represented governments, and it was criticized for political bias. In 2006 the UN replaced the Commission with the Human Rights Council in an attempt to improve its human rights performance. The UN employs independent experts as members of working groups or as rapporteurs on specific themes (such as torture) and countries. The members of the committees that monitor the various treaties are also independent experts. **Non-governmental organizations** (NGOs)—consisting of citizen activists and experts—play an important role in providing information. It is difficult to evaluate the effectiveness of the international regime, but the consensus of scholars is that it is rather weak. The future of the regime after the creation of the Human Rights Council remains to be seen.

Regional and national regimes

There are regional human rights regimes in Europe, the Americas, and Africa. The European is the most effective, and the African the least. Many scholars believe that the most important location for the protection of human rights is national law. The international regime is fairly effective in *promoting* human rights, but relatively ineffective in *implementing* them. Regional regimes are generally effective only when supervising relatively effective national regimes.

National constitutions often include human rights. Some theorists have said that economic and social rights are not 'justiciable'—that is, they are not suited to judicial decision-making. However, a recent study found almost 2,000 judicial and quasi-judicial decisions on social rights from 29 national and international jurisdictions. These included numerous cases decided by courts in developing countries. Courts have ordered the reconnection of water supplies, the halting of forced evictions, the provision of medical treatment, the reinstatement of social security benefits,

the enrolment of poor and minority children in schools, and the development of state programmes to address homelessness, disease and starvation (Langford 2008). A World Bank study of five developing countries concluded that the legalization of social rights may have prevented thousands of deaths and improved the lives of millions. The contribution of such cases to global human rights protection may be limited, but they are probably most effective when they form part of a political strategy on behalf of the poor and marginalized.

Legal regimes and power politics

Developing countries frequently complain that the international human rights regime is a smokescreen behind which powerful Western states pursue their interests. There is undoubtedly truth in this charge, but many governments of developing countries have terrible human rights records, and this has in most cases probably hindered rather than promoted development. The powerful states of the West, and the UN itself, have been criticized both for not intervening to prevent human rights violations, as in the Rwandan **genocide** of 1994, and for intervening too forcefully or for dubious motives, as in Iraq in 2003.

Key points

- The human rights conduct of states is regulated, with varying degrees of effectiveness, by legal and political regimes at international, regional, and national levels.

- The international human rights regime is fairly effective regarding promotion but relatively ineffective regarding implementation; the European regime is the most effective regional regime but human rights are best protected by national laws.

- The international human rights regimes are predominantly legal, and, behind them, international power politics dominates the human rights agenda, which for developing countries makes them matters of intense controversy.

There is a widely held view that developing countries must give development priority over human rights. The fundamental intuition underlying this view is that starving people cannot benefit from, say, the right to free speech, and that, without development, human rights are not possible, and perhaps not even desirable. 'Human rights begin at breakfast', Léopold Senghor, the former President of Senegal, is supposed to have said. Various arguments support this position. It is claimed, for example, that human rights—especially economic and social rights—are simply too expensive for poor countries. It is also maintained that, especially in less developed countries with problematic ethnic divisions, human rights subvert social order and thus hinder development: the government of Singapore, for example, has often made this argument. Even if this is not so, free societies tend to divert resources from savings and investment to consumption, and this slows down long-term development. Empirically, the so-called Asian 'tigers'—South Korea, Taiwan, Malaysia, and Singapore, in particular—and, more recently, China, are cited as examples of successful economic development under authoritarian rule. The idea that human rights are *necessary* for development—an idea commonly promoted by the West—is thereby falsified. Most Western countries developed their economies and human rights over long periods of time, and generally recognized human rights only when they had sufficiently developed economies to support them.

Conceptions of development

'Development' is often assumed to mean economic development, and economic development has often been measured by per capita income. Recently, however, development has been reconceptualized as 'human development', with emphasis on the quality of life. The economic development of states is compatible with the misery of many people. The new conception of development sees human rights and development as *conceptually* overlapping. There is, for example, a human right to an adequate standard of living. If development is defined in terms of the standard of living, then human rights and development are positively correlated *by definition*. The new conceptualization has had practical implications: the UN Development Programme, for example, has recently included the protection of human rights in its policies. This new conception of development has been closely associated with an increased emphasis on gender equality.

Are human rights and development interdependent?

The Vienna Declaration asserted that human rights and development are 'interdependent': is this true?

The arguments that restrictions of human rights are either *necessary* or *sufficient* for development are not well supported by the evidence. The arguments often rely on very selective use of case studies, especially from East Asia. South Korea and Taiwan achieved rapid economic development under authoritarian governments, but both developed into liberal democracies. Singapore has also been economically successful with a so-called 'soft authoritarian' regime. Other cases are ambiguous. Some Latin American countries—such as Pinochet's Chile—had some economic growth, but also some economic setbacks, under authoritarian rule, while China has achieved rapid economic growth combined with serious human rights violations in recent years. Authoritarian regimes can sometimes achieve rapid economic development. Most repressive regimes, however, have failed to deliver development. This suggests that violating human rights as such does not explain economic development. The causal connection between human rights violations and development has never been established. Some countries that have combined economic development with restrictions of civil and political rights—such as South Korea, Singapore, and China—have relatively good records with respect to economic and social rights, such as education and health. Some development economists believe that democratic political rights and social rights, such those to health and education, are conducive to success in development.

The relations between development and human rights may well be mediated by other factors, including the economic strategies adopted by governmental elites and the country's security situation. Taiwan, South Korea, and Singapore all faced external and/or internal security threats that made authoritarian government more likely, if not strictly necessary, and all were able to locate themselves favourably within the global economic system.

Respect for human rights is, therefore, not generally *necessary* for economic development, and violation of human rights is certainly not *sufficient* for economic development. *Most countries that have persistently and seriously violated human rights have been unsuccessful in developing their economies.* The increasing political repression in Zimbabwe, for example, has been accompanied by economic collapse, and the former is certainly a cause of the latter. It is very difficult to generalize about the relations between development and human rights, however, and we should be very cautious about inferring policies for particular countries from generalizations, and, a fortiori, from the experience of selected countries.

Attempts to establish statistical relations between human rights and development in large numbers of countries have also produced inconclusive and sometimes apparently contradictory results. The famous Indian economist, Amartya Sen, has argued that the evidence suggests little correlation, positive or negative, between respect for civil and political rights and economic growth, and that the violation of such rights is not *necessary* to economic development. He reminds us that human rights have a value that is independent of development,

in so far as we believe in 'the dignity and worth of the human person', and argues consequently that the available evidence is no barrier to the policy of pursuing development-with-human-rights (Sen 1999b). But if the relation between human rights and development is unclear, and developed states have far from perfect records in respecting human rights, then the most grave human-rights disasters of recent years—such as the tyranny of Idi Amin in Uganda (1972–78), the mass killings by the Khmer Rouge in Cambodia (1975–79), the terror regime of Saddam Hussein in Iraq (1979–2003), and the genocide in Rwanda (1994)—have taken place in developing countries. Why is this?

Developing countries are mostly poor, and are economically vulnerable to the power of rich states. This makes economic development difficult. Without economic development, the resources for implementing human rights are scarce. Paradoxically, where resources are not scarce (as in oil-producing countries, such as Nigeria, Saudi Arabia, Iraq, and Iran), the temptations of corruption and authoritarianism may also be great. This has come to be known as 'the resource curse'.

The achievement of independence from colonial rule, the ethos of the United Nations and world culture, and the spread of information and images through modern media of communication have raised expectations of economic progress among the peoples of the developing countries. Then the persistent inability of governments to meet them has created widespread and intense social frustration, active opposition to governments, and consequent repression. These problems are aggravated in many developing countries by ethnic divisions. Although ethnic diversity does not necessarily lead to conflict and human rights violations, such divisions are difficult to manage, where ethnicity is a potent source of competition, and can therefore lead to serious human rights violations.

Developing countries should not be seen simply as dependent victims of domination by rich states, international institutions, multinational corporations, or global capitalism. They have some autonomy, however limited, as the success of the

Asian tigers demonstrates. Corrupt and incompetent government has contributed to the economic failures of many developing countries, and human rights violations are partly explained by the desire of powerful and corrupt rulers to remain in power, as for instance in China, Indonesia, Iraq, Saudi Arabia, Nigeria, and Zimbabwe.

Most developing countries lack traditions of human rights (see Box 18.2). They may have traditional cultures with morally admirable features, such as mutual solidarity, and they may also have active human rights organizations—which are found throughout much of Asia, Africa, and Latin America—and even individual 'human rights heroes' (such as Aung San Suu Kyi in Burma/Myanmar). But, in contrast with Europe, the value of human rights may not be deeply embedded in the public culture of the society. Even where the government has ratified international human rights treaties, and human rights are written into national constitutions, human rights may not be a strong feature of the political culture.

The Vienna Declaration maintained that democracy, development, and human rights were interdependent. This claim, however, oversimplifies a complex set of relations. Democracy is probably not necessary to development, but may improve its chances (see Chapter 14). The problem is that it is very difficult to establish democracy at very low levels of development. Empirically, democracies respect human rights better than other forms of government do, but all democracies violate human rights sometimes, and so-called 'facade democracies', which hold formally fair and free elections, but exclude sections of the population from effective political participation, are likely to have fairly poor human rights records. The protection of human rights by legal institutions may run counter to the democratic will of the people. The human rights of suspected criminals, refugees, and ethnic and political minorities are particularly vulnerable to democratic violations, in developed and developing countries. Finally, in developing countries with ethnic divisions and weak human rights traditions, the process of democratization itself may lead to serious human rights violations. Democratization played a role in ethnic conflict and genocide in Rwanda, for example. In both the Philippines and Indonesia, democratization has led to new forms of human rights violations, as space is made for ethnic demands that are met by repressive responses. The **war on terrorism** has led to human rights violations in some democracies as well in some authoritarian countries.

Box 18.2 Barriers to Human Rights Implementation by Developing Countries

- Most developing countries are poor and cannot afford the full implementation of human rights.

- Most developing countries have little power in the global economic system, and are consequently vulnerable to the policies of powerful states and non-state actors that are often unfriendly to human rights.

- In the conditions of contemporary global culture and media of mass communication, where the expectations of many people in developing countries for economic progress are high, the inability of governments to meet those expectations stimulates protest and repression.

- Most developing countries have ethnic divisions that predispose them to conflict in conditions of scarcity, and consequently to repression.

- Corrupt and incompetent government has been common in developing countries, and human rights are explained in part by the desire of corrupt rulers to remain in power.

- Many developing countries have had traditional cultures, wherein human rights enjoyed little place, and have developed a modern human rights culture only in a weak form.

Key points

- It is commonly argued that development should have priority over human rights, although when development is defined as quality of life it overlaps with the concept of human rights.

- Although the empirical relationship between human rights and development is not well understood, the available evidence suggests that it is weak. There are independent reasons for valuing human rights.

- Democracies generally respect human rights better than authoritarian regimes do, but sometimes violate them. The US war on terrorism has led to human rights violations by both democratic and authoritarian governments.

Universalism and Cultural Diversity

The Preamble to the Universal Declaration of Human Rights refers to 'the equal and inalienable rights of all members of the human family', and the Declaration proclaims itself to be 'a common standard of achievement for all peoples'. Article 1 states that all human beings 'are born free and equal in dignity and rights'. The Vienna Declaration reaffirmed the universality of human rights.

This universalism of human rights beliefs derives from the liberal Enlightenment doctrine of eighteenth-century Europe that the 'Rights of Man', as human rights were then called, were the rights of everyone, everywhere, at all times. This doctrine derived in turn from Christian teaching that there was only one God, and that the divine law applied to everyone, equally, everywhere, and at all times. One source of Christian philosophy was the Graeco-Roman theory of natural law, which taught that all human beings formed a single moral community, governed by a common law that was known to human reason. The philosophical school of the Stoics was the proponent of pre-Christian, natural-law philosophy. The natural-law philosophical tradition that runs from the Stoics through medieval Christianity to Enlightenment liberalism and the contemporary concept of human rights forms a powerful, although controversial, component of Western, and to some extent global, culture.

Cultural imperialism and cultural relativism

The belief that human rights are universal appears to conflict with the obvious cultural diversity of the world. Moral and political ideas, many people say, derive from culture, and different societies have different cultures. To impose human rights on everyone in the world is therefore intolerant, imperialistic, and unjustified. This moral logic may be supported by the *historical* claims that: (1) the concept of human rights is a Western concept; and (2) the West has a history of political, economic, and cultural imperialism that is not yet over. Some non-Western critics of human rights argue that not only is human rights a concept alien to non-Western cultures, but its use by the West is part of a project of global political and economic domination. The 2003 war in Iraq might be cited as an example of the use of human rights to legitimate political expansionism.

In the 1990s a number of governments and intellectuals from East and South-East Asian countries that had achieved considerable economic success called into question the dominant interpretation of human rights by appealing to what they claimed were distinctively Asian values. This claim was somewhat puzzling, as the cultures of East Asia are extremely diverse, ranging from officially atheist China to predominantly Muslim Indonesia and Malaysia. One of the leading proponents of 'Asian values'—Dr Mahathir Mohamad, then Prime Minister of Malaysia—acknowledged that Asian values were similar to *conservative* Western values: order; harmony; respect for authority. The Asian values argument was partially acknowledged by the Vienna Declaration, which reaffirmed the universality of human rights, but conceded that 'the significance of national and regional particularities and various historical, cultural and religious backgrounds should be borne in mind'. Read literally, this statement is uncontroversial, for it would be foolish to interpret and implement human rights without bearing in mind the significance of these cultural differences. However, many Asian NGOs continued to affirm the universalist orthodoxy without qualifications. Thus two different Asian approaches to human rights were produced during this controversy. Some human rights scholars and activists saw the appeal to Asian values as an ideological attempt to justify authoritarian government, but it did provoke a debate about how the universal values of human rights should be reconciled with the world's cultural traditions.

This issue requires careful analysis. Much of the *moral* critique of human rights derives from the claim that it constitutes **cultural imperialism**, and relies on the intuition that imperialism is obviously wrong. If we ask *why* imperialism is wrong, however, we may say that it violates the rights of those who are its victims. If we next ask *which* rights of the victims are violated by imperialism, the most common answer is the **right to self-determination**. At this point, the objection to moral universalism depends on a universal principle (the right to self-determination) and is therefore self-contradictory. If there is at least one universal right (the right to self-determination), there may also be others. It is difficult to argue that the right to self-determination is a universal right without accepting that the right not to be enslaved is also a universal right. This appeal to universalism does not necessarily justify the full list of rights in the Universal Declaration,

but it does refute one common line of argument against universalism.

Another approach would be to reject all forms of universalism, and rely on the claim that all moral principles derive from *particular* cultures, particular cultures are *diverse*, some cultures reject at least some human rights principles (gender equality is a common example), and human rights are valid only within the culture of the modern West. On this view, there is a human rights culture. But it is only one culture among many, and, because it derives from Western (secular) liberalism, it is not particularly appealing, still less *obligatory*, for those who, perhaps on the basis of their religious beliefs, subscribe to non-liberal moral and political codes. This argument has been proposed by some (but not all) Muslims, who believe that Islam requires submission to the will of God, and this must have priority over any secular obligations, such as those of human rights.

This argument avoids the self-contradiction of the anti-imperialist approach, but at a considerable cost. The first difficulty is that the argument that all actual moral principles are justified by the cultures of which they form a part is another universal principle that cannot be used against universalism as such without self-contradiction. The next difficulty is that, if all principles are justified by their cultures, then imperialism would be justified by imperialistic cultures—a view that is anathema to critics of human rights universalism. They could argue that, according to the criteria of their culture, imperialism is wrong, but not show would-be imperialists why they should act according to these criteria. In practice, most critics of human rights universalism accept that racism is universally wrong, and cannot be justified by racist cultures like that of apartheid South Africa. A further difficulty with the 'culturalist' conception of morality is that actual cultures are complex, contested, and overlapping. There are, for examples, many schools of Islamic thought, there are disputes about the requirements of the religion, and Islamic ideas have mixed with other ideas in different ways in different societies. The idea of a homogeneous culture that justifies particular moral ideas is a myth. The world is full of a great diversity of complex moral ideas, some of which cohere in different ways, with different degrees of uniformity and solidarity, into patterns that are themselves subject to change, in part as the result of interaction with other cultures.

These arguments do not themselves provide a justification of human rights. Only a justificatory theory of human rights could do that, and any such theory is likely to be controversial, not just between the West and the rest, but within Western thought, and even among human rights supporters. They also imply no disrespect for culture as such. Culture provides meaning, value, and guidance to human life, and there is a human right to participate in the cultural life of one's community. They do show that cultures are not self-justifying, and that we commit no logical or moral error in subjecting actual cultures to critical scrutiny. Feminist human rights scholars have argued that the appeal to culture has often been made in an attempt to justify the oppression of women.

Islam, human rights, and the war on terrorism

The rise in oil prices in the early 1970s, the Islamic Revolution of Iran (1979), the persistence of corrupt, authoritarian governments, and extreme poverty in many Muslim countries, and the continuing Israel–Palestine conflict contributed to the development of fundamentalist Islamic parties and movements.

As Soviet troops withdrew from Afghanistan in 1988, Osama bin Laden, son of a rich Saudi businessman, who had recruited non-Afghans to support the Afghan resistance to the Soviet occupiers, formed al-Qaeda to continue a *jihad* (holy war) against the perceived enemies of Islam. In 1991 the forces of the secular Iraqi regime of Saddam Hussein invaded Kuwait, the population of which is almost wholly Muslim. A US-led force, acting with UN authority, and based in Saudi Arabia, expelled the Iraqi invaders from Kuwait. Following this war,

several attacks on US and other targets were attributed to al-Qaeda, culminating in the attacks on the USA on 11 September 2001. The USA responded by invading Afghanistan, the extreme Islamic government of which, the Taliban, was believed to have protected al-Qaeda. President Bush declared a war on terrorism (Box 18.3). The USA set up a detention camp in Guantanamo Bay, Cuba, where it held several hundred suspected terrorists without due process of law. Many countries introduced new anti-terrorists laws, which were criticized by NGOs for their neglect of human rights protections. After the USA and some of its allies invaded Iraq, in 2003, many allegations of human rights violations by US troops became common. Allegations of torture by US forces in Afghanistan, Iraq, and at Guantanamo Bay, and charges of the 'rendition' (transportation) of suspects to other countries in which torture was common, were commonplace and were usually denied by the US government. However, pictures of the mistreatment of Iraqi prisoners in the Abu Ghraib prison in Baghdad created an international scandal.

These events changed the context of the global human rights struggle because the USA had become the only superpower; administration officials had, both in internal memoranda and public pronouncements, shown contempt for the UN, international law, and human rights. Many governments have used the war on terrorism as an excuse for increasing human rights violations. Although most Muslims oppose terrorism, the use of Islam by al-Qaeda to justify its actions, the widespread targeting of Muslims as suspected terrorists, the election of the Islamist terrorist group, Hamas, as the government of the Palestinians, the election of a hard-line Islamist President of Iran, and the publication of cartoons highly offensive to Muslims in a Danish newspaper all contributed to a crisis in the relations between Islam and the West. Human rights activists had to come to terms both with the war on terrorism and their own relations with Islam. There are many schools of thought within Islam, some incompatible with human rights in important respects (especially relating to the rights of women), while others seek reconciliation between Islam and human rights. Some experts believe that the question of Islam and human rights is not fundamentally one of religion, but of the political and economic problems of the Middle East. These problems derive in part, but by no means wholly, from the history of Western imperialist intrusions into the Middle East. The election of Barack Obama as President of the USA in November 2008 was based in part on promises to end the human rights violations associated with the 'war on terror'. Whether these promises will be fully implemented remains to be seen. In the autumn of 2009 it was reported that al-Qaeda had been seriously weakened, although terrorist groups with a similar ideology were still active.

Box 18.3 Islam and the War on Terrorism

" For more than seven years the United States has been occupying the lands of Islam in the holiest of places, the Arabian Peninsula, plundering its riches, dictating to its rulers, humiliating its people, terrorizing its neighbours and turning its bases in the peninsula into a spearhead through which to fight the neighbouring Muslim peoples.... These crimes and sins committed by the Americans are a clear declaration of war on God, his messenger and Muslims. And *ulema* [Muslim scholars] have throughout Islamic history unanimously agreed that the *jihad* is an individual duty if the enemy destroys the Muslim countries. On that basis, and in compliance with God's order, we issue the following *fatwa* [decree] to all Muslims: The ruling is to kill the Americans and their allies is an individual duty for every Muslim who can do it, in order to liberate the Al Aqsa mosque [in Jerusalem] and the Holy Mosque [in Mecca]...
" (*al-Qaeda*, February 1998)

" I also want to speak tonight directly to Muslims throughout the world. We respect your faith.... Its teachings are good and peaceful, and those who commit evil in the name of Allah blaspheme the name of Allah. The terrorists are traitors to their own faith, trying, in effect, to hijack Islam itself. The enemy is not our many Muslim friends. It is not our many Arab friends. Our enemy is a radical network of terrorists and every government that supports them. Our war on terror begins with al-Qaeda, but it does not end there. It will not end until every terrorist group of global reach has been found, stopped and defeated.
" (President George W. Bush, 20 September 2001)

" The Muslim Council of Britain utterly condemns today's indiscriminate acts of terror in London.... We must and will be united in common determination that terror cannot succeed...
" (Muslim Council of Britain, 7 July 2005, the day on which 52 people were killed by terrorists bombs on the London transport system)

" Each day brings more information about the appalling abuses inflicted upon men and women held by the United States in Iraq, Afghanistan, and elsewhere around the world. U.S. forces have used interrogation techniques including hooding, stripping detainees naked, subjecting them to extremes of heat, cold, noise and light, and depriving them of sleep.... This apparently routine infliction of pain, discomfort, and humiliation has expanded in all too many cases into vicious beatings, sexual degradation, sodomy, near drowning, and near asphyxiation. Detainees have died under questionable circumstances while incarcerated.... In the course of 2005, it became indisputable that U.S. mistreatment of detainees reflected not a failure of training, discipline, or oversight, but a deliberate policy choice. The problem could not be reduced to a few bad apples at the bottom of the barrel.
" (Human Rights Watch)

Key points

- The argument that attempts to universalize human rights are imperialistic fails because it presupposes the universal right to self-determination.

- The argument that all values are relative to culture is unconvincing because cultures are not self-justifying, and hardly anyone believes that anything done in the name of culture is justified.

- The concept of human rights includes the right to practise one's culture, and thus human rights and culture may be compatible. Some cultural practices may, however, violate human rights standards.

- The rise of political Islam and the US war on terrorism have raised new challenges for the human rights movement.

The New Political Economy of Human Rights

Marxists have traditionally argued that human rights conceal real inequalities of wealth and power. The inclusion of economic and social rights in the list of human rights has been intended to meet this criticism, but its success has been very problematic. First, economic and social rights have been relatively neglected in international politics compared with civil and political rights. Second, great inequalities of wealth and power persist worldwide. Nevertheless, some attempts have been made recently to integrate human rights with development, and to improve poverty-reduction strategies.

Globalization

Globalization is a contested concept in social science. Global trade is ancient, and there is a dispute as to how it may have changed in recent times. However, whatever economic historians may say about global trends, it is obvious that we live in a dynamic, interrelated world that is changing rapidly in certain important respects. What is the impact of globalization on human rights?

Globalization has been opposed by a worldwide protest movement expressing diverse concerns, including world poverty, environmental degradation, and human rights. This has replaced, to a considerable extent, the earlier socialist movement opposing capitalism. The targets of this movement are primarily rich states, associations of rich states (such as the so-called G8), and multinational corporations (MNCs). The human rights movement has recently increased its concern about the role of MNCs in human rights violations, either directly (for example, by the employment of child labour) or in collaboration with repressive governments. Issues of globalization, development, the environment, and human rights have often come together as MNCs seek to develop natural resources in ways that damage the environment (see Chapter 17) and local ways of life, and popular protests (see Chapter 11) are sometimes met by governmental repression.

The relations between human rights and globalization are complex, however. The idea of human rights claims to be universal, and the human rights movement seeks global reach, and achieves it to some extent by global means of communication (email, Internet, mobile phones). Meyer (1998) has conducted an empirical investigation into the impact of MNCs on human rights in developing countries, and concluded that there is a positive correlation between MNC investment in developing countries and human rights. He does not deny that some MNCs are involved in human rights violations in these countries. Other scholars, using different methods, have reached different conclusions (Smith, Bolyard, and Ippolito 1999). Globalization, some say, increases inequality, drives the vulnerable to the margins of survival, and thereby feeds religious and nationalist extremism. After the financial crisis in South-East Asia at the end of the 1990s, for example, the International Monetary Fund imposed strict conditions on Indonesia that led to ethnic and religious riots. On the other hand, it has been argued that neo-liberal globalization has tended to undermine the caste system in India, thereby emancipating the untouchables and advancing the cause of human rights (Sikand 2003: 112).

Global capitalism is a dynamic process that probably has positive and negative consequences for human rights. There is also a global economic regime—consisting of organizations such as the G8, the European Union, the North American Free Trade Agreement (NAFTA), the World Bank, the International Monetary Fund (IMF), and the World Trade Organization (WTO)—that regulates global capitalism and the economies of the developing countries. The World Bank and the IMF are powerful actors in the international economy, and have traditionally been unconcerned with human rights. Critics have alleged that their policies have often been very harmful to human rights, especially economic and social rights. The World Bank has recently opened up a dialogue with NGOs and independent experts on human rights, but it remains to be seen whether this will change its policies significantly. The WTO is also accused of working to the disadvantage of the developing countries (Pogge 2002: 17–19). The UN conception of human rights is a statist, social democratic idea, whereas the global economy, and the international financial institutions that are supposed to regulate it, are based on a neo-liberal ideology that prefers vibrant markets and weak states. Recently, extreme neo-liberalism has been somewhat modified by the belief that 'good governance' and poverty reduction are necessary to development.

A new approach to globalization and human rights is based on the concept of **human security**. This idea first appeared in the 1994 Report of the UN Development Programme. Canada promoted the idea in the Security Council during its membership from 1998 to 2000. It was adopted by the UN Millennium Summit, which focused on freedom from fear and freedom from want. An independent Commission on Human Security was established, and its report was presented to the UN Secretary-General on 1 May 2003. It invites us to consider the security of individuals as well as that of states. It invites us also to consider, not only threats of violence from both political and criminal actors, but also the insecurity arising from extreme poverty, disease, and lack of access to food. The special vulnerability of women and children to the effects of conflict and poverty are often emphasized. The concept of 'human security' seeks to investigate in an integrated, interdisciplinary way the connections between human rights, poverty, conflict, global crime and terrorism, and development (see Box 18.4). The protection of human rights is central to the idea of human security, but the new concept may throw light on important connections that traditional approaches to human rights have ignored (see Chapter 19 for further discussion).

MICHAEL FREEMAN

Box 18.4 Human Security: The Case of Darfur

" It took three months for Fatouma Moussa to collect enough firewood to justify a trip to sell it in the market town of Shangil Tobayi, half a day's drive by truck from here. It took just a few moments on Thursday for janjaweed militiamen, making a mockery of the new cease-fire, to steal the $40 she had earned on the trip and rape her. Speaking barely in a whisper, Ms. Moussa, who is 18, gave a spare account of her ordeal. 'We found janjaweed at Amer Jadid,' she said, naming a village just a few miles north of her own. 'One woman was killed. I was raped.' Officially, the cease-fire in Darfur went into effect last Monday. But the reality was on grim display in this crossroads town, where Ms. Moussa and other villagers were attacked Thursday as they rode home in a bus from Shangil Tobayi. The Arab militiamen who attacked them killed 1 woman, wounded 6 villagers and raped 15 women, witnesses and victims said.

" (*New York Times* correspondent, Lydia Polgreen, 12 May 2006)

Darfur is a region of western Sudan, about the size of France, with a population of approximately 6 million. After a long and brutal civil war between the Sudanese government and the Muslim north against the Christian south, a peace agreement was signed in January 2005. Darfur, composed of many ethnic groups, all Muslim, has suffered from extreme economic and social neglect since colonial times. The relative stability of Darfur was undermined by increased competition for diminishing land resources as a result of desertification, the emergence of a racist Arab ideology in Sudan, expansionist policies by Libya's Colonel Gaddafi in neighbouring Chad, and the intrusion of southern Sudanese rebels into Darfur. Darfurian self-defence organizations developed into a number of rebel forces. The Sudanese government sought to repress these rebellions by a savage counter-insurgency, called by some, including the US government, a 'genocide', employing Arab militias known as the *Janjaweed* (evil horsemen). A peace agreement was signed in Abuja, Nigeria, on 5 May 2006 by the Sudanese government and the largest rebel group, but not by other rebels. Estimates of those killed in the period 2003–06 range from 200,000 to 500,000, those displaced more than 2 million, and those suffering deprivation nearly 4 million. The UN Secretary-General, Kofi Annan, compared Darfur to the Rwandan genocide of 1994. By July 2006 the UN and the European Union had passed various resolutions, a few rich countries had supplied some, but insufficient, humanitarian aid, and the peace agreement remained empty words. In the period 2006–09 the level of violence appeared to decrease, but, according to some well-informed sources, the humanitarian catastrophe remained.

Key points

- Marxists have criticized human rights for obscuring inequalities of wealth and power inherent in capitalism, while more recently the anti-globalization movement criticizes globalization's implications for human rights.

- Global capitalist institutions are quite frequently involved in human rights violations but the general relations between global capitalism and human rights are complex.

- The global economic regime that seeks to regulate global capitalism almost certainly has a major impact on human rights, but this is yet to be studied in detail.

- A new concept of human security seeks to integrate our understanding of conflict, crime, human rights, and development.

The concept of human rights became important in world politics only with the adoption of the United Nations Charter in 1945. Although it was derived from Western moral, legal, and political philosophy, it was declared to be universal. On the foundation of the UN Universal Declaration of Human Rights (1948) a large body of international human rights law has been elaborated. Most of this is legally binding on most states, and the principles of the Declaration have been reaffirmed by all UN members. Nevertheless, international procedures for implementing human rights are weak, human rights violations are common, and the concept of human rights is not universally accepted as culturally legitimate.

The main question raised by human rights in the developing countries is the relationship between development and human rights. This is a complex issue. There is more than one definition of 'development', and some definitions include human rights. There is, however, a widespread view that some restriction of human rights is a precondition of development, and that development should take priority over human rights. There is no doubt that some countries have achieved rapid rates of economic development while violating civil and political rights. However, most rights-violating countries have poor records of development. The relations between human rights and development are still not well understood, but the evidence suggests that, generally, factors other than human rights are more important in promoting or obstructing development. The case for violating human rights for the sake of development is therefore much weaker than it has often been thought to be. The view that human rights are necessary for economic development is, however, not well supported by the evidence. There are also strong reasons for respecting human rights independently of their relation to development. Recently, international efforts have been made to integrate human rights and development.

Developing countries are generally poor, which makes it difficult to fund the implementation of human rights. They may not want to do so because their governments are corrupt and unconcerned with human rights. They may not be able to because external agents—for example, donor governments and/or international financial institutions—limit their capacity to do so by insisting on the reduction of state budgets.

The United Nations is right in seeing development and human rights as interdependent, not in the sense that each always helps the other, but in so far as improvements in each makes the achievement of the other easier. Crises of development are often accompanied by crises of human rights, as countries like Somalia, the Democratic Republic of Congo, and Liberia show. Development success is good news for human rights—as South Korea and Taiwan illustrate—although the interests of elites and local cultures may limit human rights achievements, as in Singapore. Rwanda and Zimbabwe show that apparent initial success in development accompanied by human rights violations may lead to disaster for both human rights and development.

The process of globalization has been associated with the assertion of cultural difference. This has meant that the claim that human rights are universal, although reaffirmed by UN member states in 1993, is constantly challenged. Some of these challenges express the interests of the powerful, who are reluctant to allow a voice to dissenters. Others raise difficult questions about legitimating universal principles in a culturally diverse world. Debates about Asian values in the 1990s have been succeeded by debates about Islam and terrorism, but the underlying problems may be political and economic, rather than cultural or religious.

Arguments that the concept of human rights expresses the interests of the West or the rich are generally not convincing. Taking human rights seriously would benefit most the poorest and most oppressed. There is a danger, however, that Western states may discredit the concept by associating it with their own foreign policies motivated by their own interests. The cause of human rights will be damaged if it is, or is perceived to be, a new form of imperialism. Although human rights are now well established in great power politics, it may be that the best hope for their future lies with the increasing number of grass-roots movements in the developing countries.

? Questions

1. Is there now a global consensus on human rights?

2. What are the best arguments for human rights?

3. What are the prospects for the success of the UN Human Rights Council?

4. What are the main problems raised by the idea of the rights-based approach to development?

5. Can Islam be reconciled with human rights?

6. Can the idea of Asian values be reconciled with universal human rights?

7. What are the implications of human rights for global poverty-reduction strategies?

8. Can poor countries afford human rights?

→ Further reading

■ Alston, P. and Robinson, M. (eds) (2005), *Human Rights and Development: Towards Mutual Reinforcement* (Oxford: Oxford University Press). A useful collection of essays on the integration of human rights and development.

■ Brownlie, I. and Goodwin-Gill, G. S. (eds) (2006), *Basic Documents on Human Rights*, 5th edn (Oxford: Oxford University Press). An authoritative collection of international legal texts.

■ Donnelly, J. (2003), *Universal Human Rights in Theory and Practice*, 2nd edn (Ithaca, NY: Cornell University Press). An excellent introduction to the international conception of human rights and the principal issues of human rights implementation.

■ Forsythe, D. P. (2006), *Human Rights in International Relations*, 2nd edn (Cambridge: Cambridge University Press). An authoritative introduction to the topic.

■ Freeman, M. A. (2002), *Human Rights: An Interdisciplinary Perspective* (Cambridge: Polity Press). A comprehensive introduction for social science students and law students who want a non-legal approach.

■ Kaldor, M. (2007), *Human Security* (Cambridge: Polity Press). A stimulating introduction to human security issues.

■ Langford, M. (ed.) (2008), *Social Rights Jurisprudence: Emerging Trends in International and Comparative Law* (Cambridge: Cambridge University Press). A comprehensive survey of legal decisions on social rights.

■ Office of the United Nations High Commissioner for Human Rights (2004), *Human Rights and Poverty Reduction* (New York/Geneva: United Nations). An influential analysis of the relations between human rights and development.

■ Pogge, T. (2002; 2nd edn 2008), *World Poverty and Human Rights* (Cambridge: Polity Press). An influential collection of philosophical essays on various aspects of development and human rights.

■ Sen, A. (1999), *Development as Freedom* (Oxford: Oxford University Press). A thought-provoking argument for the mutual relations between development and freedom.

■ Uvin, P. (2004), *Human Rights and Development* (Bloomfield, CT: Kumarian Press). A provocative critique of various attempts to integrate human rights and development.

Web links

■ www.ohchr.org   The website of the Office of the UN High Commissioner for Human Rights, which is the best way into the UN human rights system.

■ www.hri.ca   Excellent website for communication about, and among, human rights activists.

■ www.amnesty.org   Amnesty International.

■ www.unglobalcompact.org   Human Rights Watch.

■ www.unglobalcompact.org   Website of UN Global Compact, which coordinates international efforts for global corporate social responsibility, including human rights protection.

■ www.humansecurity-chs.org   Information about the Commission on Human Security.

■ www.humansecuritycentre.org   Useful source for the academic study of human security.

Online Resource Centre

For additional material and resources, please visit the Online Resource Centre at:
www.oxfordtextbooks.co.uk/orc/burnell3e/

Security

Nicole Jackson

 Overview

This chapter examines the contested concept of security and its application to issues in the developing world. The study of security today has widened to include far more than an examination of military issues and threats to states. It now includes a range of real and perceived threats to peoples, societies, regions, networks, and the global community. The topic generates scholarly debates about the definition of security and the impact of globalization on security issues. Three key security issues that concern us here are: violent conflict (including state and non-state); international organized crime; and infectious disease. To varying degrees, these issues pose threats to much of the developing world and have provoked a wide range of local, regional, and Western policy responses. The challenge for both the developed and developing worlds is to adopt a more holistic approach to security policy, one that bridges the artificial divide between traditional security and development studies.

Introduction

Security is a highly contested term and there is considerable debate over its definition. The study of security has traditionally taken place within international relations (IR), and especially in its subfield 'security studies'. Only relatively recently has it been considered within development studies. In its more traditional form, the discipline of security studies examines military issues and the interplay among 'great powers'. It has therefore been criticized for being Western-centric and dismissing or marginalizing the weaker developing world and the so-called 'real threats' to its people and societies.

The term 'security' is derived from the Latin *se* (without) and *cura* (care), suggesting the absence of a threat. Security is the absence of threat—to the stability of states, regions, the global community, networks, and/or human lives. For a nuanced understanding of security, issues must be considered at different levels of analysis. There are many security issues in the developing world that threaten, to various degrees, peoples, societies, and states. They include violent conflict (state and non-state), international organized crime (trafficking in persons, narcotics, and small arms), and disease (human immunodeficiency virus/acquired immune deficiency syndrome, or HIV/AIDS, and severe acute respiratory syndrome, or SARS). How these issues are perceived and acted upon form the subject of this chapter. These three issues are chosen for examination here because they pose immediate and pervasive security concerns across the developed and developing worlds.

The chapter begins with an overview of major scholarly debates about security. It identifies key Western-defined security concepts that are applicable or useful to understanding the developing world. It then examines the impact of globalization on security issues. Today, many issues in one area of the world increasingly affect security in another. Globalization also allows the West to have a major influence on how security issues around the world are perceived and challenged. The rest of the chapter is divided into three parts to examine the following key security issues in the developing world: violent conflict; international organized crime; and infectious disease. Each section asks what is the geographical distribution of the so-called threat, who or what is threatened, and explores variations in perceptions and key policy responses.

> **Key points**
>
> - Security is a contested term.
> - Security is the absence of threat—to the stability of states, regions, the global community, networks, and/or human lives.

Scholarly Debates about Security

Realists, who dominated international relations from 1940 to 1990, define security as 'national security'. Stephen M. Walt (1991: 212) says 'security studies may be defined as the study of the threat, use and control of military force'. The focus is on military threats to the state, and inter-state conflict. The traditional understandings of security have thus emphasized states and their competition for power in the international system. Today, this approach continues to be popular and is generally termed 'strategic studies'.

After the cold war, new approaches in security studies proliferated with the aim of challenging traditional and **realist** theories. This debate began in response to the claim that the security agenda must be broadened to examine threats beyond state and military security. For example, in 1983, Buzan (1991) defined security as including military, social, economic, political, and environmental 'sectors' or dimensions.

Today, other threats to the security of states are termed non-traditional issues or **non-traditional** security threats (that is, non-military). These issues include: environmental problems (ozone depletion and global warming); threats from nationalism; migration; international crime (narcotic trafficking, human trafficking); and disease, such as AIDS and SARS. This expansion of the concept of security does not undermine the realist logic of traditional security studies as the main focus is still on the state system. Nevertheless, many traditionalists argue that this widening makes the concept redundant, and dilutes the important task of analysing military threats and inter-state conflict. Other scholars within IR ask *whose* security is threatened. And the reply is that it is not just states that are threatened.

These 'new security' scholars deepen the concept to include global, network, regional, societal, and individual security. There are many issues, such as wars, **terrorism**, crime, and health epidemics, each of which can affect security at many different levels. Threats also change over time; they vary depending on context, and the perceptions of peoples and states. Perceptions themselves may even be undefined or ambiguous. Security issues defined by the peoples and states in the developing world are often different than those defined by peoples and states in the developed world.

Concepts of security and the developing world

Security studies as a discipline is mostly Western-oriented and defined by Western theories (see Box 19.1). Although its practitioners increasingly note unique political and cultural conditions, they rarely draw on the rich variety of other philosophical traditions, such as Islamic thought, Indian or Chinese philosophy. In the developing world, academic work on specific security issues tends to occur within traditional policy-oriented circles that are often dominated by strategic studies. However, this is changing as more scholars and practitioners recognize a misfit between wider IR theory and developing world realities. Traditional security thinking, with its focus on sovereignty, inter-state war, and abstract theory, is increasingly confronted by the reality of interlinked political, economic, and social systems, and internal and transnational conflicts, particularly seen in the developing world.

Box 19.1 Approaches to Security Studies

Realism: Classical realists define security as national security. These traditionalists emphasize military threats to the state and inter-state conflict.

Modified realism: These scholars continue to emphasize the state, however some broaden the focus away from military threats while others move the focus away from the 'great powers' towards the developing world.

Constructivism: Mainstream constructivists examine the role of ideas, identity, and other cultural factors in our understanding or 'construction' of security.

The Copenhagen School: The Copenhagen School broadens the security agenda to five 'sectors': military; political; economic; societal; and ecological. The state remains the referent object.

The Aberystwyth School: These scholars conceptualize security not in terms of its relation with the state but in terms of that with its people. Scholars attempt to identify victims of social exclusion and to evaluate strategies for their emancipation.

Feminist perspectives: Feminists range from liberal to critical but are united in their view that security has generally been presented as gender-neutral, when in fact it is infused with gendered assumptions and representations.

Critical security studies, in its broadest sense, is a collection of approaches all united by dissatisfaction with so-called traditional security studies and in particular its state- and military-centrism. Critical approaches range from conventional constructivists, through the Copenhagen and Aberystwyth schools to feminist and more radical post-modern positions.

Recent Western concepts about security may be more applicable to the developing world. For example, the Aberystwyth School of critical security studies differs from traditional security studies in its focus on the lives of people and in its concept of **emancipation** or freedom (of people from threats) and may be understood as particularly relevant to the developing world where the states themselves are often the source of the threat. Realists, however, counter that the focus should remain on the state and that critical security studies imposes 'a model of contemporary Western polities . . . that are far removed from Third World realities' (Ayoob 1995: 97).

The **human security** perspective, with its focus on individuals and the protection of lives from critical and pervasive threats, also attempts to move the focus away from realist, state-centred concerns to those that are more salient to the peoples of the developing world. The 'broad' concept of human security, first outlined in the 1994 United Nations Human Development Report, argues that human security rests on two pillars: freedom from want and freedom from fear. An even broader view of human security includes food security, adequate shelter, security from poverty, and for some, 'threats to human dignity'. Poverty is a central concern for most of those who adhere to a 'broad' or 'broader' approach to human security. For them, security is a priori about human beings, and they understand poverty and insecurity to be mostly synonymous. Others, however, argue that these definitions are too encompassing to be helpful in policy development. In contrast, they adopt a narrow concept of human security focusing on freedom from violence, including the role of criminal and political violence on individuals.

The broad concept of human security is increasingly being considered by scholars in Asia and Africa, and even adopted in some regional security arrangements, for example the Association of South-East Asian Nations (ASEAN). Generally, however, the difficulty with putting the human security concept into practice is that its focus on individuals and human rights appears threatening to many authoritarian leaders, and is contrary to the emphasis many societies place on community and the state. Most states in the developing world are the providers of security the power of which is predicated on the concepts of absolute sovereignty and non-interference in domestic affairs.

Feminists adopt many varied perspectives on security, however they are united in their understanding that security has generally been presented as gender-neutral, when in fact it is infused with gendered assumptions and representations. Liberal feminists, for example, are interested in notions of equality and tend to focus on questions of women's representations within the public sphere. Radical feminists focus more on notions of difference. Feminist perspectives on war have focused on the impact of war and conflict on women and men, their active roles in armed conflict, and how assumptions about masculinity and femininity figure into conflict and decision-making. A notable consequence of the recent increase of scholarship and awareness about gender and security is the UN Security Council Resolution 1325 on 'Women, Peace and Security' adopted in October 2000, which states that women and girls are affected by armed conflict in different ways than men and boys, and argues the importance of incorporating a 'gender perspective' into peace operations. The details of these differences, and how they should inform policy is, as we shall see below, controversial.

Another Western-defined concept that has applicability to the developing world is **securitization**, defined as 'the move that takes politics beyond the established rules of the game and frames the issue either as a special kind of politics or as above politics' (Buzan, Waever, and de Wilde 1998: 23). The securitization framework highlights how language is used to construct threats. Although it is a helpful descriptive and explanatory tool, particularly in understanding how states elevate particular threats, again there are difficulties with putting this concept into practice. There are fears that securitization arguments (that is, the labelling of an issue as a security threat) could be misused by rulers for domestic purposes. For example, in Latin America there is a widespread consciousness about how security rhetoric has been used by military governments in the past against their own people, and there is therefore distrust about how it may be applied.

Finally, within the developing world, new (and non-Western) thinking about security is being developed and put into practice. For example, China's multilateral cooperation and dialogue through the Shanghai Cooperation Organization (SCO) on a range of new security issues (such as terrorism and trafficking) demonstrates a unique type of cross-regional cooperative thinking and action on non-traditional security issues.

Globalization of security

The study of security has evolved largely in tandem with globalization. **Globalization**, understood as a state of interdependence, accelerated by advances in technology, trade, political relationships, transboundary communication, and movement of peoples, goods, and services, has created new channels for exercising power outside the state. The state is not about to disappear but is confronted by new global forces, transborder flows (financial, population, environmental, viral), international regimes, and complex networks (media, criminal, terrorist). Thus, globalization has heightened new security priorities such as terrorism, organized crime, narcotic trafficking, and disease. Globalization can turn essentially local problems into regional or global security challenges. It allows issues and events in the developing world to reach the developed world, and vice versa.

This process should not be overstated however. The interrelatedness of the world is not new; the degree is simply greater. There is also a real danger that globalization is facilitating new forms of interaction (or power) that increasingly allow the West to dominate the security agenda and to structure the way in which security issues around the world are perceived and challenged. This is of particular concern for the developing world and is reflected in the partial merging of security and development policy agendas.

The merging of security and development agendas?

There has been an increasingly vigorous debate among scholars and practitioners over efforts to link development and security agendas, most recently over the controversial linking of development aid to the **war on terror**. A serious concern is that development goals based on humanitarian principles, poverty reduction for instance, could be increasingly subordinated to Western foreign and security policy objectives. Some countries well known for human rights abuses have been offered US aid to take a supportive position on the war on terror. Examples include Pakistan and Uzbekistan. From the perspective of many development studies scholars, development concerns should not be subordinated to international security issues, and the securitization of aid does not address real development issues.

Of course, the merging of security and development agendas is not new. During the cold war, development aid was linked with the geopolitical power struggles of the US and the Soviet Union. Today, economic prosperity and growth are generally viewed as co-dependent on security, and linked as policy issues by many Western governments. Underdevelopment is, however, often viewed more in terms of the potential threat it poses to the security of powerful countries than in terms of the well-being of affected populations. Underdevelopment is thus considered by many Western governments and organizations as threatening national and global security, for example by fuelling illicit drug-trafficking, or supporting the spread of terrorism. The World Bank report, *Breaking the Conflict Trap* (2003d), for example, describes conflict and its associated security problems as a failure of development.

Realists would argue that Western governments have always linked their aid policies to their strategic interests, relatively neglecting countries of lesser economic or political interest to them. Countries deemed to be of direct interest, for example Afghanistan, Iraq, and Israel, receive favourable consideration. However, there currently seems to be a movement towards a more overt and instrumental securitization of the development agenda.

Key points

- Security cannot be fully understood through a single level of analysis. Security issues may include threats to individuals, societies, states, networks, and/or the global community.

- Approaches to security studies are predominantly Western-defined and include realist, constructivist, feminist, critical, and post-modern interpretations.

- Concepts from wider security studies such as emancipation, human security, and securitization have some benefits for understanding the developing world, as well as some limits in their practical application.

- Globalization and the increased interrelatedness of the world, mean that local issues can affect any combination of national, regional, and global security.

- Development goals based on humanitarian principles are increasingly subordinated to Western-defined security objectives. This is particularly the case with the link of development aid to the war on terror.

Violent Conflict: War and Terrorism in the Developing World

One of the key security issues in the developing world is violent conflict. Most of the world's poorest countries are suffering, or have recently suffered, from large-scale, violent conflict. Traditionally, security analyses of the developing world focused on inter-state wars, with a particular focus on the role of the colonizers or superpowers in fuelling the conflicts. However, since the end of the cold war, there has been an acknowledgement in the discipline that much of the violence in the world actually occurs within states, and that civilians have been the victims of violence perpetrated by both state and non-state groups (see Chapter 13). Therefore, the previously dominant state-level of analysis is increasingly being supplemented by other levels—individual, regional, network, or global.

Traditional and non-traditional violent conflict

Traditional security studies examine violence between states. However, since the end of the cold war, the number of inter-state wars around the world has declined. Even in the region with the greatest number of ongoing inter-state wars, Central and West Africa, many of these inter-state tensions and conflicts have arisen from spillovers of interethnic conflict and civil war, and are therefore different from traditional wars between states. For example, in former Zaire from 1998 to 2003 approximately 3 million people died in a civil war that ended up involving nine other countries: Angola; Zimbabwe; Namibia; Chad; Sudan; Uganda; Burundi; Rwanda; and Tanzania.

Scholars of traditional security studies quantify military power. The developing world spends a comparatively high proportion of its gross domestic product (GDP) on defence. Of course, military power is a double-edged sword. It may undermine rather than enhance a country's security. Arms expenditures divert resources and often have an enormous economic as well as human drain on a country. Moreover, when states become trapped in arms races that consume a great percentage of their resources, war may become more likely.

Despite the 2008 global recession, the US increased its overall arms sales to US$37.8 billion or 64 per cent of all business in global arms trade (Grimmett 2009). The primary focus of global arms sales is to the developing world, with overall sales reaching US$42.4 billion and US sales reaching US$29.6 billion or 70 per cent. In 2008, Russia was a distant second with sales to the developing world down to US$3.3 billion, with China and India, and Venezuela as its key partners. The overall top buyers in the developing world were the United Arab Emirates, Saudi Arabia, and Morocco.

Increasingly, much of the developing world is also confronted with the traditional threat of the use of nuclear weapons. In October 2006, North Korea alarmed its regional neighbours and the great powers when it joined India, Pakistan, China, Israel, Russia, the US, Britain, and France in the nuclear club. Other potential members, who in the past have shown interest in developing a nuclear programme or who are suspected of pursuing nuclear ambitions, include South Africa, Brazil, Iran, and Venezuela.

While traditional wars between states have been declining, intra(within)-state conflict is common, particularly in the developing world. Internal security problems are pervasive in many areas of Asia, the Middle East, Latin America, and especially Africa, where interethnic conflicts, insurgencies, and civil wars have been endemic and prolonged (see Chapter 13). In contrast to the traditional approach, the human security approach is helpful in stressing internal dynamics and the human costs of war. This includes issues such as child soldiers and landmines, which pose considerable threats to the lives of peoples of the developing world. The use of children in war is not new but is believed to be rapidly growing. Children fight in almost 75 per cent of today's armed conflicts (Human Security Report Project 2005: 35). They have been used in terrorist operations in Northern Ireland, Columbia, and Sri Lanka.

The human security approach also highlights that the greatest human costs of war are not the battle deaths but the 'indirect' deaths caused by disease, lack of access to food, clean water, and heathcare services. The lives of refugees, who commonly result from wars, are often at great risk—for example the 1.5 million refugees who fled the Rwandan genocide of 1994 into neighbouring Zaire (now the Democratic Republic of Congo), Tanzania, and Burundi.

Distribution of the conflicts and Western response

Overall, the number of active major armed conflicts has gone down. However, many small wars have erupted as others have died down, and currently many groups are rearming. Most violent conflicts in Asia, the Middle East, Africa, and Latin America are geographically separate and often unrelated. However, linkages within regions are common, as are ties with the developed world, particularly because of the involvement of great powers. In just one of many examples, the US and North Atlantic Treaty Organization (NATO) are at the time of writing (August 2010) engaged in **robust peacekeeping** in Afghanistan. This allows them much more leeway to make peace as opposed to keeping and monitoring it. Meanwhile, the UN currently has approx. 116,000 personnel serving on 17 peace operations led by the UN Department of Peacekeeping Operations (DPKO) on four continents. This represents eight times more peacekeepers than 1999. The percentage of women deployed as civilians in peacekeeping operations has reached 30 per cent (UN Department of Peacekeeping Operations 2009).

Increasingly, the **international community** perceives the need for a unified global agenda, rather than unilateral approaches, to resolve these conflicts. However, international action continues to be mostly limited and very selectively applied. Western approaches have ranged from outright neglect to preventative measures to (unilateral and multilateral) military intervention. From the perspective of most developing countries, international involvement, and in particular military intervention, is highly problematic and an infringement of their state sovereignty. Increasingly, they perceive the developed world as posing security threats to the developing world, in particular through the threat of military intervention, and the projection of Western or Northern power through the process of globalization.

In this spirit, the Non-Aligned Movement (NAM), originally developed to combat colonialism and avoid competing superpower alliances, is becoming increasingly influential. NAM is now made up of 118 developing countries that are increasingly concerned with reasserting their influence in a world largely still dominated by the United States, as well as by specific issues like globalization, HIV/AIDS, and international crime. The current challenge for NAM is to move beyond anti-Western rhetoric and to gain world attention in order to effectively promote the interests of the developing world.

Gender and conflict

Recently, as mentioned above, there have been attempts to bring a gendered perspective to the study of armed conflict, and this has led to a focus on the unique threats that women and girls face in conflict zones. There is, for example, more attention paid to the widespread phenomenon of wartime sexual violence. Although more men are killed in battle than women, we know that women are more vulnerable to sexual violence and predatory behaviour. The difficulty, however, is that there is little or no reliable data to help determine whether sexual violence

in war is increasing or not. This lack of reliable statistics also exists, for example, when we look at whether it is men or women who are more affected by 'collateral damage', war-exacerbated disease and malnutrition, or long-term psychological trauma. This means that policies relating to gender and conflict are rarely based on robust evidence, because good data is either not available or, where available, not accessible to non-specialists. It also means that many analyses underestimate the gender-based violence directed against males, and pay little heed to the active roles that women play in all types of warfare, from national militaries to terrorist groups (see forthcoming Human Security Report 2011).

The securitization of terrorism in the developing world

Despite the variety of ongoing violence in much of the developing world, there has been a recent shift of Western attention towards global terrorism in that part of the world. Terrorism is an asymmetrical strategy available to weak actors seeking to level the strategic playing field. It is a tactic designed to achieve an objective (usually political) by using violence against innocent civilians to generate fear. Terrorism has been widely used in both the developed and developing worlds.

After 2001 and the beginning of the war on terror, the West focused particularly on transnational terrorist violence rather than other types of internal or inter-state conflict. The declining capacity of some states to meet basic human needs and enforce the rule of law is increasingly perceived to provide fertile conditions or training areas for global terrorist sympathizers. For example, in Afghanistan, some areas of Pakistan and Somalia and other very weak or collapsed states, groups with links to al-Qaeda are commonly understood to have developed, and now pose transnational or global threats. Western security focus has therefore increasingly shifted to organizations and groups at the network and global levels that are considered to require networked and global responses.

While a causal relationship between poverty and terrorism has not been established, it is clear that non-state armed groups are able to exploit the dehumanizing conditions that result from poverty. The militarization of society and the context of violent occupation and war, which characterize many developing states, can be used by terrorists to gather sympathy for violent acts against perceived oppressors and their supporters. Globalization has also provided them new means to finance, carry out, and publicize attacks, as well as to forge alliances or networks with other groups around the world. Nevertheless, most terrorist actions remain localized. Non-state groups view terrorism as cheap and effective, and thus a weapon of choice for their wars against oppressive states. For example, until it was defeated by the Sri Lankan military in May 2009, the Liberation Tigers of Tamil Eelam (LTTE) has fought the Sri Lankan government since the 1970s with a well-organized terror campaign, pursuing objectives ranging from greater autonomy to complete secession.

When the war on terror became the West's first global priority in 2001, states with large Muslim populations and insurgency movements became priorities for US assistance. The US substantially increased its foreign aid to Pakistan, India, the Philippines, Indonesia, and Uzbekistan as part of its anti-terrorism efforts. US military and security aid to Africa have also increased—and, as Bermeo (2009) argues, serves to undercut US efforts at democracy promotion too. The post-9/11 war on terror, by its very definition, took a primarily military approach consistent with traditional security. However, it is increasingly acknowledged that unless social, economic, and political contexts are addressed, and other tactics such as diplomacy and intelligence are deployed, problems will not disappear and global terrorism could escalate.

The West's perceived abuse of power and neglect of certain issues is also felt strongly in the developing world. Examples given of Western hypocrisy include when the West acted to protect the abuse of Kurds in Iraq, but not Kurds in Turkey, and when the US and UK provided military support for regimes with very poor human rights records (as in Uzbekistan), while preaching the need for democracy and human rights. Ironically, such hypocrisy creates fertile ground for organizations in the developing world that advocate terror and the rejection of the West, together with its agenda of **good governance** and democracy (see Chapters 14 and 15).

Key points

- Today, violence between states, the traditional subject of security studies, is less common than intra-state violence.

- Human security focuses on individual lives and the human costs of war.

- Violent conflict in the developed world is diverse and specific to regions and particular states and localities.

- Western involvement in conflicts ranges from neglect to outright military intervention.

- Western hypocrisy and focus on the military approach to counter global terrorism creates fertile ground for a growing anti-Western approach in the developing world.

International organized crime (IOC), a significant threat to peoples, societies, and states, is often overlooked when examining the developing world. However, the movement of illicit goods across borders is not new, and around the world organized crime has always presented a variety of threats. What is new today is the scale of the problem and the growing power and capability of organized crime. IOC includes activities such as trafficking in narcotics, small arms, nuclear materials, and people, smuggling of illegal aliens, and money laundering. Few of these activities are confined to specific areas of the globe; rather they have taken on a transnational character. The global aspect of the drug trade, for example, mirrors the global divisions of labour found in other economic realms, where production in the developing areas has risen largely to meet the demand in advanced industrial states.

Criminals have benefited significantly from globalization—that is, from the rise of information technology, the development of stronger political and economic linkages, and the shrinking importance of global distance. Globalization has expanded illegal markets and increased the size and resources of criminal networks. Some IOC groups operate within strategic alliances like firms; some work in globally coordinated networks; others have looser and more ad hoc affiliations. Global criminal organizations vary in terms of their cohesion, longevity, degree of hierarchical control, degree of penetration, and acceptance within society. IOC groups based in the developing world include, for example, the Triad gangs of Hong Kong, China, and various overseas ports, and the Colombian cocaine cartels.

Securitization of crime

Traditionally crime has been categorized as an economic activity, a 'low politics' topic best suited to disciplines such as economics or criminology. However, increasingly, it has become obvious that crime may threaten individual, societal, state, regional, and even global security. The network level is particularly relevant here because while criminals often act in interconnected groups across borders, there is similarly a need for international cooperation (or networks) to counter them.

As described above, the determination by governments that an issue constitutes a security problem is generally driven more by realist, state-centred calculations than by humanitarianism. Drugs and arms are thus considered by states to be security issues in part because of their connection to violence. From a traditional standpoint, they may threaten the stability of governments. However, IOC also impacts on human security directly at the individual level in specific national, regional, or local contexts.

IOC poses a considerable challenge to states in the developed and developing world. At its most extreme, it can control territory, extract rents, provide services for local populations, and even wage war, as in Colombia and Afghanistan. It can also pose long-term structural damage such as the erosion of rule of law. The direct threat to state control is exacerbated by the relative weakness or low levels of political institutionalization of the state (as in Nigeria, Laos, and Tajikistan). IOC also erodes faith in democratic institutions depending on the degree to which criminality pervades the political, institutional, and financial infrastructure of the state, a significant problem in the post-Soviet states. Finally, IOC can undermine the state by destroying trust between people and state, eroding the tax basis and diverting resources.

IOC poses specific problems for developing countries. Crime is perceived as a sign of social instability, which may drive away foreign investment, foreign aid, and business. For example, in some African states, investment levels are low partly because of the perception that the rule of law does not prevail. IOC can also undermine the ability of a state to promote development. Finally, crime can harm social and human capital and is associated with increased violence. It can have a far greater impact on human lives in countries in which the state is less able to intervene to protect individuals, for example in Brazil and South Africa.

Three key types of IOC that, to varying extent, impact on security at all levels of analysis are trafficking in persons, narcotics, and small arms.

Trafficking in persons

Trafficking in persons is a highly complex phenomenon that includes recruitment, movement, and exploitation. It is a threat to human security because, in its many forms, it violates human rights by depriving people of basic human dignity and jeopardizing individual and public health. Human rights violations include the lack of freedom of movement, and physical, sexual, or mental abuse. Trafficking in persons may also be perceived as a threat to global security because it is often part of a larger phenomenon of illegal migration and transnational organized crime.

There are many types of human trafficking: forced labour including that of children (for example in South Asia, where people are forced to work in sweat shops); slavery (Sudan); selling of organs (Latin America and Asia); selling of orphans (for example, following the Tsunami disaster in south Asia, December 2004). However, the most common and most lucrative is sex trafficking. Sex trafficking is global in scope, but particularly affects peoples in the developing world, from Tajikistan and Nigeria to Thailand.

Narcotic trafficking

Narcotic trafficking similarly affects, to varying extents, the security of peoples and states around the world. Traditionally, Asia and Latin America have been key source regions, while Europe and North America have been key regions of demand.

However, overall narcotic consumption is increasing around the world. There is also evidence that transit states eventually become consumer and distributor states, as is currently happening in much of the post-Soviet Union and Africa.

Narcotic trafficking activity in places like Colombia and Afghanistan damages economies, corrupts institutions, and affects regional stability and security. Colombia epitomizes the security threats posed by crime. There, drug trafficking represents a direct security threat to people, while criminal organizations, as well as violent political organizations such as the Revolutionary Armed Forces of Colombia (FARC) and National Liberation Army (ELN) in Colombia, have undermined the capacity of the government to rule the country. Narcotic trafficking also affects human security because individuals suffer the negative health effects of drugs such as cocaine and heroin, and the spread of **HIV/AIDS** associated with intravenous drug use. The United Nations Office on Drugs and Crime (UNODC) suggests that there were between 18 million and 38 million 'problem drug users' aged 15–64 in 2007 (UNODC World Drug Report 2009). Of course, different drugs pose unique problems for different regions. Encouragingly, a UNODC survey shows that in 2008 there was a reduction in opium poppy cultivation in Afghanistan of 19 per cent and a reduction in coca cultivation in Colombia of 18 per cent.

Narcotic trafficking also tends to be associated with other types of crime. For example, in Colombia, incidents of murder and kidnapping are among the highest in the world, with 2 million out of 6 million people being displaced by guerrillas or kidnappers. Throughout Latin America drug trafficking undermines civil society through pervasive corruption and intimidation of politicians, and through the breakdown of law and order.

Small arms trafficking

The third IOC security issue is small arms trafficking. At the end of the cold war, there was a surplus of weapons that became ready stockpiles for legal and illicit markets. Today, over two-thirds of the world's legitimate arms sales (and likely more of the illegal sales) are directed towards developing states. This both reflects and contributes to violence in the developing world. Worldwide, small arms and light weapons are responsible for the majority of direct conflict deaths. The new conflicts that characterize the post-cold war world tend to be fought using small arms and light weapons, and not conventional weapons or the threat of weapons of mass destruction, which characterized the cold war.

The widespread availability of small arms has been a factor in facilitating and sustaining wars and violence and is thus a concern to human and state security. In the developing world, small arms are inexpensive and widely available, which makes them very difficult to regulate. Their small size and the fact that they are relatively easy to use make them ideal for untrained combatants and children. They have thus contributed to the tragic growth in numbers of child soldiers, particularly in Africa.

The ability of developing countries to obtain an abundance of weapons has often been facilitated by great power struggles, through direct or illegal sales. During the cold war, rival powers armed regional antagonists such as India and Pakistan, Iran and Iraq, Israel and Syria, Ethiopia and Somalia. However, increasingly, producers of arms are selling them simply for commercial profit in many conflicts throughout the developing world and especially in Africa.

International policies

In the past, illicit trades and trafficking were most often perceived to be the responsibility of the state harbouring the clandestine transnational activities. Today, there is a broad consensus among the international community that these are global security threats and that the international community must be actively engaged to counter them. Criminal (and terrorist) networks are believed to increasingly pose distributed and mobile threats. There is often no obvious source that is easy to target and thus international cooperation is required to effectively counter them.

Some developing states are perceived by international organizations as having become transhipment regions for organized crime activities, and there is a fear that they are becoming safe havens for them. Overall, governments in developed and developing countries have obsolete tools, inadequate laws, ineffective bureaucratic arrangements, and ineffective strategies to deal with IOC. However, the situation in many developing countries is comparatively worse. There, power generally rests in the hands of a small group of elites who have ambiguous attitudes towards crime.

Box 19.2 United Nations Conventions on Organized Crime

Year	Convention title
2000	UN Convention against Transnational Organized Crime
2000	UN Convention against Transnational Organized Crime: Protocol against the Smuggling of Migrants by Land, Sea and Air
2000	UN Convention against Transnational Organized Crime: Protocol to Prevent, Suppress and Punish Trafficking in Persons, Especially Women and Children
2001	UN Convention against Transnational Organized Crime: Protocol against the Illicit Manufacturing of and Trafficking in Firearms, Their Parts and Components and Ammunition
2003	UN Convention against Corruption

In this context, international organizations are currently taking steps to securitize (defined as 'push to the top of the political agenda') these activities. UN Conventions have been signed, but difficulties in implementation remain (see Box 19.2). Another major challenge is that in many regions of the world criminal groups are either tolerated, or more directly supported, by governments. IOC may pose **security dichotomies** for peoples and states. As well as the negative effects on individual and state security, trafficking activities may provide work for people when the state can not help them, and may contribute to a state's economy, especially in times of crisis or transition.

The effectiveness of many of the policies initiated by the international community against IOC is questionable. The securitization of crime has meant that several specific strategies—in particular border management and law enforcement—have been adopted. These strategies are important but limited. The most extreme examples of securitization include the use of special military forces in the 1990s by the UK and USA in tackling South American drug cartels, and the use of NATO today to counter trafficking in Afghanistan. The continuing flow of cocaine and heroin shows the limitations of such traditional security approaches.

Finally, once again Western governments are generally not as interested in the root causes or the effects of crime on individuals (the human security approach), as in the effects of transnational or global effects on Western states and peoples. Western states are therefore often viewed as hypocritical by the developing world for lecturing them, for example, to do more to decrease narcotic trade, when the trade is mostly driven by Western demand.

Key points

- IOC groups pose a variety of levels of threat to peoples, states, and regions in the developing world, as well as to the global community.

- IOC operates in transnational groups, demands transnational responses, and thus can be usefully considered at the network or global level of analysis.

- While trafficking in persons is predominantly a human security threat, narcotic and arms trafficking pose threats to individuals, societies, and states. All three types of trafficking are increasingly perceived by the international community as global security threats because of their real and perceived negative effects on Western peoples and states.

- IOC poses security dichotomies for developing states, in that their activities may be perceived, by states and peoples, positively as well as negatively.

Infectious Disease

Health and disease have traditionally not been understood as security issues. Most often, they have been viewed within the framework of development studies and human rights, with health and freedom from disease being key goals of local and state socio-economic development efforts. However, recently, health is also being examined as one of many factors that contribute to human security, while the dangers to health are perceived as new threats to state security. At the global level, health security is increasingly framed within foreign and security policy concerns, for example the transnational threat of HIV/AIDS, SARS, and bioterrorism.

In the course of history the threat posed by disease to human security and well-being has been at least comparable to the effects of war. In just one example, the Spanish Flu in 1918–19 killed between 40 million and 50 million people worldwide, compared to approximately 15 million people killed during the Second World War. Today, throughout the world, infectious diseases kill more people than all other causes combined (Kassalow 2001: 6). Compounding the tragedy is the fact that each year, millions of people die from preventable, curable, and treatable diseases. Most of these deaths occur in the developing world, where there is a lack of vaccines and basic sanitation.

The securitization of transnational diseases

The increasingly high-level attention given to global health since the mid-1990s is largely due to the recognition that there is a strong relationship between health and development. People in the developing world suffer greater ill health and shorter life expectancy compared with the West, partly as a result of higher than average child and maternal mortality, as well as inequitable access to health care and social protection. However, more recently, health has also come to be linked to the security agenda, both in the traditional state sense, and with the human security agenda and its focus on individuals.

Although modern medicine has made great advances, it has achieved only limited success in halting the spread of infectious diseases. Across the world, cures for some of the older diseases are even at risk of being reversed, for example tuberculosis, cholera, and malaria. Meanwhile, new diseases have emerged, such as HIV/AIDS, Ebola virus, hepatitis C, SARS, and avian flu. The increase in globalization, particularly the ease of travel, has made it more difficult to prevent deadly pathogens from spreading across borders.

These diseases are therefore currently perceived by many world leaders, and many international organizations, as threats to global security. For example, the avian influenza virus (H5N1) broke out in 1997 in Hong Kong, killing six of the 18 people infected with it. In 2002, SARS was first identified in southern China. During the next two years, 9,000 cases were identified and 900 people died, mostly in Asia but also Canada. Apart from its threat to human lives, it negatively affected the economies of those states. In mid-2009 we contended with a worldwide epidemic of H1N1, or swine flu.

Of course, even localized diseases can spread fear around the world, such as the outbreak in 2000 of the Ebola haemorrhagic fever in Uganda, which remained relatively contained, but caused panic due to the rapid spread of the disease and its horrific symptoms. Finally, particularly since the events of September 2001, there has been a heightened concern that terrorist or other groups could use diseases such as plague, anthrax, and smallpox to raise attention for their cause, by creating panic and instilling fear. This particular concern has most greatly contributed to the recent Western attempts to securitize some infectious diseases.

HIV/AIDS

HIV/AIDS is an example of a disease no longer seen as just a health or public policy issue. Increasingly, it is perceived as a security issue at many levels. It challenges human security, the political, economic, and social stability of states and regions, and the broader global security.

HIV/AIDS directly threatens the lives and health of individuals and communities around the world. In 2007, an estimated 33 million people were living with HIV. There were 2.7 million new HIV infections and 2 million AIDS-related deaths that year (Joint United Nations Programme on HIV/AIDS (UNAIDS) 2008). Ninety-five per cent of those infected with HIV are in the developing world. Africa is the epicentre of the pandemic with approximately 22 million people living with HIV in sub-Saharan Africa.

Beyond Africa, the rest of the developing world has witnessed a dramatic increase in HIV infection across Asia, and throughout the former Soviet States, Central Asia, and Latin America. Nevertheless, globally, the HIV incidence rate is believed to have peaked in the late 1990s. After decades of increasing mortality, the annual number of AIDS deaths globally has declined in the past two years, in part as a result of greater access to treatment (UNAIDS 2008).

Access to treatment has dramatically expanded over the past seven years in developing countries, notably in Botswana, Namibia, Rwanda, Kenya, South Africa, Uganda, and Zambia. Nearly 3 million people were receiving antiretroviral treatment in low- and middle-income countries at the end of 2007. This represents 31 per cent of estimated global need and 48 per cent improvement over 2006. However, antiretroviral coverage varies considerably within regions.

As well as the horrific toll on human lives, HIV/AIDS also weakens social and state security. It can affect family, community, and social cohesion. It often harms the productive members of society, including teachers and healthcare workers. HIV/AIDS is a risk to human capital, natural resource development, and business investment, and thus an economic liability to national economies.

HIV/AIDS may also be perceived as a traditional military security threat. Singer (2002) and Elbe (2002) have analysed the high rate of AIDS in the military forces, as well as its relation to conflicts in Africa. The average rate of infection for African militaries is 30 per cent and AIDS is a primary cause of death in many African armies. The weakening of militaries can make states more vulnerable to attack, and make it more difficult for them to keep stability or order. HIV/AIDS has also been used as a weapon of war, for example, in the Rwandan genocide, between 200,000 and 500,000 women and children were raped, increasing the risk of the spread of diseases.

One of the many difficulties in responding effectively to the HIV/AIDS crisis in the developing world is concern that it may draw resources away from other health challenges or infectious diseases, such as malaria, which, despite some recent advances, still kills more than 1 million Africans a year, or tuberculosis, which is the leading cause of death of AIDS victims. There is an ongoing debate within the global health community about whether health investment should be targeted at trying to improve the entire health system, or on specific programmes aimed at improvement in particular areas, like AIDS. Another grave difficulty is the great diversity in response to HIV by different countries and the unwillingness of certain state leaders to acknowledge the seriousness of the issue. For example, former South African President Mbeki had questioned the scientific conclusion that HIV causes AIDS and had refused to sanction public funding of antiretroviral drugs—a policy that his successor President Zuma now supports.

International policy responses

Globalization may be a cause of global health concerns, but it also offers opportunities to enhance health security through the dissemination of medical knowledge, and to empower organizations such as the World Health Organization to coordinate policy. In 2000, the UN Security Council adopted a resolution calling on UN agencies to collaborate in response to the HIV/AIDS pandemic.

World leaders are increasingly recognizing that global health and global security are intertwined. In 2000, the US formally identified HIV/AIDS as a security threat by, controversially, linking it to violence and state failure. According to the US National Intelligence Council (NIC), dramatic declines in life expectancy due to this disease are strong risk factors for revolutionary wars, ethnic wars, genocides, and disruptive regime transitions in the developing world. The social consequences of HIV/AIDS have particularly strong correlations with the likelihood of state failure in partial democracies (NIC 2000).

Health issues thus have become linked with traditional security agendas and human security. From the perspective of the international development community, closer linking of foreign aid with traditional security policy shifts the referent object away from the most vulnerable/those with greatest need, to individuals or populations that pose the greatest perceived threat to the strategic interests of selected states. Some fear that health is becoming a tool of foreign and security policy. Meanwhile, many of those within the security sector fear that broadening the definition of security means that they are, or will be, forced to deal with issues best left to state social policy.

The human security approach supports broadening the responsibility for health security. It shifts responsibility down from the national level to communities, civil organizations, and individuals, and upwards to international institutions and networks. In 2002, the Global Fund to Fight HIV/AIDS, Tuberculosis and Malaria was created to fulfil commitments by G8 countries to improve the health of populations in low-income countries. Three of eight **Millennium Development Goals** (MDG) call for: specific health improvements by 2015: reducing child deaths; reducing maternal mortality; and

slowing the spread of HIV/AIDS, malaria, and tuberculosis.

A serious cause of concern is that Western and international concern for health issues in the developing world is primarily focused on transnational diseases, not those specific to developing countries. In this regard, a recent positive step is that the World Health Organization (WHO) has set up new guidelines to launch a preventative and treatment programme to tackle specific diseases that affect hundreds of millions of people in the developing world, such as river blindness and bilharziasis (a disease caused by parasitic worms). This is the first large-scale attempt to use drugs on healthy (as well as infected) people to offer quasi-immunization in an attempt to eliminate the diseases. At the same time, the WHO, along with funds from United States Agency for International Development (USAID) and the Bill and Melinda Gates Foundation, supports preventative chemotherapy in several countries including Tanzania, Uganda, Burkina Faso, Mali, Niger, and Ghana. These are significant, if still small, steps in global cooperation on health in the developing world.

Key points

- Infectious diseases pose a variety of different threats to human, state, and global security.
- Africa is the epicentre of an HIV/AIDS pandemic. Ninety-five per cent of those infected with HIV/AIDS are in the developing world.
- Globalization, especially the ease of travel, has made it more difficult to prevent the spread of diseases across borders. However, it also offers opportunities to share knowledge and to coordinate policy.

Conclusion

Key issues in current debates about security and the developing world include: what is security? Are Western-defined concepts and approaches about security applicable to the developing world? What have been the ramifications of globalization

on security issues? Are development goals based on humanitarianism increasingly subordinated to Western foreign and security policy objectives?

Security is a contested concept and this chapter argues that security must be examined through different levels of analyses. Today, the discipline of security studies increasingly includes not only state-centred analyses and the study of military threats and inter-state conflict, but also intra-state conflicts and direct threats to individual lives. Critical security studies, including feminist, normative, and post-structuralist approaches, all question the concept of security and critique of the realist/traditionalist approach. This chapter adopts a comprehensive definition of security that entails examination at the individual, state, regional, network, and global levels.

Many security issues impact strongly on developing states. The three key issues examined in this chapter—violent conflict, international organized crime, and disease—all affect security at many levels of analysis. Security threats are perceived differently in the developed and developing worlds. They change over time, depending on context and the perceptions of peoples and states. The developing world, similar to the developed world, is not monolithic and different issues affect different countries, areas, and regions.

Western states and organizations have often structured global priorities according to their own, generally traditionally defined, security interests. Those interests are mostly focused on the transnational effects of so-called threats to Western peoples and states, rather than on the issues that directly threaten developing states and their peoples. For example, the preoccupation with global terrorism after 2001 initially diverted attention and funding from many development issues, but this is changing and, among many states and organizations, there is now a renewed focus on them (and a greater focus on their relationship to terrorism).

From the perspective of many developing countries, the developed world itself poses many security threats, in particular the threat of military intervention, and the projection of Western or Northern power through the process of globalization. Developing countries have limited means available to make their voices heard and little bargaining power. In the absence of a conventional military balance, some developing states with sufficient economic and technical capacity have sought weapons of mass destruction to level the playing field. Less well-off state and non-state actors have increasingly turned to terrorism as a potential equalizer; others engage in 'bandwagoning' with the dominant power, or join regional organizations and the NAM to pool resources and project a unified response. The current question for the developing world is how to promote its interests effectively in a world in which few listen to its voice. The challenge for both worlds is to adopt a more holistic approach to security policy, one that bridges the increasingly artificial divide between traditional security and development studies.

? **Questions**

1. What are the key approaches to the study of security?

2. What is the impact of globalization on human security in the developing world?

3. What is the benefit of bringing a gendered perspective to the study of armed conflict?

4. Does the West's 'securitization' of terrorism have any specific implications for state security in the developing world?

5. How does international organized crime affect the security of peoples and states in the developing world? Explain with reference to either narcotic trafficking or human trafficking.

6. What are the dangers in securitizing or conversely not securitizing health?

7. From a critical security perspective, explain why Western governments are not responding appropriately to security challenges in the developing world?

Further reading

■ Ayoob, M. (1995), *The Third World Security Predicaments: State Making, Regional Conflict and the International System* (Boulder, CO: Lynne Rienner). An important book examining security in the developing world from a state-centric perspective.

■ Chen, L., Fukuda-Parr, S., and Seidensticker, E. (eds) (2003), *Human Insecurity in a Global World* (Cambridge, MA: Global Equity Initiative, Asia Center, Harvard University). Examines global issues from the human security perspective.

■ Friman, R. and Andreas, P. (eds) (1999), *The Illicit Global Economy and State Power* (New York: Rowman and Littlefield). Offers a solid introduction to the subject of transnational organized crime.

■ Human Security Report Project (2005), *Human Security Report 2005; War and Peace in the 21st Century* (Oxford: Oxford University Press). A ground-breaking report that defines human security as freedom from violence. It provides data and analysis about the effects of violence on peoples around the world.

■ Kay, S. (2006), *Global Security in the Twenty-First Century: The Quest for Power and the Search for Peace* (Oxford: Rowman and Littlefield). An excellent introduction to global security and to the liberal and realist perspectives.

■ Kegley, C. W. Jr (ed.) (2003), *The New Global Terrorism: Characteristics, Causes, Controls* (Saddle River, NJ: Pearson Education). An excellent edited volume of major academic articles on non-state violence.

■ Pettiford, L. and Curley, M. (1999), *Changing Security Agendas and the Third World* (London/New York: Pinter). This thought-provoking book examines security from a developing world perspective, countering traditional international relations theory.

■ Singer, P. (2002), 'AIDS and International Security', *Survival*, 44/1: 45–158.

■ Tickner, J. A. (1992), *Gender in International Relations: Feminist Perspectives on Achieving Global Security* (New York: Columbia University Press). A ground-breaking book introducing feminist perspectives on global security.

■ United Nations (2004), *A More Secure World: Our Shared Responsibility, Report of the UN Secretary General's High Level Panel on Threats, Challenges and Change* (London: Stationery Office). This UN-commissioned report outlines the key security challenges facing the world today and gives proposals for their resolution.

Web links

■ www.humansecuritygateway.info/ The Human Security Gateway, an excellent research and information database on human security issues.

■ www.crisisgroup.org/ Site of the International Crisis Group (ICG), a non-profit NGO that provides high quality reports and briefs on deadly conflicts around the world.

- www.isn.ethz.ch/   The site of the International Relations and Security Network, which shares specialized information among international relations and security professionals worldwide.

- http://first.sipri.org/   Facts on International Relations and Security Trends (FIRST) gives access to a large number of databases on traditional and non-traditional security issues.

- www.unodc.org   The website of the United Nations Office on Drugs and Crime.

- www.who.int/en/   The website of the World Health Organization.

 Online Resource Centre

For additional material and resources, please visit the Online Resource Centre at:

www.oxfordtextbooks.co.uk/orc/burnell3e/

PART 5

Case Studies: Experiences Compared

In this part, we deploy a range of case studies to add 'thick description' to the 'thin description' provided by the wide selections of examples that have been cited in the discussions in the earlier parts. There are two main aims. *First*, to illustrate in depth many of the larger themes that have been introduced and discussed in the earlier parts, by reference to countries carefully chosen as cases for their capacity to reveal the complexity of the issues involved. Our *second* aim is to demonstrate the great diversity of experience through a combination of cases drawn from the main developing regions, with some countries showing what might be considered positive developments or genuine achievements and others displaying more troublesome features. The intention to illustrate good news as well as less attractive features was a primary criterion in the selection process. Space limitations mean it is not possible to provide a comprehensive overview of the politics in these countries. But basic data for socio-economic and political indicators for them and their globalization rankings can be found in Appendix 1 and Appendix 2.

While the country cases each tell their own story the combinations supply evidence of some contrasting experiences. At the same time the evidence shows that often we must be qualified when making judgements. Indeed, what counts as, for instance, good news is to some extent in the eye of the beholder: the country analysts were encouraged to bring their own views to bear and apply their own interpretation of the evidence. Moreover, the political dynamics of developing countries are such that the way and extent to which a country illustrates a particular politics, for example state-building or conversely state failure, can change over time, sometimes more quickly than the time it takes for a book to move from one published edition to another. Put differently, the country cases do illustrate specific themes from Part 1 through to Part 4, but no one should expect them to do so permanently or in straightforward black-and-white fashion.

Thus in Chapter 20, 'Reconfiguring the Political Order', Indonesia's far-flung archipelago and diverse peoples might seem like a country in which increasing fragmentation is only to be expected, given the transition from political authoritarianism and the decentralization that followed the fall of President Suharto. And it is true that some secessionist tendencies have been in evidence, most dramatically in the acquisition of independence by East Timor in 2002. And yet the account of Indonesia while documenting the tensions inside Indonesia also presents a more complex picture. In contrast, South Africa's recent past is suggestive of an unambiguously positive experience in nation-building, coming as it did after forecasts of political disintegration on the attainment of black majority rule. Even so, the remarkable story of national reconciliation and racial harmony since the end of apartheid appears to indicate that class-based inequalities could soon come to pose a greater challenge to national unity or at least reduce the political dominance of the African National Congress. Indonesia and South Africa together illustrate the potential and the limitations of state reshaping and nation-building in countries in which European imperial expansion and the colonial legacy have left a major impact, and the possible pitfalls of making predictions about the same. Yet so far both can be presented as successful examples of democratic advance, in contrast to the third case, Iraq. Under Saddam Hussein's strong centralized state, social order was guaranteed by heavy repression. Those days are now gone. And the multiple challenges of national reconciliation, state reconstruction, and institutionalization of some measure of democracy against a background of economic destruction and massive external interference all weigh heavily on the Iraqi people and their leaders.

In Chapter 21, 'Military in Politics Versus Democratic Advance', three countries illustrate contrasting versions of a global contest between the different overarching principles of political organization that have occupied much of the developing world. It is a contest in which different countries exhibit diverse trajectories, and the position a country holds in relation to the different categories and subcategories of authoritarian, democratic, and hybrid forms of rule is not always obvious. The first case, Pakistan, a country that is deemed critical to international efforts to combat terrorism by radical Islamic groups, cannot be viewed as politically very stable. The political role of the armed forces has been fundamental in the past and even now should not be discounted. This chapter explains why. Nigeria appears to tell a different story. Although like Pakistan it has a history of military intervention, since 1999 it has sustained a return to elected civilian rule. But how precarious is this development? Nigeria is a multiethnic society that has known civil war. Regional and religious differences are strongly felt, and Nigeria's political leaders continue to be criticized both at home and abroad for not doing enough to end corruption and not facing up to other serious weaknesses in governance. And yet by virtue of its size, oil wealth, and importance to inter-state politics on the African continent, Nigeria cannot be ignored.

Mexico is an example of yet a third political path, in this case from what Schedler calls 'electoral authoritarianism' to 'democratization by elections'. And yet Mexico shows that even where the military seem extremely unlikely to intervene in politics the process of consolidating a civil democratic peace may not be smooth. The disputes occasioned by the 2006 presidential election and ongoing deterioration in public security, fuelled by an explosive increase in narco-violence, provide examples.

Chapter 22, 'Underdevelopment and Development', provides further examples of both success and failure in developmental terms and its political coordinates. Guatemala shows how difficult it can be to break away from the structural cycle of underdevelopment, notwithstanding modest reform of the formal political institutions. The continuing abuse of human rights as well as human development failings more generally come out strongly. South Korea by comparison is a success story not just in terms of its strong overall record of economic and social development but also because of the embedding of stable democracy. Development has proceeded on all fronts, then. But what made this possible? And what new political challenges does the country now face? While Guatemala in Central America and South Korea in East Asia may represent extremes of underdevelopment and development, the perhaps more typical experience of the many countries that lie somewhere between the extremes is illustrated in the shape of Zambia, on the Online Resource Centre to this book.

Finally, in Chapter 23, 'South–South Relations and the Changing Landscape of International Development Cooperation', the rapidly developing external engagement by India and China with countries in the developing world offers a powerful demonstration that old stereotypes of the international system based on 'First World' and 'Third World', 'North' and 'South', are being fundamentally transformed.

All told, the chapters in the book's final part underline that to understand politics in the developing world a detailed historical knowledge acquired on a case-by-case basis is an indispensable complement to the larger theorizing. This part can help us to decide which theoretical approaches offer the most insight into a specific case. And although the case studies are brought together here they can be read on a free-standing basis; readers are also recommended to consult the case or cases that are most relevant to a big issue or theme immediately after reading the preceding chapter or chapters on that issue or theme. The brief introduction to the cases here is offered as a guide to matching up the different parts of the book in this way.

To round off the country studies, the Online Resource Centre also includes specially commissioned new material, ranging from the theme of political parties, to individual studies of Zambia, Iran, and Brazil.

Reconfiguring the Political Order

20

20a Indonesia: Redistributing Power

Edward Aspinall

» Chapter contents

- Introduction
- Making Indonesia
- Democratization and National Disintegration
- Toward Reintegration
- Conclusion

＊ Overview

This chapter focuses on the crisis of 'national disintegration' (as it was sometimes known) in Indonesia in the years following the collapse of President Suharto's authoritarian regime in 1998. After decades of militaristic and centralized rule, there was a sudden eruption of fragmentary and contentious politics based around ethnic, regional, and religious identities. Civil disturbances, inter-communal warfare, and separatist insurgencies occurred in several regions. Government leaders feared that decades of nation-building efforts were unravelling. This chapter surveys the historical experiences that led to this outcome, outlines the main dimensions of the crisis, and discusses alternative explanations for it. Some accounts point to the intractable nature of Indonesia's problems, ultimately deriving from the heterogeneity of the population and the 'artificiality' of the country's colonial origins, while others emphasize the role of the post-colonial state in generating ethnic tensions and violence. Figure 20a.1 is a map of Indonesia and Box 20a.1 provides an overview of key dates in Indonesia's history.

Figure 20a.1 Indonesia

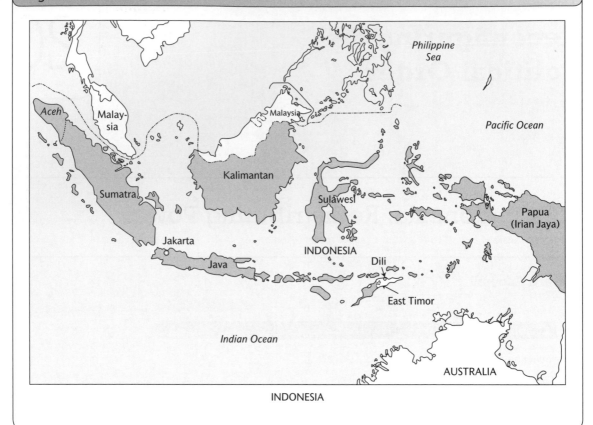

INDONESIA

Box 20a.1 Key Dates in Indonesia's History

1942	Japanese military occupies the Netherlands East Indies
1945	Nationalist leaders proclaim Indonesian independence
1945–49	Independence revolution: armed conflict and negotiations with the Dutch
1955	Indonesia's first parliamentary elections produce a fractured political map
1959	President Sukarno dissolves parliament and establishes 'Guided Democracy'
1965	Failed coup attempt in Jakarta, army begins massacre of communists
1966	President Suharto's 'New Order' regime begins
1997	Asian financial crisis
1998	Nationwide student protests force resignation of President Suharto
	B. J. Habibie takes over and initiates political reform
1999	Democratic elections
	East Timor votes to become independent
	Major violence in Maluku and Aceh
2003	Martial law aims at eradicating separatist insurgency in Aceh
2005	Helsinki peace agreement signed by Acehnese rebel leaders and government representatives
2009	Third post-Suharto democratic elections

Introduction

When President Suharto's military-based regime collapsed in 1998, hopes were high in Indonesia that the country was entering a new democratic era. However, democratization was accompanied by a surge of mobilization along ethnic and religious lines. In the worst instances, communal conflicts caused thousands of deaths. In three provinces, long-standing separatist movements re-emerged, leading to the independence of one province, East Timor, which became an internationally recognized sovereign state in May 2002. Many Indonesians began to fear that their country would break up.

Indonesia's political trajectory over recent decades mirrors broad trends in the developing world. The country has faced nation-building challenges similar to those experienced by other post-colonial states, and it has experimented with solutions resembling those tried elsewhere. In the post-independence years of the 1950s, Indonesia adopted a political format (parliamentary democracy) and a development strategy (economic nationalism and state-led industrialization) similar to those of many other African and Asian post-colonies. Also, as in many other newly independent states, democratic rule did not long survive the divisions unleashed by independence, social transformation, and the cold war. From the late 1960s, Indonesia approximated more to the model of authoritarian developmentalism pioneered by states in East Asia such as South Korea and Taiwan.

Even the communal mobilization and fragmentation from 1998 mirrors developments elsewhere over the last two decades (India is one example).

As well as outlining the main trends, this chapter surveys the alternative explanations for the fragmentary pressures. With some simplification, it can be seen that there are two basic schools of thought. On the one hand are those who see fragmentation as virtually an inevitable product of Indonesia's great ethnic and religious heterogeneity. In this view, the post-1998 violence was merely the latest explosion of tensions that first surfaced in the early post-independence years. President Suharto's authoritarian rule kept the lid on centrifugal forces, but once repressive constraints were removed, these forces reasserted themselves. A second set of explanations takes a less pessimistic view of Indonesian society, instead pointing to the disruptive effects of the state's own political and economic policies as causes of fragmentation. Broadly speaking, this debate mirrors larger ones in the fields of political science, history, and sociology, about whether contemporary ethnic and national political identities and conflicts arise naturally from deep-seated social divisions ('primordialism'), or whether they are produced by modern phenomena, such as economic development, state formation, the impacts of post-colonial states, and communication technologies ('modernism') (Smith 1998). This chapter finds the second set of explanations for Indonesia's post-1998 crises more convincing.

Making Indonesia

A starting point for understanding Indonesia's post-1998 fragmentation is noting the great ethnic and religious diversity of the country. Indonesia consists of approximately 17,000 islands, about

6,000 of which are populated. There are over 700 languages, and perhaps 1,000 ethnic or sub-ethnic groups (depending on how they are defined). By far the largest ethnic group is the Javanese, at about 42 per cent of the population. Approximately 88 per cent of Indonesians are Muslims, alongside significant Christian, Hindu, and Buddhist minorities. While almost all Indonesian Muslims are Sunni, they are themselves divided, notably between 'traditionalists', who are followers of *ulama* (religious scholars) in rural areas, and the more urban 'modernists'. Like many post-colonial states, Indonesia is not heir to any long-standing pre-colonial polity (indeed, the word 'Indonesia' was not coined until the nineteenth century and became popular only in the early twentieth century). Instead, it was the Dutch colonialists who united the diverse societies of what is now thought of as Indonesia into a single colony, the Netherlands East Indies.

For scholars who argue that durable nations arise out of ethnic affinity or belief in common descent (for example Connor 1994: 90–100), it would follow logically that Indonesia is not a true nation-state. In fact, the Indonesian experience demonstrates the historical processes by which a sense of nationhood may come into being and, over time, strike deep roots.

In the early twentieth century, a new Indonesian nationalist movement emerged, led by Western-educated elites. Early nationalist leaders stressed the need for unity among the diverse peoples of the archipelago. For example, they relabelled the Malay language (already a lingua franca in colonial times) as Indonesian, the 'language of unity'. Experiences of struggle and sacrifice during the early nationalist movement (c. 1912–42) and independence revolution (1945–49) popularized the ideas of Indonesian unity and independence and sanctified them in blood. In the early years of independence, nation-building became the theme par excellence of the country's leaders, especially its first president, Sukarno.

Despite the emphasis on unity, the transition to independence was fractious. Elections in 1955 produced a Parliament divided between secular-nationalists, communists, traditionalist Muslims, and modernist Muslims. Cabinets rose and fell in quick succession. Tensions between Muslims and secularists over whether the state should oblige Muslims to observe Islamic law caused deadlock in a constituent assembly. Armed revolts in several regions expressed regionalist, Islamic, and anti-communist urges. Rapid growth of the communist party threatened Indonesia's elites.

President Sukarno tried to overcome these divisions by a system of left-populist but authoritarian rule, which he labelled 'Guided Democracy' (1959–65). However, this system did not prevent polarization between the massive Communist Party on the left and the military and its allies on the right. The military was ultimately victorious, cementing its triumph with the massacre of approximately 500,000 leftists in 1965–66, an event that was enthusiastically welcomed by the United States and its allies. Subsequently, under Suharto's leadership, the military established an authoritarian regime, the 'New Order', which lasted from 1966 to 1998.

The New Order still focused on nation-building, but whereas Sukarno had tried to unify Indonesia by mobilizing and channelling popular passions, Suharto and the military tried to suppress them. They proclaimed that they aimed at 'accelerated modernization', which would gradually eliminate 'primordial' divisions. They believed they had to limit political mobilization in order to create a stable environment for economic development. Indonesia experienced almost three decades of rapid growth. Gross domestic product (GDP) and income per capita tripled between 1970 and 2000 and the number of people inhabiting urban areas doubled to around 40 per cent of the total, with the proportion employed in agriculture falling by a third. In this context, a tiny but wealthy capitalist class emerged, as did a larger middle class, and there were gradually rising living standards for many of the poor. The regime also encouraged national cohesion by pursuing economic integration and propagating unifying national symbols and cultural habits. For example, it developed a *Pancasila* ideology, to which all citizens were expected to adhere, and expanded uniform national education for school students (Drake 1989).

Rapid economic and social change was not matched by political evolution. Suharto remained in power, ageing and inflexible. His regime still aimed to constrain, control, and repress popular pressures rather than to accommodate them. Political strains increased in the early 1990s, as speculation grew about presidential succession and rising social forces became more assertive. The collapse of the regime, however, was triggered not by economic growth, but by economic crisis. When the Asian financial collapse of 1997 hit Indonesia, it triggered student-led protests, which, in May 1998, forced Suharto to resign.

At this point, Indonesia did not seem to be facing elemental crisis. There had been separatist unrest in some provinces, but it had been militarily suppressed. Some communal violence accompanied rising anti-Suharto sentiment, but it was of secondary importance to the anti-Suharto protests, the leaders of which wanted to solve the country's national problems by introducing political reform (*reformasi*). Overall, their mood was optimistic.

Key points

- Indonesia is an ethnically diverse nation-state formed within the boundaries of the Dutch colony, the Netherlands East Indies.

- Early post-independence governments stressed nation-building but faced difficulties in managing conflicts generated by the transition to independence.

- Suharto's New Order regime (1966–98) pursued highly authoritarian and centralized solutions to Indonesia's nation-building challenges, suppressing independent politics and emphasizing economic development.

- The collapse of this regime did not result from communal conflict.

Democratization and National Disintegration

Responding to popular discontent, post-Suharto governments pursued rapid democratization. Defying predictions, this process proceeded smoothly. The military withdrew from national political management. New political parties and **civil society** organizations multiplied. The press became one of the most free in Asia. Democratic elections were held in 1999 and again in 2004 and 2009, producing a fragmented political map (see Box 20a.2).

In many regions, anti-government *reformasi* protests seamlessly gave way after Suharto fell to a new **localism**, meaning the tendency to prioritize local cultural, economic, and political interests and identities over national ones. Many demonstrators wanted to replace discredited local officials

and voiced long-suppressed local grievances. Often, their protests were framed in terms of reassertion of local cultural identities. In some regions, there were demands that only *putra daerah* (sons of the region) should obtain political posts, government contracts, or civil service employment. This process accelerated after the government of President Habibie (1998–99) introduced regional autonomy legislation, which devolved wide-ranging political powers and financial responsibility to several hundred district governments (Aspinall and Fealy 2003). In one of the world's most radical experiments in decentralization, political and economic power shifted massively to the local level.

In some places, localism took violent form. There were two main categories of violence. First, was conflict *within* local societies, between rival re-ligious or ethnic communities. Sometimes this involved one-sided attacks on largely defenceless minority groups. A series of mob attacks against ethnic Chinese (a group that makes up about 2 per cent of the population—the figure is dis-puted—but which is prominent in trade) coincided with the fall of Suharto (Purdey 2006). Violence in

Kalimantan (Borneo) was directed largely against migrants from the island of Madura. Some hostile communities were more evenly matched. The worst inter-communal violence occurred in Maluku (the Moluccas), where the population was almost equally divided between Muslims and Christians, resulting in virtual civil war and approximately 5,000–6,000 deaths.

Box 20a.2 Fragmentation: Indonesia's Party System

Major vote winners in post-Suharto legislative elections

	1999 (%)	2004 (%)	2009 (%)
Secular nationalist parties			
Gerindra, Greater Indonesia Movement Party, personal vehicle for former general Prabowo Subianto			4
Golkar, the ruling party under Suharto's New Order regime	22	22	14
Hanura, People's Conscience Party, personal vehicle for former general Wiranto			4
PDI-P, Indonesia Democracy Party—Struggle, led by Megawati Soekarnoputri and heir to Sukarnoist nationalist traditions	34	19	14
PD, Democrat Party, personal vehicle for president Susilo Bambang Yudhoyono	—	7	21
Pluralist Islamic parties			
PKB, National Awakening Party, aligned with the main traditionalist Islamic organization, Nadhatul Ulama	13	11	5
PAN, National Mandate Party, aligned with the main modernist Islamic organization, Muhammadiyah	7	6	6
Islamist parties			
PPP, United Development Party, Islamic party first formed under the New Order	11	8	5
PKS, Justice and Welfare Party, party of puritanical, urban intellectuals	1	7	8

Source: Author's calculations taken from Komisi Pemilihan Umum, General Elections Commission: www.kpu.go.id

---

A second category of violence involved local com-munities confronting state authority. These con-flicts mostly involved separatist movements fighting with (or being repressed by) security forces. The best-known case internationally was East Timor, which had long been a site of conflict and source of diplomatic difficulties for Indonesia. President Habibie unexpectedly allowed a UN-supervised

vote on independence there in 1999, prompting the military to organize militias to terrorize the pop-ulation. They caused approximately 1,500 deaths during a wave of destruction after 78.5 per cent of the population voted for independence. Violence was worse in Aceh, in northern Sumatra, where a long-running insurgency reignited after Suharto fell. For a time, the guerrillas of GAM (Free Aceh

Movement) controlled much of the countryside. Between 1999 and 2005, approximately 7,200 persons were killed in the ensuing conflict and counter-insurgency operations. In Papua, the western half of the island of New Guinea, support for independence was also great among the indigenous Melanesian population, although here most independence supporters used non-violent means (Chauvel 2003).

Observers have offered many different explanations for post-Suharto disintegrative tendencies and violence. Given the variety of the processes involved and the complexity of the debates, it is possible to give only a schematic overview here. In general terms, the debates mirrored broader ones between advocates of primordialist and modernist interpretations of ethnic and nationalist conflicts.

First, some argued that violence reflected deep-seated, primordial, and even ancient identities and enmities. This view was mostly discredited among scholars (Mote and Rutherford 2001). However, it was popular among some journalists and commentators, who sometimes used the metaphor of the 'seething cauldron' to describe Indonesia. Western journalists were often fascinated with seemingly exotic or pre-modern manifestations of violence (such as head-hunting by Dayak fighters in Kalimantan — Parry 2005). A few foreign analysts suggested that these conflicts were occurring because (as one anonymous Western diplomat explained to a journalist) Indonesia was 'an artificial country held together by artificial means' during the Suharto years (Gaouette 1999). Suharto's exit had taken the lid off the cauldron.

Similar views were also held by many actors directly or indirectly involved in violence. Participants in ethnic or separatist violence invariably described their enemies in absolutist and essentialist terms. For example, Hasan Tiro, the founder of GAM, claimed that Indonesia was a fabrication designed to cover Javanese dominance and that Indonesians were a 'non-existent human species' (Tiro 1984: 68). GAM leaders believed that Indonesia's old ethnic groups were beginning to reassert themselves and that the country would inevitably disintegrate. Ironically, some in the military and national government agreed that Indonesia was fragile (although they obviously did not think it was inherently flawed) and might collapse if they loosened political controls too much.

The second set of arguments, more dominant in the scholarly literature, held that post-Suharto violence did not result from immutable enmities or from Indonesia's 'artificiality', but stemmed instead from recent processes of economic development, social change, state formation, and repression. In particular, most analysts stressed the legacies of Suharto's authoritarian rule. For example, they argued that popular support for independence in Aceh resulted from inequitable resource exploitation in the province under Suharto (Aceh had major natural gas reserves and had been a big contributor to national income) and from the military violence used to eliminate what had initially been a tiny separatist movement there (Robinson 1998). Analysts of violence in Maluku pointed to the accumulation of tensions in that province under Suharto, caused by migration and competition between Muslims and Christians for bureaucratic positions and economic resources, in conditions under which such tensions could not be resolved by democratic means (Bertrand 2002).

Such analyses did not see Indonesia as inherently flawed, but rather looked for specific causes of violence in each case. It was invariably possible to identify grievances that had developed or accumulated under authoritarian rule. Such analyses thus viewed the Suharto regime not as having held Indonesia together in the face of intrinsic disintegrative pressures, but rather as having generated latent grievances that erupted once authoritarian rule was relaxed.

Examination of the extent and variety of post-Suharto violence makes this second group of explanations more convincing, and does not justify the 'seething cauldron' image. Overall, the death toll in post-Suharto violence (approximately 20,000 in an overall population of 200 million), while very great, was far less than in many other recent internal conflicts in the developing world. The media concentrated on places where violence was worst, and tended to overlook that most regions remained peaceful. The image of a country on the verge of disintegration also loses force if we remember that it was in only three provinces (out of a total of 27 in 1998) that there was significant support for independence. In some other provinces (notably Riau, Bali, and Maluku) a few intellectuals argued for independence but failed to rally popular enthusiasm.

Analysis of the three 'separatist provinces' (Aceh, Papua, and East Timor), however, requires us to qualify the view that disintegrative pressures arose only because of Suharto's authoritarianism. It is certainly true that repression under Suharto increased support for independence in each place. But repression in these provinces was also a *response* to popular resistance as much as being a cause of it. Aceh, for example, was not notably more militarized than other provinces prior to the establishment of GAM in 1976. Understanding the origins of separatism requires us to extend our historical inquiry to before Suharto's rule, back to the colonial origins of Indonesia.

One distinguishing feature of each separatist province was that its mode of incorporation into the Indonesian nation-state produced a strong regional identity at least partly defined against Indonesia. East Timor was the obvious example: it had never been part of the Netherlands East Indies but was instead a Portuguese colony. Against a backdrop of cold war tensions, Suharto's army violently invaded the territory in 1975, causing great loss of life. Many East Timorese never accepted the Indonesian presence, viewing it instead as an occupying power. Papua had been ruled by the Dutch, but it also had a distinct history. The Indonesian nationalist movement had not struck deep roots there in the early twentieth century. Crucially, when Indonesia became independent in 1949, Holland retained control over Papua and began to groom a layer of local leaders for independence. Following US pressure on Holland, Papua was incorporated into Indonesia in the 1960s, but by then most politically conscious Papuans already imagined a future separate to Indonesia. Incorporation involved Indonesian military action and intimidation, causing lasting resentment. Aceh was different again: its population enthusiastically supported Indonesia's independence struggle in 1945–49, so much so that Aceh was the only part of their former colony that the Dutch did not dare to try to reconquer. As a result, Aceh's leaders had unfettered control over local affairs during that period. When Indonesia became independent, they lost much of that autonomy, causing bitterness and gradual evolution of a distinct identity. GAM built on this underlying resentment when it called for Aceh's independence.

Exploring how recent separatist conflicts originated in colonization and decolonization does not validate primordialist arguments that Indonesia, as a post-colonial state containing diverse ethnic groups, was congenitally flawed. Ethnic differences alone did not motivate these conflicts. For example, the East Timorese are very similar ethno-linguistically to their neighbours in Indonesian West Timor. Rather than arising out of the mere fact of ethnic difference, separatism arose out of interactions between local populations and processes of state formation. Where those interactions gave rise to identities that were defined in opposition to an overarching Indonesian identity, they became bases for separatist mobilization.

Key points

- Democratization unleashed fragmentation pressures, including communal conflicts and revived separatist movements in some regions.

- One set of explanations for this unrest stresses the artificiality of Indonesia due to its social heterogeneity, and its colonial origins.

- A second group of arguments blames violence on state actions, especially during Suharto's rule. It views this period of authoritarianism not as having

saved Indonesia from disintegrative pressures, but as having generated them.

- The second set of arguments is more convincing. Communal and other violence did not occur in most areas of Indonesia. In places where it did occur, it was always possible to identify specific societal grievances generated by state behaviour.

- The roots of recent violence in the three main separatist provinces can also be traced to experiences of colonization and decolonization.

Toward Reintegration

By about 2003, Indonesia no longer appeared to be on the verge of disintegration. The worst violence was passing: for instance, leaders of the warring communities in Maluku reached a peace agreement in February 2002. Even in Aceh, GAM leaders agreed to give up their independence goal and signed an accord with the government in August 2005.

In part, the crisis ended because violence had simply exhausted itself. But the state's own response also contributed. The crisis had prompted two contradictory policy approaches from national elites. First, it had triggered toughening of views and a return to hard-line, even militaristic, policies in some instances. This reflected the view in some elite circles, especially in the military, that Indonesian unity was fragile and should be maintained with constant vigilance. After the 'loss' of East Timor, from 2000 post-Suharto governments once again suppressed separatist movements. In Papua, security forces harassed, arrested, and (in one case) assassinated pro-independence leaders, while in Aceh a full-scale military assault on rebels was launched in May 2003. Military and

government leaders were adamant that such steps were needed to stop a domino effect whereby the separatist contagion would spread to other provinces. Critics argued that violent methods would fan separatist sentiment in the long run, as in the past. Yet the return to military solutions in the short term ended the sense of possibility that had arisen in separatist provinces after Suharto fell. In Aceh, for example, GAM rebels abandoned independence partly because they realized their guerrilla campaign had reached an impasse.

The return to hard-line policies was not the dominant response, however, and it does not provide the main explanation for how the crisis ended. Most of Indonesia's new leaders knew that Suharto's old centralized and authoritarian system could not be revived, and they blamed it for the crisis. Instead, they saw democratization and decentralization as the means to ensure national survival, believing such policies would empower local communities to redress their own grievances. Even in Papua and Aceh therefore, alongside military operations, the government offered concessions in the form of

Special Autonomy laws (Box 20a.3). In most regions of Indonesia, democratization and the nationwide decentralization laws had the desired effect. Most local leaders no longer concerned themselves with challenging Jakarta, but instead busied themselves with local affairs.

Box 20a.3 Special Autonomy in Aceh and Papua

Key Points of the Papua Special Autonomy Law 2001 and the Government of Aceh Law 2006

- Wide-ranging grant of powers, covering everything except foreign affairs, defence, security, judiciary, monetary and fiscal matters, and religion, which are retained by the central government

- Both provinces retain a larger share of natural resource revenues than other provinces, including from oil and gas (80 per cent for Papua; 70 per cent for Aceh)

- Both provinces may have their own symbols, including a flag and an anthem

- Human Rights Courts and Truth and Reconciliation Commissions

Papua	*Aceh*
• Establishment of a Papuan People's Council, consisting of representatives of women, traditional communities, and religious groups; charged with ensuring indigenous rights are upheld	• Application of Islamic law (*Sharia*) to Muslims in Aceh; establishes a *Sharia* court with authority over both civil and criminal matters
• Indigenous Papuans granted certain special rights, for instance only an indigenous Papuan may become governor	• Establishment of a council of *ulama* (religious scholars) with special advisory powers
• Provincial government charged with protecting customary law, land rights, and local culture	• Independent candidates (that is, those not nominated by political parties) can run in elections for governor and district heads; formation of local political parties, to run in local elections from 2009

Source: Author's compilation

This change does not mean that Indonesia experienced a sudden and miraculous transition to **good governance**, as some of the international agencies promoting decentralization had hoped. On the contrary, old elites adapted to the new system. In most regions **corruption** proliferated, as local leaders used state funds to enrich themselves and their supporters. But the transformation did mean that the axis of political contention, including struggles to control economic resources, shifted from the national level to the regions. Localism still flourished, but not in ways that directly undermined the idea of Indonesia.

Although the crisis of the post-Suharto years has passed, the new dispensation raises other possibilities: not of sudden disintegration, but rather of gradual decline in national cohesion. Whatever ordinary citizens thought about the former regimes of Presidents Sukarno and Suharto, they could see that each articulated a clear set of national goals and had concrete ideas about how to achieve them. Evidence of nation-building was visible everywhere: ubiquitous mass mobilization under Sukarno; economic development, infrastructure projects, and ideological indoctrination under Suharto. A uniform national political culture was developing. Even today, there are still factors creating a sense of commonality (such as the national electronic media, especially television). Now, in a new era of decentralized politics, for the first time for fifty years there are also strong countervailing pressures. In one perspective, Indonesia is becoming a patchwork of regions, in which local interests and dynamics predominate over national ones.

An example is the contest over the political role of Islam. In the 1950s, division over whether the constitution should require Muslims to observe Islamic law rent the body politic at the national level. After the fall of Suharto, Islamic parties made only token efforts to revive the national constitutional debate. Instead, by late 2006, several dozen local administrations had begun to introduce regulations that included elements of Islamic law (for example, making the Islamic dress code mandatory for women) piecemeal. Secular-oriented groups tried to oppose such initiatives nationally, but failed to gain much traction in the regions concerned.

And yet, it would be rash to pass a negative judgement on the future of Indonesia's national project. For many Indonesians, the new diversity produced by democratic politics and regional autonomy does not signify loss of national cohesion, but simply readjusts a political formula that had been tilted too far in favour of uniformity. Although localism is vigorous, many factors still underpin national unity, including widely shared pride in national history and symbols. Belief that diversity is integral to Indonesian identity is itself a core element in Indonesian nationalism. Finally, certain safeguards have been built into Indonesia's new institutional framework to constrain disintegrative tendencies (for instance, to register for elections, political parties must prove that they have a broad national presence).

Key points

- The extreme post-Suharto fragmentary pressures and violence lasted for a brief period (approximately five years). Indonesia is currently undergoing reconsolidation.
- State violence played a role in overcoming this crisis, especially in ending (at least for a time) separatist challenges.
- More significant were decentralization and democratization. These policies assuaged local grievances and encouraged regional elites to engage in local political processes rather than to challenge the central state.
- The major challenge facing Indonesia today, therefore, is not dramatic disintegration but rather gradual decline of cohesion.

Conclusion

This chapter has surveyed the crisis of national disintegration experienced by Indonesia from the late 1990s, and discussed two sets of explanations for it: those that locate the source of these problems in the country's multi-ethnic make-up and its origins as heir to an artificial colonial state, and those that instead focus on grievances caused by state action, especially under the Suharto regime. The brief survey of the evidence in the chapter suggests that the second group of explanations is more convincing.

Indeed, it should be stressed that while the country has great ethnic and linguistic diversity, Indonesia is no more artificial than any post-colonial, or indeed any other, modern state. Modern nation-states did not arise seamlessly from pre-existing ethnic communities, but were instead produced by long processes of state- and nation-building. In most cases, these processes involved force, as well as the creation over generations of political institutions, standardized education, and other mechanisms for generating national cohesion.

The fragmentation pressures experienced by Indonesia from the late 1990s were similar to those experienced in many developing countries over the last two decades. For instance, ethnic and religious identity politics have in many places stepped into the vacuum created by declining popular enthusiasm for early post-independence nation-building policies. The suddenness and scale of the crisis in Indonesia resulted from the steady build-up of social tensions during Suharto's authoritarian rule, and their sudden release with democratization. Indonesia was not inherently flawed. Instead, authoritarianism was an unsustainable method of managing the country's diversity.

? Questions

1. What is meant by fragmentation in a country like Indonesia? Are all forms of fragmentation equally damaging or dangerous?

2. Is it accurate to describe fragmentation pressures in Indonesia after 1998 as being a product of democratization? What roles did earlier experiences—notably colonialism and authoritarianism—play in producing those pressures?

3. What role can or should force play in holding together highly diverse developing countries like Indonesia?

4. Is fragmentation a greater challenge for developing or developed countries? Why?

5. National political leaders in highly diverse countries often say that policies of decentralization will accelerate fragmentation. Are they correct?

→ Further reading

■ Aspinall, E. and Fealy, G. (eds) (2003), *Local Power and Politics in Indonesia: Democratisation and Decentralisation* (Singapore: Institute of Southeast Asian Affairs). An early survey of the flowering of local politics prompted by regional autonomy.

■ Bertrand, J. (2004), *Nationalism and Ethnic Conflict in Indonesia* (Cambridge: Cambridge University Press). Overview of the ethnic conflicts that accompanied and followed the fall of Suharto. The author explains the grievances that motivated each conflict and links them to the broader institutional shifts associated with democratization.

■ Robison, R. and Hadiz, V. R. (2004), *Reorganizing Power in Indonesia: The Politics of Oligarchy in an Age of Markets* (London/New York: Routledge). An account of the democratic transition, emphasizing political economy and the preservation of elite authority and privilege.

■ Van Klinken, G. (2007), *Communal Violence and Democratization in Indonesia: Small Town Wars* (London: Routledge). Uses a sociological approach to explain six key episodes of post-Suharto communal violence.

Web links

■ www.insideindonesia.org Australia-based quarterly magazine that focuses on human rights and political and environmental issues.

■ www.thejakartapost.com Indonesia's premier daily English-language newspaper, complete with a useful search engine and archives.

■ http://cip.cornell.edu/Indonesia Produced by Cornell University, *Indonesia* has, since the late 1960s, been the premier academic journal on Indonesian affairs.

Online Resource Centre

For additional material and resources, please visit the Online Resource Centre at: www.oxfordtextbooks.co.uk/orc/burnell3e/

20b South Africa: From Divided Society to New Nation

Robert A. Schrire

Chapter contents

- Introduction: The Historical Legacy
- The Struggle
- Negotiations
- The New Order: From Apartheid to the Rainbow Nation
- Political Transformation and Nation-Building
- Leadership, National Identities, and the Future
- Conclusion

Overview

If ever a country's history made it seem predestined to fail, South Africa would be such a country. From its creation in 1910 to the first democratic elections in 1994, South Africa was ruled by a white minority determined to maintain power and privileges irrespective of the costs to nation-building or other social groups. Many discriminatory economic and political policies were implemented over several decades. In time the white regime began to meet the growing black challenge with increased ruthlessness, which frequently transcended even **apartheid** legality. This created a powerful black response, increasing from the 1970s onwards. Few observers prior to 1990, then, believed in the possibility of relatively peaceful deracialization. Even fewer would have predicted that an African National Congress-controlled South Africa would be able to manage peacefully the massive historical cleavages, based upon class, ethnic, and racial interests. Yet with stunning speed, power was transferred from white to black hands. And far from collapsing, South Africa, a genuine democracy since 1994, has experienced uninterrupted economic growth until 2008, and relative internal peace. This chapter explains the paradox by exploring the historical legacy of apartheid, the armed struggle, the negotiation process, the complex question of identity, and the significant role of leadership in shaping nation-building in South Africa. Figure 20b.1 is a map of South Africa and Box 20b.1 provides an overview of key dates in South African history.

Figure 20b.1 South Africa

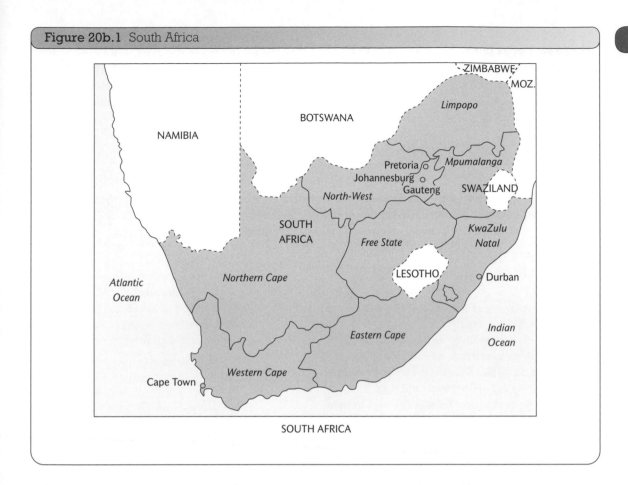

SOUTH AFRICA

Introduction: The Historical Legacy

The Union of South Africa, established in 1910, faced many problems, none more important than the issues of nationality and political rights. The Union Constitution reflected a compromise between the different 'native' policies of the former colonies and in general reduced the limited black political rights exercised previously. English- and Afrikaans-speaking whites competed fiercely for power up to the decisive victory of Afrikaner nationalism in 1948. The English, as a demographic minority, tended to advocate the politics of white unity, while many Afrikaner leaders advocated the politics of exclusive Afrikaner nationalism. After 1948, the National Party (NP) representing Afrikaner nationalism consolidated its political dominance. White unity took precedence in response to growing pressures from the outside world and black South Africans, accelerating after the establishment of a republic in 1961. The key dilemma—never resolved—was to create a morally acceptable political framework that did not endanger the Afrikaner's grasp of power. Meeting the political aspirations of the African majority was an intractable problem. The government's answer was the policy of grand apartheid, which constituted the African population as ten ethnic nations, each entitled to sovereign independence. Every African, irrespective of culture, birthplace, residence, or personal preferences, was assumed to be an immutable member of one of these ethnic communities. The ostensible aim was to create ten independent African nations in which Africans would have full citizenship rights. However, most of the homeland leaders, most notably KwaZulu's Mangosuthu Buthelezi, rejected the proposals, in part because of their normative vision of an undivided South Africa under democratic control, although some traditional leaders agreed to the creation of four independent homelands. Box 20b.1 provides an overview of key dates in South Africa's history.

Box 20b.1 Key Dates in South Africa's History

1652	Dutch settlement under Jan van Riebeck at the Cape	1991	Convention for a Democratic South Africa (CODESA) begins
1795	First British occupation at the Cape	1992	De Klerk wins a whites-only referendum to approve negotiations with the ANC
1836	Beginning of the Great Trek by Afrikaners into the interior	1992	(May) CODESA 2 convenes, then breaks down over deadlock in negotiations
1910	Union of South Africa founded, with merging of conquered Boer Republics of Transvaal and Orange Free State and the British Colonies of the Cape of Good Hope and Natal	1993	(March) A new negotiating council convenes (November) National Council adopts Interim Constitution
1912	African National Congress founded to resist Native Land Act	1994	(April) South Africa's first democratic election, ANC wins large majority
1948	Nationalist–Afrikaner Party coalition wins election on apartheid platform		(May) Nelson Mandela inaugurated President Government of National Unity takes (GNU) office
1960	Sharpeville massacre; state of emergency declared; ANC and PAC banned	1995	Truth and Reconciliation Commission formed
1976	Soweto student uprisings	1996	(May) Constitutional Assembly adopts final SA Constitution
1982	Period of tentative informal negotiations between the Apartheid government and ANC leaders, first in exile and then in prison, begins	1997	National Party under F. W. De Klerk withdraws from GNU
1984	Mass black township uprisings begin; government declares state of emergency	1999	South Africa's second democratic election. ANC again wins a large majority
1989	F. W. De Klerk becomes leader of National Party	2004	ANC wins a two-thirds majority in the third democratic election

| 1990 | (2 February) Nelson Mandela released from prison | 2005 | New National Party disbands and many of its leaders join the ANC |
| 1990 | ANC and NP leaders meet to sign historic Groote Schuur Accord charting the way to negotiations | 2009 | Fourth democratic election repeats high voter turnout of previous elections |

The Struggle

The African National Congress (ANC) was founded in 1912 to oppose the Land Acts, which were designed to ensure that most of South Africa's land resources remained permanently in white hands. Until the 1950s it was marginal to the great dramas taking place in white politics. Its strategy of seeking allies in the white, coloured, and Indian communities and especially from the ranks of the South African Communist Party (SACP) had mixed results, and caused the government to view it increasingly as an enemy of the state; repression escalated, polarizing national politics even further. The Pan Africanist Congress (PAC) split from the ANC in 1958 and fierce competition for African support ensued, including mass protests, the burning of passes that restricted movement, and attempts to force the police to engage in mass arrests, culminating in 1960 in the Sharpeville 'massacre'. Both the ANC and PAC were banned (the SACP had already been proscribed) and went underground and began to plan an armed insurrection. Nelson Mandela was chosen by the ANC to organize an armed struggle. That said, the commitment to violence was taken only with great reluctance by a largely Christian leadership, and by the early 1960s the insurrection

was smashed, its leaders either imprisoned or in exile. Peace returned to South Africa for another decade, but the illusion was shattered in 1976 by another massacre, at Soweto. Violence and protests spread rapidly throughout the country, forcing the government to declare yet another state of emergency. In 1983 new constitutional proposals by the government unexpectedly brought massively increased politicization and anger, leading the National Party to embark on modest reform initiatives for urban Africans, coloureds, and Indians. Widely resented by the black population, the proposals nevertheless opened up political space for public debate and greater participation. The founding of the United Democratic Front (UDF) in 1983 to oppose the government's proposals was highly significant. It brought together a wide range of civil society groups into the political arena, supported by the ANC in exile. Its membership and leaders were drawn from all segments: white, African, coloureds, and Indian; rural and urban; middle class and poor. The UDF was an important and successful experiment in non-racial political cooperation. The new tricameral system failed to gain legitimacy despite gaining the support of a whites-only referendum.

ROBERT A. SCHRIRE

Negotiations

The factors favouring a negotiated outcome included national economic decline, white divisions, sanctions, and other global pressures, which seriously dented the economy, increasing unemployment and the tax burden especially on whites. Three additional factors are of pivotal importance: first, the government failed to restore 'normality' after the unrest resumed in the early 1980s. The country was far from being ungovernable, but there seemed no end in sight to the turmoil in black areas, the industrial unrest, and the implosion in black education. Second, once the negotiations began, very strong forces worked to make failure to reach an accommodation very costly because it would destroy the leaderships in both parties. White politics would at best have seen a move to the ultra-reactionary right and at worst a military takeover. In the ANC, failure would have discredited the moderate leadership of Mandela and Thabo Mbeki. The country would have faced escalating violence—consequences 'too dreadful to contemplate' in the words of former Prime Minister Vorster.

Finally, and perhaps paradoxically, the negotiations, once initiated, did not take the form of white versus black. Although there were racially exclusive splinter groups, including the fragmented Afrikaner right, the key players—the ANC and the NP—fielded multi-racial delegations. The ANC,

in partnership with the UDF and SACP, had a significant and influential non-African component including communist leader Joe Slovo. Similarly, the NP led a heterogeneous grouping, which included conservative coloureds and African tribal leaders. Although the core of the historical conflict was the issue of political power and the consequent struggle between Afrikaner and African nationalism, the negotiations themselves involved teams of multi-racial delegates seeking to determine the broad principles, which would regulate a post-apartheid South Africa.

The informal discussions initiated by the Convention for a Democratic South Africa (CODESA) began, and in 1992 President De Klerk won a whites-only referendum on the reform policy, which he interpreted as a mandate for legitimizing the final proposals. The alienation of the conservative Zulu Inkatha Freedom Party (IFP) under Mangosuthu Buthelezi, who threatened violence and the boycott of elections, was not easily defused. Eventually, in 1994 broad agreement was reached around the principles embodied in an interim Constitution. Ad hoc arrangements were put in place to ensure that the ruling NP did not use the advantages of incumbency to advance its cause, including an independent electoral commission. Elections were held; all major groups and interests, including the white right and Zulu traditionalists, took part. The newly elected Parliament, acting as a constituent assembly, prepared a final Constitution based upon the principles already agreed and it was ratified by the legislature and the Constitutional Court in 1996. The country's second general election in 1999 was thus the first election held in terms of the new Constitution. The results resembled 1994.

Key points

- Although not yet ungovernable, entrenched structural weaknesses in the South African economy, growing internal unrest, a changed regional context and hardening international attitudes created a stalemate.

- The leadership on both sides realized that failure to reach a negotiated compromise would ensure a devastatingly violent future.

- Negotiations culminated in multi-party elections (1994) in which groups on the margins—the white right and Zulu traditionalists—participated.

The New Order: From Apartheid to the Rainbow Nation

The emergence of a non-racial and democratic South Africa constituted a dramatic and unforeseen reversal of centuries of history. Perhaps the real miracle was the transformation of the political discourse away from race and ethnicity. Both the ANC and the NP espoused a vision for South Africa that transcended their historical race/ethnic constituencies. Although the core of ANC support came from the African population, the party was greatly influenced by the minority of coloureds and Indians and a few notable whites. Yet it is still surprising how rapidly the ideal of a non-racial and non-ethnic society captured the reform process. The initial leanings of the NP and the largely Zulu-based IFP towards a society in which ascriptive group rights were to be constitutionally entrenched were soon thrust aside. The negotiations produced, in Mandela's words, a 'normal democracy'. And Africanist proponents of an African-only state exercised even less influence on the deliberations.

South Africa is constitutionally a non-racial democracy but it has based itself upon a very liberal notion of nationality. The so-called rainbow nation has been built upon a rejection of the model of a nation conceptualized as a people united around one identity, language, and set of national symbols. To give institutional content to this vision, new institutions were profoundly different from the former centralized, monocultural state. The foundation of a stable order thus recognized both a common nationality and important diversities: the national coat of arms' motto is 'Diverse People Unite'; the national anthem is composed of a combination of the old Afrikaner (South African) national anthem and a traditional African unity anthem. The country was divided into nine provinces, reflecting the historical continuities of history and ethnicity. Although not genuinely federal it creates a power structure outside the centre. Each province is headed by a premier and may draw up its own constitution. The divisive issue of the allocation of resources between provinces was taken out of the political arena with the creation of a technocratic Financial and Fiscal Commission, which employs fixed criteria such as population and poverty levels in its decisions. The country has 11 official languages; English is the language of record. Each province may determine which languages will be used officially. The national Parliament has two chambers—the popularly elected National Assembly, constituted on the basis of strict proportional representation, and the 90-member National Council of Provinces, in which each province has ten members, including *ex officio* the premiers of all the provinces or their representatives.

A critical problem has been how to deal with the past. Would perpetrators of human rights abuses face legal retribution? Would victims receive reparations? The political solution devised was to pass the Promotion of National Unity and Reconciliation Act, which created the Truth and Reconciliation Commission (TRC). This proceeded to antagonize almost all key parties including the ANC and NP; a consensus in favour of ignoring many of its findings ensued! Perhaps this liberated the polity to focus on issues of contemporary public policies. The resolution of amnesty and other contentious issues eased adoption of the interim Constitution, which mandated a government of national unity (GNU), embracing all parties that received at least 10 per cent of the vote. The GNU under President Mandela worked quite harmoniously for two years until De Klerk led a divided NP out of the coalition. After the 1999 elections, in which the ANC effectively won a two-thirds majority, its coalition partner the IFP remained in the cabinet. For elections, the strict system of proportional representation with no threshold ensures that even minor interests that can mobilize some support can be represented in Parliament.

Key points

- The 'real miracle' of South African transition is transformation of the political discourse from one based on race and ethnicity to one founded on a common national identity based on important diversities.

- An institutional framework was created to reflect the principle of inclusiveness, by creating a quasi-federal system, proportional representation, formal and informal power-sharing, all designed to ensure significant space and legitimacy for cultural and political minorities.

Political Transformation and Nation-Building

Had South Africa disintegrated into ethnic and racial conflicts, analysts would have had many explanations: the legacy of white domination; traditional ethnic animosities; high levels of inequality; and many others. So, why has South Africa thus far confounded many critics? In multi-ethnic societies, several types of conflict may threaten the state; easily the most serious by far is directly related to the central issue of nation-building—whose country is it? What symbols and values should dominate?

Indeed, who is a citizen of the state? Today the issue seems to have been decisively resolved in favour of a broad South Africanism. The threats from Zulu and Afrikaner nationalists have been decisively defeated. There is no **clash of civilizations** in South Africa; most of the population is predominantly Christian and Western-oriented in core value systems. Politics, then, revolves largely around issues of who gets what, when, and how. The issue of citizenship is illustrative. South Africa has been an independent state for almost a century; even before union (1910) many of the provinces had lengthy experiences of centralized administration, producing substantial acceptance of an identity that transcended in part traditional ethnicities. The vast majority of Africans and coloureds became converts to Christianity. The emergence of a capitalist economy too created powerful integrating forces. All who resided legally in the country were accepted as South Africans—at least until the social engineering of the 1960s.

Then the NP policy of apartheid and ethnic mobilization created a powerful reaction in black politics against race and ethnicity and helped to legitimize the demand for a non-ethnic and non-racial South Africa. The manipulation of ethnicity by whites proved counter-productive, securing an African leadership committed to the ideals of one nation. White racism did not create black racism and the only major black parties with a race-based policy, the PAC and Azanian People's Organization (AZAPO), have virtually disappeared as an electoral and political force. The racial/ethnic composition of the ANC leadership reflects its normative commitment to a united South Africa, and the vital importance of utilizing the skills of all sectors of the population to address often intractable problems. Thus, following the 1994 elections, the ANC's parliamentary delegation included 170 Africans, 40 whites, 23 Indians, and 19 coloureds. After the 1999 elections, the composition was 193 Africans, 31 whites, 27 coloureds, and 15 Indians. Racial minorities are strongly represented in executive positions in the party, Parliament, and the government.

A second set of factors contributing to national unity and a decline in the politics of ethnic mobilization is the political arithmetic of race and ethnicity. If the salient divisions are seen to be African (79 per cent), white (9 per cent), coloured (8.8 per cent), and Indian (2.5 per cent), then it is unnecessary for an African-oriented party to emphasize race for political ends. Similarly, parties with traditional support bases in the white, coloured, and Indian communities have strong incentives to seek African support if they wish to play a major role in national politics. If, however, language and ethnicity are seen as constituting the prime elements of political identity, as the old NP used proudly to proclaim when it described South Africa as a nation of minorities, then the political arithmetic also contributes to nation-building. No political party with national aspirations can build a powerful constituency by mobilizing ethnicity, as the most recent statistics in Table 20b.1 confirm.

Table 20b.1 South African Linguistic Groups, 2001

	Number (m.)	%
Zulu	10.7	23.8
Xhosa	7.9	17.6
Afrikaans[a]	6.0	13.6
Sepedi	4.2	9.4
English	3.7	8.2
Tswana	3.7	8.2
Sesotho	3.6	7.4
Tsonga	2.0	4.4
Swazi	1.2	2.7
Venda	1.0	2.3
Ndebele	0.7	1.6

[a] The most important components are 2.9 million coloured people and 2.6 million whites.

The dynamics of the political economy reinforce the demographic implications. The core of South Africa's industrial wealth lies in Gauteng, which includes Johannesburg, the largest city, and Pretoria, the executive capital. This area has the largest concentration of wealth and second largest population, and is the most ethnically mixed. The rise of large urban centres from the late nineteenth century weakened the ethnic allegiances of the new urban migrants, creating a significant non-ethnic community. The economic heart of the country is thus national. It has played an important role in integrating the country, not least through channelling revenues to the other provinces, especially the impoverished rural homelands. The Western Cape, the second wealthiest region, similarly has no dominant ethnic community, with large populations of whites, coloureds, and Xhosas.

Race and inequality

Although the most important aspect of nation-building turns on competing nationalisms in a single territory, the relationship between ascriptive groups is also significant. Historically, race and class coincided to a significant degree. Of course, this was no accident but reflected deliberate colonial and white policies over many centuries. The claim that South Africa was divided into two nations—a poor black and an affluent white nation—rang true up to the end of the 1980s. However, this relationship is now being undermined through public policy especially, as ANC leaders recognized the urgent need to move away from a racialized economy. Labour legislation, increased social expenditures, the deracialization of educational institutions, affirmative action especially in the public sector, and black empowerment policies have all contributed. As a consequence, there are now three nations: a wealthy white nation; a wealthy black nation; and an impoverished black nation. Although the poor constitute about half of the total, what is politically important is that the sizes of the wealthy black and white groups are about equal. The trends confirm that black wealth will in time overtake white wealth. Race and class are becoming delinked.

However, the critical problem of a large black underclass remains unresolved by the upward mobility of privileged blacks. Indeed, inequality within the black community has increased dramatically. Whereas in 1975 the top 20 per cent of African household income was eight times higher than the bottom 40 per cent, today this may be 40 times as great. Meanwhile, vast inequalities between whites and Africans remain: in 1995 whites earned on average more than seven times African incomes and five times coloured incomes. In 2009 a major study concluded that between 1995 and 2005 African incomes actually declined in real terms while the incomes of whites increased significantly. A notable cause is unemployment: today nearly 40 per cent of Africans are unemployed, while white unemployment is around 5 per cent.

These inequalities produce two sets of political problems. Policy measures such as affirmative action and black empowerment risk alienating whites, provoking emigration and export of capital. Given the inevitably slow rate of change, black frustration could express itself in mass protests, violence, and increasing support for populist and radical parties and movements.

Key points

- The history of the South African state, the political arithmetic of race and ethnicity, and the political economy all help to explain why there is neither a public demand for separate nationalities nor a set of elite-driven political strategies based upon ethnic/race mobilization.

- Historically, race and class have coincided in South Africa, dividing it into two nations. The emergence today of a rapidly expanding black middle class undermines this conception, delinking race and inequality.

- Strategies to address historical inequalities potentially could frustrate both blacks and whites.

South Africa has developed a remarkable tradition since 1989 of resolving apparently intractable problems through often tough negotiations. Part of the explanation lies in a mix of both history and personalities, which produced such remarkable leaders as Mandela, Oliver Tambo, and De Klerk.

Mandela took office with the recognition that his advanced years made a one-term presidency probable. He made reconciliation his central mission; his personality and message of one nation with many cultures gave the new democracy an encouraging beginning.

Mandela's successor, Thabo Mbeki, faced a more difficult task. If symbolism could inspire the first democratic government, the second administration had to deliver. Mbeki himself, and the ANC in general, remain wedded to the Mandela paradigm of the rainbow nation. Mbeki and now his successor Zuma say that all who live in South Africa have a claim to being Africans (see Box 20b.2). The ruling party remains wedded to the ideal of inclusivity. Personalities alone cannot explain the quality of leadership. Mandela and Mbeki came into power at a very favourable historical juncture. The implosion of Marxism and the failures of grand apartheid heralded the final discrediting of social engineering and macro-planning. The lesson from elsewhere in post-colonial Africa was that ambitious state-led projects to create nations by destroying indigenous customs and traditions were doomed to failure. When in exile key ANC leaders personally witnessed such failures.

Box 20b.2 The Zuma Saga

1997	Elected Deputy President of the ANC
1999	Appointed by President Mbeki to the post of Deputy President of South Africa
2001	Investigated by the state for possible corrupt involvement in a major arms deal
2005	Financial adviser and close friend Schabir Shaik found guilty of 'a generally corrupt relationship' with Zuma Mbeki fires Zuma from his government but not party position Zuma charged with corruption Turmoil in the ANC over the issue of presidential succession, with the ANC Youth League and COSATU strongly supporting Zuma for the presidency
2006	Zuma charged with rape but found not guilty Charges of corruption dropped but the Supreme Court of Appeal unanimously upholds Shaik's conviction Growing polarization within the ANC, with many Zulu traditionalists joining with the left to claim that Zuma is a victim of a plot
2007	Zuma elected ANC president at the party's national congress, in Polokwane
2009	Zuma becomes South Africa's president

In addition, the magnitude of the contained challenges of poverty, inequality, and HIV/AIDS was almost overwhelming. In a world of financial and economic globalization, encouraging multinational corporations to invest in South Africa seems imperative. South Africa's elites recognized very quickly that without rapid development the country faced increasing poverty and social unrest. Government leaders have had to repress their own personal prejudices and racial/ethnic attitudes in order not to alienate important domestic and foreign economic players.

On almost every major issue with cultural implications, the government has compromised rather than asserted its authority, in areas from minority rights of Afrikaners to traditional authorities and ethnic symbols. Of course, an ANC that is not threatened from the left or from Africanist forces can afford to be magnanimous. It has had the political space in which to adopt nation-building policies. It is impossible to predict how it would react to a genuine threat to its power base.

It is not inevitable that the South African miracle will continue. But the historical factors discussed above have created a common web of identities, in which a transcendent South African identity is prominent. Survey research confirms that although most South Africans have multiple identities, more than nine out of ten Africans are nonetheless proud to be called 'South Africans'.

Key points

- Individual leadership has contributed to shaping the conception of a non-racial and democratic South Africa.

- The process of nation-building is ongoing.

Conclusion

In contemporary South Africa, no important political party is asking the critically destructive question 'whose country is this?' The struggle cry 'one settler, one bullet' has disappeared from debate. Historically the two major threats to nation-building have come from the Afrikaner right and Zulu traditionalists. The former has almost totally disintegrated; Zulu alienation was largely ended when Zuma — a Zulu with considerable support in rural areas and amongst traditionalists — became president of ANC and then South Africa.

Class and nationality conflicts are not the same. There is clearly a possibility of a black populist party emerging from the poorest sections of the population. But although it might contain anti-white elements, it would be unlikely to challenge the core identity of the South African nation.

Although the electoral position of the ANC remains unchallenged with 65.9 per cent of the electorate supporting the party in the 2009 elections, this is deceptive. The firing of Mbeki from the presidency in 2008 created a party split: several prominent leaders defected, establishing a new party, Congress of the People (COPE). However, COPE lacked a credible policy and resources, and in the 2009 election won only 7.4 per cent of the vote. The future challenge to the ANC will more likely come from the class-oriented trade union movement under the banner of the Congress of Trade Unions (COSATU) and the SACP.

The other opposition parties are widely viewed as historically tainted by their history under apartheid. The Democratic Alliance, the official parliamentary opposition, is perceived to be a 'white' party notwithstanding significant coloured support. The IFP is seen as a party of Zulu traditionalists. Other new parties like the Independent Democrats also experience difficulties over resources and their image.

However, the ANC's broad church is under increased pressure as class and ethnic tensions grow. A new leader might be able to reduce these tensions, already aggravated by the leadership succession race. However, it is inevitable that the alliance will fragment, perhaps sooner rather than later.

South Africa's political leadership reflects the sophistication of the country's large First World economic and administrative systems. A recognition of the mutual dependency of all ethnic and racial communities and its importance is perhaps the most powerful factor shaping elite policies and attitudes. But South Africa continues to face major problems of race and class. Indeed, almost all problems—from HIV/AIDS to job creation—are exacerbated by high levels of inequality. The high levels of unemployment have also produced an explosion in crime, especially violent crimes such as armed robbery. Brutal attacks have taken place against foreigners (mostly Zimbabweans) competing for jobs with desperately poor local people, but crime and violence threaten all social sectors of society, especially the poor. These issues could yet destroy growth prospects by discouraging investment. The lack of a strong parliamentary opposition poses a real danger to the quality of democracy and creates both the temptation and the opportunity for corruption and authoritarianism in the ruling party. This was compounded by the centralizing tendencies of the Mbeki presidency. A weak parliamentary opposition makes policy conflicts and leadership choices within the ruling party very important. However, it could still be argued that nation-building and democracy remain fragile and robust politics could tear the nation apart. As Mandela frequently claimed, popular black opinion was frequently a good deal less moderate on economic and racial issues than the more broad-based ANC leadership. But these challenges should not be confused with the issue of nation-building. Whatever other problems South Africa faces, there is little debate over the definition of citizenship. The future debate will be over how this citizenship is to be given meaning.

? **Questions**

1. What key realities forced the ANC and the NP to begin the negotiation process?

2. What factors contributed to the decline of black versus white conflict during the transition to a non-racial democracy in South Africa?

3. How important in relative terms were internal and external factors in contributing to the end of apartheid in South Africa?

4. What are the key features of nation-building in South Africa?

5. How does the nature of the democratic system in post-apartheid South Africa relate to the principles of nation-building?

6. What are the implications of class and race coinciding in South Africa for the future of nation-building?

7. Is the alliance between the ruling ANC and its partners COSATU and the SACP an obstacle to the consolidation of democracy?

8. Does democracy in South Africa need a more competitive party system?

9. Can South African democracy continue to survive in a region dominated by turmoil, conflict, and poverty?

10. Can South Africa be considered the equal of so-called BRICs states?

→ Further reading

■ Butler, A. (2008), *Contemporary South African Politics*, 2nd edn (Basingstoke: Palgrave). An introduction to emerging patterns of economic, social, and political life in South Africa with reference also to its place in the regional and wider environment.

■ Daniel, J., Southall, R., and Lutchman, J. (eds) (2005), *State of the Nation: South Africa 2004–* (Cape Town: HSRC Press).

■ Giliomee, H. and Schlemmer, L. (1989), *From Apartheid to Nation Building* (Cape Town: Oxford University Press). Analysis of the roots of apartheid and of the possibilities for conflict resolution in South Africa as seen from the vantage point of the late 1980s, before the system reached the point of collapse.

■ Ishikawa, K. (1999), *Nation Building and Development Assistance in Africa: Different but Equal?* (New York: St Martin's Press).

■ Lodge, T. (2003), *Politics in South Africa: From Mandela to Mbeki* (Cape Town: David Philip, 2002; Bloomington, IN: Indiana University Press). Thirteen detailed essays on contemporary politics starting with the Mandela presidency.

■ Simkins, C. (1988), *The Prisoners of Tradition and the Politics of Nation Building* (Johannesburg: South African Institute of Race Relations).

■ Terreblanche, S. (2004), *A History of Inequality in South Africa 1652–* (Pietermartizburg: University of Natal Press). Historical examination of the economic exploitation of the indigenous peoples by settler groups. Argues that society in South Africa is more unequal than ever, with social democracy offering a more appropriate solution than 'neo-liberal democratic capitalism'.

■ Venter, A. and Landsberg, C. (2006), *Government and Politics in the New South Africa* (Pretoria: Van Schaik).

:// Web links

■ www.anc.org.za The website of the African National Congress.

■ www.elections.org.za The website of the South African Independent Electoral Commission.

■ www.gov.za The official website of the South African government.

■ www.hsrc.ac.za The site of the Human Sciences Research Council, Pretoria.

■ www.idasa.org.za The Institute for Democracy in South Africa (Cape Town), an independent, non-profit, public interest organization.

■ www.iol.co.za Independent Online, a South African news website.

■ www.mg.co.za The *Mail & Guardian* online.

- **www.nedlac.org.za**   The National Economic Development and Labour Council—'South Africa's primary institute for social dialogue'.
- **www.parliament.gov.za**   The site of the Parliament of South Africa.
- **www.polity.org.za**   Policy and Law Online News.

 Online Resource Centre

For additional material and resources, please visit the Online Resource Centre at:
www.oxfordtextbooks.co.uk/orc/burnell3e/

20c Iraq's Triple Challenge: State, Nation, and Democracy

Nadje Al-Ali and Nicola Pratt

 Chapter contents

- Introduction
- The Political Process
- The Post-Invasion Security Situation
- Human and Economic Development
- Conclusion

 Overview

This chapter examines the challenges facing Iraq since the US and UK invasion in March 2003, how these have been addressed, and with what effect for Iraqis. The chapter focuses on three areas: the political process; the security situation; and human and economic development. It also provides some information about the composition of the Iraqi population. This chapter examines how the political process has contributed to political and violent conflict. This, in turn, has limited the effectiveness of the Iraqi government. The poor security situation coupled with a weak central government has been a major obstacle to the reconstruction of Iraq's infrastructure, basic services, and economy, leaving many Iraqis disillusioned and impoverished and undermining democracy building. Figure 20c.1 is a map of Iraq and Box 20c.1 provides an overview of key dates in Iraq's history.

Figure 20c.1 Iraq

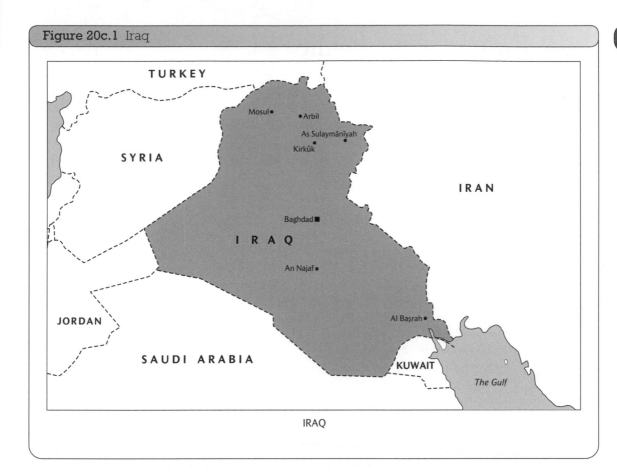

IRAQ

Box 20c.1 Key Dates in Iraq's History

1831–1914	Ottoman rule of Iraq
1914	British invasion of Iraq
1921	British install Faisal Ibn Husain al-Hashemi as first king of Iraq
1932	Independence formally granted to Iraq by League of Nations
July 1958	Military coup against monarchy and British presence; establishment of republic; 'Abdel Karim Qasim becomes prime minister
February 1963	Military coup against Qasim by Ba'thists and Arab nationalists
November 1963	President 'Abd al Salam 'Arif and allies sideline Ba'thists
July 1968	Ba'thist military coup
1972	Nationalization of oil industry
1974–75	Iraqi government puts down Kurdish revolt for greater autonomy in northern Iraq
July 1979	Saddam Hussein becomes president
1980	Following Iranian revolution, Iraqi government cracks down on Shi'a Islamist groups, including Da'wa party; expels 40,000 Shi'a to Iran
1980–88	Iran–Iraq War
1988	Iraqi government wages Al-Anfal campaign, which includes chemical warfare, in Kurdish areas in northern Iraq, resulting in up to 60,000 deaths
August 1990	Iraq invades and annexes Kuwait; UN imposes strict sanctions regime against Iraq (until April 2003)

January–February 1991	'Desert Storm'—US-led international military coalition forces Iraqi troops out of Kuwait through air bombardment of Iraq	8 March 2004	Signing of Transitional Administrative Law (laying out timeline for elections and constitution drafting)
March 1991	Iraqi government crushes popular uprisings in north and south of country; UN creates 'safe haven' in north; UN weapons inspections begin	28 June 2004	Abolition of CPA and IGC and handover of US power to Iraqi Interim Government
May 1992	Elections in Kurdish areas	Jan 2005	Elections to Iraqi Transitional National Assembly
July 1992	Kurdish Democratic Party (KDP) and PUK (Patriotic Union of Kurdistan) form Kurdish Regional Government but maintain respective areas of control	May–September 2005	Drafting of the Permanent Constitution
May–August 1994	Armed conflict between PUK and KDP	October 2005	Referendum on the Permanent Constitution
September 1998	Fighting between PUK and KDP ended by Washington Agreement	December 2005	Elections to the Council of Representatives
December 1998	'Operation Desert Fox'—air bombardment of Iraq by US and UK in retaliation for Iraq's non-cooperation with weapons inspectors	February 2006	Attack on the Al-Askari Mosque in Samarra escalates sectarian tensions and triggers widespread violence
March 2003	US and UK invade Iraq	September 2006	Constitutional Review Committee formed
April 2003	US forces enter Baghdad; toppling of Ba'th regime	January 2007	US President Bush announces the deployment of a further 30,000 US troops to Iraq (generally called 'the surge')
1 May 2003	Coalition Provisional Authority (CPA) replaces Office for Reconstruction and Humanitarian Assistance (ORHA)	February 2009	US President Obama announces that all US combat operations in Iraq will end by 31 August 31, 2010, and that he intends to fully withdraw all American troops by the end of 2011
23 July 2003	Establishment of 25-member Iraqi Governing Council (IGC) (responsible for advising CPA)	April 2009	UK withdraws all troops from Iraq
		March 2010	Elections to the Council of Representatives take place

Introduction

On 20 March 2003, in the face of significant opposition, the US, supported by the UK, launched a 'pre-emptive' military attack on Iraq in order to disarm the country of its weapons of mass destruction and end its support for international terrorism. (Since then, the evidence for these claims has been discredited by, amongst others, Zunes 2006.) The dictatorial regime of Saddam Hussein was toppled on 20 April 2003 and by 1 May 2003 US President George Bush declared the end of hostilities, designating Iraq a 'post-conflict' zone. Yet, in reality, Iraq was entering a new phase of conflict—one that has combined elements of anti-colonial insurgency with the 'new wars' of the post-Cold War period (see

Chapter 13). The violence has been a huge obstacle to Iraq's reconstruction. However, the way in which reconstruction has taken place, largely under the direction of the international community, seems to confirm the argument made by Edward Newman, Roland Paris, and Oliver Richmond (2009) that the liberal premises of post-conflict peacebuilding may exacerbate rather than mitigate conflict.

The Political Process

Before the invasion, the US administration of President George Bush had assumed that it would hand over power to an Iraqi government within a short time frame. By May 2003 it became clear to the US that this would not be straightforward and it was obliged to construct a political process that would establish a stable and legitimate Iraqi government without having planned for such a task. Following much discussion between the US and Iraqi political and religious leaders, with involvement from the UN, a plan for the introduction of democracy to Iraq was agreed according to which multi-party elections to a Transitional National Assembly (TNA) took place in January 2005. The TNA was responsible for drafting the permanent Constitution for the new Iraq. The Constitution was ratified by popular referendum in October 2005, despite significant opposition (see, amongst others, Hiltermann 2005). Nationwide elections to a new legislature—the Council of Representatives—took place in December 2005.

The political transition has faced a number of criticisms with regards to the timing of the elections, the Constitution-drafting process, and the involvement of the US.

With regards to electoral timing, there are criticisms that the political transition was too rapid, enabling the monopolization of the process by the former opposition in exile, which returned to Iraq with the US/UK invasion, in addition to the two main Iraqi Kurdish nationalist parties that had taken control of Northern Iraq after the Gulf War of 1990–91. Research suggests that only 26.8 per cent of the post-invasion ruling elite had stayed

in Iraq under Ba'thist rule (Marr 2006). The returning exiles were largely unknown to Iraqis and were viewed with suspicion (Melia and Katulis 2003). Yet these groups dominated the temporary governing institutions appointed by the US-led Coalition Provisional Authority (CPA) in 2003 and were able to use their access to state resources to dominate the election campaigning process. Meanwhile, two groups inside Iraq that organized resistance to the US occupation—the followers of Shi'a cleric, Muqtada al-Sadr, and local Sunni leaders—were excluded from these institutions. The US came under pressure to hold elections at the earliest possible moment as a means of appeasing its Iraqi allies as well as undercutting the anti-US insurgency (the elections failed to meet the latter objective).

Not only electoral timing, but also the nature of the electoral system poses difficulties in post-conflict situations. Following UN recommendations, the electoral system adopted for the elections of January 2005 was that of single constituency proportional representation ('closed list'). The advantages of this system was that it did not require the drawing of constituency boundaries (that is, all of Iraq was to be treated as one constituency) and, therefore, would allow elections to take place sooner. The threshold for nominating candidates was low in order to encourage independent candidates to compete in the elections, whilst the list system was supposed to encourage alliances between candidates and/or parties.

Rather than producing alliances and encouraging inclusivity, the January 2005 elections produced a TNA that was dominated by the Shi'i and Kurdish parties that had also been in the majority in the interim governing institutions. Those areas of the country in which voter turnout was low (that is, predominantly Sunni areas in which the insurgency was strongest and Sunni politicians boycotted the elections) ended up without any elected representation. In addition, violence and intimidation, by insurgents as well as militias linked to the major political parties, prevented candidates from the smaller (and more anti-sectarian parties) campaigning freely.

The results of the elections of January 2005 also determined the composition of the Constitution-drafting process in the summer of 2005, giving the Shi'a and Kurdish parties a free hand in writing the Constitution. Unelected Sunni representatives were brought into the process later on as the US realized that their marginalization would de-legitimize the Constitution. Yet, there was little consultation with civil society over the contents of the Constitution, as had been practised in other post-conflict countries.

US pressure on the drafting committee to finish writing the Constitution and put it to referendum by the originally agreed October 2005 deadline meant that difficult issues were not resolved by the drafting process and, consequently, continued to harm the political process. These may be summarized as struggles over the distribution of power and resources in Iraq. The main issues concern: the exploitation of oil resources and distribution of oil revenues; defining the boundaries of Iraqi Kurdistan; federal arrangements; some reversal in the de-Baathification law; and reintegration of former insurgent fighters, many of whom are Sunnis (for more details of these issues, see International Crisis Group 2008).

The design of political institutions has also proved ineffective in producing necessary political compromise. Attempts at power-sharing within the cabinet, through the allocation of ministerial posts to different parties in proportion to seats in Parliament, has been a source of antagonisms, greatly delaying the formation of governments following the January and December 2005 elections, and presenting obstacles to effective decision-making. This is not helped by the closed-list system of voting, which made politicians less accountable to the voters and more accountable to their parties.

Consequently, the legitimacy of the government is not evenly spread throughout Iraq. With the exception of the Kurdish region in the north and the Shi'a-dominated south of the country, many Iraqis feel that their lives have not improved and, in many cases, have deteriorated since the fall of the Ba'th regime (Page and Salih 2007; Juburi 2009; Lendman 2010).

The general lack of security is a major problem, in addition to the limited supply of basic services, such as electricity and clean water. This has led a significant number of Iraqis to view the political process negatively and to regard their political leaders with scepticism. Meanwhile, violence continues to affect parts of Iraq.

Key points

- Following the overthrow of the Ba'th regime, the US helped to establish a multi-party democracy through the organizing of elections and the drafting of a constitution. However, the timing and pace of this process has been criticized as failing to build peace and trust amongst Iraqis and their leaders.

- Elections did not engender widespread legitimacy of the government due to their limited inclusiveness.

- Power-sharing arrangements in government increased conflict between the major parties and made central government ineffective.

- The Constitution process failed to mediate conflicting interests between the major parties over how power and resources would be distributed in the new Iraq.

There are several explanations for the violence and lawlessness that broke out following the US-led invasion: poor planning and poor decisions by the US administration and CPA, anti-occupation resistance, and sectarianism. Several writers point to the failure of the US and its allies to plan sufficiently for the post-invasion situation (for example, Dodge 2005; von Hippel 2004). The Pentagon did not consider the general security of Iraq, believing that policing was not its duty. The failure of the US to curb general criminality, including widespread looting, in the early days following the fall of the Ba'th regime not only damaged US credibility in the eyes of Iraqis, but provided a fertile environment for the increase in violence against the occupation forces. The US exacerbated the security problem through 'two strategic miscalculations' (Diamond 2004): the 'de-Ba'thification' policy, which removed people from government on the basis of their membership of the Ba'th party—regardless of their past conduct; and the dissolution of the Iraqi army, which may have pushed some Iraqis towards the insurgency, whilst depriving the CPA of help in restoring order (ibid.). Coalition programmes to rebuild the army and police force through training new recruits met with multiple problems as they became overrun by sectarian militias, seeking to pursue their own agendas and take revenge on their opponents (Wong 2006).

Much of the violence in post-invasion Iraq has been directed against the US-led occupation, including the multinational forces, Iraqi police force, as well as Iraqi and foreign civilians working for Iraqi state institutions and foreign agencies. This insurgency is made up of different groups (mainly Iraqi, with some foreign fighters) that combine, to different degrees, patriotic and political Islamist motivations. Their aim is to eject US forces from Iraq and protect the unity of Iraq (International Crisis Group 2006). All have been able to take advantage of the lack of general security in the post-invasion period, as well as the availability of small weapons and links to Iraq's neighbouring countries (all of whom have a vested interest in how events unfold in Iraq). The surge in US troop numbers in 2008, combined with divisions between insurgent groups over tactics and the gradual withdrawal of US troops from urban areas led to a decrease in anti-US insurgency-related violence in early 2009.

In 2006–08, sectarian violence by different militia groups—either those linked to political parties in government, such as the Badr Brigade, Mahdi Army, and *Peshmerga* or neighbourhood militia—resulted in daily deaths on the streets of Baghdad and other cities in central Iraq, with individuals being summarily executed and their bodies dumped in sewage plants, irrigation canals, or even in the middle of the street (Abdul-Ahad 2006). The majority of killings occurred on a 'tit-for-tat' basis between Shi'i and Sunni groups. In 2009, sectarian violence shifted to Ninewa province in northern Iraq, as Arab and Kurdish nationalists competed for control of the province. Sectarian violence is largely linked to the failures of the political process, as well as the absence of a reconciliation process between Iraqis of different communities. More than 40,000 families have been displaced as a result of sectarian violence.

Whilst men constitute the majority of victims of violence, the lack of security impacts upon women in particular ways. Women have been abducted by gangs, raped, beaten, and their bodies dumped, or they are sold into prostitution. If they manage to survive the ordeal, the stigma attached to rape deters women from reporting cases of sexual violence, since they could be killed by their families in order to protect their 'honour'. As a result of the security situation, many women have stopped going to work or university and young girls have been pulled out of school (Box 20c.2).

Box 20c.2 The Iraqi Population

Iraq's population, like other countries in the Middle East, is very young, with about 40 per cent of the population under 15 years of age. Relatively high birth rates (about 4 per woman) as well as high death rates of adult males due to wars, violence, and political oppression over the past decades has created not only a young population but also a demographic imbalance between men and women. While no official statistics are available, estimates range between 55–65 per cent of the population is female. The more recent violence linked to the invasion and occupation of Iraq has increased this demographic imbalance both in terms of age and gender. During 2006 and 2007, over 90 civilians died violently every day (United Nations Assistance Mission for Iraq (UNAMI) 2007). Men have been the main victims of these violent deaths.

In terms of ethnic and religious make-up, Iraq has historically been diverse and mixed. Shi'a Arabs make up the majority of the Iraqi population, followed by Sunni Arabs, Kurds (predominantly Sunni), Iraqi Turkmen, Assyrian and Chaldean Christians, as well as Yazidis. Historically Iraq also had a large indigenous Jewish population, the majority of whom migrated from Iraq in the 1950s and 1960s. Arabic (Iraqi dialect) is the most widely spoken language, followed by Kurdish, Turkish, Aramaic, Syriac,

and Armenian. While the south has been predominantly Arab Shi'i and the north mainly inhabited by Sunni Kurds (there is also a minority of Shi'a Kurds called Faili Kurds) as well as Iraqi Turkmen, and Assyrian and Chaldean Christians, central and southern Iraq has always been very mixed. Sectarianism, especially in its overt violent form, is predominantly a post-invasion phenomenon as Iraqis have been living as neighbours and even inter-marrying for decades.

However, since Saddam Hussein's assumption of the presidency in 1979, divide-and-rule tactics increased sectarian divisions inside Iraq (Farouk-Sluglett and Sluglett 2003). There is no doubt that Kurds and Shi'a bore the brunt of the atrocities committed by the regime (see chronology of key events above). Yet, Sunni Arabs in political opposition parties and, increasingly, even within the Ba'th party, were also subjected to arrests, torture, and executions, as were members of other minorities such as Chaldeans, Assyrians, Turkmen, and Mandaeans if they were part of opposition groups or, at least, suspected to be so. Based on accounts of Iraqis of different ethnic and religious backgrounds, social class played a more important role in terms of defining social difference (Al-Ali 2007).

Key points

- The sources of violence in Iraq are multiple and include the insurgency against the US-led occupation, sectarian violence between militias representing different Iraqi communities and general lawlessness and organized crime.

- In 2008, the US managed to decrease the violence through tactical alliances with Sunni tribes and other, predominantly, Sunni insurgent groups

fighting al-Qaeda. However, 2009 saw another increase in violence, principally as a result of conflict between Arab nationalists and Kurdish nationalists over control of disputed territories.

- The causes of violence are the result of the power vacuum left by the fall of the Ba'th regime, coupled with problems in the political process and in rebuilding the security forces.

Human and Economic Development

The current post-invasion economic conditions and humanitarian crisis need to be addressed in the context of the legacy of the UN economic sanctions (1990–2003). Sanctions froze Iraqi financial assets abroad and banned all imports and exports, except for medical supplies and, 'in humanitarian circumstances, foodstuffs' (Graham-Brown 1999: 57). The most devastating effects of economic sanctions were dramatically increased child mortality rates, widespread malnutrition, deteriorating health care and general infrastructure, as well as widespread poverty and economic crisis. But sanctions also led to the breakdown of the welfare state, which had a disproportionate effect on women, who had been its main beneficiaries. It was clearly not the Iraqi regime but the majority of the Iraqi population that paid a heavy price for the sanctions regime. When asked on a US television news show, *60 Minutes*, in May 1996 what she thought about the reported deaths of half a million Iraqi children as a result of UN sanctions, then US ambassador to the UN, Madeleine Albright, famously answered: 'We think the price is worth it.'

Following the invasion, Iraq was in dire need of rebuilding and humanitarian assistance. However, reconstruction has been undermined by a range of factors. The first few years after the downfall of Saddam Hussein were punctuated by changes in state personnel. Many experienced civil servants were either dismissed from their jobs as part of the de-Baathification orders or fled the country as a result of the widespread violence. Meanwhile, staff were hired and fired with the changes in interim governments in the first few years following the invasion. In many cases, the political parties dominating national politics used state institutions to build up networks of patronage and nepotism, rather than hiring the most competent people to implement much-needed reconstruction (Al-Ali and Pratt 2009: 66).

Slow disbursement of funding due to the dire security situation as well as lack of expertise also contributed to undermine reconstruction. One obvious failure has been in relation to the rehabilitation of the healthcare system. Despite the dire need to rebuild the system after the war, less than US $1 billion of US funds was allocated to the health sector. Moreover, by April 2007, less than half of planned projects had been completed.

The CPA promoted neo-liberal economic reforms, such as liberalizing prices and removing subsidies, which often ran counter to economic reconstruction and human development (Herring and Rangwala 2006). The Brookings Institute estimates unemployment figures falling from an initial rate of 50–60 per cent in June 2003 to 25–40 per cent in 2007 (O'Hanlon and Campbell 2007: 40)—although anecdotal evidence would suggest that unemployment remains higher than this. Unemployment was exacerbated by de-Baathification and the dissolution of the military, which, it is estimated, put 430,000 individuals out of work. This has fuelled poverty as well as increasing potential recruits to armed groups.

In addition, it has emerged that there is a significant problem of corruption. A report by the international watchdog Transparency International claimed that Iraq could 'become the biggest corruption scandal in history' (2005: 87). The corruption ranges from petty bribery of civil servants, which was already increasingly common under the sanctions regime, to the misuse of millions of dollars of reconstruction funds due to a lack of oversight by donors. In addition to evidence of unaccounted expenditures, kickbacks, and bribes, there has also been criticism that large projects for the rehabilitation of essential services and infrastructure have been awarded to US contracting companies, which have often inflated costs and failed to achieve their objectives (Herring and Rangwala 2006; Al-Ali and Pratt 2009).

According to Oxfam (2007), 'eight million people are in urgent need of emergency aid'; that figure includes over 2 million who are displaced within the country, and more than 2 million refugees. According to the United Nations High Commissioner for Refugees (UNHCR) fact sheet for June 2009, over 90 per cent of Iraqis residing in Jordan and 86 per cent of those in Syria have no intention to return to Iraq in the foreseeable future (Iraq Inter-Agency Information and Analysis Unit (IAU) 2009). Poverty has become extremely widespread and endemic, with 54 per cent of Iraqis living on less than US $1 per day. Food is scarce and malnutrition rampant.

Twenty-two per cent of children (0–5 years old) are suffering from malnutrition (IAU 2009). While lawlessness, violence, and sectarianism have been subject to much debate, Iraq's humanitarian crisis has received less public attention. Yet, entire communities are extremely vulnerable and need immediate protection and humanitarian assistance. Paradoxically, humanitarian aid fell alarmingly during the past years despite the widespread evidence of an increase in need (Oxfam 2007: 5).

Key points

- Iraq already experienced a humanitarian crisis and deterioration of infrastructure due to 13 years of economic sanctions.

- While national security has been high on the agenda, human security has been neglected.

- Lack of expertise on behalf of the occupation forces, the promotion of neo-liberal economic reforms, widespread corruption, poor security, and the marginalization of local engineers and professionals have been obstacles to economic reconstruction and human development.

- The lack of proper reconstruction has contributed to the increase in violence.

- Iraqi society continues to experience a humanitarian crisis.

Conclusion

Since the toppling of the Ba'th regime in April 2003, Iraq has faced multiple challenges that are interconnected and not yet resolved. The political process, rather than reducing conflict, has contributed to increasing it due to its limited inclusiveness and failure to resolve key issues about the future of the country. Failures in the political process have fuelled sectarian violence and done little to reduce the insurgency. The ongoing violence, as well as the weakness and corruption of Iraq's government, have presented huge obstacles to the economic reconstruction process, thereby impacting upon human and economic development. Simultaneously, the failure of human and economic development feeds grievances against the government and the political process more generally, and provides potential recruits to violent groups.

The experience of Iraq illustrates the complex relationship between the political process, law and order, and socio-economic development (Burnell 2009). The Iraq case also underlines the significant role played by external actors, particularly the US, in shaping the post-conflict reconstruction process. US belief that democracy promotion and neo-liberal economic reforms were the panacea to Iraq's problems has yet to be proven correct.

? Questions

1. Why is Iraq often referred to as 'post-conflict'? Is this a useful term?

2. What are the sources of sectarian conflicts in Iraq? Does democracy help or hinder?

3. Why have Iraqis been unable to rebuild their country to the levels experienced before 1991?

4. To what degree has violence in Iraq since the US-led invasion been fuelled by inadequate socio-economic development?

5. How do Iraqis' views of the previous regime shape their views of how post-invasion Iraqi institutions should be crafted?

6. To what degree has the international community, including the US and Iraq's neighbours, played a positive role in the development of Iraq?

→ **Further reading**

■ Abdullah, T. (2003), *A Short History of Iraq* (London: Pearson-Longman). A concise, insightful and rigorous history of Iraq since the Iran–Iraq war by a well-respected Iraqi intellectual.

■ Al-Ali, N. (2009), *Iraqi Women: Untold Stories from 1948 to the Present* (London/New York: Zed Books). An accessible modern history of Iraqi women and Iraqi society more generally, based on oral histories as well as relevant historical sources.

■ —— and Pratt, N. (2009), *What Kind of Liberation? Women and the Occupation of Iraq* (Berkeley, CA: University of California Press). Exploration of political and socio-economic impacts of the US-led invasion on Iraqi women, as well as their participation in reconstruction.

■ Dodge, T. (2005), *Iraq's Future: The Aftermath of Regime Change*, Adelphi Paper No. 372 (London: International Institute for Strategic Studies). An incisive and insightful essay outlining the major challenges facing post-invasion Iraq.

■ Farouk-Sluglett, M. and Sluglett, P. (2003), *Iraq Since 1958: From Revolution to Dictatorship* (London/New York: I.B. Tauris). Provides the political, social, and economic background to some of the key developments in the post-invasion period.

■ Fawn, R. and Hinnebusch, R. (eds) (2006), *The Iraq War* (Boulder, CO: Lynne Rienner). A collection that explores the international dimensions of the invasion of Iraq, including the reasons why the US went to war and the impact of the war on international and Middle East regional relations.

■ Hashim, A. (2006), *Insurgency and Counter-Insurgency in Iraq* (London: Hurst and Company). An insider's account of the insurgency and the failure of US policy to defeat it.

■ Herring, E. and Rangwala, G. (2006), *Iraq in Fragments: the Occupation and its Legacy* (London: Hurst and Company). A detailed account of political developments in Iraq during the first few years following the invasion, focusing on the ways in which the US occupation shaped political outcomes.

■ Tripp, C. (2000), *A History of Iraq* (Cambridge: Cambridge University Press). A history of modern Iraq that focuses on the development of Iraqi state structures and their implications for how politics has played out. A very important background to understanding post-invasion developments.

:// **Web links**

■ www.iwpr.net/ Institute for War and Peace Reporting, Iraqi Crisis Report.

■ www.crisisgroup.org/ International Crisis Group reports on Iraq.

■ http://gulfanalysis.wordpress.com/ Iraq and Gulf Analysis: a periodic commentary on Iraqi politics by Reidar Visser of the Norwegian Institute of International Affairs.

 Online Resource Centre

For additional material and resources, please visit the Online Resource Centre at:
www.oxfordtextbooks.co.uk/orc/burnell3e

Military in Politics Versus Democratic Advance

21a Pakistan: The Military as a Political Fixture

David Taylor

* Overview

Since its creation in 1947, Pakistan has struggled to develop a system of sustainable democratic government, and for more than half its history the country has been under either military or quasi-military rule. From 1999 to 2008, the country was ruled by General Pervez Musharraf. This is in stark contrast to India, despite sharing the same colonial background. Ironically, the reintroduction of military rule has usually been welcomed in Pakistan as a relief from the factional disputes among the civilian political leaders and accompanying high levels of corruption. This chapter explains how and why the military continues to be central to the political process in Pakistan. Figure 21a.1 is a map of Pakistan and Box 21a.1 provides an overview of key dates in Pakistan's history.

Figure 21a.1 Pakistan

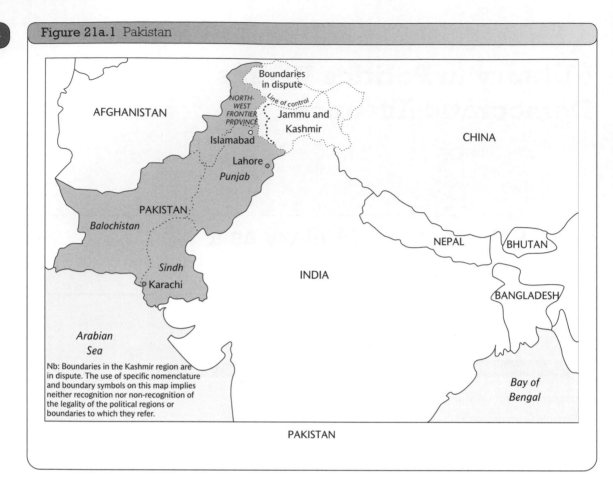

PAKISTAN

Box 21a.1 Key Dates in Pakistan's History

14 August 1947	Pakistan independence
11 September 1948	Independence leader Muhammad Ali Jinnah dies
February 1954	Pakistan joins a US-led cold war military alliance
March 1956	First constitution passed (but never fully implemented)
October 1958	General Ayub Khan carries out first military coup
February 1960	Ayub Khan elected president through indirect election
March 1961	Muslim Family Laws Ordinance
March 1962	New constitution passed
September 1965	Indecisive war with India
March 1969	Military coup led by General Yahya Khan deposes Ayub Khan

December 1970	Elections give absolute majority to East Pakistan-based Awami League
December 1971	Indian intervention brings about defeat of Pakistan army and separation of Bangladesh
January 1972	Zulfikar Ali Bhutto, leader of the Pakistan People's Party (PPP), becomes president (later prime minister)
April 1977	General election returns Bhutto to power but opposition launches agitation claiming the results were rigged
July 1977	Military coup led by General Zia-ul-Haq
April 1979	Bhutto executed
December 1984	Referendum gives Zia the basis to become president
February 1985	Elections held on non-party basis
November 1985	Constitutional amendments strengthen Zia's discretionary power
August 1988	Zia killed when his plane is blown up
November 1988	Elections return Benazir Bhutto to power
May 1998	Pakistan tests nuclear devices
October 1999	Military coup led by General Pervez Musharraf topples government of Nawaz Sharif
April 2002	Referendum makes Musharraf president
October 2002	Elections bring to power the Pakistan Muslim League (Quaid) (PML(Q)), a party sympathetic to Musharraf
December 2003	Constitutional changes strengthen Musharraf's position
March 2007	Chief Justice of Pakistan suspended
October 2007	Musharraf stands down as Army Chief in favour of General Ashfaq Kayani
December 2007	Benazir Bhutto assassinated
February 2008	Elections bring PPP back to power
August 2008	Musharraf resigns as President

Introduction: From Independence to State Breakup in 1971

Pakistan's military forces (principally the army, which numerically and politically has always been the key player) have dominated the country for most of its history since independence. This has meant not only political power but the pre-emption of a substantial share of economic resources. According to International Institute of Strategic Studies' estimates, defence expenditure was 3.16 per cent of gross domestic product (GDP) in 2007, a figure that has been declining in the past few years, but remains the highest in the region. Defence consumes almost as much as the total federal expenditure on social and economic development. The army is 550,000-strong, and many more depend on the army directly or indirectly for employment. Internationally, the image of Pakistan as a **garrison state**, although acceptable at times to the USA, has often created difficulties, for example the country's suspension from the Commonwealth after the 1999 military coup until 2004. A garrison state is a state maintained by military power and, in some definitions, is a state organized to secure primarily its own need for military security.

The dominance of the military in Pakistan has been explained in different ways. Some note the way in which Pakistan inherited a strong army from the colonial state; others see it as an aspect of a social order still dominated by landowning groups. The two arguments come together in the fact that the army is recruited very heavily from the Punjab—the most populous of the country's four provinces and with a strong representation of landlord politicians—although the officer corps is increasingly coming from more middle-class families. The army thus tends to share a strong sense of Pakistan as a unitary state. Regional and international factors are also important, with Pakistan's long-running conflict with India over Kashmir and the cold war both influential.

Pakistan inherited its state structures from the colonial period. The Indian army played a key role in sustaining British power, and in turn the government took steps to ensure the soldiers' loyalty, for example through generous treatment in the allocation of land and through the racially based classification of Indians into martial and non-martial groups. The Punjab and to a lesser extent the North-West Frontier Province (renamed Khyber Pakhtunkhwa in April 2010) were the main areas of army recruitment.

When British India became independent in 1947, and was simultaneously divided into the two successor states of India and Pakistan, the armed forces were similarly divided. As a result of previous recruitment policies, Pakistan got more than its proportionate share of soldiers. It also inherited a social structure in which control of land and of the people who worked the land was the single most important basis of political power. Political parties were weak.

At first the unchallenged authority wielded by Muhammad Ali Jinnah, who had led the Pakistan movement from its inception, kept tensions between provinces and between locals and newcomers in check. However, after his death in 1948, the country lacked political leadership of national standing. While popular leaders emerged in the eastern wing of the country (now Bangladesh), in the west (from where the army was recruited), provincial politicians battled for local control with little regard to national issues.

At the same time as Pakistan was facing difficulties in establishing stable structures of government, there was a belief that India's leaders had agreed to the partition of British India grudgingly and would miss no opportunity to sabotage its new neighbour. The distrust soon found a focus in the conflict over the princely state of Jammu and Kashmir. As a Hindu ruler with a powerful Hindu minority dominating the upper ranks of the bureaucracy, but with an overall Muslim majority, the Maharaja, Hari Singh, prevaricated over to which new state to affiliate. War ensued between India and Pakistan, until a truce under United Nations auspices was negotiated in August 1948.

The weakness of Pakistan's political institutions and perceived need for security against a more powerful India meant the army as an institution became increasingly important in Pakistan's public life and took on a prominent political role. The first Pakistani Commander-in-Chief of the army, General Ayub Khan, became minister of defence for a period in 1954 and played a key role in bringing Pakistan into the US-led military alliance system that was constructed in Asia in the early 1950s. A complementary development was the assertion of the role of the bureaucracy as a guardian of the state in the absence of strong national leadership and in the face of challenges to the dominance of the established social order, in particular of the Punjab. While not identical, the social base of the army and the bureaucracy overlapped, and their perceptions of Pakistan were similar.

Under the Constitution that had been adopted in 1956, Pakistan's first parliamentary elections were due in 1958. To avoid the accession to power of H. S. Suhrawardy, an East Bengal-based politician, the then president, Iskander Mirza, declared martial law. Shortly after, Ayub Khan assumed political control, sending Mirza into exile. Ayub Khan was anxious to ensure his own formal legitimacy in terms of Pakistan's legal institutions, and was able to obtain a judgment from the Supreme Court authorizing his rule. He also conducted a campaign against the political leaders he had displaced. Hundreds of politicians were disqualified from further political activity, on the grounds of corruption. This was complemented by an analysis of the situation that seemed to draw both on colonial assumptions and on some of the contemporary thinking in the USA, for example by the political scientist Samuel P. Huntington, about economic and political development. Pakistan was seen as a society that needed firm leadership and guidance from the top if it was to move along a trajectory towards healthy national development.

Building on this analysis, Ayub Khan initiated what was called the Basic Democracies system, which brought around 80,000 local leaders and notables into politics on a non-party basis. As well as electing a National Assembly, they also formed an electoral college for the presidency, and in 1960 Ayub Khan was duly elected president. This enabled him to dispense with martial law and to formulate a new Constitution for the country—duly brought into effect in 1962. This defined Pakistan as a progressive Muslim state, pursuing policies that reflected a dynamic interpretation of religious values. In line with this, Ayub Khan's government in 1961 issued the Family Laws Ordinance, which introduced reforms in the area of marriage and divorce, significantly improving the rights of women. Although Ayub Khan eventually permitted the re-establishment of political parties in order to provide a safety valve, and in fact placed himself at the head of one of them so as to attract many of the local leaders who had dominated rural politics in the past, he was unable to cope with the increasing alienation of East Bengal, and in basic democrat and presidential elections held in 1964–65 he was unable to gain a majority there.

Growing discontent in both parts of the country, especially after an abortive attempt to seize Kashmir led to war with India in September 1965, paved the way for the then army chief, General Yahya Khan, to displace Ayub Khan in March 1969 and declare a fresh period of martial rule. He promised direct parliamentary elections, which eventually took place in December 1970. East Pakistan, which held a demographic majority, voted overwhelmingly for the Awami League, led by Sheikh Mujibur Rahman; Zulfikar Ali Bhutto, a former protégé of Ayub Khan who had established his own Pakistan People's Party (PPP) in 1967, won convincingly in the west but on a smaller scale. Sheikh Mujibur Rahman's insistence on his right to the prime ministership and on his power to write a constitution that would give full autonomy to the east was rejected by the army and West Pakistan's politicians, and in March 1971 the army deployed force to assert the authority of the (West) Pakistan state. Indian intervention led to a decisive military defeat for Pakistan, providing the opportunity for Bhutto to take over in the west, and ushering in the creation of Bangladesh in the east.

> **Key points**
>
> - Pakistan has been dominated by the army since its creation in 1947. Social and political factors, as well as the cold war context, have contributed to this situation.
>
> - Pakistan's state structures derive from the colonial period; the colonial army was recruited heavily from the areas of British India that became Pakistan in 1947, especially the Punjab.
>
> - Because conflict with India, especially over Kashmir, has fostered insecurity, the army has been able to place its needs and requirements at the centre of political life.
>
> - Ayub Khan, Pakistan's first military ruler following the 1958 coup, attempted to develop an alternative political structure based on mobilization of rural leadership.
>
> - The unsuccessful 1965 war with India ultimately led to Ayub Khan's downfall. The failure of his successor, General Yahya Khan, over Bangladesh led to his displacement by Zulfikar Ali Bhutto.

DAVID TAYLOR

The Bhutto era represented an attempt at a politics of **populism**, but by using the apparatus of the state to achieve his ends, Bhutto remained caught within its folds. The army as an institution remained a central actor, being used in 1974 to put down an internal rising in the province of Balochistan. The personalization of power by Bhutto alienated many army officers. In 1977, he faced a political crisis largely of his own making when he was accused by the opposition parties of rigging elections. Following three months of continuous agitation in the main cities, the army, headed by General Zia-ul-Haq (whom Bhutto had promoted ahead of more senior generals in the belief that he had no political ambitions) intervened and called for fresh elections.

Bhutto's evident popularity among his supporters persuaded General Zia to have him re-arrested and the elections postponed. Bhutto was arraigned on murder charges and executed in April 1979, although the judicial decision was not unanimous. At the same time, Zia began to take steps to reconstruct Pakistan's institutions in a generally Islamic direction, with the support of a growing number of officers who were taking a prominent role in helping those Afghan forces that were fighting against the Soviet-backed government in Kabul during the 1980s. Other officers too held the civilian politicians in general, and the PPP in particular, in contempt, and had no difficulty with the continuation of military rule.

During the early 1980s, Zia pressed ahead with the Islamization of the country's institutions on several fronts, for example introducing changes to the banking system to eliminate the payment of interest. One major series of initiatives that attracted worldwide attention was a redefinition of the legal position of women. Their standing as witnesses in legal cases was reduced to half that of men, and rules on pre- and extra-marital sexual relations made more punitive in ways that especially disadvantaged women. In 1985, Zia felt strong enough to end the period of direct martial rule, reintroducing a heavily modified Constitution that gave the president sweeping discretionary powers. This had been preceded by a referendum that was widely regarded as bogus, but which enabled him to claim a five-year term as president. Elections held under the new Constitution on a non-party basis then allowed the choice of a traditional landlord politician, Mohammad Khan Junejo, as the prime minister. Nearly three years later, Zia dismissed the prime minister, claiming that Islamization was proceeding too slowly. Zia seemed set to continue to rule through a civilian facade but with strong presidential powers retained by himself, until in August 1988 he was killed by a bomb planted on his plane. Many theories have been advanced, but it is still not certain who the perpetrators were.

After Zia's death the elections brought back to power the PPP under Bhutto's daughter Benazir, and she alternated in office with the other major civilian political leader, Nawaz Sharif, whose power base lay in the Punjab. In 11 years there were four elections but throughout effective power was in fact shared between the political leadership, the army, and sections of the civilian bureaucracy. This uneasy arrangement produced constant difficulty. In 1993, a deadlock between the president, Ghulam Ishaq Khan, a former senior civil servant who had been close to Zia, and the then prime minister Nawaz Sharif, was eventually resolved through the intervention of the army chief, who insisted that both resign prior to new elections under a neutral, caretaker prime minister. Nawaz Sharif returned to power in 1997, and succeeded in amending the Constitution to restrict the powers of the president, which had been abused by both Ghulam Ishaq Khan and his successor. He also forced General Jehangir Karamat, the army chief, to resign in 1998 and appointed as his successor General Pervez Musharraf, who was born in India and had come to Pakistan as a refugee at independence. Musharraf reasserted the right of the army to take part in policymaking by unilaterally embarking on a military adventure in the Kargil district of Kashmir in 1999. The fighting — the most intense since 1971 — was brought to an end through US diplomatic pressure and without any gains by Pakistan. This left the army and the government deeply suspicious of each other. In October, General Musharraf launched a military coup to prevent his own dismissal.

Key points

- Bhutto's failed attempt at populist politics, bypassing the military, triggered a coup by General Zia-ul-Haq in 1977 and his own execution in 1979.
- Zia's political strategy relied heavily on presenting himself and the army as the guardians of Pakistan's Islamic goals: he retained sweeping powers as head of state but in 1985 introduced changes to the Constitution enabling restoration of the political process.

- Following Zia's assassination, the period 1988 to 1999 saw unstable civilian governments alternating between Benazir Bhutto and Nawaz Sharif, with the army and the bureaucracy continuing to exercise power behind the scenes.
- A failed military adventure over Kashmir in 1999 ultimately generated a further military coup led by General Pervez Musharraf.

General Musharraf's Rule from 1999 to 2008

Coming after a period of instability, Musharraf began with substantial popular support. He promised action against the more notoriously corrupt politicians and bureaucrats and seemed in tune with the aspirations of many of Pakistan's urban population for a more liberal lifestyle. The question he had to resolve, however, was how quickly to return to civilian rule while maintaining his own and the army's decisive power to intervene in areas that were deemed critical to national interests.

Musharraf's initial political move was to hold a referendum to make himself president, but the exercise was seen as manipulated and lacking legitimacy. In another echo of previous military rulers' strategies, Musharraf also increased devolution of administration to the local level and matched it with non-party elections to local councils. Elections later in 2002 were fought on a party basis, but the leaders of the two main parties, who were both abroad, were unable to participate directly. A breakaway faction of the Pakistan Muslim League (PML(Q)),

known popularly as the 'King's Party', was able, with strong official support, to win a plurality of seats and form a government. In advance of the elections, Musharraf introduced the Legal Framework Order (LFO) (echoing Yahya Khan's innovation), which strengthened the power of the president and sought to establish a National Security Council, in which the military chiefs would have representation. The constitutional status of the LFO was unclear, and for the whole of 2003 the opposition brought the National Assembly to an effective halt over the issue, questioning Musharraf's entitlement to remain as army chief while also posing as a civilian president. At the end of 2003 a deal was struck with the main Islamist parties to allow an amended LFO to be adopted, but, given Musharraf's own liberal leanings, this was a tactical deal (for the Islamists, the quid pro quo was a clear run for their government in the North-West Frontier Province) and served only to heighten the contradictions in his efforts to remain above civilian politics. It also acted as a brake on his efforts to reform the law on sexual offences, in which regard only a very modest measure could be passed in 2006.

In March 2007 Musharraf took the dramatic step of suspending the Chief Justice of Pakistan, allegedly because of abuse of power, but in reality for fear that the Supreme Court would rule against him on key political and constitutional issues. The decision provoked nationwide protests led by the lawyers, and Musharraf's position began to weaken. In July the Chief Justice was reinstated and in October Musharraf appointed General Ashfaq Kayani to succeed him as army chief, thus conceding a key demand of his opponents. In November, however, he again imposed a state of emergency, enabling him to once more dismiss the Chief Justice. The assassination of Benazir Bhutto at the end of the year, apparently by Islamist militants, changed the political landscape yet again and the PPP won the elections that were eventually held in February 2008. In August Musharraf was forced to resign and Benazir Bhutto's widower, Asif Ali Zardari, succeeded him. One major factor in this decision was the evident desire by Kayani to withdraw the army from direct political involvement.

One major reason for Musharraf's long survival was that he enjoyed the political and financial support of the USA, even though the latter clearly saw India as an emerging major power. In return, he supported US actions in Afghanistan, including incursions into Pakistani territory along the frontier, where the Taliban and other groups enjoy significant local support. While he constantly faced pressure to do more, substantial sections of public opinion resented subordination to a US agenda that is widely perceived as anti-Muslim. Towards the end of his period in office, the USA put increasing pressure on him for a negotiated handover of power to civilian parties.

Another reason for his survival was the relatively strong performance of the economy, buoyed by increased inflows of funds both from official donors, following Pakistan's strategic importance

in the wake of 9/11, and from diaspora Pakistanis. Inflation was brought under control and industrial production picked up, so that significant real growth in the economy became evident. However, poverty levels remained stubbornly high, and Pakistan failed to match the economic transformation taking place in India.

While initially staunch in his support for Pakistan's long-standing positions on Kashmir, at the beginning of 2004 Musharraf set in motion fresh talks with India over Kashmir, partly in response to pressure from the international community, and perhaps partly in the hope that a breakthrough would win back much of the civilian electorate. However, these talks and negotiations moved very slowly, largely because of India's reluctance to make matching concessions, and eventually proved fruitless. Nevertheless, the fact that Musharraf was able to initiate them at all demonstrates that in some circumstances military-led governments have greater freedom of manoeuvre.

A key challenge that Musharraf was unable to settle was the rising tide of Islamist militancy. This had taken firm root in the 1980s, when during the Zia period militants had been encouraged to fight against Soviet forces in Afghanistan. A network of religious schools (*madrasahs*) had developed, which trained a generation of fiercely committed young men willing to sacrifice themselves in a fight against what were perceived as oppressive and un-Islamic regimes. While Islamic militancy in itself received only a limited degree of support from Pakistani society, Musharraf's room for manoeuvre was restricted by the way in which the issue became embroiled in the realpolitik of Afghanistan and Kashmir. Army intelligence agencies, notably the Inter-Services Intelligence (ISI), had long maintained contacts with militant groups. In July 2007 the government was forced to take strong action to close down a mosque in the capital Islamabad that had become closely associated with an Islamist group. Fierce fighting led to over fifty deaths.

Key points

- Musharraf enjoyed substantial support for his coup, seen as promising relief from corrupt and incompetent civilian governments.
- Musharraf responded to 9/11 by giving full support to the USA, although this was unpopular with some sections of the population.
- Like his predecessors, Musharraf sought to discredit existing political leaders and to build a party loyal to himself; he amended the Constitution to increase his discretionary powers as president.
- Musharraf's popular support declined steadily; he tried to divide the political parties but in the end was unable to maintain his juggling act.

Conclusion

Zia was in power for 11 years; Ayub Khan for ten; and Musharraf for nine. The three military rulers differed in social background and personal agenda, yet each followed similar strategies to stay in power. Rather than trying to rule in a wholly despotic and arbitrary manner, they have all sought to ground themselves in Pakistan's history and institutions.

A discourse on politics has developed that is shared not just by the military but to some degree by other sections of society. Politics as it has commonly been practised is conceived as an aspect of the 'feudal' phase of Pakistani history. To break its hold and to usher in a new phase (the precise lineaments of which have been specific to each leader), the army may need to intervene to help the process along. The 'ordinary' Pakistani is a key figure in this discourse, and is brought into politics through carefully tailored institutions from which party politics are excluded, at least on the surface. At the same time, politicians are seen as people who may for their own selfish reasons betray Pakistan's key national interests, particularly over Kashmir. The acquisition by Pakistan of nuclear weapons in the late 1990s, carefully guarded by the army, has heightened the sense that the armed forces have a unique role to play in the survival of the state.

While the army leadership projects itself as the guardian of the national interest, it is often seen by others as primarily concerned with its own interests. Army officers are often appointed to senior administrative positions after retirement and are given preferential treatment in many different areas, most significantly the allocation of prime rural and urban land. Nothing has changed in this respect in recent years. A further issue is the extent to which the army is committed to preserving the existing social structure. There has so far been little desire to challenge the status quo, either in terms of property ownership or the power of the central government versus the provinces.

A key challenge to the army that has developed since the beginning of the 2000s is the initiation of internal security operations against Islamic militant groups who have, since the end of 2007, fought under the banner of the Tehrik-i-Taliban Pakistan. The losses the army is suffering in these campaigns, and its evident difficulty in bringing the insurgency under control are themselves worrisome, but more serious is the risk they pose to the internal coherence of the army itself. It is evident that some members of the armed forces are sympathetic to Islamist ideas, and also resent the actions of the Americans in Iraq and Afghanistan, especially the targeting of militants on Pakistani territory. The possibility of a coup within the army (as against the pattern to date where all four coups have been carried out by the army as an institution) cannot be ruled out.

Repeated cycles of political instability and military intervention have led some army leaders to the belief that Pakistan cannot sustain a political system that does not give a major role to the armed forces. Turkey is often cited as a parallel example. The weakness of civil society and of the civilian political process and the special security needs not only of Pakistan itself but of the Muslim world more gen-

erally are seen as justifications for this view. Some civilians share this view but many more reject it, especially in the smaller provinces. However, until there has been a lengthy spell of civilian rule under a prime minister or president who has the skills to wean the army away from its current set of assumptions without provoking a backlash, the present situation is likely to continue. Circumstances in Pakistan are not likely to lead to this outcome in the immediate future, and further direct or indirect military intervention in politics remains a constant possibility.

? Questions

1. What policies did the colonial state pursue that prepared the way for recurrent military intervention in politics after independence?

2. To what extent was the cold war a factor in facilitating the dominance of the army in Pakistan?

3. What analysis do army leaders make of Pakistan's politics, and how do they see their own role within it?

4. Compare and contrast the political strategies of Generals Ayub Khan, Zia-ul-Haq, and Pervez Musharraf.

5. What have been the consequences for Pakistani society of prolonged periods of military dominance?

6. What has been the impact of military rule on Pakistan's relations with India, especially in the light of the dispute over Kashmir?

7. How helpful is the idea of a 'garrison state' in understanding the place the military occupies within Pakistan's political and social structures?

8. Explore the contribution that Pakistan makes to our understanding of the relation between military rule and social change.

9. What factors constrain the Pakistan army's ability to repress Islamist militancy?

10. Is Pakistan likely to see further military interventions in the future, and if so, why?

→ Further reading

■ Ali, T. (1983), *Can Pakistan Survive? The Death of a State* (Harmondsworth: Penguin Books). Highly critical analysis by a leading journalist and political activist.

■ Aziz, M. (2007), *Military Control in Pakistan: The Parallel State* (London: Routledge). A recent work that focuses on the extent to which the military intervene to protect their institutional interests.

■ Cloughley, B. (2000), *A History of the Pakistan Army: Wars and Insurrections* (Karachi: Oxford University Press Pakistan). A history of the army that details its role at various stages of Pakistan's history. The author has known many of the key personalities involved.

■ Cohen, S. P. (2002), *The Pakistan Army* (Karachi: Oxford University Press). Based on extensive interactions with the Pakistan army's leadership, this carefully documented analysis of the history and development of the army is coupled with a discussion of its political attitudes.

■ Dewey, C. (1999), 'The Rural Roots of Pakistani Militarism', in D. A. Low (ed.), *The Political Inheritance of Pakistan* (Basingstoke: Macmillan), 255–83. The author is a historian of the Punjab, and relates the persistence of military influence to the army's embeddedness in the structures of power in rural society.

■ Jaffrelot, C. (ed.) (2002), *A History of Pakistan and its Origins* (London: Anthem Press). An up-to-date collection on different aspects of Pakistan's history and social structure. The contributions by the editor are especially valuable.

■ Jalal, A. (1990), *State of Martial Rule: The Origins of Pakistan's Political Economy of Defence* (Cambridge: Cambridge University Press). A detailed study of the process by which the Pakistan army became central to the Pakistan state. The author locates internal processes within the general cold war context.

■ Musharraf, P. (2006), *In the Line of Fire* (London: Simon and Schuster). General Musharraf's own (ghostwritten) account of his life and times.

■ Rizvi, H.-A. (1986), *The Military and Politics in Pakistan* (Lahore: Progressive Publishers). Detailed study of civil–military relations by a leading Pakistani scholar.

■ Siddiqa, A. (2007), *Military Inc.: Inside Pakistan's Military Economy* (London: Pluto Press). This work by a Pakistani political scientist caused a huge stir in the country when first published. It documents and analyses the extent of the Pakistan army's involvement in the civilian economy.

■ Talbot, I. (1998), *Pakistan: A Modern History* (London: Christopher Hurst). The most reliable of recent histories of the country. Talbot has a strong sense of the provincial roots of contemporary Pakistan.

Web links

■ http://countrystudies.us/Pakistan/ A detailed US-based compilation of information on the history, economy, society, and politics of Pakistan.

■ www.sacw.net/ The South Asia Citizens Web is an independent space that provides exchanges of information between and about citizen initiatives in South Asia.

Online Resource Centre

For additional material and resources, please visit the Online Resource Centre at: www.oxfordtextbooks.co.uk/orc/burnell3e/

21b Nigeria: Building Political Stability with Democracy

Stephen Wright

  Chapter contents

- Introduction
- The Political Economy of Oil
- Social Change, Democracy, and Instability
- Regional Influence in Foreign Policy
- Conclusion

  Overview

Since independence from Britain in 1960, Nigeria has struggled to maintain stability in the face of significant ethnic, regional, and religious divisions. Military governments ruled the country for almost thirty years, but there is hope that the successive civilian governments of President Olusegun Obasanjo (1999–2007) and President Umaru Yar'Adua (2007–May 2010) have consolidated democracy, even though significant societal problems remain. Despite these, Nigeria has continued to promote a forceful foreign policy, shaped by its demographic size as Africa's largest country, as well as by its significant petroleum exports. Figure 21b.1 is a map of Nigeria and Box 21b.1 provides an overview of key dates in Nigeria's history.

Figure 21b.1 Nigeria

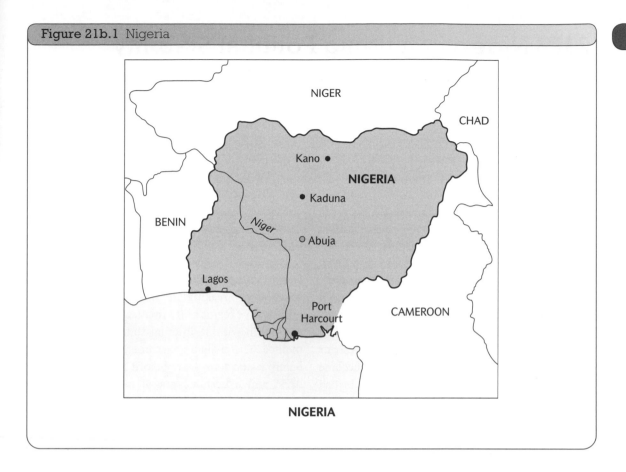

NIGERIA

Box 21b.1 Key Dates in Nigeria's History

1914	Britain pulls together various territories into the colony of Nigeria
1960	Independence from Britain
1966	Two military coups end the first civilian republic
1967	The start of the three-year civil war over Biafran secession
1976	Murtala Muhammed assassinated, and Olusegun Obasanjo takes over as military head of state, supervising a transition to civilian rule
1979	Second civilian republic inaugurated, under Presi ShehuShagari
1983	Military coup on New Year's Eve ushers in 16 years of military rule
1985	Ibrahim Babangida takes over in palace coup, and postpones multiple attempts to return to civilian government
1993	Moshood Abiola wins the presidency, but elections annulled by Babangida; later that year Sani Abacha seizes power in a coup

1999	Following the death of Abacha in 1998, a new transition is undertaken, which elects Obasanjo to the presidency, and a new civilian republic begins
2003	Obasanjo re-elected for a further term amid allegations of electoral irregularities
2007	Umaru Yar'Adua elected president in a disputed election; the first successful civilian transfer of power
2010	Vice-President Goodluck Johnson succeeds to the presidency, following Yor' Adua's death

Introduction

The West African state of Nigeria offers an interesting case study of a country that has struggled since its independence with chronic political instability, resulting in the longest period of unbroken civilian rule being the most recent since 1999. Prior to colonial rule, the territory that was to become Nigeria consisted of numerous empires, but British colonists gradually absorbed these into three administrative regions. In turn, these regions were amalgamated into the colony of Nigeria in 1914, although each maintained a strong degree of identity and separation. Tensions between the three regions deepened in the 1950s, as ethnicity became a political vehicle in the jostling for power in a post-independent Nigeria. This struggle to manage ethnic tensions has been a constant feature and has significantly contributed to the country's instability.

Despite efforts to ease ethnic and religious tensions, notably by breaking up the three powerful administrative regions into smaller units—eventually ending up with 36 internal states—instability remained. The civilian government installed in 1979 barely lasted four years before the military swept back, and a despotic era of military rule lasted until 1999, when the civilian government of President Olusegun Obasanjo (himself a former military head of state) was elected to office. His re-election in 2003 was considered a hopeful sign of a maturing democratic system, as was the election of President Umaru Yar'Adua in 2007. Obasanjo had attempted to change the Constitution in 2006 to allow him to contest a third term in office, but was defeated by the Senate. All this is indicative of the challenge of building democracy in a severely fractured state.

Instability

The British installed a parliamentary democracy in Nigeria prior to their departure in 1960, but the system could not function effectively in the highly combative political environment. The first of many military *coups d'état* took place in January 1966, sweeping the civilians from office. A second coup later in the year slid the country towards a brutal civil war between 1967 and 1970, and civilian government was not allowed to return again until 1979.

Regional influence

Nigeria's regional prominence stems largely from two key factors: population and petroleum. Ethnicity politicizes the census process and makes an accurate headcount problematic, but the population is estimated to be around 150 million, a little under one-sixth of the continent's total population, and places the country as the world's 15th largest. Geological good fortune enabled Nigeria to be a prominent producer and exporter of oil and gas, making Nigeria's the largest economy in the region, and one of the largest in Africa. Currently, Nigeria stands as the world's 15th largest producer of oil, and the sixth largest in the Organization of Petroleum Exporting Countries (OPEC), with 4 per cent of the world's proven reserves. Nigeria has been the leading member of the Economic Community of West African States (ECOWAS) since its founding in 1975, and has often taken up leadership causes on behalf of the continent as a whole. Its demographic and economic prowess has assured close foreign policy linkages with countries outside Africa, notably the United States, Britain, and the European Union, with China also becoming an important oil trading partner since 2005.

> ## Key points
>
> - British colonization created a 'new' country of Nigeria, the people of which had lived separately prior to colonial rule.
> - Nigeria's population is the largest in Africa.
> - Nigeria is the leading country in the 15-member ECOWAS, and its influence is based on population size and oil revenues.

The Political Economy of Oil

Transformation of the economy

At independence, agriculture dominated the economy. The British had created export production of single crops for each region—groundnuts in the north, palm oil in the south-east, and cocoa in the south-west. Oil production, focused in south-eastern Nigeria, began in earnest in the 1960s and proved to be a contributing factor in the country's civil war. Once peace was attained, oil production accelerated rapidly, contributing to an economic boom in the 1970s, helped significantly by soaring prices after 1973. Agriculture quickly lost its prominence as oil revenues contributed more than 90 per cent of export revenues, a figure that has remained fairly constant ever since. Massive development schemes were started, including dams, roads, airports, universities, and hospitals, but some of these projects were of more political significance than economic benefit.

The combination of oil wealth and a large consumer population led to considerable foreign investment. By the end of the 1970s, Nigeria was widely touted as the champion of Africa, both in diplomatic and economic terms, and utilized this status to pursue important foreign policy initiatives, notably working for the 'liberation' of Zimbabwe and South Africa, and attempting to represent the views of developing countries in their call for a transformed global political economy.

Elusive development

The hopes and ambitions of the 1970s were undermined after 1980 by a series of events. The most important of these was the glut of oil in world markets, which contributed to the collapse of Nigerian revenues. An economy distorted by the oil bonanza was now undermined by the rapid bust of the market. Development projects quickly became expensive white elephants, and import dependence racked up large national debt. Oil revenues had not only been squandered, but were siphoned off to corrupt civilian and military elites, taking billions of dollars out of the development process. The governments of the 1980s, civilian and military, were forced to relinquish their outspoken role in world politics and take up the very different challenge of seeking structural adjustment funding and debt support from the World Bank and International Monetary Fund.

The 1990s was arguably the most difficult decade in Nigeria's political and economic development. Continuing low oil revenues served to debilitate social and human development. Infrastructure and transport crumbled, despite efforts at privatization and liberalization of critical sectors. External debt rose to a level of US$34 billion, then the largest in Africa. Compounding the problem was the country's military leader between 1993 and 1998, General Sani Abacha, whose brutal rule led to Nigeria's ostracism from most international bodies.

The election of Obasanjo in 1999 helped to stabilize the economic environment. His attempt to crack down on corruption brought some limited success. Obasanjo was able to engage the international financial community, paying down the country's debt considerably, as well as facilitating large investment inflows into the oil and gas sectors.

of which feel cheated out of a greater share of resources. These actions have reduced Nigerian oil production by 20–40 per cent, with an average daily production of 2.1 million barrels, so undermining revenue. Little progress has been made to maximize the potential of the substantial gas reserves, although plans to prevent gas flaring will provide significant environmental improvement in the delta. Social and educational development remains stifled, and the gross domestic product (GDP) per capita stalled at US$1,415. Despite well-publicized efforts by the Obasanjo and following Yar'Adua administrations, corruption continues, where lucrative contracts are still in the hands of patrimonial elites. The more democracy is explored, the more entrenched the forces of corruption appear to be, as elites seek to take advantage while they can.

Current political economy challenges

Many challenges remain to promote a more balanced, stable, and equitable political economy. Diversification away from a dependence upon oil has not occurred, and is unlikely in the foreseeable future. The thorny problem of revenue allocation within Nigeria still pits communities against the federal government, most notably in the oil-producing areas of the delta region, in which an insurgency has been led by the Movement for the Emancipation of the Delta (MEND), the members

> **Key points**
>
> - The mainstay of the Nigerian economy is oil, accounting for about 90 per cent of export revenue.
> - Following the collapse of the oil market in the early 1980s, Nigeria struggled to maintain development projects, and was forced to seek loans and debt rescheduling from the international financial institutions.
> - The 2000s witnessed a slight upturn in economic conditions, partly helped by the presence of civilian government, although still with ethnic divisions and social inequalities.

Social Change, Democracy, and Instability

Social fabric

Nigeria is made up of a complex mosaic of ethnic, regional, and religious identities, all of which have served at some time or other to undermine the country's stability. British colonialism forged together a country of disparate people, and also helped to create a heightened sense of ethnic identity and competition. The three regions—north, west, and east—of colonial Nigeria contained a single dominant ethnic group in each—Hausa, Yoruba, and Igbo respectively—who increasingly viewed politics as a battle for resources between the ethnic groups. The fledgling federal state at independence could not contain this animosity, and the early experiment was brought to a close in the 1966 military coup. Tensions between these three powerful ethnic groups form only a part of the story. Minority ethnic groups, particularly from the centre of the country and the country's oil belt, have increasingly become a major factor in politics. Superimposed upon this ethnic tension is religion. A rough division sees the country divided into a Muslim north and a Christian south, although the reality is much more complex. Religious differences have become increasingly politicized since the 1980s, and the establishment of *Sharia* (or Islamic) law in 12 northern states exacerbated an already tense situation. Religious riots, often led by unemployed and disaffected youth, killing hundreds at a time are now commonplace, the most recent being Muslim–Christian clashes in Jos in March 2010. These provide a problem that no Nigerian government has been able to puzzle out (see also Chapter 8).

It is probably fair to say that Nigeria's political elites, both civilian and military, have failed the country. Politics is based upon patrimonial inclinations, where access to political office normally translates into corrupt access to the nation's wealth. Elections are routinely and blatantly rigged. Even though the country is one of the continent's wealthiest, social development has remained poor, as money often does not make its way into productive usage. The most obvious example of this skewed development can be seen in the oil-producing areas of the Niger River delta. Potentially the wealthiest of all the regions, the people inhabiting the delta have the lowest indicators of social development, and the environmental degradation of the region is staggering. This has led to massive social protests over the past decade, led most recently by MEND. These have consistently been met with force by the federal government, arguably with the connivance of the oil corporations. However, President Yar'Adua offered an amnesty in June 2009 to those fighting, and promised greater revenue allocation to the region. This new approach seemed to make ground initially, with 15,000 people turning themselves in, and with MEND calling a ceasefire in October 2009.

Institutions and parties

Since 1960, Nigeria has had just under thirty years of military government, four different constitutions and republics, both parliamentary and presidential forms of government, at least eight governments overthrown by the military, and numerous different sets of political parties. The internal federal structure has evolved from three regions to 36 states in an effort to undermine the strength of regional and ethnic politics (and to offer more politicians the opportunity to extract wealth). In this environment of experimentation and instability, it is little surprise that democratic institutions and structures of government have found it difficult to establish themselves.

At independence, Nigeria was bestowed the **Westminster model** of government. This failed to contain the conflicts between government and 'opposition', which were exacerbated by the power struggle between fledgling federal government and established ethnically driven regional governments. With hindsight, this system perhaps only effectively operated for two or three years, but it lingered until the 1966 military coup. Military governments ruled for all but four years between 1966 and 1999, and ranged considerably in capability and probity. Political parties were proscribed during much of military rule, and little progress was made in solving the social, ethnic, and religious problems facing the country. The civilian Second Republic (1979–83) was, like the first, dominated by northern power groups, and fizzled out in extreme corruption, ethnic bias, and electoral fraud before being swept from office on New Year's Eve 1983. This republic was very much fashioned upon the American presidential model, with an executive president, a Senate, and a House of Representatives. This political model is perhaps better suited to Nigerian political life, and was adopted for the Fourth Republic in 1999.

The 1990s proved to be the darkest period of political development, as the federal government became the personal plaything of one leader, Sani Abacha. In elections for the Third Republic in 1993, results pointed to a win by Chief Moshood Abiola, a Yoruba Muslim businessman. Alarmed at the possible consequences, the military government under Ibrahim Babangida — perhaps prompted by Abacha as the powerful minister of defence — annulled the elections and transferred power to a military and civilian coalition that lasted a few months before being overthrown by Abacha. When Abiola returned from exile in 1994, he was detained by Abacha, and eventually died in prison (his wife was assassinated). Plans for a return to civilian government were repeatedly postponed, as civilian political leaders were hand-picked and dropped by Abacha. By 1998, Abacha had manipulated the political process to the extent that he was the sole presidential candidate of all five parties allowed by his regime. Upon his surprise death, yet another transition was started, and a new slate of political parties created. The success of Obasanjo, a former military head of state, indicates the residual power of military leaders in the political process. In 2003, the presidential election was contested by two former military heads of state, Obasanjo and Muhammadu Buhari.

The April 2007 presidential election provided the first-ever transfer of power from one civilian government to another. Tensions within the ruling People's Democratic Party (PDP) were rife during Obasanjo's second term, with the president and vice president Atiku Abubakar trading barbs and, by 2006, each calling for the other's resignation. Abubakar accepted the presidential nomination from the opposition Action Congress in December 2006, sparking further conflict. The PDP selected a relatively unknown governor from the northern state of Katsina, Umaru Yar'Adua, to be its presidential candidate. The 2007 elections were marred by widespread fraud and violence, with Yar'Adua unsurprisingly winning. He largely continued Obasanjo's policies, although in a more subdued, low-profile manner, possibly because of his poor health. Tensions are high prior to the 2011 elections, spurred on by uncertainty over whether Yar'Adua's successor as president, Goodluck Jonathan, will stand in his party's primaries for the presidential nomination. Previous to becoming vice president and then president, Goodluck Jonathan, who hails from a southern state, was little known.

Civil society

Despite long periods of oppressive rule, civil society groups have remained active and strong. The media have been outspoken during even the darkest times, and have helped to maintain a healthy dialogue about national and local policies. The universities have also played a strong role in voicing opinions about governments and policies, and student and faculty protests are a common feature. Similarly trade unions have been relatively well organized and not afraid to take action when their interests were threatened, and judges strove to maintain their independence. During the Abacha administration, repression of these groups was at its maximum, but many of them fought back against the regime, often from exile. Human rights and democracy organizations flourished, and worked with external groups to maintain pressure upon the regime. Unfortunately, these groups were sometimes divided upon ethnic lines, but nevertheless indicated the strength and vitality of civilian society, resisting blatant oppression. Prominent Nigerian writers such as Chinua Achebe, Ken Saro-Wiwa, and Wole Soyinka were also important in maintaining pressure upon the corrupt regimes. With such a vibrant civil society, one perhaps might expect significant advances in the political arena in terms of **good governance** and accountability. Unfortunately, to date, this has not fully transpired

Women's groups are also well represented in civil society, although their focus is often shaped along regional lines. For example, the Federation of Muslim Women's Associations in Nigeria (FOMWAN) focuses upon education and health within an Islamic framework. Nationally, women's groups argue that they are worse off than in pre-colonial times, as their economic and political rights have been usurped by men. Few women reach the highest rungs of politics, especially in the north of the country. A United Nations report in December 2009 stated that only 10 per cent of women are tested for HIV, and that 90 per cent of pregnant women with HIV are not accessing treatment. Much work still needs to be done to improve the status of women, even though they do play significant roles within the formal and informal economies.

Key points

- The military has played a dominant role in the political history of Nigeria.

- Significant political experimentation with institutions and structures of government has occurred, but with only modest success in containing societal strains

- Civil society groups have maintained a consistently strong role in Nigerian political life.

- The re-election of Obasanjo in 2003, and the election of Yar'Adua in 2007, gave hope to the idea that the cycle of military rule has been broken.

Regional Influence in Foreign Policy

Although opinions differ over the extent of Nigeria's influence in the international arena, it is evident that the country exerts considerable influence in the West African region, and has an important role to play in many African issues. The factors shaping this role are fairly evident. Nigeria's population size, market potential, military capability, oil and gas revenues, and OPEC membership provide important resources for the projection of influence. Its GDP is equivalent to the other 14 ECOWAS members combined, as most of its neighbours are small, and lack the demographic and economic resources to be very active in the foreign policy arena.

West Africa has been the most important focus of foreign policy, although this has often been an unsympathetic arena for Nigerian endeavours. All of its neighbours are former French colonies, and the residual linkages of **la francophonie** have at times undermined Nigerian initiatives. In 1975, Nigeria's lead in diplomacy with Benin brought about ECOWAS as an attempt to check French influence in the region. During its 35 years, ECOWAS has attempted to improve trade and movement of people within the region. Official trade figures remain low, as vital trade partners are in Europe, but unofficial (illegal) trade has flourished, with the porosity of the Nigerian borders being an important contributory factor. The role of Nigeria in the region's trade is important, either way.

Nigerian governments have often taken on the role of African champion, promoting causes on behalf of the continent. During the 1960s and 1970s, these focused upon non-alignment, African independence, liberation in southern Africa, and economic rights. In 1973, for example, the administration of General Gowon was a leader of the **New International Economic Order** as well as in negotiations leading to the agreement signed in 1975 between the European Union and the African, Caribbean, and Pacific (ACP) States, which issued in the first of four Lomé Conventions. After 1980, as economic problems weakened Nigerian leverage, the country's global impact was less certain.

During the 1990s, Nigeria's position as Africa's proclaimed champion was further undermined by several factors. First, the achievement of majority rule by South Africa meant that Nigeria's somewhat unchallenged 'leadership' of the continent was now rivalled by a stronger economic power. Second, whereas Nelson Mandela was, and remains, an icon to the world, the despotic military leaders in Nigeria left the country increasingly isolated. Nigeria's isolation peaked during the mid-1990s, when minor sanctions were imposed by the West, and Nigeria was suspended from the Commonwealth. Third, the failure to democratize until 1999 and the overall frailty of democracy served to undermine its legitimacy to lead.

The new era opened up by the election of Obasanjo in 1999 helped to restore some credibility, and also repaired frayed relations with the United States, the European Union, and the international financial institutions. Investment in the oil and gas sectors increased considerably, although they had not been affected much during the 1990s. The Obasanjo government helped to restore the country's battered image, sending peacekeepers to African Union missions in Darfur and Sierra Leone. Nigeria played an important role in helping to establish the New Economic Partnership for Africa's

Development (NEPAD) in 2001, a major development initiative for the continent in partnership with the UN and industrialized countries. Nigeria also benefited from the US's strategy to lessen its dependence upon Middle Eastern oil, and by 2006 some 40 per cent of Nigeria's oil exports went to the US. This positive direction was maintained by the Yar'Adua government, and vindicated by Nigeria's election to serve on the UN Security Council for 2010–11. Unfortunately, the global recession and collapse of oil prices in 2009 undermined Nigeria's economic strength.

Key points

- Nigerian governments in the 1970s were extremely active in promoting foreign policy objectives on behalf of the African continent.
- Nigeria championed the ACP group of countries during negotiations leading to the Lomé Convention in 1975.
- In recent years, Nigeria's attempts to lead African opinion have been somewhat undermined by the leadership and economic strength of South Africa.

Conclusion

Probably the best way to describe Nigeria is as a country of unfulfilled promise. Despite its demographic size and economic potential, the country has been dogged by numerous political and social problems, although it has scored some modest foreign policy successes. So how should we view Nigeria? In a positive outlook, Nigeria still remains a strong state with viable potential. Unlike some of its neighbours, the federal government exerts considerable power internally, and the country's borders remain relatively secure. The election of Yar'Adua in 2007 provided optimism that the country has finally turned away from military government, and

may be moving closer to improving its political development. Continuing large inflows of foreign investment into the oil and gas sectors indicate that the economic profile can remain strong.

Conversely, it is possible to pull together a number of negative factors that create a more pessimistic forecast. Instability and corruption remain endemic, with fraud being an important element of all elections. Ethnic and religious intolerance and violence remain problematic, with the government showing small gains. Violent unrest in the critical oilfields spells problems unless this can be resolved. Human development indicators remain relatively poor. Democracy's quality is flawed and its future not yet secure.

Which Nigeria do we see? On the one hand, many of these problems are not new, and Nigeria has weathered them quite effectively. On the other hand, there appears to be scant progress over five decades in solving these endemic issues. Nigeria is often seen as a bellwether for other countries across the continent, and so how it develops over the coming years, and especially in the 2011 elections, is of vital importance to the West African region, if not to the continent as a whole.

? Questions

1. Was the breakdown of the new Nigerian state in the early 1960s almost inevitable?
2. What policies have been adopted to try to build national cohesion and identity in Nigeria?
3. To what extent has oil benefited and detracted from development in Nigeria?
4. How effective are civil society groups in promoting democracy in Nigeria?
5. Does the transition of power from one civilian government to another confirm that democracy is entrenched in Nigeria today?
6. What factors contribute to Nigeria's influence in West Africa, and the wider African continent?

→ Further reading

■ Balogun, M. (2009), *The Route to Power in Nigeria* (New York: Palgrave Macmillan). An empirical analysis of failed leadership in Nigeria.

■ Falola, T. and Heaton, M. (2008), *A History of Nigeria* (Cambridge: Cambridge University Press). An overview of the historical development of Nigeria, and the legacies of history faced today.

■ Maier, K. (2000), *This House Has Fallen: Midnight in Nigeria* (New York: Public Affairs). A more informal account of the political and social demise of Nigeria during the 1990s.

■ Okonta, I. and Oronto, D. (2003), *Where Vultures Feast: Shell, Human Rights, and Oil* (London: Verso). An account of oil issues in the Nigerian delta.

■ Osaghae, E. (1998), *Crippled Giant: Nigeria Since Independence* (Bloomington, IN: Indiana University Press). An overview of Nigerian political and economic development since independence.

■ Smith, D. J. (2007), *A Culture of Corruption: Everyday Deception and Popular Discontent in Nigeria* (Princeton, NJ: Princeton University Press). An examination of the methods and impact of corruption in Nigeria.

■ Soyinka, W. (1996), *The Open Sore of a Continent: A Personal Narrative of the Nigerian Crisis* (New York: Oxford University Press). The Nobel laureate's bitter account of the failings of the Abacha regime.

■ Wright, S. (1998), *Nigeria: Struggle for Stability and Status* (Boulder, CO: Westview Press). An analysis of Nigeria since independence, focusing upon domestic instability and efforts to promote a strong external policy.

STEPHEN WRIGHT

 Web links

- www.onlinenewspapers.com/nigeria.htm Numerous news sources.
- www.newswatchngr.com *Newswatch* magazine.
- www.ngrguardiannews.com *Guardian* (Lagos) newspaper.
- www.vanguardngr.com *Vanguard* news media.
- www.tribune.com.ng *Tribune* (Ibadan) newspaper.

 Online Resource Centre

For additional material and resources, please visit the Online Resource Centre at:
www.oxfordtextbooks.co.uk/orc/burnell3e/

21c Mexico: Democratic Transition and Beyond

Andreas Schedler

Chapter contents

- Introduction: From Independence to Revolution
- The Foundations of Electoral Authoritarianism
- The Structural Bases of Regime Change
- Democratization by Elections
- After Transition
- Conclusion

Overview

With a population of over 100 million, a vast and heterogeneous territory, an extended common border with the United States, Mexico commands the attention of international policymakers. Traditionally classified as part of Mesoamerica, in 1994 Mexico was formally admitted into North America following the enactment of the North American Free Trade Agreement with the USA and Canada. In 2000, the victory of conservative opposition candidate Vicente Fox in Mexico's presidential election sealed the end of more than seven decades of uninterrupted single-party rule. For most of the twentieth century, the country was ruled by a broadly inclusive hegemonic party seeking to ratify its monopoly hold on power through controlled, non-competitive elections at all levels. In contrast to much of the literature, this chapter presents Mexico's post-revolutionary political system not as a regime *sui generis*—a unique, idiosyncratic form of authoritarianism—but rather as a prototypical case of 'electoral authoritarianism'. Similarly, it interprets the country's trajectory of regime change not as a transition *sui generis*—as a unique, idiosyncratic path to democracy—but as a prototypical case of 'democratization by elections'. Figure 21c.1 shows a map of Mexico and Box 21c.1 provides an overview of key dates in Mexico's history.

Figure 21c.1 Mexico

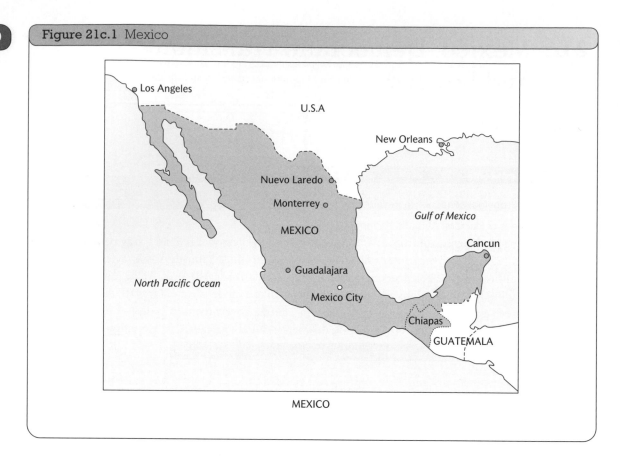

MEXICO

Box 21c.1 Key Dates in Mexico's History

1810–21	War of Independence against Spain
1846–8	War between Mexico and the United States
1857	New republican constitution
1876–1910	Presidency of Porfirio Díaz
1910–20	Mexican Revolution
1917	New constitution (still in force)
1929	Foundation of the National Revolutionary Party, later changed to PRI, that was to rule Mexico for seven decades
1934–40	Land redistribution, social reforms, and oil nationalization under President Lázaro Cárdenas
1982	Debt crisis
1988	'Earthquake election': unprecedented competitiveness at a presidential election; the PRI candidate obtains a bare majority of valid votes; the opposition charges fraud
1990	Foundation of the Federal Electoral Institute (IFE)
1994	North American Free Trade Agreement; Zapatista rebellion
1996	The 'definitive' electoral reform
1997	In mid-term election, PRI loses its absolute majority in the Chamber of Deputies

| 2000 | Conservative opposition candidate Vicente Fox wins the presidency |
| 2006 | In a close and contested election, Felipe Calderón from the conservative PAN wins the presidency; left-wing candidate López Obrador rejects the election as fraudulent |

Introduction: From Independence to Revolution

As Mexico reached independence from Spain after a decade of war in 1821, it faced the triple challenge of redefining its political regime, constructing a modern state, and laying the foundations of a capitalist economy. Failure in establishing a regime — in institutionalizing accepted rules of access to power and exercise of power — precluded success in building a state and developing a market. In its first thirty years of political independence, the country fell prey to the vicissitudes of *caudillismo*. Between 1821 and 1850, the country was (nominally) ruled by fifty different governments, most of them delivered by military rebellions. Internal instability was matched by external vulnerability. In the war against the United States (1846–48), Mexico lost around half its territory. At home, civilian politics was increasingly driven by the major cleavage common to most of nineteenth-century Latin America: conflict between conservatives and liberals. Conservatives sought to protect the inherited political, economic, and cultural power of the Catholic Church. Liberals strove to limit it and to create an autonomous sphere of secular politics.

The developmental dictatorship under Porfirio Díaz (1876–1910), while harshly repressive, brought an unprecedented measure of stability and institutional modernization. Having taken power by a coup, General Díaz proceeded to set up an early variant of **electoral authoritarianism** (Box 21c.2). Regular (indirect) presidential elections confirmed his continuity in power by acclamation. Regular legislative contests between extremely personalized and fragmented political parties produced mostly weak, even if nominally representative, legislatures. At the same time, something like a modern state started to take shape, with a central government, a national military, and a professional bureaucracy extending its reach to the country's periphery. In addition, foreign investment aided by public infrastructure (railways) enabled some incipient, dependent industrialization through the development of an extractive enclave economy.

Box 21c.2 Electoral Authoritarianism

Electoral autocracies display a nominal adherence to the principle of democratic rule, while denying democracy in practice. Particularly, they hold regular multiparty elections, yet constrain and subvert them so deeply as to render them instruments not of democracy, but of authoritarian rule. Modern examples are the presidencies of Fujimori (Peru), Mugabe (Zimbabwe), and Suharto (Indonesia).

The Mexican Revolution (1910–20) is customarily explained as a response to the growing impoverishment of the rural masses. Its first impulse, however, was entirely political. After three decades of developmental dictatorship, liberal reformer Francisco I. Madero demanded democratic elections (*sufragio efectivo*) and alternation in power (*no-reelección*). In the 1911 (indirect) elections, he won the presidency with 99.3 per cent of total votes. He was murdered two years later in a military coup. The ensuing civil war is commonly described as the first social revolution of the twentieth century, and about 1.4 million people out of a total population of 15.2 million lost their lives.

The revolutionary Constitution, enacted in 1917 and still in force today, enshrined a mixture of political liberalism and social reformism. It copied almost the full set of political institutions from the US Constitution: presidential government; federalism; bicameralism; and plurality elections at all levels. In addition, it limited the scope of the market economy by reserving 'strategic sectors' to the state while stipulating extensive social rights for peasants and workers. Ironically, under the one-party hegemony that emerged after the revolution, the Constitution proved ineffective in its procedural as well as in its substantive aspects. It worked neither as an effective institutional constraint on politics nor as an effective policy programme.

> **Key points**
>
> - During much of the nineteenth century, Mexico's difficulties in institutionalizing a political regime frustrated its efforts at state-building and economic development.
> - The revolutionary 1917 Constitution established (on paper) a liberal division of power, while locking in substantive policies in the fields of public education, labour rights, and control over national resources.

The Foundations of Electoral Authoritarianism

Post-revolutionary politics continued to be disorderly and violent. The bullet, alongside the ballot, enjoyed acceptance as a valid currency for gaining and losing public office. Violent protest, military rebellion, and the physical elimination of adversaries remained common. But regular elections took place at all levels, although nothing resembling a structured party system existed. Political parties were ephemeral collections of followers around local notables or military leaders. Politics remained a game of elite competition mediated by force, not by formal institutions.

The crisis of presidential succession in 1928 marked a turning point. After the assassination of president elect Alvaro Obregón in July, the outgoing president, Plutarco Elías Calles (1924–28), announced his intention to institutionalize the revolutionary government. In Spring 1929, he founded the National Revolutionary Party (PRN) as an umbrella organization of all revolutionary leaders, factions, and parties.

Twin institutionalization

The PRN was to pacify electoral disputes by providing a transparent mechanism of electoral coordination: it would select winning candidates from among the 'revolutionary family', reward their followers, and crush their opponents. By the mid-1930s, the PRN was able to centralize candidate selection by dissolving local parties and prohibiting the immediate re-election of deputies. Within a few years, what was initially a loose alliance of local factions established itself as a centralized hegemonic party that was to rule Mexico for the rest of the century.

Before quitting power peacefully in the 2000 presidential elections, the successor party of the PRN, the Institutional Revolutionary Party (PRI), was the longest-ruling political party in the world. It had clearly excelled in fulfilling its original mission of pacifying and stabilizing the country. How did the PRI achieve this extraordinary success in party and regime institutionalization? Like all institutions, it had to accomplish two basic objectives: 'stability' and 'value' (Huntington 1968). The former is a matter of expectations; the latter one of evaluations. People had to know that the PRI was there to stay—that the revolutionary game it played was 'the only game in town'. But they had to value it, too. One-party hegemony had to appear as a fact of life as well as moral achievement.

The institutional infrastructure

Over seven decades, the PRI sustained a regime that looked as exceptional as its longevity. Scholars commonly described it as a civilian, inclusive, corporatist, and hyper-presidential authoritarian regime held together by a pragmatic, patronage-based state party. In essence, Mexico's 'authoritarianism with adjectives' rested upon three institutional pillars: a hierarchical state party; state corporatism; and electoral gatekeeping.

On the first, the hegemonic party operated as a big 'linkage mechanism' that turned the Mexican state into a unitary hierarchical organization. By controlling all branches and levels of government, the hegemonic party effectively cancelled the constitutional distribution of state power. It annulled the horizontal division of power between the executive, legislative, and judicial branches as well as the vertical division of power between central government, federal states, and municipalities. The fusion between state and party granted almost unlimited powers to the president who acted as the supreme patron at the peak of a **clientelist** pyramid; the Mexican state.

The state in turn controlled civil society by co-opting and corrupting potential dissidents and opponents. The party patronized, and at the same time domesticated, labour unions, peasant organizations, and popular movements by incorporating them into tightly controlled corporatist arrangements. It kept business people content with subsidies, market protection, and informal access to power. Through a mixture of material incentives

and political constraints it kept the mass media quiet. Finally, the Catholic Church was persuaded to observe its constitutional mandate of keeping out of politics by reminders of the possible alternative: oppression by the state of religious institutions, as in the 1920s.

Electoral autocracies like the PRI regime reproduce and legitimate themselves on the basis of periodic elections that show some measure of pluralism but fall short of minimum democratic standards. In such regimes, multi-party elections are not embedded in the 'surrounding freedoms' essential to **liberal democracy**. Instead, they are constrained through a variety of authoritarian controls. The violations of liberal-democratic norms may be manifold (see Schedler 2002b), and post-revolutionary Mexico had nearly all of them in place: limitations of civil and political liberties; restrictions on party and candidate registration; discriminatory rules of representation; electoral fraud; corruption; and coercion; as well as an uneven playing field, with the incumbent enjoying close to monopolistic access to media and campaign resources.

The ideological infrastructure

Following Sartori (1976), scholars commonly portray Mexico's post-revolutionary regime as 'pragmatic' authoritarianism. True, the PRI did not institute a mobilizational dictatorship that tried to coerce its subjects into ideological uniformity. It accepted some measure of economic and civil liberties, including religious freedom, encouraged political opposition parties to its left and right (as long as they remained harmless), and accommodated considerable programmatic diversity within the party. The relative tolerance of pluralism, however, should not be mistaken for the absence of ideology. Its revolutionary nationalism was not a mere echo chamber.

Actually, the PRI was remarkably successful in creating what Antonio Gramsci called cultural 'hegemony'. The state party defined lasting coordinates of national identity—the national history, national foes and heroes, national symbols and rituals, and, last but not least, the promise of progress and justice. The official party effectively managed to turn its ideology—a combination of liberalism, nationalism, and the corporative defence of the welfare state—into the foundations of national political correctness. Even today, the language and ideology of revolutionary nationalism continues to constrain Mexican politics. It still sets the terms of public debate in numerous policy spheres, such as the management of natural resources, public education, and foreign policy.

Key points

- Post-revolutionary Mexico developed an electoral authoritarian regime held together by a hegemonic party, the PRI.

- The party commandeered the state as well as civil society. Through its centralized control of elections, it acted as the sole gatekeeper to public office.

- The PRI did not exercise its power 'naked' but draped in national-revolutionary ideology. Non-democratic rule lived off popular legitimacy.

The Structural Bases of Regime Change

The relationship between economic development and political democracy has been subject to intense debate (see Chapter 14). But although for long a democratic underachiever, Mexico seems to confirm the elective affinity between socio-economic and political modernization.

Societal transformation

Not unlike Porfirio Díaz—even if less personalistic, repressive, and exclusionary—the PRI established its own version of developmental dictatorship. Especially during the 'Mexican miracle' between 1940 and 1970, it achieved steady rates of economic growth and expanding public services. Notwithstanding the economic crises that irrupted at each presidential succession from 1976 to 1994, seven decades of modernizing authoritarian rule by the PRI produced profound societal transformations. Mexico at the end of the revolution was a country dramatically different from Mexico at the turn of the century. In 1930, Mexico's population stood at 16.5 million, the annual per capita income stood at US$166 (in 1960 terms), 70.2 per cent of the workforce was employed in agriculture, and the

illiteracy rate among the population of age 10 and higher was 61.5 per cent. In 1995, by contrast, the population had jumped to 93.7 million, annual per capita income reached US$2,790 (current), primary sector employment was only 22.3 per cent, and illiteracy down to 10.6 per cent (figures from Banco de México, Instituto Nacional de Estadística, Geografía e Informática, and World Bank). Although about half of the population still counts as poor, and the country displays one of the most unequal income distributions in the world, the structural transformation from poor and rural to middle-income and urban was bound to create strong pressures for democratization. The widening gap between socio-economic and political modernization was difficult to sustain. Societal pluralism could not be contained within the confinements of a single party. In addition, the structural dissociation between a hegemonic party and a complex society was deepened by economic mismanagement and crisis.

Economic crises

After 1970, a mixture of structural disequilibria and performance failure pushed Mexico into periodic economic recessions. Each presidential succession from 1976 to 1994 was marked by economic crisis. The oil boom and external debt first postponed, and then aggravated, the big crash of 1982. In 1983, per capita gross domestic product (GDP) fell 4.2 per cent, annual inflation reached 80.5 per cent, and real minimum wages plummeted by 25.2 per cent (Banco de México). Popular discontent sky-rocketed.

In retrospect, the debt crisis of the early 1980s was the starting point of democratization. There was nothing inevitable about it, however. Neither structural incongruence nor cyclical stress translate smoothly and automatically into democratizing progress. During the 1970s and 1980s, the talk of the day was about *crisis*—a situation of change

and anxiety, without any clear sense of where the country was heading. Anything seemed possible, including a return to the violence of the past. It was only in the late 1980s that this diffuse sense of alarm receded. Actors and analysts started talking about democratic *transition*. And they started playing the game of transition—the game of peaceful, incremental political democratization.

> **Key points**
>
> - Socio-economic modernization created multiple pressures for democratization.
> - Cycles of economic crisis eroded the regime's legitimacy.

Democratization by Elections

Under electoral autocracies like the PRI regime, elections are not 'instruments of democracy' (Powell 2000) but battlefields of democratization. Unlike democratic elections, manipulated elections unfold as two-level games in which parties compete for votes at the same time as they struggle over basic rules. Electoral competition goes hand in hand with institutional conflict. Democratization 'by elections' ensues when opposition parties succeed at both levels, when they manage to undermine both pillars of authoritarian rule: its popular support as well as its anti-democratic institutions (Schedler 2002a). Mexico's emergent opposition parties—the right-wing National Action Party (PAN), a tenacious regime opponent since the late 1940s, and the left-wing Party of the Democratic Revolution (PRD), founded in 1989—were able to start just such a self-reinforcing spiral of rising competitiveness and democratic reform. As they turned into serious contenders, they were able to remove successive layers of authoritarian control, in five negotiated electoral reforms following 1987.

Electoral competition

Historic turnout figures indicate the hegemonic party's capacity for electoral mobilization was modest. Its official election results, by contrast, were impressive. Until 1982, all Mexican revolutionary and post-revolutionary presidents were elected by acclamation (except for 1946 and 1952 when they faced relatively popular splinter candidates). Plurality elections prevented opposition parties from winning legislative seats until the early 1960s. In 1963, the PRI introduced some element of proportional representation to keep the PAN in the electoral game, yet without jeopardizing its two-thirds majority—a condition to enact constitutional changes.

In the wake of the 1982 debt crisis, however, the governing party's hegemony began to crumble. First, the PAN started to win, and to defend its victories, in a series of post-electoral confrontations, at the municipal and state levels in northern Mexico. Then, in the 1988 presidential election, the performance of PRI dissident Cuauhtémoc Cárdenas shattered the image of PRI invincibility at the national level. His followers continued to think he had actually won the contest, only being denied victory by blatant electoral fraud. Afterwards, opposition parties conquered more and more sites of sub-national power, at the same time as they strengthened their presence in the bicameral national legislature. In 1997, the official party lost its absolute majority in the Chamber of Deputies, inaugurating an unprecedented period of divided government. Finally, in 2000 PAN candidate Vicente Fox won the really big prize in Mexican politics — the presidency.

Electoral reform

The rising competitiveness of the party system made possible (and was made possible by) profound changes in the institutions of electoral governance. Today, vote-rigging and the state control of elections belong to the past. Within less than a decade, Mexico effectively remodelled its electoral institutions. The electoral reforms, negotiated under the pressure of hundreds of local post-electoral conflicts, and enacted in 1990, 1993, 1994, and culminating in 1996, added up to a veritable institutional revolution within the (self-denominated) regime of the institutional revolution.

The new electoral system rested upon three institutional columns: a new independent election body; the judicialization of conflict resolution; and comprehensive oversight by parties. Consonant with an international trend, Mexican parties decided to delegate the organization of elections to a permanent and independent election management body, the Federal Electoral Institute (IFE), founded in 1990. Electoral reformers have also set up a new system for the judicial resolution of election disputes: the Electoral Tribunal of the Judicial Power of the Federation (TEPJF) now has the last say in all electoral disputes, national as well as sub-national. Finally, parties have institutionalized a 'panoptic regime' of

surveillance that allows them to monitor closely the entire electoral process step by step.

Outside the electoral arena

While political parties are the lead actors in democratization by elections, they have to be responsive to shocks and actors outside the electoral arena. Given the civilian nature of the Mexican regime, political actors have not had to worry much about the military, but nevertheless faced a complex configuration of other domestic and international players.

Business people — for long supportive of electoral authoritarianism — began to disown the PRI after 1982. Economic crisis and nationalization of the banks taught them authoritarian discretion was bad for business. By contrast, organized labour remained bound to the PRI even as individual workers and dissident unions grew autonomous. Until recently, the party could count as well on the green vote of the rural poor. The 1994 uprising by the Zapatistas in the southern state of Chiapas opened the door for the entry of indigenous people into the arena of politics. Initially, as it forced political parties to resume reform negotiations (in early 1994), it played out a recurrent irony of history: the threat of violence acting as a midwife of democratizing consensus.

Undoubtedly, international factors carried weight as well. Historically, the United States, much like the Mexican middle class, has been more interested in Mexican stability than democracy. It started to distance itself from the PRI to the extent that the party lost its ability to guarantee the country's political and economic stability. The North American Free Trade Agreement (NAFTA), in force since 1994, did little to promote democracy directly. But by locking in liberal market reforms it made Mexican economic policies essentially immune to democratic alternation in power. Democracy, rendered conservative in this way, stopped frightening economic liberals in Washington as well as in Mexico City.

Key points

- Mexico's democratic advance resulted from the interplay between democratizing reform and increasing inter-party competition.

- The NAFTA constrains the macro-economic policies of future democratic governments.

After Transition

Often, after the excitement of transition, political boredom and disenchantment set in. With the 2000 alternation in power, Mexico has turned into a 'normal' Latin American democracy operating in the context of a weak state and an unequal society. Mexican elites and citizens now face the triple challenge of democratic consolidation, democratic deepening, and democratic performance.

Democratic consolidation

The loss of the presidency by the PRI in 2000 marked the symbolic end of the democratic transition. It also seemed to mark the instantaneous accomplishment of democratic consolidation. Clearly, it seemed, democracy had come to stay, recognized and practised by all relevant actors as 'the only game in town' (Linz and Stepan 1996). The contested 2006 presidential election did not shatter expectations of democratic stability entirely. Yet it did introduce serious question marks.

Left-wing candidate Andrés Manuel López Obrador lost by barely 0.58 per cent of valid votes against the conservative Felipe Calderón. He revived the dramatic rhetoric of past democratizing struggles, claimed fraud, and took his followers to the streets. As the federal electoral tribunal denied his demand of a full vote recount, he sent existing political institutions 'to the devil' and had a crowd of followers proclaim him 'legitimate president' of Mexico. Upon close examination, the election could be considered clean, fair, and democratic. Still, several coinciding factors allowed the losing candidate to mobilize institutional distrust: a defective system of ballot accounting; logical inconsistencies in the electoral tribunal's final ruling; the memory of past electoral fraud; the general context of weak legality; his firm expectation of victory; as well as the long-standing fear that his adversaries were willing to transgress democratic rules in order to keep him out of the presidential office (Schedler 2007).

To appease the PRD and start healing the wounds of the acrimonious presidential election, in late 2007 and early 2008, political parties passed a broad package of electoral reforms that translated López Obrador's complaints about unfair campaigning into new networks of bureaucratic regulation. The reform introduced provisions that threaten the freedom of expression, curtail the participation of civil society in electoral campaigns, loosen the accountability of political parties, strengthen elite control over internal party affairs, weaken the IFE's political independence, and overall render electoral administration more bureaucratic, expensive, and contentious. Besides, somewhat ironically, the reform failed to address the central demand of the PRD in 2006. The new legislation does not foresee the possibility of conducting a national recount of votes in case of close outcomes (see Serra 2009).

While party politicians have tried to amend the fissured democratic consensus among political parties, new threats have emerged outside the party system. Upon taking office, president Calderón mobilized the military into a full-scale war against the production and distribution of drugs. While this policy change responded to a pressing problem his predecessor had neglected, it was carried out without previous public debate, without a strategic understanding of the logic of organized violence, and without a functioning police and justice system in place. In consequence, it has contributed to escalate the violent competition between drug enterprises as well as their warfare against the intrusive, market-repressing state. During the first two-and-a-half years of the Calderón presidency, the national newspaper *Reforma* counted over 10,000 assassinations attributed to drug cartels, an average of 11 per day (see Guerrero 2009).

This must be considered a full-fledged civil war. Given the contending groups' almost unlimited access to financial resources, arms, and personnel, it goes for the long haul. It is a post-modern war for sure, driven by no other ideology than material gain. In principle, illicit drug enterprises have only one political goal: keeping the state out of their business. Their quarrels are with the state, not the political regime. Yet the war carries the constant threat of spilling into the arena of democratic politics and already exerts a chilling effect on civil liberties and political rights.

Democratic deepening

In 2000, for the first time ever, Freedom House classified Mexico as an 'electoral democracy' (and has continued to do so up to now, despite the recent erosion of civil liberties). This could be misleading if it implies that democratizing progress had been limited to the electoral arena. True enough, struggles for democratization have revolved around the conduct of elections. Yet, as political actors were rebuilding the electoral arena they transformed other spheres of politics as well. Constructing new rules of *access* to power as well as new realities of

inter-party competition had profound implications for the *exercise* of power as well.

The mere introduction of opposition at all levels changed the political system without the need to change its constitutional underpinnings. Thanks to the new pluralism of the party system, the constitutional division of power, once a formality, is now meaningful reality. Today both the legislature and the judiciary impose tangible limits on the executive, and federalism is no longer hollow. Both state and municipal governments are real sites of power. A host of autonomous administrative, regulatory, and jurisprudential bodies complement the classic division of power. Contemporary Mexico may not be a fully liberal democracy, but it is not a purely minimal democracy either. Given the dense web of formal and political constraints officeholders face, the country cannot be described as an **illiberal or delegative democracy**.

That said, there is considerable scope for democratic completion and deepening. The rule of law is incomplete and fragile. Despite recent reforms, the realm of criminal law continues to form a theatre of tragic corruption and injustice, procedural as well as substantive. The prohibition of immediate re-election of legislators and mayors renders electoral accountability ineffective. High public officials are obscenely well paid, while corruption is widespread at lower and sub-national levels of public administration. Citizen participation is shallow, instruments of direct democracy are inexistent, and discontent runs deep.

Democratic performance

Democratic deficits are joined by policy failures. Mexico's multiple free-trade agreements have allowed a sustained expansion of exports, while they have contributed little to alleviate the plight of the rural poor. Persistent widespread poverty and socio-economic inequality betray the democratic promise of equal participation in public life. Powerful private monopolies and unaccountable public-sector unions perpetuate wasteful systems of rent-seeking. Political incompetence, ideological polarization, and the constitutional fragmentation of power block urgent policy reforms.

The balance of democracy's first decade is sobering, in terms of the quality of democracy as well as the effectiveness of democratic policymaking. Of course, democracy never is the solution to all problems; it is an institutional framework for seeking solutions and resolving conflicts in a peaceful way. Yet democratizing democracy and improving its substantive performance are clearly among the big assignments of Mexico's fledgling democratic regime.

Key points

- Mexico faces the triple challenge of consolidating and deepening its fledgling democracy, while improving its policy effectiveness.

- With the 2000 alternation in power and no extremist parties threatening the democratic system, Mexican democracy seemed to have achieved instantaneous consolidation.

- The close and contested presidential election of 2006, however, involved various threats to Mexico's democratic advances. The losing candidate did not concede defeat, and a third of citizens continue to believe the election was fraudulent.

- Over the past decade, violent competition over the illicit market of drugs has evolved into a non-recognized civil war that undermines the state and threatens the fledgling democratic regime.

Conclusion

At the turn of the twenty-first century, after traumatic experiences of instability and violence, followed by seven decades of authoritarian stability, Mexico finally seemed to have found a way of reconciling political stability and democracy. After the tranquil alternation in power of the year 2000, few things seemed to be capable of upsetting the new-found equilibrium of democratic politics. A close outcome in presidential elections was one of them. In the 2006 presidential elections, this feared scenario came true, and it involved a true test for Mexico's fledgling democracy. Fortunately, the democratic system proved resilient to the aggressive anti-political and anti-institutional discourse of the losing candidate. However, the only way of guaranteeing democracy is by not taking it for granted. If Mexican democracy is to be saved from a frustrating period of stagnation and disorder fuelled by the drugs war, it may only be through an audacious programme of democratizing democracy. To secure the democratic advances of the past, politicians as well as citizens, rather than ceding to illiberal impulses, will have to push for further democratic advances.

? Questions

1. What were the central political and economic challenges of post-independence Mexico?

2. How do you account for the institutional and ideological foundations of Mexico's post-revolutionary authoritarianism?

3. How did Mexico's socio-economic modernization in the twentieth century create pressures for political democratization?

4. Which were the core features of 'democratization by elections'? What are its political legacies?

5. What are the implications of the contested 2006 presidential election for Mexico's democratic consolidation?

6. What are the main democratic deficiencies of Mexican democracy today? How does the war on drugs affect the quality of Mexican democracy?

→ Further reading

■ Bruhn, K. et al. (2007), 'The 2006 Election and its Aftermath', *PS Political Science and Politics* 40/1 (January). Symposium on parties and voters in the 2006 elections.

■ Casar, M. A. and Marván, I. (eds) (2002), *Gobernar sin Mayoría: México 1867–1997* (Mexico City: Taurus and CIDE). An insightful series of studies on historical and sub-national experiences of divided government.

■ Eisenstadt, T. (2003), *Courting Democracy in Mexico: Party Strategies and Electoral Institutions* (Cambridge: Cambridge University Press). A comprehensive study of the judicialization of post-electoral conflicts in the 1990s.

■ Elizondo, C. and Nacif, B. (eds) (2003), *Lecturas sobre el Cambio político en México* (Mexico City: Fondo de Cultura Económica). A fine collection of essays on political change in Mexico.

■ Guerrero, E. (2009), 'Las Tres Guerras: Violencia y Narcotráfico en México,' *Nexos* 381 (September), 33–37. A spatial analysis of the logic of drug-related violence in Mexico.

■ Lawson, C. H. (2002), *Building the Fourth Estate: Democratization and the Rise of a Free Press in Mexico* (Berkeley, CA: University of California Press). A systematic study of media opening and democratization.

■ Levy, D. C. and Bruhn, K. (2006), *Mexico: The Struggle for Democratic Development*, 2nd edn (Berkeley, CA: University of California Press). Broad introduction to Mexican politics.

■ Magaloni, B. (2006), *Voting for Autocracy: Hegemonic Party Survival and its Demise in Mexico* (New York: Cambridge University Press). A theoretical and empirical analysis of voting behaviour in the last two decades of PRI rule.

■ Schedler, A. (2004), 'From Electoral Authoritarianism to Democratic Consolidation', in R. Crandall, G. Paz, and R. Roett (eds), *Mexico's Democracy at Work: Political and Economic Dynamics* (Boulder, CO/London: Lynne Rienner), 9–37. An overview of democratic transition and consolidation with a synthesis of electoral reforms 1977–96.

■ —— (2007), 'Mexican Standoff: The Mobilization of Distrust', *Journal of Democracy*, 18/1: 88–102. A resumé and critical analysis of the 2006 post-electoral conflict.

■ Serra, G. (2009), 'Una Lectura Crítica de la Reforma Electoral en México a Raíz de 2006', *Política y Gobierno* 16/2: 411–427. A critique of the 2007–08 electoral reforms.

■ Weldon, J. A. (1997), 'The Political Sources of Presidencialismo in Mexico', in S. Mainwaring and M. S. Shugart (eds), *Presidentialism and Democracy in Latin America* (Cambridge: Cambridge University Press), 225–58. Much-cited analysis of the partisan foundations of Mexico's 'hyper-presidentialism'.

:// Web links

■ http://directorio.gob.mx   Web directory of the Mexican government, includes links to ministries, legislatures, courts, sub-national governments, embassies, media, universities, and civic associations.

■ www.gob.mx   Citizen portal of the Federal government contains legal and other information across a wide range of policy fields.

■ www.ife.org.mx   Federal Electoral Institute (IFE).

■ www.trife.gob.mx   Federal Electoral Tribunal (TEPJF).

■ www.ifai.org.mx   Federal Institute for Access to Public Information (IFAI).

■ www.unam.mx   National Autonomous University (UNAM).

■ www.laneta.apc.org   LaNeta—'alternative' civil society information.

Online Resource Centre

For additional material and resources, please visit the Online Resource Centre at:
www.oxfordtextbooks.co.uk/orc/burnell3e/

22

Underdevelopment and Development

22a Guatemala: Enduring Underdevelopment

Rachel Sieder

» **Chapter contents**

- Introduction: Guatemala's Poverty and Multiple Inequalities
- Patterns of State Formation
- The Peace Accords: A Turning Point?
- Lack of Domestic Commitment
- Conclusion

* **Overview**

This study examines Guatemala as a persistent case of underdevelopment, defining development in terms of social, economic, cultural, and political rights. The principal features of underdevelopment in contemporary Guatemala are described. The account analyses historical patterns of state formation and economic development before examining the attempts to reverse historical trends and 'engineer development' represented by the 1996 peace agreement. The final section signals the main contemporary causes of the country's persistent underdevelopment: a **patrimonialist** and **predatory state** linked in turn to the strength and conservatism of the private sector, the weakness of the party system, the continuing influence of the armed forces, and extremely high levels of crime and impunity.Figure 22a.1 is a map of Guatemala and Box 22a.1 provides an overview of key dates in Guatemala's history.

Figure 22a.1 Guatemala

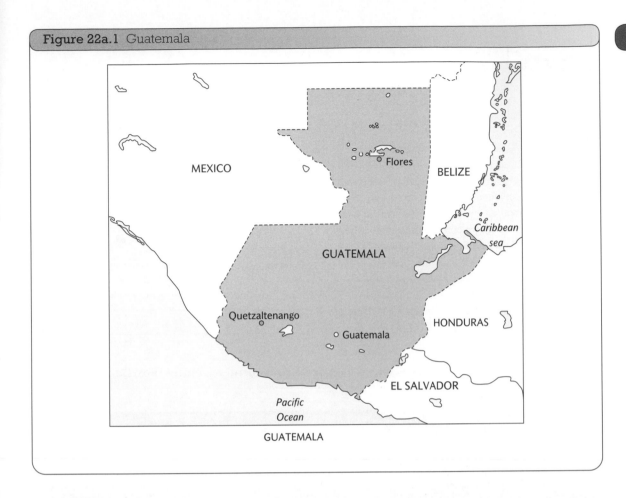

GUATEMALA

Introduction: Guatemala's Poverty and Multiple Inequalities

The influence of rights-based approaches to development (see also Chapter 18) in recent years has ensured that our understanding of 'development' and 'underdevelopment' has become more holistic. Where previously development was measured simply in terms of economic variables, today assessments tend to include composite measures of the socio-economic, cultural, and political rights enjoyed by its inhabitants, and the extent to which their inclusion and well-being is secured. Thinking on development policy has evolved accordingly (see Chapter 16).

Box 22a.1 Key Dates in Guatemala's History

1944	Forced labour abolished, universal male suffrage introduced
1952	Agrarian reform law approved
1954	Democratically elected government of Jacobo Arbenz overthrown in CIA-backed coup
1960	First guerrilla insurgency
1978–83	Height of counter-insurgency war; 100,000 civilians killed or disappeared 1981–83
1984–5	Military oversee guided transition to elected, civilian government
1990	Oslo Accord between government and URNG establishes framework for national peace negotiations
1993	Attempted executive coup by President Serrano fails
1994–6	UN mediates peace process; agreements reached on human rights, indigenous rights and identity, re-settlement of displaced populations, clarification of human rights violations, agricultural modernization, and reform of the military and the state
1996	Final peace settlement signed
1999	United Nations Truth Commission finds Guatemalan state guilty of acts of genocide during armed conflict; recommends prosecutions
2007	Frente Repúblicano Guatemalteco (FRG), led by former dictator Rios Montt, wins presidential elections
2007	Social democrat candidate Álvaro Colom wins presidential elections

Guatemala can be characterized as a country with persistent underdevelopment (Box 22a.2).

Box 22a.2 Key Development Indicators for Guatemala

UN Human Development Index	0.704 (122nd out of 182 countries)
UN Human Poverty Index (HPI-1)	19.7% (76th out of 135 countries)
Gini Index	55.1
Share of national income of top quintile of population	63%
Share of income of bottom quintile of population	2.9%
Percentage of population in poverty	50.9%
Percentage of population in extreme poverty	15.2%
Numbers of people living in poverty	6.6 million (of total population of 13 million)

Source: PNUD 2008

Ethnic, regional, and gender inequality

Economic differences between different regions of the country and between ethnic groups—in a country in which indigenous people constitute around half the population—are huge. The predominantly rural indigenous areas of the country have the worst conditions of poverty, health, education, and land shortages (see Box 22a.3). Government spending on welfare provision is lower in rural areas, although has increased in recent years.

Box 22a.3 Key Inequality Indicators for Guatemala

Percentage of overall population in poverty	50.9%
Percentage of indigenous population in poverty	73%
Percentage of non-indigenous population in poverty	35%
Percentage of indigenous population in extreme poverty	26.4%
Percentage of non-indigenous population in extreme poverty	7.3%
Percentage of rural population in poverty	74.5%
Percentage of urban population in poverty	27%
Percentage of rural population in extreme poverty	24.4%
Percentage of urban population in extreme poverty	5%

Source: PNUD 2008

Guatemala is classified as a middle-income country, but has a long history of low social spending. This is partly accounted for by historically low rates of tax collection: Guatemala's tax coefficient was 9.7 per cent of gross domestic product (GDP) in 2004, despite commitments in the peace accords of 1996 to increase it to 12 per cent by 2002. Public spending on education, health and infrastructure improved somewhat after the mid-1990s, but remains low by regional standards. The legacy of gender and ethnic discrimination is evident in literacy statistics: although literacy rates for women improved between 1989 (when 67.5 per cent of women were literate) to 2006 (when 84.8 per cent of women were in this category), women still lag behind men (91.4 per cent of whom are literate), and indigenous women in the rural areas have even lower literacy rates (68.9 per cent). However, overall literacy rates and the number of years students stay in school have improved during the 2000s (PNUD 2008). Women also occupy more precarious and less well-paid jobs: in 2006, 75.7 per cent of women worked in the informal sector, and 53.4 per cent of these earned less than the basic minimum wage (PNUD 2008).

Growth and employment

For much of its recent history, Guatemala has enjoyed relative macro-economic stability and reasonable growth — an annual average of 2.7 per cent between 1986 and 2007. Growth reached 5.7 per cent in 2007, but fell to 3.3 per cent in 2008 due to the global economic crisis. Nonetheless, with one of the highest population growth rates in the region (around 2.6 per cent per annum) income per capita growth rates were significantly lower (and even negative during the 1980s), averaging around 1 per cent annually over the past fifty years. Economic development has not generated sufficient low-skilled jobs to absorb the poor. Consequently between 700,000 and 1 million Guatemalans are forced to migrate for seasonal harvest work. Working conditions for migrant workers are extremely tough; they are often paid less than the minimum wage and have little or no access to health and educational facilities. In recent years the structural crisis of coffee and sugar markets (two of Guatemala's main agro-exports) has drastically reduced national and regional employment opportunities for migrant workers and the numbers of those attempting to reach the USA as illegal migrants increased. Poor families increasingly rely on dollar remittances from family members working in the USA, which represent around 10 per cent of overall GDP. In 2007 average remittances per person were US$319, compared with the average for Latin America and the Caribbean of US$114 (UNDP 2007).

Democratic disenchantment

Like most of Latin America, Guatemala is now formally a democracy. However, while respect for political and human rights has undoubtedly improved compared to the 1980s, these rights are still far from secure and democracy remains fragile. Since restoration of electoral rule in 1986 elections have become freer and fairer and an increasingly broad spectrum of political opinion has been represented at the polls, particularly following the successful conclusion of a negotiated settlement to the armed conflict in December 1996. During the 1990s, decentralization and electoral reforms increased opportunities for citizen participation in municipal government.

Yet Guatemalans' levels of political participation and faith in the institutions of government are low compared to other countries in the region. Voter turnout is comparatively poor and regional public opinion surveys such as the Latinobarometer regularly find that Guatemalans have some of the lowest regard for democratic norms in the region. One explanation could be corruption, endemic both at national and local level. Another is chronic impunity and citizen insecurity: Guatemala has one of the highest homicide rates in the region and extremely high levels of so-called common, especially violent, crime. Crime and gender-based violence are a common occurrence for many citizens, particularly the poor. The judicial system is weak, impunity is routine, and those responsible for criminal acts are rarely prosecuted. Respect for indigenous peoples' rights was a cornerstone of the peace accords (see below) but despite some advances, progress has been extremely slow. For most Guatemalans democracy clearly has yet to deliver.

Key points

- Guatemala has among the highest rates of poverty and inequality in Latin American and Caribbean.

- In 2006, 50.9 per cent of the population lacked sufficient income to meet their minimum subsistence requirements.

- Indigenous people, rural inhabitants, women, and children are amongst the poorest and most disadvantaged sectors of the population.

- Despite relative macro-economic stability, tax collection and social spending rates over the last three decades have been low.

- A return to electoral democracy occurred in 1986, but citizen disenchantment with democratic performance is high.

Patterns of State Formation

Guatemala's economic fortunes were built on agro-exports and based on a highly exploitative form of rural capitalism, which in turn was reflected in authoritarian and exclusive forms of politics and development. The dispossession of indigenous people from their historic lands began with colonization in the sixteenth century and accelerated during the late nineteenth-century coffee boom. New laws were introduced to stimulate coffee production and agro-exports, and inequality of access to land grew rapidly. Colonial forms of labour coercion were replaced by such mechanisms as forced indebtedness and vagrancy laws, which remained on the statute books until the mid-twentieth century. The capitalist planter class in Guatemala relied on forced wage-labour, becoming increasingly dependent on the coercive power of the central state, dominated by the armed forces, to ensure its supply of workers. Economic downturns necessitated repression by the military to quell wage demands and ensure profitability margins. Ruling elites did not view the poor and particularly the indigenous as citizens, but rather as subjects to be disciplined, controlled, and 'civilized'. The richest families traced their descent to European settlers and viewed themselves as 'white'; indeed in the early twentieth century many still held *certificados de raza* — documents that supposedly proved they had no Indian blood. Race and class discrimination were mutually reinforcing and underpinned the economic system.

The cold war: Reform reversed

Between 1944 and 1954, reformist governments were elected, following a coup by junior military officers. The administration of Juan José Arévalo (1944–51) introduced universal male suffrage, abolished forced labour and indentured servitude, and sponsored progressive labour and social security legislation. The more radical government of Jacobo Arbenz (1952–54) introduced an agrarian reform law in an effort to stimulate agricultural production and address rural poverty. However, the expropriation of large, underutilized estates and their distribution to landless peasants angered both rich landowners and the US-based United Fruit Company, one of the largest landowners in Guatemala. United Fruit conspired with US President Eisenhower's administration and elements of Guatemala's armed forces to overthrow the reformers, accusing the Arbenz government of communist sympathies. In 1954, Guatemala gained the dubious distinction of being the second country subject to a CIA-sponsored 'cold war coup' (Iran being the first in 1953).

Following the overthrow of Arbenz the agrarian reform was reversed and peasant organizers persecuted. The Guatemalan armed forces received significant support from the USA within the regional framework of counter-insurgency training. The state became increasingly dominated by the military, which by the 1970s had become a powerful economic actor in its own right. Espousing a virulent anti-communism, the private sector relied on the army to repress workers' demands for improved wages or better working conditions. Delegating the business of government to the military, it nonetheless exercised a permanent veto on social reform. Regular elections took place but the spectrum was confined to transient centre-right and right-wing parties, which invariably fielded military officers as presidential candidates. Participation was low and levels of political violence and intimidation high.

Insurgency, counter-insurgency, and genocide

Such acute socio-economic and political exclusion contributed to the emergence of a guerrilla insurgency in the 1960s. This was brutally repressed by the army. State violence increased throughout the 1970s targeting trade unionists, social activists, and reformist politicians, reaching a peak in the early 1980s when de facto military regimes fought an all-out war against the civilian population to stamp out a second guerrilla insurgency. This involved hundreds of army-led massacres, 'scorched earth' measures, forced displacement of thousands of Guatemalans, mandatory paramilitary 'civil patrols' for all indigenous men in the countryside, and the militarization of the entire state apparatus; it constituted one of the most extreme cases of state repression in twentieth-century Latin America. In total during 36 years of armed conflict, some 200,000 people were killed (2 per cent of the 1980 population), nearly a quarter of whom 'disappeared'. Another million were displaced, either internally or into Mexico. In 1999, the United Nations found that the Guatemalan state was responsible for over 90 per cent of gross human rights violations documented throughout the armed conflict and was guilty of acts of genocide against the indigenous population between 1981 and 1983. This massive destruction of human and social capital had significant negative consequences for Guatemala's development prospects.

Electoral democracy and peace negotiations

In the mid-1980s, the military returned the country to civilian rule in a 'guided transition' to democracy designed to improve the country's standing before the international community, while perpetuating effective control by the armed forces over national affairs. The return to elected government, encouraged by US President Reagan's administration, permitted restoration of US military aid—suspended since 1978 by US President Carter in protest at human rights violations. Presidential elections held in 1985 were won by the centre-right Christian Democrat party; a new Constitution was adopted in 1986. Yet political parties remained weak and fragmented, the influence of the military was undiminished, and state-perpetrated political repression of political opponents and trade union and human rights activists continued. In 1993, gridlock between executive and congress led President Jorge Serrano to attempt a 'self-coup', closing down Congress and dismissing the Supreme Court. Serrano was thwarted by a combination of popular mobilization and opposition from the domestic private sector, the international community, and sectors of the armed forces, representing an important step in the strengthening of Guatemala's weak democracy.

The armed conflict was not resolved until December 1996, when the pro-business sector government of President Alvaro Arzú signed a definitive peace settlement with the insurgent Unidad Revolucionaria Nacional Guatemalteca (URNG), bringing nine years of stop–start peace talks to a successful conclusion. The international community exerted considerable pressure to secure a settlement: the final phase of the negotiations was overseen by the United Nations, and after 1994 an on-site UN mission was charged with verification and supervision of the peace accords. Through its sponsorship of the peace settlement the international community became highly involved in attempts to kick-start development in Guatemala.

Key points

- Guatemala's republican history is characterized by authoritarian rule, coercive rural capitalism, and racist discrimination.

- A reformist democratic regime was overthrown in 1954 at the height of the cold war by a US-backed military coup.

- In response to guerrilla challenges, the armed forces militarized the state and used extreme violence against the civilian population.

- The country returned to elected civilian government in 1986, but the military continued to dominate politics and repress opponents.

- Thirty-six years of civil war finally ended with a UN-sponsored negotiated settlement in 1996.

The peace accords aimed not only to formally end the armed conflict, but also to reverse the country's historically exclusionary pattern of development. They comprised 13 separate accords, involving four main areas:

- resettlement of displaced populations, reincorporation of former guerrillas, and reconciliation regarding past violations of human rights;

- an integrated programme for human development, which mandated a 50 per cent increase over five years in health and education spending;

- goals for productive and sustainable development, including market-led reform of the agricultural sector;

- modernization of the democratic state, including reduction in the role of the armed forces, strengthening the rule of law and increasing civil society participation, particularly in implementing the accords themselves.

Three cross-cutting elements were emphasized: the rights of indigenous communities; commitments regarding the rights and position of women; and greater social participation. The international community pledged more than US$3.2 billion in aid—over 60 per cent as grants to implement the accords.

Lack of Domestic Commitment

The peace accords constituted important achievements in their own right, but implementation was slow and uneven. Given the country's violent past and history of socio-economic and ethnic and gender exclusion, meeting the comprehensive goals of the peace settlement was bound to be challenging. However, lack of commitment by key domestic actors further constrained prospects for success. While the international community and civil society organizations backed the agreements, the commitment of the main political parties, the military, and the private sector to the settlement was weak. The powerful and conservative private sector staunchly defended its privileges, despite the more progressive stance of certain reformist elements within the business community. During the negotiating process, the private sector association CACIF (Comité de Asociaciones Agricolas, Comerciales, Industriales y Financieras)—dominated by large landowners—steadfastly vetoed attempts at

land reform, insisting on the sanctity of private property. In the wake of the settlement, CACIF has successfully blocked far-reaching fiscal reform or tax reforms, especially any increase in direct taxes.

Implementation: A mixed record

Other aspects of the peace settlement were more successful. The guerrillas (all but decimated as a military force by the violence of the early 1980s) were reincorporated into civilian life—the ceasefire was not breached and the URNG became a political party. Displaced and returned refugee populations were resettled, although many complained of being allocated poor land and of insufficient access to credit. A UN-led truth commission was completed in 1999, a major achievement that signalled army responsibility for gross violations of human rights and recommended legal prosecutions. Yet, despite the efforts of human rights organizations to secure justice, impunity remains the norm. Attacks have occurred against human rights organizations and indigenous communities trying to secure exhumations of mass graves and bring perpetrators to trial. Spending on health and education did increase and a number of important structural reforms were implemented, particularly in education. However, this has not yet had an appreciable impact on social indicators. Social spending was supposed to be redirected towards the poorer regions, but the record has been mixed. The global economic downturn in 2000–01 combined with the global fall in agro-export prices severely hampered even the limited development plans for the rural sector set out in the peace accords. The rural poor continue to lack access to land. In some cases large landowners made a healthy profit from the peace funds provided by the international community by selling unproductive lands at inflated prices to the national peace fund. Landless peasants settled on these lands found they were unable to feed themselves and saddled with debt repayment obligations they could not meet.

A patrimonialist state and weak party system

In addition to private sector intransigence, the failure to modernize the state and the weakness of democratic institutions provide clues to Guatemala's continuing underdevelopment. The internationally prescribed formula of institutional strengthening and 'civil society strengthening' contained in the peace accords failed to transform an exclusive, **patrimonialist** state into a developmental state. This reflects the balance of political forces and inherent difficulty of changing historically entrenched patterns. The nature of Guatemala's party system is both cause and effect of the patrimonialist state.

During the 1960s and 1970s, Guatemalan political parties were highly dependent on the armed forces; elections regularly took place but most presidential candidates were military officers from different factions backed by one or another group of private sector interests. During the transition to democracy in the 1980s, the Christian Democrat party rose to national prominence and enjoyed mass support, but its fortunes subsequently declined due to corruption and intra-party factionalism. A core nucleus of political parties on the right and centre-right of the political spectrum contested elections throughout the 1990s signalling a degree of stability of the party system, but these parties continued to be dominated by personalist politics within the private sector. Some centre-left parties, including the former guerrilla URNG, gained ground after 1995, but their share of the vote remains limited and the parties themselves far from consolidated.

In general, Guatemalan political parties tend to be dominated by powerful individuals who campaign on the strength of their personal, clientelist networks, rather than by programmatic coherence or the representation of different groups in society. They are subject to continuous division and fragmentation; indeed, many are little more than electoral alliances of convenience formed to support the interests of one or another economic sector. Traditions of coalition government and inter-party cooperation within congress are weak. In the absence of congressional majorities, governments are forced to rely on opportunistic coalitions between the different parties in Congress. Party discipline is extremely lax, elected deputies often switching their allegiance during their term of office, and **clientelism** is rife.

In November 1999, the right-wing populist Frente Republicano Guatemalteco (FRG), led by former military dictator Ríos Montt, won national elections, fielding Alfonso Portillo as their presidential candidate. The FRG's electoral victory represented the displacement of the Guatemalan private sector from control of government for the first time since the return to democracy in 1986 and signalled the rise to power of a new economic elite linked to the military and organized crime. While in government, the FRG manipulated state institutions for its own political and economic advantage: accusations of government corruption, kickbacks, and clientelism mounted, and confrontation between government and civil society groups increased. Following the return of traditional private sector interests to government with the election of Oscar Berger in 2003, some members of the former administration were imprisoned on charges of corruption. Portillo was stripped of his parliamentary immunity and fled the country following indictment for embezzlement of state funds. In 2007 Social Democrat candidate Álvaro Colom won the presidency. However, his administration lacks a congressional majority and has proved unable to advance tax reforms or to improve the appalling record of public security.

Military power, weak civil society, and continued human rights abuses

The Guatemalan armed forces largely retained their power following the peace settlement. In contrast to neighbouring El Salvador, the armed challenge from the guerrilla forces in Guatemala was negligible and the leverage of the USA over the armed forces limited. Troop numbers were reduced during the late 1990s, but the military budget increased, directly contravening the peace accords. While efforts to consolidate a civilian police force have advanced, the police remain weak, corrupt, and underfunded, and the army has again been employed in public security functions, once more in contravention of the peace settlement.

In addition to the slowness of institutional reform of the armed forces, more sinister manifestations of military power are evident. Serving and former military officers form part of a network of so-called 'parallel powers', which has influence within the highest spheres of government. These mafia-style networks are implicated in corruption scandals, organized crime, and maintaining impunity for those guilty of gross violations of human rights. Police and army units are implicated in extrajudicial executions of suspected gang members and in so-called social cleansing operations, including one

notorious massacre of prison inmates in 2006. A United Nations Commission to investigate abuses by clandestine groups operating in the country was finally approved in late 2006, in part in response to consistent failure of the Guatemalan state to effectively tackle this problem, although its implementation was blocked for a year by the Guatemalan Congress. In 2009 the UN Secretary General extended the mandate of the commission to 2011.

Civil society organizations have become more vocal advocates of government transparency and accountability in recent years, but face adverse conditions. Violence and intimidation against rights activists continue and popular awareness of the historically high costs of dissent means that Guatemalan civil society remains comparatively weak. Indigenous Mayan organizations gained a national presence after the early 1990s and have advanced important national and local development initiatives, but their influence has recently declined. According to the framework for peace negotiations, all reforms to the constitution had to be approved by Congress and then passed by a majority in a national referendum. A poll held in May 1999 (with a turnout of less than 20 per cent) rejected a package of constitutional reforms that included the official recognition of Guatemala as a multicultural and multi-ethnic nation-state. Elements of the private sector campaigned vociferously against recognition of indigenous peoples' rights, arguing it would lead to 'reverse discrimination' and **balkanization** of the country. Unlike other Latin American countries with large indigenous populations—for example, Bolivia or Ecuador—multicultural reforms of the Guatemalan state have been relatively limited to date. Guatemala has ratified the International Labour Organization's Convention 169 on the rights of indigenous and tribal peoples, but has largely failed to honour its international commitments to respect indigenous rights.

Despite some decentralization and greater involvement of non-governmental organizations (NGOs) in delivery of public services during the 1990s, state–civil society relations remain conflictive. Whilst in some cases more participatory local government has been strengthened, in others local administration is characterized by corruption and clientelism. Instead of working with the state, civil society organizations often go *around* the state in an effort to secure their demands. For example, echoing what has been called the 'boomerang effect', human rights organizations work through transnational networks to persuade foreign governments and donors to put pressure on the Guatemalan state to meet its human rights obligations.

In spite of the end of the armed conflict, the human rights situation in Guatemala remains extremely bleak. High levels of violent crime, continued impunity, and the ineffectiveness of the police and the judiciary mean weak civil rights protection. The growth of rival armed gangs linked to drug-trafficking during the 1990s worsened the security situation for ordinary Guatemalans, many of whom live in marginal urban settlements controlled by drug barons. Male homicide rates are amongst the highest in Latin America and the Caribbean; violent murders of women also increased in the 2000s, leading some Guatemalan human rights campaigners to talk about 'femicide'. More than 5,000 murders a year are committed in Guatemala, more than during the final years of the armed conflict; most are never investigated. United Nations officials have accused the Guatemalan government of fostering a culture of impunity, and have pointed to the costs of violence for development: the UN's Development Programme for Guatemala estimated in 2006 that violence cost 7.3 per cent of GDP, costs associated with health care, lost production, and public and private security. Public security and violence constitute major priorities for government and continue to weigh negatively on Guatemala's development prospects.

Key points

- The 1996 peace accords set out a programme aiming to reverse exclusionary development and improve social participation, especially of women and indigenous peoples.

- The accords were backed by the international community and civil society groups, but the commitment of the armed forces, private sector, and political parties to the settlement was low.

- Some progress on implementation has been made, but targets have not been met. Private sector resistance to raising fiscal revenues remains high.

- Key factors impeding emergence of a developmental state include opportunist, clientelist, and fragmented political parties, a powerful and autonomous military and relatively weak civil society.

- Confrontational party politics and the rise of organized crime and 'parallel powers' pose serious threats to Guatemalan democracy and obstacles to development.

Conclusion

Guatemala is a predatory state rather than a developmental state. The US-supported derailing of the reformist administration of Jacobo Arbenz produced one of the most violent and authoritarian regimes in the region. The state lacked autonomy and was effectively colonized by powerful private interests to the detriment of the majority of the population. During the cold war, it was supported by the regional superpower under the aegis of anti-communism. Despite transition to electoral rule two decades ago, such predatory tendencies have not disappeared—indeed, many now point to the increasingly mafia-style operation of the Guatemalan state.

The peace process of the 1990s provided an important space for reorienting historically exclusionary patterns of development. However, without the political commitment of the most powerful domestic actors, international pressure and the support of civil society organizations were unable to secure such a shift. Guatemala today is a weak and illiberal democracy—the population may enjoy suffrage or political rights, but civil rights are not enforced and the rule of law is routinely flouted by powerful actors within and outside government. Historical patterns of ethnic and economic exclusion combined with the legacy of extreme levels of state violence against the civilian population mean that citizen participation is relatively weak. The strength and conservatism of the private sector, its historic reliance on the armed forces, and the systematic persecution of the left and centre-left has engendered a particularly weak and venal political class and party system constituting another impediment to development. More progressive elements secured a foothold during the 1990s, but they face powerful opposition and have yet to consolidate effective parties capable of winning elections.

Finally, long-term structural factors have not favoured the Guatemalan economy. Historically reliant on a particularly exploitative form of rural capitalism, the private sector has largely failed to adapt to new global conditions despite the relative decline of traditional agro-exports. High commodity prices have helped secure macro-economic stability, but the historic lack of investment in human capital remains a serious impediment to future economic development. Prevailing economic policies have proved singularly incapable of generating greater development and equality.

Questions

1. Critically examine Guatemala's performance in terms of rights-based measures of development.

2. What impact did the end of armed conflict have on development prospects?

3. Can international intervention address the historical causes of underdevelopment, and if so, under what circumstances?

4. Are the main causes of underdevelopment in Guatemala largely economic or mainly political?

Further reading

■ Jonas, S. (2000), *Of Centaurs and Doves: Guatemala's Peace Process* (Boulder, CO/London: Westview Press). A comprehensive overview of the peace process and of contemporary Guatemalan politics.

■ PNUD (Programa de las Naciones Unidas para el Desarrollo) (2008), *Guatemala: ¿Una economía al Servicio del Desarrollo Humano?*, Informe Nacional de Desarrollo Humano 2007–08, Guatemala, available at http://desarrollohumano.org.gt

■ Sieder, R. (ed.) (1998), *Guatemala after the Peace Accords* (London: Institute of Latin American Studies). Academics and practitioners consider the challenges following the peace agreements.

■ ——, Thomas, M., Vickers, J., and Spence, J. (2002), *Who Governs? Guatemala Five Years after the Peace Accords* (Washington DC: Hemisphere Initiatives/Washington Office on Latin America). Reports on the progress of the peace settlement after five years.

■ UNDP (2007), *Human Development Report*, available at http://hdrstats.undp.org/es/countries/data_sheets/cty_ds_GTM.html [accessed 8 January 2010].

Web links

■ www.desarrollohumano.org.gt   United Nations Human Development Report for Guatemala 2007–08.

■ http://lnweb18.worldbank.org   World Bank Guatemala Poverty Assessment (GUAPA) 2003.

Online Resource Centre

For additional material and resources, please visit the Online Resource Centre at:
www.oxfordtextbooks.co.uk/orc/burnell3e/

22b South Korea: From Development to New Challenges

Peter Ferdinand

＊ Overview

This chapter concentrates on the role of the state in directing and leading development in the Republic of Korea since the end of the Korean War in 1953. It falls into six main parts, beginning with three legacies from recent Korean history that favoured success. The second part identifies key institutions of Korea's developmental state, with 'embedded autonomy' from societal pressures. The third part assesses the success of Korea's development policies: land reform; industrialization that from the mid-1960s was increasingly export-led; and investment in education. The fourth part considers the reforms of the developmental state since 1998. The fifth part examines the transition to democracy since 1987. The final part identifies new challenges for South Korea in a world of increasing globalization. Figure 22b.1 is a map of South Korea and Box 22b.1 provides an overview of key dates in South Korea's history.

Figure 22b.1 South Korea

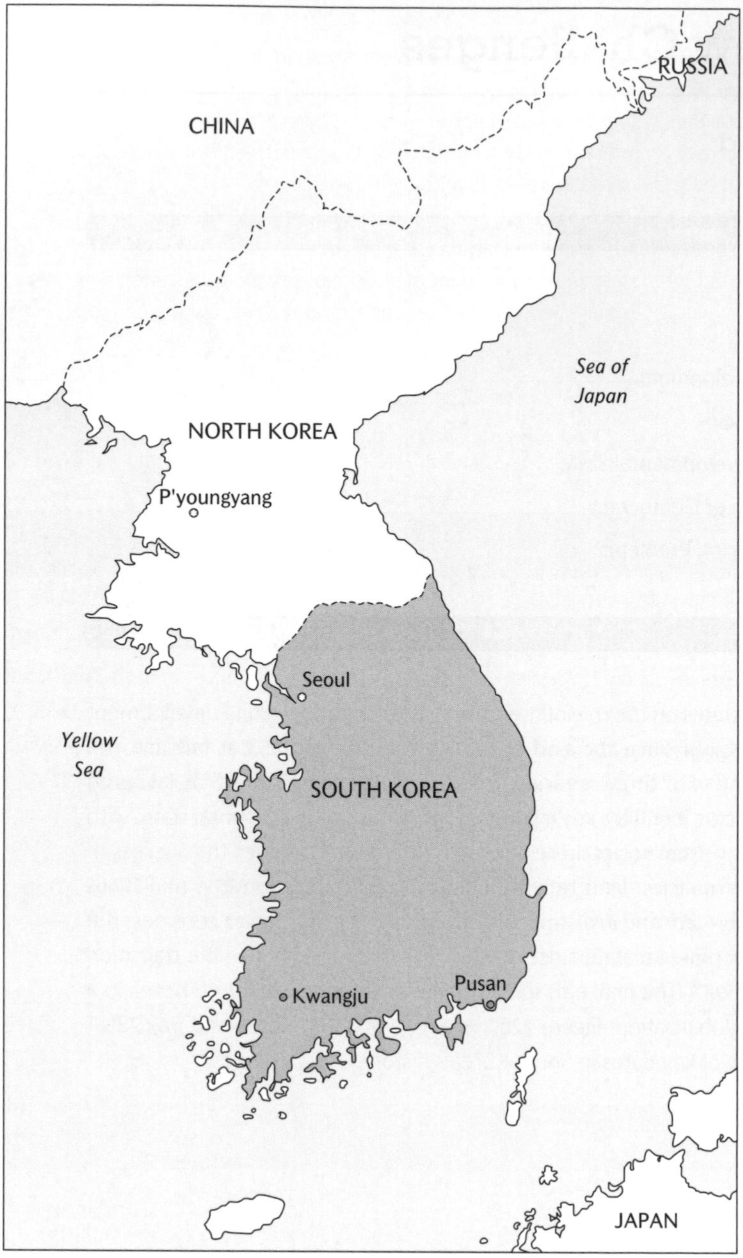

SOUTH KOREA

Box 22b.1 Key Dates in Modern Korea's History

1910	Colonized by Japan
1945	Creation of two separate independent Korean states in the north and the south
1950–53	Korean War
1961	General Park Chung Hee seizes power in South Korea
1987	Democracy re-emerges as General Roh Tae Woo allies with former oppositionist Kim Young Sam to form the Democratic Liberal Party and rule through it
1992	Kim Young Sam becomes the first civilian president since 1961
1997	Asian financial crisis and Kim Dae Jung is elected president
2002	Roh Moo Hyun's election as president marks rise of new political generation
2007	Lee Myung Bak is elected president from the Grand National Party (inauguration February 2008)

Introduction

In 1945 the Korean peninsula was freed from Japanese colonial rule by the USA and the Soviet Union. It was divided into two states—one communist in the north and one capitalist in the south. In 1950, North Korea (the Democratic People's Republic of Korea, or DPRK) invaded the south (Republic of Korea, or ROK). In three years over 11 million people died as a result of the conflict, and it left per capita income in the south, approximately US$67 per year (in 1996 dollars), among the lowest in the world. By 2001, that figure had risen to around US$9,400. In 1995, it became only the second Asian state after Japan and the second former colony after Mexico to be admitted to the Organisation for Economic Co-operation and Development (OECD).

Key points

- On all conventional measures, South Korea's record of development since the early 1950s is highly impressive.

Historical Legacies

Three legacies from before 1953 contributed to the drive for national economic development, especially after 1961: social traditions; the impact of Japanese colonialism, partition, and civil war; South Koreans' perception of their place in the East Asian region and the world.

First, South Korea has the distinct advantage of being ethnically homogeneous. The *ius sanguinis* determines Korean nationality and until 1997 this could only be transmitted from a Korean father, not a Korean mother, other than in exceptional circumstances.

Also, over the centuries Confucianism became the dominant ideology of social organization. According to the 1995 census about a quarter of the population are Christian and slightly fewer are Buddhists, but principles of Confucian social organization are deeply embedded in Korean society. These respect a hierarchy of relationships within the family, in which everyone knows their obligations towards everyone else, as the basis for a well-ordered society. The patriarchal head of the family was entitled to absolute respect. So too was the emperor or ruler. Filial piety—the devotion of the son to the father—was the core relationship.

Second, colonialism launched Korean modernization and development. Until the twentieth century, the Korean peninsula—the 'hermit kingdom'—was a poor backwater, largely ignored by its neighbours. After 1910, Japanese colonialism introduced a wider set of regional relations and industrialization in the north, but the Japanese occupied all the important managerial and administrative posts. The resentment over colonial experiences generated a very powerful sense of patriotism among Koreans, both in the north and the south.

Third, a hunger to remake the country after the civil war underlay the development drive in both north and south, where both were conscious of the immense size of their near neighbours and wary of their respective superpower protectors.

Key points

- A unique combination of three distinct historical legacies has exercised a powerful influence on South Korea's distinctive developmental success over the last fifty years.

Institutions of Development

South Korea's government was determined to pursue industrialization vigorously, for security's sake as much as prosperity.

Politics in South Korea was dominated by the military from the 1960s up until the 1990s. General Park Chung Hee (Korean family names come first) staged a coup in 1961, and from then until 1992 generals dominated government, committed to making the nation 'rich and strong'. General Park declared: 'The Asian peoples want to obtain economic equality first and build a more equitable political machinery afterward' (in Jones and Il 1980: 43).

He laid the basis for what has subsequently been termed a **developmental state**. Its main endogenous features have been described as: (a) a nationalist agenda; (b) state direction of finance for priority development projects; (c) an effective and technocratic bureaucracy; (d) partnership between the state and business; and (e) authoritarianism (Woo-Cummings 1999: 1–31). The major development decisions were formulated by the Economic Planning Board (EPB), founded in 1961. For the next 15 years the economy grew faster than 'planned'.

Table 22b.1 South Korea's Average Annual Growth Rate of Gross Domestic Product (%)

1950–59	1960–69	1970–79	1980–89	1990–2000	2001–08
5	8.5	9.5	9.4	5.7	4.4

Source: World Bank, *World Development Report* (various years)

A key factor was the state's **embedded autonomy** (Evans 1995): aimed at developing capitalist enterprises, the state was insulated from excessive pressure by those interests, freeing it to pursue long-term national development goals. The military's political domination helped with firm decision-making. During the 1960s and 1970s, a solid, merit-based bureaucracy was created. Favoured businessmen were allowed to build empires, the most successful putting together *chaebols*—business groups or conglomerates. These were family-based companies with cross-holdings of shares in subsidiaries. These families grew exceedingly rich and were widely resented (Eckert 1990). They benefited from government favouritism; financing remained the preserve of state banks, although this limited their experience of assessing genuine commercial risks. Cartels were encouraged but the state demanded energetic competition between them.

Chaebols were compensated if the government misdirected them into financial losses (Lee 1997). The government also tightly controlled the labour unions, calling up memories of the civil war and military service, and fear of communist infiltration (Janelli 1993).

According to the World Bank, average annual per capital gross national income (GNI) growth between 1960 and 1995 was around 7.5 per cent (see Table 22b.1).

> **Key points**
>
> • An intensive period of economic development and industrialization between 1961 and 1979 created a powerful business sector but also solidified business dependence upon the state. Later the state became more dependent upon big business.

Development Policies

In 1953, the economy was still overwhelmingly agricultural. The first task was land reform, to introduce greater fairness into the size of landholdings and free up capital and workers for industrialization. The second priority was rebuilding the country. The government strongly encouraged

'patriotic' savings, also imposing punitive taxes on expensive consumer imports. The results were impressive (see Table 22b.2), and the savings were channelled towards government-determined investment priorities.

Table 22b.2 Gross Domestic Savings as a Percentage of South Korea's Growing GDP

1960	1970	1980	1990	2000	2008
2	16.2	20.8	36.1	33	30.3

Source: World Bank, *World Development Report* (various years)

Initially the government pursued **import-substitution industrialization**, as much for reasons of national security as for the prevailing orthodoxy of development economics. After 1965, however, the government changed strategy and concentrated more upon exports. The selective targeting of industries for national development succeeded handsomely. Then Japan's revaluation of the yen, in 1985, created new export opportunities, leading to a doubling of exports to the

USA between 1985 and 1988. Also, Korean corporations were now able to create their own non-bank financial institutions and to tap international financial markets for investments, all of which allowed them to resist government demands when it suited.

The government's commitment to education had considerable long-term economic significance. Illiteracy was virtually eliminated by 1963; by 1978 the proportion of secondary-school-age pupils actually in school was higher than in Singapore, Argentina, Mexico, Turkey, or India. By the 1990s, the proportion of students in higher education was higher than in Japan. Amsden (1989: 219) remarked: 'Korea, therefore, is both a general case of a well-educated late industrializing country and a special case of an exceptionally well-educated one.'

South Korea's achievements stand in stark contrast with those of the north or Myanmar. Both were traumatized by war and had similar levels of development in the 1950s. Both, however, pursued socialist policies and minimized contact with the world economy. South Korea's economic performance has been vastly superior. According to the Asian Development Bank, in 2004 per capita GNI was US$220 in Myanmar and US$14,000 in South Korea. While Burma remains predominantly an agricultural society, and whilst North Korea is predominantly an industrial country, South Korea's workforce now more closely resembles the post-industrial societies of the West. But perhaps the most striking feature of South Korea's development has been its high degree of income equality. The **Gini coefficient** for income inequality was 0.312 in 1985 and fell as low as 0.283 in 1997 on the verge of the Asian financial crisis. That crisis led to increased inequality and by 2007 it had risen back to 0.316—although still low by international standards.

Key points

- South Korea's adoption of a state-led strategy for development, supported by universal primary education, has been outstandingly successful, especially by comparison with others in the region who pursued more socialist and inward-looking policies.

Reforming the Developmental State

Korea's run of nearly forty years of high economic growth was interrupted by the Asian financial crisis of 1997. Although the crisis first broke in Thailand, it spread to Korea. It revealed that Korea had undertaken financial liberalization in the 1990s without adequate state regulation, and then the Bank of Korea almost exhausted the national reserves in trying to prop up the currency. So the state no longer had the resources to bail out the corporate sector. The weakness in the financial sector infected manufacturing. In 1998 the Korean economy shrank by almost 7 per cent, and unemployment rose by 7 per cent. Korea had to turn to the International Monetary Fund (IMF) for stand-by credit of US $57 billion, at that time the largest that the IMF had made.

The next few years saw a transformation in the ownership and management of Korean banks. Initially the only solution was for the state to increase its support—state ownership of banks rose from 33 per cent in 1996 to 54 per cent in 2000. Overall the state spent the equivalent of 28 per cent of gross domestic product (GDP) in 2000 in stabilizing the banking sector (Kalinowski and Cho 2009: 230–1). Once these emergency measures had taken effect, however, the state decided that the only way to make banking more secure was through investments from foreign banks, which could transfer Western experience and methods.

The state was less successful in pushing through reforms in industry. For years Korean leaders had reiterated the need to rebalance the economy with small and medium-sized enterprises (SMEs) playing a greater role in wealth creation at the expense of the *chaebols*, but the latter had consistently fought off the challenges. The 1997 crisis offered a much better opportunity. The interests of President Kim, labour unions and non-governmental organizations (NGOs), the IMF and potential foreign investors all converged. Half of the 30 largest *chaebols* either went bankrupt or had to introduce state-backed reforms to ensure survival. The state demanded a rationalization of production in key sectors such as car manufacturing and electronics to reduce overcapacity. And the state ordered a reduction in cross-holding of shares within *chaebols*. All this opened up the economy to foreign investors. However, as the economy and the re-structured *chaebols* recovered, the state's leverage over them subsided again. Corporations such as Samsung, Hyundai, and LG developed into global brands of technological excellence. Firms began to generate more funds for new investment from their own profits. They depended less upon banks, whether state- or foreign-run, for credit (Kalinowski and Cho 2009). The state's efforts to tame them have largely failed.

Korea was able to restore economic success remarkably quickly. It increased its export/GDP ratio from 39 per cent in 2000 to 53 per cent in 2008. Between 1998 and 2007 Korea consistently ran significant foreign trade surpluses, the longest period in its history. Throughout the previous forty years it had only achieved trade surpluses between 1986 and 1990. China's market in particular offered enormous potential. Where in 1992, when the two states exchanged diplomatic recognition, there had been virtually no trade, by 2003 China had become Korea's number one export destination. Korea also retained relatively high import duties on agriculture and significant non-tariff barriers. Korean foreign exchange reserves soared to US$264.2 billion in Autumn 2009, the seventh largest in the world. And whilst foreign direct investment (FDI) in Korea certainly increased, it still remained at a relatively low level by OECD standards.

In one respect the economy did see significant change. Welfare expenditures grew—partly to ease the hardship of the much greater numbers of unemployed. According to the OECD, in 2005 the share of GDP represented by public social expenditure had risen to 6.9 per cent, where in 1995 it had been 3.3 per cent. Nevertheless this was still the lowest figure within the OECD and far below the average.

Thus the decade from the Asian Financial Crisis had seen the economy significantly open up and liberalize. The state had guided the transformation—by 2005 the Ministry of Commerce, Industry and Energy employed 25 per cent more officials than it did in 1998 (Kim and Kim 2005: 61)—but it failed to achieve all its restructuring objectives.

Key points

- The Asian financial crisis provided an opportunity to restructure the developmental state.
- The state transformed the financial sector by collaborating with globalizing foreign investors.
- In industry, however, the *chaebols* were able to recover from dependence upon state aid and resume their pre-eminence.

The Consolidation of Democracy

During the 1990s, Korea turned into a functioning multi-party democracy. In elections in 1997 power changed hands from one party to another for the first time, and peacefully, despite the Asian financial crisis, allowing Kim Dae Jung, a veteran oppositionist to the military's rule, to become president without any response from the military.

Thus Korea's growing prosperity was followed by democratization, seeming to bear out theories that suggest a sequential link between the two (see Chapter 14). Such was the country's economic development in the 1980s that in 1988 GDP exceeded US$3,000 per capita—the threshold beyond which, for Huntington (1996b: 7–8), military coups rarely succeed.

The main catalysts for change were workers and students. The labour unions saw democracy as essential to asserting their members' interests, after decades of repression. And although students benefited from the massive expansion of the education system, they were less deferential to their elders than previous generations. There were also now 1.4 million of them, far more than in the 1960s. When riot police violently dispersed their demonstrations, this antagonized parents too, especially middle-class ones. And organized religion became a more potent factor in democratization. Both Protestant and Catholic churches openly challenged the military leaders and became a key forum for political protest.

In 1987 General Chun Doo Hwan provoked widespread public anger by nominating General Roh Tae Woo as the next president. The decision needed ratification by general election, but the regime failed to win an overall majority. Although the precedent of direct presidential rule was an option, the regime wanted more sympathetic treatment from the international media, especially in the USA, as the 1988 Seoul Olympics approached. President Reagan specifically telephoned President Chun to warn against bloodletting. So the authorities embarked upon protracted secret negotiations with the divided opposition, at the end of which Roh Tae Woo made a pact with the leader of the largest opposition party, Kim Young Sam, to form the Democratic Liberal Party (DLP) with the understanding that Kim would become the next president after Roh.

The 1990s saw democratic consolidation as power passed peacefully from one party to another.

The military withdrew from politics. Kim Young Sam became president as planned and launched an anti-corruption campaign, which then ensnared the two preceding presidents, Chun Doo Hwan and Roh Tae Woo. Both were sentenced to long prison terms.

From 1997 liberal political leaders held the state presidency for ten years—Kim Dae Jung and Roh Moo Hyun. This contributed to the stabilization of the democratic system. The victory of President Roh also marked the advent of a new generation of leaders, the so-called '386 generation'—that is those who were in their thirties in the 1990s, attended college in the 1980s, and were born in the 1960s. Yet neither presidency lived up to the expectations of their supporters, let alone the public more generally.

The Asia Barometer survey of 2003 showed that 88 per cent of respondents believed that democracy was 'fairly good' or 'very good' for Korea. On the other hand only 11 per cent had confidence in parliament, the lowest figure for any public institution and much less than the 59 per cent who had confidence in the army (Shin and Lee 2006: 280, 299).

One factor in this was the state's inability to safeguard the livelihood of many workers who lost their jobs after 1997, as well as the sale of shares in many *chaebols* to foreigners. But another was the persisting issue of political corruption (Ferdinand 2003). Despite their promises, the terms of all three democratically elected presidents have ended in ignominy surrounded by charges of corruption—most tragically leading to the suicide of Roh Moo Hyun after the defeat of his party's nominee as successor for president in the 2007 elections. According to the surveys of Transparency International, South Korea was ranked 27th out of 41 countries in 1995, and 40th out of 180 countries in 2009 (first place being least corrupt), with almost identical raw scores. During the 1990s, there was a widespread perception that democracy had actually exacerbated the problem, by multiplying the number of decision-makers who needed to be 'squared'. Of course, the problem is not just one of bribery or greed. It also involves Koreans' sense of family-based identity. As long as Korean politicians are expected to perform social roles of giving gifts on constituents' family occasions when their official salaries are insufficient, this problem will persist, but so will the dissatisfaction.

In 2007 the first former *chaebol* head was elected president, Lee Myung Bak, although he also had previous political experience as a member of the Korean parliament and as mayor of Seoul. The economic achievements of the *chaebols* in restoring the economy have to some extent rehabilitated their political image. Now popular fears about the dangers of combined business and political power seem to have dissipated, along with hopes for a cleaner politics under liberal politicians. President Lee promised to revive the economy, as former Hyundai Engineering and Construction. However, the cycle of allegations of corruption by presidential aides has again resurfaced.

Gradually the party system has become more stable, at least among conservatives, where the Grand National Party (the successor to the DLP) has established itself as the main protagonist. Opposing them, however, has been a string of parties that have collapsed through factionalism and regrouped under new names every few years. Parties tend still to be dominated by fractious individual leaders.

Party instability is exacerbated by the constitution in two ways. First, it allows the president only one term of office of five years. In practice this limits his effective control over the political system to at best three to four years, before would-be successors begin to assert themselves. The fact that there is no vice-president aggravates this problem. Second, the constitution lays down different electoral cycles for the presidency and the National Assembly, which regularly leads to cohabitation and gridlock, with different parties controlling the two institutions.

One other political development needs to be noted because it also makes politics more turbulent. Korea is now one of the most 'wired' societies. By 2008, according to the International Telecommunications Union, South Korea had the seventh highest figure for broadband penetration and the highest for any non-European state. This has affected the media's reporting of politics. Whilst most of the main national newspapers are conservative, the online *Ohmynews* has attracted a wide following because of the alternative coverage that it offers. It relies upon large numbers of 'citizen reporters' to file stories.

Key points

- Economic development reconfigured social forces and gradually constrained military rule. Then a changing external environment acted as a key catalyst in South Korea's transition to democracy.

- Democracy emerged as a pact between elites and above all key leaders.

- Widespread acceptance of democracy in general persists, although it was shaken by the financial crisis.

- The party system remains fragile.

- Democratic consolidation has yet to witness a marked decrease in high-level corruption.

Conclusion: Emerging Problems

South Korea has come a long way since 1953. It is now a moderately prosperous and economically developed country with an apparently consolidated democracy. The new Confucian ethic has incorporated dimensions that promote patriotism and prosperity, whilst assimilating Western values such as individualism, material success, and pragmatism. Thus while traditional values continue to shape society, they are themselves reshaped by development. Korea is now qualitatively different from both the Korea of 1945 and much of the developing world. Yet the country does face substantial new challenges. Some of them stem from globalization. Others are more typical of developed political economies.

An emerging challenge concerns the impact of Korea's development on the environment. Although Korea uses energy fairly efficiently, energy production has doubled since 1990 — the same rate of increase as China's. The Lee administration recognizes the international and domestic pressure to improve environmental protection. Although, as a recently more-developed economy, it could claim, like many developing states, that it had made virtually no contribution to global warming, this administration has decided on serious action. It has agreed to reduce its greenhouse gas emissions, even though it was not required to do so under the Kyoto Protocol. The administration has a five-year plan to increase its spending on low-carbon green growth to 2 per cent of GDP by 2013, which is double the figure generally advocated by the UN.

A second challenge is to involve more women in political life. According to the Inter-Parliamentary Union, women held 41 seats (13.7 per cent) in the Korean National Assembly in 2009. This put it 85th out of 136 (www.ipu.org/wmn-e/classif.htm). This is certainly an improvement on 1997 when only nine women (3 per cent) held seats. Nevertheless it is still low by regional as well as global standards.

A third challenge follows from the global financial crisis. Korea maintained its developmental momentum after 1998 through increasing exports. Whilst many of these went to new markets in China and Asia, a significant proportion continued to go to the US and Europe. Consumers there will be less able to buy Korean consumer goods since the 2008–09 global financial crisis, which means that the country will need to focus more on internally generated growth.

A fourth challenge concerns the provision of welfare, where until 1997 the Korean state spent relatively little. It thought that supporting industrial and agricultural production would generate the income to support the needy, and relied upon the family for distribution. The financial crisis has changed all that. This is no longer politically sustainable. Even the more conservative Grand National Party programme promises a universal social safety net.

Then there are expressly political challenges. Collective action remains a problem. Civil society is still relatively underdeveloped. Political parties lack deep grass-roots commitment and the party system remains fragile.

Last, there is the challenge of relations with the US. Until the 1980s, Koreans had a very positive image of the US. This was based upon intervention in the Korean War and subsequent US aid. That has changed significantly. Many increasingly regard China as a more important economic partner. Many younger people now feel closer to North Korea than before. All this means that external relations complicate Korean domestic politics.

? Questions

1. To what extent has Korea's traditional political culture shaped democracy and how far has it adapted to democracy?

2. Is Korea's developmental state still viable? If not, why not?

3. Why is Korean civil society still weak and does this matter for politics?

4. Does the personalization of political leadership in Korea have any specific implications for politics, society, and economy?

5. Has Korea developed a stable competitive political party system characterized by parties with coherent and distinctive ideologies? If not, why not?

6. In what main ways and in what direction do globalization and external relations have an influence on domestic South Korean politics and political economy?

7. Does South Korea's example of combining development and democratization have any particular lessons for other developing countries in the region and is it relevant to countries elsewhere in the developing world?

→ Further reading

■ Amsden, A. H. (1989), *Asia's Next Giant: South Korea and Late Industrialization* (Oxford: Oxford University Press). Examines how and why Korea got prices 'wrong' and yet achieved dramatic economic growth.

■ Eckert, C. J. (1990), 'The South Korean Bourgeoisie: A Class in Search of Hegemony', *Journal of Korean Studies*, 7: 115–48. Outlines the rise of the families owning *chaebols*.

■ Evans, P. (1995), *Embedded Autonomy: States and Industrial Transformation* (Princeton, NJ: Princeton University Press). Focuses on a key element of the developmental state.

■ Janelli, R. L. (1993), *Making Capitalism* (Stanford, CA: Stanford University Press). The internal life of a Korean *chaebol* based on extended fieldwork.

■ Jones, L. P. and SaKong Il (1980), *Government, Business and Entrepreneurship in Economic Development: The Korean Case* (Cambridge, MA: Harvard University Press). A revealing early account of the key role of government in Korean development.

■ Kalinowski, T. and Hyekyung C. (2009), 'The Political Economy of Financial Liberalization in South Korea: State, Big Business, and Foreign Investors', *Asian Survey*, 49/2: 221–42. An up-to-date account of the complex progress of the economic reforms.

■ Lee, Y.-H. (1997), *The State, Society and Big Business in South Korea* (London/New York: Routledge). A very good account of this key relationship.

■ Pirie, I. (2005), 'Better by Design: Korea's Neoliberal Economy', *Pacific Review*, 18/3: 355–74. A good and provocative summary of the changes in Korean political economy since 1997.

■ Shin, Doh C. (1999), *Mass Politics and Culture in Democratizing Korea* (Cambridge: Cambridge University Press). The best single account of the emergence of Korea's democracy.

■ —— and Lee, J. (2006), *The Korea Democracy Barometer Surveys 1997–2004: Unraveling the Cultural and Institutional Dynamics of Democratization* (Aberdeen: Centre for the Study of Public Policy, University of Aberdeen). An interesting comparison of various political opinion surveys.

■ Woo-Cummings, M. (ed.) (1999), *The Developmental State* (Ithaca, NY/London: Cornell University Press). Outlines the basic principles and their realization in various countries around the world.

:// Web links

■ www.korea.net   The South Korean government's official homepage.

■ www.kdi.re.kr   Korean Development Institute.

■ **www.ohmynews.com** A purely online news service that relies upon citizen journalists for material, but the English-language version is only a pale shadow of the Korean.

■ **http://english.yonhapnews.co.kr** The Yonhap news service; much fuller coverage in English.

■ **www.hannara.or.kr/** Website of the Grand National Party (the site of the opposition United New Democratic Party is still under construction).

■ **www.nec.go.kr/english** National Election Commission.

■ **www.kicac.go.kr/PORTAL/Eng/index.jsp** Korean Independent Commission Against Corruption.

■ **www.onlinewomeninpolitics.org/Statistics.htm** A website devoted to increasing women's participation in politics.

 Online Resource Centre

For additional material and resources, please visit the Online Resource Centre at:
www.oxfordtextbooks.co.uk/orc/burnell3e/

South–South Relations and the Changing Landscape of International Development Cooperation

23

23a India as a 'Post-Colonial Donor'

Emma Mawdsley

 Overview

Many countries of the global South have established 'development cooperation' policies and programmes with other low- and middle-income countries. A few started as long ago as the 1950s, while others are more recent entrants to the field. Often bundled closely with trade, investment and diplomatic agendas, this South–South foreign aid includes debt relief, concessional loans, grants, humanitarian assistance, technical support, and educational and training provision. Until recently, most Western commentators on foreign aid and development largely overlooked these 'non-traditional' donors, but for various reasons they are now firmly on the radar. The '(re-)emerging donors' raise a series of challenges for the mainstream aid community, and the direct and indirect impacts of their development cooperation programmes will have implications for the world's poor, and for the politics of development. This chapter outlines the main trends and issues of South–South development cooperation, using India as a case study. Figure 23a.1 is a map of India and Box 23a.1 provides an overview of key dates in India's history.

Figure 23a.1 India

Area claimed by India and Pakistan

Area claimed by India and China

line of control

Jammu & Kashmir

CHINA

Himachal Pradesh

Punjab · Uttaranchal

PAKISTAN

Haryana

○ Delhi

Sikkim

Arunachal Pradesh

NEPAL

Uttar Pradesh

Bhutan

Rajasthan

Ayodhya
○

Bihar

Assam

Meghalaya

Nagaland

Manipur

BANGLADESH

Tripura

Jharkhand

West
Bengal

Mizoram

Gujarat

INDIA

Madhya Pradesh

Chattisgarh

Kolkata
(Calcutta)

Mumbai
(Bombay)

Orissa

Maharashtra

Arabian
Sea

Andhra
Pradesh

Bay
of
Bengal

Karnataka

Goa

Bangalore

Nb: Boundaries in the Kashmir region are in dispute. The use of specific nomenclature and boundary symbols on this map implies neither recognition nor non-recognition of the legality of the political regions or boundaries to which they refer.

Tamil
Nadu

Kerala

Indian Ocean

SRI
LANKA

INDIA

Box 23a.1 Key Dates in India's History

1858 India comes under direct rule of the British Crown, which takes it over from the East India Company

1885 The Indian National Congress is formed by emerging nationalists

1920–22 A civil disobedience movement against British rule is launched by Congress, led by Mahatma Gandhi

1947 India achieves independence, but the country is violently split by the Partition; East Pakistan (later

	Bangladesh) and West Pakistan (later Pakistan) are also created out of the former colony; Jawaharlal Nehru becomes independent India's first Prime Minister	1989	Congress loses the national elections to a coalition of other parties
1949–52	The Constitution of India is drawn up, declaring it to be a secular, federal Republic	1991	Major economic reforms implemented by Prime Minister Narasimha Rao mark a decisive shift towards neo-liberalism
1962	India loses a short border war with China, despite earlier declarations of friendship	1998	The Bharatiya Janata Party (BJP), a Hindu nationalist party, wins national elections; controversial nuclear tests carried out shortly afterwards
1964	Jawaharlal Nehru dies		
1966	Indira Gandhi, Nehru's daughter (no relation to Mahatma Gandhi), becomes Prime Minister, leading the ruling Indian National Congress Party	2000	India's population reaches 1 billion
		2006	Hu Jintao visits India, the first Chinese President to do so for a decade
		2007	Launch of India's first commercial space rocket
1971	Third war with Pakistan, this time over the secession of East Pakistan to form Bangladesh	2008	Closer US–India ties signalled by a nuclear deal
1984	Indira Gandhi assassinated; her son Rajiv Gandhi elected Prime Minister	2009	Indian National Congress, with Manmohan Singh as Prime Minister, re-elected to central government

Introduction

Over the last few years, India has been involved in all sorts of development activities with other countries. These include debt cancellation, loans and credits, humanitarian and emergency responses, as well as various forms of technical assistance. But in all of these instances, India is not the *recipient* of such aid, it is the *donor*—or to use its preferred term, 'development partner'. This chapter explores how and why a country that has more absolutely poor people than the whole of sub-Saharan Africa, gives development assistance to poor countries in Asia and Africa. It will start with a brief introduction to the issue of the '(re-)emerging donors' and then move to a more detailed analysis of India's foreign aid.

Foreign Aid and the 'Non-DAC Donors'

Commentators tend to disagree—often virulently —about every conceivable aspect of foreign aid, including stated and real motivations, effective and appropriate modalities, desirable recipients, direct and indirect impacts, and much more. The depth and range of disagreement is not surprising given the enormous complexity of the global foreign aid architecture, the vast range of actors (from the World Bank, to bilateral aid agencies, to global non-governmental organizations (NGOs), right down to small grass-roots local organizations), and its multiple, contingent and often conflicting stated rationales—humanitarian, developmental, commercial, and diplomatic. But what almost all of these contending evaluations share is a dominant geographical imaginary that views foreign aid as given by rich industrialized countries to poorer countries—that is to say, most people in the West imagine that development and humanitarian aid is its preserve and its gift. Until recently, with few exceptions, Western analysts almost entirely overlooked the large number of other countries that offer official 'development assistance' to other poorer countries. Six (2009) suggests that this represents a form of amnesia concerning these 'Other' donors. However, this is a situation that has changed rapidly, and the non-Development Assistance Committee (DAC) donors, or NDDs (see Box 23a.2 for a discussion of terminology), are now very much on the agenda.

Box 23a.2 Terminological Dilemmas

'Emerging' or 'new' donors? Some countries are embarking upon development assistance programmes for the first time, but many have a long history of development partnership.

'Post-colonial' donors? In some ways this is an attractive term as it explicitly reverses Orientalist binaries that set up the North as giver and the South as receiver. However, if the term is used in the sense of 'countries that were once formally colonized but which are now independent', it is not universally accurate.

'Non-DAC' donors? Although accurate, as a residual category (i.e. something is defined by what it is *not*) this term appears to promote the centrality of DAC—what unites all of the other donors is their non-DAC status, suggesting a peripheral location, or even an unfulfilled aspiration. It does not signal the active critique of DAC ideologies and practices, and the wider discontent with the dominant structures of foreign aid, felt by many around the world, and especially within the global South.

Moreover, many NDDs are cautious about the label of 'donor', with some firmly rejecting it. 'Donor' is burdened with associations of paternalism, hierarchy and neo-colonial interference. Similarly, some reject the term 'foreign aid', preferring 'development assistance.

The DAC donors

The Organisation for Economic Co-operation and Development (OECD) is made up of 30 countries, all of which are relatively industrialized and high income. Of these, 23 are members of the Development Assistance Committee (DAC), while the 24th member is the European Commission (Box 23a.3). All are Western, with the exception of Japan (which at one point was the largest aid donor in the world) and, since January 2010, South Korea. The DAC acts as a powerful forum for formulating dominant aid policies and practices around the world.

Box 23a.3 DAC and Non-DAC Donors

DAC members	**The main non-DAC donors**
Australia, Austria, Belgium, Canada, Denmark, European Commission, Finland, France, Germany, Greece, Ireland, Italy, Japan, Luxemburg, New Zealand, Norway, Portugal, South Korea, Spain, Sweden, Switzerland, The Netherlands, United Kingdom, United States	Brazil, Bulgaria, China, Cuba, Cyprus, Czech Republic, Estonia, Hungary, Iceland, India, Israel, Kuwait, Latvia, Lithuania, Malta, Mexico, Poland, Romania, Russia, Saudi Arabia, Slovak Republic, Slovenia, South Africa, Taiwan, Thailand, Turkey, United Arab Emirates, Venezuela

Although the 1990s was a decade in which the contribution of many of the NDDs declined sharply, at times in the past they have accounted for a substantial share of official development flows. In 1978, for example, the Organization of Petroleum Exporting Countries (OPEC) donors alone provided one third of all official foreign aid. Current calculations suggest that the NDDs contribute around 10 per cent of 'foreign aid', although extreme difficulties with both definitions and the availability and robustness of data means this can estimated only with considerable caution. Although dwarfed by the DAC total, this is still a significant absolute and relative amount. Moreover, for some countries, aid from the NDDs constitutes a high proportion of the total, notably the Occupied Palestinian Territories and North Korea. Another way of looking at it is to compare absolute amounts with those of DAC donors. Harmer and Cotterell (2005) calculate that in 2003 Saudi Arabia, South Korea, Qatar, India, and South Africa all gave more in humanitarian aid that a number of DAC donors. The growing numbers of Southern donors was starkly demonstrated after the Indian Ocean tsunami of 2004, when over seventy countries offered humanitarian assistance.

Some countries are embarking upon development assistance programmes for the first time, but many have a long history of development partnership.

In the post-WWII era, a large number of communist countries provided various forms of development assistance to other communist countries and to 'friendly' regimes, as well as those they hoped to influence and bring into the Soviet orbit, including Vietnam, Yemen, and Indonesia, amongst others. The Arab OPEC donors set up their development cooperation institutions following the oil price rises of the 1970s, which led to a massive boost in their economic resources. Driven by regional geo-political considerations, and shaped by Islamic cultures of charitable giving, they have been major donors for more than thirty years.

The historical lineages of other donors lie in more specific interests. For example, the origins of Taiwan foreign aid activities are highly specific to its competition with the People's Republic of China (PRC) for diplomatic recognition, but they also reflect its achievement of rapid and very successful industrial development and economic growth, and the view that it has valuable experiences to share. But it is only in the last few years that the broader development community has really woken up to these 'other' development actors.

What has jolted Western academics and policymakers out of their amnesia in the last few years has much to do with the growing role and presence of China (Bräutigam 2009). China is a major, long-standing development assistance partner to many countries, notably in Africa, and its growing 'aid' activities actively complement its wider economic, diplomatic and geo-political ambitions (see Chapter 23b). The recent visibility of the NDDs has also been driven by Venezuela's substantial aid programmes under Hugo Chávez, which are openly constructed as a challenge to US hegemony, as well as simply the growing numbers of NDDs. Furthermore, in 2004, ten new states joined the European Union. Most had previous experience of foreign aid as in the socialist period, but they are now in the process of re-establishing their aid institutions and policies in compliance with the EU's norms and standards (Grimm and Harmer 2005).

We can now observe within the heavily Western-dominated 'global' foreign aid architecture, including DAC, its member states, the World Bank Group, and various UN bodies, a new interest in the NDDs. This chapter offers a case study of India as a 'post-colonial donor'. Although India is obviously not 'representative' of the non-DAC donors—they are simply too diverse in their origins, histories, interests, capabilities, ideologies and cultures—what we sacrifice in breadth we gain in some depth.

Key points

- There is no easy way to capture or categorize the diversity of the 'non-DAC donors'.
- Although the NDDs have historically contributed a significant share of official aid, Western academic

and policy analysts have tended to overlook their roles and activities—something that is now changing.

India and South–South Relations

Over the last sixty years India has been at the centre of a series of attempts to contest the ordering of the world along the economic and political hierarchies established during the colonial period, and which often deepened during the Cold War. India was a key architect of the Non-Aligned Movement (NAM), for example, which started in the 1950s and which insisted the sovereign right of the newly decolonizing nations to resist subordination to the cold war giants. At the Bandung Conference of 1955, the principles of South–South solidarity were set out, centring on:

- mutual respect for each other's territorial integrity and sovereignty;
- mutual non-aggression;
- mutual non-interference in domestic affairs;
- equality and mutual benefit;
- peaceful coexistence.

Although aid was never a major aspect of the Non-Aligned Movement, these discourses of non-interference and mutual benefit remain the stated values underlying much South–South development cooperation programmes (although like other aspects of NAM, practices sometimes depart from principles).

Over the last ten to fifteen years, sustained high economic growth (albeit very socially and regionally uneven in its rewards) has enabled India to put greater financial and diplomatic weight behind these assertions of global stature. Whereas

in the first few decades of Independence India had to mobilize other strengths—Prime Minister Nehru's charisma and the exercise of 'soft power', India's size, its ability to play off the US and USSR, and its technological and scientific strengths—now its growing wealth, and the confidence of its increasingly assertive middle classes and elites are underpinning a new vigour in its foreign policy (Raja Mohan 2004). During the 1990s and twenty-first century, for example, India has been a controversially disruptive voice in the World Trade Organization, demanding a better deal for developing countries. However, despite claims to Third World leadership, as Varun Sahni points out:

> India's foreign policy has always exhibited a dichotomy between principle and practice: an ideological opposition to formal institutionalized discrimination in the international system—such as UNSC [United Nations Security Council] permanent membership and nuclear weapon status in the Nuclear Non-Proliferation Treaty—has gone hand-in-hand with a pragmatic willingness to seek the best possible deal for India within a hierarchical international system that is not egalitarian   (Sahni, 2007: 23).

This would suggest that India's claim to leadership, and to South–South partnership and solidarity, must be critically and carefully appraised in all arenas, including its development cooperation efforts.

Singh (2007:10), for example, argues that 'ever since economic liberalization started in 1991 India's foreign policy has been increasingly driven towards finding export markets, and attracting foreign capital and technological know-how', and observes the growing place of development cooperation in facilitating these trends. As I shall argue below, while there are indeed many potential direct and indirect benefits from India's development cooperation efforts, it would be naive to see these as necessarily positive simply by virtue of India's post-colonial status and rhetoric, as some less critical commentators claim.

Key points

- India has long positioned itself as a leader of the 'Third World', and has been an active and sometimes effective challenger of neo-imperialistic hierarchies that characterize the current world order.

- However, India's strategic imperatives (as with any other state) mean the pursuit of its interests may clash with the interests of other Southern states.

India as a Development Assistance Partner

After Independence in 1947, India was very quickly targeted by both the US and the USSR as a potential cold war ally, although over the succeeding decades the US was to turn much more strongly to India's neighbour and rival, Pakistan. Even so, both offered substantial amounts of aid to India, and it became one of the largest aid recipients in the world. Despite this status, India rapidly took on a donor mantle, starting in the 1950s with its northern Himalayan neighbour, Nepal. In the early 1960s India also started providing development assistance to another northern neighbour, Bhutan. Price (2005) notes that India was the sole external contributor to Bhutan's Second Five-Year Plan, and India remains a key contributor to Bhutan's economy.

A process that also started in the 1950s was the provision of technical experts in a wide range of fields to partner countries, and the offer of training. Despite budget constraints, Nehru was determined that India would invest in science and technology, and to that end he made sure that scarce funding was directed towards universities and research institutions—expertise that India has been able to deploy abroad. In 1964, India created the Indian Technical and Economic Cooperation scheme (ITEC). ITEC supports projects, deputations of experts, and study tours, but its main focus is on providing training programmes in areas as diverse as small and medium enterprises, rural credit programmes, food processing, textiles, information technology (IT), and women's entrepreneurship. The scheme now runs in 156 countries, and through it the Indian government offers about 4,000 placements a year.

What explains India's early entry into donor activities? Clearly it was in part motivated by the desire to create regional goodwill, especially given the hostile embrace of West Pakistan (now Pakistan) and East Pakistan (now Bangladesh) following Partition in 1947. Moreover, after Sino–Indian friendship crumbled (the nadir being the 1962 border invasion), India wished to promote strong and stable buffer states between itself and China. Thus, India looked to secure regional allies, and foreign aid played some part in that. A second incentive was energy security, which helps to explain the early focus on hydropower projects in Bhutan and Nepal. A third motivation arose from India's desire to take its place in the world not just as a regional, but as an international, power. Being an aid donor helped to build relations of solidarity with other newly independent countries, and signalled India's aspirant status to international stature.

Whereas infrastructure has been the main focus of development assistance to its Asian neighbours, historically India's development partnership with Africa has been heavily oriented towards the provision of technical skills and training, principally delivered through ITEC. In part this reflects the government of India's relatively limited financial capacity, which means that it simply cannot provide large grants and/or loans on the scale of many Western countries (or, increasingly, China). But this role also reflects the expertise and high quality provision available in many Indian universities, training centres, and institutes noted above, and it is emblematic of the discourse of South–South partnership in which India claims that it does not seek to copy the Western model of financing, with all of the implications of a donor–recipient relationship. One of India's flagship technology transfer programmes, for example, is the pan-Africa e-network. The scheme aims to provide facilities for tele-education, tele-medicine, and network video conferencing for heads of state in all 53 members of the African Union (AU). The network will also connect 53 learning centres, ten super-speciality hospitals (three of which are in India), 53 other hospitals, and five universities (two in India). India has committed at least US$100 million to this scheme. Other forms of development assistance include debt write-offs and a substantial set of contributions to food aid and peacekeeping personnel.

However, the last few years have witnessed some significant changes in the modalities of India's development cooperation. In particular, lines of credit are becoming an increasingly favoured route of channelling 'development assistance'. Since 2003 these have been managed by the Export-Import Bank of India, which is managed indirectly by the Ministry of Finance. The Ministry of Commerce is also playing a growing role—indicative of the increasingly economically strategic profile of Indian aid. For many commentators, this represents a relatively new departure. The pursuit of 'soft power' continues to be a major incentive for development cooperation, as a resurgent India acts as a key player in the growing challenge to current hegemonies.

Development assistance, in other words, can be a useful means of promoting good diplomatic relations around the world. However, India's development cooperation is evidently also being newly leveraged to support commercial and trade objectives. Mutual benefits with 'partner' countries are entirely possible within this new dispensation (and in many ways are more desirable than the West's dubious claims to ethically motivated foreign aid), but the claims to a 'win–win' alternative model are going to be harder to substantiate in some cases.

The changing geography of Indian development cooperation is also suggestive of its increasingly strategic intent. After Asia, Africa has long been a major destination for India's developmental assistance, with the anglophone Commonwealth countries historically the favoured partners. However, one of the interesting shifts in India's engagement with Africa has been its growing interest in West Africa (Singh 2007). While India has had long linkages with Nigeria and Ghana, it has tended to have less diplomatic affinity and trade relations with francophone countries. What has changed is the growing demand for resources—above all oil—and the search for investment opportunities. Reflecting these new imperatives, in 2004 the 'Techno-Economic Approach for Africa-India Movement' (TEAM-9) initiative was launched by the government of India together with eight resource and energy-rich West African countries.

India also contributes to regional and global development institutions, and is now a net creditor to the International Monetary Fund, and a major contributor to the World Food Programme and to UN peacekeeping forces. In the last few years India has also engaged in development cooperation with other donors, although so far only in a limited number of arenas, notably Afghanistan, in which it is a member of the Afghanistan Donors Group. India was also one of the 'Group of Four', together with Australia, Japan, and the US, which coordinated the post-tsunami emergency relief response in 2005. One area in which there has been little change to date has been that of NGOs and other civil society organizations. Aside from the Indian Red Cross (which in any case stands in a unique position in relation to the Indian government and its district administration), India has not sought to make use of NGOs as a channel for development funding and assistance. The government has an uneasy relationship with its own NGO community, and appears reluctant to devolve any overseas functions in this direction.

India has also been involved in what appear to be emerging pressures on the global architecture of foreign aid. In 2007, for example, India helped promote the creation of the Development Cooperation Forum in ECOSOC (the United Nations Economic and Social Council), which, unlike DAC, represents a grouping of donors *and* recipients, and which seeks to identify *mutually* acceptable principles and priorities. India, like other NDDs, has signalled its independence from dominant aid ideologies and practices, deliberately articulating different principles of development engagement. Moreover, in 2003 India announced that it no longer needed the assistance of the majority of its own donors, although they are still able to fund NGOs in India, under government supervision, and through multilateral organizations. The remaining donors (Germany, Japan, Russia, the UK, the US, and the European Union) are subject to considerable scrutiny and direction from the government. India has recently paid off its debts to 15 bilateral funders, and large parts of its debt to the Asian Development Bank and the World Bank. India is making the transition from recipient to donor, as befits a country with aspirations to global status, a key member of the 'BRIC' grouping, and an 'Asian Driver'. While aid is a rather small part of this process in comparison to trade, investment and diplomatic relations, it is by no means insignificant. However, the paradox on India's own vast levels of poverty remains unresolved. For some commentators, India's development cooperation is all about diplomatic and commercial support for the 'rising power' constituency of India—the politicians, policymakers, and increasingly affluent middle classes who benefit most from its booming neo-liberal economy and increasingly assertive global presence. At present, these benefits appear not to be tricking down to the mass of India's poor.

Key points

- India has a long history of development assistance in Asia and Africa, dating back to the 1950s.
- India argues that it differs from Western donors in that it promotes 'genuine' partnership and mutual benefit—although similarities of style and incentives have certainly been identified in some contexts.
- Many commentators suggest that the motivations for Indian development assistance are increasingly tilting from promoting South–South solidarity and diplomatic alliances, to more commercial and resource-oriented needs. However, these are not necessarily mutually exclusive.
- The benefits to 'India' of its development cooperation are shared very unevenly.

Conclusion

Political analysts of foreign aid are becoming increasingly aware of the opportunities and problems raised by the diverse set of 'non-DAC donors'. For their supporters, the NDDs represent a break from and alternative to the discredited intentions and outcomes of Western-dominated foreign aid. As Woods (2008: 1220) suggests:

"
In Africa and elsewhere, governments needing development assistance are skeptical of promises of more aid, wary of conditionalities associated with aid, and fatigued by the heavy bureaucratic and burdensome delivery systems used for delivery of aid. Small wonder that the emerging donors are being welcomed with open arms.
"

However, this is not to deny the strategic goals of South–South development cooperation. Despite claims by some to a selfless post-colonial solidarity, there is no doubt that the NDDs share the complex mix of motivations that characterize Western donors—humanitarian, geo-political, and commercial. The differences reside more in the modalities, recipients, and discourses of NDD foreign aid. The relative lack of conditionalities is key here—no structural adjustment programmes or insistence on 'good governance' accompany the bulk of NDD assistance. Supporters argue that this more honest relationship represents a much more genuine partnership than the hollow use of the term by the World Bank and others, allowing partner countries to benefit much more from investment in training opportunities, infrastructure development, trade growth, and local investment. Critics, on the other hand, fear that the NDDs will contribute to an unravelling of the fragile process towards greater transparency, effectiveness and well-targeted anti-poverty efforts. Moreover, in wider terms, although aid is generally dwarfed by trade and investment flows, there are questions about its role in promoting the sorts of shifting geographies of economic growth and power that the world is witnessing (Wilson and Purushothaman 2003).

Most analytical attention is understandably directed at China, but India, like other NDDs, provides a fascinating example of a challenge to Western-dominated institutions, practices, and ideologies of foreign aid. The politics of the developing world is changing, and development cooperation is one constituent element and reflection of this.

? Questions

1. What will be the impacts of the NDDs on humanitarian intervention, longer-term development, poverty reduction, and economic growth in poorer countries?

2. What will be the impacts of the NDDs on the existing architecture of foreign aid—the ideologies, policies, and practices of the dominant institutions?

3. What part will NDD development assistance play in the changing global geographies of economic and geopolitical power that are taking place and predicted to accelerate?

4. What challenges does the (re-)emergence of the NDDs have for theorizing politics and development?

→ Further reading

■ Agrawal, S. (2007), *Emerging Donors in International Development Assistance: The India Case*, Partnership in Business and Development Working Paper.

■ Manning, R. (2006), 'Will 'Emerging' Donors Challenge the Face of International Co-operation? *Development Policy Review*, 24/4: 371–83. A view on the emerging donors from the former Director of DAC.

■ Price, G. (2005), *Diversity in Donorship: The Changing Landscape of Official Humanitarian Aid: India's Official Aid Programme* (London: Overseas Development Institute HPG Background Paper) available at www.globaleconomicgovernance.org/wp-content/uploads/ChinaNew donorsIA.pdf. A detailed and very useful analysis of India as a donor.

■ Woods, N. (2008), 'Whose Aid? Whose Influence? China, Emerging Donors and the Silent Revolution in Development Assistance', *International Affairs*, 84/6: 1205–21. Critically summarizes the 'emerging donors' and the response of the 'traditional' donor community.

:// Web links

■ www.africa-union.org/root/au/Conferences/2008/april/India-Africa/India-Africa.html   Website for the Africa-India Forum Summit.

■ www.soas.ac.uk/africaasia/   Homepage of the Africa–Asia centre.

■ http://ssc.undp.org/   Homepage of the UN's special unit for South–South cooperation.

 ## Online Resource Centre

For additional material and resources, please visit the Online Resource Centre at:
www.oxfordtextbooks.co.uk/orc/burnell3e/

23b China and the Developing World

Deborah Bräutigam

Chapter contents

- Introduction
- A Brief History
- Instruments of Engagement
- Going Global: Fuelling the Chinese Economy
- Controversies
- Conclusion

Overview

China's rise as a world power marks the coming of age of a country that has in recent years been considered part of—and yet different from—the rest of the developing world. China's South–South relations are shaped by the nature of the Chinese state: a highly capable, developmental state that uses an array of instruments to promote its interests. In addition to foreign investment and commercial loans, the Chinese have developed **soft power** tools to engage other developing countries. Chinese ties are shaped by long-standing foreign policy principles, including non-interference in the internal affairs of others, equality, and mutual benefit. China's need for raw materials and resources, the political imperative of reassuring other developing countries that China's rise will not preempt their opportunities, and China's embrace of globalization and the growth of its own multinational companies also condition its ties with other developing countries. Some applaud the rise of China as an investor and financier, noting that China provides an alternative to the **Washington consensus**. Others worry that Chinese competition, and lower concern for environmental, social, and governance standards, may set back progress in other developing countries. Figure 23b.1 is a map of China and Box 23b.1 provides an overview of key dates in China's history.

Figure 23b.1 China

CHINA

Box 23b.1 Key Dates in China's history

1949:	Founding of the People's Republic of China	1972:	War with Vietnam (February–March)
1950:	China intervenes on North Korea's side in Korean War	1976:	Tanzania–Zambia Railway opens
1955:	Bandung Afro-Asian Conference in Indonesia	1978:	Chinese pragmatists win over radicals; economic reforms begin
1958–59:	Great Leap Forward	1979:	One-child policy imposed
1959:	China sends troops to suppress revolt in Tibet, tightening control	1982–83:	Chinese premier Zhao Ziyang visits 11 countries in Africa
1960:	Soviet Union withdraws aid and advisers from China	1989:	Tiananmen Square demonstrations violently suppressed
1962:	Border war with India over Tibet	1989:	Taiwan begins diplomatic offensive
1963:	Chinese premier Zhou Enlai visits ten African countries	1993:	China begins to import oil
		1996:	President Jiang Zemin state visit to six African countries, the first Chinese president to visit Africa
1966–76:	Cultural Revolution led by Mao Zedong and the 'Gang of Four'	1997:	Britain returns Hong Kong to China

2000:	Forum on China–Africa Cooperation (FOCAC) established	2006:	Beijing Summit of FOCAC; 44 African heads of state participate
2004:	President Hu Jintao state visit to Brazil, Argentina, Chile and Cuba	2008:	Beijing hosts summer Olympics; unrest in Tibet
2005:	President Hu Jintao pledges US$10 billion finance for MDGs		

Introduction

At least since the founding of the People's Republic of China in 1949, the Chinese have considered themselves to be part of the developing world. China lost portions of its territory to the colonial ambitions of others, suffered armed invasion and revolution, and endured more than a decade as a failed state in the 'warlord period' between 1916 and 1928. Yet China's history as a developing country is also quite different from most other parts of the global South.

China has been an effective regional power in the past. The roots of its capable state bureaucracy can be traced back to the third century B.C. China has long had the capacity to extend its reach far beyond its borders. Agriculture was relatively productive and well beyond the level of subsistence, while manufacturing was fairly well developed in areas like Shanghai, even before World War II. Although after 1949, China was subjected to political sanctions, and trade embargos, it has never been dominated by foreign multinational corporations, grown dependent on foreign aid, or felt the weight of external pressure to liberalize its economy or to democratize.

In recent decades, as China has moved to regain its historic prominence as a centre of world trade, culture, and political influence, these differences have helped to shape the framework for its contemporary South–South engagement. In addition, China is both a centralized **developmental state** in the mode of Japan or South Korea, and a socialist country still undergoing economic liberalization. This tension means that while Beijing continues to plan its overseas engagements, and has many tools with which to promote its interests, it no longer exercises complete control over state-owned companies and provincial governments. It has even less influence with the growing number of private Chinese and Hong Kong firms operating overseas (Gill and Reilly 2007).

Chinese foreign policy is influenced by the 'five principles of peaceful coexistence' (Box 23b.2). These principles emphasize sovereignty, non-interference in each other's internal affairs, non-aggression, equality, and mutual benefit. With some notable exceptions, such as Chinese support for left-wing rebellions abroad during the Cultural Revolution (1966–76), or sporadic clashes along the borders with the former Soviet Union, Vietnam, and India, Chinese leaders have shied away from political or military intervention overseas and promote non-interference as a standard that prizes sovereignty over newer norms such as universal human rights or the **responsibility to protect (R2P)**.

Box 23b.2 Five Principles of Peaceful Coexistence (1954)

1. Mutual respect for each other's territorial integrity and sovereignty

2. Mutual non-aggression

3. Mutual non-interference in each other's internal affairs

4. Equality and mutual benefit

5. Peaceful coexistence

Too weak to stand as a counterweight to the hegemony of the Soviet Union or the Western powers during the cold war, China emphasized the equality of nations as promised by the United Nations and advocated multilateral forums for international negotiations concerning the rules of world order. Concerned itself about the vulnerabilities and inequalities associated with dependence on the Soviet Union during the 1950s, and with a relatively small budget for external assistance, China emphasized economic cooperation and mutual assistance, rather than the one-way transfer of resources through foreign aid. However, as China grows in power and influence, and as Chinese loans and investments are put at risk in politically tense environments, assumptions of equality, and the principles of mutual benefit and non-interference, are increasingly difficult to maintain.

China's South–South partnerships today build on a substantial history of foreign aid and economic cooperation, new instruments of soft power, and skyrocketing increases in trade, loans, and investment over the past decade. This involvement with other developing countries has at least four overarching goals.

First, China aims to preserve its own sovereignty and territorial integrity. This security concern also helps explain why Chinese assistance has always been concentrated in Asia, particularly in the countries on its border: North Korea, Cambodia, Burma, and Pakistan, for example.

Second, China has long used economic diplomacy to counter efforts by its breakaway province of Taiwan to gain international standing. This explains Beijing's emphasis on the 'One China' policy: a consistent practice of cutting off formal ties with all countries that give official diplomatic recognition to the government in Taiwan as 'China'.

Third, China wants to maintain its long-standing role as a leader among developing countries, while assuaging fears that its rise will threaten other countries. Knitting together regional groupings, ratcheting up communications and assistance, and building up the tools of public diplomacy are part of this effort.

Finally, Beijing is keen to create a stable global environment that will allow China to focus on its own economic development. This includes secure access to raw materials, new markets, and opportunities for Chinese companies overseas.

Key points

- China considers itself to be a developing country, yet there are many differences between China's history and that of others in the global South.

- China is a developmental state and has many instruments with which to reach its national goals. But as China liberalizes its economy it has less control over its companies and their behaviour overseas.

- The five policies of peaceful coexistence influence Chinese foreign policy and economic cooperation. These stress non-interference in internal affairs of other countries, and mutual benefit.

Ethnic Chinese traders and labourers have ventured abroad for many centuries, settling in dense communities in South-East Asia, and establishing Chinatowns in many other parts of the developing world. During most of its imperial history, however, the Chinese state was uninterested in venturing abroad, with the exception of the voyages of the Muslim admiral Zheng He who travelled to Africa between 1418 and 1433.

In the mid-nineteenth and early twentieth centuries, the Chinese lost portions of their territory: the island of Taiwan to Japan; Macao to Portugal; Hong Kong to Great Britain. The last imperial dynasty ended in 1911 with the founding of the Republic of China (ROC). Battles with warlords between 1916 and 1928 gave way to a civil war between the ROC and the Chinese communists. In 1949, with the communists close to victory, the government of the ROC fled to the island of Taiwan, where it remains today. The United States intervened in the conflict by sending the Seventh Fleet to patrol the waters between Taiwan and the mainland. The US was also able to muster enough international support to keep the ROC (that is, Taiwan) in China's Security Council seat at the United Nations until 1971.

At first the Chinese communists had close ties with the Soviet Union, which sent advisers and helped to build China's economy. Deteriorating ties led Moscow to cut its assistance in 1960, just as the Chinese had begun to back away from the Great Leap Forward (1958–59), a disastrous effort to mobilize the population to create collective farms, rural mines, and rudimentary, small-scale industries. More than 20 million Chinese are believed to have died as a result of the Great Leap, combined with several natural disasters.

At the same time, the break with the Soviet Union helped China to solidify a role as part of the 'Third World' — not in the capitalist camp, but not in the Soviet camp either. The origins of this idea of non-alignment can be traced to the 1955 Afro-Asian Solidarity Conference in Bandung, Indonesia where Chinese leaders met with those from India, Egypt, and others just emerging from colonialism. Bandung helped mark out a space for countries that wished to avoid the two cold war camps. The five principles of peaceful coexistence proposed by China's premier Zhou Enlai were later espoused by the Non-Aligned Movement, even though there were notable exceptions: China's 1962 border war with India sparked by the Chinese military's suppression of the Tibet uprising, for example.

During the 1950s and even in the 1960s, Chinese engagement with other developing countries emphasized advancing the cause of socialism. When Zhou Enlai visited Africa in 1964, he declared the continent 'ripe for revolution'. Chinese assistance to communist North Vietnam, locked in combat with the United States, took up 40 per cent of China's aid budget during this period. However, the goal of regaining China's seat in the United Nations (UN) became an equally important objective. This required assuaging the fears of non-socialist countries in places like Africa. Aid was an important tool in China's economic diplomacy. In 1975, four years after winning its seat back in the UN, China had aid programmes in more African countries than did the United States (Bräutigam 2009). In contrast, Chinese ties are newer in Latin America, a legacy of the cold war and of American hegemony. Chile, under socialist president Salvador Allende, was the first Latin American country to switch diplomatic ties from Taipei to Beijing (in 1972). Taiwan retained diplomatic ties with much of Central America until very recently.

In the late 1970s, under reformist leader Deng Xiaoping, the Chinese began a long road of gradual economic reforms. In 1982, Chinese premier Zhao Ziyang embarked on a trip to 11 African countries to discuss what China's economic reforms would mean for its relationships on the continent.

Instead of aid, he said, China would now emphasize 'South–South cooperation' in a diversity of forms. It would experiment, beginning with joint ventures, construction projects, and other forms of engagement aimed at mutual benefit and practical results.

Nearly thirty years later, Chinese companies were making headlines with multi-billion dollar business deals in developing countries. China's relationship with other developing countries had evolved a great deal. The world had begun to see a small group of powerful countries—Brazil, Russia, India, and China as the 'BRICs' (see Chapter 5): not as developed as the West and Japan, but not 'Third World' either (Glosny 2010: 129). Being part of this group allowed China to follow Deng Xiaoping's advice: 'Keep a low profile and be patient.'

> **Key points**
>
> - Like many other developing countries, China suffered colonial incursions, periods as a failed state, and civil war during the twentieth century.
> - After the founding of the People's Republic of China in 1949, the Chinese communists broke away from the Soviet Union and tried to build a Non-Aligned Movement.
> - In the 1970s aid shifted from being primarily a tool to support other socialist countries to being primarily a tool to win diplomatic recognition.
> - As China shifted toward the market, its overseas engagement began to stress business opportunities and economic cooperation.

Instruments of Engagement

Although it attracted little notice until after the millennium, Chinese business engagement in Asia, Africa, and elsewhere in the developing world had been steadily growing since the 1990s. As that decade began, Chinese construction companies were already starting to win contracts in countries around the world. In a separate trend, in 1993 China's oil imports exceeded its oil exports for the first time (Downs 2007). By the end of the 1990s, it was clear that South–South cooperation would need to be vastly increased if China was going to find the new markets and access to resources required to sustain its rapid modernization.

Following in the footsteps of Japan and other developmental states, the Chinese established new instruments to meet these goals. China Export Import Bank (China Eximbank), set up in 1994, offered preferential government loans to facilitate trade and investment, particularly in poorer countries. It would also manage a new foreign aid instrument: low-interest (concessional) loans. China Development Bank (CDB), set up in 1994, primarily to serve development needs within China, gradually began to support China's efforts to go global. In 2006, CDB set up the China–Africa Development Fund an equity fund targeted to reach US$5 billion, to promote Chinese investment. CDB has also extended very large lines of credit to Chinese companies active overseas. The telecoms company Huawei, for example, received a US$10 billion line of credit in 2004, and another US$20 billion five years later in 2009.

Beijing also began to set up new regional organizations to boost political, cultural, and economic ties. The Forum on China–Africa Cooperation (FOCAC) was established in 2000, and the Shanghai Cooperation Organization (SCO) emphasizing mutual security concerns, in 2001. The SCO comprises China, Russia, Uzbekistan, Kazakhstan, Kyrgyzstan, and Tajikistan. Forums were founded for the Caribbean, Portuguese-speaking countries, Arab states, and the Pacific Islands. These have many similar features, often including promises of aid, trade benefits, and debt relief. In Latin America,

Chinese engagement has focused mainly on business. China's first free trade agreement, with Chile, went into effect in 2006, and the Chinese are negotiating free trade agreements with Peru and Costa Rica.

The selection of regions for engagement reflected three goals: (1) the drive to secure access to resources, in particular oil; (2) the diplomatic isolation of Taiwan and the protection of Chinese interests in the many small countries in Africa, the South Pacific, and the Caribbean, where the competition with Taiwan remained a factor; (3) promoting business—for example, business networks in the Portuguese-speaking Chinese enclave of Macao were enlisted to give Chinese companies an important comparative advantage in concluding deals with countries like Brazil.

Soft power

In addition, China's **soft power** expanded. Just as the French promote their language and culture and influence through the Alliance Française, and the Germans through Goethe Institutes, so the Chinese have been setting up Confucius Institutes to teach the Chinese language and sponsor cultural events. Between 2004 and 2009, more than 282 Confucius Institutes were set up in 88 countries. Since 1963, more than 65 countries have hosted Chinese medical teams. Between 2006 and 2012, university scholarships for African students were to increase from 2,000 to 5,500 per year. The Chinese established a Youth Volunteer Programme in 2002, sending the first volunteers to countries on China's border: Laos and Burma. In 2006, Beijing pledged to send 300 youth volunteers to Africa.

As they moved up in international influence and power, Chinese leaders also became increasingly visible as benefactors in multilateral situations. For example, in a speech at the United Nations in September 2005, Chinese President Hu Jintao made a pledge to provide US$10 billion in finance for the Millennium Development Goals (MDGs) and training opportunities in China for 30,000 people

from developing countries. The Chinese joined the Africa Development Bank and the Latin American Development Bank, and in 2008, they became a donor to the World Bank with a modest pledge of US$30 million.

China's effort to position itself as a 'responsible power' was reflected in its unprecedented response to the Indian Ocean tsunami disaster and the Pakistan earthquake in 2005. Chinese humanitarian aid that year came to about US$250 million, half from the government, and half from Chinese non-governmental organizations (NGOs) like the Red Cross, and the private sector (Qi 2007: 5).

Arms and peacekeeping: China's military presence

Chinese arms in world export markets, and the emergence of Chinese peacekeepers are two other sides of Chinese involvement in the developing world. Small arms made in China have been a feature of most conflicts in the developing world in recent years. Yet the restructuring of China's defence industry and the divestiture of enterprises formerly owned by the military means that it is difficult to track the dimensions of this trade. Beijing has not published information on its export of arms, while arms traders have sometimes mislabelled shipments of Chinese arms as agricultural equipment in order to slip past arms embargoes (Taylor 2009: 126). It is likely that more than half of China's arms exports go to Asia, with Africa receiving about 17 per cent. China is estimated to be third behind France and Russia as a supplier of arms to Africa (Taylor 2009: 119–120).

Although Chinese spokesmen insist that they respect the UN arms embargo on southern Sudan, military equipment of Chinese make has been recovered from sites in the troubled province of Darfur. In 2008, on the eve of landlocked Zimbabwe's controversial presidential election, South African unions in the port of Durban refused to unload the An Yue Jiang, a ship carrying arms intended for the Mugabe government, in power since 1980.

This portrait of China as arms supplier to rogue regimes is offset by another picture: China's role as a supplier of United Nations peacekeepers. At the end of 2009, according to UN figures, some 2143 Chinese were serving in the UN police or military missions, mainly in Lebanon, Sudan, Liberia, and the Democratic Republic of the Congo. Of UN Security Council members, China was second only to France as a supplier of UN peacekeepers (Taylor 2009: 133). In 2009, responding to a sharp rise in attacks by Somali pirates on ships moving through the Arabian Gulf, the Chinese dispatched two naval ships to help escort merchant vessels

through the troubled waters. These modest moves abroad by China's military are being watched with some concern in the developing world, particularly in Asia.

Key points

- Chinese policy banks were established to provide finance to meet government objectives. This follows the 'developmental state' model pioneered by Japan.

- China set up a number of regional organizations as strategic forums for interaction. Soft power and China's military presence also increased.

Going Global: Fuelling the Chinese Economy

Above all, China's growing partnerships with other developing countries today are based on economic interests. China's rapidly growing economy and position as the 'world's workshop' require raw materials and markets. Since 2001, under the 'Going Global' policies, Chinese companies have expanded their efforts to diversify their markets and assure a supply of raw materials to the Chinese economy. Chinese firms are encouraged to invest abroad, helping Chinese industries at home to move up the value chain, and to shift away from labour and energy-intensive manufacturing. The Chinese state also wants a select group of its companies to become global leaders.

Trade is central in this effort. In 2004, visiting Latin America and the Caribbean, and in 2006, during a large summit of African leaders in Beijing, Chinese President Hu Jintao announced targets of US$100 billion in trade by 2010—with both regions. China succeeded early. In 2000, trade between China and Africa was only US$10.5 billion, and in Latin America, US$12.2 billion. By 2008, African trade surpassed US$106 billion and in Latin America, US$140 billion. This surge was partly due

to high prices for natural resources, stimulated by China's growing demand. However, in both regions, Chinese exports made up nearly half of this trade, demonstrating the success of Chinese companies in diversifying their markets. In Africa, some small-scale Chinese traders are competing with African traders in local markets, leading to complaints.

Chinese banks have ratcheted up their loans in developing countries, and some of these large loans are linked to natural resource exports. In Brazil, newly discovered oil deposits locked between layers of deep-sea salt beds will require billions for state-owned Petrobras to unlock. CDB offered Petrobras a line of credit of US$10 billion to be repaid by regular exports of oil (valued at the market price). In 2009, Venezuela received a similar CDB oil-backed loan, for US$4 billion. Chile's state-owned copper company formed a joint venture in 2006 with China's Minmetals, receiving a US$550 million loan from CDB to expand copper production, to be repaid from copper proceeds. The Democratic Republic of the Congo signed a deal in 2008 with China Eximbank and a Chinese consortium to develop a copper/cobalt mine. Output from the mine will repay US$3 billion (and possibly more) worth of infrastructure (roads, rail, hospitals, water systems, universities), to be built mainly by Chinese companies. War-torn Angola has received at least US$4.5 billion in similar oil-backed infrastructure credits from China Eximbank since 2004.

In resource-backed construction deals like this, and by winning contracts financed by the World Bank, other donors, and African governments, Chinese companies have earned billions of dollars in recent years: US$12.7 billion in Africa; US$23.8 billion in Asia and the Middle East; and US$47.9 worldwide in 2007 alone. Many of these construction contracts were secured by telecoms companies such as Huawei, as the Chinese state helped them to profit by assisting Africans to bypass the era of fixed line telephones and jump directly into wireless.

Key points

- The 'Going Global' policies involve trade diversification, secure access to raw materials, overseas investment and contracting, and the building up of Chinese multinational corporations.

- Chinese trade has risen enormously, crossing the US$100 billion annual mark in 2006 in Latin America, and in 2008 in Africa.

- Chinese banks have made very large, long-term loans, many linked to repayment in natural resources. In Africa, some of these loans pay for much needed infrastructure.

Controversies

Chinese engagement with other developing countries is more controversial than that of any of the other BRICs. Some worry that large new loans will exacerbate debt burdens. Particularly in Latin America and Africa, critics charge that Chinese economic engagement replicates 'colonial' patterns: exports of manufactured goods, and imports of raw materials. Chinese textiles, plastic products, and other simple manufactured goods threaten the weak industrial sectors in some countries. Colombia imposed tariffs on Chinese textiles, and South Africa asked China for temporary voluntary export restraints. While Chinese demand benefits commodity exporters through higher prices, Chinese goods have provided devastating competition for many manufacturers. To counter the political frictions caused by these trade patterns, the Chinese have announced programmes like the planned construction of at least ten overseas economic zones, in which Chinese companies will be encouraged to invest in manufacturing.

Social and environmental complaints about Chinese companies are common. Many Chinese companies, particularly in Africa, use Chinese nationals for management and technical positions—on average, about 20 per cent of employment in a project or investment will be Chinese. In 2008, at least 140,000 Chinese were officially working in Africa and these numbers have been rising steadily (Editorial Board of the China Commerce Yearbook 2009). Others have criticized Chinese companies' low environmental, safety and labour standards. In one infamous case, an explosion in a Chinese-owned factory killed more than fifty Zambian workers. Poor work conditions have led to strikes and host government reprimands from Peru to Papua New Guinea. Chinese companies are blamed for overfishing in the coastal waters of other developing countries, or for illegal timber harvesting. In 2005, Chile banned Chinese fishing trawlers from its ports, while coastal African countries have raised similar concerns. These problems may increase. The rise of Chinese private companies, provincial firms, and increased independence for non-state actors (including Hong Kong companies) means that Beijing now has fewer levers to control the actions of its companies overseas (Gill and Reilly 2007).

Finally, civil society groups in developing countries and in the global North (along with northern governments) charged that Chinese policies of aid and commercial engagement with 'no strings attached' propped up rogue regimes in places like Sudan, Myanmar (Burma), and Zimbabwe. The Chinese response is that active engagement works better than embargoes, that they abide by sanctions when imposed by the United Nations, and that their diplomats have played constructive roles in getting warring parties to agree to peace talks over thorny issues like the Darfur rebellion in oil-rich Sudan. They also point out that when it is convenient for them, Western companies and governments themselves engage with many reviled regimes.

> **Key points**
>
> - Chinese patterns of trade in many developing countries often follow 'colonial' patterns, with China exporting manufactured goods, and importing raw materials.
> - Concerns raised about Chinese companies overseas include their tendency to employ Chinese in management and skilled labour roles, and low social and environmental standards.
> - China's policy of investment and aid without political conditions means that it actively engages some pariah regimes such as Sudan, Zimbabwe, and Myanmar (Burma).
> - Western reporting on Chinese economic engagement is often inaccurate. Misinformation travels quickly through cyberspace, lingering on websites without being corrected.

Conclusion

Beijing is careful not to position China as the leader of the developing world. At the same time, Chinese leaders want their country to be seen as a 'responsible power' the rise of which will provide more opportunities than threats to other developing countries. As it grows wealthier, Beijing does not want to replicate the familiar 'North–South' relations based on foreign aid. And yet it runs the risk of being seen as reproducing 'neo-colonialism' through patterns of trade and investment based on raw materials and low-level manufactured goods. Because China's engagement with other developing countries has grown so rapidly, it is difficult to find more than anecdotal evidence of the impact of China's ties on governance, debt, environment, employment, or social standards. This makes it challenging to find balanced and accurate analysis, but it also means that the field is open for evidence-based research on an important new phenomenon.

? **Questions**

1. In what ways have changes within China affected its relations with other developing countries over time?

2. Is China's rise a threat, or an opportunity for other developing countries? Why?

3. What kind of evidence would we want to see in order to answer question 2?

4. Is China's experience as a developing country a useful role model for other developing countries?

5. Should China become more like the more developed countries in its pattern of aid and economic engagement? Why or why not?

 Further reading

■ Bräutigam, D. (2009), *The Dragon's Gift: The Real Story of China in Africa* (Oxford: Oxford University Press). A comparative introduction to Chinese aid and economic engagement in Africa. Tackles the myths and misunderstandings as well as the dimensions of engagement and how it works.

■ Congressional Research Service (2008), *China's Foreign Policy and 'Soft Power' in South America, Asia, and Africa*, Study prepared for the Committee on Foreign Relations, United States Senate, April. Official United States government study, with a comprehensive overview. Provides a useful comparison of US and Chinese soft power; evidence on US engagement is stronger than that on China.

■ Ellis, R. E. (2009), *China and Latin America: The Whats and Wherefores* (Boulder, CO: Lynne Rienner Publishers). A new and very comprehensive look at China's engagement in Latin America. Chapters range from economic to military topics.

■ Sutter, R. G. (2005), *China's Rise in Asia: Promises and Perils* (New York: Rowman and Littlefield). A useful overview of China's engagement in Asia. Outlines the threats and opportunities.

 Web links

■ www.chinaafricarealstory.com   Blog exploring Chinese aid, investment, and economic engagement.

■ www.geography.dur.ac.uk/projects/china-africa/Home/tabid/2486/Default.aspx   The website of an ESRC funded research project on the political implications of China's role in sub-Saharan Africa, based at the Open University.

■ http://ssc.undp.org/   Homepage of the UN's special unit for South–South cooperation.

@ Online Resource Centre

For additional material and resources, please visit the Online Resource Centre at:
www.oxfordtextbooks.co.uk/orc/burnell3e/

APPENDIX 1

Case Study Countries: Basic Indicators

	Population million 2007	Average annual population growth 2000–08, %	GNI 2008, US$ billion, PPP	GNI per capita 2008, US$ PPP	GDP: per capita average % growth 2007–08	% of population on less than US$1.25 a day, PPP	GINI Index (most recent)	HDI (value), 2007	Political rights 2008	Civil liberties 2008
China	1326	0.6	7984	6020	8.4	15.9	41.5	0.772	7	6
Guatemala	14.0	2.5	64	4690	1.5	11.7	53.7	0.704	3	4
India	1140	1.4	3375	2960	5.7	41.6	32.5	0.612	2	3
Indonesia	228	1.3	875	3830	4.9	n.a.	39.4	0.734	2	3
Mexico	106	1.0	1517	14270	0.8	2.0	48.1	0.854	2	3
Nigeria	151	2.4	293	1940	3.0	64.4	42.9	0.511	5	4
Pakistan	166	2.3	449	2700	3.7	22.6	31.2	0.572	4	5
South Africa	49	1.3	476	9780	1.3	26.2	57.8	0.683	2	2
South Korea	49	0.4	1367	28120	1.9	n.a.	31.6	0.937	1	2
UK	61	0.5	2218	36130	0.1	n.a.	36.0	0.947	1	1
USA	304	0.9	14283	46970	0.2	n.a.	40.8	0.956	1	1

Notes: GDP (gross domestic product); GNI (gross national income); PPP (purchasing power parity); GINI index (income/expenditure inequality–0 = *perfect* equality and 100 = *perfect* inequality); HDI (Human Development Index—a composite of education, longevity, and GDP per capita); n.a. (not available); political rights and civil liberties on scale 1 (most free)–7 (least free). No data available for Iraq apart from 6 for political rights and civil liberties. United States (USA) and United Kingdom (UK) are included in the list for comparison.

Sources: United Nations Development Programme 2009, *Human Development Report 2009* (columns 7, 8); World Bank 2009, *World Development Report 2010* (columns 1–6); Freedom House 2009, *Annual Freedom House Survey* (columns 9, 10)

Case Study Countries: Globalization Rankings and Scores, 2004

	Overall globalization ranking	Economic globalization ranking	Political globalization ranking	Social globalization ranking	Political globalization index (score)
China	23	25	4	96	0.775
Guatemala	78	114	67	94	0.333
India	34	42	13	113	0.656
Indonesia	51	38	44	98	0.462
Iraq	n.a.	n.a.	99	n.a.	0.245
Mexico	61	56	62	70	0.344
Nigeria	45	110	18	132	0.624
Pakistan	39	92	16	121	0.635
South Africa	48	60	35	85	0.510
South Korea	20	46	32	26	0.513
UK	4	34	5	11	0.769
USA	5	74	2	18	0.873

Note: The CSGR Globalization Index, which presents data from 1982 to 2004, is explicitly designed to be comparable across countries and time. It measures economic globalization as a function of trade (exports plus imports), foreign direct investment (inflows plus outflows), portfolio investment (inflows plus outflows), and international income flows (payments to non-resident workers and investment income from assets owned by non-residents). All these are assessed as a proportion of gross domestic product (GDP). Social globalization is assessed mainly in terms of the movement of people across borders including worker remittances and tourist arrivals and departures, together with the flow of ideas via telephone and Internet usage, films and book imports and exports. The volume of international mail per capita is also taken into account. The index obtains its measurements for political globalization from the number of foreign embassies in a country, its participation in United Nations peacekeeping operations, and membership of international organizations. n.a. means not available.

Sources: Lockwood and Redoano 2005

Glossary

aid selectivity determining aid allocations between countries on the basis of demonstrable commitment to pro-developmental policies and institutions rather than on the basis of future promises or conditionalities

apartheid an Afrikaans word meaning separateness, in South Africa expressed as the official government policy of racial segregation, between 1948 and 1989

ascriptive identities groupings to which people belong by birth rather than by choice

autonomy of politics/political autonomy the extent to which politics as a level or sphere of social life is determined by economic and/or social/cultural dimensions of society or is able independently to impact on those dimensions

balkanization referring to the breaking up of a region or country into small territorial units, often as a means to 'divide and rule'

Bretton Woods consensus *see* Washington consensus

caste a system of social stratification characterized by hereditary status, endogamy, and social barriers sanctioned by custom or law

caste associations organizations to represent the interests of a caste group or cluster of closely related caste groups, largely confined to India

caudillismo historically referring to the organization of political life in parts of Latin America by local 'strongmen' (*caudillos*) competing for power and its spoils

chaebols the family-based business groups or conglomerates, many of them with cross-ownership, that have been South Korea's primary source of capital accumulation

Christian democracy the application of Christian precepts to electoral politics

civic nationalism involving unity among citizens of an autonomous state

civil regulation in the environmental arena referring to a range of activities undertaken by civil society actors aimed at creating new frameworks of expectation and obligation for companies

civil society a term highly contested, and concerning the realm of voluntary citizen associations that exists between the family and the state, enjoying independence of the latter, and seeking to influence public policy without aspirations to public office. **Modern civil society** comprises formal, professionalized non-governmental organizations typical of the late twentieth century; **traditional civil society** is organized more informally, and may follow patterns with deep and enduring roots in history and society

clash of civilizations referring to Samuel P. Huntington's prediction that after the end of the cold war international conflicts would increasingly have cultural characteristics, most notably setting the Christian 'West' against the mostly Muslim, mostly Arab 'East'

clientelism/clientelist referring to the exchange of specific services or resources (usually publicly funded) between individuals in return for political support such as votes, and essentially a relationship between unequals

collapsed state *see* state collapse

commodification the transformation of something into a commodity to be bought and sold on the market

comparative advantage the economic theory that countries should specialize in the production and export of those goods and services that they have a *relative* cost advantage in producing compared to other countries

competitive authoritarianism a kind of 'illiberal democracy' in which formal democratic institutions are widely viewed as the principal source of political authority but rulers violate the rules so strikingly that the regime fails to meet conventional minimum standards of democracy

conditionality/conditionalities referring to the attachment of policy and/or other conditions to offers of financial and other assistance, with the possibility of aid sanctions for non-compliance

constructive programmes challenge systemic and structural violence by finding and applying solutions at the local level and in everyday life; they restructure power relations so that the oppressed are no longer dependent upon the oppressors but instead become self-reliant and autonomous from exploitive state or market relations

corruption involving the private use of public office and resources and generally considered illegal

cross-conditionality exists where one lender makes its aid offers conditional on the recipient meeting conditions laid down by one or more other lenders

critical security studies refers to approaches united by dissatisfaction with the so-called 'traditional' security studies and in particular its state and military centrism

cruel choice Jagdish Bhagwati's term for the dilemma he believed faced developing countries: either concentrate on economic development, or emulate the political systems of the West

cultural imperialism the domination of vulnerable peoples by the culture of economically and politically powerful societies

decentralized despotism a pattern of colonial and post-colonial government identified by Mahmood Mamdani (1996) as arising from the colonial practice of indirect rule

delegative democracy according to Guillermo O'Donnell, resting on the premise that whoever wins election to the presidency is thereby entitled to govern as he or she thinks fit, constrained only by the hard facts of existing power relations and a constitutionally limited term of office

democracy assistance comprises largely consensual and concessionary international support to democratic reform chiefly by way of specific projects and programmes, for instance civil society capacity-building endeavours

democracy promotion encompasses a wide range of approaches including not only democracy assistance but also diplomatic pressure and in some accounts much more coercive forms of intervention where democratization is the stated goal

democratic peace theory the claim that democracies do not go to war with one another

democratization backwards describing situations in which largely free elections are introduced in advance of such basic institutions of the modern state as the rule of law, full executive accountability, and a flourishing civil society

dependency theory an argument that the weak structural position of developing countries in the international capitalist system influences important variables in their political life as well as explains their failure to achieve stronger development

deprivation according to Nancy Fraser (1997), 'being denied an adequate material standard of living'

despotic power the power to control and suppress (as Michael Mann has called it), as opposed to **infrastructural power**, the power to penetrate and transform society

developing world a term conventionally referring to the predominantly post-colonial regions of Africa, Asia, Latin America and the Caribbean, and the Middle East, perceived to be poorer, less economically advanced, and less 'modern' than the developed world

development administration a field of study aimed at providing an understanding of administrative performance in the specific economic and cultural contexts of poor, non-Western societies

developmental state according to Adrian Leftwich, concentrating sufficient power, autonomy, and capacity at the centre to bring about explicit developmental objectives, whether by encouraging the conditions and direction of economic growth or by organizing it directly. The hallmarks include a competent bureaucracy and the insulation of state institutions from special interests in society, in other words, the state enjoys **embedded autonomy**. While there are significant differences among the cases commonly cited as examples of the development state, the most successful examples in East Asia have tended to be authoritarian

direct democracy exists where citizens can vote directly on public policy and decide what is to be done on other important political issues, through devices such as referenda

discourse theory an interpretative approach closely associated with Michel Foucault that analyses power in terms of the dominant discourses, or chains of meaning, which shape understanding and behaviour

eco-colonialism an argument that the imposition of environmental conditions on financial and economic support for developing countries restricts their development

economic growth the rate of growth in a country's national output or income, often measured by its gross domestic product (GDP) or gross national product (GNP) and often presented on a per capita basis

economic marginalization 'being confined to undesirable or poorly paid work' (Fraser 1997)

economic rents incomes derived from the possession of a valuable licence or permit, particularly for the import of foreign goods

electoral authoritarianism/autocracy where elections are an instrument of authoritarian rule, an alternative to both democracy and naked repression

electoral democracy a fairly minimalist conception of democracy that highlights electoral competition and a degree of popular participation but understates the civil liberties and some other distinguishing features associated with liberal democracy

emancipation in IR theory comes from the Aberystwyth School of **critical security studies** that defines security in terms of 'emancipation' or freedom of people from threats

embedded autonomy according to Peter Evans, characterized by the relative facility of the developmental state to transcend sectional interests in society, providing a sound basis for pursuing national industrial transformation

entitlements justified rights or claims belonging to individuals or groups

equality of outcome an approach that aims to make people equal whatever their original differences

ethnic identities socially constructed identities that follow when people self-consciously distinguish themselves from others on the basis of perceived common descent and/or shared culture. Many but not all such identities are politicized

ethnic morphology refers to the form and structure of groups

ethnonational identities defining the nation in ethnic terms, attaining unity through the merger of ethnic and national identities, and demanding autonomy for ethnic nations

ethnopolitical identities those ethnic identities that have been politicized—that is, made politically relevant

evaluation research research into the outcomes of programme intervention or policy change

evangelical Christianity usually refers to conservative, nearly always Protestant, Christian religious practices and traditions that emphasize evangelism, a personal experience of conversion, faith rooted in the Holy Bible, and a belief in the relevance of Christian faith to cultural issues

exploitation in Nancy Fraser's (1997) words, 'having the fruits of one's labour appropriated for the benefit of others'

extents of freedom in Amartya Sen's terminology, the capabilities or the *freedom* to achieve whatever functionings an individual happens to value

extractive state the idea that the extraction of the nation's (natural resource) wealth for the benefit of its ruler(s) becomes the primary goal of the ruler(s)

extraversion a theory of African political behaviour developed by Jean-François Bayart (1993) that argues that, historically, the relatively weak development of the continent's productive forces and its internal social struggles made African political actors more disposed to mobilize resources from their relationship with the external environment

failing state a state that is failing in respect of some or all of its functions without yet having reached the stage of 'collapse'

fallacy of electoralism privileging electoral contestation as if that were a sufficient condition for democracy to exist

fatwa a religious edict issued by an Islamic leader

feminism/feminist comprising recognition and action on women's common bonds and inequalities between men and women

garrison state a state maintained by military power and in some definitions a state organized to secure primarily its own need for military security

gatekeeper state a term coined by the African historian Frederick Cooper (2002) to denote a form of state focused on controlling the intersection of the territory with the outside world, collecting and distributing the resources that that control brought

gender referring to ideas about male and female and the relations between them as social constructions rather than the product of biological determinants only

genocide referring to deliberate extermination of a social group selected on grounds of culture, ethnicity, or race

Gini coefficient a commonly used measure of inequality (household income or consumption)—the higher the figure, the more unequal the distribution

global justice movement a loose, increasingly transnational network of non-governmental and social movement organizations opposed to neo-liberal economic globalization, violence, and North–South inequalities; they support participatory democracy, equality, and sustainable development

global stewardship referring to resources that are said to be part of the common heritage of humankind and should be managed for the benefit of all

globalization a highly contested term, defined in different ways that range from increasing global economic integration, in particular international trade, to processes whereby many social relations become relatively delinked from territorial geography and human lives are increasingly played out in the world as a single place

globalization theory focusing on a process of accelerated communication and economic integration that transcends national boundaries and increasingly incorporates all parts of the world into a single social system

good governance originated in World Bank discourse to mean the sound management of public affairs with a bias towards neo-liberal conceptions of the state's role in the economy, but went on to acquire broader connotations sharing many of the ideas and institutions associated with democracy, and hence democratic governance

governance an omnibus term with a variety of meanings that reflects its usage in diverse disciplines and practices ranging from new public management to international development cooperation, and spanning institutions at both the local and the global level. Best defined contextually, and best understood with reference to both the objective and normative purposes of the definer, as exemplified in, for instance, the similarly wide-ranging but nevertheless contrasting accounts offered by the Governance Matters Project of the World Bank and the World Governance Assessment, which lies closer to the thinking of the UNDP

heavily indebted poor countries *see* 'Heavily Indebted Poor Countries Initiative'

Heavily Indebted Poor Countries Initiative (HIPC) arranged by the World Bank and International Monetary Fund, has the objective of bringing the countries' debt burden to sustainable levels, subject to satisfactory policy performance, so as to ensure that adjustment and reform efforts are not put at risk by continued high debt and debt service burdens

Hindu caste system a complex and ancient, although evolving, system of social stratification in which people's caste status is determined at birth

HIV/AIDS refers to human immunodeficiency virus, a retrovirus that infects cells of the human immune system. It is widely accepted that infection with HIV causes AIDS (acquired immunodeficiency syndrome), a disease characterized by the destruction of the immune system

human capital referring to the knowledge, skills, and capabilities of individuals

human development according to the United Nations Development Programme, about freedom, well-being, and dignity of people everywhere; the UNDP's human development index measures longevity, educational attainment, and standard of living

human rights either the rights everyone has because they are human or those generally recognized as such by governments or in international law

human security is an emerging paradigm that links development studies and national security and is defined as the protection of human lives from critical and pervasive threats. A wide-ranging version claims human security is 'freedom from want': extreme poverty precludes real security. More narrowly, human security is 'freedom from fear': the emphasis is on safety from violence including wars and violent crime

Ikhwan The brethren, religious followers of *Wahhabism*

illiberal democracy Fareed Zakaria's term for polities in which governments are elected but have little respect for constitutional liberalism—the rule of law, separation of powers, and such basic liberties as speech, assembly, religion, and property

import-substitution industrialization (ISI) referring to the economic strategy of protecting the growth of manufacturing industry by reserving the home market for domestic producers ('infant industries'), through introducing barriers to imports

indirect rule a mode of rule developed especially, although not only, by Britain under which the colonial power allowed native rulers and chiefs to exercise limited authority

informal economy referring to employment and wealth creation that is not captured by the official data, offering opportunities for people who are unable to participate in the formal economy; governments find it difficult to regulate and tax the informal sector

informal institutions rules and procedures that are created, communicated, and enforced outside the officially sanctioned channels. They may undermine, reinforce, or even override the formal institutions

infrastructural power the power to penetrate and transform society

institutions collections of (broadly) agreed norms, rules, procedures, practices, and routines, either formally established or written down and embodied in organizations or as informal understandings embedded in culture

international community a loose term denoting the main Western powers and the international organizations in and over which they exert considerable influence, for example in the United Nations

international human rights regime a large body of international law and a complex set of institutions to implement it

intentional institutional design refers to situations in which political institutions are deliberately, consciously, and explicitly designed or reformed, often with a particular object in view

la francophonie the international organization of French-speaking communities, given a formal institutional basis in 1970

legitimacy a psychological relationship between the governed and their governors, which engenders a belief that the state's leaders and institutions have a right to exercise political authority over the rest of society

liberal democracy embodying a combination of political rights and civil liberties that go beyond **electoral democracy's** more limited attachment to civil freedoms and minority rights

liberal imperialism the idea that powerful advanced Western states should intervene, if necessary by force, in other countries to spread good government and liberal democratic values.

liberalism a political philosophy that gives priority to individual freedom

liberation theology a school of theological thought with widespread influence in Latin America beginning in the 1960s, which explores the relation between Christian theology and political activism in the areas of poverty, social justice, and human rights

localism the tendency to prioritize local cultural, economic, and political interests and identities over national ones

mainstreaming in the context of gender and environment, infusing public policies with a gender or environmental focus

majlis a traditional tribal forum for male elders and has evolved into an institution for consultation between ruler and ruled (Saudi Arabia)

micro-credit the provision of small loans to poor people who cannot obtain normal commercial credit for entrepreneurial activities

Millennium Development Goals (MDGs) established by the United Nations Millennium Declaration (September 2000) in the following eight areas: eradicate extreme poverty and hunger; achieve universal primary education; promote gender equality and empower women; reduce child mortality; improve maternal health; combat HIV/AIDS, malaria, and other diseases; ensure environmental sustainability; develop a global partnership for development

modern civil society *see* civil society

modernization referring to a complex set of changes in culture, society, and economy characterized by urbanization, industrialization, and in some cases secularization, although one response to it may be religious revival

modernization revisionism a critique of **modernization theory**, centred on its oversimplified notions of tradition, modernity, and their interrelationship

multi-ethnic or multicultural national identities defining the nation in terms of several ethnic or cultural identities contained within citizenship, political interaction, and an overarching national identity in an autonomous state

national identities inherently political, emphasizing the autonomy and unity of the nation as an actual or potential political unit

nation-building referring to building a sense of national belonging and unity

natural capital comprising nature's free goods and services

neo-liberalism stressing the role of the market in resource allocation and a correspondingly reduced role for the state, together with integration into the global economy. Aspects of the neo-liberal agenda are exhibited in the **Washington consensus** associated with the Bretton Woods institutions

neo-patrimonialism combining patrimonialism and legal-rational bureaucratic rule, which gives formal recognition to the distinction between the public and the private

new institutional economics (NIE) an approach that focuses on the way in which society's institutions affect economic performance

New International Economic Order comprising a set of reform proposals for the international financial and trading systems, to help the economic development of the developing countries, first proposed at a summit meeting of the Non-Aligned Movement (1973) and incorporated in a Declaration of the UN General Assembly in 1974

new protectionism referring to the measures of developed countries to reserve their domestic markets for home producers by means of non-tariff barriers such as imposing environmental standards

newly (or new) industrialized(izing) countries (NICs) referring to those developing countries primarily but not exclusively in East Asia (also sometimes called 'dragon' or 'tiger' economies) that experienced dramatic industrialization soonest after 1945

non-governmental organizations (NGOs) organizations that operate in civil society and are not part of government or the state (although sometimes dependent, in part, on government for funding)

non-traditional security threats non-military issues such as environmental problems, threats from migration, international organized crime, and disease

non-violent action refers to methods of political action that do not involve violence or the threat of violence against living beings; instead, they involve an active process of bringing political, economic, social, emotional, or moral pressure to bear in the wielding of power in contentious interactions between collective actors, through methods such as protest demonstrations, marches, civil disobedience, and land occupations

official development assistance (ODA) comprising resources transferred on concessional terms with the promotion of the economic development and welfare of the developing countries as the main objective

only game in town when applied to a perception that democratic elections are a permanent institution, often said to mark out democratic consolidation

ontological equality the assumption that all people are born equal

Orientalism referring to Edward Said's influential account (1978) of Western dominance of the East and how images of the Orient (the 'other') helped to define the West as its contrasting image

outward-oriented development looking to the global economy as a driving force for economic growth, through the creation of a favourable policy environment for exports

overpopulation referring to birth rates that exceed death rates, producing growth that is difficult to sustain with the given resource base

pacted transition where transition to democracy comes about by agreement among political elites integral to the precursor regime

Pancasila the official ideology of Soeharto's Indonesia, enjoining belief in a supreme being, humanitarianism, national unity, consensus democracy, and social justice

path dependence claiming that where you come from, the method of change, and choices made or not made along the way significantly influence the outcome and final destination

patriarchy referring to the ideology and institutions of male rule, male domination, and female subordination

patrimonialism treating the state as the personal patrimony or property of the ruler (hence **patrrimonialist** state), and all power relations between ruler and ruled are personal relations

patronage the politically motivated distribution of favours, intended to create and maintain political support among groups

patron–client relations connecting **patronage** and **clientelism**

people power movements comprise popular civilian-based challenges to oppression and injustice that depend primarily on methods of non-violent action rather than on armed methods

political culture embracing the attitudes, beliefs, and values that are said to underlie a political system

political development understood in the 1960s as a process of political change associated with increasing equality, political system capability, and differentiation of political roles and structures

political Islam refers to a political movement with often diverse characteristics that at various times has included elements of many other political movements, while simultaneously adapting the religious views of Islamic fundamentalism or Islamism

politicide referring to extermination of political enemies

politics on a narrow understanding, a kind of activity associated with the process of government, and in modern settings also linked with the 'public' sphere. On a broader understanding, it is about 'power' relations and struggles not necessarily confined to the process of government or restricted to the public domain

politics of order a critique of political development theory that focused on the need for strong government and political order

polyarchy Robert Dahl's influential idea of democracy that rests on the two pillars of public contestation and the right to participate

populism a political ideology or approach that claims to be in the interests of 'the people'

post-colonial state a state that came into being as a consequence of the dissolution of the European colonial empires

post-structuralism/post-structuralist sometimes also referred to as post-modernism, a broad philosophical approach that questions the epistemological foundations of 'rational' enlightenment thinking

predatory state close to the idea of an **extractive state**, one that exploits the people for the benefit of the rulers and holds back development

privatization the transformation of something that is communally or publicly owned to private property

process conditionality refers to the requirement of the poverty reduction strategy process that a government formulates (pro-poor) development policy itself through the consultation of local stakeholders, civil society in particular, so as to secure 'local ownership', in principle thereby avoiding the failings of conditionality

pro-natalism/pro-natalist referring to policies or values that motivate high birth rates

proxy wars conflicts carried out on behalf of, and supported by, the great powers, as was often the case in developing areas during the cold war era

pseudo-democracy existing where there is not a sufficiently fair arena of electoral contestation to allow the ruling party to be turned out of power

public goods goods such as defence that if supplied to anybody are necessarily supplied to everybody, and in consequence the market is unlikely to provide them in sufficient quantity

public institutions the institutions of the modern state are all 'public' institutions and include 'the government' and legislature, the courts, civil service, army and police, plus any state-owned agencies

rational choice theory a deductive approach that argues from the premise that in making choices individual political actors behave rationally in terms of the objectives they pursue. The quest for individual utility maximization is assumed to be paramount

realists in IR theory include classical realists who define security as national security. They emphasize military threats to the state and inter-state conflict

regime a set of rules and practices that regulate the conduct of actors in a specified field (as distinct from political regime understood as a system of government)

regime change came to be applied to the practice of removing a government by external force, as in the military invasion of Afghanistan and Iraq to topple the Taliban and Saddam Hussein's government, respectively. Some opponents of international intervention in developing countries choose to identify it with the aspirations behind democracy promotion and democracy assistance from the West

religio-politics political activity with religious dimensions

religious fundamentalism a disputed term applied most often to groups of Islamic, Hindu, and Christian worshippers who place strong emphasis on a return to their faith's fundamentals and resistance to secularization, often through political means

rentier state a state the income of which takes the form primarily of rents from a resource such as oil, or from foreign aid, rather than from taxing the subjects, which gives it high autonomy from society and may restrain citizens from demanding democratically accountable government

rent-seeking referring to the pursuit of gains (**economic rents**) to be derived from control over scarce goods or services—a scarcity that might be artificially created for the purpose

responsibility to protect refers both to states' responsibility to protect their own citizens and the international community's responsibility to engage in humanitarian intervention where a state fails in its responsibilities

right to self-determination the claimed right of a distinct group of people to determine their own political, economic, and cultural destinies

robust peacekeeping used by NATO to define the new type of peacekeeping in which its troops in Afghanistan are engaged. There they have more leeway to make peace as well as peacekeeping and monitoring functions

rule of law the idea that all citizens including the lawmakers and all other government officials are bound by the law and no one is above the law

scramble for Africa a name given to the late nineteenth-century territorial expansion of European powers in Africa, leading to the Congress of Berlin (1884–85), which formally adopted the division of the new colonies and protectorates

secularization the gradual diminution of the influence of religion on public affairs. Liberal secularism advocates separation of church and state, with the second power being dominant and no one religion having official priority

securitization occurs when an issue is presented as posing an existential threat to a designated object, traditionally but not necessarily the state. The designation of the threat in this way is used to justify the use of extraordinary measures in response

security dichotomies refer to a duality of perceptions, a division into two contradictory understandings of a security issue, one negative and one positive

Sharia law Islamic religious law, incorporated to varying degrees in the legal systems of states with large Islamic populations

shura an Islamic term used for consultation between the people and the ruler

social capital referring to social networks, norms, and trust, which enable participants to function more effectively in pursuing a common goal. Arguably high levels are valuable both for political and economic cooperation

social movements loose networks of informal organizations that come about in response to an issue, crisis, or concern and seek to influence social and other public policy, such as environmental policy, often through using direct action, which may or may not employ violence

societal collapse occurring where the fabric of linkages and feedback mechanisms between state and society and within society are irreparably ruptured

soft power in its original formulation by Joseph Nye Jnr, the ability of a country's culture, ideals, and policies to influence others by attraction and without deliberate resort to bribery or coercion

soft state Gunnar Myrdal's term for states with low enforcement capacity such as those with lax bureaucracy and corruption

state collapse occurring where a functioning state system ceases to exist

state failure indicating a less-than-complete collapse of the state system

state–church relations the interactions in a country between the state and the leading religious organization(s)

stateless societies societies that do not have a state but which may still enjoy a measure of social and economic order

status a quality of social honour or a lack of it, which is mainly conditioned as well as expressed through a specific style of life

structural adjustment programmes (SAPs) designed to shift economic policy and management in the direction of the **Washington consensus**, sometimes leading to more narrowly focused sectoral adjustment programmes, and often associated with **structural adjustment loans** (SALs) from the Bretton Woods institutions and other aid donors

subsistence economy referring to activity outside the cash economy for barter or home use

sustainable development a disputed term, which was defined by the Brundtland Report (1987) as development that meets the needs of the present without compromising the ability of future generations to meet their own needs; environmental degradation is minimized while ecological sustainability is maximized

terrorism a tactic designed to achieve an objective (usually political) by using violence against innocent civilians to generate fear

third wave of democracy Samuel P. Huntington's term for democratization in the late twentieth century

traditional civil society *see* civil society

transaction costs the costs of doing business in a market economy, including the cost of finding market information as well as the costs incurred when parties to a contract do not keep to their agreement

ulema Islamic clergy or body consisting of those educated in Islam and *Sharia* (Islamic law) with the function of ensuring the implementation of Islamic precepts

underdevelopment lack of development, according to dependency theory, which is a consequence of capitalist development elsewhere

unequal exchange the idea that international trade between developed and developing countries is an instrument whereby the former exploit the latter and capture the greater part of the benefits

unsecularization a global religious revitalization

urban bias bias in public policy and spending against the rural areas in favour of urban areas or urban-based interests, due to their greater political influence

war on terrorism is the term given by the USA and its allies to an ongoing campaign with the stated goal of ending global terrorism. It was launched in response to the 11 September 2001 terrorist attacks on the USA

warlords powerful regional figures possessing coercive powers, inside a country

Washington consensus the term applied (by John Williamson, in 1989) to a package of liberalizing economic and financial policy reforms deemed essential if Latin America (and subsequently other parts of the developing world) are to escape debt and rejuvenate their economic performance. The term quickly became attached to the policy approach in the 1990s of the Bretton Woods Institutions especially, namely the International Monetary Fund and World Bank. The central elements are fiscal discipline, reorientation of public expenditures, tax reform, financial liberalization, openness to foreign direct investment, privatization, deregulation, and secure property rights

weak states according to Joel Migdal, states lacking the capability to penetrate society fully, regulate social relations, extract and distribute resources, or implement policies and plans

wealth theory of democracy claiming that the prospects for stable democracy are significantly influenced by economic and socio-economic development

Westminster model referring to the institutional arrangement of parliamentary government bequeathed by Britain to many of its former colonies

women's (or gender) policy interests referring to official decisions or practices in which women have a special stake because of need, discrimination, or lack of equality

women's policy machinery units within government such as women's bureaux, commissions of women, ministries of women, and women's desks

References

Abdelal, R. et al. (2009), 'Identity as a Variable', in R. Abdelal et al. (eds), *Measuring Identity: A Guide for Social Scientists* (New York: Cambridge University Press).

Abdul-Ahad, G. (2006), 'Inside Iraq's Hidden War', *The Guardian* (London), 20 May.

Acharya, A. (1999), 'Developing Countries and the Emerging World Order', in L. Fawcett and Y. Sayigh (eds), *The Third World Beyond the Cold War* (Oxford: Oxford University Press), 78–98.

Ackerman, P. and DuVall, J. (2000), *A Force More Powerful: A Century of Nonviolent Conflict* (New York: Palgrave MacMillan).

Adeney, K. and Wyatt, A. (2004), 'Democracy in South Asia: Getting beyond the Structure–Agency Dichotomy', *Political Studies*, 52/1: 1–18.

Afrobarometer (2009), *Neither Consolidating nor Fully Democratic*, Briefing Paper No. 67.

Ahluwalia, P. (2001), *Politics and Post-Colonial Theory. African Inflections* (London: Routledge).

Ake, C. (1996), *Democracy and Development in Africa* (Washington DC: Brookings Institution).

—— (2000), *The Feasibility of Democracy in Africa* (Senegal: CODESRIA).

Alavi, H. (1979), 'The State in Post-Colonial Societies', in H. Goulbourne (ed.), *Politics and the State in the Third World* (London: Macmillan), 38–69.

—— (1988), 'Pakistan and Islam: Ethnicity and Ideology', in F. Halliday and H. Alavi (eds), *State and Ideology in the Middle East and Pakistan* (New York: Monthly Review Press), 64–111.

Alden, C. (2007), *China in Africa* (London: Zed).

Allison, R. and Williams, P. (1990), *Superpower Competition and Crisis Prevention in the Third World* (Cambridge: Cambridge University Press).

Almond, G. (1987), 'The Development of Political Development', in M. Weiner and S. P. Huntington (eds), *Understanding Political Development* (New York: Harper Collins), 437–90.

—— and Bingham Powell, G. (1966), *Comparative Politics: A Developmental Approach* (London: Little, Brown).

—— and Verba S. (eds) (1965), *The Civic Culture: Political Attitudes and Democracy in Five Nations* (Newbury Park, CA: Sage Publications).

Anderson, B. (1991), *Imagined Communities: Reflections on the Origin and Spread of Nationalism*, rev. edn (London: Verso).

Aspinall, E. and Fealy G. (eds) (2003), *Local Power and Politics in Indonesia: Democratization and Decentralization* (Singapore: Institute of Southeast Asian Affairs).

Baker, C. (2003), 'Thailand's Assembly of the Poor: Background, Drama, Reaction', *South East Asia Research*, 8/1: 5–29.

Banégas, R. (2008), 'Introduction: Rethinking the Great Lake Crisis, War, Violence and Political Recomposition in Africa', in. J.-P. Chrétien and R. Banégas (eds), *The Recurring Great Lakes Crisis: Identity, Violence and Power* (London: Hurst), 1–26.

Barton, J. R. (1997), *A Political Geography of Latin America* (London: Routledge).

Bastian, S. and Luckham, R. (eds) (2003), *Can Democracy Be Designed? The Politics of Institutional Choice in Conflict-Torn Societies* (London: Zed).

Bastos, S. and Camus, M. (2003), *Entre el Mecapal y el Cielo: Desarrollo del Movimento Maya en Guatemala* (Guatemala: FLASCO).

Bates, R. H. (1981), *Markets and States in Tropical Africa: The Political Basis of Agricultural Policy* (Berkeley, CA: University of California Press).

—— (1989), *Beyond the Miracle of the Market. The Political Economy of Agrarian Development in Kenya.* (Cambridge: Cambridge University Press).

—— (2001), *Prosperity and Violence: The Political Economy of Development* (New York: W. W. Norton).

Bauer, P. T. (1981), *Equality, the Third World and Economic Delusion* (London: Methuen).

Bayart, J.-F. (1993), *The State in Africa. The Politics of the Belly* (London: Longman).

Baylis, J. and Smith, S. (eds) (2001), *The Globalization of World Politics*, 2nd edn (Oxford: Oxford University Press).

Bayly, S. (1999), *The New Cambridge History of India, IV.3. Caste, Society and Politics in India from the Eighteenth Century to the Modern Age* (Cambridge: Cambridge University Press).

BBC (2008), 'Profile Mercosur = Common Market of the South', available at http://news.bbc.co.uk/1/hi/world/americas/5195834.stm

Beetham, D. (1997), 'Market Economy and Democratic Polity', *Democratization*, 4/1: 76–93.

——, Bracking, S., Kearton, I., and Weir, S. (2002), *International IDEA Handbook on Democracy Assessment* (The Hague/London/New York: Kluwer Law International).

Berdal, M. (2009), *Building Peace after War* (London: The International Institute for Strategic Studies).

Berger, M. (1994), 'The End of the "Third World"?', *Third World Quarterly*, 15/2: 257–75.

Berman, B. (1998), 'Ethnicity, Patronage and the African State: The Politics of Uncivil Nationalism', *African Affairs*, 97/388: 35–341.

Bermeo, N. (2003), *Ordinary People in Extraordinary Times: The Citizenry and the Breakdown of Democracy* (Princeton, NJ: Princeton University Press).

—— (2009), 'Democracy Assistance and the Search for Security', in P. Burnell and R. Youngs (eds), *New Challenges to Democratization* (London and New York: Routledge), 73–94.

Bertrand, J. (2002), 'Legacies of the Authoritarian Past: Religious Violence in Indonesia's Moluccan Islands', *Pacific Affairs*, 75: 57–85.

Béteille, A. (ed.) (1969), *Social Inequality* (Harmondsworth: Penguin).

Beynon, J. and Dunkerley, D. (eds) (2000), *Globalization: The Reader* (London: Athlone Press).

Bhalla, S. S. (2002), *Imagine There's No Country: Poverty, Inequality and Growth in the Era of Globalization* (Washington DC: Institute for International Economics).

Billig, M. (1995), *Banal Nationalism* (London: Sage).

Birmingham, D. (1995), *The Decolonization of Africa* (London: UCL Press).

BIS (2007), *Triennial Bank Survey* (Basle: Bank for International Settlements).

Boege, V. et al. (2008), *On Hybrid Politic Orders and Fragile States: State Formation in the Context of Fragility* (Berlin: Berghof Research Center for Constructive Conflict Management).

Boserup, E. (1989), *Women's Role in Economic Development*, rev. edn (London: Earthscan).

BP (2009), *Statistical Review of World Energy 2009*, available at www.bp.com

Branford, S. and Rocha, J. (2002), *Cutting the Wire: The Story of the Landless Movement in Brazil* (London: Latin America Bureau).

Bratton, M. (1997), *Democratic Experiments in Africa* (Cambridge: Cambridge University Press).

—— and van de Walle, N. (1994), 'Neopatrimonial Regimes and Political Transitions in Africa', *World Politics*, 46/4: 453–89.

——, Mattes, R., and Gyimah-Boadi, E. (2004), *Public Opinion, Democracy and Market Reform in Africa* (Cambridge: Cambridge University Press).

Braunstein, E. (2006), *Foreign Direct Investment, Development and Gender Equity: A Review of Research and Policy* (Geneva: United Nations Research Institute for Social Development).

Bräutigam, D. (2004), 'The People's Budget? Politics, Participation and Pro-Poor Policy', *Development Policy Review*, 22/6: 653–6.

—— (2009), *The Dragon's Gift: The Real Story of China in Africa* (Oxford: Oxford University Press).

Brennan, G. and Buchanan, J. M. (1985), *The Reason of Rules: Constitutional Political Economy* (Cambridge. Cambridge University Press).

Brown, J. (1985), *Modern India: The Origins of an Asian Democracy* (Oxford: Oxford University Press).

Brundtland, G. (ed.) (1987), *Our Common Future: The World Commission on Environment and Development* (Oxford: Oxford University Press) (The Brundtland Report).

Burnell, P. (2009), 'The Coherence of Democratic Peace Building', in T. Addison and T. Brück (eds), *Making Peace Work* (Houndmills: Palgrave Macmillan), 51–74.

—— and Calvert, P. (eds) (1999), *The Resilience of Democracy. Persistent Practice, Durable Idea* (London: Frank Cass).

Buzan, B. (1991), *People, States and Fear: an Agenda for International Security Studies in the Post-Cold War Era* (Boulder, CO: Lynne Rienner).

——, Wæver, O., and de Wilde, J. (1998), *Security: A New Framework for Analysis* (Boulder, CO: Lynne Reinner).

Calvert, P. and Calvert, S. (2001), *Politics and Society in the Third World*, 2nd edn (Harlow: Pearson Education).

Cammack, P., Pool, D., and Tordoff, W. (1993), *Third World Politics: A Comparative Introduction* (Basingstoke: Macmillan).

Campbell, H. (2008), 'China in Africa: Challenging US Global Hegemony, *Third World Quarterly*, 29/1: 89–105.

Cardoso, F. H. (1973), 'Associated Dependent Development: Theoretical and Practical Implications', in A. Stepan (ed.), *Authoritarian Brazil* (New Haven, CT: Yale University Press), 142–76.

—— and Faletto, E. (1979), *Dependency and Development in Latin America* (Berkeley, CA: University of California Press).

Carey, J. M. and Siavelis, P. (2006), 'Electoral Insurance and Coalition Survival: Formal and Informal Institutions in Chile', in G. Helmke and S. Levitsky (eds), *Informal Institutions and Democracy: Lessons from Latin America*

(Baltimore, MD: The Johns Hopkins University Press), 160–77.

Carillo, S. (2007), *Assessing Governance and Strengthening Capacity in Haiti* (Washington, DC: World Bank Development Brief).

Carranza, M. (2004), 'Mercosur and the End Game of the FTAA Negotiations: Challenges and Prospects after the Argentine Crisis', *Third World Quarterly*, 25/2: 319–37.

Casanova, J. (1994), *Public Religions in the Modern World* (Chicago, IL/London: University of Chicago Press).

Cavanagh, J., and Mander, J. (2004), *Alternatives to Economic Globalization: Another World is Possible*, 2nd ed. (San Francisco: Berrett-Koehler).

Chabal, P. (2009), *Africa: The Politics of Suffering and Smiling* (London: Zed Books).

——and Daloz, J. P. *Africa Works: Disorder as Political Instrument* (London: James Currey).

Chakrabarty, D. (2003), 'Postcoloniality and the Artifice of History: Who Speaks for "Indian" Pasts?', in J. D. LeSueur (ed.), *The Decolonization Reader* (London: Routledge), 428–48.

Chandra, B., Mukherjee, M., and Mukherjee, A. (1999), *India after Independence* (New Delhi: Viking Penguin India).

Chandra, K. and S. Wilkinson (2008), 'Measuring the Effect of "Ethnicity", *Comparative Political Studies*, 41/4/5: 515–63.

Chaney, E. M. and Castro, M. G. (eds) (1989), *Muchachas No More: Household Workers in Latin America and the Caribbean* (Philadelphia, PA: Temple University Press).

Chang, H. (2002), *Kicking Away the Ladder* (London: Anthem Press).

Chatterjee, P. (1986), *Nationalist Thought and the Colonial World: A Derivative Discourse?* (London: Zed Books).

Chauvel, R. (2003), 'Papua and Indonesia: Where Contending Nationalisms Meet', in D. Kingsbury and H. Aveling (eds), *Autonomy and Disintegration in Indonesia* (London: RoutledgeCurzon), 115–27.

Chen, S. and Ravallion, M. (2008), *The Developing World is Poorer than We Thought, But No Less Successful in the Fight Against Poverty*, Policy Research Working Paper 4703 (Washington, DC: World Bank).

Chenery, H., et al. (1974), *Redistribution with Growth* (New York: Oxford University Press).

Chibber, V. (2005), 'The Good Empire: Should We Pick Up Where the British Left Off?', *Boston Review*, 30/1, available at http://bostonreview.net/BR30.1/chibber.html

Clapham, C. (2000), 'Failed States and Non-States in the Modern International Order', Paper presented at 'Failed States III: Globalization and the Failed State', Florence, Italy, 7–10 April, available at www.comm.ucsb.edu/Research/mstohl/failed_states/2000/papers/clapham.htm

——(2002), 'The Challenge to the State in a Globalized World', *Development and Change*, 33/5: 775–95.

Cohn, B. S. (1996), *Colonialism and Its Forms of Knowledge. The British in India* (Princeton, NJ: Princeton University Press).

Collier, D. and Levitsky, S. (1997), 'Democracy with Adjectives', *World Politics*, 49: 430–51.

Collier, P. et al. (2003), *Breaking the Conflict Trap* (Washington DC: The World Bank).

Commission for Africa (2005), *Our Common Interest* (London: Penguin).

Connor, W. (1994), *Ethnonationalism: The Quest for Understanding* (Princeton, NJ: Princeton University Press).

Cooper, F. (2003), 'Conflict and Connection: Rethinking Colonial African History', in J. D. Le Sueur (ed.), *The Decolonization Reader* (London: Routledge), 23–44.

——(2005), *Colonialism in Question. Theory, Knowledge, History* (Berkeley, CA: University of California Press).

Cooper, R. (2004), *The Breaking of Nations: Order and Chaos in the Twenty-First Century* (London: Atlantic).

Cornia, G. A. and Court, J. (2001), *Inequality, Growth and Poverty in the Era of Liberalization and Globalization*, UNU Policy Brief No. 4 (Helsinki: UNU/WIDER).

Coulon, C. (1983), *Les Musulmans et le Pouvoir en Afrique Noire* (Paris: Karthala).

Craig, A. L. and Cornelius, W. A. (1995), 'Mexico', in A. Mainwaring and T. R. Scully (eds), *Building Democratic Institutions* (Stanford, CA: University of California Press).

Crook, R. C. (2005), 'The Role of Traditional Institutions in Political Change and Underdevelopment', Center for Democratic Development/Overseas Development Institute Policy Brief No. 4 (Accra: Ghana Center for Democratic Development).

Croucher, S. L. (2003), 'Perpetual Imagining: Nationhood in a Global Era', *International Studies Review*, 5: 1–24.

Dahl, R. (1971), *Polyarchy: Participation and Opposition* (New Haven, CT/London: Yale University Press).

Dauvergne, P. (1997), *Shadows in the Forest: Japan and the Politics of Timber in South East Asia* (Cambridge, MA: MIT Press).

Davidson, B. (1992), *The Black Man's Burden: Africa and the Curse of the Nation-State* (New York: Times Books).

Davis, M. (2001), *Late Victorian Holocausts: El Nino Famines and the Making of the Third World* (London: Verso).

De Tocqueville, A. (2000), *Democracy in America* (Chicago, IL/London: University of Chicago Press).

Diamond, L. (1996), 'Is the Third Wave Over?', *Journal of Democracy*, 7/3: 20–37.

——(2002), 'Thinking About Hybrid Regimes', *Journal of Democracy* 13/2: 21–35.

——(2004), 'What Went Wrong in Iraq', *Foreign Affairs* (September/October) 83/5: 34–56.

Dicken, P. (2003), *Global Shift: Reshaping the Global Economic Map in the 21st Century* (London: Sage).

Dickson, A. K. (1997), *Development and International Relations: A Critical Introduction* (Cambridge: Polity).

Dirks, N. (2001), *Castes of Mind: Colonialism and the Making of Modern India* (Princeton, NJ: Princeton University Press).

—— (2004), 'Colonial and Postcolonial Histories: Comparative Reflections on the Legacies of Empire', Global Background Paper for United Nations Development Programme, Human Development Report, *Cultural Liberty in Today's Diverse World*.

Dodge, T. (2003), *Inventing Iraq* (London: Hurst).

Dollar, D. and Burnside, C. (1998), *Assessing Aid: What Works, What Doesn't and Why* (Washington DC: World Bank).

Doorenspleet, R. (2009), 'Public Support versus Dissatisfaction in New Democracies?', in P. Burnell and R. Youngs (eds), *New Challenges to Democratization* (London and New York: Routledge), 95–117.

Doornbos, M. (2006), *Global Forces and State Restructuring: Dynamics of State Formation and Collapse* (Houndmills: Palgrave Macmillan).

Dorr, S. (1993), 'Democratization in the Middle East', in R. Slater, B. Schutz, and S. Dorr (eds), *Global Transformation and the Third World* (Boulder, CO: Lynne Rienner), 131–57.

Downs, E. (2007), 'The Fact and Fiction of Sino–African Energy Relations', *China Security*, 1 June 2007: 42–68.

Doyle, M.W. and Sambanis, N. (2006), *Making War and Building Peace: United Nations Peace Operations* (Princeton, NJ: Princeton University Press).

Drake, C. (1989), *National Integration in Indonesia: Patterns and Policies* (Honolulu: University of Hawaii Press).

Driscoll, R., with Evans, A. (2005), 'Second-Generation Poverty Reduction Strategies: New Opportunities and Emerging Issues', *Development Policy Review*, 23/1: 5–25.

Duffield, M. (2001), *Global Governance and the New Wars: The Merging of Development and Security* (London: Zed Press).

—— (2006), 'Racism, Migration and Development: The Foundations of Planetary Order', *Progress in Development Studies*, 6/1: 68–79.

Dunn, R. M., and Mutti, J. H. (2004), *International Economics*, 6th edn (London: Routledge).

Dupuy, A. (2007), *The Prophet and Power: Jean-Bertrand Aristide, the International Commmunity, and Haiti* (Lanham, MD. : Rowman & Littlefield).

Easton, D. (1965), *A Systems Analysis of Political Life* (New York: Wiley).

Eckert, C. J. (1990), 'The South Korean Bourgeoisie: A Class in Search of Hegemony', *Journal of Korean Studies*, 7: 115–48.

Editorial Board of the China Commerce Yearbook (2009), *China Commerce Yearbook 2009* (Beijing: China Commerce and Trade Press).

Ehrlich, P. (1972), *The Population Bomb* (London: Pan/Ballantine).

Elbe, S. (2002), 'HIV/AIDS and the Changing Landscape of War in Africa', *International Security*, 27/2: 157–77.

Elliot, L. (1993), 'Fundamentalists Prepare for Holy War in Nigeria', *The Guardian*, 14 April.

Elson, D. and Pearson, R. (1981), 'Nimble Fingers Make Cheap Workers: An Analysis of Women's Employment in Third World Export Manufacturing', *Feminist Review*, 7: 87–107.

Escobar, A. (1995), *Encountering Development: The Making and Unmaking of the Third World* (Princeton, NJ: Princeton University Press).

Evans, P. (1995), *Embedded Autonomy: States and Industrial Transformation* (Princeton, NJ: Princeton University Press).

Fanon, F. (1967), *The Wretched of the Earth* (Harmondsworth: Penguin).

Fawcett, L. and Sayigh, Y. (eds) (1999), *The Third World Beyond the Cold War: Continuity and Change* (Oxford: Oxford University Press).

Ferdinand, P. (2003), 'Party Funding and Political Corruption in East Asia: The Cases of Japan, South Korea and Taiwan', in International IDEA, *Funding of Political Parties and Election Campaigns* (Stockholm: International Institute for Democracy and Electoral Assistance), 55–69.

Ferguson, J. (1997), *The Anti-Politics Machine* (Minneapolis, MN: University of Minnesota Press).

Ferguson, N. (2004), *Colossus: The Rise and Fall of the American Empire* (London: Allen Lane).

Fink, C. (2009), 'The Moment of the Monks: Burma, 2007', in A. Roberts and T. Garton Ash (eds), *Civil Resistance and Power Politics: The Experience of Non-Violent Action from Gandhi to the Present* (Oxford: Oxford University Press).

Foster-Carter, A. (1978), 'The Modes of Production Controversy', *New Left Review*, 177: 47–77.

Frank, A. G. (1969), *Capitalism and Underdevelopment in Latin America: Historical Studies of Chile and Brazil* (New York: Monthly Review Press).

—— (1971), *The Sociology of Development and the Underdevelopment of Sociology* (London: Pluto Press).

—— (1998), *Reorient: Global Economy in the Asian Age* (Berkeley, CA: University of California Press).

Freston, P. (2004), *Protestant Political Parties. A Global Survey* (Aldershot: Ashgate).

Friedman, T. L. (2006), 'The First Law of Petropolitics', *Foreign Policy*, 154: 28–36.

Fukuyama, F. (1992), *The End of History and the Last Man* (Harmondsworth: Penguin).

Gaouette, N. (1999), 'Indonesian Togetherness at Stake', *Christian Science Monitor*, 18 May.

Garcia-Johnson, R. (2000), *Exporting Environmentalism: US Chemical Corporations in Brazil and Mexico* (Cambridge, MA: MIT Press).

Gerring, J. and Mahoney, J. (2007), 'Colonialism and its Legacies: A Comparative Historical Dataset', available at www. bu.edu/polisci/people/faculty/gerring/unpublishedpapers. html

Ghosh, A. (2002), *The Imam and the Indian* (New Delhi: Ravi Dayal & Permanent Black).

Gill, B. and Reilly, J. (2007),'The Tenuous Hold of China, Inc. in Africa', *The Washington Quarterly*, 30/3: 37–52.

Gilmartin, D. (2003), 'Democracy, Nationalism and the Public. A Speculation on Colonial Muslim Politics', in J. D. Le Sueur (ed.), *The Decolonization Reader*, (London: Routledge), 191–203.

Glosny, M. (2010), 'China and the BRICs', *Polity*, 42/1: 100–129.

Go, J. (2003), 'Global Perspectives on the US Colonial State in the Philippines', in J. Go and A. L. Foster (eds), *The American Colonial State in the Philippines. Global Perspectives* (Durham, NC: Duke University Press), 1–42.

Gopin, M. (2000), *Between Eden and Armageddon: The Future of World Religions, Violence and Peacemaking* (New York/London: Oxford University Press).

——(2005), 'World Religions, Violence, and Myths of Peace in International Relations', in G. Ter Haar and J. Busutill (eds), *Bridge or Barrier? Religion, Violence and Visions for Peace* (Leiden: Brill), 35–56.

Graham-Brown, S. (1999), *Sanctioning Saddam: The Politics of Intervention in Iraq* (London/New York : I.B.Tauris).

Gramsci, A. (1992), *Prison Notebooks* (New York: Columbia University Press).

Granovetter, M.S. (1985), 'Economic Action and Social Structure: The Problem of Embeddedness', *American Journal of Sociology*, 91/3: 481–510.

Gray, J. (2003), *Al Qaeda and What it Means to be Modern* (London: Faber & Faber).

Green, E. D. (2005), 'Understanding Ethnicity and Nationhood in Pre-Colonial Africa: The Case of Buganda' (London: Development Studies Institute, London School of Economics), available at http://personal.lse.ac.uk/greened/ Ethnicity%20and%20Nationhood%20in%20Pre-Colonial%20 Africa.pdf

Grimm, S. and Harmer, A. (2005), *Diversity in Donorship: The Changing Landscape of Official Humanitarian Aid—Aid: Donorship in Central Europe* (London: HPG Background Paper of the Overseas Development Institute, September 2005.

Grimmett, R. F. (2009), *Conventional Arms Transfers to Developing Nations, 1998–2005* (Washington DC: Congressional Research Service, US Library of Congress).

Guha, R. (1989), 'Dominance without Hegemony and its Historiography', in R. Guha (ed.), *Subaltern Studies VI: Writings on South Asian History and Society* (New Delhi: Oxford University Press).

Hakim, P. (2003), 'Latin America's Lost Illusions. Dispirited Politics', *Journal of Democracy*, 14/2: 108–22.

Hallencreutz, C. and Westerlund, D. (1996), 'Anti-Secularist Policies of Religion', in D. Westerlund (ed.), *Questioning the Secular State: The Worldwide Resurgence of Religion in Politics* (London: Hurst).

Halliday, F. (1989), *Cold War, Third World: An Essay on Soviet–US Relations* (London: Hutchinson).

——(1993), 'Orientalism and its Critics', *British Journal of Middle Eastern Studies*, 20/2: 145–63.

——(2002), *Two Hours that Shook the World: September 11, 2001, Causes and Consequences* (London: Saqi).

Harff, B. (2003), 'No Lessons Learned from the Holocaust? Assessing Risks of Genocide and Political Mass Murder since 1955', *American Political Science Review*, 97/1: 57–73.

Harmer, A. and Correrell, L. (2005), 'The Currency of Humanitarian Reform', HPG Briefing Note of Overseas Development Institute, London, November.

Harris, K. (2005), 'Still Relevant: Claude Ake's Challenge to Mainstream Discourse on African Politics and Development', *Journal of Third World Studies*, 22/2: 73–88.

Harrison, G. (2001), 'Post-Conditionality Politics and Administrative Reform: Reflections on the Cases of Uganda and Tanzania', *Development and Change*, 32/4: 657–79.

——(2004), 'Sub-Saharan Africa', in A. Payne (ed.), *The New Regional Politics* (Basingstoke: Palgrave), 218–47.

Haynes, J. (1993), *Religion in Third World Politics* (Buckingham: Open University Press).

——(1996), *Religion and Politics in Africa* (London: Zed Books).

——(2007), *Introduction to Religion and International Relations* (Harlow: Pearson Education).

Hegel, G. W. F. (1942), *Philosophy of Right*, trans. with notes by T. M. Knox (Oxford: Clarendon Press).

Hegre, H. et al. (2001), 'Democracy, Political Change and Civil War,' *American Political Science Review*, 95/1: 16–33.

Hellman, J. S., Jones, G., and Kaufmann, D. (2000), ' "Seize the State, Seize the Day", State Capture, Corruption and Influence in Transition', World Bank Policy Research Working Paper 2444 (Washington DC: World Bank Institute, World Bank).

Herbst, J. (2000), *States and Power in Africa* (Princeton, NJ: Princeton University Press).

Herring, R. J. (1979), 'Zulfikar Ali Bhutto and the "Eradication of Feudalism" in Pakistan', *Comparative Studies in Society and History*, 21/4: 519–57.

Higgott, R. A. and Ougaard, M. (eds) (2002), *Towards a Global Polity* (London: Routledge).

Hiltermann, J. (2005) 'Make-up or Break-up? The Impact of the Draft Constitution on Iraq's Divided Communities', available at www.crisisgroup.org/home/index.cfm?id=3707 [accessed 11 July 2008].

Hirst, P. et al. (2009), *Globalization in Question*, 3rd edn (Cambridge: Polity).

Hobson, J. A. (2004), *The Eastern Origins of Western Civilization* (Cambridge: Polity).

Hoogvelt, A. (1997), *Globalization and the Postcolonial World* (Baltimore, MD: The John Hopkins University Press).

Horowitz, D. (1985), *Ethnic Groups in Conflict* (Berkeley, CA: University of California Press).

Human Security Report Project (2005), *Human Security Report 2005: War and Peace in the 21st Century* (New York/Oxford: Oxford University Press).

Huntington, S. P. (1968), *Political Order in Changing Societies* (New Haven, CT: Yale University Press).

—— (1971), 'The Change to Change', *Comparative Politics*, 3/3: 283–332.

—— (1991), *The Third Wave: Democratization in the Late Twentieth Century* (Norman, OK/London: University of Oklahoma Press).

—— (1993), 'The Clash of Civilizations?', *Foreign Affairs*, 72/3: 22–49.

—— (1996a), *The Clash of Civilizations and the Remaking of World Order* (New York: Simon and Schuster).

—— (1996b), 'Democracy for the Long Haul', *Journal of Democracy*, 7/2: 3–14.

Hurrell, A. and Narliker, A. (2006), 'A New Politics of Confrontation? Brazil and India in Multilateral Trade Negotiations', *Global Society*, 20/4: 415–33.

Ibrahim, Y. (1992), 'Islamic Plans for Algeria on Display'. *New York Times*, 7 January.

ILO (2009), *Global Employment Trends for Women, March 2009* (Geneva: International Labour Organization).

Inter-Agency Information and Analysis Unit (IAU) and United Nations Office for the Coordination of Humanitarian Affairs (OCHA) (2009), 'The Humanitarian Situation in Iraq: Inter-Agency Fact Sheet', available at www.iauiraq.org/reports/Factsheet-EnglishR.pdf

International Crisis Group (2006), *In Their Own Words: Reading the Iraqi Insurgency* (Amman/Brussels: International Crisis Group).

—— (2008), *Iraq after the Surge II: The Need for a New Political Strategy* (Baghdad/Istanbul/Damascus/Brussels: ICG).

International Energy Agency (2008), *Key World Energy Statistics 2008*, available at www.iea.org

International Monetary Fund and World Bank (2009), *Global Monitoring Report 2009: A Development Emergency* (Washington, DC).

Isaak, R. A. (2005), *The Globalization Gap: How the Rich Get Richer and the Poor Get Left Further Behind* (London: FT Prentice Hall).

Jackson, R. H. (1990), *Quasi-States: Sovereignty, International Relations and the Third World* (Cambridge: Cambridge University Press).

Jalal, A. (1995), *Democracy and Authoritarianism in South Asia: A Comparative and Historical Perspective* (Cambridge: Cambridge University Press).

James, C. L. R. (1977), *Nkrumah and the Ghana Revolution* (London: Allison and Busby).

Janelli, R. L. (1993), *Making Capitalism* (Stanford, CA: Stanford University Press).

Johnson, M. and Blas, J. (2009), 'China Drives Commodity Price Rises', FT.com, 19 June, available at www.ft.com/cms/s/0/e7e10432–5b29–11de-be=be3f-00144feabdc0html/

Jones, L. P. and Il, S. (1980), *Government, Business and Entrepreneurship in Economic Development: The Korean Case* (Cambridge, MA: Harvard University Press).

Juburi, S. (2009) 'Iraqi Doctors in Britain and the War on Terror', available at www.opendemocracy.net/opensecurity/shatha-al-juburi/iraqi-doctors-in-britain-and-war-on-terror

Kalyvas, S. (2001), '"New' and 'Old' Civil Wars: A Valid Distinction?', *World Politics*, 54: 99–118.

Kapstein, E. and Converse, N. (2009), 'Why Democracies Fail', *Journal of Democracy*, 19/4: 57–68.

Karl, T. L. (1990), 'Dilemmas of Democratization in Latin America', *Comparative Politics*, 23/1: 1–21.

Kashyap, S. C. (1989), *Our Parliament. An Introduction to the Parliament of India* (New Delhi: National Book Trust).

Kassalow, J. S. (2001), *Why Health is Important to US Foreign Policy* (New York: Council on Foreign Relations).

Kaufman, R. and Segura-Ubiergo, A. (2001), 'Globalization, Domestic Politics, and Social Spending in Latin America', *World Politics*, 53/4: 553–87.

Keck, M.E. and Sikkink, K. (1998), *Activists Beyond Borders: Advocacy Networks in International Politics* (Ithaca, NY: Cornell University Press).

Keen, D. (2005), *Conflict & Collusion in Sierra Leone* (New York: Palgrave).

Khanna, P. (2009), *The Second World: How Emerging Powers are Redefining Global Competition in the Twenty-first Century* (London: Penguin).

Killick, T., with Gunatilaka, R. and Marr, A. (1998), *Aid and the Political Economy of Policy Change* (London/New York: Routledge).

Kim, E. and Kim, J. (2005), 'Developmental State vs Globalization: South Korea's Developmental State in the Aftermath of the Asian Financial Crisis of 1997–98', *Korean Social Science Journal*, 32/2: 43–70.

Kipling, R. (1987), 'Tods' Amendment', in *Plain Tales from the Hills* (London: Penguin, first pub. 1890), 179–84.

Krauthammer, C. (1991), 'The Unipolar Moment', *Foreign Affairs*, 70/1: 23–33.

Lal, D. (2004), *In Praise of Empires: Globalization and Order* (Basingstoke: Palgrave).

Landman, T. (2003), *Issues and Methods in Comparative Politics*, 2nd edn (London: Routledge).

Lange, M. (2009,) *Lineages of Despotism and Development: British Colonialism and State Power* (Chicago, IL: Chicago University Press).

Large, D. (2008, 'All Over in Africa', in C. Alden et al. (eds), *China Returns to Africa: A Rising Power and a Continent Embrace* (London: Hurst and Co.), 371–6

Lauth, H. J (2000), 'Informal Institutions and Democracy', *Democratization*, 7/4: 21–50.

Lawson, L. (2009), 'The Politics of Anti-Corruption Reform in Africa', *Journal of Modern African Studies*, 47/1: 73–100.

Lee, Y. H. (1997), *The State, Society and Big Business in South Korea* (London/New York: Routledge).

Leftwich, A. (1993), 'Governance, Democracy and Development in the Third World', *Third World Quarterly*, 14/3: 603–24.

——(1995), 'Bringing Politics Back In: Towards a Model of the Developmental State', *Journal of Development Studies*, 31/3: 400–27.

Lendman, S. (2010), 'Iraq Today: Afflicted by Violence, Devastation, Corruption and Desperation', Global Policy Forum, available at www.globalpolicy.org/iraq/humanitarian-issues-in-iraq/iraqs-humanitarian-crisis/49013.html

Le Sueur, J. D. (ed.) (2003), *The Decolonization Reader* (London: Routledge).

Levitsky, S. and Way, L. A. (2002), 'The Rise of Competitive Authoritarianism', *Journal of Democracy*, 13/2: 51–65.

Lewis, P. (2009), 'Growth without Prosperity in Africa', *Journal of Democracy*, 19/4: 95–109.

Lindberg, S. (2006), *Democracy and Elections in Africa* (Baltimore, MO: The Johns Hopkins University Press).

Linz, J. J. and Stepan, A. (1996), *Problems of Democratic Transition and Consolidation: Southern Europe, South America, and Post-Communist Europe* (Baltimore, MD: Johns Hopkins University Press).

Lipset, S. M. (1994), 'The Social Requisites of Democracy Revisited', *American Sociological Review*, 53/1: 1–22.

Lockwood, B. and Redoano, M. (2005), *The CSGR Globalization Index: An Introductory Guide*, Centre for the Study of Globalization and Regionalization Working Paper 155/04, available at www2.warwick.ac.uk/fac/soc/isgr/index

Lodgaard, S. (2007), 'Iran's Uncertain Nuclear Ambitions', in M. Bremer Maerli and S. Lodgaard (eds), *Nuclear Proliferation and International Security* (London: Routledge).

Lucas, R. E., Jr (1988), 'On the Mechanics of Economic Development', *Journal of Monetary Economics*, 22/1: 3–42.

Lugard, Lord (1965), *The Dual Mandate in British Tropical Africa* (London: Frank Cass, first pub. 1922).

McEwan, C. (2009), *Postcolonialism and Development* (London: Routledge).

McGrew, A. (1992), 'A Global Society?', in S. Hall, D. Held, and A. McGrew (eds), *Modernity and Its Future* (Cambridge: Polity Press), 62–102.

McMichael, P. (2008), *Development and Social Change: A Global Perspective*, 4th edn (Los Angeles, CA: Pine Forge).

Mainwaring, S. and Scully, T. (1995), *Building Democratic Institutions: Party Systems in Latin America* (Stanford, CA: Stanford University Press).

Mair, P. (1996), 'Comparative Politics: An Overview', in R. E. Goodin and H. Klingemann (eds), *A New Handbook of Political Science* (Oxford: Oxford University Press), 309–35.

Malek, C. (2004), 'International Conflict: The Conflict Resolution Information Service', available at http://v4.crinfo.org/CK_Essays/ck_international_conflict.jsp

Mamdani, M. (1996), *Citizen and Subject: Contemporary Africa and the Legacy of Late Colonialism* (London: James Currey).

Mann, M. (1986), *The Sources of Social Power*, Vol. I (Cambridge: Cambridge University Press).

March, J. (2006), 'Elaborating the "New Institutionalism"', in R.A.W. Rhodes et al. (eds), *The Oxford Handbook of Political Institutions* (Oxford University Press).

——and Olsen, J. (1984), 'The New Institutionalism: Organisational Factors in Political Life', *American Political Science Review*, 78/3: 734–49.

Marr, P. (2006), *Who Are Iraq's New Leaders? What Do They Want?*, United States Institute of Peace Special Report, Washington DC, March, p. 8, available at www.usip.org/pubs/specialreports/sr160.pdf

Martin, B. (2006), 'Paths to Social Change: Conventional Politics, Violence and Nonviolence', in R. Summy (ed.), *Nonviolent Alternatives for Social Change*, in the *Encyclopedia of Life Support Systems* (Oxford: Eolss Publishers).

Marty, M. E. and Appleby, R. S. (1993), 'Introduction', in M. and S. Appleby (eds), *Fundamentalism and the State: Remaking Polities, Economies, and Militance* (Chicago, IL: University of Chicago Press).

Marx, K. (1970), *The German Ideology* (London: Lawrence and Wishart).

Mawdsley, E. and McCann, G. (2010), 'The Elephant in the Corner? Reviewing India–Africa Relations in the New Millennium', *Geography Compass*, 4/2: 81–93.

Mayall, J. and Payne, A. (eds) (1991), *The Fallacies of Hope: The Post-Colonial Record of the Commonwealth Third World* (Manchester: Manchester University Press).

Mazrui, A. (1986), *The Africans: A Triple Heritage* (London: BBC Publications).

Mearsheimer, J. (2005), 'Clash of the Titans', *Foreign Policy*, 146: 46.

Mehta, L. (2006), 'Do Human Rights Make a Difference to Poor and Vulnerable People? Accountability for the Right to Water in South Africa', in P. Newell and J. Wheeler (eds), *Rights, Resources and the Politics of Accountability* (London: Zed Books), 63–79.

Melia, T. O. and Katulis, B. M. (2003), *Iraqis Discuss their Country's Future: Post-War Perspectives from the Iraqi Street* (Washington, DC: National Democratic Institute).

Mendoza, A. Jr. (2009), '"People Power" in the Philippines, 1983–86', in A. Roberts and T. Garton Ash (eds), *Civil Resistance and Power Politics: The Experience of Non-Violent Action from Gandhi to the Present* (Oxford: Oxford University Press).

Menkhaus, K. (2006–07), 'Governance without Government in Somalia: Spoilers, State Building, and the Politics of Coping', *International Security*, 31/3: 74–106.

Merrill, D. (1994), 'The United States and the Rise of the Third World', in G. Martel (ed.), *American Foreign Relations Reconsidered, 1890–1993* (London: Routledge), 166–86.

Mesbahi, M. (ed.) (1994), *Russia and the Third World in the Post-Soviet Era* (Gainesville, FL: University Press of Florida).

Meyer, W. H. (1998), *Human Rights and International Political Economy in Third World Nations* (Westport, CT: Praeger).

Migdal, J. S. (1988), *Strong Societies and Weak States: State–Society Relations and State Capabilities in the Third World* (Princeton, NJ: Princeton University Press).

Mill, J. S. (1888), *A System of Logic* (New York: Harper and Row).

Missingham, B. D. (2003), *The Assembly of the Poor in Thailand: From Local Struggles to National Protest Movement* (Chiang Mai: Silkworm Books).

Moore, M. (2004), 'Revenues, State Formation, and the Quality of Governance in Developing Countries', *International Political Science Review*, 25/3: 297–329.

Morris-Jones, W. H. (1987), *The Government and Politics of India* (Huntingdon: Eothen Press).

Mosley, L. (2005), 'Globalization and the State: Still Room to Move?', *New Political Economy*, 10/3: 355–62.

Mosley, P., Harrigan, J., and Toye, J. (1995), *Aid and Power: The World Bank and Policy-Based Lending*, 2nd edn (London: Routledge).

Mote, O. and Rutherford, D. (2001), 'From Irian Jaya to Papua: The Limits of Primordialism in Indonesia's Troubled East', *Indonesia*, 72: 115–40.

Mozaffar, S. (1995), 'The Institutional Logic of Ethnic Politics: A Prolegomenon', in H. Glickman (ed.), *Ethnic Conflict and Democratization in Africa* (Atlanta, GA: African Studies Association Press), 34–69.

——, Scarritt, J. R., and Galaich, G. (2003), 'Electoral Institutions, Ethnopolitical Cleavages, and Party Systems in Africa's Emerging Democracies', *American Political Science Review*, 97/3: 379–90.

Mutua, M. (2008), *Kenya's Quest for Democracy: Taming Leviathan* (Boulder, CO: Lynne Rienner).

National Intelligence Council (USA) (2000), 'The Global Infectious Disease Threat and its Implications for the United States', NIE 99–17D, available at www.fas.org/irp/threat/nie99–17d.htm

Nehru, J. (1942), *An Autobiography* (London: The Bodley Head).

—— (1961), *The Discovery of India* (Bombay: Asia Publishing House).

Neuman S. G. (ed.) (1998), *International Relations Theory and the Third World* (Basingstoke: Macmillan).

Newell, P. (2001), 'Environmental NGOs, TNCs and the Question of Governance', in D. Stevis and V. Assetto (eds), *The International Political Economy of the Environment: Critical Perspectives* (Boulder, CO: Lynne Rienner), 85–107.

—— (2007), 'Trade and Environmental Justice in Latin America', *New Political Economy*, 12/2, 237–59.

Newman, E., Richmond, O., and Paris, R. (2009), *New Perspectives on Liberal Peacebuilding* (Tokyo: United Nations University Press).

Ngũgĩ wa Thiong'o (1986), *Decolonising the Mind: The Politics of Language in African Literature* (London: James Currey).

Nkrumah, K. (1965), *Neo-Colonialism: The Last Stage of Imperialism* (London: Panaf Books).

Nolutshungu, S. C. (1991), 'Fragments of a Democracy: Reflections on Class and Politics in Nigeria', in J. Mayall and A. Payne (eds), *The Fallacies of Hope* (Manchester: Manchester University Press), 72–105.

North, D. C. (1990), *Institutions, Institutional Change and Economic Performance* (Cambridge: Cambridge University Press).

Norval, A. (1996), *Deconstructing Apartheid Discourse* (London: Verso).

Nozick, R. (1974), *Anarchy, State and Utopia* (Oxford: Blackwell).

O'Donnell, G. (1994), 'Delegative Democracy', *Journal of Democracy*, 5/1: 55–69.

O'Hanlon, M. E. and Campbell, J. H. (2007), *Iraq Index: Tracking Variables of Reconstruction and Security in Post-Saddam Iraq*, 28 June (Washington, DC, The Brookings Institution).

Olson, M. (2001), *Power and Prosperity: Outgrowing Communist and Capitalist Dictatorships* (New York: Basic Books).

Organisation for Economic Co-operation and Development (2001), *Strategies for Sustainable Development: Practical Guidance for Development Cooperation* (Paris: OECD).

O'Rourke, D. (2004), *Community-Based Regulation: Balancing Environment and Development in Vietnam* (Cambridge, MA: MIT Press).

Ottaway, M. (2003), *Democracy Challenged: The Rise of Semi-Authoritarianism* (Washington DC: Carnegie Endowment for International Peace).

—— (2009), 'Ideological Challenges to Democratization: Do They Exist?', in P. Burnell and R. Youngs (eds), *New Challenges to Democratization* (London: Routledge), 42–58.

Oxfam International (2007), *Rising to the Humanitarian Challenge in Iraq*, Briefing Paper 105 (Oxford: Oxfam).

Page, S. and Omar, S. (2007), 'Iraqis see Hope Drain Away', *USA Today*, 20 March, available at www.usatoday.com/news/world/iraq/2007–03–18-poll-cover_N.htm

Parente, S. L. and Prescott, E. C. (2000), *Barriers to Riches* (Cambridge, MA: MIT Press).

Parry, J. H. (1966), *The Spanish Seaborne Empire* (London: Hutchinson).

Parry, R. L. (2005), *In the Time of Madness: Indonesia on the Edge of Chaos* (London: Jonathan Cape).

Parsons, T. (1960), *Structure and Process in Modern Societies* (Glencoe: Free Press).

Payne, A. (2004), 'Rethinking Development Inside International Political Economy', in A. Payne (ed.), *The New Regional Politics of Development* (Basingstoke: Palgrave), 1–28.

—— (2005), 'The Study of Governance in a Global Political Economy', in N. Phillips, (ed.), *Globalizing International Political Economy* (Houndmills: Palgrave Macmillan), 55–81.

Perham, M. (1963), *The Colonial Reckoning: The Reith Lectures 1961* (London: Fontana).

Phillips, N. (ed.) (2005), *Globalizing International Political Economy* (Houndmills: Palgrave Macmillan).

Pierson, P. (2000), 'The Limits of Design: Explaining Institutional Origins and Change', *Governance*, 13/4: 475–99.

—— and Skocpol, T. (2002), 'Historical Institutionalism in Contemporary Political Science', in I. Katznelson and H. V. Miller (eds), *Political Science: State of the Discipline* (New York : Norton).

Pieterse, J. N. (1992), 'Christianity, Politics and Gramscism of the Right: Introduction', in J. Pieterse (ed.), *Christianity and Hegemony. Religion and Politics on the Frontiers of Social Change* (Oxford: Berg), 1–31.

PNUD (Programa de las Naciones Unidas para el Desarrollo) (2008), *Guatemala: Una Economia al Servicio del Desarrollo Humano?*, Informe Nacional de Desarrollo Humano 2007–08, available at http://desarrollohumano.org.gt

Porter, B. (1996), *The Lion's Share: A Short History of British Imperialism 1850–1995*, 3rd edn (London: Longman).

Posner, D. (2005), *Institutions and Ethnic Politics in Africa* (Cambridge: Cambridge University Press).

—— and Young, D. J. (2007), 'The Institutionalization of Political Power in Africa', *Journal of Democracy*, 18/3: 126–40.

Powell, G. B. (2000), *Elections as Instruments of Democracy: Majoritarian and Proportional Visions* (New Haven, CT: Yale University Press).

Prakash, G. (1999), *Another Reason: Science and the Imagination of Modern India* (Princeton, NJ: Princeton University Press).

Przeworski, A., Alvarez, M., Cheibub, J., and Limongi, F. (1996), 'What Makes Democracies Endure?', *Journal of Democracy*, 7/1: 39–55.

Purdey, J. (2006), *Anti-Chinese Violence in Indonesia, 1996–1999* (Singapore: Singapore University Press).

Putnam, R. (1993), *Making Democracy Work: Civic Traditions in Modern Italy* (Princeton, NJ: Princeton University Press).

Pye, L. W. (1966), *Aspects of Political Development* (Boston, MA: Little, Brown).

Qi Guoqiang (2007), 'China's Foreign Aid: Policies, Structure, Practice and Trend', Paper delivered to Oxford University Conference on New Directions in Foreign Aid, Oxford, June 2007.

Rai, S. M. (ed.) (2003), *Mainstreaming Gender, Democratizing the State? Institutional Mechanisms for the Advancement of Women* (Manchester/New York: Manchester University Press).

Raja Mohan, C. (2004), *Crossing the Rubicon: The Shaping of India's New Foreign Policy* (Basingstoke: Palgrave Macmillan).

Ramagundam, R. (2001), *Defeated Innocence: Adivasi Assertion, Land Rights and The Ekta Parishad Movement* (New Delhi: Grassroots India Publishers).

Ram-Prasad, C. (1993), 'Hindutva Ideology Extracting the Fundamentals', *Contemporary South Asia*, 2/3: 285–309.

Randall, V. (2004), 'Using and Abusing the Concept of the Third World: Geopolitics and the Comparative Study of Development and Underdevelopment', *Third World Quarterly*, 25/1: 41–53.

—— and Svåsand, L. (2002), 'Party Institutionalization in New Democracies', *Party Politics*, 8/1: 6–29.

Ravallion, M. (2001), 'Growth, Inequality and Poverty: Looking Beyond Averages', *World Development*, 29/11: 1803–15.

Rawls, J. (1971), *A Theory of Justice* (Oxford: Oxford University Press).

Reilly, B. and Nordlund, P. (eds) (2008), *Political Parties in Conflict-Prone Societies: Regulation, Engineering and Democratic Development* (Tokyo: United Nations University Press).

Remmer, K. (1997), 'Theoretical Decay and Theoretical Development: The Resurgence of Institutional Analysis', *World Politics*, 50/1: 34–61.

Robinson, G. (1998), 'Rawan Is as Rawan Does: The Origins of Disorder in New Order Aceh', *Indonesia*, 66: 127–56.

Robinson, W. I. (1996), *Promoting Polyarchy: Globalization, US Intervention, and Hegemony* (New York/Cambridge: Cambridge University Press).

Roett, R. and Paz, G. (eds) (2008), *China's Expansion into the Weatern Hemisphere: Implications for Latin America and the United States* (Washington DC: Brookings Institute Press).

Rondinelli, D. A. and Montgomery, J. D. (2005), 'Regime Change and Nation Building: Can Donors Restore Governance in Post-Conflict States?', *Public Administration and Development*, 25/1: 15–24.

Ross, M. (1999), 'The Political Economy of the Resource Curse', *World Politics*, 51/2: 297–322.

Rotberg, R. I. (ed.) (2004), *When States Fail* (Princeton, NJ: Princeton University Press).

Rousseau, J.J. (1755), *Discourse on Equality* (London: Everyman/Dent).

Rudolph, L. I. and Rudolph, S. H. (1967), *The Modernity of Tradition: Political Development in India* (Chicago, IL: University of Chicago Press).

Rueschemeyer, D. (2004), 'Addressing Inequality', *Journal of Democracy*, 15/4: 76–90.

——, Stephens, E. H., and Stephens, J. D. (1992), *Capitalist Democracy and Development* (Cambridge: Polity Press).

Sahni, V. (2007), 'India's Foreign Policy: Key Drivers', *South African Journal of International Affairs*, 14/2: 21–35.

Said, E. W. (1993), *Culture and Imperialism* (London: Chatto & Windus).

—— (1995), *Orientalism* (Harmondsworth: Penguin, first pub. 1978).

Samatar, A. I. (1999), *An African Miracle: State and Class Leadership and Colonial Legacy in Botswana's Development* (Portsmouth, NH: Heinemann).

Sangmpam, S. N. (2007), 'Politics Rules: The False Primacy of Institutions in Developing Countries', *Political Studies*, 55/1, 201–24.

Sartori, G. (1976), *Parties and Party Systems: A Framework for Analysis* (Cambridge: Cambridge University Press).

Scarritt, J. R. (2003), 'Why Do Multi-Ethnic Parties Predominate in Africa and Ethnic Parties Do Not?', Unpublished paper.

—— and Mozaffar, S. (1999), 'The Specification of Ethnic Cleavages and Ethnopolitical Groups for the Analysis of Democratic Competition in Contemporary Africa', *Nationalism and Ethnic Politics*, 5/1: 82–117.

Schedler, A. (1998), 'What Is Democratic Consolidation?', *Journal of Democracy*, 9/2: 91–107.

—— (2002a), 'The Nested Game of Democratization by Elections', *International Political Science Review*, 23/1: 103–22.

—— (2002b), 'Elections Without Democracy: The Menu of Manipulation', *Journal of Democracy*, 13/2: 36–50.

——, Diamond, L. and Plattner, M. (eds) (1999), *The Self-Restraining State* (Boulder, CO: Lynne Reinner).

Scheper-Hughes, N. (1992), *Death Without Weeping: The Violence of Everyday Life in Brazil* (Berkeley, CA: University of California Press).

Schneider, B. R. (1999), 'The *Desarrollista* State in Brazil and Mexico', in M. Woo-Cummings (ed.), *The Developmental State* (Ithaca, NY/London: Cornell University Press) 276–305.

Schock, K. (1999), 'People Power and Political Opportunities: Social Movement Mobilization and Outcomes in the Philippines and Burma', *Social Problems*, 46/3: 355–75.

—— (2006), 'Nonviolent Social Movements', in G. Ritzer (ed.), *The Blackwell Encyclopedia of Sociology* (Boston/London: Blackwell Publishing), 4458–63.

Scott, J. C. (1998), *Seeing Like a State* (New Haven, CT: Yale University Press).

Secretariat of the Convention on Biological Diversity (2000), *Cartagena Protocol on Biosafety* (Montreal: Secretariat of the Convention on Biological Diversity).

Selznick, P. (1948), 'Foundations of the Theory of Organization', *American Sociological Review*, 13/1: 25–35.

Sen, A. (1992), *Inequality Re-examined* (Oxford: Oxford University Press).

—— (1999a), *Development as Freedom* (Oxford: Oxford University Press).

—— (1999b), 'Human Rights and Economic Achievements', in J. R. Bauer and D. A. Bell (eds), *The East Asian Challenge for Human Rights* (Cambridge: Cambridge University Press), 88–99.

—— (2006), *Identity and Violence: The Illusion of Destiny* (London: Allen Lane).

Sethi, H. (1999), 'Review of Pradeep Chhibber, Democracy Without Associations', *Seminar 480* (August): 90–4.

Sharkey, H. (2003), *Living with Colonialism: Nationalism and Culture in the Anglo-Egyptian Sudan* (Berkeley, CA: University of California Press).

Sharp, G. (1973), *The Politics of Nonviolent Action*, 3 vols. (Boston: Porter Sargent).

Shepsle, K. A.(2006), 'Rational Choice Institutionalism', in R. A. W. Rhodes, S. A. Binder, and B. A. Rockman (eds), *The Oxford Handbook of Political Institutions* (Oxford: Oxford University Press), 23–38.

Siavelis, P. (2006), 'Accomodating Informal Institutions and Chilean Democracy', in G. Helmke and S. Levitsky (eds), *Informal Institutions and Democracy: Lessons from Latin America* (Baltimore, MD: The Johns Hopkins University Press), 33–55.

Sikand, Y. (2003), 'Response to Shiva', in M. J. Gibney (ed.), *Globalizing Rights* (Oxford: Oxford University Press) 109–14.

Silverman, S. F. (1977), 'Patronage and Community–Nation Relationships in Central Italy', in S. Schmidt, J. C. Scott, C. Landé, and L. Guasti (eds), *Friends, Followers and Factions: A Reader in Political Clientelism* (Berkeley, CA/London: University of California Press).

Singh, S. K. (2007), *India and West Africa: A Burgeoning Relationship* (London: Chatham House Africa Programme, Briefing Paper, April 2007).

Sisk, T. D. (2009), 'Pathways of the Political: Election Processes after Civil War', in R. Paris and T. D. Sisk (eds), *The Dilemmas of Statebuilding* (New York: Routledge), 196–224.

Six, C. (2009) 'The Rise of Postcolonial States as Donors: A Challenge to the Development Paradigm', *Third World Quarterly*, 30/6: 1103–21.

Sklair, L. (1991), *Sociology of the Global System* (London: Prentice-Hall).

Skocpol, T. (1979), *States and Social Revolutions* (New York: Cambridge University Press).

Slater, D. (2004), *Geopolitics and the Postcolonial: Rethinking North–South Relations* (Oxford: Blackwell).

Smith, A. D. (1991), *National Identity* (Harmondsworth: Penguin).

—— (1998), *Nationalism and Modernism: A Critical Survey of Recent Theories of Nations and Nationalism* (London: Routledge).

Smith, D. (1990), 'Limits of Religious Resurgence', in E. Sahliyeh (ed.), *Religious Resurgence and Politics in the Contemporary World* (Albany, NY: State University of New York Press).

Smith, J., Bolyard, M., and Ippolito, A. (1999), 'Human Rights and the Global Economy: A Response to Meyer', *Human Rights Quarterly*, 21/1: 207–19.

Snyder, J. (2000), *From Voting to Violence: Democratization and Nationalist Conflict* (New York: W.W. Norton).

Stapenhurst, R., Pelizzo, R., Olson, D., and von Trapp, L. (2008) *Legislative Oversight and Budgeting: a World Perspective* (Washington, DC: World Bank).

Staudt, K. (1997), *Women, International Development and Politics: The Bureaucratic Mire*, 2nd edn (Philadelphia, PA: Temple University Press).

—— (1998), *Policy, Politics and Gender: Women Gaining Ground* (West Hartford, CT: Kumarian Press).

—— and Coronado, I. (2002), *Fronteras No Más: Toward Social Justice at the US–Mexico Border* (New York: Palgrave USA).

Stiglitz, J. (2003), 'Democratizing the IMF and the World Bank: Governance and Accountability', *Governance*, 16/1: 111–39.

Suberu, R. J (2008), 'The Supreme Court and Federalism in Nigeria', *Journal of Modern African Studies*, 46/3: 451–85.

Suhrke A. and Samset, I. (2007), 'What's in A Figure? Estimating Recurrence of Civil War', *International Peacekeeping*, 14/2: 195–2003.

Sutton, P. (1991), 'Constancy, Change and Accommodation: The Distinct Tradition of the Commonwealth Caribbean', in J. Mayall and A. Payne (eds), *The Fallacies of Hope: The Post-Colonial Record of the Commonwealth Third World* (Manchester: Manchester University Press), 106–17.

Swatuk, L. A. and Shaw, T. M. (1994), *The South at the End of the Twentieth Century* (New York: St Martin's Press).

Tarrow, S. (1998), *Power in Movement: Social Movements and Contentious Politics*, 2nd edn (Cambridge: Cambridge University Press).

Tawney, R. H. (1952), *Inequality* (London: Allen and Unwin).

Taylor, I. (2009), *China's New Role in Africa* (Boulder, CO: Lynne Rienner).

Ter Haar, G. and Busutill J. (eds) (2005), *Bridge or Barrier? Religion, Violence and Visions for Peace* (Leiden: Brill).

Thelen, K. (2004), *How Institutions Evolve: The Political Economy of Skills in Germany, Britain, the United States and Japan* (New York: Cambridge University Press).

Thomas, C. and Wilkin, P. (2004), 'Still Waiting After All These Years: The Third World on the Periphery of International Relations', *British Journal of Politics and International Relations*, 6/2: 241–58.

Tilly, C. (1999), *Durable Inequality* (London: University of California Press).

Tiro, H. (1984), *The Price of Freedom (The Unfinished Diary)* (Norsberg, Sweden: Information Dept, National Liberation Front Acheh Sumatra).

Tomlinson, B. R. (1993), *The New Cambridge History of India, III.3: The Economy of Modern India, 1860–1970* (Cambridge: Cambridge University Press).

Tordoff, W. (1997), *Government and Politics in Africa* (London: Macmillan).

Toye, J. (1987), *Dilemmas of Development* (Oxford: Blackwell).

Transparency International (2005), *Global Corruption Report* (Cambridge: Cambridge University Press).

Tsai, K. S. (2006), 'Adaptive Informal Institutions and Endogenous Institutional Change in China', *World Politics*, 59/1: 116–141.

UNAIDS (2006), *Report on the Global AIDS Epidemic* (Geneva: UNAIDS).

—— (2008), *2008 Report on the Global AIDS Epidemic*, available at www.unaids.org

UNCTAD (2001), *World Investment Report 2001* (New York/Geneva: United Nations).

—— (2003), *Economic Development in Africa: Trade Performance and Commodity Dependence* (New York/Geneva: United Nations).

—— (2008a), *UNCTAD Handbook of Statistics* (Geneva: United Nations Conference on Trade and Development).

—— (2008b), *World Investment Report 2008* (Geneva: United Nations Conference on Trade and Development).

—— (2009a), *Economic Development in Africa Report 2009* (Geneva: United Nations Conference on Trade and Development).

—— (2009b), *Keeping ODA Afloat: No Stone Unturned* (Geneva: United Nations Conference on Trade and Development).

UNODC (2006), *Trafficking in Human Beings: Global Patterns* (Vienna: UNODC).

—— (2009), *World Drug Report* (New York: United Nations).

UNSCN (2009), *Global Recession Increases Malnutrition for the Most Vulnerable People in Developing Countries* (United Nations Standing Committee on Nutrition), available at www.unscn.org

United Nations (2004), *A More Secure World: Our Shared Responsibility—Report of the Secretary-General's High-Level Panel on Threats, Challenges and Change* (New York: The United Nations).

United Nations Assistance Mission for Iraq (UNAMI) (2007), *Human Rights Report: 1 January–31 March*, available at www.uniraq.org [accessed 1 March 2010]

United Nations Department of Peacekeeping Operations (2009), Background Notes 32 October 2009, available at www.un.org/en/peacekeeping/bnote.htm [accessed November 2009].

United Nations Development Programme (various years), *Human Development Reports* (New York/Oxford: Oxford University Press).

Viswanathan, G. (1990), *Masks of Conquest: Literary Study and British Rule in India* (London: Faber & Faber).

Vogel, D. (1997), *Trading Up: Consumer and Environmental Regulation in the Global Economy*, 2nd edn (Cambridge, MA: Harvard University Press).

von Hippel, K. (2004), 'Post-Conflict Reconstruction in Iraq: Lessons Unlearned', in. P. Cornish (ed.), *The Conflict in Iraq 2003* (London: Palgrave MacMillan): 200–13.

Wallerstein, I. (1979), 'The Rise and Future Demise of the World Capitalist System: Concepts for Comparative Analysis', in *The Capitalist World-Economy* (Cambridge: Cambridge University Press), 1–36.

—— (2003), *The Decline of American Power* (New York: The New Press).

Walt, S. M. (1991), 'The Renaissance of Security Studies', *International Studies Quarterly*, 35/2: 211–39.

Weber, M. (1964), *The Theory of Social and Economic Organization*, ed. by T. Parsons (New York: Free Press).

—— (1970), *From Max Weber: Essays in Sociology*, ed. H. H. Gerth and C. Wright Mills (London: Routledge).

Weiss, J. (2002), *Industrialisation and Globalisation: Theory and Evidence from Developing Countries* (London: Routledge).

Weiss, L. (2005), 'The State-Augmenting Effects of Globalization', *New Political Economy*, 10/3: 345–53.

—— and Hobson, J. M. (1995), *States and Economic Development* (Cambridge: Polity Press).

Weldon, S. L. (2002), *Protest, Policy, and the Problem of Violence Against Women: A Cross-National Comparison* (Pittsburgh, PA: University of Pittsburgh Press).

White House (2002), 'The National Security Strategy of the United States of America', September 2002, available at www.georgewbush-whitehouse.archives.gov/nsc/nss/2002/nss.pdf

Wickramasinghe, N. (2006), *Sri Lanka in the Modern Age* (London: Hurst).

Wilson, P. and Purushothaman, R. (2003), *Dreaming with BRICs: The Path to 2050*, Goldman Sachs Global Economics Paper 99, available at www2.goldmansachs.com/ideas/brics/book/99-dreaming.pdf

Wolf-Phillips, L. (1979), 'Why Third World?', *Third World Quarterly*, 1/1: 105–13.

Wong, E. (2006), 'US Faces Latest Trouble with Iraqi Forces: Loyalty', *International Herald Tribune*, 6 March [accessed 1 October 2006].

Woo-Cummings, M. (ed.) (1999), *The Developmental State* (Ithaca, NY/London: Cornell University Press).

Woodberry, R.D. (2004), 'The Shadow of Empire: Christian Missions, Colonial Policy, and Democracy in Postcolonial Societies' (unpublished Ph.D. dissertation, University of North Carolina at Chapel Hill).

Woodhead, L. and Heelas, P. (eds) (2000), *Religions in Modern Times* (Oxford: Blackwell).

World Bank (1990), *World Development Report 1990* (Washington DC: World Bank).

—— (1994), *Adjustment in Africa: Reforms, Results and the Road Ahead* (Washington, DC: World Bank Policy Research Report).

—— (1997), *World Development Report 1997: The State in a Changing World* (New York: Oxford University Press).

—— (2000), *Greening Industry: New Roles for Communities, Markets and Governments* (Washington DC: World Bank).

—— (2001), *World Development Report 2001* (Washington DC: World Bank).

—— (2003), *World Development Indicators 2003* (Washington DC: World Bank).

—— (2003d), *Breaking the Conflict Trap: Civil War and Development Policy* (Washington/Oxford: World Bank and Oxford University Press).

—— (2006), *World Bank Development Report: Equity and Development* (New York: World Bank and Oxford University Press).

—— (2009), *World Development Report 2010: Development and Climate Change* (Washington DC: World Bank).

World Trade Organization (2008), *International Trade Statistics 2008* (Geneva: WTO).

Wright, A. and Wolford, W. (2003), *To Inherit the Earth: The Landless Movement and the Struggle for a New Brazil* (Oakland, CA: Food First Books).

Yadav, Y. (1996), 'Reconfiguration in Indian Politics: State Assembly Elections, 1993–95', *Economic and Political Weekly*, 13–20 January: 95–104.

Young, C. (1994), *The African Colonial State in Comparative Perspective* (New Haven, CT: Yale University Press).

——(1998), 'Country Report: The African Colonial State Revisited', *Governance: An International Journal of Policy and Administration*, 11/1: 101–20.

——(2001), 'Nationalism and Ethnic Conflict in Africa', in M. Guibernau and J. Hutchinson (eds), *Understanding Nationalism* (Cambridge: Polity Press), 164–81.

Youngs, R. (2009), 'Energy: A Reinforced Obstacle to Democratization?', in P. Burnell and R. Youngs (eds), *New Challenges to Democratization* (London/New York: Routledge), 173–90.

Zakaria, F. (1997), 'The Rise of Illiberal Democracy', *Foreign Affairs*, 76/6: 22–43.

Zunes, S. (2006). 'The United States: Belligerant Hegemon', in R. Fawn and R. Hinnebusch (eds), *The Iraq War* (Boulder, CO: Lynne Rienner).

Index